20TH-CENTURY POETRY & POETICS

Fourth Edition

Edited by
GARY GEDDES

OXFORD
UNIVERSITY PRESS

Oxford University Press
70 Wynford Drive, Don Mills, Ontario M3C 1J9
http://www.oupcan.com

Oxford New York
Athens Auckland Bangkok Calcutta
Cape Town Chennai Dar es Salaam Delhi
Florence Hong Kong Istanbul Karachi
Kuala Lumpur Madrid Melbourne
Mexico City Mumbai Nairobi Paris
Singapore Taipei Tokyo Toronto Warsaw

and associated companies in
Berlin Ibadan

Canadian Cataloguing in Publication Data

Main entry under title:

20th-century poetry & poetics

4th ed.
Includes index.
ISBN 0–19–541015–7

1. English poetry – 20th century. 2. American poetry – 20th century 3. Canadian poetry (English) – 20th century.* 4. Poetics. I. Geddes, Gary, 1940– . II. Title: Twentieth-century poetry and poetics.

PN6101.T84 1996 821'.9108 C95–933330–4

Cover and text design: Brett Miller

3 4 5 6 – 02 01 00

This book is printed on permanent (acid-free) paper. ∞

Printed in Canada

Table of Contents

Poetics

Preface

Living Doubly

1

Sophie conducts reconnaissance from her bunker. After fifteen years of worrying three children towards a safe and healthy independence, she is back in school. It's crazy. She hasn't chosen engineering so she can ape the career of her ex-husband; nor has she enrolled in secretarial or data-processing courses in order to find in the marketplace the same domination she experienced at home. Later, when the healing has begun, she may consider social work or one of the soft sciences that will allow her to share with others what she herself has taken so long to learn. Now she's intent on survival, which means listening to her heart.

She sits, as inconspicuously as possible, in the third row of a classroom where a lecture is in progress on the poetry of John Milton. I'm hopelessly ill-prepared for this adventure, she thinks. I'm twice the age of the girls on either side of me, one of whom is dressed in combat pants and a tie-dyed singlet so loose and skimpy that her unfettered breasts are partially visible. I've been out of school so long I can't remember the difference between a gerund and a geranium, never mind a participle; and I'm afraid my brain has atrophied from all those years of domestic management and small-talk. I don't understand the terminology and can't shake my feelings of guilt for not being at someone's beck and call. Yet I'm strangely elated.

The instructor, a recent graduate with her doctorate in critical theory, a field Sophie refers to as *demolition*, is reading from *Paradise Lost*. Ms Winnifred's nasal voice is abrasive and the students have nicknamed her The Whinery. Sophie feels she should disapprove of such disrespectful behaviour, but, without realizing how it happened, has put her own spin on the naming process by whispering to the semi-nude militia-woman next to her that she likes Dry White's accent.

'Dry White? Hey, that's cool.' As the alternate nickname makes its way across the classroom, from bunker to foxhole, Sophie experiences a guilty surge of excitement and power.

Dry White usually walks back and forth in front of the class when she lectures, perhaps on the assumption that eyes with constantly adjusting lenses are less likely to close shop, but today she plunks herself down on the spindly table and lets her legs swing back and forth underneath. She is wearing a long denim skirt and Dutch clogs that peek out from under the hem with each pendulum swing. In the course of reading, the instructor is transformed and becomes the vehicle for something beautiful that Sophie can feel happening, a shiver that begins in the back of her neck and spreads like the sensation of warm tea throughout her body. Or, if she can remember that far back, like good sex.

'Hurled headlong flaming from the ethereal sky,/To bottomless perdition down.' Sophie had not started out as a great sympathizer with Satan, the fallen angel, since the squabble in the largely masculine heaven of Milton's poem is faintly reminiscent of arguments in her own kitchen. As the words flow over her, she can feel her resistance erode, slip away, her flesh naked as that of Adam and Eve. She could tell them all—Dry White and her audience—a thing or two about lost paradises, if it came to that, all the expulsions from grace, the fall from a too brief childhood, the unexpected and scarcely immaculate conception, constant unfaithfulness, and the aftermath of her own cheap revenge.

'Can I help you—Sophie, isn't it?' Dry White is sitting beside her, rummaging in her briefcase for a tissue, the classroom entirely deserted. Sophie's face is streaming, but she manages to respond, through a mouth that is half grimace, half smile.

'Words—they're only words. How does the blind old sonofabitch do it?'

2

What is it about poetry that has the power to cut through all the crap we accumulate in our lives and touch us to the quick, to make us not only recall our childhood, but also re-experience the less complicated joys and sensations of that not always guileless time?

I believe, with the Czech poet Cseslaw Milosz, that *poetry is as essential as bread*. When the physical needs of the body have been satisfied, we begin to look around us to discover meaning, to satisfy the spirit's hunger. The infant, mother's milk still glistening on its cheek, begins to make imitative sounds in order to organize and manipulate its world. Without being decipherable, these sounds give the infant pleasure and seem, astonishingly, to please the faces gathered around, some of which have set up a symphony of rather silly but nonetheless meaningful responses. A few weeks later, the six-month-old resembles a diminutive Columbus or Magellan setting foot on new continents of sound and meaning; two- or three-syllable words, phrases of varying length and complexity, at first launched shakily from the tongue, soon enough fly off with ease to weave their magic.

The child who has begun to love language, to suck the syllables and consonants in each new word as if they were candy, will have no trouble with hyper-athletic cows that insist on pole-vaulting over the moon or amorous pieces of china and cutlery that run off together for clandestine weekends. The child's world is not yet ruled by logic or empiricism; anything can still happen and, hopefully, does. This is the golden age, when the word *mother* can be used to summon that tireless, smiling, sweet-smelling provider from the far end of the house; or, if she doesn't show up promptly, offer consolation by providing a label under which to collect and organize a myriad of comforting images and sensations.

The Australian poet and psychiatrist Craig Powell, who spent ten years practising both of these vocations in Canada, argues that poetry is so deeply rooted in our childhood experiences of life that it is 'the language of the body-self and of dreaming'. In an article called 'On Poetry and Weeping', published in the journal *Free Associations*, he writes: 'Poetry, as the language of the unconscious and of dreaming, has its roots in primary process experience and is closer to the primordial union with the mother than the secondary process language of prose. The poems that move us most deeply are those which evoke the poignancy of that lost union, when in fantasy the boundaries of self and other were melted away.' A more elaborate statement of Powell's argument comes later in the same essay:

> Poetry, by the very regressive nature of its language, has the potential to evoke tears even when the manifest content of the poem has nothing to do with loss. Linear and logical progressions of thought belong to prose, which is the proper medium for philosophical discourse, for law, government and commerce. Poetry lives in tactile images of the body and the sensual world. The associations do not progress in an 'orderly' fashion but leap about, sometimes gently, as in the nineteenth-century romantics (Keats, Shelley, Coleridge) and sometimes frenetically, as in some modern Hispanic surrealists (Lorca, Vallejo, Neruda). When Auden wrote, in his elegy for W.B. Yeats, that 'poetry makes nothing happen', he might have been saying that poetry cannot be used to advance an argument or impose a solution, as prose can. It is not an instrument for lawgivers, and when Shelley wrote of poets as the 'unacknowledged legislators of mankind', he referred rather to their intuiting 'the before unapprehended relations of things'. Poetry reaches experience earlier than the Oedipal Law.

Powell's position is shared by many poets and scholars of poetry. One of these, the Russian émigré poet Joseph Brodsky, said in *The Paris Review* (1979): 'In the works of the better poets you get the sensation that they're not talking to people anymore, or to some seraphical creature. What they're doing is simply talking back to the language itself—as beauty, sensuality, wisdom, irony—those aspects of language of which the poet is a clear mirror. Poetry is not an art or branch of art, it's something more. If what distinguishes us from other species is speech, then poetry, which is the supreme linguistic operation, is our anthropological, indeed genetic, goal.'

The child in us is that part which continues to relate to the world in terms of poetic language, in terms of sound, rhythm, and metaphor. No one understood this more intimately than Wordsworth, who describes in his 'Ode: Intimations of Immortality', how the child comes 'trailing clouds of glory' only to find that 'shades of the prison-house begin to close' as it grows older. These shades include not only the inevitable separation from the mother, the painful shift from innocence to experience which that other romantic poet William Blake dramatized in his work, but also separation from the primary language of poetry. In short, and this is perhaps the greatest price to pay for growing up in our particular societies, we dwindle into prose.

Surely this is too high a price for us to pay, individually and collectively. Alienation from any of the true sources of spiritual nourishment and health leaves us spiritually and emotionally crippled, unable to function effectively as social or economic beings. Albert Camus observed in *The Rebel* that 'creating is living doubly.' He may have found the idea in Byron, who said ''T is to create, and in creating live, a being more intense, that we endow with form our fancy, gaining as we give the life we image.' Without poetry, we are doomed to act out half-lives.

In a talk entitled 'An End to Audience?' (*Second Words*, 1982), Margaret Atwood insists that 'poetry is the heart of language, the activity through which language is renewed and kept alive.' To get a clear picture of the price to be paid for not keeping language alive, we have only to turn to Octavio Paz: 'If society abolishes poetry, it commits spiritual suicide.' Paz laments the low status of poetry in most societies: 'But poetry today is like a secret cult whose rites are celebrated in the catacombs, on the fringes of society. Consumer society and commercial publishers pay little attention to poetry. I think this is one of society's diseases. I don't think we can have a good society if we don't also have good poetry. I'm sure of it.' And how can we continue to have good poetry—the question must be asked—if newspapers don't feature and review it, if publishers cease to publish it, if booksellers refuse to stock it, if professors, teachers, and boards of eduction conspire to devalue poetry by removing it from the curriculum or reducing its status to that of a mere option?

Paz speaks of poetry as fundamental even to the evolution of newer and fairer political structures. 'We need more social justice. Free market societies produce unjust and very stupid societies. I don't believe that the production and consumption of things can be the meaning of human life. All great religions and philosophies say that human beings are more than producers and consumers. We cannot reduce our lives to economics. If a society without social justice is not a good society, a society without poetry is a society without dreams, without words, and, most importantly, without that bridge between one person and another that poetry is.'

3

How do we avoid dwindling into prose and all the spiritual loss that entails? In 1964, Northrop Frye wrote an article entitled 'Elementary Teaching and Elemental Scholarship' that bears directly on this question. Claiming that 'Most of our difficulties in teaching English result from an immature scholarship that has not properly worked out its own elementary teaching principles', he asserts that poetry is our first language and that this fact is central to all literary study.

'The greatest fallacy', Frye insists, 'in the present conception of literary education is the notion that prose is the normal language of ordinary speech, and should form the centre and staple of literary teaching. From prose in this sense we move out to utilitarian English on one side and to the more specialized study of poetry on the other. Few subjects can be more futile than a prose-based approach to poetry, an approach which treats poems as documents, to be analyzed or summarized or otherwise translated into the language of communication. The root of the fallacy is the assumption that prose represents the only valid form of thought, and that poetry, considered as thought, is essentially decorated or distorted prose. When we suggest that young people try writing poetry, what most of them immediately produce are discontinuous prose statements about their emotions, or what they think their emotions ought to be, when confronted with the outside world. This is not merely because they have been taught to read poetry as a series of statements of this kind—"all that guff about nature", as one freshman expressed it—it is rather that they assume that all verbal expression derives from the attempt to describe something, and that poetry differs from prose, as a mode of thought, in being an attempt to describe subjective feelings.'

It might surprise readers who think of Frye as a rather dry, non-political thinker to see how passionate he can be on the subject of poetry in literary education. 'The primary function of education is to make one maladjusted to ordinary society', he insists, 'and literary education makes it more difficult to come to terms with the barbarizing of speech, or what *Finnegans Wake* calls the jinglish-janglage.' Frye describes poetry as 'a method of thought as well as a means of expression' and praises it for its rhythmical energy, its link with song and dance, and its power to create vivid pictures that make their appeal through concrete sensory images. 'The speech of a child is full of chanting and singing', he writes, 'and it is clear that the child understands what many adults do not, that verse is a more direct and primitive way of conventionalizing speech than prose is. This principle, that the physical energy and concrete vividness of verse should normally be presented earlier than the more complex and adulterated rhythm of prose, affects the training in both reading and writing.'

Frye's article, which is a touchstone for educators, ends on a high moral note that is worth recalling in these increasingly prosaic and materialistic times:

> What I do urge as a final word, is that teachers should understand something of the practicality of literary training, at every stage of development. We begin by teaching children to read and write, on the ground that that is the most practical subject in the world, illiteracy being a problem on the same plane as starvation and exposure. But when we get to literature we tend to talk about it as though it were one of the ornaments of life, necessary for the best life, but a luxury for the ordinary one. It is essential for the teacher of literature, at every level, to remember that in a modern democracy a citizen participates in society mainly through his imagination. We often do not realize this until an actual event with some analogy to literary form takes place; but surely we do not need to wait for a president to be assassinated before we can understand what a tragedy is and what it can do in creating a community of response. Literature, however, gives us not only a means of understanding, but a power to fight. All around us is a society which demands that we adjust or come to terms with it, and what that society presents to us is a social mythology. Advertising, propaganda, the speeches of politicians, popular books and magazines, the clichés of rumour, all have their own kind of pastoral myths, quest myths, hero myths, sacrificial myths, and nothing will drive these shoddy constructs out of the mind except the genuine forms of the same thing. We all know how important reason is in an irrational world, but the imagination, in a society of perverted imaginations, is far more essential in making us understand that the phantasmagoria of current events is not real society but only the transient appearance of real society. Real society, the total body of what humanity has done and can do, is revealed to us only by the arts and sciences; nothing but the imagination can apprehend that reality as a whole, and nothing but literature, in a culture as verbal as ours, can train the imagination to fight for the sanity and the dignity of mankind.

4

Sophie's rediscovery of poetry, let's admit it, is not a return ticket to some lost Eden of childhood; in fact, childhood was never that simple or innocent. What she has regained access to is the language through which she savoured and made sense of events and feelings that were to remain central throughout her life. The rhythms of poetry, not very different from the rhythms of the heart-beat and breathing, reach back to primal feelings just as surely as its images open windows to that larger experience whose existence she only dimly remembers.

Who can tell Sophie how a blind and, at times, embittered Milton managed to construct so vast and wonderful a verbal edifice as *Paradise Lost*, or such subtle and evocative sonnets, elegies, and meditations? Something had kept alive in him the language of first experience—the rhymes, the metres, the ballads, the biblical stories, the great sweeps of poetic and dramatic narrative—so that, as his sight grew dim, his tongue and ears, committed to double-duty, took on the task of sounding the moral depths of Western society. In the end he did not, as he had hoped, justify the ways of God to man; poetry is not a vehicle for winning arguments. He did, however, offer proof positive of that other dictum, that *the word* stands at the beginning of all things, that it predates and underwrites creation itself, that poetry is the source and foundation of our well-being.

This knowledge, this flame that flickers in the puns and jokes and homely figures of our speech, that flashes out all too rarely in the lyrics of our best poets and song-writers and story-tellers, is what we must preserve, as if our lives depended on it; and they do.

Gary Geddes
Dunvegan, Ontario
1996

A BRIEF NOTE TO THE FOURTH EDITION:

I have added twenty-five poets, as well as new poetics materials. The new poets from Canada, Ireland, the United Kingdom, the Caribbean, and the United States are Denise Levertov, Derek Walcott, Eavan Boland, Gwendolyn MacEwen, Robert Bly, Philip Levine, Galway Kinnell, John Ashbery, Louise Glück, Sharon Olds, Robert Hass, Patrick Lane, bpNichol, Gary Geddes, Daphne Marlatt, Erin Mouré, Lorna Crozier, Robert Kroetsch, Sharon Thesen, Carol Ann Duffy, Don McKay, Rita Dove, Roo Borson, Bronwen Wallace, and

Tim Lilburn. The inclusion of bpNichol not only makes available a fine poet, but also brings back a modest sampling of concrete poetry, which figured more prominently in the first edition.

I am delighted to be able to bring together further examples of the long poem, the book-length poem, and the extended meditation, in complete or partial form, including 'An Interim', *Seed Catalogue*, *Steveston*, *The T.E. Lawrence Poems*, *Thomas and Beulah*, *The Wild Iris*, *Hong Kong*, *Water & Light*, and 'My Mother's Nipples'. Like *Journals of Susannah Moodie* and *Collected Works of Billy the Kid*, these poems build on, or against, the work of the *Cantos*, *Four Quartets*, *Paterson*, and *Dream Songs*.

The inclusion of so many new poets has required the pruning of some poets and poems from the previous edition. There is no point listing all the poets whose work I would like to have included, since they constitute an even larger 'shadow' anthology. I want, simply, to make the point that the present selection, like the original, is intended to provide a fascinating cross-section of some of the best poetry written in English during the twentieth century.

At the request of a number of users of the anthology, the poems have been dated, using the date of first book publication, which is easy to determine exactly, rather than the date of composition, which is often difficult, if not impossible, to determine. Exceptions have been made in the cases of Earle Birney, who dated all of his poems precisely, and Sylvia Plath, where posthumous publication seriously distorts the chronology of her work.

I would like to thank all those who took the time to give me suggestions for a fourth edition, including Ron Smith, Lisa Potvin, and Jay Ruzesky at Malaspina College, Ross Leckie at the University of Northern British Columbia, S. Partridge at the University of British Columbia, Bob Sherrin, Crystal Hurdle, and Sharon Thesen at Capilano College, Margot Louis and Doug Beardsley at the University of Victoria, Nathalie Cook at McGill University, David Mazoff, formerly of McGill and the University of Northern British Columbia, and especially my research assistant Kevin Bushell at Concordia University, who, as well as excellent taste, has the nose of a bloodhound and the tenacity of a ferret.

G.G.

Poetry

William Butler Yeats (1865-1939)

Yeats was born at Sandymount, near Dublin, and educated in London and Dublin, spending his summers at his parents' birthplace in Sligo. After the publication of his first book, *Mosada: A Poem* (1886), Yeats lived for a time in London, where he founded the Rhymers' Club and associated with writers such as William Morris, Oscar Wilde, and Arthur Symons (who introduced him to the poetry of Mallarmé and the French Symbolists). In 1902 he helped found the Irish National Theatre Society, out of which the Abbey Theatre grew. He was greatly interested in the myths and legends of Ireland and became the leading figure of the Irish renaissance, which revived the ancient lore and traditions of Ireland in works of literature. Yeats's role in the Irish rebellions was largely insignificant; he was more of a cultural than a political force, although later, as a senator, he promoted Ireland's liberal copyright laws. Yeats received the Nobel Prize for Literature in 1923.

Perhaps the most subtle and provocative tribute to Yeats's genius is W.H. Auden's elegy 'In Memory of W.B. Yeats'. To many Europeans the death of Yeats must have seemed symbolic of the death of all that is best in civilization. Yeats had looked clearly at the myths of 'science' and 'progress', which we have created to justify the dehumanization of our fellow man, and the myth of 'self-determination', by which we justify exploitation and mass murder. Years before the Second World War, Yeats had warned that 'Things fall apart; the centre cannot hold / Mere anarchy is loosed upon the world.' Above all, Yeats had integrity—as a man and as an artist. He continually demonstrated the critical intelligence and natural skepticism without which freedom is impossible.

Although he admitted that his poetry 'all comes from rage or lust', Yeats directed his rage towards truths *outside* the self: 'all that is personal soon rots; it must be packed in ice or salt.' He believed that in order to escape the limitations of purely subjective statement the poet must write out of his 'antithetical self', that he must explore the tension that exists between opposing ideas. Much of the success of 'The Second Coming' stems from the superb coincidence of simple diction, passionate syntax, and contending opposites (Christ and anti-Christ, order and anarchy, etc.). In order to achieve an indirect mode of expression, Yeats often experimented with the mask, or persona, and, in 'Sailing to Byzantium', with Symbolist techniques. He also made use of literary and historical allusion, as in 'Leda and the Swan', where contemporary history is illuminated through reference to events in classical mythology.

Yeats had no use for sloppiness of sentiment or expression. He was an untiring craftsman, a self-critic who respected his own observations and emotions enough to give them artistic shape. He revised all that he wrote, took great care in the placement of his poems in collections, and strove constantly for simplicity. 'I tried to make the language of poetry coincide with that of passionate, normal speech,' he wrote in 'A General Introduction to My Work' (*Essays and Introductions*). 'Because I need a passionate syntax for passionate subject-matter I compel myself to accept those traditional metres that have developed with the language.' Most poets aim for diction and rhythms reflecting ordinary speech, but few can claim to have achieved in their verse the unusual degree of intensity that Yeats's poems support.

In discussing the work of his contemporary, the poet Lionel Johnson (*Autobiographies*, 1926, revised in 1938), Yeats stressed the symbiosis between the life and art of the poet: 'A poet is by the very nature of things a man who lives with entire sincerity, or rather, the better his poetry the more sincere his life. His life is an experiment in living and those that come after have a right to know it. Above all it is necessary that the lyric poet's life should be known, that we should understand that his poetry is no rootless flower but the speech of a man, that it is not a little thing to achieve anything in any art, to stand alone perhaps for many years, to go a path no other man has gone, to accept one's own thought when the thought of others has the authority of the world behind it. . . . to give one's life as well as one's words which are so much nearer to one's soul to the criticism of the world. Why should we honour those that die upon the field of battle, a man may show as reckless a courage in entering into the abyss of himself.'

In 'Anima Hominis', an essay on masks and the anti-self that appeared in Yeats's *Per Amica Silentia Lunæ* (1918), he made his famous distinction between poetry and rhetoric: 'We make out of the quarrel with others, rhetoric, but of the quarrel with ourselves, poetry. Unlike the rhetoricians, who get a confident voice from remembering the crowd they have won or may win, we sing amid our uncertainty; and, smitten even in the presence of the most high beauty by the knowledge of our solitude, our rhythm shudders.'

Yeats's poems are available in *The Poems of W.B. Yeats* (edited by Richard J. Finneran, 1983) and in the variorum edition of P. Allt and R.K. Alspach (1957); his plays in *The Collected Plays of William Butler Yeats* (1952); and much of his important prose, in *A Vision* (revised in 1937), *Autobiography* (1938), *Letters* (edited by Allan Wade, 1954), and *Essays and Introductions* (1961).

WHEN YOU ARE OLD

When you are old and grey and full of sleep,
And nodding by the fire, take down this book,
And slowly read, and dream of the soft look
Your eyes had once, and of their shadows deep;

How many loved your moments of glad grace,
And loved your beauty with love false or true,
But one man loved the pilgrim soul in you,
And loved the sorrows of your changing face;

And bending down beside the glowing bars,
Murmur, a little sadly, how Love fled
And paced upon the mountains overhead
And hid his face amid a crowd of stars.

[1892]

WHO GOES WITH FERGUS?

Who will go drive with Fergus now,
And pierce the deep wood's woven shade,
And dance upon the level shore?
Young man, lift up your russet brow,
And lift your tender eyelids, maid,
And brood on hopes and fear no more.

And no more turn aside and brood
Upon love's bitter mystery;
For Fergus rules the brazen cars,
And rules the shadows of the wood,
And the white breast of the dim sea
And all dishevelled wandering stars.

[1893]

THE FOLLY OF BEING COMFORTED

One that is ever kind said yesterday:
'Your well-belovèd's hair has threads of grey,
And little shadows come about her eyes;
Time can but make it easier to be wise
Though now it seems impossible, and so
All that you need is patience.'
                    Heart cries, 'No,
I have not a crumb of comfort, not a grain.
Time can but make her beauty over again:
Because of that great nobleness of hers
The fire that stirs about her, when she stirs,
Burns but more clearly. O she had not these ways
When all the wild summer was in her gaze.'

O heart! O heart! if she'd but turn her head,
You'd know the folly of being comforted.

[1902]

The Wild Swans at Coole

The trees are in their autumn beauty,
The woodland paths are dry,
Under the October twilight the water
Mirrors a still sky;
Upon the brimming water among the stones
Are nine-and-fifty swans.

The nineteenth autumn has come upon me
Since I first made my count;
I saw, before I had well finished,
All suddenly mount
And scatter wheeling in great broken rings
Upon their clamorous wings.

I have looked upon those brilliant creatures,
And now my heart is sore.
All's changed since I, hearing at twilight,
The first time on this shore,
The bell-beat of their wings above my head,
Trod with a lighter tread.

Unwearied still, lover by lover,
They paddle in the cold
Companionable streams or climb the air;
Their hearts have not grown old;
Passion or conquest, wander where they will,
Attend upon them still.

But now they drift on the still water,
Mysterious, beautiful;
Among what rushes will they build,
By what lake's edge or pool
Delight men's eyes when I awake some day
To find they have flown away?

[1917]

The Fisherman

Although I can see him still,
The freckled man who goes
To a grey place on a hill
In grey Connemara clothes
At dawn to cast his flies,
It's long since I began
To call up to the eyes
This wise and simple man.
All day I'd looked in the face
What I had hoped 'twould be
To write for my own race
And the reality;

The living men that I hate,
The dead man that I loved,
The craven man in his seat,
The insolent unreproved,
And no knave brought to book
Who has won a drunken cheer,
The witty man and his joke
Aimed at the commonest ear,
The clever man who cries
The catch-cries of the clown,
The beating down of the wise
And great Art beaten down.

Maybe a twelvemonth since
Suddenly I began,
In scorn of this audience,
Imagining a man,
And his sun-freckled face,
And grey Connemara cloth,
Climbing up to a place
Where stone is dark under froth,
And the down-turn of his wrist
When the flies drop in the stream;
A man who does not exist,
A man who is but a dream;

And cried, 'Before I am old
I shall have written him one
Poem maybe as cold
And passionate as the dawn.'

[1919]

EASTER 1916

I have met them at close of day
Coming with vivid faces
From counter or desk among grey
Eighteenth-century houses.
I have passed with a nod of the head
Or polite meaningless words,
Or have lingered awhile and said
Polite meaningless words,
And thought before I had done
Of a mocking tale or a gibe
To please a companion
Around the fire at the club,
Being certain that they and I
But lived where motley is worn:
All changed, changed utterly:
A terrible beauty is born.

That woman's days were spent
In ignorant good-will,
Her nights in argument
Until her voice grew shrill.
What voice more sweet than hers
When, young and beautiful,
She rode to harriers?
This man had kept a school
And rode our wingèd horse;
This other his helper and friend
Was coming into his force;
He might have won fame in the end,
So sensitive his nature seemed,
So daring and sweet his thought.

This other man I had dreamed
A drunken, vainglorious lout.
He had done most bitter wrong
To some who are near my heart,
Yet I number him in the song;
He, too, has resigned his part
In the casual comedy;
He, too, has been changed in his turn,
Transformed utterly:
A terrible beauty is born.

Hearts with one purpose alone
Through summer and winter seem
Enchanted to a stone
To trouble the living stream.
The horse that comes from the road,
The rider, the birds that range
From cloud to tumbling cloud,
Minute by minute they change;
A shadow of cloud on the stream
Changes minute by minute;
A horse-hoof slides on the brim,
And a horse plashes within it;
The long-legged moor-hens dive,
And hens to moor-cocks call;
Minute by minute they live:
The stone's in the midst of all.

Too long a sacrifice
Can make a stone of the heart.
O when may it suffice?
That is Heaven's part, our part
To murmur name upon name,
As a mother names her child
When sleep at last has come
On limbs that had run wild.
What is it but nightfall?
No, no, not night but death;
Was it needless death after all?
For England may keep faith

For all that is done and said.
We know their dream; enough
To know they dreamed and are dead;
And what if excess of love
Bewildered them till they died?
I write it out in a verse—
MacDonagh and MacBride
And Connolly and Pearse
Now and in time to be,
Wherever green is worn,
Are changed, changed utterly:
A terrible beauty is born.

[1916]

THE SECOND COMING

Turning and turning in the widening gyre
The falcon cannot hear the falconer;
Things fall apart; the centre cannot hold;
Mere anarchy is loosed upon the world,
The blood-dimmed tide is loosed, and everywhere
The ceremony of innocence is drowned;
The best lack all conviction, while the worst
Are full of passionate intensity.

Surely some revelation is at hand;
Surely the Second Coming is at hand.
The Second Coming! Hardly are those words out
When a vast image out of *Spiritus Mundi*
Troubles my sight: somewhere in sands of the desert
A shape with lion body and the head of a man,
A gaze blank and pitiless as the sun,
Is moving its slow thighs, while all about it
Reel shadows of the indignant desert birds.
The darkness drops again; but now I know
That twenty centuries of stony sleep
Were vexed to nightmare by a rocking cradle,
And what rough beast, its hour come round at last,
Slouches towards Bethlehem to be born?

[1920]

A Prayer for my Daughter

Once more the storm is howling, and half hid
Under this cradle-hood and coverlid
My child sleeps on. There is no obstacle
But Gregory's wood and one bare hill
Whereby the haystack- and roof-levelling wind,
Bred on the Atlantic, can be stayed;
And for an hour I have walked and prayed
Because of the great gloom that is in my mind.

I have walked and prayed for this young child an hour
And heard the sea-wind scream upon the tower,
And under the arches of the bridge, and scream
In the elms above the flooded stream;
Imagining in excited reverie
That the future years had come,
Dancing to a frenzied drum,
Out of the murderous innocence of the sea.

May she be granted beauty and yet not
Beauty to make a stranger's eye distraught,
Or hers before a looking-glass, for such,
Being made beautiful overmuch,
Consider beauty a sufficient end,
Lose natural kindness and maybe
The heart-revealing intimacy
That chooses right, and never find a friend.

Helen being chosen found life flat and dull
And later had much trouble from a fool,
While that great Queen, that rose out of the spray,
Being fatherless could have her way
Yet chose a bandy-leggèd smith for man.
It's certain that fine women eat
A crazy salad with their meat
Whereby the Horn of Plenty is undone.

In courtesy I'd have her chiefly learned;
Hearts are not had as a gift but hearts are earned
By those that are not entirely beautiful;

Yet many, that have played the fool
For beauty's very self, has charm made wise,
And many a poor man that has roved,
Loved and thought himself beloved,
From a glad kindness cannot take his eyes.

May she become a flourishing hidden tree
That all her thoughts may like the linnet be,
And have no business but dispensing round
Their magnanimities of sound,
Nor but in merriment begin a chase,
Nor but in merriment a quarrel.
O may she live like some green laurel
Rooted in one dear perpetual place.

My mind, because the minds that I have loved,
The sort of beauty that I have approved,
Prosper but little, has dried up of late,
Yet knows that to be choked with hate
May well be of all evil chances chief.
If there's no hatred in a mind
Assault and battery of the wind
Can never tear the linnet from the leaf.

An intellectual hatred is the worst,
So let her think opinions are accursed.
Have I not seen the loveliest woman born
Out of the mouth of Plenty's horn,
Because of her opinionated mind
Barter that horn and every good
By quiet natures understood
For an old bellows full of angry wind?

Considering that, all hatred driven hence,
The soul recovers radical innocence
And learns at last that it is self-delighting,
Self-appeasing, self-affrighting,
And that its own sweet will is Heaven's will;
She can, though every face should scowl
And every windy quarter howl
Or every bellows burst, be happy still.

And may her bridegroom bring her to a house
Where all's accustomed, ceremonious;
For arrogance and hatred are the wares
Peddled in the thoroughfares.
How but in custom and in ceremony
Are innocence and beauty born?
Ceremony's a name for the rich horn,
And custom for the spreading laurel tree.

[1921]

SAILING TO BYZANTIUM

I
That is no country for old men. The young
In one another's arms, birds in the trees
—Those dying generations—at their song,
The salmon-falls, the mackerel-crowded seas,
Fish, flesh, or fowl, commend all summer long
Whatever is begotten, born, and dies.
Caught in that sensual music all neglect
Monuments of unageing intellect.

II
An aged man is but a paltry thing,
A tattered coat upon a stick, unless
Soul clap its hands and sing, and louder sing
For every tatter in its mortal dress,
Nor is there singing school but studying
Monuments of its own magnificence;
And therefore I have sailed the seas and come
To the holy city of Byzantium.

III
O sages standing in God's holy fire
As in the gold mosaic of a wall,
Come from the holy fire, perne in a gyre,
And be the singing-masters of my soul.
Consume my heart away; sick with desire
And fastened to a dying animal
It knows not what it is; and gather me
Into the artifice of eternity.

IV
Once out of nature I shall never take
My bodily form from any natural thing,
But such a form as Grecian goldsmiths make
Of hammered gold and gold enamelling
To keep a drowsy Emperor awake;
Or set upon a golden bough to sing
To lords and ladies of Byzantium
Of what is past, or passing, or to come.

[1927]

LEDA AND THE SWAN

A sudden blow: the great wings beating still
Above the staggering girl, her thighs caressed
By the dark webs, her nape caught in his bill,
He holds her helpless breast upon his breast.

How can those terrified vague fingers push
The feathered glory from her loosening thighs?
And how can body, laid in that white rush,
But feel the strange heart beating where it lies?

A shudder in the loins engenders there
The broken wall, the burning roof and tower
And Agamemnon dead.
Being so caught up,
So mastered by the brute blood of the air,
Did she put on his knowledge with his power
Before the indifferent beak could let her drop?

[1924]

AMONG SCHOOL CHILDREN

I
I walk through the long schoolroom questioning;
A kind old nun in a white hood replies;
The children learn to cipher and to sing,
To study reading-books and histories,

To cut and sew, be neat in everything
In the best modern way—the children's eyes
In momentary wonder stare upon
A sixty-year-old smiling public man.

II
I dream of a Ledaean body, bent
Above a sinking fire, a tale that she
Told of a harsh reproof, or trivial event
That changed some childish day to tragedy—
Told, and it seemed that our two natures blent
Into a sphere from youthful sympathy,
Or else, to alter Plato's parable,
Into the yolk and white of the one shell.

III
And thinking of that fit of grief or rage
I look upon one child or t'other there
And wonder if she stood so at that age—
For even daughters of the swan can share
Something of every paddler's heritage—
And had that colour upon cheek or hair,
And thereupon my heart is driven wild:
She stands before me as a living child.

IV
Her present image floats into the mind—
Did Quattrocento finger fashion it
Hollow of cheek as though it drank the wind
And took a mess of shadows for its meat?
And I though never of Ledaean kind
Had pretty plumage once—enough of that,
Better to smile on all that smile, and show
There is a comfortable kind of old scarecrow.

V
What youthful mother, a shape upon her lap
Honey of generation had betrayed,
And that must sleep, shriek, struggle to escape
As recollection or the drug decide,
Would think her son, did she but see that shape

With sixty or more winters on its head,
A compensation for the pang of his birth,
Or the uncertainty of his setting forth?

VI
Plato thought nature but a spume that plays
Upon a ghostly paradigm of things;
Solider Aristotle played the taws
Upon the bottom of a king of kings;
World-famous golden-thighed Pythagoras
Fingered upon a fiddle-stick or strings
What a star sang and careless Muses heard:
Old clothes upon old sticks to scare a bird.

VII
Both nuns and mothers worship images,
But those the candles light are not as those
That animate a mother's reveries,
But keep a marble or a bronze repose.
And yet they too break hearts—O Presences
That passion, piety or affection knows,
And that all heavenly glory symbolise—
O self-born mockers of man's enterprise;

VIII
Labour is blossoming or dancing where
The body is not bruised to pleasure soul,
Nor beauty born out of its own despair,
Nor blear-eyed wisdom out of midnight oil.
O chestnut-tree, great-rooted blossomer,
Are you the leaf, the blossom or the bole?
O body swayed to music, O brightening glance,
How can we know the dancer from the dance?

[1927]

FOR ANNE GREGORY

'Never shall a young man,
Thrown into despair
By those great honey-coloured

Ramparts at your ear,
Love you for yourself alone
And not your yellow hair.'

'But I can get a hair-dye
And set such colour there,
Brown, or black, or carrot,
That young men in despair
May love me for myself alone
And not my yellow hair.'

'I heard an old religious man
But yesternight declare
That he had found a text to prove
That only God, my dear,
Could love you for yourself alone
And not your yellow hair.'

[1931]

Crazy Jane Talks with the Bishop

I met the Bishop on the road
And much said he and I.
'Those breasts are flat and fallen now,
Those veins must soon be dry;
Live in a heavenly mansion,
Not in some foul sty.'

'Fair and foul are near of kin,
And fair needs foul,' I cried.
'My friends are gone, but that's a truth
Nor grave nor bed denied,
Learned in bodily lowliness
And in the heart's pride.

'A woman can be proud and stiff
When on love intent;
But love has pitched his mansion in
The place of excrement;
For nothing can be sole or whole
That has not been rent.'

[1932]

LONG-LEGGED FLY

That civilisation may not sink,
Its great battle lost,
Quiet the dog, tether the pony
To a distant post;
Our master Caesar is in the tent
Where the maps are spread,
His eyes fixed upon nothing,
A hand under his head.
Like a long-legged fly upon the stream
His mind moves upon silence.

That the topless towers be burnt
And men recall that face,
Move most gently if move you must
In this lonely place.
She thinks, part woman, three parts a child,
That nobody looks; her feet
Practise a tinker shuffle
Picked up on a street.
Like a long-legged fly upon the stream
Her mind moves upon silence.

That girls at puberty may find
The first Adam in their thought,
Shut the door of the Pope's chapel
Keep those children out.
There on that scaffolding reclines
Michael Angelo.
With no more sound than the mice make
His hand moves to and fro.
Like a long-legged fly upon the stream
His mind moves upon silence.

[1939]

THE CIRCUS ANIMALS' DESERTION

I

I sought a theme and sought for it in vain,
I sought it daily for six weeks or so.
Maybe at last, being but a broken man,
I must be satisfied with my heart, although
Winter and summer till old age began
My circus animals were all on show,
Those stilted boys, that burnished chariot,
Lion and woman and the Lord knows what.

II

What can I but enumerate old themes?
First that sea-rider Oisin led by the nose
Through three enchanted islands, allegorical dreams,
Vain gaiety, vain battle, vain repose,
Themes of the embittered heart, or so it seems,
That might adore old songs or courtly shows;
But what cared I that set him on to ride,
I, starved for the bosom of his faery bride?

And then a counter-truth filled out its play,
The Countess Cathleen was the name I gave it;
She, pity-crazed, had given her soul away,
But masterful Heaven had intervened to save it.
I thought my dear must her own soul destroy,
So did fanaticism and hate enslave it,
And this brought forth a dream and soon enough
This dream itself had all my thought and love.

And when the Fool and Blind Man stole the bread
Cuchulain fought the ungovernable sea;
Heart-mysteries there, and yet when all is said
It was the dream itself enchanted me:
Character isolated by a deed
To engross the present and dominate memory.
Players and painted stage took all my love,
And not those things that they were emblems of.

III

Those masterful images because complete
Grew in pure mind, but out of what began?
A mound of refuse or the sweepings of a street,
Old kettles, old bottles, and a broken can,
Old iron, old bones, old rags, that raving slut
Who keeps the till. Now that my ladder's gone,
I must lie down where all the ladders start,
In the foul rag-and-bone shop of the heart.

[1939]

POLITICS

'In our time the destiny of man presents its meaning in political terms.'

—THOMAS MANN

How can I, that girl standing there,
My attention fix
On Roman or on Russian
Or on Spanish politics?
Yet here's a travelled man that knows
What he talks about,
And there's a politician
That has read and thought,
And maybe what they say is true
Of war and war's alarms,
But O that I were young again
And held her in my arms!

[1939]

Ezra Pound (1885-1972)

Pound was born in Hailey, Idaho, 'in a half savage country, out of date', to use his own words, and attended the University of Pennsylvania and Hamilton College, taking his M.A. in romance languages. Too much of a bohemian for the Indiana authorities, Pound was asked to resign his teaching post, after which he left for Europe on a cattle ship. In England, he married Dorothy Shakespear, edited, with Richard Aldington, the first imagist anthology, and was active in literary circles. In the 1920s, he lived in Paris before settling in Rapallo, Italy, where he worked on the *Cantos* and tried to advance the reputations of several artists, including James Joyce. In 1945 Pound was imprisoned in Rome by American troops for his support of the fascists. He was removed to the United States to be tried for treason, but instead of facing trial he was declared insane and committed (an experience described in Pound's the *Pisan Cantos* and in William Carlos Williams's *Autobiography*). In 1948 Pound was awarded the Bollingen Prize for Poetry, a much-disputed and long-overdue recognition of his genius and contribution to literature. Following his release from hospital in 1958, he returned to Italy, where he remained in relative seclusion.

As a poet, Pound is often accused of being both 'archaic' and self-consciously 'modern'. He was a constant innovator, not only inventing new forms but also reviving old forms and introducing into English elements from the poetry of other languages. Paradoxically, when Pound's poetry is most 'archaic' it is most modern in its psychology, for he seems to have achieved in his historical subjects a freedom and objectivity that were denied to him in the pressing matters of his own age. Pound brought about a revolution in poetic attitudes and practice. He anticipated the objectivism of Williams, the rhythmical preoccupations of Olson and Creeley, and the technical experimentation that characterizes poetry in this century. His own verse is lyrical, crudely didactic, satirical, esoteric, rambling, witty, and colloquial, ranging in form from the epic to the epigram, in manner from the autobiographical to the classically objective. With the imagists, he sought for concentration and clarity of expression, to reduce poetry to its essentials. His poetry bears the mark of his early interest in the Chinese ideogram, which he describes as 'a vivid shorthand picture of the operations of nature'. On the other hand, his poetry can also be vast and sprawling, as in the *Cantos*, a profoundly moving and, at times, amusing case-history of our civilization.

Pound believed 'in technique as the test of a man's sincerity'; but he also insisted that in art 'only emotion endures'. His own poetry, if one travels from the epigrams to the translations to the *Cantos*, reveals at every turn both his technical virtuosity and his emotional intensity. Pound was a born teacher, but one who had little use for institutions of learning. *ABC of Reading* (1960), for example, is a repository of wisdom and invective: 'Literature does not exist in a vacuum. Writers as such have a definite social function exactly in proportion to their ability AS WRITERS. This is their main use. . . . Language is the main means of human communication. If an animal's nervous system does not transmit sensations and stimuli, the animal atrophies. . . . The greatest barrier is probably set up by teachers who know a little more than the public, who want to exploit their fractional knowledge, and who are thoroughly opposed to making the least effort to learn anything more. . . . There is one quality which unites all great and perdurable writers, you don't NEED schools and colleges to keep 'em alive. Put them out of the curriculum, lay them in the dust of libraries, and once in every so often a chance reader, unsubsidized and unbribed, will dig them up again, put them in the light again, without asking favours.'

Pound claims that he never 'read half a page of Homer without finding melodic invention, I mean melodic invention that I didn't already know.' In his 'Treatise on Metre' (*ABC of Reading*), he insists that 'Rhythm is a form cut into time.' When it comes to specific details, however, he says: 'You can make a purely empiric list of successful manoeuvres, you can compile a catalogue of your favourite poems. But you cannot hand out a [recipe] for making a Mozartian melody on the basis of take a crochet, then a quaver, then a semi-quaver, etc. . . . The answer is: LISTEN to the sound that it makes.'

Pound was an exacting task-master who, in an essay on Whitman in *ABC of Reading*, expresses the view that 'More writers fail from lack of character than from lack of intelligence.' Whitman had intelligence and character, but, even then, his real writing only occurs 'when he gets free of all this barbed wire', by which Pound means outmoded literary conventions. While many of his followers repudiated narrative, Pound asserts in the same essay that 'narrative sense, narrative power can survive ANY truncation. If a man have the tale to tell and can keep his mind on that and refuses to worry about his own limitations, the reader will, in the long or short run, find him, and no amount of professorial abuse or theoretical sniping will have any real effect on the author's civil status.'

Much of the vitriol in his attack on money-lending and his attraction to the theories of Social Credit may be attributed to his life-long poverty and his frustration over the low status afforded to the arts in the twentieth century. Towards the end of the *ABC of Reading*, he writes: 'The chief cause of false writing is economic. Many writers need or want money. These writers could be cured by an application of banknotes.' Few of his counterparts would disagree.

Since *A Lume Spento* (1908), Pound's publications include *Personae* and *Exultations* (both in 1909), *Canzoni* (1911), *Ripostes* (1912), *Lustra* (1916), *Hugh Selwyn Mauberley* (1920), *Homage to Sextus Propertius* (1934), a series of drafts of the *Cantos* dating from 1925, *Selected Poems* (1928, up to and including *Mauberley*), *Personae: Collected Shorter Poems* (1971), *The Cantos of Ezra Pound* (1970), and *Collected Early Poems* (1976). Also available are *Letters of Ezra Pound, 1907-41* (1950), *The Literary Essays of Ezra Pound* (1954), and *The Translations of Ezra Pound* (1954).

PORTRAIT D'UNE FEMME

Your mind and you are our Sargasso Sea,
London has swept about you this score years
And bright ships left you this or that in fee:
Ideas, old gossip, oddments of all things,
Strange spars of knowledge and dimmed wares of price.
Great minds have sought you—lacking someone else.
You have been second always. Tragical?
No. You preferred it to the usual thing:
One dull man, dulling and uxorious,
One average mind—with one thought less, each year.

Oh, you are patient, I have seen you sit
Hours, where something might have floated up.
And now you pay one. Yes, you richly pay.
You are a person of some interest, one comes to you
And takes strange gain away:
Trophies fished up; some curious suggestion;
Fact that leads nowhere; and a tale or two,
Pregnant with mandrakes, or with something else
That might prove useful and yet never proves,
That never fits a corner or shows use,
Or finds its hour upon the loom of days:
The tarnished, gaudy, wonderful old work;
Idols and ambergris and rare inlays,
These are your riches, your great store; and yet
For all this sea-hoard of deciduous things,
Strange woods half-sodden, and new brighter stuff:
In the slow float of differing light and deep,
No! there is nothing! In the whole and all,
Nothing that's quite your own.
Yet this is you.

[1912]

THE GARDEN

'En robe de parade.'—SAMAIN

Like a skein of loose silk blown against a wall
She walks by the railing of a path
in Kensington Gardens,
And she is dying piece-meal
of a sort of emotional anæmia.

And round about there is a rabble
Of the filthy, sturdy, unkillable infants of the very poor.
They shall inherit the earth.

In her is the end of breeding.
Her boredom is exquisite and excessive.
She would like some one to speak to her,
And is almost afraid that I
will commit that indiscretion.

[1916]

COMMISSION

Go, my songs, to the lonely and the unsatisfied,
Go also to the nerve-racked, go to the enslaved-by-convention,
Bear to them my contempt for their oppressors.
Go as a great wave of cool water,
Bear my contempt of oppressors.

Speak against unconscious oppression,
Speak against the tyranny of the unimaginative,
Speak against bonds.
Go to the bourgeoise who is dying of her ennuis,
Go to the women in suburbs.
Go to the hideously wedded,
Go to them whose failure is concealed,
Go to the unluckily mated,
Go to the bought wife,
Go to the woman entailed.

Go to those who have delicate lust,
Go to those whose delicate desires are thwarted,
Go like a blight upon the dullness of the world;
Go with your edge against this,
Strengthen the subtle cords,
Bring confidence upon the algæ and the tentacles of the soul.

Go in a friendly manner,
Go with an open speech.
Be eager to find new evils and new good,
Be against all forms of oppression.
Go to those who are thickened with middle age,
To those who have lost their interest.

Go to the adolescent who are smothered in family—
Oh how hideous it is
To see three generations of one house gathered together!
It is like an old tree with shoots,
And with some branches rotted and falling.

Go out and defy opinion,
Go against this vegetable bondage of the blood.
Be against all sorts of mortmain.

[1916]

Dance Figure

For the Marriage in Cana of Galilee

Dark eyed,
O woman of my dreams,
Ivory sandalled,
There is none like thee among the dancers,
None with swift feet.
I have not found thee in the tents,
In the broken darkness.
I have not found thee at the well-head
Among the women with pitchers.

Thine arms are as a young sapling under the bark;
Thy face as a river with lights.

White as an almond are thy shoulders;
As new almonds stripped from the husk.
They guard thee not with eunuchs;
Not with bars of copper.

Gilt turquoise and silver are in the place of thy rest.
A brown robe, with threads of gold woven in patterns, hast thou
gathered about thee,
O Nathat-Ikanaie, 'Tree-at-the-river'.

As a rillet among the sedge are thy hands upon me;
Thy fingers a frosted stream.

Thy maidens are white like pebbles;
Their music about thee!

There is none like thee among the dancers;
None with swift feet.

[1916]

In a Station of the Metro

The apparition of these faces in the crowd;
Petals on a wet, black bough.

[1916]

ALBA

As cool as the pale wet leaves
of lily-of-the-valley
She lay beside me in the dawn.

[1916]

L'ART, 1910

Green arsenic smeared on an egg-white cloth,
Crushed strawberries! Come, let us feast our eyes.

[1916]

THE TEA SHOP

The girl in the tea shop
Is not so beautiful as she was,
The August has worn against her.
She does not get up the stairs so eagerly;
Yes, she also will turn middle-aged,
And the glow of youth that she spread about us
As she brought us our muffins
Will be spread about us no longer.
She also will turn middle-aged.

[1916]

THE RIVER-MERCHANT'S WIFE: A LETTER

While my hair was still cut straight across my forehead
I played about the front gate, pulling flowers.
You came by on bamboo stilts, playing horse,
You walked about my seat, playing with blue plums.
And we went on living in the village of Chokan:
Two small people, without dislike or suspicion.

At fourteen I married My Lord you.
I never laughed, being bashful.
Lowering my head, I looked at the wall.
Called to, a thousand times, I never looked back.

At fifteen I stopped scowling,
I desired my dust to be mingled with yours
For ever and for ever and for ever.
Why should I climb the look out?

At sixteen you departed,
You went into far Ku-to-yen, by the river of swirling eddies,
And you have been gone five months.
The monkeys make sorrowful noise overhead.

You dragged your feet when you went out.
By the gate now, the moss is grown, the different mosses,
Too deep to clear them away!
The leaves fall early this autumn, in wind.
The paired butterflies are already yellow with August
Over the grass in the West garden;
They hurt me. I grow older.
If you are coming down through the narrows of the river Kiang,
Please let me know beforehand,
And I will come out to meet you
                As far as Cho-fu-Sa.

By Rihaku [Li Bai]
A.D. 800

[1916]

FROM HUGH SELWYN MAUBERLEY

E.P. ODE POUR L'ÉLECTION DE SON SÉPULCRE

I

For three years, out of key with his time,
He strove to resuscitate the dead art
Of poetry; to maintain 'the sublime'
In the old sense. Wrong from the start—

No, hardly, but seeing he had been born
In a half-savage country, out of date;
Bent resolutely on wringing lilies from the acorn;
Capaneus; trout for factitious bait;

'Ἴδμεν γάρ τοι πάνθ', ὅσ' ἐνὶ Τροίῃ
Caught in the unstopped ear;
Giving the rocks small lee-way
The chopped seas held him, therefore, that year.

His true Penelope was Flaubert,
He fished by obstinate isles;
Observed the elegance of Circe's hair
Rather than the mottoes on sundials.

Unaffected by 'the march of events',
He passed from men's memory in *l'an trentiesm*
De son eage; the case presents
No adjunct to the Muses' diadem.

II
The age demanded an image
Of its accelerated grimace,
Something for the modern stage,
Not, at any rate, an Attic grace;

Not, not certainly, the obscure reveries
Of the inward gaze;
Better mendacities
Than the classics in paraphrase!

The 'age demanded' chiefly a mould in plaster,
Made with no loss of time,
A prose kinema, not, not assuredly, alabaster
Or the 'sculpture' of rhyme.

III
The tea-rose tea-gown, etc.
Supplants the mousseline of Cos,
The pianola 'replaces'
Sappho's barbitos.

Christ follows Dionysus,
Phallic and ambrosial
Made way for macerations;
Caliban casts out Ariel.

All things are a flowing,
Sage Heracleitus says;
But a tawdry cheapness
Shall outlast our days.

Even the Christian beauty
Defects—after Samothrace;
We see τὸ καλὸν
Decreed in the market-place.

Faun's flesh is not to us,
Nor the saint's vision.
We have the Press for wafer;
Franchise for circumcision.

All men, in law, are equals.
Free of Pisistratus,
We choose a knave or an eunuch
To rule over us.

O bright Apollo,
τίν' ἀνδρα, τίν' ἣρωα, τίνα θεὸν,
What god, man, or hero
Shall I place a tin wreath upon!

[1920]

MR NIXON

In the cream gilded cabin of his steam yacht
Mr Nixon advised me kindly, to advance with fewer
Dangers of delay. 'Consider
Carefully the reviewer.

I was as poor as you are;
When I began I got, of course,
Advance on royalties, fifty at first,' said Mr Nixon,
'Follow me, and take a column,
Even if you have to work free.

'Butter reviewers. From fifty to three hundred
I rose in eighteen months;
The hardest nut I had to crack
Was Dr Dundas.

'I never mentioned a man but with the view
Of selling my own works.
The tip's a good one, as for literature
It gives no man a sinecure.

'And no one knows, at sight, a masterpiece.
And give up verse, my boy,
There's nothing in it.'

. . .

Likewise a friend of Blougram's once advised me:
Don't kick against the pricks,
Accept opinion. The 'Nineties' tried your game
And died, there's nothing in it.

[1920]

CANTO I

And then went down to the ship,
Set keel to breakers, forth on the godly sea, and
We set up mast and sail on that swart ship,
Bore sheep aboard her, and our bodies also
Heavy with weeping, so winds from sternward
Bore us out onward with bellying canvas,
Circe's this craft, the trim-coifed goddess.
Then sat we amidships, wind jamming the tiller,
Thus with stretched sail, we went over sea till day's end.
Sun to his slumber, shadows o'er all the ocean,
Came we then to the bounds of deepest water,
To the Kimmerian lands, and peopled cities

Covered with close-webbed mist, unpiercèd ever
With glitter of sun-rays
Nor with stars stretched, nor looking back from heaven
Swartest night stretched over wretched men there.
The ocean flowing backward, came we then to the place
Aforesaid by Circe.
Here did they rites, Perimedes and Eurylochus,
And drawing sword from my hip
I dug the ell-square pitkin;
Poured we libations unto each the dead,
First mead and then sweet wine, water mixed with white flour.
Then prayed I many a prayer to the sickly death's-heads;
As set in Ithaca, sterile bulls of the best
For sacrifice, heaping the pyre with goods,
A sheep to Tiresias only, black and a bell-sheep.
Dark blood flowed in the fosse,
Souls out of Erebus, cadaverous dead, of brides,
Of youths and of the old who had borne much;
Souls stained with recent tears, girls tender,
Men many, mauled with bronze lance heads,
Battle spoil, bearing yet dreory arms,
These many crowded about me; with shouting,
Pallor upon me, cried to my men for more beasts;
Slaughtered the herds, sheep slain of bronze;
Poured ointment, cried to the gods,
To Pluto the strong, and praised Proserpine;
Unsheathed the narrow sword,
I sat to keep off the impetuous impotent dead,
Till I should hear Tiresias.
But first Elpenor came, our friend Elpenor,
Unburied, cast on the wide earth,
Limbs that we left in the house of Circe,
Unwept, unwrapped in sepulchre, since toils urged other.
Pitiful spirit. And I cried in hurried speech:
'Elpenor, how art thou come to this dark coast?
Cam'st thou afoot, outstripping seamen?'
And he in heavy speech:
'Ill fate and abundant wine. I slept in Circe's ingle.
Going down the long ladder unguarded,
I fell against the buttress,
Shattered the nape-nerve, the soul sought Avernus.

But thou, O King, I bid remember me, unwept, unburied,
Heap up mine arms, be tomb by sea-board, and inscribed:
"A man of no fortune and with a name to come."
And set my oar up, that I swung mid fellows.'

And Anticlea came, whom I beat off, and then Tiresias Theban,
Holding his golden wand, knew me, and spoke first:
'A second time? why? man of ill star,
Facing the sunless dead and this joyless region?
Stand from the fosse, leave me my bloody bever
For soothsay.'
                    And I stepped back,
And he strong with the blood, said then: 'Odysseus
Shalt return through spiteful Neptune, over dark seas,
Lose all companions.' And then Anticlea came.
Lie quiet Divus. I meant that is Andreas Divus,
In officina Wecheli, 1538, out of Homer.
And he sailed, by Sirens and thence outward and away
And unto Circe.
                    Venerandam,
In the Cretan's phrase, with the golden crown, Aphrodite,
Cypri munimenta sortita est, mirthful, oricalchi, with golden
Girdles and breast bands, thou with dark eyelids
Bearing the golden bough of Argicida. So that:

[1930]

CANTO XIII

Kung walked
                    by the dynastic temple
and into the cedar grove,
                    and then out by the lower river,
And with him Khieu Tchi
                    and Tian the low speaking
And 'we are unknown,' said Kung,
You will take up charioteering?
                    'Then you will become known,
Or perhaps I should take up charioteering, or archery?
Or the practice of public speaking?'
And Tseu-lou said, 'I would put the defences in order,'

And Khieu said, 'If I were lord of a province
I would put it in better order than this is.'
And Tchi said, 'I should prefer a small mountain temple,
With order in the observances,
            with a suitable performance of the ritual,'
And Tian said, with his hand on the strings of his lute
The low sounds continuing
            after his hand left the strings,
And the sound went up like smoke, under the leaves,
And he looked after the sound:
            'The old swimming hole,
And the boys flopping off the planks,
Or sitting in the underbrush playing mandolins.'
            And Kung smiled upon all of them equally.
And Thseng-sie desired to know:
            'Which had answered correctly?'
And Kung said, 'They have all answered correctly,
That is to say, each in his nature.'
And Kung raised his cane against Yuan Jang,
            Yuan Jang being his elder,
For Yuan Jang sat by the roadside pretending to
            be receiving wisdom.
And Kung said
            'You old fool, come out of it,
Get up and do something useful.'
            And Kung said
'Respect a child's faculties
From the moment it inhales the clear air,
But a man of fifty who knows nothing
            Is worthy of no respect.'
And 'When the prince has gathered about him
All the savants and artists, his riches will be fully employed.'
And Kung said, and wrote on the bo leaves:
            'If a man have not order within him
He cannot spread order about him;
And if a man have not order within him
His family will not act with due order;
            And if the prince have not order within him
He cannot put order in his dominions.'
And Kung gave the words 'order'
and 'brotherly deference'

And said nothing of the 'life after death'.
And he said
          'Anyone can run to excesses,
It is easy to shoot past the mark,
It is hard to stand firm in the middle.'

And they said: 'If a man commit murder
          Should his father protect him, and hide him?'
And Kung said:
          'He should hide him.'

And Kung gave his daughter to Kong-Tchang
          Although Kong-Tchang was in prison.
And he gave his niece to Nan-Young
          although Nan-Young was out of office.
And Kung said, 'Wang ruled with moderation,
          In his day the State was well kept,
And even I can remember
A day when the historians left blanks in their writings,
I mean for things they didn't know,
But that time seems to be passing.'
And Kung said, 'Without character you will
          be unable to play on that instrument
Or to execute the music fit for the Odes.
The blossoms of the apricot
          blow from the east to the west,
And I have tried to keep them from falling.'

[1930]

WILLIAM CARLOS WILLIAMS (1883-1963)

Williams was born in Rutherford, New Jersey, to an English father and a Puerto Rican mother of French and Basque parentage. Educated in New York and Paris, and at the University of Pennsylvania (where he met Ezra Pound in 1906), and in Leipzig (where he did postgraduate work in pediatrics), he practised medicine in Rutherford until a few years before his death. From the publication of *Poems* (1909), he went on to become one of the most prolific and influential American poets. His chief poetical works are *Collected Earlier Poems* (1951), *Collected Later Poems* (1950), *Journey to Love* (1955), the long poem *Paterson* (1946-58), and *Pictures from Breughel and Other Poems* (1962, Pulitzer Prize). His prose includes *In the American Grain* (1925), *The Autobiography of William Carlos Williams* (1951), *Make Light of It: Collected Stories* (1950), *Selected Essays* (1954), and *Yes, Mrs Williams* (1959). Also available is *The Selected Letters of William Carlos Williams* (1957).

Nurtured in the same soil of revolutionary Romanticism as Whitman and cummings, Williams began by rejecting the expatriate life and the preoccupation with tradition that characterized Pound and Eliot. In reaction to what he described as 'the order that cuts off the crab's feelers to make it fit into the box', he immersed himself in the American scene, in search of a distinctly American idiom and measure. In *Paterson*, an epic poem to be placed alongside *The Waste Land* and Hart Crane's *The Bridge*, he worked out his linguistic and stylistic theories and attempted the 'rediscovery of a primary impetus, the elemental principle of all art, in the local conditions'.

There can be little doubt about the extent to which Williams's ideas—his assertion of the importance of feeling and physical environment as shaping factors in a poet's work, and his rejection of poetic formalism—have influenced the directions of modern poetry. One has only to look at the work of Olson and Creeley and the poets of the Black Mountain group. But his early desire to write in a fashion that appeared 'anti-poetic' reveals a preoccupation with form that would persist throughout his life. He soon tired of free verse and the so-called objectivity of imagism, developing instead the 'variable foot', to be used in creating what he referred to as *versos sueltos*, or loose verses. 'The key to modern poetry is measure,' he finally admitted, 'which must reflect the flux of modern life. You should find a variable measure for the fixed measure; for man and the poet must keep pace with this world.' Williams's own triadic stanza and measured line enabled him during the last ten years of his life to produce some of his finest poems, those in *Pictures from Breughel*.

In *The Autobiography*, he argues that 'The poem, like every other form of art, is an object, an object that in itself formally presents its case and its meaning by the very form it assumes . . . . It must be the purpose of the poet to make of his words a new form: to invent, that is, an object consonant with his day.' While he was a careful craftsman, he had no use for the careerist mentality of so many of his contemporaries, who had lost touch with the real world of human suffering that confronted Williams daily as a doctor. In another section of *The Autobiography*, called 'The Practice', he recommends: 'Forget writing;

it's a trivial matter. . . . As far as writing itself is concerned, it takes next to no time at all. Much too much is written every day of our lives. We are overwhelmed by it. But when at times we see through the welter of evasive or interested patter, when by chance we penetrate to some moving detail of a life, there is always time to bang out a few pages. The thing isn't to find the time for it—we waste hours every day doing absolutely nothing at all—the difficulty is to catch the evasive life of the thing, to phrase the words in such a way that stereotype will yield a moment of insight. There is where the difficulty lies.'

The problem for the writer, according to Williams, is to tune out the trivial, the 'common news of the day' with its 'lying dialectics' and stereotypical nature, in favour of hidden streams of feeling, 'the hunted news I get from some obscure patient's eyes'. Then, if we listen, 'a new meaning begins to intervene. For under that language to which we have been listening all our lives a new, a more profound language underlying all the dialectics offers itself. It is what they call poetry. That is the final phase. . . . We begin to see that the underlying meaning of all they want to tell us and have always failed to communicate is the poem, the poem which their lives are being lived to realize.' The gift to hear and recognize and transmit those words longing for poetic form has little or nothing to do with conventional notions of poetry and reputation. 'You cannot recognize it from past appearances—in fact it is always a new face. It knows all that we are in the habit of describing. It will not use the same appearance for any new materialization. And it is our very life. It is we ourselves, at our rarest moments, but inarticulate for the most part except when in the poem one man, every five or six hundred years, escapes to formulate a few gifted sentences.'

AUX IMAGISTES

I think I have never been so exalted
As I am now by you,
O frost bitten blossoms,
That are unfolding your wings
From out the envious black branches.

Bloom quickly and make much of the sunshine
The twigs conspire against you!
Hear them!
They hold you from behind!

You shall not take wing
Except wing by wing, brokenly,
And yet—
Even they
Shall not endure for ever.

[1914]

DANSE RUSSE

If I when my wife is sleeping
and the baby and Kathleen
are sleeping
and the sun is a flame-white disc
in silken mists
above shining trees,—
if I in my north room
dance naked, grotesquely
before my mirror
waving my shirt round my head
and singing softly to myself:
'I am lonely, lonely.
I was born to be lonely,
I am best so!'
If I admire my arms, my face
my shoulders, flanks, buttocks
against the yellow drawn shades,—

Who shall say I am not
the happy genius of my household?

[1917]

THIS IS JUST TO SAY

I have eaten
the plums
that were in
the icebox

and which
you were probably
saving
for breakfast

Forgive me
they were delicious
so sweet
and so cold

[1934]

To Waken an Old Lady

Old age is
a flight of small
cheeping birds
skimming
bare trees
above a snow glaze.
Gaining and failing
they are buffetted
by a dark wind—

But what?
On harsh weedstalks
the flock has rested,
the snow
is covered with broken
seedhusks
and the wind tempered
by a shrill
piping of plenty.

[1921]

Tract

I will teach you my townspeople
how to perform a funeral—
for you have it over a troop
of artists—
unless one should scour the world—
you have the ground sense necessary.

See! the hearse leads.
I begin with a design for a hearse.
For Christ's sake not black—
nor white either—and not polished!
Let it be weathered—like a farm wagon—
with gilt wheels (this could be
applied fresh at small expense)
or no wheels at all:
a rough dray to drag over the ground.

Knock the glass out!
My God—glass, my townspeople!
For what purpose? Is it for the dead
to look out or for us to see
how well he is housed or to see
the flowers or the lack of them—
or what?
To keep the rain and snow from him?

He will have a heavier rain soon:
pebbles and dirt and what not.
Let there be no glass—
and no upholstery! phew!
and no little brass rollers
and small easy wheels on the bottom—
my townspeople what are you thinking of!
A rough plain hearse then
with gilt wheels and no top at all.
On this the coffin lies
by its own weight.

No wreaths please—
especially no hot-house flowers.
Some common memento is better,
something he prized and is known by:
his old clothes—a few books perhaps—
God knows what! You realize
how we are about these things,
my townspeople—
something will be found—anything—
even flowers if he had come to that.
So much for the hearse.

For heaven's sake though see to the driver!
Take off the silk hat! In fact
that's no place at all for him
up there unceremoniously
dragging our friend out to his own dignity!
Bring him down—bring him down!
Low and inconspicuous! I'd not have him ride
on the wagon at all—damn him—

the undertaker's understrapper!
Let him hold the reins
and walk at the side
and inconspicuously too!

Then briefly as to yourselves:
Walk behind—as they do in France,
seventh class, or if you ride
Hell take curtains! Go with some show
of inconvenience; sit openly—
to the weather as to grief.
Or do you think you can shut grief in?
What—from us? We who have perhaps
nothing to lose? Share with us
share with us—it will be money
in your pockets.
                                        Go now
I think you are ready.

[1917]

Spring and All

By the road to the contagious hospital
under the surge of the blue
mottled clouds driven from the
northeast—a cold wind. Beyond, the
waste of broad, muddy fields
brown with dried weeds, standing and fallen

patches of standing water
the scattering of tall trees

All along the road the reddish
purplish, forked, upstanding, twiggy
stuff of bushes and small trees
with dead, brown leaves under them
leafless vines—

Lifeless in appearance, sluggish
dazed spring approaches—

They enter the new world naked,
cold, uncertain of all
save that they enter. All about them
the cold, familiar wind—

Now the grass, tomorrow
the stiff curl of wildcarrot leaf
One by one objects are defined—
It quickens: clarity, outline of leaf

But now the stark dignity of
entrance—Still, the profound change
has come upon them: rooted, they
grip down and begin to awaken

[1923]

The Red Wheelbarrow

so much depends
upon

a red wheel
barrow

glazed with rain
water

beside the white
chickens.

[1923]

Nantucket

Flowers through the window
lavender and yellow

changed by white curtains—
Smell of cleanliness—

Sunshine of late afternoon—
On the glass tray

a glass pitcher, the tumbler
turned down, by which

a key is lying—And the
immaculate white bed

[1934]

THE YACHTS

contend in a sea which the land partly encloses
shielding them from the too heavy blows
of an ungoverned ocean which when it chooses

tortures the biggest hulls, the best man knows
to pit against its beatings, and sinks them pitilessly.
Mothlike in mists, scintillant in the minute

brilliance of cloudless days, with broad bellying sails
they glide to the wind tossing green water
from their sharp prows while over them the crew crawls

ant like, solicitously grooming them, releasing,
making fast as they turn, lean far over and having
caught the wind again, side by side, head for the mark.

In a well guarded arena of open water surrounded by
lesser and greater craft which, sycophant, lumbering
and flittering follow them, they appear youthful, rare

as the light of a happy eye, live with the grace
of all that in the mind is fleckless, free and
naturally to be desired. Now the sea which holds them

is moody, lapping their glossy sides, as if feeling
for some slightest flaw but fails completely.
Today no race. Then the wind comes again. The yachts

move, jockeying for a start, the signal is set and they
are off. Now the waves strike at them but they are too
well made, they slip through, though they take in canvas.

Arms with hands grasping seek to clutch at the prows.
Bodies thrown recklessly in the way are cut aside.
It is a sea of faces about them in agony, in despair

until the horror of the race dawns staggering the mind,
the whole sea become an entanglement of watery bodies
lost to the world bearing what they cannot hold. Broken,

beaten, desolate, reaching from the dead to be taken up
they cry out, failing, failing! their cries rising
in waves still as the skillful yachts pass over.

[1935]

THE DANCE

When the snow falls the flakes
spin upon the long axis
that concerns them most intimately
two and two to make a dance

the mind dances with itself,
taking you by the hand,
your lover follows
there are always two,

yourself and the other,
the point of your shoe setting the pace,
if you break away and run
the dance is over

Breathlessly you will take
another partner
better or worse who will keep
at your side, at your stops

whirls and glides until he too
leaves off
on his way down as if
there were another direction

gayer, more carefree
spinning face to face but always down
with each other secure
only in each other's arms

But only the dance is sure!
make it your own.
Who can tell
what is to come of it?

in the woods of your
own nature whatever
twig interposes, and bare twigs
have an actuality of their own

this flurry of the storm
that holds us,
plays with us and discards us
dancing, dancing as may be credible.

[1962]

THE REWAKING

Sooner or later
we must come to the end
of striving

to re-establish
the image the image of
the rose

but not yet
you say extending the
time indefinitely

by
your love until a whole
spring

rekindle
the violet to the very
lady's-slipper

and so by
your love the very sun
itself is revived

[1962]

TO A DOG INJURED IN THE STREET

It is myself,
        not the poor beast lying there
                yelping with pain
that brings me to myself with a start—
        as at the explosion
                of a bomb, a bomb that has laid
all the world waste.
        I can do nothing
                but sing about it
and so I am assuaged
        from my pain.

A drowsy numbness drowns my sense
        as if of hemlock
                I had drunk. I think
of the poetry
        of René Char
                and all he must have seen
and suffered
        that has brought him
                to speak only of
sedgy rivers,
        of daffodils and tulips
                whose roots they water,

even to the free-flowing river
that laves the rootlets
of those sweet-scented flowers
that people the
milky
way

I remember Norma
our English setter of my childhood
her silky ears
and expressive eyes.
She had a litter
of pups one night
in our pantry and I kicked
one of them
thinking, in my alarm,
that they
were biting her breasts
to destroy her.

I remember also
a dead rabbit
lying harmlessly
on the outspread palm
of a hunter's hand.
As I stood by
watching
he took a hunting knife
and with a laugh
thrust it
up into the animal's private parts.
I almost fainted.

Why should I think of that now?
The cries of a dying dog
are to be blotted out
as best I can.
René Char
you are a poet who believes

in the power of beauty
to right all wrongs.
I believe it also.
With invention and courage
we shall surpass
the pitiful dumb beasts,
let all men believe it,
as you have taught me also
to believe it.

[1954]

ROBERT FROST (1874-1963)

Robert Lee Frost was born in San Francisco to a Scottish mother and an outspoken father who championed the South and states' rights. This combination may explain the mixture of rebelliousness and restraint that was to characterize Frost's life and art. After his father's death, Frost and his mother moved to Lawrence, Massachusetts, where he worked as a bobbin-boy and reporter before marrying his childhood sweetheart, Elinor White. After two years at Harvard, Frost tried farming, which he hated, and teaching, for which he was temperamentally unsuited. In 1912 he went to England with his wife and four children, where he moved in literary circles and where his poetry first found recognition. With the success of *A Boy's Will* (1913) and *North of Boston* (1914), he returned to America, serving as poet-in-residence at Amherst College from 1916 to 1938. Frost spent his last years in New England, widely known and honoured as a poet and lecturer.

In 'The Figure a Poem Makes' Frost declared that a poem 'begins in delight and ends in wisdom'. Initially, few readers progressed in their appreciation beyond the deceptively simple surfaces of his poems. But Frost writes symbolic poetry; to arrive at certain basic truths about life, he explores feelings and thoughts *obliquely* through the use of simple bucolic incidents. Poems as immediately accessible as 'Stopping by Woods', 'Mending Wall', and 'Birches' possess levels of meaning that are dark and profound—like subtle literary parables. Although few of his early readers ever went beyond the delight to the wisdom of Frost's poetry, the notion that he was merely the singer of a benevolent nature is no longer accepted. He was a passionate and troubled man, who sought in his poems 'a momentary stay against confusion'; and his skilfully constructed poems testify to his mastery over that confusion. As he said in an interview with John Ciardi (*Saturday Review*, 21 March 1959), 'Each poem clarifies something. But then you've got to do it again. You can't get clarified to stay so: let you not think that. In a way, it's like nothing more than blowing smoke rings. Making little poems encourages a man to see that there is shapeliness in the world. A poem is an arrest of disorder.'

Frost's chief poetic means of attaining that 'momentary stay' was sound. While suspicious of analogies between poetry and music, he nonetheless felt that the 'vocal imagination' was of paramount importance: 'There are only three things, after all, that a poem must reach: the eye, the ear, and what we may call the heart, or the mind. It is the most important to reach the heart of the reader. And the surest way to reach the heart is through the ear. The visual images thrown up by a poem are important, but it is more important still to choose and arrange words in a sequence so as virtually to control the intonations and pauses of the reader's voice. By the arrangement and choice of words on the part of the poet, the effects of humor, pathos, hysteria, anger, and in fact, all effects, can be indicated or obtained' (quoted in Elaine Barry, *Robert Frost on Writing*, 1973).

While privileging sound in his work, Frost was not an advocate of sound-for-sound's-sake; he insisted on sound as the essential ingredient of grammatical utterance. As he said in a letter to Edward Garnett, 'There's something in the living sentence (in the shape of it) that is more imporant than any phrasing or chosen word.' His most elaborate statement about 'sentence sounds' appears in a letter to John T. Bartlett, 22 February 1914 (*Frost on Writing*). 'A sentence,' he insists, 'is a sound in itself on which other sounds called words may be strung. . . . The number of words you may string on one sentence-sound is not fixed but there is always danger of over loading.' He goes on to emphasize the role of the ear in reading, dismissing journalism and other writing meant to be skimmed by the eye as work that is pitched for oblivion. 'To judge a poem or piece of prose you go the same way to work—apply the one test—greatest test. You listen for the sentence sounds. If you find some of those not bookish, caught fresh from the mouths of people, some of them striking, all of them definite and recognizable, so recognizable that with a little trouble you can place them and even name them, you know you have found a writer.'

As the above remarks suggest, Frost cultivated a spoken, as opposed to a written, language, promoting use of the vernacular. He described style as 'that which indicates how the writer takes himself and what he is saying. . . . It is the mind skating circles around itself as it moves forward.' As this famous excerpt from a letter to Louis Untermeyer suggests, Frost rejected poetic exercises, or the writing of set-pieces: 'A poem is never a put-up job so to speak. It begins as a lump in the throat, a sense of wrong, a homesickness, a lovesickness. It is never a thought to begin with. It is at its best when it is a tantalizing vagueness.' He also placed less value on 'originality' and 'politics' than many modern poets do: 'If you want to play with the word revolution, every day and every new poem of a poet is a revolution of the spirit: that is to say it is a freshening. But it leads to nothing on the lower plane of politics. On the lower plane of thought and opinion the poet is a follower. Generally he keeps pretty well off that plane for that reason' (both quotations from *Frost on Writing*).

Most of Frost's poetry is available in *Collected Poems of Robert Frost* (1930, Pulitzer Prize; new edition, 1939), *Complete Poems of Robert Frost* (1949), and a more recent and comprehensive edition of his work, *Collected Poems of Robert Frost* (1983).

Mending Wall

Something there is that doesn't love a wall,
That sends the frozen-ground-swell under it,
And spills the upper boulders in the sun;
And makes gaps even two can pass abreast.
The work of hunters is another thing:
I have come after them and made repair
Where they have left not one stone on a stone,
But they would have the rabbit out of hiding,
To please the yelping dogs. The gaps I mean,
No one has seen them made or heard them made,
But at spring mending-time we find them there.
I let my neighbor know beyond the hill;
And on a day we meet to walk the line
And set the wall between us once again.
We keep the wall between us as we go.
To each the boulders that have fallen to each.
And some are loaves and some so nearly balls
We have to use a spell to make them balance:
'Stay where you are until our backs are turned!'
We wear our fingers rough with handling them.
Oh, just another kind of outdoor game,
One on a side. It comes to little more:
There where it is we do not need the wall:
He is all pine and I am apple orchard.
My apple trees will never get across
And eat the cones under his pines, I tell him.
He only says, 'Good fences make good neighbors.'
Spring is the mischief in me, and I wonder
If I could put a notion in his head:
'*Why* do they make good neighbors? Isn't it
Where there are cows? But here there are no cows.
Before I built a wall I'd ask to know
What I was walling in or walling out,
And to whom I was like to give offense.
Something there is that doesn't love a wall,
That wants it down.' I could say 'Elves' to him,
But it's not elves exactly, and I'd rather
He said it for himself. I see him there
Bringing a stone grasped firmly by the top

In each hand, like an old-stone savage armed.
He moves in darkness as it seems to me,
Not of woods only and the shade of trees.
He will not go behind his father's saying,
And he likes having thought of it so well
He says again, 'Good fences make good neighbors.'

[1914]

AFTER APPLE-PICKING

My long two-pointed ladder's sticking through a tree
Toward heaven still,
And there's a barrel that I didn't fill
Beside it, and there may be two or three
Apples I didn't pick upon some bough.
But I am done with apple-picking now.
Essence of winter sleep is on the night,
The scent of apples: I am drowsing off.
I cannot rub the strangeness from my sight
I got from looking through a pane of glass
I skimmed this morning from the drinking trough
And held against the world of hoary grass.
It melted, and I let it fall and break.
But I was well
Upon my way to sleep before it fell,
And I could tell
What form my dreaming was about to take.
Magnified apples appear and disappear,
Stem end and blossom end,
And every fleck of russet showing clear.
My instep arch not only keeps the ache,
It keeps the pressure of a ladder-round.
I feel the ladder sway as the boughs bend.
And I keep hearing from the cellar bin
The rumbling sound
Of load on load of apples coming in.
For I have had too much
Of apple-picking: I am overtired
Of the great harvest I myself desired.
There were ten thousand thousand fruit to touch,

Cherish in hand, lift down, and not let fall.
For all
That struck the earth,
No matter if not bruised or spiked with stubble,
Went surely to the cider-apple heap
As of no worth.
One can see what will trouble
This sleep of mine, whatever sleep it is.
Were he not gone,
The woodchuck could say whether it's like his
Long sleep, as I describe its coming on,
Or just some human sleep.

[1914]

Birches

When I see birches bend to left and right
Across the lines of straighter darker trees,
I like to think some boy's been swinging them.
But swinging doesn't bend them down to stay
As ice-storms do. Often you must have seen them
Loaded with ice a sunny winter morning
After a rain. They click upon themselves
As the breeze rises, and turn many-colored
As the stir cracks and crazes their enamel.
Soon the sun's warmth makes them shed crystal shells
Shattering and avalanching on the snow-crust—
Such heaps of broken glass to sweep away
You'd think the inner dome of heaven had fallen.
They are dragged to the withered bracken by the load,
And they seem not to break; though once they are bowed
So low for long, they never right themselves:
You may see their trunks arching in the woods
Years afterwards, trailing their leaves on the ground
Like girls on hands and knees that throw their hair
Before them over their heads to dry in the sun.
But I was going to say when Truth broke in

With all her matter-of-fact about the ice-storm
I should prefer to have some boy bend them
As he went out and in to fetch the cows—
Some boy too far from town to learn baseball,
Whose only play was what he found himself,
Summer or winter, and could play alone.
One by one he subdued his father's trees
By riding them down over and over again
Until he took the stiffness out of them,
And not one but hung limp, not one was left
For him to conquer. He learned all there was
To learn about not launching out too soon
And so not carrying the tree away
Clear to the ground. He always kept his poise
To the top branches, climbing carefully
With the same pains you use to fill a cup
Up to the brim, and even above the brim.
Then he flung outward, feet first, with a swish,
Kicking his way down through the air to the ground.
So was I once myself a swinger of birches.
And so I dream of going back to be.
It's when I'm weary of considerations,
And life is too much like a pathless wood
When your face burns and tickles with the cobwebs
Broken across it, and one eye is weeping
From a twig's having lashed across it open.
I'd like to get away from earth awhile
And then come back to it and begin over.
May no fate willfully misunderstand me
And half grant what I wish and snatch me away
Not to return. Earth's the right place for love:
I don't know where it's likely to go better.
I'd like to go by climbing a birch tree,
And climb black branches up a snow-white trunk
Toward heaven, till the tree could bear no more,
But dipped its top and set me down again.
That would be good both going and coming back.
One could do worse than be a swinger of birches.

[1916]

FIRE AND ICE

Some say the world will end in fire,
Some say in ice.
From what I've tasted of desire
I hold with those who favor fire.
But if it had to perish twice,
I think I know enough of hate
To say that for destruction ice
Is also great
And would suffice.

[1923]

STOPPING BY WOODS ON A SNOWY EVENING

Whose woods these are I think I know.
His house is in the village though;
He will not see me stopping here
To watch his woods fill up with snow.

My little horse must think it queer
To stop without a farmhouse near
Between the woods and frozen lake
The darkest evening of the year.

He gives his harness bells a shake
To ask if there is some mistake.
The only other sound's the sweep
Of easy wind and downy flake.

The woods are lovely, dark and deep,
But I have promises to keep,
And miles to go before I sleep,
And miles to go before I sleep.

[1923]

ACQUAINTED WITH THE NIGHT

I have been one acquainted with the night.
I have walked out in rain—and back in rain.
I have outwalked the furthest city light.

I have looked down the saddest city lane.
I have passed by the watchman on his beat
And dropped my eyes, unwilling to explain.

I have stood still and stopped the sound of feet
When far away an interrupted cry
Came over houses from another street,

But not to call me back or say good-bye;
And further still at an unearthly height,
One luminary clock against the sky

Proclaimed the time was neither wrong nor right.
I have been one acquainted with the night.

[1928]

DEPARTMENTAL

An ant on the tablecloth
Ran into a dormant moth
Of many times his size.
He showed not the least surprise.
His business wasn't with such.
He gave it scarcely a touch,
And was off on his duty run.
Yet if he encountered one
Of the hive's enquiry squad
Whose work is to find out God
And the nature of time and space,
He would put him onto the case.
Ants are a curious race;
One crossing with hurried tread
The body of one of their dead

Isn't given a moment's arrest—
Seems not even impressed.
But he no doubt reports to any
With whom he crosses antennae,
And they no doubt report
To the higher up at court.
Then word goes forth in Formic:
'Death's come to Jerry McCormic,
Our selfless forager Jerry.
Will the special Janizary
Whose office it is to bury
The dead of the commissary
Go bring him home to his people.
Lay him in state on a sepal.
Wrap him for shroud in a petal.
Embalm him with ichor of nettle.
This is the word of your Queen.'
And presently on the scene
Appears a solemn mortician;
And taking formal position
With feelers calmly atwiddle,
Seizes the dead by the middle,
And heaving him high in air,
Carries him out of there.
No one stands round to stare.
It is nobody else's affair.

It couldn't be called ungentle.
But how thoroughly departmental.

[1936]

DESERT PLACES

Snow falling and night falling fast, oh, fast
In a field I looked into going past,
And the ground almost covered smooth in snow,
But a few weeds and stubble showing last.

The woods around it have it—it is theirs.
All animals are smothered in their lairs.
I am too absent-sprited to count;
The loneliness includes me unawares.

And lonely as it is that loneliness
Will be more lonely ere it will be less—
A blanker whiteness of benighted snow
With no expression, nothing to express.

They cannot scare me with their empty spaces
Between stars—on stars where no human race is.
I have it in me so much nearer home
To scare myself with my own desert places.

[1936]

NEITHER OUT FAR NOR IN DEEP

The people along the sand
All turn and look one way.
They turn their back on the land.
They look at the sea all day.

As long as it takes to pass
A ship keeps raising its hull;
The wetter ground like glass
Reflects a standing gull.

The land may vary more;
But wherever the truth may be—
The water comes ashore,
And the people look at the sea.

They cannot look out far.
They cannot look in deep.
But when was that ever a bar
To any watch they keep?

[1936]

DESIGN

I found a dimpled spider, fat and white,
On a white heal-all, holding up a moth
Like a white piece of rigid satin cloth—
Assorted characters of death and blight
Mixed ready to begin the morning right,
Like the ingredients of a witches' broth—
A snow-drop spider, a flower like a froth,
And dead wings carried like a paper kite.

What had that flower to do with being white,
The wayside blue and innocent heal-all?
What brought the kindred spider to that height,
Then steered the white moth thither in the night?
What but design of darkness to appall?—
If design govern in a thing so small.

[1936]

PROVIDE, PROVIDE

The witch that came (the withered hag)
To wash the steps with pail and rag,
Was once the beauty Abishag,

The picture pride of Hollywood.
Too many fall from great and good
For you to doubt the likelihood.

Die early and avoid the fate.
Or if predestined to die late,
Make up your mind to die in state.

Make the whole stock exchange your own!
If need be occupy a throne,
Where nobody can call you crone.

Some have relied on what they knew;
Others on being simply true.
What worked for them might work for you.

No memory of having starred
Atones for later disregard,
Or keeps the end from being hard.

Better to go down dignified
With boughten friendship at your side
Than none at all. Provide, provide!

[1936]

One Step Backward Taken

Not only sands and gravels
Were once more on their travels,
But gulping muddy gallons
Great boulders off their balance
Bumped heads together dully
And started down the gully.
Whole capes caked off in slices.
I felt my standpoint shaken
In the universal crisis.
But with one step backward taken
I saved myself from going.
A world torn loose went by me.
Then the rain stopped and the blowing
And the sun came out to dry me.

[1947]

Directive

Back out of all this now too much for us,
Back in a time made simple by the loss
Of detail, burned, dissolved, and broken off
Like graveyard marble sculpture in the weather,
There is a house that is no more a house
Upon a farm that is no more a farm
And in a town that is no more a town.
The road there, if you'll let a guide direct you
Who only has at heart your getting lost,
May seem as if it should have been a quarry—

Great monolithic knees the former town
Long since gave up pretense of keeping covered.
And there's a story in a book about it:
Besides the wear of iron wagon wheels
The ledges show lines ruled southeast northwest,
The chisel work of an enormous Glacier
That braced his feet against the Arctic Pole.
You must not mind a certain coolness from him
Still said to haunt this side of Panther Mountain
Nor need you mind the serial ordeal
Of being watched from forty cellar holes
As if by eye pairs out of forty firkins.
As for the woods' excitement over you
That sends light rustle rushes to their leaves,
Charge that to upstart inexperience.
Where were they all not twenty years ago?
They think too much of having shaded out
A few old pecker-fretted apple trees.
Make yourself up a cheering song of how
Someone's road home from work this once was,
Who may be just ahead of you on foot
Or creaking with a buggy load of grain.
The height of the adventure is the height
Of country where two village cultures faded
Into each other. Both of them are lost.
And if you're lost enough to find yourself
By now, pull in your ladder road behind you
And put a sign up closed to all but me.
Then make yourself at home. The only field
Now left's no bigger than a harness gall.
First there's the children's house of make believe,
Some shattered dishes underneath a pine,
The playthings in the playhouse of the children.
Weep for what little things could make them glad.
Then for the house that is no more a house,
But only a belilaced cellar hole,
Now slowly closing like a dent in dough.
This was no playhouse but a house in earnest.
Your destination and your destiny's
A brook that was the water of the house,
Cold as a spring as yet so near its source,

Too lofty and original to rage.
(We know the valley streams that when aroused
Will leave their tatters hung on barb and thorn.)
I have kept hidden in the instep arch
Of an old cedar at the waterside
A broken drinking goblet like the Grail
Under a spell so the wrong ones can't find it,
So can't get saved, as Saint Mark says they mustn't.
(I stole the goblet from the children's playhouse.)
Here are your waters and your watering place.
Drink and be whole again beyond confusion.

[1947]

T.S. ELIOT (1888-1965)

Eliot was born in St Louis, Missouri. After completing his M.A. at Harvard, he studied philosophy, Sanskrit, and Pali at the Sorbonne, Harvard, and Merton College, Oxford. Before joining the publishing house of Faber & Faber in London, he taught briefly at Highgate School and worked in Lloyd's Bank, publishing his first volume of poetry, *Prufrock and Other Observations* in 1917, and editing *Criterion*, a quarterly review. Eliot became a British subject in 1927. He achieved distinction as a poet, dramatist, and critic and won the Nobel Prize for Literature in 1948.

Yeats once said of Eliot: 'He wrings the past dry and pours the juice down the throats of those who are either too busy, or too creative, to read as much as he does. I believe that in time he will be regarded as an interesting symptom of a sick and melancholy age.' Although Yeats's statement is limited in the extreme, it anticipates the reaction against Eliot's poetry that has begun to be felt in critical circles. We now feel less obliged, for example, to understand *all* of Eliot's French sources and esoteric references. In fact, many readers have come to regard *The Waste Land* (1922) less as a sacred text and more as an interesting literary collage. It remains true, however, that there are many levels on which Eliot's poetry may be appreciated. For the literati, there is his relation to tradition, his insistence that the poet exists not only in the present but also in 'the present moment of the past'. From this stems his deliberate quotation from, and allusion to, great literature and events of the past, his ironic juxtaposition of past and present—of Prufrock and John the Baptist, or Hamlet. For the less eclectic, there is the interest and challenge of Eliot's image-puzzles. In this respect it is perhaps useful to see him as a Tennyson strained through the filter of imagism: that is, he is essentially a narrative poet, but one who has (for reasons of economy and suggestiveness) removed most of the logical connectives from his narratives, leaving only the 'distillation' of his original conception. Keeping this in mind, readers who immerse themselves in the highly charged imagery of 'The Love Song of J. Alfred Prufrock' cannot fail to perceive the emotional state that it dramatizes.

Indeed, Eliot reveals something of the theory behind this method of writing in his essay 'Hamlet': 'The only way of expressing emotion in the form of art is by finding an "objective correlative"; in other words, a set of objects, a situation, a chain of events which shall be the formula of that *particular* emotion; such that when the external facts, which must terminate in sensory experience, are given, the emotion is immediately evoked.' This theory, as central to modern poetry as it was to imagism—which says, in short, *Show, don't tell*—not only privileged the image, or the visual dimension of poetry, but also served notice to discursiveness. However, as we have been reminded by Wayne Booth in *The Rhetoric of Fiction*, telling is itself a significant means of showing.

Eliot's verse has its own peculiar music—nursery rhymes, jazz rhythms, dissonance, prose rhythms. Most striking is the sense of the *speaking* voice that characterizes such poems as 'Journey of the Magi' and the cycle that constitutes *Four Quartets*. The strength of this speaking voice comes, in part, from Eliot's intellectual confidence, but also from his assured use of the persona and his sense of the dramatic play of feelings and ideas.

Eliot's vision and language have become part of the consciousness of this age. He has made a spiritual pilgrimage from alienation and solitude in *The Waste Land* and 'The Hollow Men' to liberation and community in *Ash Wednesday* (1930) and finally to the vision of God attained through self-knowledge in *Four Quartets* (1943). But it is the Eliot of 'Prufrock', who has measured out his life with coffee spoons, that still speaks to us most convincingly.

In his essay 'The Social Function of Poetry' (written in 1945, reprinted in *On Poetry and Poets*, 1961) Eliot argued that 'poetry is much more local than prose' and that 'no art is more stubbornly national than poetry.' Poetry, he says, is not the language of information—that is prose—but the language of feeling, and that is not easily translated. The poet's first responsibility is to preserve, extend, and improve the language, because 'in the long run, it makes a difference to the speech, to the sensibility, to the lives of all the members of a society, to all the members of the community, to the whole people, whether they read and enjoy poetry or not: even, in fact, whether they know the names of their greatest poets or not. . . . So if you follow the influence of poetry, through those readers who are most affected by it, to those people who never read at all, you will find it present everywhere. At least you will find it if the national culture is living and healthy, for in a healthy society there is a continuous reciprocal influence and interaction of each part on the others. And this is what I mean by the social function of poetry in its largest sense: that it does, in proportion to its excellence and vigour, affect the speech and the sensibility of the whole nation.'

Eliot's poetry is available in *Complete Poems and Plays* (1969). Of his plays, the most famous are *Murder in the Cathedral* (1935), *The Family Reunion* (1939), and *The Cocktail Party* (1950). His literary criticism includes *Selected Essays* (1932, 1951), *The Use of Poetry and the Use of Criticism* (1933), and *On Poetry and Poets* (1957).

The Love Song of J. Alfred Prufrock

S'io credesse che mia risposta fosse
A persona che mai tornasse al mondo,
Questa fiamma staria senza più scosse.
Ma perciocche giammai di questo fondo
Non tornò vivo alcun, s'i'odo il vero,
Senza tema d'infamia ti rispondo.

Let us go then, you and I,
When the evening is spread out against the sky
Like a patient etherised upon a table;
Let us go, through certain half-deserted streets,
The muttering retreats
Of restless nights in one-night cheap hotels
And sawdust restaurants with oyster-shells:
Streets that follow like a tedious argument
Of insidious intent
To lead you to an overwhelming question...
Oh, do not ask, 'What is it?'
Let us go and make our visit.

In the room the women come and go
Talking of Michelangelo.

The yellow fog that rubs its back upon the window-panes,
The yellow smoke that rubs its muzzle on the window-panes
Licked its tongue into the corners of the evening,
Lingered upon the pools that stand in drains,
Let fall upon its back the soot that falls from chimneys,
Slipped by the terrace, made a sudden leap,
And seeing that it was a soft October night,
Curled once about the house, and fell asleep.

And indeed there will be time
For the yellow smoke that slides along the street
Rubbing its back upon the window-panes;
There will be time, there will be time
To prepare a face to meet the faces that you meet;

There will be time to murder and create,
And time for all the works and days of hands
That lift and drop a question on your plate;
Time for you and time for me,
And time yet for a hundred indecisions,
And for a hundred visions and revisions,
Before the taking of a toast and tea.

In the room the women come and go
Talking of Michelangelo.

And indeed there will be time
To wonder, 'Do I dare?' and, 'Do I dare?'
Time to turn back and descend the stair,
With a bald spot in the middle of my hair—
[They will say: 'How his hair is growing thin!']
My morning coat, my collar mounting firmly to the chin,
My necktie rich and modest, but asserted by a simple pin—
[They will say: 'But how his arms and legs are thin!']
Do I dare
Disturb the universe?
In a minute there is time
For decisions and revisions which a minute will reverse.

For I have known them all already, known them all—
Have known the evenings, mornings, afternoons,
I have measured out my life with coffee spoons;
I know the voices dying with a dying fall
Beneath the music from a farther room.
    So how should I presume?

And I have known the eyes already, known them all—
The eyes that fix you in a formulated phrase,
And when I am formulated, sprawling on a pin,
When I am pinned and wriggling on the wall,
Then how should I begin
To spit out all the butt-ends of my days and ways?
    And how should I presume?

And I have known the arms already, known them all—
Arms that are braceleted and white and bare
[But in the lamplight, downed with light brown hair!]

Is it perfume from a dress
That makes me so digress?
Arms that lie along a table, or wrap about a shawl.
    And should I then presume?
    And how should I begin?
    . . .

Shall I say, I have gone at dusk through narrow streets
And watched the smoke that rises from the pipes
Of lonely men in shirt-sleeves, leaning out of windows?...

I should have been a pair of ragged claws
Scuttling across the floors of silent seas.
. . .

And the afternoon, the evening, sleeps so peacefully!
Smoothed by long fingers,
Asleep...tired...or it malingers,
Stretched on the floor, here beside you and me.
Should I, after tea and cakes and ices,
Have the strength to force the moment to its crisis?
But though I have wept and fasted, wept and prayed,
Though I have seen my head [grown slightly bald]
    brought in upon a platter
I am no prophet—and here's no great matter;
I have seen the moment of my greatness flicker,
And I have seen the eternal Footman hold my coat, and snicker,
And in short, I was afraid.

And would it have been worth it, after all,
After the cups, the marmalade, the tea,
Among the porcelain, among some talk of you and me,
Would it have been worth while,
To have bitten off the matter with a smile,
To have squeezed the universe into a ball
To roll it toward some overwhelming question,
To say: 'I am Lazarus, come from the dead,
Come back to tell you all, I shall tell you all'—
If one, settling a pillow by her head,
    Should say: 'That is not what I meant at all.
    That is not it, at all.'

And would it have been worth it, after all,
Would it have been worth while,
After the sunsets and the dooryards and the sprinkled streets,
After the novels, after the teacups, after the skirts that
    trail along the floor—
And this, and so much more?—
It is impossible to say just what I mean!
But as if a magic lantern threw the nerves in patterns on a screen:
Would it have been worth while
If one, settling a pillow or throwing off a shawl,
And turning toward the window, should say:
    'That is not it at all,
    That is not what I meant, at all.'
    . . .

No! I am not Prince Hamlet, nor was meant to be;
Am an attendant lord, one that will do
To swell a progress, start a scene or two,
Advise the prince; no doubt, an easy tool,
Deferential, glad to be of use,
Politic, cautious, and meticulous;
Full of high sentence, but a bit obtuse;
At times, indeed, almost ridiculous—
Almost, at times, the Fool.

I grow old...I grow old...
I shall wear the bottoms of my trousers rolled.
Shall I part my hair behind? Do I dare to eat a peach?
I shall wear white flannel trousers, and walk upon the beach.
I have heard the mermaids singing, each to each.

I do not think that they will sing to me.

I have seen them riding seaward on the waves
Combing the white hair of the waves blown back
When the wind blows the water white and black.

We have lingered in the chambers of the sea
By sea-girls wreathed with seaweed red and brown
Till human voices wake us, and we drown.

[1917]

Preludes

I

The winter evening settles down
With smell of steaks in passageways.
Six o'clock.
The burnt-out ends of smoky days.
And now a gusty shower wraps
The grimy scraps
Of withered leaves about your feet
And newspapers from vacant lots;
The showers beat
On broken blinds and chimney-pots,
And at the corner of the street
A lonely cab-horse steams and stamps.
And then the lighting of the lamps.

II

The morning comes to consciousness
Of faint stale smells of beer
From the sawdust-trampled street
With all its muddy feet that press
To early coffee-stands.
With the other masquerades
That time resumes,
One thinks of all the hands
That are raising dingy shades
In a thousand furnished rooms.

III

You tossed a blanket from the bed,
You lay upon your back, and waited;
You dozed, and watched the night revealing
The thousand sordid images
Of which your soul was constituted;
They flickered against the ceiling.
And when all the world came back
And the light crept up between the shutters
And you heard the sparrows in the gutters,
You had such a vision of the street

As the street hardly understands;
Sitting along the bed's edge, where
You curled the papers from your hair,
Or clasped the yellow soles of feet
In the palms of both soiled hands.

IV
His soul stretched tight across the skies
That fade behind a city block,
Or trampled by insistent feet
At four and five and six o'clock;
And short square fingers stuffing pipes,
And evening newspapers, and eyes
Assured of certain certainties,
The conscience of a blackened street
Impatient to assume the world.

I am moved by fancies that are curled
Around these images, and cling:
The notion of some infinitely gentle
Infinitely suffering thing.

Wipe your hand across your mouth, and laugh;
The worlds revolve like ancient women
Gathering fuel in vacant lots.

[1917]

THE HOLLOW MEN

Mistah Kurtz—he dead.

A penny for the Old Guy

I
We are the hollow men
We are the stuffed men
Leaning together
Headpiece filled with straw. Alas!
Our dried voices, when
We whisper together

Are quiet and meaningless
As wind in dry grass
Or rats' feet over broken glass
In our dry cellar

Shape without form, shade without colour,
Paralysed force, gesture without motion;

Those who have crossed
With direct eyes, to death's other Kingdom
Remember us—if at all—not as lost
Violent souls, but only
As the hollow men
The stuffed men.

II

Eyes I dare not meet in dreams
In death's dream kingdom
These do not appear:
There, the eyes are
Sunlight on a broken column
There, is a tree swinging
And voices are
In the wind's singing
More distant and more solemn
Than a fading star.

Let me be no nearer
In death's dream kingdom
Let me also wear
Such deliberate disguises
Rat's coat, crowskin, crossed staves
In a field
Behaving as the wind behaves
No nearer—

Not that final meeting
In the twilight kingdom

III

This is the dead land
This is the cactus land
Here the stone images
Are raised, here they receive
The supplication of a dead man's hand
Under the twinkle of a fading star.

Is it like this
In death's other kingdom
Waking alone
At the hour when we are
Trembling with tenderness
Lips that would kiss
Form prayers to broken stone.

IV

The eyes are not here
There are no eyes here
In this valley of dying stars
In this hollow valley
This broken jaw of our lost kingdoms

In this last of meeting places
We grope together
And avoid speech
Gathered on this beach of the tumid river

Sightless, unless
The eyes reappear
As the perpetual star
Multifoliate rose
Of death's twilight kingdom
The hope only
Of empty men.

V

Here we go round the prickly pear
Prickly pear prickly pear
Here we go round the prickly pear
At five o'clock in the morning.

Between the idea
And the reality
Between the motion
And the act
Falls the Shadow

For Thine is the Kingdom

Between the conception
And the creation
Between the emotion
And the response
Falls the Shadow

Life is very long

Between the desire
And the spasm
Between the potency
And the existence
Between the essence
And the descent
Falls the Shadow

For Thine is the Kingdom

For Thine is
Life is
For Thine is the

This is the way the world ends
This is the way the world ends
This is the way the world ends
Not with a bang but a whimper.

[1925]

JOURNEY OF THE MAGI

'A cold coming we had of it,
Just the worst time of the year
For a journey, and such a long journey:
The ways deep and the weather sharp,
The very dead of winter.'

And the camels galled, sore-footed, refractory,
Lying down in the melting snow.
There were times we regretted
The summer palaces on slopes, the terraces,
And the silken girls bringing sherbet.
Then the camel men cursing and grumbling
And running away, and wanting their liquor and women,
And the night-fires going out, and the lack of shelters,
And the cities hostile and the towns unfriendly
And the villages dirty and charging high prices:
A hard time we had of it.
At the end we preferred to travel all night,
Sleeping in snatches,
With the voices singing in our ears, saying
That this was all folly.

Then at dawn we came down to a temperate valley,
Wet, below the snow line, smelling of vegetation;
With a running stream and a water-mill beating the darkness,
And three trees on the low sky,
And an old white horse galloped away in the meadow.
Then we came to a tavern with vine-leaves over the lintel,
Six hands at an open door dicing for pieces of silver,
And feet kicking the empty wine-skins.
But there was no information, and so we continued
And arrived at evening, not a moment too soon
Finding the place; it was (you may say) satisfactory.

All this was a long time ago, I remember,
And I would do it again, but set down
This set down
This: were we led all that way for
Birth or Death? There was a Birth, certainly,
We had evidence and no doubt. I had seen birth and death,
But had thought they were different; this Birth was
Hard and bitter agony for us, like Death, our death.
We returned to our places, these Kingdoms,
But no longer at ease here, in the old dispensation,
With an alien people clutching their gods.
I should be glad of another death.

[1927]

Burnt Norton

τοῦ λόγου δ᾽ ἐόντος ξυνου ζώουσιν
οἱ πολλοὶ ὡς ἰδίαν ἔχοντες φρό–
νησιν.
I. p. 77. Fragment 2.
ὁδὸς ἄνω κάτω μία καὶ ὡυτή
I. p. 89. Fragment 60.
—Diels: *Die Fragmente der Vorsokratiker*
(Herakleitos).

I

Time present and time past
Are both perhaps present in time future,
And time future contained in time past.
If all time is eternally present
All time is unredeemable.
What might have been is an abstraction
Remaining a perpetual possibility
Only in a world of speculation.
What might have been and what has been
Point to one end, which is always present.
Footfalls echo in the memory
Down the passage which we did not take
Towards the door we never opened
Into the rose-garden. My words echo
Thus, in your mind.
But to what purpose
Disturbing the dust on a bowl of rose-leaves
I do not know.
Other echoes
Inhabit the garden. Shall we follow?
Quick, said the bird, find them, find them,
Round the corner. Through the first gate,
Into our first world, shall we follow
The deception of the thrush? Into our first world.
There they were, dignified, invisible,
Moving without pressure, over the dead leaves,
In the autumn heat, through the vibrant air,
And the bird called, in response to

The unheard music hidden in the shrubbery,
And the unseen eyebeam crossed, for the roses
Had the look of flowers that are looked at.
There they were as our guests, accepted and accepting.
So we moved, and they, in a formal pattern,
Along the empty alley, into the box circle,
To look down into the drained pool.
Dry the pool, dry concrete, brown edged,
And the pool was filled with water out of sunlight,
And the lotos rose, quietly, quietly,
The surface glittered out of heart of light,
And they were behind us, reflected in the pool.
Then a cloud passed, and the pool was empty.
Go, said the bird, for the leaves were full of children,
Hidden excitedly, containing laughter.
Go, go, go, said the bird: human kind
Cannot bear very much reality.
Time past and time future
What might have been and what has been
Point to one end, which is always present.

II

Garlic and sapphires in the mud
Clot the bedded axle-tree.
The trilling wire in the blood
Sings below inveterate scars
Appeasing long forgotten wars.
The dance along the artery
The circulation of the lymph
Are figured in the drift of stars
Ascend to summer in the tree
We move above the moving tree
In light upon the figured leaf
And hear upon the sodden floor
Below, the boarhound and the boar
Pursue their pattern as before
But reconciled among the stars.

At the still point of the turning world. Neither flesh nor fleshless;
Neither from nor towards; at the still point, there the dance is,
But neither arrest nor movement. And do not call it fixity,

Where past and future are gathered. Neither movement from nor towards,
Neither ascent nor decline. Except for the point, the still point,
There would be no dance, and there is only the dance.
I can only say, there we have been: but I cannot say where.
And I cannot say, how long, for that is to place it in time.

The inner freedom from the practical desire,
The release from action and suffering, release from the inner
And the outer compulsion, yet surrounded
By a grace of sense, a white light still and moving,
Erhebung without motion, concentration
Without elimination, both a new world
And the old made explicit, understood
In the completion of its partial ecstasy,
The resolution of its partial horror.
Yet the enchainment of past and future
Woven in the weakness of the changing body,
Protects mankind from heaven and damnation
Which flesh cannot endure.
                              Time past and time future
Allow but a little consciousness.
To be conscious is not to be in time
But only in time can the moment in the rose-garden,
The moment in the arbour where the rain beat,
The moment in the draughty church at smokefall
Be remembered; involved with past and future.
Only through time time is conquered.

III

Here is a place of disaffection
Time before and time after
In a dim light: neither daylight
Investing form with lucid stillness
Turning shadow into transient beauty
With slow rotation suggesting permanence
Nor darkness to purify the soul
Emptying the sensual with deprivation
Cleansing affection from the temporal.
Neither plenitude nor vacancy. Only a flicker
Over the strained time-ridden faces
Distracted from distraction by distraction

Filled with fancies and empty of meaning
Tumid apathy with no concentration
Men and bits of paper, whirled by the cold wind
That blows before and after time,
Wind in and out of unwholesome lungs
Time before and time after.
Eructation of unhealthy souls
Into the faded air, the torpid
Driven on the wind that sweeps the gloomy hills of London,
Hampstead and Clerkenwell, Campden and Putney,
Highgate, Primrose and Ludgate. Not here
Not here the darkness, in this twittering world.

Descend lower, descend only
Into the world of perpetual solitude,
World not world, but that which is not world,
Internal darkness, deprivation
And destitution of all property,
Desiccation of the world of sense,
Evacuation of the world of fancy,
Inoperancy of the world of spirit;
This is the one way, and the other
Is the same, not in movement
But abstention from movement; while the world moves
In appetency, on its metalled ways
Of time past and time future.

IV

Time and the bell have buried the day,
The black cloud carries the sun away.
Will the sunflower turn to us, will the clematis
Stray down, bend to us; tendril and spray
Clutch and cling?
Chill
Fingers of yew be curled
Down on us? After the kingfisher's wing
Has answered light to light, and is silent, the light is still
At the still point of the turning world.

V

Words move, music moves
Only in time; but that which is only living
Can only die. Words, after speech, reach
Into the silence. Only by the form, the pattern,
Can words or music reach
The stillness, as a Chinese jar still
Moves perpetually in its stillness.
Not the stillness of the violin, while the note lasts,
Not that only, but the co-existence,
Or say that the end precedes the beginning,
And the end and the beginning were always there
Before the beginning and after the end.
And all is always now. Words strain,
Crack and sometimes break, under the burden,
Under the tension, slip, slide, perish,
Decay with imprecision, will not stay in place,
Will not stay still. Shrieking voices
Scolding, mocking, or merely chattering,
Always assail them. The Word in the desert
Is most attacked by voices of temptation,
The crying shadow in the funeral dance,
The loud lament of the disconsolate chimera.

The detail of the pattern is movement,
As in the figure of the ten stairs.
    Desire itself is movement
    Not in itself desirable;
Love is itself unmoving,
Only the cause and end of movement,
Timeless, and undesiring
Except in the aspect of time
Caught in the form of limitation
Between un-being and being.
Sudden in a shaft of sunlight
Even while the dust moves
There rises the hidden laughter
Of children in the foliage
Quick now, here, now, always—
Ridiculous the waste sad time
Stretching before and after.

[1936]

WILFRED OWEN (1893-1918)

Owen was born in Shropshire and educated at Birkenhead and the University of London. From 1913 to 1915 he worked as tutor for a French family near Bordeaux. He seems to have been particularly sensitive to the suffering around him and to the contradictions he perceived between accepted values and corrupt social practice. On 4 January 1913, he recorded his loss of faith in conventional religion: 'I have murdered my false creed. If a true one exists, I shall find it. If not, adieu to the still false creeds that hold the hearts of nearly all my fellow men' (*The Collected Poems of Wilfred Owen*, 1963). On 28 August 1914, just after the outbreak of war, he expressed his dismay in a letter home about the terrible waste of human life: 'I feel my own life all the more precious and more dear in the presence of this deflowering of Europe. While it is true that the guns will effect a useful weeding, I am furious with chagrin to think that the Minds, which were to have excelled the civilization of two thousand years, are being annihilated—and bodies, the product of aeons of Natural Selection, melted down to pay for political statues' (quoted in *Collected Poems*, 1963).

After two years in the British army Owen would no longer be able to write naïvely of 'useful weeding' or use a trite phrase such as 'deflowering' to describe the horrors he saw. In a letter home on 4 February 1917, he would write of 'the universal perversion of Ugliness. Hideous landscapes, vile noises, foul language . . . everything unnatural, broken, blasted; the distortion of the dead, whose unburiable bodies sit outside the dug-outs all day, the most execrable sights on earth. In poetry we call them the most glorious' (*Collected Poems*, 1963). The reference to poetry here is instructive, for the war made a poet of Owen. Although he was interested in writing before the war, it was his contact at the front with the poet Siegfried Sassoon that gave Owen the greatest impetus to make poetry his voice and comfort. He was killed at the Sambre Canal just seven days before the Armistice in 1918.

Owen's poetry addresses one of the fundamental issues of twentieth-century life: the madness and inhumanity of war. His descriptions of the mutilation of body and mind are shocking and immediate, even in an age accustomed to a steady diet of violence and obsessed with the atrocities of war. That he should have experienced war from the trenches rather than the administrative offices makes all the more remarkable his capacity to respond to it with such profound pity and restraining irony.

'The poetry's in the Pity,' Owen wrote in the draft of a preface he was preparing (it was quoted years later in *Poems*, 1949). His works first came to the attention of the public with the 1933 edition, but it influenced several generations of poets writing about war, including W.H. Auden, Earle Birney, and Randall Jarrell, whose 'The Death of the Ball Turret Gunner' was to become a classic of the Second World War: 'From my mother's sleep I fell into the State, / And I hunched in its belly till my wet fur froze. / Six miles from earth, loosed from its dream of life, / I woke to black flak and the nightmare fighters. / When I died they washed me out of the turret with a hose.'

However, the lasting quality of Owen's poetry lies not so much in its content as in its verbal mastery, particularly the naturalness of his idiom and his attention to sound, or prosody. While the war imagery and narrative elements give his work a rugged, startling beauty, Owen's poems make their principal claim at the level of verbal music. His experiments with assonance, internal half-rhymes and other kinds of layered and interlocking sound patterns are the work of an original and skilled technician. The restraint and control evident in what are essentially prologues to dying result in a poignancy and tension that are unavoidably passionate.

Owen's collected poems were first published in 1920 with an introduction by Siegfried Sassoon. A second edition, edited by the poet Edmund Blunden, including a number of previously unpublished pieces and notices of his life and work, was published in 1931. A third edition, published in 1963, was edited with an introduction by the poet C. Day Lewis.

STRANGE MEETING

It seemed that out of battle I escaped
Down some profound dull tunnel, long since scooped
Through granites which titanic wars had groined.
Yet also there encumbered sleepers groaned,
Too fast in thought or death to be bestirred.
Then, as I probed them, one sprang up, and stared
With piteous recognition in fixed eyes,
Lifting distressful hands as if to bless.
And by his smile, I knew that sullen hall,
By his dead smile I knew we stood in Hell.
With a thousand pains that vision's face was grained;
Yet no blood reached there from the upper ground,
And no guns thumped, or down the flues made moan.
'Strange friend,' I said, 'here is no cause to mourn.'
'None,' said the other, 'save the undone years,
The hopelessness. Whatever hope is yours,
Was my life also; I went hunting wild
After the wildest beauty in the world,
Which lies not calm in eyes, or braided hair,
But mocks the steady running of the hour,
And if it grieves, grieves richlier than here.
For of my glee might many men have laughed,
And of my weeping something had been left,
Which must die now. I mean the truth untold,
The pity of war, the pity war distilled.
Now men will go content with what we spoiled,
Or, discontent, boil bloody, and be spilled.
They will be swift with swiftness of the tigress.

None will break ranks, though nations trek from progress.
Courage was mine, and I had mystery,
Wisdom was mine, and I had mastery:
To miss the march of this retreating world
Into vain citadels that are not walled.
Then, when much blood had clogged their chariot-wheels,
I would go up and wash them from sweet wells,
Even with truths that lie too deep for taint.
I would have poured my spirit without stint
But not through wounds; not on the cess of war.
Foreheads of men have bled where no wounds were.
I am the enemy you killed, my friend.
I knew you in this dark: for so you frowned
Yesterday through me as you jabbed and killed.
I parried; but my hands were loath and cold.
Let us sleep now. . . .

[1920]

Greater Love

Red lips are not so red
As the stained stones kissed by the English dead.
Kindness of wooed and wooer
Seems shame to their love pure.
O Love, your eyes lose lure
When I behold eyes blinded in my stead!

Your slender attitude
Trembles not exquisite like limbs knife-skewed,
Rolling and rolling there
Where God seems not to care;
Till the fierce love they bear
Cramps them in death's extreme decrepitude.

Your voice sings not so soft,—
Though even as wind murmuring through raftered loft,—
Your dear voice is not dear,
Gentle, and evening clear,
As theirs whom none now hear,
Now earth has stopped their piteous mouths that coughed.

Heart, you were never hot
    Nor large, nor full like hearts made great with shot;
And though your hand be pale,
Paler are all which trail
Your cross through flame and hail:
    Weep, you may weep, for you may touch them not.

[1920]

ARMS AND THE BOY

Let the boy try along this bayonet-blade
How cold steel is, and keen with hunger of blood;
Blue with all malice, like a madman's flash;
And thinly drawn with famishing for flesh.

Lend him to stroke these blind, blunt bullet-heads
Which long to nuzzle in the hearts of lads,
Or give him cartridges of fine zinc teeth,
Sharp with the sharpness of grief and death.

For his teeth seem for laughing round an apple.
There lurk no claws behind his fingers supple;
And God will grow no talons at his heels,
Nor antlers through the thickness of his curls.

[1920]

ANTHEM FOR DOOMED YOUTH

What passing-bells for these who die as cattle?
    Only the monstrous anger of the guns.
    Only the stuttering rifles' rapid rattle
Can patter out their hasty orisons.
No mockeries now for them; no prayers nor bells,
    Nor any voice of mourning save the choirs,—
The shrill, demented choirs of wailing shells;
    And bugles calling for them from sad shires.

What candles may be held to speed them all?
Not in the hands of boys, but in their eyes
Shall shine the holy glimmers of good-byes.
The pallor of girls' brows shall be their pall;
Their flowers the tenderness of patient minds,
And each slow dusk a drawing-down of blinds.

[1920]

Dulce Et Decorum Est

Bent double, like old beggars under sacks,
Knock-kneed, coughing like hags, we cursed through sludge,
Till on the haunting flares we turned our backs
And towards our distant rest began to trudge.
Men marched asleep. Many had lost their boots
But limped on, blood-shod. All went lame; all blind;
Drunk with fatigue; deaf even to the hoots
Of tired, outstripped Five-Nines that dropped behind.

Gas! Gas! Quick, boys!—An ecstasy of fumbling,
Fitting the clumsy helmets just in time;
But someone still was yelling out and stumbling
And flound'ring like a man in fire or lime...
Dim, through the misty panes and thick green light,
As under a green sea, I saw him drowning.

In all my dreams, before my helpless sight,
He plunges at me, guttering, choking, drowning.

If in some smothering dreams you too could pace
Behind the wagon that we flung him in,
And watch the white eyes writhing in his face,
His hanging face, like a devil's sick of sin;
If you could hear, at every jolt, the blood
Come gargling from the froth-corrupted lungs,
Obscene as cancer, bitter as the cud
Of vile, incurable sores on innocent tongues,—
My friend, you would not tell with such high zest
To children ardent for some desperate glory,
The old Lie: Dulce et decorum est
Pro patria mori.

[1920]

e.e. cummings (1894-1962)

cummings wrote many kinds of poetry: the delicate, almost sentimental lyricism in 'somewhere i have never travelled gladly beyond'; the engaging puns and humour in 'may i feel'; and the savage criticism of cant and hypocrisy in 'i sing of Olaf.' His poetic experiments—dispensing with punctuation, distorting typography, using lower-case type, ignoring the rules of grammar and syntax—are an important aspect of his fight against established ideas and systems that threaten the spontaneity and joy cummings valued most in his life. His painter's preoccupation with the visual dimensions of poetry and his curiosity about the letter and the syllable as units of meaning look forward to the work of the concrete poets and have been a liberating force in modern poetry. His humour and his unabashed celebration of the simple pleasures of the body and emotions of the heart are antidotes to the cynicism and despair so evident in the work of his contemporaries.

'The poems to come are for you and for me and are not for mostpeople,' he wrote in 'An Introduction' to *Poems 1932-1954*. 'Life,for eternal us,is now;and now is much too busy being a little more than everything to seem anything,catastrophic included. Life,for mostpeople, simply isn't. . . . Miracles are to come. With you I leave a remembrance of miracles: they are by somebody who can love and who shall be continually reborn,a human being;somebody who said to those near him,when his fingers would not hold a brush "tie it into my hand"—.' As this linguistic play, including the jammed prose with no spaces after punctuation, makes clear, cummings does not let up on his 'Only how measureless cool flames of making,' but pushes readers continually into new territory where growth is inevitable and where they may discover 'Always the beautiful answer who asks a more beautiful question.'

James Dickey's famous review of cummings's *95 Poems* (in *Babel to Byzantium*, 1968) is worth considering here, if only to put the work in some sort of perspective. While he rejected most of cummings's typographical gymnastics, word-fracturing, and 'unwords', Dickey nonetheless had high praise for those moments of lyric grace for which cummings will be most remembered: 'Let me make my own position clear right away. I think that Cummings is a daringly original poet, with more virility and more sheer, uncompromising talent than any other living American writer. I cannot and would not want to deny, either, that he dilutes even the finest of his work with writing that is hardly more than the defiant playing of a child, though the fact that he does this with the superb arrogance of genius has always seemed to me among the most attractive of his qualities. I love Cummings's verse, even a great deal of it that is not lovable or even respectable, but it is also true that I am frequently and thoroughly bored by its continuous attitudinizing and its dogmatic preaching.'

cummings was born in Cambridge, Massachusetts, and educated at Harvard before joining an ambulance corps in France during the First World War. His imprisonment in a detention camp for three months, due to the error of a military censor, is recorded in his novel *The Enormous Room* (1922). After studying art in Paris, cummings lived with his wife, the photographer and fashion model Marion

Morehouse, in Greenwich Village and at Silver Lake, New Hampshire, where he wrote poetry and painted. He delivered the Charles Eliot Norton Lectures at Harvard in 1952-53 and received the Bollingen Prize for Poetry in 1957.

In addition to the poetry available in *Poems, 1923-1954* (1954), *95 Poems* (1958), *100 Selected Poems* (1959), and *Complete Poems* (1972), cummings wrote a play, *him* (1927), and a book about his travels in Russia, *Eimi* (1933).

CHANSONS INNOCENTES

I

in Just-
spring   when the world is mud-
luscious the little
lame balloonman

whistles   far   and wee

and eddieandbill come
running from marbles and
piracies and it's
spring

when the world is puddle-wonderful

the queer
old balloonman whistles
far   and   wee
and bettyandisbel come dancing

from hop-scotch and jump-rope and
it's
spring
and
    the
        goat-footed

balloonMan   whistles
far
and
wee

II
hist   whist
little ghostthings
tip-toe
twinkle-toe

little twitchy
witches and tingling
goblins
hob-a-nob   hob-a-nob

little hoppy happy
toad in tweeds
tweeds
little itchy mousies

with scuttling
eyes   rustle and run   and
hidehidehide
whisk

whisk   look out for the old woman
with the wart on her nose
what she'll do to yer
nobody knows

for she knows the devil   ooch
the devil   ouch
the devil
ach   the great
green
dancing
devil
devil

devil
devil
    wheeEEE

III
Tumbling-hair
                    picker of buttercups
                                        violets
dandelions
And the big bullying daisies
                                        through the field wonderful
with eyes a little sorry
Another comes
                    also picking flowers

[1922]

my sweet old etcetera

my sweet old etcetera
aunt lucy during the recent

war could and what
is more did tell you just
what everybody was fighting

for,
my sister
isabel created hundreds
(and
hundreds) of socks not to
mention shirts fleaproof earwarmers
etcetera wristers etcetera, my
mother hoped that

i would die etcetera
bravely of course my father used
to become hoarse talking about how it was
a privilege and if only he
could meanwhile my
self etcetera lay quietly
in the deep mud et

cetera
(dreaming,
et
        cetera, of
Your smile
eyes knees and of your Etcetera)

[1926]

i sing of Olaf

i sing of Olaf glad and big
whose warmest heart recoiled at war:
a conscientious object-or

his wellbelovéd colonel (trig
westpointer most succinctly bred)
took erring Olaf soon in hand;
but—though an host of overjoyed
noncoms (first knocking on the head
him) do through icy waters roll
that helplessness which others stroke
with brushes recently employed
anent this muddy toiletbowl,
while kindred intellects evoke
allegiance per blunt instruments—
Olaf (being to all intents
a corpse and wanting any rag
upon what God unto him gave)
responds, without getting annoyed
'I will not kiss your f.ing flag'

straightway the silver bird looked grave
(departing hurriedly to shave)
but—though all kinds of officers
(a yearning nation's blueeyed pride)
their passive prey did kick and curse
until for wear their clarion
voices and boots were much the worse,
and egged the firstclassprivates on
his rectum wickedly to tease

by means of skilfully applied
bayonets roasted hot with heat—
Olaf (upon what were once knees)
does almost ceaselessly repeat
'there is some s. I will not eat'

our president,being of which
assertions duly notified
threw the yellowsonofabitch
into a dungeon,where he died

Christ(of His mercy infinite)
i pray to see;and Olaf,too

preponderatingly because
unless statistics lie he was
more brave than me:more blond than you.

[1931]

somewhere i have never travelled,gladly beyond

somewhere i have never travelled,gladly beyond
any experience,your eyes have their silence:
in your most frail gesture are things which enclose me,
or which i cannot touch because they are too near

your slightest look easily will unclose me
though i have closed myself as fingers,
you open always petal by petal myself as Spring opens
(touching skilfully, mysteriously)her first rose

or if your wish be to close me,i and
my life will shut very beautifully,suddenly,
as when the heart of this flower imagines
the snow carefully everywhere descending;

nothing which we are to perceive in this world equals
the power of your intense fragility:whose texture
compels me with the colour of its countries,
rendering death and forever with each breathing

(i do not know what it is about you that closes
and opens;only something in me understands
the voice of your eyes is deeper than all roses)
nobody,not even the rain,has such small hands

[1931]

anyone lived in a pretty how town

anyone lived in a pretty how town
(with up so floating many bells down)
spring summer autumn winter
he sang his didn't he danced his did.

Women and men(both little and small)
cared for anyone not at all
they sowed their isn't they reaped their same
sun moon stars rain

children guessed(but only a few
and down they forgot as up they grew
autumn winter spring summer)
that noone loved him more by more

when by now and tree by leaf
she laughed his joy she cried his grief
bird by snow and stir by still
anyone's any was all to her

someones married their everyones
laughed their cryings and did their dance
(sleep wake hope and then)they
said their nevers they slept their dream

stars rain sun moon
(and only the snow can begin to explain
how children are apt to forget to remember
with up so floating many bells down)

one day anyone died i guess
(and noone stooped to kiss his face)
busy folk buried them side by side
little by little and was by was

all by all and deep by deep
and more by more they dream their sleep
noone and anyone earth by april
wish by spirit and if by yes.

Women and men(both dong and ding)
summer autumn winter spring
reaped their sowing and went their came
sun moon stars rain

[1940]

my father moved through dooms of love

my father moved through dooms of love
through sames of am through haves of give,
singing each morning out of each night
my father moved through depths of height

this motionless forgetful where
turned at his glance to shining here;
that if(so timid air is firm)
under his eyes would stir and squirm

newly as from unburied which
floats the first who,his april touch
drove sleeping selves to swarm their fates
woke dreamers to their ghostly roots

and should some why completely weep
my father's fingers brought her sleep:
vainly no smallest voice might cry
for he could feel the mountains grow.

Lifting the valleys of the sea
my father moved through griefs of joy;
praising a forehead called the moon
singing desire into begin

joy was his song and joy so pure
a heart of star by him could steer
and pure so now and now so yes
the wrists of twilight would rejoice

keen as midsummer's keen beyond
conceiving mind of sun will stand,
so strictly(over utmost him
so hugely)stood my father's dream

his flesh was flesh his blood was blood:
no hungry man but wished him food;
no cripple wouldn't creep one mile
uphill to only see him smile.

Scorning the pomp of must and shall
my father moved through dooms of feel;
his anger was as right as rain
his pity was as green as grain

septembering arms of year extend
less humbly wealth to foe and friend
than he to foolish and to wise
offered immeasurable is

proudly and(by octobering flame
beckoned)as earth will downward climb,
so naked for immortal work
his shoulders marched against the dark

his sorrow was as true as bread:
no liar looked him in the head;
if every friend became his foe
he'd laugh and build a world with snow.

My father moved through theys of we,
singing each new leaf out of each tree
(and every child was sure that spring
danced when she heard my father sing)

then let men kill which cannot share,
let blood and flesh be mud and mire,
scheming imagine,passion willed,
freedom a drug that's bought and sold

giving to steal and cruel kind,
a heart to fear,to doubt a mind,
to differ a disease of same,
conform the pinnacle of am

though dull were all we taste as bright,
bitter all utterly things sweet,
maggoty minus and dumb death
all we inherit,all bequeath

and nothing quite so least as truth
—i say though hate were why men breathe—
because my father lived his soul
love is the whole and more than all

[1940]

love is more thicker than forget

love is more thicker than forget
more thinner than recall
more seldom than a wave is wet
more frequent than to fail

it is most mad and moonly
and less it shall unbe
than all the sea which only
is deeper than the sea

love is less always than to win
less never than alive
less bigger than the least begin
less littler than forgive

it is most sane and sunly
and more it cannot die
than all the sky which only
is higher than the sky

[1940]

dying is fine)but Death

dying is fine)but Death

?o
baby
i

wouldn't like

Death if Death
were
good:for

when(instead of stopping to think)you

begin to feel of it,dying

's miraculous
why?be

cause dying is

perfectly natural;perfectly
putting
it mildly lively(but

Death

is strictly
scientific
& artificial &

evil & legal)

we thank thee
god
almighty for dying

(forgive us,o life!the sin of Death

[1950]

i thank You God for most this amazing

i thank You God for most this amazing
day:for the leaping greenly spirits of trees
and a blue true dream of sky;and for everything
which is natural which is infinite which is yes

(i who have died am alive again today,
and this is the sun's birthday;this is the birth
day of life and of love and wings:and of the gay
great happening illimitably earth)

how should tasting touching hearing seeing
breathing any—lifted from the no
of all nothing—human merely being
doubt unimaginable You?

(now the ears of my ears awake and
now the eyes of my eyes are opened)

[1950]

WALLACE STEVENS (1879-1955)

Stevens was born in Reading, Pennsylvania. Educated at Harvard and the New York Law School, he was admitted to the bar in 1904. After practising in New York City, he joined the legal department of the Hartford Accident and Indemnity Company in 1916 and became vice-president in 1934. In the years between the publication of his first volume, *Harmonium* (1923, reissued 1931), and his death in 1955, he published *Ideas of Order* (1935), *Owl's Clover* (1936), *The Man With the Blue Guitar* (1937), *Parts of a World* (1942), *Notes Toward a Supreme Fiction* (1942), *Esthétique du Mal* (1944), *Transport to Summer* (1947), and *The Auroras of Autumn* (1950). His *Selected Poems* first appeared in England in 1953. Two further publications are *Collected Poems* (1954) and the prose work *The Necessary Angel: Essays on Reality and the Imagination* (1951). *Opus Posthumous*, a collection of plays, essays, some poems, and epigrams, was published in 1957.

Stevens is a philosophical poet. His poems are primarily analytical rather than descriptive, pressing towards discovery, towards a more profound apprehension of reality. As he explains in 'A Collect of Philosophy' (*Opus Posthumous*): 'Theoretically, the poetry of thought should be the supreme poetry. . . . A poem in which the poet has chosen for his subject a philosophic theme should result in the poem of poems. That the wing of poetry should also be the rushing wing of meaning seems to be an extreme aesthetic good; and so in time and perhaps, in other politics, it may come to be.' Stevens shares with Coleridge a conviction that imagination is the 'sum of all our faculties' and an interest in defining that particular intersection of imagination and reality that is the poetic process. His poems have their base in reality, the familiar world of feelings and objects and events, but they move towards the unreal, the unfamiliar: 'one may find intimations of immortality in an object on the mantelpiece; and these intimations are as real in the mind in which they occur as the mantelpiece itself.' He writes, as he explains, about 'a particular of life thought of for so long that one's thoughts have become an inseparable part of it or a particular of life so intensely felt that the feeling has entered into it.'

In 'The Noble Rider and the Sound of Words' (*The Necessary Angel*), Stevens describes poetry as 'the supreme use of language' and insists that 'what makes the poet the potent figure that he is, or was, or ought to be, is that he creates the world to which we turn incessantly and without knowing it and that he gives to life the supreme fictions without which we are unable to conceive of it.' Poetry serves as a bastion against what Stevens calls the 'pressure of reality', the quotidian world of advertising, consumerism, belief systems or ideologies, vested sexual, emotional, or political interests; imagination, using language non-referentially, identifies and extracts the nobility in things, in events, in people, gives us distance and perspective. This nobility, he says, is 'a violence from within that protects us from a violence without. It is the imagination pressing back against the pressure of reality. It seems, in the last analysis, to have something to do with our self-preservation; and that, no doubt, is why the expression of it, the sound of its words, helps us live our lives.'

In the same essay, Stevens expresses admiration for Croce's view of language as perpetual creation and claims that poetry is our chief means of 'escaping' into a deeper and richer realm of experience. 'A poet's words are of things that do not exist without the words. Thus, the image of the charioteer and of the winged horses, which has been held to be precious for all of time that matters, was created by words of things that never existed without the words. . . . Poetry is a revelation in words by means of the words.'

Ultimately it is not the naturalistic subject-matter in his poems that interests the reader, but the language-centred sensibility that perceives and defines it. Stevens writes with wit and elegance. His meditative poems have the depth and insight one associates with the paintings of the Dutch masters, a close acquaintance with light and shadow, intense concentration on detail, and a profund compassion for human life in all its forms. 'One of the consequences of the ordination of style,' he insists, 'is not to limit it, but to enlarge it, not to impoverish it, but to enrich and liberate it.' Considering the beauty and control of such poems as 'Sunday Morning' and 'The Idea of Order at Key West', it is difficult not to agree with Stevens that, if liberty is attainable in life and art, it will not be far removed from the 'idea of order'.

The Emperor of Ice-Cream

Call the roller of big cigars,
The muscular one, and bid him whip
In kitchen cups concupiscent curds.
Let the wenches dawdle in such dress
As they are used to wear, and let the boys
Bring flowers in last month's newspapers.
Let be be finale of seem.
The only emperor is the emperor of ice-cream.

Take from the dresser of deal,
Lacking the three glass knobs, that sheet
On which she embroidered fantails once
And spread it so as to cover her face.
If her horny feet protrude, they come
To show how cold she is, and dumb.
Let the lamp affix its beam.
The only emperor is the emperor of ice-cream.

[1923]

Sunday Morning

I
Complacencies of the peignoir, and late
Coffee and oranges in a sunny chair,
And the green freedom of a cockatoo

Upon a rug mingle to dissipate
The holy hush of ancient sacrifice.
She dreams a little, and she feels the dark
Encroachment of that old catastrophe,
As a calm darkens among water-lights.
The pungent oranges and bright, green wings
Seem things in some procession of the dead,
Winding across wide water, without sound.
The day is like wide water, without sound,
Stilled for the passing of her dreaming feet
Over the seas, to silent Palestine,
Dominion of the blood and sepulchre.

II

Why should she give her bounty to the dead?
What is divinity if it can come
Only in silent shadows and in dreams?
Shall she not find in comforts of the sun,
In pungent fruit and bright, green wings, or else
In any balm or beauty of the earth,
Things to be cherished like the thought of heaven?
Divinity must live within herself:
Passions of rain, or moods in falling snow;
Grievings in loneliness, or unsubdued
Elations when the forest blooms; gusty
Emotions on wet roads on autumn nights;
All pleasures and all pains, remembering
The bough of summer and the winter branch.
These are the measures destined for her soul.

III

Jove in the clouds had his inhuman birth.
No mother suckled him, no sweet land gave
Large-mannered motions to his mythy mind.
He moved among us, as a muttering king,
Magnificent, would move among his hinds,
Until our blood, commingling, virginal,
With heaven, brought such requital to desire
The very hinds discerned it, in a star.
Shall our blood fail? Or shall it come to be
The blood of paradise? And shall the earth

Seem all of paradise that we shall know?
The sky will be much friendlier then than now,
A part of labor and a part of pain,
And next in glory to enduring love,
Not this dividing and indifferent blue.

IV
She says, 'I am content when wakened birds,
Before they fly, test the reality
Of misty fields, by their sweet questionings;
But when the birds are gone, and their warm fields
Return no more, where, then, is paradise?'
There is not any haunt of prophecy,
Nor any old chimera of the grave,
Neither the golden underground, nor isle
Melodious, where spirits gat them home,
Nor visionary south, nor cloudy palm
Remote on heaven's hill, that has endured
As April's green endures; or will endure
Like her remembrance of awakened birds,
Or her desire for June and evening, tipped
By the consummation of the swallow's wings.

V
She says, 'But in contentment I still feel
The need of some imperishable bliss.'
Death is the mother of beauty; hence from her,
Alone, shall come fulfilment to our dreams
And our desires. Although she strews the leaves
Of sure obliteration on our paths,
The path sick sorrow took, the many paths
Where triumph rang its brassy phrase, or love
Whispered a little out of tenderness,
She makes the willow shiver in the sun
For maidens who were wont to sit and gaze
Upon the grass, relinquished to their feet.
She causes boys to pile new plums and pears
On disregarded plate. The maidens taste
And stray impassioned in the littering leaves.

VI
Is there no change of death in paradise?
Does ripe fruit never fall? Or do the boughs
Hang always heavy in that perfect sky,
Unchanging, yet so like our perishing earth,
With rivers like our own that seek for seas
They never find, the same receding shores
That never touch with inarticulate pang?
Why set the pear upon those river-banks
Or spice the shores with odors of the plum?
Alas, that they should wear our colors there,
The silken weavings of our afternoons,
And pick the strings of our insipid lutes!
Death is the mother of beauty, mystical,
Within whose burning bosom we devise
Our earthly mothers waiting, sleeplessly.

VII
Supple and turbulent, a ring of men
Shall chant in orgy on a summer morn
Their boisterous devotion to the sun,
Not as a god, but as a god might be,
Naked among them, like a savage source.
Their chant shall be a chant of paradise,
Out of their blood, returning to the sky;
And in their chant shall enter, voice by voice,
The windy lake wherein their lord delights,
The trees, like serafin, and echoing hills,
That choir among themselves long afterward.
They shall know well the heavenly fellowship
Of men that perish and of summer morn.
And whence they came and whither they shall go
The dew upon their feet shall manifest.

VIII
She hears, upon that water without sound,
A voice that cries, 'The tomb in Palestine
Is not the porch of spirits lingering.
It is the grave of Jesus, where he lay.'

We live in an old chaos of the sun,
Or old dependency of day and night,
Or island solitude, unsponsored, free,
Of that wide water, inescapable.
Deer walk upon our mountains, and the quail
Whistle about us their spontaneous cries;
Sweet berries ripen in the wilderness;
And, in the isolation of the sky,
At evening, casual flocks of pigeons make
Ambiguous undulations as they sink,
Downward to darkness, on extended wings.

[1923]

THE IDEA OF ORDER AT KEY WEST

She sang beyond the genius of the sea.
The water never formed to mind or voice,
Like a body wholly body, fluttering
Its empty sleeves; and yet its mimic motion
Made constant cry, caused constantly a cry,
That was not ours although we understood,
Inhuman, of the veritable ocean.

The sea was not a mask. No more was she.
The song and water were not medleyed sound
Even if what she sang was what she heard,
Since what she sang was uttered word by word.
It may be that in all her phrases stirred
The grinding water and the gasping wind;
But it was she and not the sea we heard.

For she was the maker of the song she sang.
The ever-hooded, tragic-gestured sea
Was merely a place by which she walked to sing.
Whose spirit is this? we said, because we knew
It was the spirit that we sought and knew
That we should ask this often as she sang.

If it was only the dark voice of the sea
That rose, or even colored by many waves;
If it was only the outer voice of sky
And cloud, of the sunken coral water-walled,
However clear, it would have been deep air,
The heaving speech of air, a summer sound
Repeated in a summer without end
And sound alone. But it was more than that,
More even than her voice, and ours, among
The meaningless plungings of water and the wind,
Theatrical distances, bronze shadows heaped
On high horizons, mountainous atmospheres
Of sky and sea.
It was her voice that made
The sky acutest at its vanishing.
She measured to the hour its solitude.
She was the single artificer of the world
In which she sang. And when she sang, the sea,
Whatever self it had, became the self
That was her song, for she was the maker. Then we,
As we beheld her striding there alone,
Knew that there never was a world for her
Except the one she sang and, singing, made.

Ramon Fernandez, tell me, if you know,
Why, when the singing ended and we turned
Toward the town, tell why the glassy lights,
The lights in the fishing boats at anchor there,
As the night descended, tilting in the air,
Mastered the night and portioned out the sea,
Fixing emblazoned zones and fiery poles,
Arranging, deepening, enchanting night.

Oh! Blessed rage for order, pale Ramon,
The maker's rage to order words of the sea,
Words of the fragrant portals, dimly-starred,
And of ourselves and of our origins,
In ghostlier demarcations, keener sounds.

[1936]

THE MAN ON THE DUMP

Day creeps down. The moon is creeping up.
The sun is a corbeil of flowers the moon Blanche
Places there, a bouquet. Ho-ho...The dump is full
Of images. Days pass like papers from a press.
The bouquets come here in the papers. So the sun,
And so the moon, both come, and the janitor's poems
Of every day, the wrapper on the can of pears,
The cat in the paper-bag, the corset, the box
From Esthonia: the tiger chest, for tea.

The freshness of night has been fresh a long time.
The freshness of morning, the blowing of day, one says
That it puffs as Cornelius Nepos reads, it puffs
More than, less than or it puffs like this or that.
The green smacks in the eye, the dew in the green
Smacks like fresh water in a can, like the sea
On a cocoanut—how many men have copied dew
For buttons, how many women have covered themselves
With dew, dew dresses, stones and chains of dew, heads
Of the floweriest flowers dewed with the dewiest dew.
One grows to hate these things except on the dump.

Now, in the time of spring (azaleas, trilliums,
Myrtle, viburnums, daffodils, blue phlox),
Between that disgust and this, between the things
That are on the dump (azaleas and so on)
And those that will be (azaleas and so on),
One feels the purifying change. One rejects
The trash.
That's the moment when the moon creeps up
To the bubbling of bassoons. That's the time
One looks at the elephant-colorings of tires.
Everything is shed; and the moon comes up as the moon
(All its images are in the dump) and you see
As a man (not like an image of a man),
You see the moon rise in the empty sky.

One sits and beats an old tin can, lard pail.
One beats and beats for that which one believes.
That's what one wants to get near. Could it after all
Be merely oneself, as superior as the ear
To a crow's voice? Did the nightingale torture the ear,
Pack the heart and scratch the mind? And does the ear
Solace itself in peevish birds? Is it peace,
Is it a philosopher's honeymoon, one finds
On the dump? Is it to sit among mattresses of the dead,
Bottles, pots, shoes and grass and murmur *aptest eve*:
Is it to hear the blatter of grackles and say
Invisible priest; is it to eject, to pull
The day to pieces and cry *stanza my stone*?
Where was it one first heard of the truth? The the.

[1942]

THE MOTIVE FOR METAPHOR

You like it under the trees in autumn,
Because everything is half dead.
The wind moves like a cripple among the leaves
And repeats words without meaning.

In the same way, you were happy in spring,
With the half colors of quarter-things,
The slightly brighter sky, the melting clouds,
The single bird, the obscure moon—

The obscure moon lighting an obscure world
Of things that would never be quite expressed,
Where you yourself were never quite yourself
And did not want nor have to be,

Desiring the exhilarations of changes:
The motive for metaphor, shrinking from
The weight of primary noon,
The A B C of being,

The ruddy temper, the hammer
Of red and blue, the hard sound—
Steel against intimation—the sharp flash,
The vital, arrogant, fatal, dominant X.

[1947]

CREDENCES OF SUMMER

I

Now in midsummer come and all fools slaughtered
And spring's infuriations over and a long way
To the first autumnal inhalations, young broods
Are in the grass, the roses are heavy with a weight
Of fragrance and the mind lays by its trouble.

Now the mind lays by its trouble and considers.
The fidgets of remembrance come to this.
This is the last day of a certain year
Beyond which there is nothing left of time.
It comes to this and the imagination's life.

There is nothing more inscribed nor thought nor felt
And this must comfort the heart's core against
Its false disasters—these fathers standing round,
These mothers touching, speaking, being near,
These lovers waiting in the soft dry grass.

II

Postpone the anatomy of summer, as
The physical pine, the metaphysical pine.
Let's see the very thing and nothing else.
Let's see it with the hottest fire of sight.
Burn everything not part of it to ash.

Trace the gold sun about the whitened sky
Without evasion by a single metaphor.
Look at it in its essential barrenness
And say this, this is the centre that I seek.
Fix it in an eternal foliage

And fill the foliage with arrested peace,
Joy of such permanence, right ignorance
Of change still possible. Exile desire
For what it is not. This is the barrenness
Of the fertile thing that can attain no more.

III

It is the natural tower of all the world,
The point of survey, green's green apogee,
But a tower more precious than the view beyond,
A point of survey squatting like a throne,
Axis of everything, green's apogee

And happiest folk-land, mostly marriage-hymns.
It is the mountain on which the tower stands,
It is the final mountain. Here the sun,
Sleepless, inhales his proper air, and rests.
This is the refuge that the end creates.

It is the old man standing on the tower,
Who reads no book. His ruddy ancientness
Absorbs the ruddy summer and is appeased,
By an understanding that fulfils his age,
By a feeling capable of nothing more.

IV

One of the limits of reality
Presents itself in Oley when the hay,
Baked through long days, is piled in mows. It is
A land too ripe for enigmas, too serene.
There the distant fails the clairvoyant eye

And the secondary senses of the ear
Swarm, not with secondary sounds, but choirs,
Not evocations but last choirs, last sounds
With nothing else compounded, carried full,
Pure rhetoric of a language without words.

Things stop in that direction and since they stop
The direction stops and we accept what is
As good. The utmost must be good and is
And is our fortune and honey hived in the trees
And mingling of colors at a festival.

V

One day enriches a year. One woman makes
The rest look down. One man becomes a race,
Lofty like him, like him perpetual.
Or do the other days enrich the one?
And is the queen humble as she seems to be,

The charitable majesty of her whole kin?
The bristling soldier, weather-foxed, who looms
In the sunshine is a filial form and one
Of the land's children, easily born, its flesh,
Not fustian. The more than casual blue

Contains the year and other years and hymns
And people, without souvenir. The day
Enriches the year, not as embellishment.
Stripped of remembrance, it displays its strength—
The youth, the vital son, the heroic power.

VI

The rock cannot be broken. It is the truth.
It rises from land and sea and covers them.
It is a mountain half way green and then,
The other immeasurable half, such rock
As placid air becomes. But it is not

A hermit's truth nor symbol in hermitage.
It is the visible rock, the audible,
The brilliant mercy of a sure repose,
On this present ground, the vividest repose,
Things certain sustaining us in certainty.

It is the rock of summer, the extreme,
A mountain luminous half way in bloom
And then half way in the extremest light
Of sapphires flashing from the central sky,
As if twelve princes sat before a king.

VII

Far in the woods they sang their unreal songs,
Secure. It was difficult to sing in face
Of the object. The singers had to avert themselves
Or else avert the object. Deep in the woods
They sang of summer in the common fields.

They sang desiring an object that was near,
In face of which desire no longer moved,
Nor made of itself that which it could not find . . .
Three times the concentred self takes hold, three times
The thrice contented self, having possessed

The object, grips it in savage scrutiny,
Once to make captive, once to subjugate
Or yield to subjugation, once to proclaim
The meaning of the capture, this hard prize,
Fully made, fully apparent, fully found.

VIII

The trumpet of morning blows in the clouds and through
The sky. It is the visible announced,
It is the more than visible, the more
Than sharp, illustrious scene. The trumpet cries
This is the successor of the invisible.

This is its substitute in stratagems
Of the spirit. This, in sight and memory,
Must take its place, as what is possible
Replaces what is not. The resounding cry
Is like ten thousand tumblers tumbling down

To share the day. The trumpet supposes that
A mind exists, aware of division, aware
Of its cry as clarion, its diction's way
As that of a personage in a multitude:
Man's mind grown venerable in the unreal.

IX

Fly low, cock bright, and stop on a bean pole. Let
Your brown breast redden, while you wait for warmth.
With one eye watch the willow, motionless.
The gardener's cat is dead, the gardener gone
And last year's garden grows salacious weeds.

A complex of emotions falls apart,
In an abandoned spot. Soft, civil bird,
The decay that you regard: of the arranged
And of the spirit of the arranged, *douceurs*,
Tristesses, the fund of life and death, suave bush

And polished beast, this complex falls apart.
And on your bean pole, it may be, you detect
Another complex of other emotions, not
So soft, so civil, and you make a sound,
Which is not part of the listener's own sense.

X

The personae of summer play the characters
Of an inhuman author, who meditates
With the gold bugs, in blue meadows, late at night.
He does not hear his characters talk. He sees
Them mottled, in the moodiest costumes,

Of blue and yellow, sky and sun, belted
And knotted, sashed and seamed, half pales of red,
Half pales of green, appropriate habit for
The huge decorum, the manner of the time,
Part of the mottled mood of summer's whole,

In which the characters speak because they want
to speak, the fat, the roseate characters,
Free, for a moment, from malice and sudden cry,
Complete in a completed scene, speaking
Their parts as in a youthful happiness.

[1947]

THE POEM THAT TOOK THE PLACE OF A MOUNTAIN

There it was, word for word,
The poem that took the place of a mountain.

He breathed its oxygen,
Even when the book lay turned in the dust of his table.

It reminded him how he had needed
A place to go to in his own direction,

How he had recomposed the pines,
Shifted the rocks and picked his way among clouds,

For the outlook that would be right,
Where he would be complete in an unexplained completion:

The exact rock where his inexactnesses
Would discover, at last, the view toward which they had edged,

Where he could lie and, gazing down at the sea,
Recognize his unique and solitary home.

[1954]

W.H. AUDEN (1907-1973)

Auden led an extremely restless and productive life. Born in York, England, and educated at Oxford, he married Erika Mann (daughter of Thomas Mann) in 1936 to enable her to leave Nazi Germany, participated in the Spanish Civil War as an ambulance driver for the Loyalists in 1937, and travelled to China with Christopher Isherwood in 1938. The following year he moved to the United States, becoming a citizen in 1946, and thereafter divided his time between New York and Austria. He was elected professor of poetry at Oxford in 1956.

Associated in the 1930s with the Oxford poets C. Day Lewis, Stephen Spender, and Louis MacNiece, who turned to communism in reaction to the economic depression and the rise of fascism, Auden eventually moved from Marxism through Freudian psychoanalysis and existentialism to Anglo-Catholicism. The pressures of economic and political commitment dominated his early poetry, giving it a public rather than a private character. In this period Auden was primarily a topical poet, like Dryden, most at ease with a 'subject' upon which he could turn his unfailing eye for significant detail and his wonderful control of language. 'Musée des Beaux Arts', for example, is a masterpiece of understatement in which, through the ironic tension between stark images and a painfully matter-of-fact tone, Auden captures the tragic sense of indifference to human suffering and aspiration that informs Breughel's 'The Fall of Icarus'.

Like the confessional poetry of Robert Lowell, Auden's later verse is personal and relaxed; it is also refreshingly meditative and conversational. His analysis of the human condition may not be deep, but his evocation of the surfaces and moods of the political and intellectual life of his times is unquestionably brilliant. He wrote many provocative aphorisms on poetry as both game and knowledge, ranging from the whimsical observation in 'Writing' (*The Dyer's Hand*, 1962) that 'No poet wishes he were the only one who ever lived, but most of them wish they were the only one alive, and quite a number fondly believe their wish has been granted' to this more serious discrimination: 'A poet is, before anything else, a person who is passionately in love with language. Whether this love is a sign of his poetic gift or the gift itself—for falling in love is given not chosen—I don't know, but it is certainly the sign by which one recognizes whether a young man is potentially a poet or not. "Why do you want to write poetry?" If the young man answers: "I have important things I want to say," then he is not a poet. If he answers: "I like hanging around words listening to what they say," then maybe he is going to be a poet.'

Poetically, Auden was just as restless and experimental, exploring everything from Anglo-Saxon verse forms and ballad rhythms to epigrams and blues. In 'Writing', he insisted that 'Rhymes, metres, stanza forms, etc., are like servants. If the master is fair enough to win their affection and firm enough to command their respect, the result is an orderly, happy household. If he is too tyrannical, they give notice; if he lacks authority, they become slovenly, impertinent, drunk, and dishonest.' In the same essay, he makes a wonderfully ironic comment about free verse: 'The poet who writes "free" verse is like Robinson Crusoe on his desert island: he must do all his cooking, laundry, and darning for himself. In a few exceptional cases, this manly independence produces something original and impressive, but more often the result is squalor—dirty sheets on the unmade bed and empty bottles on the unswept floor.'

Auden is famous for his shifting views on the relation of poetry to politics, from his assertion in his elegy 'In Memory of W.B. Yeats' that 'Poetry makes nothing happen' to the argument in 'The Poet and the City' (*The Dyer's Hand*) that 'the mere making of a work of art is itself a political act.' He offers yet another slant on this question in 'Writing': 'Owing to its superior power as a mnemonic, verse is superior to prose as a medium for didactic instruction. . . . On the other hand, verse is unsuited to controversy, to proving some truth or belief which is not universally accepted, because its formal nature cannot but convey a certain skepticism about its conclusions.'

Auden refused to romanticize the poetic process: 'Poetry is not magic. Insofar as poetry, or any other of the arts, can be said to have an ulterior purpose, it is, by telling the truth, to disenchant and disintoxicate' ('Writing'). But he was well aware of its powers to move and persuade: 'Whatever its actual content and overt interest, every poem is rooted in imaginative awe. Poetry can do a hundred and one things, delight, sadden, disturb, amuse, instruct—it may express every possible shade of emotion, and describe every conceivable kind of event, but there is only one thing that all poetry must do; it must praise all it can for being as for happening.'

Auden published many volumes of poetry, including *Poems* (1930), *The Double Man* (1941), *For the Time Being, a Christmas Oratorio* (1945), *The Age of Anxiety: A Baroque Eclogue* (1948, Pulitzer Prize), *Nones* (1951), *The Shield of Achilles* (1955), and *Homage to Clio* (1960). His collections include *Collected Shorter Poems* (1967), *Collected Longer Poems* (1969), and *Collected Poems* (1976), as well as *The English Auden* (1977), which also includes several of his plays. Two important collections of his critical work are *The Enchafèd Flood: The Romantic Iconography of the Sea*, three critical essays on the romantic spirit published in 1950, and *The Dyer's Hand*, a volume of essays that appeared in 1962.

As I Walked Out One Evening

As I walked out one evening,
    Walking down Bristol Street,
The crowds upon the pavement
    Were fields of harvest wheat.

And down by the brimming river
    I heard a lover sing
Under an arch of the railway:
    'Love has no ending.

'I'll love you, dear, I'll love you
    Till China and Africa meet,
And the river jumps over the mountain
    And the salmon sing in the street,

'I'll love you till the ocean
  Is folded and hung up to dry
And the seven stars go squawking
  Like geese about the sky.

'The years shall run like rabbits,
  For in my arms I hold
The Flower of the Ages,
  And the first love of the world.'

But all the clocks in the city
  Began to whirr and chime:
'O let not Time deceive you,
  You cannot conquer Time.

'In the burrows of the Nightmare
  Where Justice naked is,
Time watches from the shadow
  And coughs when you would kiss.

'In headaches and in worry
  Vaguely life leaks away,
And Time will have his fancy
  To-morrow or to-day.

'Into many a green valley
  Drifts the appalling snow;
Time breaks the threaded dances
  And the diver's brilliant bow.

'O plunge your hands in water,
  Plunge them in up to the wrist;
Stare, stare in the basin
  And wonder what you've missed.

'The glacier knocks in the cupboard,
  The desert sighs in the bed,
And the crack in the tea-cup opens
  A lane to the land of the dead.

'Where the beggars raffle the banknotes
    And the Giant is enchanting to Jack,
And the Lily-white Boy is a Roarer,
    And Jill goes down on her back.

'O look, look in the mirror,
    O look in your distress;
Life remains a blessing
    Although you cannot bless.

'O stand, stand at the window
    As the tears scald and start;
You shall love your crooked neighbour
    With your crooked heart.'

It was late, late in the evening,
    The lovers they were gone;
The clocks had ceased their chiming,
    And the deep river ran on.

[1940]

LULLABY

Lay your sleeping head, my love,
Human on my faithless arm;
Time and fevers burn away
Individual beauty from
Thoughtful children, and the grave
Proves the child ephemeral:
But in my arms till break of day
Let the living creature lie,
Mortal, guilty, but to me
The entirely beautiful.

Soul and body have no bounds:
To lovers as they lie upon
Her tolerant enchanted slope
In their ordinary swoon,
Grave the vision Venus sends
Of supernatural sympathy,

Universal love and hope;
While an abstract insight wakes
Among the glaciers and the rocks
The hermit's carnal ecstasy.

Certainty, fidelity
On the stroke of midnight pass
Like vibrations of a bell
And fashionable madmen raise
Their pedantic boring cry:
Every farthing of the cost,
All the dreaded cards foretell,
Shall be paid, but from this night
Not a whisper, not a thought,
Not a kiss nor look be lost.

Beauty, midnight, vision dies:
Let the winds of dawn that blow
Softly round your dreaming head
Such a day of welcome show
Eye and knocking heart may bless,
Find our mortal world enough;
Noons of dryness find you fed
By the involuntary powers,
Nights of insult let you pass
Watched by every human love.

[1940]

Musée des Beaux Arts

About suffering they were never wrong,
The Old Masters: how well they understood
Its human position; how it takes place
While someone else is eating or opening a window or just walking
    dully along;
How, when the aged are reverently, passionately waiting
For the miraculous birth, there always must be
Children who did not specially want it to happen, skating
On a pond at the edge of the wood:

They never forgot
That even the dreadful martyrdom must run its course
Anyhow in a corner, some untidy spot
Where the dogs go on with their doggy life and the torturer's horse
Scratches its innocent behind on a tree.

In Brueghel's *Icarus*, for instance: how everything turns away
Quite leisurely from the disaster; the ploughman may
Have heard the splash, the forsaken cry,
But for him it was not an important failure; the sun shone
As it had to on the white legs disappearing into the green
Water; and the expensive delicate ship that must have seen
Something amazing, a boy falling out of the sky,
Had somewhere to get to and sailed calmly on.

[1940]

IN MEMORY OF W.B. YEATS

(d. Jan. 1939)

I

He disappeared in the dead of winter:
The brooks were frozen, the airports almost deserted,
And snow disfigured the public statues;
The mercury sank in the mouth of the dying day.
What instruments we have agree
The day of his death was a dark cold day.

Far from his illness
The wolves ran on through the evergreen forests,
The peasant river was untempted by the fashionable quays;
By mourning tongues
The death of the poet was kept from his poems.

But for him it was his last afternoon as himself,
An afternoon of nurses and rumours;
The provinces of his body revolted,
The squares of his mind were empty,
Silence invaded the suburbs,
The current of his feeling failed; he became his admirers.

Now he is scattered among a hundred cities
And wholly given over to unfamiliar affections,
To find his happiness in another kind of wood
And be punished under a foreign code of conscience.
The words of a dead man
Are modified in the guts of the living.

But in the importance and noise of to-morrow
When the brokers are roaring like beasts on the floor of the Bourse,
And the poor have the sufferings to which they are fairly accustomed,
And each in the cell of himself is almost convinced of his freedom,
A few thousand will think of this day
As one thinks of a day when one did something slightly unusual.
What instruments we have agree
The day of his death was a dark cold day.

II

You were silly like us; your gift survived it all:
The parish of rich women, physical decay,
Yourself. Mad Ireland hurt you into poetry.
Now Ireland has her madness and her weather still,
For poetry makes nothing happen: it survives
In the valley of its making where executives
Would never want to tamper, flows on south
From ranches of isolation and the busy griefs,
Raw towns that we believe and die in; it survives,
A way of happening, a mouth.

III

Earth, receive an honoured guest:
William Yeats is laid to rest.
Let the Irish vessel lie
Emptied of its poetry.

In the nightmare of the dark
All the dogs of Europe bark,
And the living nations wait,
Each sequestered in its hate;

Intellectual disgrace
Stares from every human face,
And the seas of pity lie
Locked and frozen in each eye.

Follow, poet, follow right
To the bottom of the night,
With your unconstraining voice
Still persuade us to rejoice;

With the farming of a verse
Make a vineyard of the curse,
Sing of human unsuccess
In a rapture of distress;

In the deserts of the heart
Let the healing fountain start,
In the prison of his days
Teach the free man how to praise.

[1940]

THE UNKNOWN CITIZEN

To JS/07/M/378
This Marble Monument
Is Erected by the State

He was found by the Bureau of Statistics to be
One against whom there was no official complaint,
And all the reports on his conduct agree
That, in the modern sense of an old-fashioned word, he was a saint,
For in everything he did he served the Greater Community.
Except for the War till the day he retired
He worked in a factory and never got fired,
But satisfied his employers, Fudge Motors Inc.
Yet he wasn't a scab or odd in his views,
For his Union reports that he paid his dues,
(Our report on his Union shows it was sound)
And our Social Psychology workers found

That he was popular with his mates and liked a drink.
The Press are convinced that he bought a paper every day
And that his reactions to advertisements were normal in every way.
Policies taken out in his name prove that he was fully insured,
And his Health-card shows he was once in hospital but left it cured.
Both Producers Research and High-Grade Living declare
He was fully sensible to the advantages of the Instalment Plan
And had everything necessary to the Modern Man,
A phonograph, a radio, a car, and a frigidaire.
Our researchers into Public Opinion are content
That he held the proper opinions for the time of year;
When there was peace, he was for peace; when there was war, he went.
He was married and added five children to the population,
Which our Eugenist says was the right number for a parent of
    his generation,
And our teachers report that he never interfered with their education.
Was he free? Was he happy? The question is absurd:
Had anything been wrong, we should certainly have heard.

[1940]

THE SHIELD OF ACHILLES

She looked over his shoulder
    For vines and olive trees,
Marble well-governed cities
    And ships upon untamed seas,
But there on the shining metal
    His hands had put instead
An artificial wilderness
    And a sky like lead.

A plain without a feature, bare and brown,
    No blade of grass, no sign of neighbourhood,
Nothing to eat and nowhere to sit down,
    Yet, congregated on its blankness, stood
    An unintelligible multitude,
A million eyes, a million boots in line,
Without expression, waiting for a sign.

Out of the air a voice without a face
    Proved by statistics that some cause was just
In tones as dry and level as the place:
    No one was cheered and nothing was discussed;
    Column by column in a cloud of dust
They marched away enduring a belief
Whose logic brought them, somewhere else, to grief.

    She looked over his shoulder
        For ritual pieties,
    White flower-garlanded heifers,
        Libation and sacrifice,
    But there on the shining metal
        Where the altar should have been,
    She saw by his flickering forge-light
        Quite another scene.

Barbed wire enclosed an arbitrary spot
    Where bored officials lounged (one cracked a joke)
And sentries sweated for the day was hot:
    A crowd of ordinary decent folk
    Watched from without and neither moved nor spoke
As three pale figures were led forth and bound
To three posts driven upright in the ground.

The mass and majesty of this world, all
    That carries weight and always weighs the same
Lay in the hands of others; they were small
    And could not hope for help and no help came:
    What their foes liked to do was done, their shame
Was all the worst could wish; they lost their pride
And died as men before their bodies died.

    She looked over his shoulder
        For athletes at their games,
    Men and women in a dance
        Moving their sweet limbs
    Quick, quick, to music,
        But there on the shining shield
    His hands had set no dancing-floor
        But a weed-choked field.

A ragged urchin, aimless and alone,
Loitered about that vacancy, a bird
Flew up to safety from his well-aimed stone:
That girls are raped, that two boys knife a third,
Were axioms to him, who'd never heard
Of any world where promises were kept,
Or one could weep because another wept.

The thin-lipped armourer,
Hephaestos hobbled away,
Thetis of the shining breasts
Cried out in dismay
At what the god had wrought
To please her son, the strong
Iron-hearted man-slaying Achilles
Who would not live long.

[1951]

Dylan Thomas (1914-1953)

Dylan Thomas was born in Swansea, Wales. After attending Swansea Grammar School he set out for London, where he worked as a reporter and broadcaster, wrote radio and movie scripts, and published his first volume of verse, *18 Poems* (1934). Thomas's unique combination of charisma, eloquence, and incorrigibility made him a sensational success on the reading and lecture circuit in America. But he could never entirely reconcile his needs as a creative artist with the destructive forces in his personality; and, consequently, he was exploited by people who had no interest in his art and was reduced to a state of constant financial and social turmoil. He died in New York on his third reading tour. The best poems of his first six volumes of poetry may be found in his *Collected Poems 1934-52* (1952). In addition to his play *Under Milk Wood* (1954), Thomas wrote a number of prose works, including *Portrait of the Artist as a Young Dog* (1940), *Quite Early One Morning* (1954), and *Adventures in the Skin Trade* (1955). *Early Prose Writings* was published in 1971.

Thomas reserved his weaknesses and buffoonery for life; in his poetry he was a conscientious craftsman. He had an unparalleled ear for language and believed that poetry must be read aloud: 'a poem on a page is only half a poem.' The magic of his words has caused the less astute critics to accuse Thomas of being 'all sound and no sense'; and it has moved many of his most enthusiastic admirers to consider his poems somehow *above* analysis. Each of Thomas's poems is carefully wrought, a 'formally watertight compartment of words', controlled by either a narrative or an associative logic. Thomas's metaphors are the most startling thing about his poetry. He has the kind of wit that Samuel Johnson ascribed to the 'metaphysical' poets of the seventeenth century, *discordia concors*: the ability to combine dissimilar images or to discover the resemblances in things apparently different. While the metaphysical poets preferred the extended metaphor (i.e., comparing two lovers to the fixed arms of a compass), Thomas's great strength lies in the *compressed* metaphor: 'green age', 'the weather of the heart,' 'windy boy', 'holy streams', 'fields of praise', 'lamb white days', 'fire green as grass'.

In a much-quoted letter (*Dylan Thomas*, by Henry Treece, 1956), Thomas argues against the pursuit of a single, central image. 'A poem by myself needs a host of images, because its centre is a host of images. I make one image—though "make" is not the word; I let, perhaps, an image be "made" emotionally in me and then apply to it what intellectual and critical forces I possess—let it breed another, let that image contradict the first, make, of the third image bred out of the other two together, a fourth contradictory image, and let them all, within my imposed formal limits, conflict. Each image holds within it the seed of its own destruction, and my dialect[ic]al method, as I understand it, is a constant building up and breaking down of the images that come out of the central seed, which is itself destructive and constructive at the same time. . . . I believe in the simple thread of action through a poem, but that is an intellectual thing aimed at lucidity through narrative. My object is, as you say, conventionally "to get things straight". Out of the inevitable conflict of images—inevitable, because of the creative, recreative, destructive and contradictory nature of the motivating centre, the womb of war—I try to make that momentary peace which is a poem.'

The Force That Through the Green Fuse Drives the Flower

The force that through the green fuse drives the flower
Drives my green age; that blasts the roots of trees
Is my destroyer.
And I am dumb to tell the crooked rose
My youth is bent by the same wintry fever.

The force that drives the water through the rocks
Drives my red blood; that dries the mouthing streams
Turns mine to wax.
And I am dumb to mouth unto my veins
How at the mountain spring the same mouth sucks.

The hand that whirls the water in the pool
Stirs the quicksand; that ropes the blowing wind
Hauls my shroud sail.
And I am dumb to tell the hanging man
How of my clay is made the hangman's lime.

The lips of time leech to the fountain head;
Love drips and gathers, but the fallen blood
Shall calm her sores.
And I am dumb to tell a weather's wind
How time has ticked a heaven round the stars.

And I am dumb to tell the lover's tomb
How at my sheet goes the same crooked worm.

[1933]

If I were tickled by the rub of love

If I were tickled by the rub of love,
A rooking girl who stole me for her side,
Broke through her straws, breaking my bandaged string,
If the red tickle as the cattle calve
Still set to scratch a laughter from my lung,
I would not fear the apple nor the flood
Nor the bad blood of spring.

Shall it be male or female? say the cells,
And drop the plum like fire from the flesh.
If I were tickled by the hatching hair,
The winging bone that sprouted in the heels,
The itch of man upon the baby's thigh,
I would not fear the gallows nor the axe
Nor the crossed sticks of war.

Shall it be male or female? say the fingers
That chalk the walls with green girls and their men.
I would not fear the muscling-in of love
If I were tickled by the urchin hungers
Rehearsing heat upon a raw-edged nerve.
I would not fear the devil in the loin
Nor the outspoken grave.

If I were tickled by the lovers' rub
That wipes away not crow's-foot nor the lock
Of sick old manhood on the fallen jaws,
Time and the crabs and the sweethearting crib

Would leave me cold as butter for the flies,
The sea of scums could drown me as it broke
Dead on the sweethearts' toes.

This world is half the devil's and my own,
Daft with the drug that's smoking in a girl
And curling round the bud that forks her eye.
An old man's shank one-marrowed with my bone,
And all the herrings smelling in the sea,
I sit and watch the worm beneath my nail
Wearing the quick away.

And that's the rub, the only rub that tickles.
The knobbly ape that swings along his sex
From damp love-darkness and the nurse's twist
Can never raise the midnight of a chuckle,
Nor when he finds a beauty in the breast
Of lover, mother, lovers, or his six
Feet in the rubbing dust.

And what's the rub? Death's feather on the nerve?
Your mouth, my love, the thistle in the kiss?
My Jack of Christ born thorny on the tree?
The words of death are dryer than his stiff,
My wordy wounds are printed with your hair.
I would be tickled by the rub that is:
Man be my metaphor.

[1934]

And death shall have no dominion

And death shall have no dominion.
Dead men naked they shall be one
With the man in the wind and the west moon;
When their bones are picked clean and the clean bones gone,
They shall have stars at elbow and foot;
Though they go mad they shall be sane,
Though they sink through the sea they shall rise again;
Though lovers be lost love shall not;
And death shall have no dominion.

And death shall have no dominion.
Under the windings of the sea
They lying long shall not die windily;
Twisting on racks when sinews give way,
Strapped to a wheel, yet they shall not break;
Faith in their hands shall snap in two,
And the unicorn evils run them through;
Split all ends up they shan't crack;
And death shall have no dominion.

And death shall have no dominion.
No more may gulls cry at their ears
Or waves break loud on the seashores;
Where blew a flower may a flower no more
Lift its head to the blows of the rain;
Though they be mad and dead as nails,
Heads of the characters hammer through daisies;
Break in the sun till the sun breaks down,
And death shall have no dominion.

[1936]

A Refusal to Mourn the Death, by Fire, of a Child in London

Never until the mankind making
Bird beast and flower
Fathering and all humbling darkness
Tells with silence the last light breaking
And the still hour
Is come of the sea tumbling in harness

And I must enter again the round
Zion of the water bead
And the synagogue of the ear of corn
Shall I let pray the shadow of a sound
Or sow my salt seed
In the least valley of sackcloth to mourn

The majesty and burning of the child's death.
I shall not murder
The mankind of her going with a grave truth
Nor blaspheme down the stations of the breath
With any further
Elegy of innocence and youth.

Deep with the first dead lies London's daughter,
Robed in the long friends,
The grains beyond age, the dark veins of her mother,
Secret by the unmourning water
Of the riding Thames.
After the first death, there is no other.

[1946]

DO NOT GO GENTLE INTO THAT GOOD NIGHT

Do not go gentle into that good night,
Old age should burn and rave at close of day;
Rage, rage against the dying of the light.

Though wise men at their end know dark is right,
Because their words had forked no lightning they
Do not go gentle into that good night.

Good men, the last wave by, crying how bright
Their frail deeds might have danced in a green bay,
Rage, rage against the dying of the light.

Wild men who caught and sang the sun in flight,
And learn, too late, they grieved it on its way,
Do not go gentle into that good night.

Grave men, near death, who see with blinding sight
Blind eyes could blaze like meteors and be gay,
Rage, rage against the dying of the light.

And you, my father, there on the sad height,
Curse, bless, me now with your fierce tears, I pray.
Do not go gentle into that good night.
Rage, rage against the dying of the light.

[1951]

IN MY CRAFT OR SULLEN ART

In my craft or sullen art
Exercised in the still night
When only the moon rages
And the lovers lie abed
With all their griefs in their arms,
I labour by singing light
Not for ambition or bread
Or the strut and trade of charms
On the ivory stages
But for the common wages
Of their most secret heart.

Not for the proud man apart
From the raging moon I write
On these spindrift pages
Nor for the towering dead
With their nightingales and psalms
But for the lovers, their arms
Round the griefs of the ages,
Who pay no praise or wages
Nor heed my craft or art.

[1946]

FERN HILL

Now as I was young and easy under the apple boughs
About the lilting house and happy as the grass was green,
        The night above the dingle starry,
                Time let me hail and climb
        Golden in the heydays of his eyes,
And honoured among wagons I was prince of the apple towns
And once below a time I lordly had the trees and leaves
                Trail with daisies and barley
        Down the rivers of the windfall light.

And as I was green and carefree, famous among the barns
About the happy yard and singing as the farm was home,
    In the sun that is young once only,
        Time let me play and be
    Golden in the mercy of his means,
And green and golden I was huntsman and herdsman, the calves
Sang to my horn, the foxes on the hills barked clear and cold,
        And the sabbath rang slowly
    In the pebbles of the holy streams.

All the sun long it was running, it was lovely, the hay
Fields high as the house, the tunes from the chimneys, it was air
    And playing, lovely and watery
        And fire green as grass.
    And nightly under the simple stars
As I rode to sleep the owls were bearing the farm away,
All the moon long I heard, blessed among stables, the nightjars
    Flying with the ricks, and the horses
        Flashing into the dark.

And then to awake, and the farm, like a wanderer white
With the dew, come back, the cock on his shoulder: it was all
    Shining, it was Adam and maiden,
        The sky gathered again
    And the sun grew round that very day.
So it must have been after the birth of the simple light
In the first, spinning place, the spellbound horses walking warm
    Out of the whinnying green stable
        On to the fields of praise.

And honoured among foxes and pheasants by the gay house
Under the new made clouds and happy as the heart was long,
    In the sun born over and over,
        I ran my heedless ways,
    My wishes raced through the house high hay
And nothing I cared, at my sky blue trades, that time allows
In all his tuneful turning so few and such morning songs
    Before the children green and golden
        Follow him out of grace,

Nothing I cared, in the lamb white days, that time would take me
Up to the swallow thronged loft by the shadow of my hand,
    In the moon that is always rising,
        Nor that riding to sleep
    I should hear him fly with the high fields
And wake to the farm forever fled from the childless land.
Oh as I was young and easy in the mercy of his means,
        Time held me green and dying
    Though I sang in my chains like the sea.

[1946]

A.M. KLEIN (1909-1972)

Abraham Moses Klein was born in the Ukraine to orthodox Jewish parents, who emigrated to Canada the following year. He graduated from McGill University in 1929 and studied law at the University of Montreal, graduating in 1933. Klein practised law, intermittently and without enthusiasm, in Montreal, edited the *Canadian Jewish Chronicle*, taught English literature part-time at McGill, worked on a study of James Joyce (published incomplete in *Accent*, x, 3, 1950 and *New Directions 13*), and in 1949 ran unsuccessfully as a CCF candidate for the federal parliament in the riding of Cartier. The previous year he had won a Governor General's Award for *The Rocking Chair and Other Poems*, a brilliant evocation of aspects of Quebec life that celebrates the shared resources of the French and English languages. There is no single reason for Klein's years of silence and withdrawal, which included suicide attempts, but his critics and acquaintances have attributed blame to insufficient recognition, to his sense of dislocation from the Jewish community, even as he was endeavouring to explore its rich heritage in both his poems and his novel *The Second Scroll* (1951), and to his demeaning relations with Samuel Bronfman, from whom he earned some of his income as a public-relations adviser and speech-writer.

There is a poignant moment in Klein's diary in 1944 (*Notebooks: Selections from the A.M. Klein Papers*, edited by Zailig Pollock and Usher Caplan, 1994), where he recorded Bronfman's reaction to hearing of the CCF nomination: 'B. himself does not know whether to be joyful or otherwise at my decision. I think he is glad about it—although has not said so. Hypocritically expressed fear lest his Liberal associations be marred by my running C.C.F. Assured him that I still would prefer professorship at McGill to House of Commons seat.' This entry, followed by an ironic observation—'Landlord fixed lavatory bowl. A seat for the future M.P.'—is a reminder of how much Klein yearned for the security and affirmation of a permanent teaching position.

Among the selected papers published in *Notebooks*, there are some wonderful fragments and cryptic comments on poetry, including the following: 'Prose is concerned with denotations; poetry with detonations'; 'In the writing of poetry it is not necessary to be sincere. It is necessary only to give the impression of sincerity. To this end, being sincere may help; but it is not sine qua non'; and 'The purpose of politics is to bend another's will to your own; the purpose of poetry is to intertwine another's mood with your own.' His humorous remarks on the sonnet are worth quoting in their entirety, as they so clearly state the modernist case against certain aspects of traditional form and, by implication, certain social practices:

'Sonnets—neat, compact, residential—like self-contained cottages. Standard Petrarchan specifications: ground floor—an octave, topped by sleeping quarters of the sestet. 14 rooms 14. Note the southern exposure of the climactic line. Apply Poetry's Suburbia.

'It is no wonder that my contemporaries sneer at the sonnet. It is part of their general antipathy to the bourgeois. To them the sonneteer is the last degradation—a man of property: a promoter of real estate developments.

'How much goodlier, O Vers Libre, are thy *tents*?

'One must admit that too many sonnets, because of the very needs of their architecture, are conspicuous more by their cloacal gadgets than by their liveableness. Nevertheless, even nomads must concede that there are sonnets which, like good addresses. . . .'

Klein's poetic heritage was extremely rich. He drew from his knowledge of the French, English, and Hebrew languages and their respective cultures and was as familiar with the writings of T.S. Eliot and James Joyce and the literature of the English Renaissance as he was with Jewish history and religious teachings. In the best of Klein's poetry these diverse elements are fused by a penetrating social consciousness, which is compounded of great rage and compassion. In his dramatic monologue 'In re *Solomon Warshawer*', the Jew who declaims against the 'unfuturity' of the S.S. men is, in fact, addressing himself to all such emanations of evil in the history of mankind: 'O I have known them all, / The dwarf dictators, the diminutive dukes, / The heads of straw, the hearts of galls, / Th' imperial plumes of eagles covering rooks!' Klein's brilliance as a poet lies not only in his exploration of 'the heart's depths, how it may sink / Down to the deep and ink of genesis', but also in his astonishing range of reference.

Klein is a master of the declamatory, but he is also capable of intense lyricism, religious rhapsody, reminiscence, confession, humour, and satire. While he suffered from what he perceived as insufficient recognition, he was able, as he illustrates in 'Portrait of the Poet as Landscape', 'to say the word that will become sixth sense', 'to bring / new form to life', and to make 'of his status as zero, a rich garland, / a halo of his anonymity'.

In addition to *The Rocking Chair*, Klein's volumes of poetry include *Hath Not a Jew* (1940), *The Hitleriad* (1944), *Poems* (1944), and *The Collected Poems of A.M. Klein* (1974), edited by Miriam Waddington. In addition to *Notebooks*, scholarly editions of his complete writings have been published by University of Toronto Press, including *Beyond Sambation: Selected Essays and Editorials 1928-1955* (1982), edited by M.W. Steinberg and Usher Caplan; *A.M. Klein: Short Stories* (1983), edited by M.W. Steinberg; and *A.M. Klein: Literary Essays and Reviews* (1986) and *A.M. Klein: Complete Poems* (1990), both edited by Zailig Pollock.

Heirloom

My father bequeathed me no wide estates;
No keys and ledgers were my heritage;
Only some holy books with *yahrzeit* dates
Writ mournfully upon a blank front page—

Books of the Baal Shem Tov, and of his wonders;
Pamphlets upon the devil and his crew;
Prayers against road demons, witches, thunders;
And sundry other tomes for a good Jew.

Beautiful: though no pictures on them, save
The Scorpion crawling on a printed track;
The Virgin floating on a scriptural wave,
Square letters twinkling in the Zodiac.

The snuff left on this page, now brown and old,
The tallow stains of midnight liturgy—
These are my coat of arms, and these unfold
My noble lineage, my proud ancestry!

And my tears, too, have stained this heirloomed ground,
When reading in these treatises some weird
Miracle, I turned a leaf and found
A white hair fallen from my father's beard.

[1943]

Autobiographical

I
Out of the ghetto streets where a Jewboy
Dreamed pavement into pleasant bible-land,
Out of the Yiddish slums where childhood met
The friendly beard, the loutish Sabbath-goy,
Or followed, proud, the Torah-escorting band
Out of the jargoning city I regret
Rise memories, like sparrows rising from

The gutter-scattered oats,
Like sadness sweet of synagogal hum,
Like Hebrew violins
Sobbing delight upon their eastern notes.

II
Again they ring their little bells, those doors
Deemed by the tender-year'd, magnificent:
Old Ashkenazi's cellar, sharp with spice;
The widow's double-parloured candy-stores
And nuggets sweet bought for one sweaty cent;
The warm fresh-smelling bakery, its pies,
Its cakes, its navel'd bellies of black bread;
The lintels candy-poled
Of barber-shop, bright-bottled, green, blue, red;
And fruit-stall piled, exotic,
And the big synagogue door, with letters of gold.

III
Again my kindergarten home is full—
Saturday night—with kin and compatriot:
My brothers playing Russian card-games; my
Mirroring sisters looking beautiful
Humming the evening's imminent fox-trot;
My uncle Mayer, of blessed memory,
Still murmuring Maariv, counting holy words;
And the two strangers, come
Fiery from Volhynia's murderous hordes—
The cards and humming stop.
And I too swear revenge for that pogrom.

IV
Occasions dear: the four-legged aleph named
And angel pennies dropping on my book;
The rabbi patting a coming scholar-head;
My mother, blessing candles, Sabbath-flamed,
Queenly in her Warsovian perruque;
My father pickabacking me to bed
To tell tall tales about the Baal Shem Tov,

Letting me curl his beard.
O memory of unsurpassing love,
Love leading a brave child
Through childhood's ogred corridors, unfear'd.

V
The week in the country at my brother's (May
He own fat cattle in the fields of heaven!)
Its picking of strawberries from grassy ditch,
Its odour of dogrose and of yellowing hay,—
Dusty, adventurous, sunny days, all seven!—
Still follow me, still warm me, still are rich
With the cow-tinkling peace of pastureland.
The meadow'd memory
Is sodded with its clover, and is spanned
By that same pillow'd sky
A boy on his back one day watched enviously.

VI
And paved again the street; the shouting boys
Oblivious of mothers on the stoops
Playing the robust robbers and police,
The corn-cob battle,—all high-spirited noise
Competitive among the lot-drawn groups.
Another day, of shaken apple-trees
In the rich suburbs, and a furious dog
And guilty boys in flight;
Hazelnut games, and games in the synagogue.
The burrs, the Haman rattle,
The Torah-dance on Simchas-Torah night.

VII
Immortal days of the picture-calendar
Dear to me always with the virgin joy
Of the first flowing of senses five
Discovering birds, or textures, or a star,
Or tastes sweet, sour, acid, those that cloy,
And perfumes. Never was I more alive.
All days thereafter are a dying-off,

A wandering away
From home and the familiar. The years doff
Their innocence.
No other day is ever like that day.

VIII
I am no old man fatuously intent
On memoirs, but in memory I seek
The strength and vividness of nonage days,
Not tranquil recollection of event.
It is a fabled city that I seek;
It stands in space's vapours and Time's haze;
Thence comes my sadness in remembered joy
Constrictive of the throat;
Thence do I hear, as heard by a Jewboy
The Hebrew violins,
Delighting in the sobbed oriental note.

[1951]

POLITICAL MEETING

for Camillien Houde

On the school platform, draping the folding seats,
they wait the chairman's praise and glass of water.
Upon the wall the agonized Y initials their faith.

Here all are laic; the skirted brothers have gone.
Still, their equivocal absence is felt, like a breeze
that gives curtains the sounds of surplices.

The hall is yellow with light, and jocular;
suddenly some one lets loose upon the air
the ritual bird which the crowd in snares of singing

catches and plucks, throat, wings, and little limbs.
Fall the feathers of sound, like *alouette*'s.
The chairman, now, is charming, full of asides and wit,

building his orators, and chipping off
the heckling gargoyles popping in the hall.
(Outside, in the dark, the street is body-tall,

flowered with faces intent on the scarecrow thing
that shouts to thousands the echoing
of their own wishes.) The Orator has risen!

Worshipped and loved, their favourite visitor,
a country uncle with sunflower seeds in his pockets,
full of wonderful moods, tricks, imitative talk,

he is their idol: like themselves, not handsome,
not snobbish, not of the *Grande Allée! Un homme!*
Intimate, informal, he makes bear's compliments

to the ladies; is gallant; and grins;
goes for the balloon, his opposition, with pins;
jokes also on himself, speaks of himself

in the third person, slings slang, and winks with folklore;
and knows now that he has them, kith and kin.
Calmly, therefore, he begins to speak of war,

praises the virtue of being *Canadien*,
of being at peace, of faith, of family,
and suddenly his other voice: *Where are your sons?*

He is tearful, choking tears; but not he
would blame the clever English; in their place
he'd do the same; maybe.

Where *are* your sons?
The whole street wears one face,
shadowed and grim; and in the darkness rises
the body-odour of race.

[1948]

LONE BATHER

Upon the ecstatic diving board the diver,
poised for parabolas, lets go
lets go his manshape to become a bird.
Is bird, and topsy-turvy
the pool floats overhead, and the white tiles snow
their crazy hexagons. Is dolphin. Then
is plant with lilies bursting from his heels.

Himself, suddenly mysterious and marine,
bobs up a merman leaning on his hills.

Plashes and plays alone the deserted pool;
as those, is free, who think themselves unseen.
He rolls in his heap of fruit,
he slides his belly over
the melonrinds of water, curved and smooth and green.
Feels good: and trains, like little acrobats
his echoes dropping from the galleries;
circles himself over a rung of water;
swims fancy and gay; taking a notion, hides
under the satins of his great big bed,—
and then comes up to float until he thinks
the ceiling at his brow, and nowhere any sides.

His thighs are a shoal of fishes: scattered: he
turns with many gloves of greeting
towards the sunnier water and the tiles.

Upon the tiles he dangles from his toes
lazily the eight reins of his ponies.

An afternoon, far from the world
a street sound throws like a stone, with paper, through the glass.
Up, he is chipped enamel, grained with hair.
The gloss of his footsteps follows him to the showers,
the showers, and the male room, and the towel
which rubs the bird, the plant, the dolphin back again
personable plain.

[1948]

PORTRAIT OF THE POET AS LANDSCAPE

I

Not an editorial-writer, bereaved with bartlett,
mourns him, the shelved Lycidas.
No actress squeezes a glycerine tear for him.
The radio broadcast lets his passing pass.
And with the police, no record. Nobody, it appears,
either under his real name or his alias,
missed him enough to report.

It is possible that he is dead, and not discovered.
It is possible that he can be found some place
in a narrow closet, like the corpse in a detective story,
standing, his eyes staring, and ready to fall on his face.
It is also possible that he is alive
and amnesiac, or mad, or in retired disgrace,
or beyond recognition lost in love.

We are sure only that from our real society
he has disappeared; he simply does not count,
except in the pullulation of vital statistics—
somebody's vote, perhaps, an anonymous taunt
of the Gallup poll, a dot in a government table—
but not felt, and certainly far from eminent—
in a shouting mob, somebody's sigh.

O, he who unrolled our culture from his scroll—
the prince's quote, the rostrum-rounding roar—
who under one name made articulate
heaven, and under another the seven-circled air,
is, if he is at all, a number, an x,
a Mr Smith in a hotel register,—
incognito, lost, lacunal.

II

The truth is he's not dead, but only ignored—
like the mirroring lenses forgotten on a brow
that shine with the guilt of their unnoticed world.
The truth is he lives among neighbours, who, though they will allow
him a passable fellow, think him eccentric, not solid,
a type that one can forgive, and for that matter, forego.

Himself he has his moods, just like a poet.
Sometimes, depressed to nadir, he will think all lost,
will see himself as throwback, relict, freak,
his mother's miscarriage, his great-grandfather's ghost,
and he will curse his quintuplet senses, and their tutors
in whom he put, as he should not have put, his trust.

Then he will remember his travels over that body—
the torso verb, the beautiful face of the noun,
and all those shaped and warm auxiliaries!
A first love it was, the recognition of his own.
Dear limbs adverbial, complexion of adjective,
dimple and dip of conjugation!

And then remember how this made a change in him
affecting for always the glow and growth of his being;
how suddenly was aware of the air, like shaken tinfoil,
of the patents of nature, the shock of belated seeing,
the lonelinesses peering from the eyes of crowds;
the integers of thought; the cube-roots of feeling.

Thus, zoomed to zenith, sometimes he hopes again,
and sees himself as a character, with a rehearsed role:
the Count of Monte Cristo, come for his revenges;
the unsuspected heir, with papers; the risen soul;
or the chloroformed prince awaking from his flowers;
or—deflated again—the convict on parole.

III

He is alone; yet not completely alone.
Pins on a map of a colour similar to his,
each city has one, sometimes more than one;
here, caretakers of art, in colleges;
in offices, there, with arm-bands, and green-shaded;
and there, pounding their catalogued beats in libraries,—

everywhere menial, a shadow's shadow.
And always for their egos—their outmoded art.
Thus, having lost the bevel in the ear,
they know neither up nor down, mistake the part
for the whole, curl themselves in a comma,
talk technics, make a colon their eyes. They distort—

such is the pain of their frustration—truth
to something convolute and cerebral.
How they do fear the slap of the flat of the platitude!
Now Pavlov's victims, their mouths water at bell,
the platter empty.
                    See they set twenty-one jewels
into their watches; the time they do not tell!

Some, patagonian in their own esteem,
and longing for the multiplying word,
join party and wear pins, now have a message,
an ear, and the convention-hall's regard.
Upon the knees of ventriloquists, they own,
of their dandled brightness, only the paint and board.

And some go mystical, and some go mad.
One stares at a mirror all day long, as if
to recognize himself; another courts
angels,—for here he does not fear rebuff;
and a third, alone, and sick with sex, and rapt,
doodles him symbols convex and concave.

O schizoid solitudes! O purities
curdling upon themselves! Who live for themselves,
or for each other, but for nobody else;
desire affection, private and public loves;
are friendly, and then quarrel and surmise
the secret perversions of each other's lives.

IV

He suspects that something has happened, a law
been passed, a nightmare ordered. Set apart,
he finds himself, with special haircut and dress,
as on a reservation. Introvert.
He does not understand this; sad conjecture
muscles and palls thrombotic on his heart.

He thinks an impostor, having studied his personal biography,
his gestures, his moods, now has come forward to pose
in the shivering vacuums his absence leaves.

Wigged with his laurel, that other, and faked with his face,
he pats the heads of his children, pecks his wife,
and is at home, and slippered, in his house.

So he guesses at the impertinent silhouette
that talks to his phone-piece and slits open his mail.
Is it the local tycoon who for a hobby
plays poet, he so epical in steel?
The orator, making a pause? Or is that man
he who blows his flash of brass in the jittering hall?

Or is he cuckolded by the troubadour
rich and successful out of celluloid?
Or by the don who unrhymes atoms? Or
the chemist death built up? Pride, lost impostor'd pride,
it is another, another, whoever he is,
who rides where he should ride.

V

Fame, the adrenalin: to be talked about;
to be a verb; to be introduced as *The*:
to smile with endorsement from slick paper; make
caprices anecdotal; to nod to the world; to see
one's name like a song upon the marquees played;
to be forgotten with embarrassment; to be—
to be.

It has its attractions, but is not the thing;
nor is it the ape mimesis who speaks from the tree
ancestral; nor the merkin joy...
Rather it is stark infelicity
which stirs him from his sleep, undressed, asleep
to walk upon roofs and window-sills and defy
the gape of gravity.

VI

Therefore he seeds illusions. Look, he is
the nth Adam taking a green inventory
in world but scarcely uttered, naming, praising,
the flowering fiats in the meadow, the
syllabled fur, stars aspirate, the pollen
whose sweet collision sounds eternally.
For to praise

the world—he, solitary man—is breath
to him. Until it has been praised, that part
has not been. Item by exciting item—
air to his lungs, and pressured blood to his heart,—
they are pulsated, and breathed, until they map,
not the world's, but his own body's chart!

And now in imagination he has climbed
another planet, the better to look
with single camera view upon this earth—
its total scope, and each afflated tick,
its talk, its trick, its tracklessness—and this,
this he would like to write down in a book!

To find a new function for the declassé craft
archaic like the fletcher's; to make a new thing;
to say the word that will become sixth sense;
perhaps by necessity and indirection bring
new forms to life, anonymously, new creeds—
O, somehow pay back the daily larcenies of the lung!

These are not mean ambitions. It is already something
merely to entertain them. Meanwhile, he
makes of his status as zero a rich garland,
a halo of his anonymity,
and lives alone, and in his secret shines
like phosphorus. At the bottom of the sea.

[1948]

Theodore Roethke (1908-1963)

Roethke's odyssey in search of the self involved many emotional and financial hardships, many painful self-revelations. As a sensitive but unfortunately vulnerable and insecure man, he suffered considerable frustration as a result of his loneliness and his initial lack of recognition as a poet. 'I learn by going where I have to go,' he admits in 'The Waking'. Roethke's poetry traces with frankness and honesty this long journey towards self-knowledge and fulfilment, recording sensations of childhood, mental breakdown, bereavement, and, finally, love. To use his own words, it is the poetry of a man 'naked to the bone'.

Roethke was born in Saginaw, Michigan, and grew up around the greenhouses and sanctuary started by his grandfather, who had been Bismarck's head forester in Prussia. From these impressionable years and, perhaps, in reaction to his own troubled life, he found power and order in the world of growing things, which he felt and loved deeply. His profound reverence for life is reflected not only in his delightfully fresh and immediate nature poems, but also in poems about friends, students, and shared experiences. Before embarking on a life of teaching and writing, Roethke attended Harvard. He taught at Lafayette, Pennsylvania State, Bennington, and the University of Washington, where he received the honorary title of poet-in-residence in 1962. His awards include a Pulitzer Prize, a Ford Foundation grant, the Bollingen Prize, two National Book Awards, and a Fulbright lectureship in Italy.

In his poetry Roethke reveals an affection (unusual in the mid-twentieth century) for formal rhythm and rhyme. He considered free verse a contradiction in terms and was continuously struggling for new rhythms and forms of expression. As he remarked in connection with a poem by Blake, 'Rhythm gives us the very psychic energy of the speaker, in one emotional situation at least.' Undoubtedly the vitality of his poetry in comparison with much of the verse now printed in literary magazines stems from his search for appropriate rhythms. Roethke's technical excellence and his depth of emotion are evident in 'Big Wind', an extended metaphor of great lyrical intensity and beauty, and 'I Knew a Woman', a love poem that is a masterpiece of wit and feeling. Each is a rhythmical *tour de force*.

Though self-defensive to a fault, Roethke was more than willing to consult and learn from other writers. As he wrote in 1939, in 'Verse in Rehearsal' (*On the Poet and His Craft: Selected Prose of Theodore Roethke*, edited by Ralph J. Mills, Jr, 1965), 'The writer who maintains that he works without regard for the opinion of others is either a jackass or a pathological liar.' In reviewing other poets, such as Louise Bogan, Roethke draws attention to 'exactitude in language', the 'inevitable image', momentum, shifts in rhythm, and fidelity to emotional particulars, all matters of craft that concerned him personally. In many respects he most resembles Rilke, in his struggle to come to a personal and poetic realization of the oneness of man and nature and in his determination to achieve 'heightened consciousness' and 'intensity in the seeing' in his poems. 'When I was young,' he writes in 1963 in 'On Identity' (*On the Poet and His Craft*) 'to make something in language, a poem that was all of a piece, a poem that could stand for what I was at the time—that seemed to be the most miraculous thing in the world. Most scholarship seemed irrelevant rubbish; most teachers seemed lacking in wisdom, in knowledge they had proved on their pulses. Certain writers called out to me: I believed them implicitly. I still do.'

Why did Roethke choose poetry, rather than some other form? 'The novel, that secondary form, can teach us how to act; the poem, and music, how to feel: and the feeling is vastly important. And the "creativity" may be vicarious. Once we begin to feel deeply, to paraphrase Marianne Moore, we begin to behave.'

Roethke published numerous volumes of poetry, including *Open House* (1941), *The Lost Son* (1948), *Praise to the End!* (1951), *The Waking: Poems, 1933-1953* (1953, Pulitzer Prize), *Words for the Wind* (1958, Bollingen Prize), *I am! Says the Lamb* (1961), and *The Far Field* (1964). Available now are *The Collected Poems of Theodore Roethke* (1966), *On the Poet and His Craft: Selected Prose of Theodore Roethke* (1965), and *Selected Letters of Theodore Roethke* (1968).

PRAYER

If I must of my Senses lose,
I pray Thee, Lord, that I may choose
Which of the Five I shall retain
Before oblivion clouds the brain.
My Tongue is generations dead,
My Nose defiles a comely head;
For hearkening to carnal evils
My Ears have been the very devil's.
And some have held the Eye to be
The instrument of lechery,
More furtive than the Hand in low
And vicious venery—Not so!
Its rape is gentle, never more
Violent than a metaphor.
In truth, the Eye's the abettor of
The holiest platonic love:
Lip, Breast, and Thigh cannot possess
So singular a blessedness.
Therefore, O Lord, let me preserve
The Sense that does so fitly serve,
Take Tongue and Ear—all else I have—
Let Light attend me to the grave!

[1941]

BIG WIND

Where were the greenhouses going,
Lunging into the lashing
Wind driving water
So far down the river
All the faucets stopped?—
So we drained the manure-machine
For the steam plant,
Pumping the stale mixture
Into the rusty boilers,
Watching the pressure gauge
Waver over to red,

As the seams hissed
And the live steam
Drove to the far
End of the rose-house,
Where the worst wind was,
Creaking the cypress window-frames,
Cracking so much thin glass
We stayed all night,
Stuffing the holes with burlap;
But she rode it out,
That old rose-house,
She hove into the teeth of it,
The core and pith of that ugly storm,
Ploughing with her stiff prow,
Bucking into the wind-waves
That broke over the whole of her,
Flailing her sides with spray,
Flinging long strings of wet across the roof-top,
Finally veering, wearing themselves out, merely
Whistling thinly under the wind-vents;
She sailed until the calm morning,
Carrying her full cargo of roses.

[1948]

DOLOR

I have known the inexorable sadness of pencils,
Neat in their boxes, dolor of pad and paper-weight,
All the misery of manilla folders and mucilage,
Desolation in immaculate public places,
Lonely reception room, lavatory, switchboard,
The unalterable pathos of basin and pitcher,
Ritual of multigraph, paper-clip, comma,
Endless duplication of lives and objects.
And I have seen dust from the walls of institutions,
Finer than flour, alive, more dangerous than silica,
Sift, almost invisible, through long afternoons of tedium,
Dropping a fine film on nails and delicate eyebrows,
Glazing the pale hair, the duplicate grey standard faces.

[1948]

PRAISE TO THE END!

I

It's dark in this wood, soft mocker.
For whom have I swelled like a seed?
What a bone-ache I have.
Father of tensions, I'm down to my skin at last.

It's a great day for the mice.
Prickle-me, tickle-me, close stems.
Bumpkin, he can dance alone.
Ooh, ooh, I'm a duke of eels.

    Arch my back, pretty-bones, I'm dead at both ends.
    Softly softly, you'll wake the clams.
    I'll feed the ghost alone.
    Father, forgive my hands.

The rings have gone from the pond.
The river's alone with its water.
All risings
Fall.

II

Where are you now, my bonny beating gristle,
My blue original dandy, numb with sugar?
Once I fished from the banks, leaf-light and happy:
On the rocks south of quiet, in the close regions of kissing,
I romped, lithe as a child, down the summery streets of my veins,
Strict as a seed, nippy and twiggy.
Now the water's low. The weeds exceed me.
It's necessary, among the flies and bananas, to keep a constant vigil,
For the attacks of false humility take sudden turns for the worse.
Lacking the candour of dogs, I kiss the departing air;
I'm untrue to my own excesses.

Rock me to sleep, the weather's wrong.
Speak to me, frosty beard.
Sing to me, sweet.

Mips and ma the mooly moo,
The likes of him is biting who,
A cow's a care and who's a coo?—
What footie does is final.

My dearest dear my fairest fair,
Your father tossed a cat in air,
Though neither you nor I was there,—
What footie does is final.

Be large as an owl, be slick as a frog,
Be good as a goose, be big as a dog,
Be sleek as a heifer, be long as a hog,—
What footie will do will be final.

I conclude! I conclude!
My dearest dust, I can't stay here.
I'm undone by the flip-flap of odious pillows.
An exact fall of waters has rendered me impotent.
I've been asleep in a bower of dead skin.
It's a piece of a prince I ate.
This salt can't warm a stone.
These lazy ashes.

III

The stones were sharp,
The wind came at my back;
Walked along the highway,
Mincing like a cat.

The sun came out;
The lake turned green;
Romped upon the goldy grass,
Aged thirteen.

The sky cracked open
The world I knew;
Lay like the cats do
Sniffing the dew.

I dreamt I was all bones;
The dead slept in my sleeve;
Sweet Jesus tossed me back:
I wore the sun with ease.

The several sounds were low;
The river ebbed and flowed:
Desire was winter-calm,
A moon away.

Such owly pleasures! Fish come first, sweet bird.
Skin's the least of me. Kiss this.
Is the eternal near, fondling?
I hear the sound of hands.

Can the bones breathe? This grave has an ear.
It's still enough for the knock of a worm.
I feel more than a fish.
Ghost, come closer.

IV
Arch of air, my heart's original knock,
I'm awake all over:
I've crawled from the mire, alert as a saint or a dog;
I know the back-stream's joy, and the stone's eternal pulseless longing.
Felicity I cannot hoard.
My friend, the rat in the wall, brings me the clearest messages;
I bask in the bower of change;
The plants wave me in, and the summer apples;
My palm-sweat flashes gold;
Many astounds before, I lost my identity to a pebble;
The minnows love me, and the humped and spitting creatures.

I believe! I believe!—
In the sparrow, happy on gravel;
In the winter-wasp, pulsing its wings in the sunlight;
I have been somewhere else; I remember the sea-faced uncles.
I hear, clearly, the heart of another singing,
Lighter than bells,
Softer than water.

Wherefore, O birds and small fish, surround me.
Lave me, ultimate waters.
The dark showed me a face.
My ghosts are all gay.
The light becomes me.

[1951]

THE WAKING

I wake to sleep, and take my waking slow.
I feel my fate in what I cannot fear.
I learn by going where I have to go.

We think by feeling. What is there to know?
I hear my being dance from ear to ear.
I wake to sleep, and take my waking slow.

Of those so close beside me, which are you?
God bless the Ground! I shall walk softly there,
And learn by going where I have to go.

Light takes the Tree; but who can tell us how?
The lowly worm climbs up a winding stair;
I wake to sleep, and take my waking slow.

Great Nature has another thing to do
To you and me; so take the lively air,
And, lovely, learn by going where to go.

This shaking keeps me steady. I should know.
What falls away is always. And is near.
I wake to sleep, and take my waking slow.
I learn by going where I have to go.

[1953]

I KNEW A WOMAN

I knew a woman, lovely in her bones,
When small birds sighed, she would sigh back at them;
Ah, when she moved, she moved more ways than one:

The shapes a bright container can contain!
Of her choice virtues only gods should speak,
Or English poets who grew up on Greek
(I'd have them sing in chorus, cheek to cheek).

How well her wishes went! She stroked my chin,
She taught me Turn, and Counter-turn, and Stand;
She taught me Touch, that undulant white skin;
I nibbled meekly from her proffered hand;
She was the sickle; I, poor I, the rake,
Coming behind her for her pretty sake
(But what prodigious mowing we did make).

Love likes a gander, and adores a goose:
Her full lips pursed, the errant note to seize;
She played it quick, she played it light and loose;
My eyes, they dazzled at her flowing knees;
Her several parts could keep a pure repose,
Or one hip quiver with a mobile nose
(She moved in circles, and those circles moved).

Let seed be grass, and grass turn into hay:
I'm martyr to a motion not my own;
What's freedom for? To know eternity.
I swear she cast a shadow white as stone.
But who would count eternity in days?
These old bones live to learn her wanton ways:
(I measure time by how a body sways).

[1958]

The Far Field

I

I dream of journeys repeatedly:
Of flying like a bat deep into a narrowing tunnel,
Of driving alone, without luggage, out a long peninsula,
The road lined with snow-laden second growth,
A fine dry snow ticking the windshield,
Alternate snow and sleet, no on-coming traffic,
And no lights behind, in the blurred side-mirror,

The road changing from glazed tarface to a rubble of stone,
Ending at last in a hopeless sand-rut,
Where the car stalls,
Churning in a snowdrift
Until the headlights darken.

II

At the field's end, in the corner missed by the mower,
Where the turf drops off into a grass-hidden culvert,
Haunt of the cat-bird, nesting-place of the field-mouse,
Not too far away from the ever-changing flower-dump,
Among the tin cans, tires, rusted pipes, broken machinery,—
One learned of the eternal;
And in the shrunken face of a dead rat, eaten by rain and
ground-beetles
(I found it lying among the rubble of an old coal bin)
And the tom-cat, caught near the pheasant-run,
Its entrails strewn over the half-grown flowers,
Blasted to death by the night watchman.

I suffered for birds, for young rabbits caught in the mower,
My grief was not excessive.
For to come upon warblers in early May
Was to forget time and death:
How they filled the oriole's elm, a twittering restless cloud,
all one morning,
And I watched and watched till my eyes blurred from the
bird shapes,—
Cape May, Blackburnian, Cerulean,—
Moving, elusive as fish, fearless,
Hanging, bunched like young fruit, bending the end branches,
Still for a moment,
Then pitching away in half-flight,
Lighter than finches,
While the wrens bickered and sang in the half-green hedgerows,
And the flicker drummed from his dead tree in the chicken-yard.

—Or to lie naked in sand,
In the silted shallows of a slow river,
Fingering a shell,
Thinking:

Once I was something like this, mindless,
Or perhaps with another mind, less peculiar;
Or to sink down to the hips in a mossy quagmire;
Or, with skinny knees, to sit astride a wet log,
Believing:
I'll return again,
As a snake or a raucous bird,
Or, with luck, as a lion.

I learned not to fear infinity,
The far field, the windy cliffs of forever,
The dying of time in the white light of tomorrow,
The wheel turning away from itself,
The sprawl of the wave,
The on-coming water.

III

The river turns on itself,
The tree retreats into its own shadow.
I feel a weightless change, a moving forward
As of water quickening before a narrowing channel
When banks converge, and the wide river whitens;
Or when two rivers combine, the blue glacial torrent
And the yellowish-green from the mountainy upland,—
At first a swift rippling between rocks,
Then a long running over flat stones
Before descending to the alluvial plain,
To the clay banks, and the wild grapes hanging from the elmtrees.
The slightly trembling water
Dropping a fine yellow silt where the sun stays;
And the crabs bask near the edge,
The weedy edge, alive with small snakes and bloodsuckers,—
I have come to a still, but not a deep center,
A point outside the glittering current;
My eyes stare at the bottom of a river,
At the irregular stones, iridescent sandgrains,
My mind moves in more than one place,
In a country half-land, half-water.

I am renewed by death, thought of my death,
The dry scent of a dying garden in September,
The wind fanning the ash of a low fire.
What I love is near at hand,
Always, in earth and air.

IV
The lost self changes,
Turning toward the sea,
A sea-shape turning around,—
An old man with his feet before the fire,
In robes of green, in garments of adieu.
A man faced with his own immensity
Wakes all the waves, all their loose wandering fire.
The murmur of the absolute, the why
Of being born fails on his naked ears.
His spirit moves like monumental wind
That gentles on a sunny blue plateau.
He is the end of things, the final man.

All finite things reveal infinitude:
The mountain with its singular bright shade
Like the blue shine on freshly frozen snow,
The after-light upon ice-burdened pines;
Odour of basswood on a mountain-slope,
A scent beloved of bees;
Silence of water above a sunken tree:
The pure serene of memory in one man,—
A ripple widening from a single stone
Winding around the waters of the world.

[1964]

In a Dark Time

In a dark time, the eye begins to see,
I meet my shadow in the deepening shade;
I hear my echo in the echoing wood—
A lord of nature weeping to a tree.
I live between the heron and the wren,
Beasts of the hill and serpents of the den.

What's madness but nobility of soul
At odds with circumstance? The day's on fire!
I know the purity of pure despair,
My shadow pinned against a sweating wall.
That place among the rocks—is it a cave,
Or winding path? The edge is what I have.

A steady storm of correspondences!
A night flowing with birds, a ragged moon,
And in broad day the midnight come again!
A man goes far to find out what he is—
Death of the self in a long, tearless night,
All natural shapes blazing unnatural light.

Dark, dark my light, and darker my desire.
My soul, like some heat-maddened summer fly,
Keeps buzzing at the sill. Which I is I?
A fallen man, I climb out of my fear.
The mind enters itself, and God the mind,
And one is One, free in the tearing wind.

[1964]

EARLE BIRNEY (1904-1995)

Born in Calgary, Birney spent most of his youth in Banff, Alberta, and Creston, BC. He graduated from the University of British Columbia in 1926. When his graduate studies in California were interrupted by difficulties, mostly financial, he went to Utah to teach, and then to New York to work for the Trotskyites. With a grant from the Royal Society he completed his doctoral studies in London and at the University of Toronto, where he lectured for several years. He served as literary editor of the *Canadian Forum* until 1940, when he went overseas as a Personnel Selection Officer. For a short time he was Supervisor of Foreign Language Broadcasts to Europe for the CBC, after which he became a Professor of English at UBC. There he established and headed the Department of Creative Writing. After his retirement, he travelled widely, settling in Toronto with his second wife, Weilan Chan, but was incapacitated by a serious stroke not long after his eightieth birthday.

Since his early radical days, Birney's poetry has exhibited a wide range and depth of social criticism, exposing instances of exploitation, such as the rape of the BC forests by industry, the suppression of minorities, or the mass murder of innocents in time of war. He considered the artist an antenna, or DEW (Distant Early Warning) system, for picking up and alerting us to the signs of society's ills. For a time Birney's primary response was that of moral outrage, as seen in his mock-heroic satire on bigotry and small-mindedness in 'Anglosaxon Street'. His notion of the ideal development for a poet consisted of finding newer and subtler ways to express contempt for injustice and concern for brotherhood. In his later poems he creates the persona of a sensitive tourist, a kind of twentieth-century Gulliver, whose curiosity and wry sense of self make him an ideal commentator on the human condition. In 'A Walk in Kyoto', for example, the poet explores his own reactions to an unfamiliar environment and, through self-analysis and careful attention to nuance and detail, discovers something fundamental about his relation to these people and places.

Birney argues in *The Creative Writer* (1966), a series of talks for the CBC radio program *Ideas*, that poetry is 'a kind of intricate and infinite play', but one which is not the exclusive preserve of poets. 'Some psychologists say, and I agree with them, that creativity in the sense of the drive to find new things, explore, discover, is basic to the human animal. I think all children who aren't born into absolute idiocy are artistically creative. With a favourable kind of environment and education, most of them, I suspect, grow up retaining some creative powers as men and women. But there's a strong social urge to conform, to become dependent on others, to accept instruction, guidance, doctrine, to stop really thinking, or even feeling deeply, for one's self. Artists are people who resist this conforming pressure, at least with part of their energies. They're helped in doing this, if I follow this psychological theorizing rightly, by having a disposition for what is called autistic thinking. That is, they can turn on a tap of free-flowing thought without much need for stimulus from external evidence. In other words, they're given to fantasy, to lively speculation, humorous or lugubrious exaggeration, games of pretending, and to uninhibited delight in images and, in the case of writers, in words themselves.'

'Living art,' Birney explains in *The Creative Writer*, 'like anything else, stays alive only by changing.' He mastered such traditional forms as the narrative, the meditative lyric, verse satire, and the descriptive nature poem, and has experimented with Anglo-Saxon verse rhythms. But he was also interested in experiments with typography and orthography and in the theories and practice of the Black Mountain and concrete poets. Birney was a constant reviser, reworking his poems extensively and often removing traditional punctuation. He complains that 'one of the things long bedevilling our literature has been the timidity of its writers to move freely from one form of writing to another' when 'the new writers in America and Europe have virtually obliterated the distinctions between prose and poetry.'

Refusing to be a 'mere worker-ant or emasculated drone in a beehive', Birney insists on remaining 'a cayuse, an unbroken horse, who will have to be dragged, or ridden and broken to arrive at the roundup or the horse butcher's. I'll even settle for the role of the coyote, that lonely yapping ornery stinking enduring snooty creature, that wild to-hell-with-conformity dog, that prototype of the damn-you-general critter we call a writer—howling alone, yet hoping at least to hear one other yip-yip start up over the next hill' (*The Creative Writer*).

Birney's reputation as a poet was established with *David and Other Poems* (1942) and *Now Is Time* (1945), both of which won Governor General's awards. Further poetry books include *The Strait of Anian* (1948), *Trial of a City and Other Verse* (1952; the narrative poem of the title was reprinted as *The Damnation of Vancouver*),

Near False Creek Mouth (1964), *Collected Poems* (1975), *Ghost in the Wheels: Selected Poems* (1977), and *Fall by Fury* (1978). He has also published two novels, *Turvey* (1949) and *Down the Long Table* (1955), and three books about his life and art: *The Creative Writer* (1966), *The Cow Jumped Over the Moon* (1972), and *Spreading Time: Book I, 1940-1949* (1980).

VANCOUVER LIGHTS

About me the night   moonless   wimples the mountains
wraps ocean   land   air   and mounting
sucks at the stars   The city   throbbing below
webs the peninsula   Streaming   the golden
strands overleap the seajet   by bridge and buoy
vault the shears of the inlet   climb the woods
toward me   falter   and halt   Across to the firefly
haze of a ship on the gulf's erased horizon
roll the spokes of a restless lighthouse

Through the feckless years we have come to the time
when to look on this quilt of lamps is a troubling delight
Welling from Europe's bog   through Africa flowing
and Asia   drowning the lonely lumes on the oceans
tiding up over Halifax   now to this winking
outpost comes flooding the primal ink

On this mountain's brutish forehead with terror of space
I stir   of the changeless night and the stark ranges
of nothing   pulsing down from beyond and between
the fragile planets   We are a spark beleaguered
by darkness   this twinkle we make in a corner of emptiness
how shall we utter our fear that the black Experimentress
will never in the range of her microscope find it?   Our Phoebus
himself is a bubble that dries on Her slide   while the Nubian
wears for an evening's whim a necklace of nebulae

Yet we must speak   we the unique glowworms
Out of the waters and rocks of our little world
we cunningly conjured these flames   hooped these sparks
by our will   From blankness and cold we fashioned stars

to our size and signalled Aldebaran This must we say
whoever may be to hear us if murk devour
and none weave again in gossamer:

These rays were ours
we made and unmade them Not the shudder of continents
doused us the moon's passion nor crash of comets
In the fathomless heat of our dwarfdom our dream's combustion
we contrived the power the blast that snuffed us
No one bound Prometheus Himself he chained
and consumed his own bright liver O stranger
Plutonian descendant or beast in the stretching night—
there was light

[1941]

ANGLOSAXON STREET

Dawndrizzle ended dampness steams from
blotching brick and blank plasterwaste
Faded housepatterns hoary and finicky
unfold stuttering stick like a phonograph

Here is a ghetto gotten for goyim
O with care denuded of nigger and kike
No coonsmell rankles reeks only cellarrot
ottar of carexhaust catacorpse and cookinggrease
Imperial hearts heave in this haven
Cracks across windows are welded with slogans
There'll Always Be An England enhances geraniums
and V's for a Victory vanquish the housefly

Ho! with beaming sun march the bleached beldames
festooned with shopping bags farded flatarched
bigthewed Saxonwives stepping over buttrivers
waddling back wienerladen to suckle smallfry

Hoy! with sunslope shrieking over hydrants
flood from learninghall the lean fingerlings
Nordic nobblecheeked not all clean of nose
leaping Commandowise into leprous lanes

What! after whistleblow!   spewed from wheelboat
after daylong doughtiness   dire handplay
in sewertrench or sandpit   come Saxonthegns
Junebrown Jutekings   jawslack for meat

Sit after supper   on smeared doorsteps
not humbly swearing   hatedeeds on Huns
profiteers politicians   pacifists Jews

Then by twobit magic   to muse in movie
unlock picturehoard   or lope to alehall
soaking bleakly   in beer skittleless
Home again to hotbox   and humid husbandhood
in slumbertrough adding   sleepily to Anglekin

Alongside in lanenooks   carling and leman
caterwaul and clip   careless of Saxonry
with moonglow and haste   and a higher heartbeat

Slumbers now slumtrack   unstinks cooling
waiting brief for milkhind   mornstar and worldrise

[Toronto 1942]

From the Hazel Bough

He met a lady
    on a lazy street
hazel eyes
    and little plush feet

her legs swam by
    like lovely trout
eyes were trees
    where boys leant out

hands in the dark and
    a river side
round breasts rising
    with the finger's tide

she was plump as a finch
 and live as a salmon
gay as silk and
 proud as a Brahmin

they winked when they met
 and laughed when they parted
never took time
 to be brokenhearted

but no man sees
 where the trout lie now
or what leans out
 from the hazel bough

[Toronto, 1945—Vancouver, 1947]

David

I

David and I that summer cut trails on the Survey,
All week in the valley for wages, in air that was steeped
In the wail of mosquitoes, but over the sunalive week-ends
We climbed, to get from the ruck of the camp, the surly

Poker, the wrangling, the snoring under the fetid
Tents, and because we had joy in our lengthening coltish
Muscles, and mountains for David were made to see over,
Stairs from the valleys and steps to the sun's retreats.

II

Our first was Mount Gleam. We hiked in the long afternoon
To a curling lake and lost the lure of the faceted
Cone in the swell of its sprawling shoulders. Past
The inlet we grilled our bacon, the strips festooned

On a poplar prong, in the hurrying slant of the sunset.
Then the two of us rolled in the blanket while round us the cold
Pines thrust at the stars. The dawn was a floating
Of mists till we reached to the slopes above timber, and won

To snow like fire in the sunlight. The peak was upthrust
Like a fist in a frozen ocean of rock that swirled
Into valleys the moon could be rolled in. Remotely unfurling
Eastward the alien prairie glittered. Down through the dusty

Skree on the west we descended, and David showed me
How to use the give of shale for giant incredible
Strides. I remember, before the larches' edge,
That I jumped a long green surf of juniper flowing

Away from the wind, and landed in gentian and saxifrage
Spilled on the moss. Then the darkening firs
And the sudden whirring of water that knifed down a fern-hidden
Cliff and splashed unseen into mist in the shadows.

III
One Sunday on Rampart's arête a rainsquall caught us,
And passed, and we clung by our blueing fingers and bootnails
An endless hour in the sun, not daring to move
Till the ice had steamed from the slate. And David taught me

How time on a knife-edge can pass with the guessing of fragments
Remembered from poets, the naming of strata beside one,
And matching of stories from schooldays. . . . We crawled astride
The peak to feast on the marching ranges flagged

By the fading shreds of the shattered stormcloud. Lingering
There it was David who spied to the south, remote,
And unmapped, a sunlit spire on Sawback, an overhang
Crooked like a talon. David named it the Finger.

That day we chanced on the skull and the splayed white ribs
Of a mountain goat underneath a cliff-face, caught
On a rock. Around were the silken feathers of hawks.
And that was the first I knew that a goat could slip.

IV
And then Inglismaldie. Now I remember only
The long ascent of the lonely valley, the live
Pine spirally scarred by lightning, the slicing pipe
Of invisible pika, and great prints, by the lowest

Snow, of a grizzly. There it was too that David
Taught me to read the scroll of coral in limestone
And the beetle-seal in the shale of ghostly trilobites,
Letters delivered to man from the Cambrian waves.

V

On Sundance we tried from the col and the going was hard.
The air howled from our feet to the smudged rocks
And the papery lake below. At an outthrust we baulked
Till David clung with his left to a dint in the scarp,

Lobbed the iceaxe over the rocky lip,
Slipped from his holds and hung by the quivering pick,
Twisted his long legs up into space and kicked
To the crest. Then grinning, he reached with his freckled wrist

And drew me up after. We set a new time for that climb.
That day returning we found a robin gyrating
In grass, wing-broken. I caught it to tame but David
Took and killed it, and said, 'Could you teach it to fly?'

VI

In August, the second attempt, we ascended The Fortress.
By the forks of the Spray we caught five trout and fried them
Over a balsam fire. The woods were alive
With the vaulting of mule-deer and drenched with clouds
    all the morning,

Till we burst at noon to the flashing and floating round
Of the peaks. Coming down we picked in our hats the bright
And sunhot raspberries, eating them under a mighty
Spruce, while a marten moving like quicksilver scouted us.

VII

But always we talked of the Finger on Sawback, unknown
And hooked, till the first afternoon in September we slogged
Through the musky woods, past a swamp that quivered
    with frog-song,
And camped by a bottle-green lake. But under the cold

Breath of the glacier sleep would not come, the moon-light
Etching the Finger. We rose and trod past the feathery
Larch, while the stars went out, and the quiet heather
Flushed, and the skyline pulsed with the surging bloom

Of incredible dawn in the Rockies. David spotted
Bighorns across the moraine and sent them leaping
With yodels the ramparts redoubled and rolled to the peaks,
And the peaks to the sun. The ice in the morning thaw

Was a gurgling world of crystal and cold blue chasms,
And seracs that shone like frozen saltgreen waves.
At the base of the Finger we tried once and failed. Then David
Edged to the west and discovered the chimney; the last

Hundred feet we fought the rock and shouldered and kneed
Our way for an hour and made it. Unroping we formed
A cairn on the rotting tip. Then I turned to look north
At the glistening wedge of giant Assiniboine, heedless

Of handhold. And one foot gave. I swayed and shouted.
David turned sharp and reached out his arm and steadied me,
Turning again with a grin and his lips ready
To jest. But the strain crumbled his foothold. Without

A gasp he was gone. I froze to the sound of grating
Edge-nails and fingers, the slither of stones, the lone
Second of silence, the nightmare thud. Then only
The wind and the muted beat of unknowing cascades.

VIII

Somehow I worked down the fifty impossible feet
To the ledge, calling and getting no answer but echoes
Released in the cirque, and trying not to reflect
What an answer would mean. He lay still, with his lean

Young face upturned and strangely unmarred, but his legs
Splayed beneath him, beside the final drop,
Six hundred feet sheer to the ice. My throat stopped
When I reached him, for he was alive. He opened his grey

Straight eyes and brokenly murmured 'over . . . over.'
And I, feeling beneath him a cruel fang
Of the ledge thrust in his back, but not understanding,
Mumbled stupidly, 'Best not to move,' and spoke

Of his pain. But he said, 'I can't move. . . . If only I felt
Some pain.' Then my shame stung the tears to my eyes
As I crouched, and I cursed myself, but he cried,
Louder, 'No, Bobbie! Don't ever blame yourself.

I didn't test my foothold.' He shut the lids
Of his eyes to the stare of the sky, while I moistened his lips
From our water flask and tearing my shirt into strips
I swabbed the shredded hands. But the blood slid

From his side and stained the stone and the thirsting lichens,
And yet I dared not lift him up from the gore
Of the rock. Then he whispered, 'Bob, I want to go over!'
This time I knew what he meant and I grasped for a lie

And said, 'I'll be back here by midnight with ropes
And men from the camp and we'll cradle you out.' But I knew
That the day and the night must pass and the cold dews
Of another morning before such men unknowing

The ways of mountains could win to the chimney's top.
And then, how long? And he knew . . . and the hell of hours
After that, if he lived till we came, roping him out.
But I curled beside him and whispered, 'The bleeding will stop.

You can last.' He said only, 'Perhaps. . . . For what? A wheelchair,
Bob?' His eyes brightening with fever upbraided me.
I could not look at him more and said, 'Then I'll stay
With you.' But he did not speak, for the clouding fever.

I lay dazed and stared at the long valley,
The glistening hair of a creek on the rug stretched
By the firs, while the sun leaned round and flooded the ledge,
The moss, and David still as a broken doll.

I hunched to my knees to leave, but he called and his voice
Now was sharpened with fear. 'For Christ's sake push me over!
If I could move. . . . Or die. . . .' The sweat ran from his forehead,
But only his eyes moved. A hawk was buoying

Blackly its wings over the wrinkled ice.
The purr of a waterfall rose and sank with the wind.
Above us climbed the last joint of the Finger
Beckoning bleakly the wide indifferent sky.

Even then in the sun it grew cold lying there. . . . And I knew
He had tested his holds. It was I who had not. . . . I looked
At the blood on the ledge, and the far valley. I looked
At last in his eyes. He breathed, 'I'd do it for you, Bob.'

IX

I will not remember how nor why I could twist
Up the wind-devilled peak, and down through the chimney's empty
Horror, and over the traverse alone. I remember
Only the pounding fear I would stumble on It

When I came to the grave-cold maw of the bergschrund . . . reeling
Over the sun-cankered snowbridge, shying the caves
In the névé . . . the fear, and the need to make sure It was there
On the ice, the running and falling and running, leaping

Of gaping greenthroated crevasses, alone and pursued
By the Finger's lengthening shadow. At last through the fanged
And blinding seracs I slid to the milky wrangling
Falls at the glacier's snout, through the rocks piled huge

On the humped moraine, and into the spectral larches,
Alone. By the glooming lake I sank and chilled
My mouth but I could not rest and stumbled still
To the valley, losing my way in the ragged marsh.

I was glad of the mire that covered the stains, on my ripped
Boots, of his blood, but panic was on me, the reek
Of the bog, the purple glimmer of toadstools obscene
In the twilight. I staggered clear to a firewaste, tripped

And fell with a shriek on my shoulder. It somehow eased
My heart to know I was hurt, but I did not faint
And I could not stop while over me hung the range
Of the Sawback. In blackness I searched for the trail by the creek

And found it. . . . My feet squelched a slug and horror
Rose again in my nostrils. I hurled myself
Down the path. In the woods behind some animal yelped.
Then I saw the glimmer of tents and babbled my story.

I said that he fell straight to the ice where they found him,
And none but the sun and incurious clouds have lingered
Around the marks of that day on the ledge of the Finger,
That day, the last of my youth, on the last of our mountains.

[1942]

BUSHED

He invented a rainbow but lightning struck it
shattered it into the lake-lap of a mountain
so big his mind slowed when he looked at it

Yet he built a shack on the shore
learned to roast porcupine belly and
wore the quills on his hatband

At first he was out with the dawn
whether it yellowed bright as wood-columbine
or was only a fuzzed moth in a flannel of storm

But he found the mountain was clearly alive
sent messages whizzing down every hot morning
boomed proclamations at noon and spread out
a white guard of goat
before falling asleep on its feet at sundown

When he tried his eyes on the lake   ospreys
would fall like valkyries
choosing the cut-throat
He took then to waiting
till the night smoke rose from the boil of the sunset

But the moon carved unknown totems
out of the lakeshore
owls in the beardusky woods derided him
moosehorned cedars circled his swamps and tossed
their antlers up to the stars
Then he knew   though the mountain slept   the winds
were shaping its peak to an arrowhead
poised

And now he could only
bar himself in and wait
for the great flint to come singing into his heart

[1951]

A Walk in Kyoto

All week   the maid tells me   bowing
her doll's body at my mat   is Boys' Day
Also please Man's Day   and gravely
bends deeper   The magnolia sprig in my alcove
is it male?   The ancient discretions of Zen were not shaped
for my phallic western eye   There is so much discretion
in this small bowed body of an empire
the wild hair of waterfalls combed straight
in the ricefields   the inn-maid retreating
with the face of a shut flower   I stand hunched
and clueless like a castaway in the shoals of my room

When I slide my parchment door to stalk awkward
through Lilliput gardens framed and untouchable
as watercolors   the streets look much the same
the Men are being pulled past on the strings of their engines
the legs of the Boys are revolved by a thousand pedals
and all the faces as taut and unfestive as Moscow's
or Toronto's   or mine

Lord Buddha help us all there is vigor enough
in these islands and in all islands reefed and resounding
with cities   But the pitch is high as the ping
of cicadas   those small strained motors concealed

in the propped pines by the dying river   and only
male as the stretched falsetto of actors mincing
the women's roles in *kabuki*   or female only
as the lost heroes womanized in the Ladies' Opera
Where in these alleys jammed with competing waves
of signs in two tongues and three scripts
can the simple song of a man be heard?

By the shoguns' palace   the Important Cultural Property
stripped for tiptoeing schoolgirls   I stare at the staring
penned carp that flail on each other's backs
to the shrunk pool's edge for the crumb this non-fish
tossed   Is this the Day's one parable?
Or under that peeling pagoda the five hundred tons
of hermaphrodite Word?

At the inn I prepare to surrender again my defeated
shoes to the bending maid   But suddenly the closed
lotus opens to a smile and she points
over my shoulder   above the sagging tiles   to where
tall in the bare sky and huge as Gulliver
a carp is rising   golden and fighting
thrusting its paper body up from the fist
of a small boy on an empty roof   higher
and higher   into the endless winds of the world

[1958]

THE BEAR ON THE DELHI ROAD

Unreal   tall as a myth
by the road the Himalayan bear
is beating the brilliant air
with his crooked arms
About him two men   bare
spindly as locusts   leap

One pulls on a ring
in the great soft nose   His mate
flicks   flicks with a stick
up at the rolling eyes

They have not led him here
down from the fabulous hills
to this bald alien plain
and the clamorous world   to kill
but simply to teach him to dance

They are peaceful both   these spare
men of Kashmir   and the bear
alive is their living   too
If   far on the Delhi way
around him galvanic they dance
it is merely to wear   wear
from his shaggy body the tranced
wish forever to stay
only an ambling bear
four-footed in berries

It is no more joyous for them
In this hot dust to prance
out of reach of the praying claws
sharpened to paw for ants
in the shadows of deodars

It is not easy to free
myth from reality
or rear this fellow up
to lurch   lurch with them
in the tranced dancing of men

[Srinagar, 1958—Île des Porquerolles, 1959]

Haiku for a Young Waitress

With dusk I am caught
peering over the holly
hedge at the dogwood

[1960]

Al Purdy (b. 1918)

Al Purdy is a maverick. Born Alfred Wellington Purdy in Wooler, Ontario, a self-confessed 'neurotic kid', he left Albert College at the age of sixteen to take up the life of a transient worker, apple-picking and riding the rods to western Canada. He enlisted in the RCAF in January 1940, but his independence of mind resulted in his being 'busted' from the rank of sergeant while in Trenton, Ontario. After the war, he started a short-lived taxi and bootlegging business. From 1949 to 1955 he lived in Vancouver with his wife, Eurithe, and organized a union in a mattress factory where he worked. After selling his first play to the CBC in 1955, Purdy moved to Montreal, where he developed friendships with Irving Layton and Milton Acorn, and then to Roblin Lake at Ameliasburg, where he lived for many years. He has travelled widely, to the Cariboo region of British Columbia, the Arctic, Greece, Mexico, Asia, and the Soviet Union, and now spends most of his time in Sidney, BC.

Purdy's first book of poetry, *The Enchanted Echo*, was self-published in 1944; *The Crafte So Long to Lerne* appeared in 1959. With the publication of *Poems for All the Annettes* (1962) and *The Cariboo Horses* (1965, Governor General's Award), Purdy's reputation was established. In these volumes he revealed a rich sense of humour and a delightful capacity for self-mockery. In *North of Summer* (1967) and *Wild Grape Wine* (1968), however, the engaging, boisterous Purdy gives way to a more restrained descriptive and meditative poet. His earlier poetry owes something to D.H. Lawrence, Earle Birney, Irving Layton, and Robert Creeley, but his more recent influences have been largely European poetry in translation. The best of Purdy's poems, such as 'Lament for the Dorsets', are historical meditations, delicate renderings of vanishing moments from the past. Like Philip Larkin, he has an unusual sensitivity to change, a time-consciousness; his imagination is attuned to the subtle ironies and nuances produced by juxtaposing past and present. 'I thought it was a fascinating concept,' he says in an interview with Alan Twigg in *Strong Voices* (1988), 'to imagine everybody living to leave lines behind on the street where they've been. . . . What it means is you're walking across the paths of the dead at all times. Everytime you cross the St Lawrence River you're crossing Champlain's path.'

Primarily self-taught, and a prodigious reader, Purdy claims to have played hookey for two months at age thirteeen to read a pile of two hundred popular novels by Frank Merriwell. He has little patience for certain schools of poetry, particularly poets such as Robert Creeley, Charles Olson, and their Canadian followers, associated with Black Mountain College: 'It's still a dead-end. They don't have any variety. The Black Mountain people talk in a certain manner in which they make under-emphasis a virtue. It's dull writing. It's far duller than conversations. I can't understand how people can write it, except kids write it and think, I too can be a poet. They can ignore a thousand years of writing poems, not read what's come before.'

When asked by Twigg if he is attracted to blemish or imperfection, Purdy replies: 'Don't you ever want to splash muddy water into a sunset? A sunset is too marvellous, how are you going to paint it? How are you going to talk about it? So there is a quality of wishing to muddy up perfection, I agree.' This view of things has its corollary in terms of form, too, particularly his use of the dash to end a poem: 'Yes, a lot of poems are in process, as if things happen after you stop looking at it. A poem is a continual revision, even if you've written it down without changing a single word. I like the thought of revision. When I copy a poem, I often change it. When I've written a poem in longhand, as I always do, I'll type, then I'll scribble it all up with changes.'

About the origins of the poetic impulse, he says: 'You have to go back to when you started to write. I think most young poets begin to write through sheer ego. Look at me, no hands, Mom. There's always going to be the element of ego, because we can't escape our egos. We don't necessarily want to. But there has to be a time when we can sit down and write and try to say a thing and the ego isn't so important. When you are just trying to tell the truth, you're not trying to write immortal lines that will go reverberating down the centuries. You're saying what you feel and think and what is important to you.'

In a memoir entitled 'The Bad Times', written in 1988, Purdy describes his transition from an inept scribbler of doggerel to a successful poet: 'But I was reading Dylan Thomas, T.S. Eliot, and others; I was growing even more interested in and curious about other people. I was also a navel-watcher, narcissistic as hell. Sure I was fascinated by myself. It's been a metamorphosis—not to produce a butterfly but, I hope, a writer. Curiosity seems to me my most salient characteristic. I'd like to use it for a few years more. I want to go on exploring my own limitations and boundaries. And in all my writing, there's a shadow self I'm trying to get in touch with, the other self who lives in all of us, friend, foe, or neutral judge. A doppelgänger of the soul, that absurd word designating something that doesn't exist. Therefore I invent him.'

Since the mid-sixties Purdy has published many books of poetry, including *Wild Grape Wine* (1968), *Love in a Burning Building* (1970), *Selected Poems* (1972), *Sex & Death* (1973), *Sundance At Dusk* (1976), *The Poems of Al Purdy* (1976), *Being Alive: Poems 1958-1978* (1978), *The Stone Bird* (1981), *Piling Blood* (1984), *The Collected Poems of Al Purdy* (1986), and *The Woman on the Shore* (1990). He has also edited the anthologies *Fifteen Winds* (1969), *Storm Warning I* (1972), and *Storm Warning II* (1976), and written a novel and several volumes of memoirs and letters, including *The Bukowski / Purdy Letters 1964-1974* (1984).

The Cariboo Horses

At 100 Mile House the cowboys ride in rolling
stagey cigarettes with one hand reining
restive equine rebels on a morning grey as stone
—so much like riding dangerous women
        with whiskey coloured eyes—
such women as once fell dead with their lovers
with fire in their heads and slippery froth on thighs
—Beaver and Carrier women maybe or
        Blackfoot squaws far past the edge of this valley
on the other side of those two toy mountain ranges
        from the sunfierce plains beyond—

But only horses
waiting in stables
hitched at taverns
standing at dawn
pastured outside the town with
jeeps and fords and chevvys and
busy muttering stake trucks rushing
importantly over roads of man's devising
over the safe known roads of the ranchers
families and merchants of the town—
On the high prairie
are only horse and rider
wind in dry grass
clopping in silence under the toy mountains
dropping sometimes and
lost in the dry grass
golden oranges of dung—
Only horses
no stopwatch memories or palace ancestors
not Kiangs hauling undressed stone in the Nile Valley
and having stubborn Egyptian tantrums or
Onagers racing thru Hither Asia and
the last Quagga screaming in African highlands
lost relatives of these
whose hooves were thunder
the ghosts of horses battering thru the wind
whose names were the wind's common usage
whose life was the sun's
arriving here at chilly noon
in the gasoline smell of the
dust and waiting 15 minutes
at the grocer's—

[1965]

SONG OF THE IMPERMANENT HUSBAND

Oh I would
I would in a minute
if the cusswords and bitter anger couldn't—
if the either/or quarrel didn't—

and the fat around my middle wasn't—
if I was young if
                I wasn't so damn sure
I couldn't find another maddening bitch
like you holding on for dear life to
all the different parts of me for
twenty or twenty
                thousand years
I'd leave in the night like
a disgraced caviar salesman
                descend the moonlight
stairs to Halifax
        (uh—no—not Halifax)
well then Toronto
                uh
I guess not Toronto either/or
nouveau riche Vancouver down
                                down
                                    down
the dark stairs to
the South Seas' sunlit milky reefs and
        the jungle's green
                unending bank account with
all the brown girls being brown
                as they can be and all
the one piece behinds stretched tight tonight
in small sarongs not to be touched tho Oh
beautiful as an angel's ass without the genitals
and me
        in Paris like a smudged Canadian postcard and
(dear me)
        all the importuning white and lily girls
of Rue Pigalle
            and stroll
the sodden London streets and
            find a sullen foggy woman who
enjoyed my odd colonial ways and send
a postcard back to you about my faithfulness and
talk about the lovely lovely English weather
I'd be the slimiest most uxorious wife deserter
            my shrunk amoeba self absurd inside

a saffron girl's geography and
hating me between magnetic nipples
but
    fooling no one in all the sad
    and much emancipated world
Why then I'll stay at least for tea for
all the brownness is too brown and
all the whiteness too damned white
and I'm afraid
        afraid of being
any other woman's man who
might be me
        afraid
the unctuous and uneasy self I glimpse
sometimes might lose my faint and yapping cry for
being anything was never quite what I intended
And you you
        bitch no irritating
questions re love and permanence only
        an unrolling lifetime here
between your rocking thighs and
        the semblance of motion

[1965]

Eskimo Graveyard

Walking in glacial litter
frost boils and boulder pavements
of an old river delta
where angry living water
changes its mind every half century
and takes a new direction
to the blue fiord
The Public Works guy I'm with
says you always find good gravel
for concrete near a graveyard
where digging is easy maybe
a footnote on human character
But wrapped in blankets
above ground a dead old woman

(for the last few weeks I'm told)
without a grave marker
And a hundred yards away
the Anglican missionary's grave
with whitewashed cross
that means equally nothing
The river's soft roar
drifts to my ears and changes
tone when the wind changes
ice debris melts at low tide
& the Public Works guy is mildly pleased
with the good gravel we found
for work on the schoolhouse
which won't have to be shipped in
from Montreal
and mosquitoes join happily
in our conversation Then
he stops to consult
with the construction foreman
I walk on
toward the tents of The People
half a mile away
at one corner of the picture
Mothers with children on their backs
in the clean white parkas
they take such pride in
buying groceries at H.B.C.
boys lounging under the store
in space where timber stilts
hold it above the permafrost
with two of them arm in arm
in the manner of Eskimo friends
After dinner
I walk down among the tents
and happen to think of the old woman
neither wholly among the dead
nor quite gone from the living
and wonder how often
a thought of hers enters the minds
of people she knew before
and what kind of flicker it is

as lights begin to come on
in nightlong twilight
and thoughts of me
occur to the mosquitoes
I keep walking
as if something ought to happen
(I don't know what)
with the sun stretching
a yellow band across the water
from headland to black headland
at high tide in the fiord
sealing in the settlement
as if there was no way out
and indeed there isn't
until the looping Cansos come
dropping thru the mountain doorway
That old woman?
it occurs to me
I might have been thinking
about human bookkeeping
debits and credits that is
or profit and loss
(and laugh at myself)
among the sealed white tents
like glowing swans
hoping
for a most improbable
birth

[1967]

ARCTIC RHODODENDRONS

They are small purple surprises
in the river's white racket
and after you've seen them
a number of times
in water-places
where their silence seems
related to river-thunder
you think of them as 'noisy flowers'

Years ago
it may have been
that lovers came this way
stopped in the outdoor hotel
to watch the water floorshow
and lying prone together
where the purged green
boils to a white heart
and the shore trembles
like a stone song
with bodies touching
flowers were their conversation
and love the sound of a colour
that lasts two weeks in August
and then dies
except for the three or four
I pressed in a letter
and sent whispering to you

[1967]

Lament for the Dorsets

(Eskimos extinct in the 14th century A.D.)

Animal bones and some mossy tent rings
scrapers and spearheads   carved ivory swans
all that remains of the Dorset giants
who drove the Vikings back to their long ships
talked to spirits of earth and water
—a picture of terrifying old men
so large they broke the backs of bears
so small they lurk behind bone rafters
in the brain of modern hunters
among good thoughts and warm things
and come out at night
to spit on the stars

The big men with clever fingers
who had no dogs and hauled their sleds
over the frozen northern oceans
awkward giants
                killers of seal

they couldn't compete with little men
who came from the west with dogs
Or else in a warm climatic cycle
the seals went back to cold waters
and the puzzled Dorsets scratched their heads
with hairy thumbs around 1350 A.D.
—couldn't figure it out
went around saying to each other
plaintively
            'What's wrong? What happened?
            Where are the seals gone?'
And died

Twentieth century people
apartment dwellers
executives of neon death
warmakers with things that explode
—they have never imagined us in their future
how could we imagine them in the past
squatting among the moving glaciers
six hundred years ago
with glowing lamps?
As remote or nearly
as the trilobites and swamps
when coal became
or the last great reptile hissed
at a mammal the size of a mouse
that squeaked and fled

Did they ever realize at all
what was happening to them?
Some old hunter with one lame leg
a bear had chewed
sitting in a caribou skin tent
—the last Dorset?
Let's say his name was Kudluk
carving 2-inch ivory swans
for a dead grand-daughter
taking them out of his mind
the places in his mind
where pictures are

He selects a sharp stone tool
to gouge a parallel pattern of lines
on both sides of the swan
holding it with his left hand
bearing down and transmitting
his body's weight
from brain to arm and right hand
and one of his thoughts
turns to ivory
The carving is laid aside
in beginning darkness
at the end of hunger
after a while wind
blows down the tent and snow
begins to cover him
After 600 years
the ivory thought
is still warm

[1968]

POEM

You are ill and so I lead you away
and put you to bed in the dark room
—you lie breathing softly and I hold your hand
feeling the fingertips relax as sleep comes

You will not sleep more than a few hours
and the illness is less serious than my anger or cruelty
and the dark bedroom is like a foretaste of other darknesses
to come later which all of us must endure alone
but here I am permitted to be with you

After a while in sleep your fingers clutch tightly
and I know that whatever may be happening
the fear coiled in dreams or the bright trespass of pain
there is nothing at all I can do except hold your hand
and not go away

[1968]

GROSSE ISLE

Look, stranger, at this island now
The leaping light for your delight discovers—
—W.H. Auden

Look stranger
a diseased whale in the St Lawrence
this other island than Auden's
dull grey when the weather is dull grey
and an east wind brings rain
this Appalachian outcrop
a stone ship foundered in the river estuary
now in the care and keeping of Parks Canada
—a silence here like no mainland silence
at Cholera Bay where the dead bodies
awaited high tide and the rough kindness
of waves sweeping them into the dark—

Look stranger
at this other island
weedgrown graves in the three cemeteries
be careful your clothes don't get hooked
by wild raspberry canes and avoid the poison ivy
—here children went mad with cholera fever
and raging with thirst they ran into the river
their parents following a little way
before they died themselves
—and don't stumble over the rusted tricycle
somehow overlooked at the last big cleanup
or perhaps left where it is for the tourists?

Look stranger
where the sea wind sweeps westward
down the estuary
this way the other strangers came
potato-famine Irish and Scotch crofters
refugees from the Highland clearances
and sailing ships waited here
to remove their corpses
and four million immigrants passed through

—now there's talk of a Health Spa and Casino
we could situate our billboard
right under the granite cross by the river:
UNLIMITED INVESTMENT OPPORTUNITIES

Look stranger
see your own face reflected in the river
stumble up from the stinking hold
blinded by sunlight and into the leaky dinghy
only half-hearing the sailors taunting you
'Shanty Irish! Shanty Irish!'
gulp the freshening wind and pinch yourself
trying to understand if the world is a real place
stumble again and fall when you reach the shore
and bless this poisoned earth
but stranger no longer
for this is home

[1994]

Robert Lowell (1917-1977)

Born in Boston into one of the famous families of New England, Robert Lowell received his formal education at Harvard, at Kenyon College, where he studied classics and worked with the writer John Crowe Ransom, and at Louisiana State University. During the Second World War Lowell was drafted, after trying twice to enlist in 1943, but he refused to serve on the grounds that the allied bombing of enemy civilians was unjustified and that America was out of danger. His imprisonment is recorded in some of his later poems ('Given a year, / I walked on the roof of West Street Jail'). Early in his poetic career Lowell became a Catholic, adding to the burden and complications of a New England Puritan conscience. He was married twice, to Jean Stafford (1940) and Elizabeth Hardwick (1948), and was an occasional teacher.

Lowell's early poetry is mannered and formal, employing rhyme and metrics, and is steeped in the lore and landscape of New England. In this environment, he found abundant correlatives for the turmoil of his young manhood: in 'The Quaker Graveyard in Nantucket' the tortuous moral terrain of New England is brilliantly realized; and in 'Mr Edwards and the Spider' the Puritan obsession with sin and damnation is rendered in the form of a dramatic monologue by the famous preacher Jonathan Edwards. In the later *Life Studies* (1959), however, Lowell's poems are confessional and conversational, without the apparent formality and objectivity of *Lord Weary's Castle* (1946). Instead of rhyme and metrics, one finds in 'For the Union Dead,' for example, continuously shifting speech rhythms in conjunction with strikingly appropriate images: 'Their monument sticks like a fish-bone / in the city's throat. / Its colonel is as lean / as a compass needle.' Such poems are neither casual nor relaxed; Lowell's early restraint is still there, but it is apparent in a new spareness, a strength and clarity of outline, that is the legacy of the imagists.

Derek Walcott has said of his friend and poetic idol (*The Paris Review*, 1985): 'The influence of Lowell on everyone, I think, is in his brutal honesty, his trying to get into poetry a fictional power that wasn't there before, as if your life was a section of a novel—not because you're the hero, but because some of the things that were not in poems, some of the very ordinary banal details, can be illumined. Lowell emphasized the banality. In a sense to keep the banality banal and still make it poetic is a great achievement.' In his own interview in the same magazine (reprinted in *Writers At Work* 2, edited by George Plimpton, 1962), Lowell said: 'I'm sure that writing isn't a craft, that is, something for which you learn the skills and go on turning out. It must come from some deep impulse, deep inspiration. That can't be taught.'

Lowell's attraction to formal difficulty and breadth of personal and historical reference underscores his interest in the novel: 'The ideal modern form seems to be the novel and certain short stories. Maybe Tolstoi would be the perfect example—his work is imagistic, it deals with all experience, and there seems to be no conflict of the form and content. So one thing is to get into poetry that kind of human richness in rather simple descriptive language. Then there's another side of poetry: compression, something highly rhythmical and perhaps wrenched into a small space. I've always been fascinated by both these things. But getting it all on one page in a few stanzas, getting it all done in as little space as possible, revising and revising so that each word and rhythm though not perfect is pondered and wrestled with—you can't do that in prose very well, you'd never get your book written.'

In mid-career, Lowell admitted, he 'began to have a certain disrespect for tight forms. . . . That regularity just seemed to ruin the honesty of sentiment, and became rhetorical; it said, "I'm a poem" . . . . But there's another point about this mysterious business of prose and poetry, form and content, and the reasons for breaking forms. I don't think there's any very satisfactory answer. I seesaw back and forth between something highly metrical and something highly free; there isn't any one way to write. But it seems to me we've gotten into a sort of Alexandrian age. Poets of my generation and particularly younger ones have gotten terribly proficient at these forms. They write a very musical, difficult poem with tremendous skill, perhaps there's never been such skill. Yet the writing seems divorced from culture somehow. It's become too much something specialized that can't handle much experience. It's become a craft, purely a craft, and there must be some breakthrough back into life.'

In terms of the relation between poetry and experience, Lowell has this to say of the poems in *Life Studies*: 'They're not always factually true. There's a good deal of tinkering with fact. You leave out a lot, and emphasize this and not that. Your actual experience is a complete flux. I've invented facts and changed things, and the whole balance of the poem was something invented. So there's a lot of artistry, I hope, in the poems. Yet there's this thing: if a poem is autobiographical—and this is true of any kind of autobiographical writing and of historical writing—you want the reader to say, this is true.'

Lowell revised endlessly and even cannibalized his earlier poems, to achieve both greater clarity and greater suggestiveness: 'I think we always bring over some unexplained obscurities by shifting lines. . . but you always want—I think Chekhov talks about this—the detail that you can't explain. It's just there. It seems right to you, but you don't have to have it; you could have something else entirely. Now if everything's like that you'd have chaos, but a few unexplained difficult things—they seem to be the life-blood of variety—they may work.'

In his final remarks to the interviewer Frederick Seidel, Lowell moves from praising Robert Frost to a personal credo: 'Almost the whole problem of writing poetry is to bring it back to what you really feel, and that takes an awful lot of maneuvering. You may feel the doorknob more strongly than some big personal event, and the doorknob will open into something that you can use as your own. A lot of poetry seems to me very good in the tradition but just doesn't move me very much because it doesn't have personal vibrance to it. I probably exaggerate the value of it, but it's precious to me. Some little image, some detail you've noticed—you're writing about a little country shop, just describing it, and your poem ends up with an existentialist account of your experience. But it's the shop that started it off.'

Lowell's books of poetry include *Land of Unlikeness* (1944), *Lord Weary's Castle* (1946, Pulitzer Prize), *Poems, 1938-49* (1950), *The Mills of the Kavanaughs* (1951), *Life Studies* (1959), *Imitations* (1961), *For the Union Dead* (1964), *Near the Ocean* (1967), *The Dolphin* (1973), *History* (1973), *Selected Poems* (1976; revised in 1977), and *Day By Day* (1977).

THE HOLY INNOCENTS

Listen, the hay-bells tinkle as the cart
Wavers on rubber tires along the tar
And cindered ice below the burlap mill
And ale-wife run. The oxen drool and start
In wonder at the fenders of a car,
And blunder hugely up St Peter's hill.
These are the undefiled by woman—their
Sorrow is not the sorrow of this world:
King Herod shrieking vengeance at the curled
Up knees of Jesus choking in the air,

A king of speechless clods and infants. Still
The world out-Herods Herod; and the year,
The nineteen-hundred forty-fifth of grace,
Lumbers with losses up the clinkered hill
Of our purgation; and the oxen near
The worn foundations of their resting-place,
The holy manger where their bed is corn
And holly torn for Christmas. If they die,
As Jesus, in the harness, who will mourn?
Lamb of the shepherds, Child, how still you lie.

[1946]

Christmas in Black Rock

Christ God's red shadow hangs upon the wall
The dead leaf's echo on these hours
Whose burden spindles to no breath at all;
Hard at our heels the huntress moonlight towers
And the green needles bristle at the glass
Tiers of defence-plants where the treadmill night
Churns up Long Island Sound with piston-fist.
Tonight, my child, the lifeless leaves will mass,
Heaving and heaping, as the swivelled light
Burns on the bell-spar in the fruitless mist.

Christ Child, your lips are lean and evergreen
Tonight in Black Rock, and the moon
Sidles outside into the needle-screen
And strikes the hand that feeds you with a spoon
Tonight, as drunken Polish night-shifts walk
Over the causeway and their juke-box booms
Hosannah in excelsis Domino.
Tonight, my child, the foot-loose hallows stalk
Us down in the blind alleys of our rooms;
By the mined root the leaves will overflow.

December, old leech, has leafed through Autumn's store
Where Poland has unleashed its dogs
To bay the moon upon the Black Rock shore:
Under our windows, on the rotten logs
The moonbeam, bobbing like an apple, snags
The undertow. O Christ, the spiralling years
Slither with child and manger to a ball
Of ice; and what is man? We tear our rags
To hang the Furies by their itching ears,
And the green needles nail us to the wall.

[1946]

After the Surprising Conversions

September twenty-second, Sir: today
I answer. In the latter part of May,
Hard on our Lord's Ascension, it began

To be more sensible. A gentleman
Of more than common understanding, strict
In morals, pious in behaviour, kicked
Against our goad. A man of some renown,
An useful, honoured person in the town,
He came of melancholy parents; prone
To secret spells, for years they kept alone—
His uncle, I believe, was killed of it:
Good people, but of too much or little wit.
I preached one Sabbath on a text from Kings;
He showed concernment for his soul. Some things
In his experience were hopeful. He
Would sit and watch the wind knocking a tree
And praise this countryside our Lord has made.
Once when a poor man's heifer died, he laid
A shilling on the doorsill; though a thirst
For loving shook him like a snake, he durst
Not entertain much hope of his estate
In heaven. Once we saw him sitting late
Behind his attic window by a light
That guttered on his Bible; through that night
He meditated terror, and he seemed
Beyond advice or reason, for he dreamed
That he was called to trumpet Judgment Day
To Concord. In the latter part of May
He cut his throat. And though the coroner
Judged him delirious, soon a noisome stir
Palsied our village. At Jehovah's nod
Satan seemed more let loose amongst us: God
Abandoned us to Satan, and he pressed
Us hard, until we thought we could not rest
Till we had done with life. Content was gone.
All the good work was quashed. We were undone.
The breath of God had carried out a planned
And sensible withdrawal from this land;
The multitude, once unconcerned with doubt,
Once neither callous, curious nor devout,
Jumped at broadnoon, as though some peddler groaned
At it in its familiar twang: 'My friend,

Cut your own throat. Cut your own throat. Now! Now!'
September twenty-second, Sir, the bough
Cracks with the unpicked apples, and at dawn
The small-mouthed bass breaks water, gorged with spawn.

[1946]

THE QUAKER GRAVEYARD IN NANTUCKET

(for Warren Winslow, dead at sea)

Let man have dominion over the fishes of the sea and the fowls of the air and the beasts and the whole earth, and every creeping creature that moveth upon the earth.

I

A brackish reach of shoal off Madaket,—
The sea was still breaking violently and night
Had steamed into our North Atlantic Fleet,
When the drowned sailor clutched the drag-net. Light
Flashed from his matted head and marble feet,
He grappled at the net
With the coiled, hurdling muscles of his thighs:
The corpse was bloodless, a botch of reds and whites,
Its open, staring eyes
Were lustreless dead-lights
Or cabin-windows on a stranded hulk
Heavy with sand. We weight the body, close
Its eyes and heave it seaward whence it came,
Where the heel-headed dogfish barks its nose
On Ahab's void and forehead; and the name
Is blocked in yellow chalk.
Sailors, who pitch this portent at the sea
Where dreadnoughts shall confess
Its heel-bent deity,
When you are powerless
To sand-bag this Atlantic bulwark, faced
By the earth-shaker, green, unwearied, chaste
In his steel scales: ask for no Orphean lute
To pluck life back. The guns of the steeled fleet
Recoil and then repeat
The hoarse salute.

II

Whenever winds are moving and their breath
Heaves at the roped-in bulwarks of this pier,
The terns and sea-gulls tremble at your death
In these home waters. Sailor, can you hear
The Pequod's sea wings, beating landward, fall
Headlong and break on our Atlantic wall
Off 'Sconset, where the yawning S-boats splash
The bellbuoy, with ballooning spinnakers,
As the entangled, screeching mainsheet clears
The blocks: off Madaket, where lubbers lash
The heavy surf and throw their long lead squids
For blue-fish? Sea-gulls blink their heavy lids
Seaward. The winds' wings beat upon the stones,
Cousin, and scream for you and the claws rush
At the sea's throat and wring it in the slush
Of this old Quaker graveyard where the bones
Cry out in the long night for the hurt beast
Bobbing by Ahab's whaleboats in the East.

III

All you recovered from Poseidon died
With you, my cousin, and the harrowed brine
Is fruitless on the blue beard of the god,
Stretching beyond us to the castles in Spain,
Nantucket's westward haven. To Cape Cod
Guns, cradled on the tide,
Blast the eelgrass about a waterclock
Of bilge and backwash, roil the salt and sand
Lashing earth's scaffold, rock
Our warships in the hand
Of the great God, where time's contrition blues
Whatever it was these Quaker sailors lost
In the mad scramble of their lives. They died
When time was open-eyed,
Wooden and childish; only bones abide
There, in the nowhere, where their boats were tossed
Sky-high, where mariners had fabled news
Of IS, the whited monster. What it cost
Them is their secret. In the sperm-whale's slick
I see the Quakers drown and hear their cry:

'If God himself had not been on our side,
If God himself had not been on our side,
When the Atlantic rose against us, why,
Then it had swallowed us up quick.'

IV

This is the end of the whaleroad and the whale
Who spewed Nantucket bones on the thrashed swell
And stirred the troubled waters to whirlpools
To send the Pequod packing off to hell:
This is the end of them, three-quarters fools,
Snatching at straws to sail
Seaward and seaward on the turntail whale,
Spouting out blood and water as it rolls,
Sick as a dog to these Atlantic shoals:
Clamavimus, O depths. Let the sea-gulls wail
For water, for the deep where the high tide
Mutters to its hurt self, mutters and ebbs.
Waves wallow in their wash, go out and out,
Leave only the death-rattle of the crabs,
The beach increasing, its enormous snout
Sucking the ocean's side.
This is the end of running on the waves;
We are poured out like water. Who will dance
The mast-lashed master of Leviathans
Up from this field of Quakers in their unstoned graves?

V

When the whale's viscera go and the roll
Of its corruption overruns this world
Beyond tree-swept Nantucket and Wood's Hole
And Martha's Vineyard, Sailor, will your sword
Whistle and fall and sink into the fat?
In the great ash-pit of Jehoshaphat
The bones cry for the blood of the white whale,
The fat flukes arch and whack about its ears,
The death-lance churns into the sanctuary, tears
The gun-blue swingle, heaving like a flail,
And hacks the coiling life out: it works and drags
And rips the sperm-whale's midriff into rags,
Gobbets of blubber spill to wind and weather,

Sailor, and gulls go round the stoven timbers
Where the morning stars sing out together
And thunder shakes the white surf and dismembers
The red flag hammered in the mast-head. Hide,
Our steel, Jonas Messias, in Thy side.

VI

OUR LADY OF WALSINGHAM

There once the penitents took off their shoes
And then walked barefoot the remaining mile;
And the small trees, a stream, and hedgerows file
Slowly along the munching English lane,
Like cows to the old shrine, until you lose
Track of your dragging pain.
The stream flows down under the druid tree,
Shiloah's whirlpools gurgle and make glad
The castle of God. Sailor, you were glad
And whistled Sion by that stream. But see:

Our Lady, too small for her canopy,
Sits near the altar. There's no comeliness
At all or charm in that expressionless
Face with its heavy eyelids. As before,
This face, for centuries a memory,
Non est species, neque decor,
Expressionless, expresses God: it goes
Past castled Sion. She knows what God knows,
Not Calvary's Cross nor crib at Bethlehem
Now, and the world shall come to Walsingham.

VII

The empty winds are creaking and the oak
Splatters and splatters on the cenotaph,
The boughs are trembling and a gaff
Bobs on the untimely stroke
Of the greased wash exploding on a shoal-bell
In the old mouth of the Atlantic. It's well;
Atlantic, you are fouled with the blue sailors,
Sea-monsters, upward angel, downward fish:
Unmarried and corroding, spare of flesh
Mart once of supercilious, wing'd clippers,

Atlantic, where your bell-trap guts its spoil
You could cut the brackish winds with a knife
Here in Nantucket, and cast up the time
When the Lord God formed man from the sea's slime
And breathed into his face the breath of life,
And blue-lung'd combers lumbered to the kill.
The Lord survives the rainbow of His will.

[1946]

MEMORIES OF WEST STREET AND LEPKE

Only teaching on Tuesday, book-worming
in pajamas fresh from the washer each morning,
I hog a whole house on Boston's
'hardly passionate Marlborough Street',
where even the man
scavenging filth in the back alley trash cans,
has two children, a beach wagon, a helpmate,
and is a 'young Republican'.
I have a nine months' daughter,
young enough to be my granddaughter.
Like the sun she rises in her flame-flamingo infants' wear.

These are the tranquillized *Fifties*,
and I am forty. Ought I to regret my seedtime?
I was a fire-breathing Catholic C.O.,
and made my manic statement,
telling off the state and president, and then
sat waiting sentence in the bull pen
beside a Negro boy with curlicues
of marijuana in his hair.

Given a year,
I walked on the roof of the West Street Jail, a short
enclosure like my school soccer court,
and saw the Hudson River once a day
through sooty clothesline entanglements
and bleaching khaki tenements.
Strolling, I yammered metaphysics with Abramowitz,
a jaundice-yellow ('it's really tan')

and fly-weight pacifist,
so vegetarian,
he wore rope shoes and preferred fallen fruit.
He tried to convert Bioff and Brown,
the Hollywood pimps, to his diet.
Hairy, muscular, suburban,
wearing chocolate double-breasted suits,
they blew their tops and beat him black and blue.

I was so out of things, I'd never heard
of the Jehovah's Witnesses.
'Are you a C.O.?' I asked a fellow jailbird.
'No,' he answered. 'I'm a J.W.'
He taught me the 'hospital tuck',
and pointed out the T-shirted back
of *Murder Incorporated*'s Czar Lepke,
there piling towels on a rack,
or dawdling off to his little segregated cell full
of things forbidden the common man:
a portable radio, a dresser, two toy American
flags tied together with a ribbon of Easter palm.
Flabby, bald, lobotomized,
he drifted in a sheepish calm,
where no agonizing reappraisal
jarred his concentration on the electric chair—
hanging like an oasis in his air
of lost connections . . .

[1959]

SKUNK HOUR
for Elizabeth Bishop

Nautilus Island's hermit
heiress still lives through winter in her Spartan cottage;
her sheep still graze above the sea.
Her son's a bishop. Her farmer
is first selectman in our village,
she's in her dotage.

Thirsting for
the hierarchic privacy
of Queen Victoria's century,
she buys up all
the eyesores facing her shore,
and lets them fall.

The season's ill—
we've lost our summer millionaire,
who seemed to leap from an L. L. Bean
catalogue. His nine-knot yawl
was auctioned off to lobstermen.
A red fox stain covers Blue Hill.

And now our fairy
decorator brightens his shop for fall,
his fishnet's filled with orange cork,
orange, his cobbler's bench and awl,
there is no money in his work,
he'd rather marry.

One dark night,
my Tudor Ford climbed the hill's skull,
I watched for love-cars. Lights turned down,
they lay together, hull to hull,
where the graveyard shelves on the town. . . .
My mind's not right.

A car radio bleats,
'Love, O careless Love . . .' I hear
my ill-spirit sob in each blood cell,
as if my hand were at its throat. . . .
I myself am hell,
nobody's here—

only skunks, that search
in the moonlight for a bite to eat.
They march on their soles up Main Street:
white stripes, moonstruck eyes' red fire
under the chalk-dry and spar spire
of the Trinitarian Church.

I stand on top
of our back steps and breathe the rich air—
a mother skunk with her column of kittens swills the garbage pail.
She jabs her wedge-head in a cup
of sour cream, drops her ostrich tail,
and will not scare.

[1959]

FOR THE UNION DEAD

'Relinquunt omnia servare rem publicam.'

The old South Boston Aquarium stands
in a Sahara of snow now. Its broken windows are boarded.
The bronze weathervane cod has lost half its scales.
The airy tanks are dry.

Once my nose crawled like a snail on the glass;
my hand tingled
to burst the bubbles
drifting from the noses of the cowed, compliant fish.

My hand draws back. I often sigh still
for the dark downward and vegetating kingdom
of the fish and reptile. One morning last March,
I pressed against the new barbed and galvanized

fence on the Boston Common. Behind their cage,
yellow dinosaur steamshovels were grunting
as they cropped up tons of mush and grass
to gouge their underworld garage.

Parking spaces luxuriate like civic
sandpiles in the heart of Boston.
A girdle of orange, Puritan-pumpkin colored girders
braces the tingling Statehouse,

shaking over the excavations, as it faces Colonel Shaw
and his bell-cheeked Negro infantry
on St Gaudens' shaking Civil War relief,
propped by a plank splint against the garage's earthquake.

Two months after marching through Boston,
half the regiment was dead;
at the dedication,
William James could almost hear the bronze Negroes breathe.

Their monument sticks like a fishbone
in the city's throat.
Its Colonel is as lean
as a compass-needle.

He has an angry wrenlike vigilance,
a greyhound's gentle tautness;
he seems to wince at pleasure,
and suffocate for privacy.

He is out of bounds now. He rejoices in man's lovely,
peculiar power to choose life and die—
when he leads his black soldiers to death,
he cannot bend his back.

On a thousand small town New England greens,
the old white churches hold their air
of sparse, sincere rebellion; frayed flags
quilt the graveyards of the Grand Army of the Republic.

The stone statues of the abstract Union Soldier
grow slimmer and younger each year—
wasp-waisted, they doze over muskets
and muse through their sideburns. . . .

Shaw's father wanted no monument
except the ditch,
where his son's body was thrown
and lost with his 'niggers'.

The ditch is nearer.
There are no statues for the last war here;
on Boylston Street, a commercial photograph
shows Hiroshima boiling

over a Mosler Safe, the 'Rock of Ages'
that survived the blast. Space is nearer.
When I crouch to my television set,
the drained faces of Negro school-children rise like balloons.

Colonel Shaw
is riding on his bubble,
he waits
for the blessèd break.

The Aquarium is gone. Everywhere,
giant finned cars nose forward like fish;
a savage servility
slides by on grease.

[1959]

MR EDWARDS AND THE SPIDER

I saw the spiders marching through the air,
Swimming from tree to tree that mildewed day
In latter August when the hay
Came creaking to the barn. But where
The wind is westerly,
Where gnarled November makes the spiders fly
Into the apparitions of the sky,
They purpose nothing but their ease and die
Urgently beating east to sunrise and the sea;

What are we in the hands of the great God?
It was in vain you set up thorn and briar
In battle array against the fire
And treason crackling in your blood;
For the wild thorns grow tame
And will do nothing to oppose the flame;
Your lacerations tell the losing game
You play against a sickness past your cure.
How will the hands be strong? How will the heart endure?

A very little thing, a little worm,
Or hourglass-blazoned spider, it is said,
Can kill a tiger. Will the dead
Hold up his mirror and affirm
To the four winds the smell
And flash of his authority? It's well
If God who holds you to the pit of hell,
Much as one holds a spider, will destroy,
Baffle and dissipate your soul. As a small boy

On Windsor Marsh, I saw the spider die
When thrown into the bowels of fierce fire:
There's no long struggle, no desire
To get up on its feet and fly—
It stretches out its feet
And dies. This is the sinner's last retreat;
Yes, and no strength exerted on the heat
Then sinews the abolished will, when sick
And full of burning, it will whistle on a brick.

But who can plumb the sinking of that soul?
Josiah Hawley, picture yourself cast
Into a brick-kiln where the blast
Fans your quick vitals to a coal—
If measured by a glass,
How long would it seem burning! Let there pass
A minute, ten, ten trillion; but the blaze
Is infinite, eternal: this is death,
To die and know it. This is the Black Widow, death.

[1946]

PHILIP LARKIN (1922-1985)

Philip Larkin was born in Coventry, Warwickshire, and educated at St John's College, Oxford. He made his living as librarian in the University of Hull. In addition to *The North Ship* (1945), he published several volumes of poems, including *The Less Deceived* (1955), *The Whitsun Weddings* (1964), and *High Windows* (1974); two novels, *Jill* (1946) and *A Girl in Winter* (1947); and a book of critical and biographical writings, *Required Reading: Miscellaneous Pieces, 1955-1982* (1984).

Larkin is the poet of the emotionally underprivileged, of the vast majority of mankind for whom life is a progressive disillusionment. His poetic personae are invariably unimposing figures: a solitary man, with bicycle clips on his trousers, ruminating in an empty church; an outsider looking in on the merrymaking of others; an unfortunate who has literally and figuratively missed the boat. If Larkin's subject was the short end of the stick, one can only say that he had a firm grasp on it; he was not a shallow cynic, but an intelligent skeptic, like Thomas Hardy, one of his early influences.

Larkin's distaste for the spectacular extended also to the *manner* of his poetry, which is traditional rather than experimental. His small output reflects his concern for careful observation, and for clarity and precision of statement—something learned from the poetry of Yeats. Larkin's is a grey world, but it is a compellingly frank and honest one, to be understood, as the title of his second volume suggests, only by the less deceived.

Interviewed by Robert Phillips (1981-2) in *The Paris Review*, Larkin was dismissive of the tendency to talk about the creative process: 'I remember saying once, I can't understand these chaps who go round American universities explaining how they write poems: it's like going around explaining how you sleep with your wife. Whoever I was talking to said, "They'd do that, too, if their agents could fix it".' At the end of the interview, he explained this reluctance: 'You must realize I've never had "ideas" about poetry. To me it's always been a personal, almost physical release or solution to a complex pressure of needs—wanting to create, to justify, to praise, to explain, to externalize, depending on the circumstances. And I've never been much interested in other people's poetry—one reason for writing, of course, is that no one's written what you want to read.

'Probably my notion of poetry is very simple. Some time ago I agreed to help judge a poetry competition—you know, the kind where they get about 35,000 entries, and you look at the best few thousand. After a bit I said, Where are all the love poems? And nature poems? And they said, Oh, we threw all those away. I expect they were the ones I should have liked.'

In an article entitled 'The Whitsun Weddings' (*Poetry Book Society Bulletin* 40, February 1964), Larkin scoffed at any notion that the poet is 'the priest of a mystery'. In 'Speaking of Writing—XIII', which appeared in *The Times*, 20 February 1974 and was reprinted in *An Enormous Yes: In Memoriam, Philip Larkin, 1922-1985* (edited by Harry Chambers, 1986), Larkin insisted that his poetic aim was not to add to the stock of poems on shelves, but to add to the stock of experience: 'What I want readers to carry away from the poem in their minds is not the poem, but the experience; I want them to live something through the poem, without necessarily being conscious of the poem as a poem.'

In 'Two poets promenading' (*An Enormous Yes*), Larkin wrote: 'Poetry is memorable speech. I write when I feel strongly, and want to tell people. . . I have no enthusiasm for obscurity. Except, of course, for luminous and wonder-generating obscurity.' Again, in an interview at Beverley Grammar School in 1976 (*An Enormous Yes*): '. . . one writes really to reproduce in other people the particular sensations or thoughts or emotions that you've had yourself. I don't know why one should do this, but that is the point of it—to construct a verbal device rather like a verbal penny-in-the-slot machine whereby, when the reader puts the penny of his attention into the machine, he gets the full sensation or emotion that provokes you to write the poem in the first place. One hopes this will go on happening long after one is dead and long after the Earth is inhabited by men from Mars and so on. . . .'

LINES ON A YOUNG LADY'S PHOTOGRAPH ALBUM

At last you yielded up the album, which,
Once open, sent me distracted. All your ages
Matt and glossy on the thick black pages!
Too much confectionery, too rich:
I choke on such nutritious images.

My swivel eye hungers from pose to pose—
In pigtails, clutching a reluctant cat;
Or furred yourself, a sweet girl-graduate;
Or lifting a heavy-headed rose
Beneath a trellis, or in a trilby hat

(Faintly disturbing, that, in several ways)—
From every side you strike at my control,
Not least through these disquieting chaps who loll
At ease about your earlier days:
Not quite your class, I'd say, dear, on the whole.

But o, photography! as no art is,
Faithful and disappointing! that records
Dull days as dull, and hold-it smiles as frauds,
And will not censor blemishes
Like washing-lines, and Hall's-Distemper boards,

But shows the cat as disinclined, and shades
A chin as doubled when it is, what grace
Your candour thus confers upon her face!
How overwhelmingly persuades
That this is a real girl in a real place,

In every sense empirically true!
Or is it just *the past*? Those flowers, that gate,
These misty parks and motors, lacerate
Simply by being over; you
Contract my heart by looking out of date.

Yes, true; but in the end, surely, we cry
Not only at exclusion, but because
It leaves us free to cry. We know *what was*
Won't call on us to justify
Our grief, however hard we yowl across

The gap from eye to page. So I am left
To mourn (without a chance of consequence)
You, balanced on a bike against a fence;
To wonder if you'd spot the theft
Of this one of you bathing; to condense,

In short, a past that no one now can share,
No matter whose your future; calm and dry,
It holds you like a heaven, and you lie
Unvariably lovely there,
Smaller and clearer as the years go by.

[1955]

WANTS

Beyond all this, the wish to be alone:
However the sky grows dark with invitation-cards
However we follow the printed directions of sex
However the family is photographed under the flagstaff—
Beyond all this, the wish to be alone.

Beneath it all, desire of oblivion runs:
Despite the artful tensions of the calendar,
The life insurance, the tabled fertility rites,
The costly aversion of the eyes from death—
Beneath it all, desire of oblivion runs.

[1955]

CHURCH GOING

Once I am sure there's nothing going on
I step inside, letting the door thud shut.
Another church: matting, seats, and stone,
And little books; sprawlings of flowers, cut
For Sunday, brownish now; some brass and stuff
Up at the holy end; the small neat organ;
And a tense, musty, unignorable silence,
Brewed God knows how long. Hatless, I take off
My cycle-clips in awkward reverence,

Move forward, run my hand around the font.
From where I stand, the roof looks almost new—
Cleaned, or restored? Someone would know: I don't.
Mounting the lectern, I peruse a few
Hectoring large-scale verses, and pronounce
'Here endeth' much more loudly than I'd meant.
The echoes snigger briefly. Back at the door
I sign the book, donate an Irish sixpence,
Reflect the place was not worth stopping for.

Yet stop I did: in fact I often do,
And always end much at a loss like this,
Wondering what to look for; wondering, too,
When churches fall completely out of use
What we shall turn them into, if we shall keep
A few cathedrals chronically on show,
Their parchment, plate and pyx in locked cases,
And let the rest rent-free to rain and sheep.
Shall we avoid them as unlucky places?

Or, after dark, will dubious women come
To make their children touch a particular stone;
Pick simples for a cancer; or on some
Advised night see walking a dead one?
Power of some sort or other will go on
In games, in riddles, seemingly at random;
But superstition, like belief, must die,
And what remains when disbelief has gone?
Grass, weedy pavement, brambles, buttress, sky,

A shape less recognisable each week,
A purpose more obscure. I wonder who
Will be the last, the very last, to seek
This place for what it was; one of the crew
That tap and jot and know what rood-lofts were?
Some ruin-bibber, randy for antique,
Or Christmas-addict, counting on a whiff
Of gown-and-bands and organ-pipes and myrrh?
Or will he be my representative,

Bored, uninformed, knowing the ghostly silt
Dispersed, yet tending to this cross of ground
Through suburb scrub because it held unspilt
So long and equably what since is found
Only in separation—marriage, and birth,
And death, and thoughts of these—for which was built
This special shell? For, though I've no idea
What this accoutred frowsty barn is worth,
It pleases me to stand in silence here;

A serious house on serious earth it is,
In whose blent air all our compulsions meet,
Are recognised, and robed as destinies.
And that much never can be obsolete,
Since someone will forever be surprising
A hunger in himself to be more serious,
And gravitating with it to this ground,
Which, he once heard, was proper to grow wise in,
If only that so many dead lie round.

[1955]

TOADS

Why should I let the toad *work*
Squat on my life?
Can't I use my wit as a pitchfork
And drive the brute off?

Six days of the week it soils
With its sickening poison—
Just for paying a few bills!
That's out of proportion.

Lots of folk live on their wits:
Lecturers, lispers,
Losels, loblolly-men, louts—
They don't end as paupers;

Lots of folks live up lanes
With fires in a bucket,
Eat windfalls and tinned sardines—
They seem to like it.

Their nippers have got bare feet,
Their unspeakable wives
Are skinny as whippets—and yet
No one actually *starves*.

Ah, were I courageous enough
To shout *Stuff your pension!*
But I know, all too well, that's the stuff
That dreams are made on:

For something sufficiently toad-like
Squats in me, too;
Its hunkers are heavy as hard luck,
And cold as snow,

And will never allow me to blarney
My way to getting
The fame and the girl and the money
All at one sitting.

I don't say, one bodies the other
One's spiritual truth;
But I do say it's hard to lose either,
When you have both.

[1955]

POETRY OF DEPARTURES

Sometimes you hear, fifth-hand,
As epitaph:
He chucked up everything
And just cleared off,
And always the voice will sound
Certain you approve
This audacious, purifying,
Elemental move.

And they are right, I think.
We all hate home
And having to be there:
I detest my room,
Its specially-chosen junk,
The good books, the good bed,
And my life, in perfect order:
So to hear it said

He walked out on the whole crowd
Leaves me flushed and stirred,
Like *Then she undid her dress*
Or *Take that you bastard*;
Surely I can, if he did?
And that helps me stay
Sober and industrious.
But I'd go today,

Yes, swagger the nut-strewn roads,
Crouch in the fo'c'sle
Stubbly with goodness, if
It weren't so artificial,
Such a deliberate step backwards
To create an object:
Books; china; a life
Reprehensibly perfect.

[1955]

IF, MY DARLING

If my darling were once to decide
Not to stop at my eyes,
But to jump, like Alice, with floating skirt into my head,

She would find no tables and chairs,
No mahogany claw-footed sideboards,
No undisturbed embers;

The tantalus would not be filled, nor the fender-seat cosy,
Nor the shelves stuffed with small-printed books for the Sabbath,
Nor the butler bibulous, the housemaids lazy:

She would find herself looped with the creep of varying light,
Monkey-brown, fish-grey, a string of infected circles
Loitering like bullies, about to coagulate;

Delusions that shrink to the size of a woman's glove
Then sicken inclusively outwards. She would also remark
The unwholesome floor, as it might be the skin of a grave,

From which ascends an adhesive sense of betrayal,
A Grecian statue kicked in the privates, money,
A swill-tub of finer feelings. But most of all

She'd be stopping her ears against the incessant recital
Intoned by reality, larded with technical terms,
Each one double-yolked with meaning and meaning's rebuttal:

For the skirl of that bulletin unpicks the world like a knot,
And to hear how the past is past and the future neuter
Might knock my darling off her unpriceable pivot.

[1955]

FAITH HEALING

Slowly the women file to where he stands
Upright in rimless glasses, silver hair,
Dark suit, white collar. Stewards tirelessly
Persuade them onwards to his voice and hands,
Within whose warm spring rain of loving care
Each dwells some twenty seconds. *Now, dear child,*
What's wrong, the deep American voice demands,
And, scarcely pausing, goes into a prayer
Directing God about this eye, that knee.
Their heads are clasped abruptly; then, exiled

Like losing thoughts, they go in silence; some
Sheepishly stray, not back into their lives
Just yet; but some stay stiff, twitching and loud
With deep hoarse tears, as if a kind of dumb
And idiot child within them still survives
To re-awake at kindness, thinking a voice
At last calls them alone, that hands have come
To lift and lighten; and such joy arrives
Their thick tongues blort, their eyes squeeze grief, a crowd
Of huge unheard answers jam and rejoice—

What's wrong! Moustached in flowered frocks they shake:
By now, all's wrong. In everyone there sleeps
A sense of life lived according to love.
To some it means the difference they could make
By loving others, but across most it sweeps
As all they might have done had they been loved.
That nothing cures. An immense slackening ache,
As when, thawing, the rigid landscape weeps,
Spreads slowly through them—that, and the voice above
Saying *Dear child*, and all time has disproved.

[1964]

Irving Layton (b. 1912)

Layton was born in Romania but has spent most of his life since early childhood in Montreal. He studied agriculture at Macdonald College and economics and political science at McGill University; taught in Montreal secondary schools and at Sir George Williams University and York University; and has travelled extensively in Europe and Asia. Through his numerous readings, outspoken opinions on current affairs, and prodigious literary output, Layton became a well-known, though little understood, public figure. He has produced a steady stream of books, including *Here and Now* (1945), *Now Is the Place* (1948), *The Long Pea-Shooter* (1954), *The Cold Green Element* (1955), *The Improved Binoculars* (1956), *A Red Carpet for the Sun* (1959, Governor General's Award), *Balls for a One-Armed Juggler* (1963), *The Laughing Rooster* (1964), *Collected Poems* (1965), *Periods of the Moon* (1967), *The Shattered Plinths* (1968), *The Collected Poems of Irving Layton* (1971), *The Pole-Vaulter* (1974), *For My Brother Jesus* (1976), *The Covenant* (1977), *Droppings from Heaven* (1979), *A Wild Peculiar Joy* (1982), and *The Gucci Bag* (1983).

In the Foreword to *A Red Carpet for the Sun* (1959), Layton dissociated himself from cynics and nay-sayers and offered this whimsical, potted autobiography: 'My extraction has made me suspicious of both literature and reality. Let me explain. My father was an ineffectual visionary; he saw God's footprint in a cloud and lived only for his books and meditations. A small bedroom in a slum tenement, which in the torrid days steamed and blistered and sweated, he converted into a tabernacle for the Lord of Israel; and here, like the patriarch Abraham, he received his messengers. Since there was nothing angelic about me or his other children, he no more noticed us than if we had been flies on a wall. Had my mother been as otherworldly as he was, we should have starved. Luckily for us, she was not; she was tougher than nails, shrewd and indomitable. Moreover, she had a gift for cadenced vituperation; to which, doubtless, I owe my impeccable ear for rhythm. With parents so poorly matched and dissimilar, small wonder my entelechy was given a terrible squint from the outset. I am not at ease in the world (what poet ever is?); but neither am I fully at ease in the world of the imagination. I require some third realm, as yet undiscovered, in which to live. My disease has spurred me on to bridge the two with the stilts of poetry, or to create inside me an ironic balance of tensions.'

To many readers, Layton remains a paradox. His poetic personæ assume violent and aggressive stances, shocking 'delicate' sensibilities with their bombast, satire, and blatantly self-conscious erotica, and espousing what he considers dark truths about mankind. This is the Layton of 'Misunderstanding' and 'Whom I Write For,' the poet who (intending no irony) dedicates a volume of poetry to Lyndon Johnson, the US president who succeeded John F. Kennedy and pursued the Vietnam war so vigorously. The more attractive and enduring side of Layton's poetry is characterized by sensitivity, nostalgia, and reflectiveness, as in the warmly elegiac 'Cain' and 'The Bull Calf' or the naturalistic 'The Cold Green Element' and 'A Tall Man Executes a Jig'.

While Layton's poetry may at times have suffered from his inability to reconcile two opposing conceptions of the poet's function—the public spokesman who storms up and down the market-place, like Christ and the prophets, railing at vice and folly, and the clear-thinking analyst and articulator of the human condition—his reputation did not. People who knew nothing of his poetry had opinions about him and his antics or pronouncements. *Engagements: The Prose of Irving Layton* (1972) is full of examples of the poet at his pugilistic and controversial best, taking on critics, former literary associates, and reviewers such as Barry Callaghan, who had accused him of lacking 'any sense of ethical affirmation'. Layton's response in his letter to *Saturday Night* (May 1972) concludes with a spirited rebuttal: 'But enough of this. Though, really, I have been poetically involved with many other things besides machismo and vulvas, Callaghan has written an essay of startling originality and eloquence. Had he but identified cunt with life or the world, he would have hit the nail on the head and saved me the embarrassment of having to explain to my girlfriends that I neither hate nor fear them but love them—something no Ontarian can be expected to ever comprehend—with all my unjoyful undivided self.'

Although he insists that the poet is a conscience for mankind, Layton makes an astonishing attempt in 1972 to redefine his socialism: 'I am a socialist for I believe in the wise husbanding of all our resources, human and material. The last thing wanted, however, is levelling down and mediocritization in the name of social justice or democracy. The myth of a proletariat seizing power and ushering in an era of universal brotherhood has been thoroughly discredited in the twentieth century; it can now take its deserved rest beside that of the Olympian gods and the God-Man of Christianity. The only truly revolutionary class in history has been the bourgeoisie; by contrast the working class and their allies among the disaffected intellectuals appear to be reactionaries yearning for the heel of a dictator. . . . The only hope for civic and world peace lies in the rapid growth and spread of multinational corporations. By a paradox Marx would have greatly appreciated, it is the Devil's pitchfork of greed, pride and egotism that is prodding the capitalist and managerial class to create a world where mutual benevolence and goodwill have become eminently profitable. The swift unstoppable development of multinational corporations will do more to eliminate wars between countries than the Sermon on the Mount or Shelley's pious hope that people can be humanized by reading poetry.'

'Can anyone explain what happens in the writing of a poem,' Layton asks in the Preface to *The Laughing Rooster* (1964). 'I doubt it. . . . Cut it any way you like, dissect it, take it apart at the seams, analyse it to your heart's content—human creativity remains a mysterious fact in our law-abiding, mechanical universe that bankrupts all the theories that wish to explain it.' And yet he does endeavour again and again to describe the origin of poems, the *données* and pressures that provide creative sparks. Central to his work is the view that emotion drives the poem and technique steers it—or tries, at least, to hang on. 'Will power, character, determination, the possession of a first-rate brain, even the knowledge that one has written great poems in the past are useless if the peculiar ferment that brings up lines, images, and rhythms from the Unconscious is lacking. No ferment, no poetry: that's the long and short of it!'

In a number of superb poems, including 'Sacrament by Water', 'Berry Picking', 'Keine Lazarovitch', and those listed above, Layton directs his anger, pain, or ecstasy towards poetic excellence rather than public utterance. The intensity of feeling and technical authority evident in these poems indicate not only that certain kinds of content stimulate Layton to do his best work and enable him to ignore the easy but fickle sirens of journalism and the public media, but also that he is one of Canada's finest craftsmen.

THE BIRTH OF TRAGEDY

And me happiest when I compose poems.
Love, power, the huzza of battle
are something, are much;
yet a poem includes them like a pool
water and reflection.
In me, nature's divided things—
tree, mould on tree—
have their fruition;
I am their core. Let them swap,
bandy, like a flame swerve
I am their mouth; as a mouth I serve.

And I observe how the sensual moths
big with odour and sunshine
dart into the perilous shrubbery;
or drop their visiting shadows
upon the garden I one year made
of flowering stone to be a footstool
for the perfect gods:
who, friends to the ascending orders,
sustain all passionate meditations
and call down pardons
for the insurgent blood.

A quiet madman, never far from tears,
I lie like a slain thing
under the green air the trees
inhabit, or rest upon a chair
towards which the inflammable air
tumbles on many robins' wings;
noting how seasonably
leaf and blossom uncurl
and living things arrange their death,
while someone from afar off
blows birthday candles for the world.

[1954]

LOOK, THE LAMBS ARE ALL AROUND US!

Your figure, love,
curves itself
into a man's memory;
or to put it the way
a junior prof
at Mount Allison might,
Helen with her thick
absconding limbs
about the waist
of Paris
did no better.

Hell, my back's sunburnt
from so much love-making
in the open air.
The Primate (somebody
made a monkey of him)
and the Sanhedrin
(long on the beard, short
on the brain)
send envoys to say
they don't approve.
You never see them, love.
You toss me in the air
with such abandon,
they take to their heels and run.
I tell you
each kiss of yours
is like a blow on the head!

What luck, what luck to be loved
by the one girl
in this Presbyterian
country
who knows how to give
a man pleasure.

[1954]

THE COLD GREEN ELEMENT

At the end of the garden walk
the wind and its satellite wait for me;
their meaning I will not know
        until I go there,
but the black-hatted undertaker

who, passing, saw my heart beating in the grass,
is also going there. Hi, I tell him,
a great squall in the Pacific blew a dead poet
        out of the water,
who now hangs from the city's gates.

Crowds depart daily to see it, and return
with grimaces and incomprehension;
if its limbs twitched in the air
        they would sit at its feet
peeling their oranges.

And turning over I embrace like a lover
the trunk of a tree, one of those
for whom the lightning was too much
        and grew a brilliant
hunchback with a crown of leaves.

The ailments escaped from the labels
of medicine bottles are all fled to the wind;
I've seen myself lately in the eyes
        of old women,
spent streams mourning my manhood,

in whose old pupils the sun became
a bloodsmear on broad catalpa leaves
and hanging from ancient twigs,
        my murdered selves
sparked the air like the muted collisions

of fruit. A black dog howls down my blood,
a black dog with yellow eyes;
he too by someone's inadvertence
        saw the bloodsmear
on the broad catalpa leaves.

But the furies clear a path for me to the worm
who sang for an hour in the throat of a robin,
and misled by the cries of young boys
        I am again
a breathless swimmer in that cold green element.

[1940]

The Bull Calf

The thing could barely stand. Yet taken
from his mother and the barn smells
he still impressed with his pride,
with the promise of sovereignty in the way
his head moved to take us in.
The fierce sunlight tugging the maize from the ground
licked at his shapely flanks.
He was too young for all that pride.
I thought of the deposed Richard II.

'No money in bull calves,' Freeman had said.
The visting clergyman rubbed the nostrils
now snuffing pathetically at the windless day.
'A pity,' he sighed.
My gaze slipped off his hat toward the empty sky
that circled over the black knot of men,
over us and the calf waiting for the first blow.

Struck,
the bull calf drew in his thin forelegs
as if gathering strength for a mad rush . . .
tottered . . . raised his darkening eyes to us,
and I saw we were at the far end
of his frightened look, growing smaller and smaller
till we were only the ponderous mallet

that flicked his bleeding ear
and pushed him over on his side, stiffly,
like a block of wood.

Below the hill's crest
the river snuffled on the improvised beach.
We dug a deep pit and threw the dead calf into it.
It made a wet sound, a sepulchral gurgle,
as the warm sides bulged and flattened.
Settled, the bull calf lay as if asleep,
one foreleg over the other,
bereft of pride and so beautiful now,
without movement, perfectly still in the cool pit,
I turned away and wept.

[1956]

SACRAMENT BY THE WATER

How shall I sing the accomplished waters
Whose teeming cells make green my hopes
How shall the Sun at daybreak marry us
Twirling these waters like a hoop.

Gift of the waters that sing
Their eternal passion for the sky,
Your cunning beauty in a wave of tumult
Drops an Eden about your thighs.

Green is the singing singing water
And green is every joyous leaf
White myrtle's in your hand and in the other
The hairy apple bringing life.

[1956]

WHATEVER ELSE POETRY IS FREEDOM

Whatever else poetry is freedom.
Forget the rhetoric, the trick of lying
All poets pick up sooner or later. From the river,
Rising like the thin voice of grey castratos—the mist;

Poplars and pines grow straight but oaks are gnarled;
Old codgers must speak of death, boys break windows;
Women lie honestly by their men at last.

And I who gave my Kate a blackened eye
Did to its vivid changing colours
Make up an incredible musical scale;
And now I balance on wooden stilts and dance
And thereby sing to the loftiest casements.
See how with polish I bow from the waist.
Space for these stilts! More space or I fail!

And a crown I say for my buffoon's head.
Yet no more fool am I than King Canute,
Lord of our tribe, who scanned and scorned;
Who half-deceived, believed; and, poet, missed
The first white waves come nuzzling at his feet;
Then damned the courtiers and the foolish trial
With a most bewildering and unkingly jest.

It was the mist. It lies inside one like a destiny.
A real Jonah it lies rotting like a lung.
And I know myself undone who am a clown
And wear a wreath of mist for a crown;
Mist with the scent of dead apples,
Mist swirling from black oily waters at evening,
Mist from the fraternal graves of cemeteries.

It shall drive me to beg my food and at last
Hurl me broken I know and prostrate on the road;
Like a huge toad I saw, entire but dead,
That Time mordantly had blacked; O pressed
To the moist earth it pled for entry.
I shall be I say that stiff toad for sick with mist
And crazed I smell the odour of mortality.

And Time flames like a paraffin stove
And what it burns are the minutes I live.
At certain middays I have watched the cars
Bring me from afar their windshield suns;

What lay to my hand were blue fenders,
The suns extinguished, the drivers wearing sunglasses.
And it made me think I had touched a hearse.

So whatever else poetry is freedom. Let
Far off the impatient cadences reveal
A padding for my breathless stilts. Swivel,
O hero, in the fleshy groves, skin and glycerine,
And sing of lust, the sun's accompanying shadow
Like a vampire's wing, the stillness in dead feet—
Your stave brings resurrection, O aggrievèd king.

[1958]

BERRY PICKING

Silently my wife walks on the still wet furze
Now darkgreen the leaves are full of metaphors
Now lit up is each tiny lamp of blueberry.
The white nails of rain have dropped and the sun is free.

And whether she bends or straightens to each bush
To find the children's laughter among the leaves
Her quiet hands seem to make the quiet summer hush—
Berries or children, patient she is with these.

I only vex and perplex her; madness, rage
Are endearing perhaps put down upon the page;
Even silence daylong and sullen can then
Enamour as restraint or classic discipline.

So I envy the berries she puts in her mouth,
The red and succulent juice that stains her lips;
I shall never taste that good to her, nor will they
Displease her with a thousand barbarous jests.

How they lie easily for her hand to take,
Part of the unoffending world that is hers;
Here beyond complexity she stands and stares
And leans her marvellous head as if for answers.

No more the easy soul my childish craft deceives
Nor the simpler one for whom yes is always yes;
No, now her voice comes to me from a far way off
Though her lips are redder than the raspberries.

[1958]

KEINE LAZAROVITCH 1870-1959

When I saw my mother's head on the cold pillow,
Her white waterfalling hair in the cheeks' hollows,
I thought, quietly circling my grief, of how
She had loved God but cursed extravagantly his creatures.

For her final mouth was not water but a curse,
A small black hole, a black rent in the universe,
Which damned the green earth, stars and trees in its stillness
And the inescapable lousiness of growing old.

And I record she was comfortless, vituperative,
Ignorant, glad, and much else besides; I believe
She endlessly praised her black eyebrows, their thick weave,
Till plagiarizing Death leaned down and took them for his mould.

And spoiled a dignity I shall not again find,
And the fury of her stubborn limited mind;
Now none will shake her amber beads and call God blind,
Or wear them upon a breast so radiantly.

O fierce she was, mean and unaccommodating;
But I think now of the toss of her gold earrings,
Their proud carnal assertion, and her youngest sings
While all the rivers of her red veins move into the sea.

[1961]

A TALL MAN EXECUTES A JIG

I

So the man spread his blanket on the field
And watched the shafts of light between the tufts
And felt the sun push the grass towards him;
The noise he heard was that of whizzing flies,
The whistlings of some small imprudent birds,

And the ambiguous rumbles of cars
That made him look up at the sky, aware
Of the gnats that tilted against the wind
And in the sunlight turned to jigging motes.
Fruitflies he'd call them except there was no fruit
About, spoiling to hatch these glitterings,
These nervous dots for which the mind supplied
The closing sentences from Thucydides,
Or from Euclid having a savage nightmare.

II

Jig jig, jig jig. Like minuscule black links
Of a chain played with by some playful
Unapparent hand or the palpitant
Summer haze bored with the hour's stillness.
He felt the sting and tingle afterwards
Of those leaving their unorthodox unrest,
Leaving their undulant excitation
To drop upon his sleeveless arm. The grass,
Even the wildflowers become black hairs
And himself a maddened speck among them.
Still the assaults of the small flies made him
Glad at last, until he saw purest joy
In their frantic jiggings under a hair,
So changed from those in the unrestraining air.

III

He stood up and felt himself enormous.
Felt as might Donatello over stone,
Or Plato, or as a man who has held
A loved and lovely woman in his arms
And feels his forehead touch the emptied sky
Where all antinomies flood into light.
Yet jig jig jig, the haloing black jots
Meshed with the wheeling fire of the sun:
Motion without meaning, disquietude
Without sense or purpose, ephemerides
That mottled the resting summer air till
Gusts swept them from his sight like wisps of smoke.
Yet they returned, bringing a bee who, seeing
But a tall man, left him for a marigold.

IV
He doffed his aureole of gnats and moved
Out of the field as the sun sank down,
A dying god upon the blood-red hills.
Ambition, pride, the ecstasy of sex,
And all circumstance of delight and grief,
That blood upon the mountain's side, that flood
Washed into a clear incredible pool
Below the ruddied peaks that pierced the sun.
He stood still and waited. If ever
The hour of revelation was come
It was now, here on the transfigured steep.
The sky darkened. Some birds chirped. Nothing else.
He thought the dying god had gone to sleep:
An Indian fakir on his mat of nails.

V
And on the summit of the asphalt road
Which stretched towards the fiery town, the man
Saw one hill raised like a hairy arm, dark
With pines and cedars against the stricken sun
—The arm of Moses or of Joshua.
He dropped his head and let fall the halo
Of mountains, purpling and silent as time,
To see temptation coiled before his feet:
A violated grass snake that lugged
Its intestine like a small red valise.
A cold-eyed skinflint it now was, and not
The manifest of that joyful wisdom,
The mirth and arrogant green flame of life;
Or earth's vivid tongue that flicked in praise of earth.

VI
And the man wept because pity was useless.
'Your jig's up; the flies come like kites,' he said
And watched the grass snake crawl towards the hedge,
Convulsing and dragging into the dark
The satchel filled with curses for the earth,
For the odours of warm sedge, and the sun,
A blood-red organ in the dying sky.
Backwards it fell into a grassy ditch

Exposing its underside, white as milk,
And mocked by wisps of hay between its jaws;
And then it stiffened to its final length.
But though it opened its thin mouth to scream
A last silent scream that shook the black sky,
Adamant and fierce, the tall man did not curse.

VII

Beside the rigid snake the man stretched out
In fellowship of death; he lay silent
And stiff in the heavy grass with eyes shut,
Inhaling the moist odours of the night
Through which his mind tunnelled with flicking tongue
Backwards to caves, mounds, and sunken ledges
And desolate cliffs where come only kites,
And where of perished badgers and racoons
The claws alone remain, gripping the earth.
Meanwhile the green snake crept upon the sky,
Huge, his mailed coat glittering with stars that made
The night bright, and blowing thin wreaths of cloud
Athwart the moon; and as the weary man
Stood up, coiled above his head, transforming all.

[1963]

ELIZABETH BISHOP (1911-1979)

Elizabeth Bishop was born in Worcester, Massachusetts, to parents of Canadian origin, and spent a number of impressionable years as a child living with her grandparents in Great Sands, Nova Scotia. Her father's early death, her mother's mental breakdown, and the unstable conditions of life with a series of relatives led her to describe herself as a 'country mouse' and to see her childhood as a series of 'tiny tragedies and grotesque grieves'; not surprisingly, she took refuge in the imaginative worlds of fantasy and books. She attended Vassar College, travelled to Paris, and lived for nine years in Key West, Florida; but, despite friendships with Marianne Moore, Randall Jarrell, and Robert Lowell, she never established permanent roots in the US and eventually settled in Brazil. She won numerous awards, including the Pulitzer Prize, the news of which she celebrated alone by eating two Oreo cookies found in her neighbour's empty house. She served as poetry consultant to the Library of Congress 1949-50 and in later years taught intermittently at Harvard, New York University, and the Massachusetts Institute of Technology. Her published works include

North & South (1946), *A Cold Spring* (1955), *Questions of Travel* (1965), *Geography III* (1977), *The Complete Poems, 1927-1979* (1980), and *The Collected Prose* (1984). She also co-edited an anthology of Brazilian poetry translated into English and wrote (with the editors of *Life*) a book about Brazil.

The search for home, 'wherever that may be', led Bishop to examine in great detail not only the bleak, almost elemental landscapes of her childhood and the exotic surfaces of the Brazil of her maturity, but also to question the function of travel and the nature of reality itself, where the world of the senses cannot always be trusted and where 'there are too many waterfalls'. Her poems have a highly charged quality that reminds one of the effect of a slowly-panning camera in a gothic film, or of the unsettling and unnerving lighting and sense of stasis or suspended animation produced by the paintings of magic realists such as Andrew Wyeth. Bishop had no program to follow. She was not a nature poet, though few poets have given so impressive an account of the colours and textures of human and physical nature; neither was she a symbolist, though her best lyrics rise to a symbolic level. She preferred 'glimpses of the always-more-successful surrealism of everyday life'. Though she often begins with the particulars of the natural world, she will occasionally reverse her process, as in '12 O'Clock News', where she makes the flotsam of her writing desk an everywhere — a complex moral and political landscape mined with meaning and significance.

Bishop is an exacting poet. She claimed that Marianne Moore's concern for felicity of sound and exactness of expression 'made me realize more than I ever had the rarity of true originality and also the sort of alienation it might involve'. She came to believe that poetry must be 'effortlessly rhetorical' and that there is 'no detail too small' for the serious poet. In other words, she found her home at last in art, in language itself, the medium that possesses a more 'watery, dazzling rhetoric' than an Amazon village, that 'resolves and dissolves' the contradictions and contrarieties of ordinary life.

In an interview conducted by Robert Seidel for *The Paris Review*, Robert Lowell praised Elizabeth Bishop's poetry, where 'a whole new world is gotten out and you don't know what will come after any one line. It's exploring. And it's as original as Kafka. She's gotten a world, not just a way of writing. She seldom writes a poem that doesn't have that exploratory quality; yet it's very firm, it's not like beat poetry, it's all controlled.' These explorations were, for Bishop, not something to be easily explained or articulated. She was terribly shy and diffident as a young poet, as she admitted in her own interview for the same magazine, conducted in 1978 by Elizabeth Spires: 'On the newspaper board they used to sit around and talk about how they could get published and so on and so on. I'd just hold my tongue. I was embarrassed by it. And still am. There's nothing more embarrassing than being a poet, really. . . . there must be an awful core of ego somewhere for you to set yourself up to write poetry. I've never *felt* it, but it must be there.'

While she was committed to poetic excellence, Bishop's life was refreshingly free of self-promotion or careerism. 'One is offered such oracular statements all the time,' she wrote in 1962, when asked to select and comment on one of her poems for *Poet's Choice* (edited by Paul Engle and Joseph Langland), 'but often misses them, gets lazy about writing them out in detail, or the meaning refuses to stay put. This poem seems to me to have stayed put fairly well—but as Fats Waller used to say, "One never knows, do one?"'

THE MAP

Land lies in water; it is shadowed green.
Shadows, or are they shallows, at its edges
showing the line of long sea-weeded ledges
where weeds hang to the simple blue from green.
Or does the land lean down to lift the sea from under,
drawing it unperturbed around itself?
Along the fine tan sandy shelf
is the land tugging at the sea from under?

The shadow of Newfoundland lies flat and still.
Labrador's yellow, where the moony Eskimo
has oiled it. We can stroke these lovely bays,
under a glass as if they were expected to blossom,
or as if to provide a clean cage for invisible fish.
The names of seashore towns run out to sea,
the names of cities cross the neighboring mountains
—the printer here experiencing the same excitement
as when emotion too far exceeds its cause.
These peninsulas take the water between thumb and finger
like women feeling for the smoothness of yard-goods.

Mapped waters are more quiet than the land is,
lending the land their waves' own conformation:
and Norway's hare runs south in agitation,
profiles investigate the sea, where land is.
Are they assigned, or can the countries pick their colors?
—What suits the character or the native waters best.
Topography displays no favorites; North's as near as West.
More delicate than the historians' are the map-makers' colors.

[1955]

THE IMAGINARY ICEBERG

We'd rather have the iceberg than the ship,
although it meant the end of travel.
Although it stood stock-still like cloudy rock
and all the sea were moving marble.

We'd rather have the iceberg than the ship;
we'd rather own this breathing plain of snow
though the ship's sails were laid upon the sea
as the snow lies undissolved upon the water.
O solemn, floating field,
are you aware an iceberg takes repose
with you, and when it wakes may pasture on your snows?

This is a scene a sailor'd give his eyes for.
The ship's ignored. The iceberg rises
and sinks again; its glassy pinnacles
correct elliptics in the sky.
This is a scene where he who treads the boards
is artlessly rhetorical. The curtain
is light enough to rise on finest ropes
that airy twists of snow provide.
The wits of these white peaks
spar with the sun. Its weight the iceberg dares
upon a shifting stage and stands and stares.

This iceberg cuts its facets from within.
Like jewelry from a grave
it saves itself perpetually and adorns
only itself, perhaps the snows
which so surprise us lying on the sea.
Good-bye, we say, good-bye, the ship steers off
where waves give in to one another's waves
and clouds run in a warmer sky.
Icebergs behoove the soul
(both being self-made from elements least visible)
to see them so: fleshed, fair, erected indivisible.

[1955]

At the Fishhouses

Although it is a cold evening,
down by one of the fishhouses
an old man sits netting,
his net, in the gloaming almost invisible,
a dark purple-brown,
and his shuttle worn and polished.

The air smells so strong of codfish
it makes one's nose run and one's eyes water.
The five fishhouses have steeply peaked roofs
and narrow, cleated gangplanks slant up
to storerooms in the gables
for the wheelbarrows to be pushed up and down on.
All is silver: the heavy surface of the sea,
swelling slowly as if considering spilling over,
is opaque, but the silver of the benches,
the lobster pots, and masts, scattered
among the wild jagged rocks,
is of an apparent translucence
like the small old buildings with an emerald moss
growing on their shoreward walls.
The big fish tubs are completely lined
with layers of beautiful herring scales
and the wheelbarrows are similarly plastered
with creamy iridescent coats of mail,
with small iridescent flies crawling on them.
Up on the little slope behind the houses,
set in the sparse bright sprinkle of grass,
is an ancient wooden capstan,
cracked, with two long bleached handles
and some melancholy stains, like dried blood,
where the ironwork has rusted.
The old man accepts a Lucky Strike.
He was a friend of my grandfather.
We talk of the decline in the population
and of codfish and herring
while he waits for a herring boat to come in.
There are sequins on his vest and on his thumb.
He has scraped the scales, the principal beauty,
from unnumbered fish with that black old knife,
the blade of which is almost worn away.

Down at the water's edge, at the place
where they haul up the boats, up the long ramp
descending into the water, thin silver
tree trunks are laid horizontally
across the gray stones, down and down
at intervals of four or five feet.

Cold dark deep and absolutely clear,
element bearable to no mortal,
to fish and to seals . . . One seal particularly
I have seen here evening after evening.
He was curious about me. He was interested in music;
like me a believer in total immersion,
so I used to sing him Baptist hymns.
I also sang 'A Mighty Fortress Is Our God'.
He stood up in the water and regarded me
steadily, moving his head a little.
Then he would disappear, then suddenly emerge
almost in the same spot, with a sort of shrug
as if it were against his better judgment.
Cold dark deep and absolutely clear,
the clear gray icy water . . . Back, behind us,
the dignified tall firs begin.
Bluish, associating with their shadows,
a million Christmas trees stand
waiting for Christmas. The water seems suspended
above the rounded gray and blue-gray stones.
I have seen it over and over, the same sea, the same,
slightly, indifferently swinging above the stones,
icily free above the stones,
above the stones and then the world.
If you should dip your hand in,
your wrist would ache immediately,
your bones would begin to ache and your hand would burn
as if the water were a transmutation of fire
that feeds on stones and burns with a dark gray flame.
If you tasted it, it would first taste bitter,
then briny, then surely burn your tongue.
It is like what we imagine knowledge to be:
dark, salt, clear, moving, utterly free,
drawn from the cold hard mouth
of the world, derived from the rocky breasts
forever, flowing and drawn, and since
our knowledge is historical, flowing, and flown.

[1955]

Cape Breton

Out on the high 'bird islands', Ciboux and Hertford,
the razorbill auks and the silly-looking puffins all stand
with their backs to the mainland
in solemn, uneven lines along the cliff's brown grass-frayed edge,
while the few sheep pastured there go 'Baaa, baaa'.
(Sometimes, frightened by aeroplanes, they stampede
and fall over into the sea or onto the rocks.)
The silken water is weaving and weaving,
disappearing under the mist equally in all directions,
lifted and penetrated now and then
by one shag's dripping serpent-neck,
and somewhere the mist incorporates the pulse,
rapid but unurgent, of a motorboat.

The same mist hangs in thin layers
among the valleys and gorges of the mainland
like rotting snow-ice sucked away
almost to spirit; the ghosts of glaciers drift
among those folds and folds of fir: spruce and hackmatack—
dull, dead, deep peacock-colors,
each riser distinguished from the next
by an irregular nervous saw-tooth edge,
alike, but certain as a stereoscopic view.

The wild road clambers along the brink of the coast.
On it stand occasional small yellow bulldozers,
but without their drivers, because today is Sunday.
The little white churches have been dropped into the matted hills
like lost quartz arrowheads.
The road appears to have been abandoned.
Whatever the landscape had of meaning appears to have
    been abandoned,
unless the road is holding it back, in the interior,
where we cannot see,
where deep lakes are reputed to be,
and disused trails and mountains of rock
and miles of burnt forests standing in gray scratches
like the admirable scriptures made on stones by stones—

and these regions now have little to say for themselves
except in thousands of light song-sparrow songs floating upward
freely, dispassionately, through the mist, and meshing
in brown-wet, fine, torn fish-nets.

A small bus comes along, in up-and-down rushes,
packed with people, even to its step.
(On weekdays with groceries, spare automobile parts, and
    pump parts,
but today only two preachers extra, one carrying his frock
    coat on a hanger.)
It passes the closed roadside stand, the closed schoolhouse,
where today no flag is flying
from the rough-adzed pole topped with a white china doorknob.
It stops, and a man carrying a baby gets off,
climbs over a stile, and goes down through a small steep meadow,
which establishes its poverty in a snowfall of daisies,
to his invisible house beside the water.

The birds keep on singing, a calf bawls, the bus starts.
The thin mist follows
the white mutations of its dream;
an ancient chill is rippling the dark brooks.

[1955]

Arrival at Santos

Here is a coast; here is a harbor;
here, after a meager diet of horizon, is some scenery:
impractically shaped and—who knows?—self-pitying mountains,
sad and harsh beneath their frivolous greenery,

with a little church on top of one. And warehouses,
some of them painted a feeble pink, or blue,
and some tall, uncertain palms. Oh, tourist,
is this how this country is going to answer you

and your immodest demands for a different world,
and a better life, and complete comprehension
of both at last, and immediately,
after eighteen days of suspension?

Finish your breakfast. The tender is coming,
a strange and ancient craft, flying a strange and brilliant rag.
So that's the flag. I never saw it before.
I somehow never thought of there *being* a flag,

but of course there was, all along. And coins, I presume,
and paper money; they remain to be seen.
And gingerly now we climb down the ladder backward,
myself and a fellow passenger named Miss Breen,

descending into the midst of twenty-six freighters
waiting to be loaded with green coffee beans.
Please, boy, do be more careful with that boat hook!
Watch out! Oh! It has caught Miss Breen's

skirt! There! Miss Breen is about seventy,
a retired police lieutenant, six feet tall,
with beautiful bright blue eyes and a kind expression.
Her home, when she is at home, is in Glens Fall

s, New York. There. We are settled.
The customs officials will speak English, we hope,
and leave us our bourbon and cigarettes.
Ports are necessities, like postage stamps, or soap,

but they seldom seem to care what impression they make,
or, like this, only attempt, since it does not matter,
the unassertive colors of soap, or postage stamps—
wasting away like the former, slipping the way the latter

do when we mail the letters we wrote on the boat,
either because the glue here is very inferior
or because of the heat. We leave Santos at once;
we are driving to the interior.

[1965]

Questions of Travel

There are too many waterfalls here; the crowded streams
hurry too rapidly down to the sea,
and the pressure of so many clouds on the mountaintops
makes them spill over the sides in soft slow-motion,

turning to waterfalls under our very eyes.
—For if those streaks, those mile-long, shiny, tearstains,
aren't waterfalls yet,
in a quick age or so, as ages go here,
they probably will be.
But if the streams and clouds keep travelling, travelling,
the mountains look like the hulls of capsized ships,
slime-hung and barnacled.

Think of the long trip home.
Should we have stayed at home and thought of here?
Where should we be today?
Is it right to be watching strangers in a play
in this strangest of theatres?
What childishness is it that while there's a breath of life
in our bodies, we are determined to rush
to see the sun the other way around?
The tiniest green hummingbird in the world?
To stare at some inexplicable old stonework,
inexplicable and impenetrable,
at any view,
instantly seen and always, always delightful?
Oh, must we dream our dreams
and have them, too?
And have we room
for one more folded sunset, still quite warm?

But surely it would have been a pity
not to have seen the trees along this road,
really exaggerated in their beauty,
not to have seen them gesturing
like noble pantomimists, robed in pink.
—Not to have had to stop for gas and heard
the sad, two-noted, wooden tune
of disparate wooden clogs
carelessly clacking over
a grease-stained filling-station floor.
(In another country the clogs would all be tested.
Each pair there would have identical pitch.)
—A pity not to have heard

the other, less primitive music of the fat brown bird
who sings above the broken gasoline pump
in a bamboo church of Jesuit baroque:
three towers, five silver crosses.
—Yes, a pity not to have pondered,
blurr'dly and inconclusively,
on what connection can exist for centuries
between the crudest wooden footwear
and, careful and finicky,
the whittled fantasies of wooden cages.
—Never to have studied history in
the weak calligraphy of songbirds' cages.
—And never to have had to listen to rain
so much like politicians' speeches:
two hours of unrelenting oratory
and then a sudden golden silence
in which the traveller takes a notebook, writes:

'Is it lack of imagination that makes us come
to imagined places, not just stay at home?
Or could Pascal have been not entirely right
about just sitting quietly in one's room?

Continent, city, country, society:
the choice is never wide and never free.
And here, or there . . . No. Should we have stayed at home,
wherever that may be?'

[1965]

SQUATTER'S CHILDREN

On the unbreathing sides of hills
they play, a specklike girl and boy,
alone, but near a specklike house.
The sun's suspended eye
blinks casually, and then they wade
gigantic waves of light and shade.
A dancing yellow spot, a pup,
attends them. Clouds are piling up;

a storm piles up behind the house.
The children play at digging holes.
The ground is hard; they try to use
one of their father's tools,
a mattock with a broken haft
the two of them can scarcely lift.
It drops and clangs. Their laughter spreads
effulgence in the thunderheads,

weak flashes of inquiry
direct as is the puppy's bark.
But to their little, soluble,
unwarrantable ark,
apparently the rain's reply
consists of echolalia,
and Mother's voice, ugly as sin,
keeps calling to them to come in.

Children, the threshold of the storm
has slid beneath your muddy shoes;
wet and beguiled, you stand among
the mansions you may choose
out of a bigger house than yours,
whose lawfulness endures.
Its soggy documents retain
your rights in rooms of falling rain.

[1965]

12 O'Clock News

	As you all know, tonight is the night of the full moon,
	half the world over. But here the moon seems to hang
gooseneck	motionless in the sky. It gives very little light; it could
lamp	be dead. Visibility is poor. Nevertheless, we shall try to
	give you some idea of the lay of the land and the
	present situation.
	The escarpment that rises abruptly from the central
	plain is in heavy shadow, but the elaborate terracing of
typewriter	its southern glacis gleams faintly in the dim light, like

fish scales. What endless labor those small, peculiarly
shaped terraces represent! And yet, on them the
welfare of this tiny principality depends.

A slight landslide occurred in the northwest about an
pile of mss. hour ago. The exposed soil appears to be of poor
quality: almost white, calcareous, and shaly. There are
believed to have been no casualties.

Almost due north, our aerial reconnaissance reports the
typed sheet discovery of a large rectangular 'field', hitherto unknown
to us, obviously man-made. It is dark-speckled. An
airstrip? A cemetery?

In this small, backward country, one of the most back-
ward left in the world today, communications are crude
envelopes and 'industrialization' and its products almost non-
existent. Strange to say, however, sign-boards are on a
truly gigantic scale.

We have also received reports of a mysterious, oddly
shaped, black structure, at an undisclosed distance to
the east. Its presence was revealed only because its
highly polished surface catches such feeble moonlight
as prevails. The natural resources of the country being
far from completely known to us, there is the possibility
that this may be, or may contain, some powerful and
ink-bottle terrifying 'secret weapon'. On the other hand, given what
we do know, or have learned from our anthropologists
and sociologists about this people, it may well be nothing
more than a *numen*, or a great altar recently erected to
one of their gods, to which, in their present historical
state of superstition and helplessness, they attribute mag-
ical powers, and may even regard as a 'savior', one last
hope of rescue from their grave difficulties.

At last! One of the elusive natives has been spotted! He
appears to be—rather, to have been—a unicyclist-
typewriter courier, who may have met his end by falling from the
eraser height of the escarpment because of the deceptive

illumination. Alive, he would have been small, but
undoubtedly proud and erect, with the thick, bristling
black hair typical of the indigenes.

From our superior vantage point, we can clearly see
into a sort of dugout, possibly a shell crater, a 'nest'
of soldiers. They lie heaped together, wearing the
camouflage 'battle dress' intended for 'winter warfare'.
They are in hideously contorted positions, all dead.
We can make out at least eight bodies. These

ashtray

uniforms were designed to be used in guerrilla warfare
on the country's one snow-covered mountain peak.
The fact that these poor soldiers are wearing them
here, on the plain, gives further proof, if proof
were necessary, either of the childishness and
hopeless impracticality of this inscrutable people,
our opponents, or of the sad corruption of their
leaders.

[1971]

SANTARÉM

Of course I may be remembering it all wrong
after, after—how many years?

That golden evening I really wanted to go no farther;
more than anything else I wanted to stay awhile
in that conflux of two great rivers, Tapajós, Amazon,
grandly, silently flowing, flowing east.
Suddenly there'd been houses, people, and lots of mongrel
riverboats skittering back and forth
under a sky of gorgeous, under-lit clouds,
with everything gilded, burnished along one side,
and everything bright, cheerful, casual—or so it looked.
I liked the place; I liked the idea of the place.
Two rivers. Hadn't two rivers sprung
from the Garden of Eden? No, that was four
and they'd diverged. Here only two
and coming together. Even if one were tempted

to literary interpretations
such as: life/death, right/wrong, male/female
—such notions would have resolved, dissolved, straight off
in that watery, dazzling dialectic.

In front of the church, the Cathedral, rather
there was a modest promenade and a belvedere
about to fall into the river,
stubby palms, flamboyants like pans of embers,
buildings one storey high, stucco, blue or yellow,
and one house faced with *azulejos*, buttercup yellow.
The street was deep in dark-gold river sand
damp from the ritual afternoon rain,
and teams of zebus plodded, gentle, proud,
and *blue*, with down-curved horns and hanging ears,
pulling carts with solid wheels.
The zebus' hooves, the people's feet
waded in golden sand,
dampered by golden sand,
so that almost the only sounds
were creaks and *shush, shush, shush*.

Two rivers full of crazy shipping—people
all apparently changing their minds, embarking,
disembarking, rowing clumsy dories.
(After the Civil War some Southern families
came here; here they could still own slaves.
They left occasional blue eyes, English names,
and oars. No other place, no one
on all the Amazon's four thousand miles
does anything but paddle.)
A dozen or so young nuns, white-habited,
waved gaily from an old stern-wheeler
getting up steam, already hung with hammocks
—off to their mission, days and days away
up God knows what lost tributary.
Side-wheelers, countless wobbling dugouts . . .
A cow stood up in one, quite calm,
chewing her cud while being ferried,
tipping, wobbling, somewhere, to be married.
A river schooner with raked masts

and violet-colored sails tacked in so close
her bowsprit seemed to touch the church
(Cathedral, rather!). A week or so before
there'd been a thunderstorm and the Cathedral'd
been struck by lightning. One tower had
a widening zigzag crack all the way down.
It was a miracle. The priest's house right next door
had been struck, too, and his brass bed
(the only one in town) galvanized black.
Graças a deus—he'd been in Belém.

In the blue pharmacy the pharmacist
had hung an empty wasps' nest from a shelf:
small, exquisite, clean matte white,
and hard as stucco. I admired it
so much he gave it to me.
Then—my ship's whistle blew. I couldn't stay.
Back on board, a fellow-passenger, Mr Swan,
Dutch, the retiring head of Philips Electric,
really a very nice old man,
who wanted to see the Amazon before he died,
asked, 'What's that ugly thing?'

[1979]

P.K. PAGE (b. 1916)

Born in England, P.K. Page was raised in Calgary and Winnipeg. She lived briefly in the Maritimes before moving to Montreal, where she worked at the National Film Board and in 1942 became associated with Patrick Anderson and F.R. Scott on the board of the 'little magazine' *Preview*. She married the diplomat Arthur Irwin and, as the wife of the Canadian ambassador, lived from 1953 to 1964 in Mexico, Brazil, and Australia. Her poetry collections are *As Ten as Twenty* (1946), *The Metal and the Flower* (1954, Governor General's Award), *Cry Ararat!* (1967), *Poems New and Selected* (1974), *Leviathan in a Pool* (1974), *Evening Dance of the Grey Flies* (1981), *The Glass Air* (1985, 1991), and *Hologram* (1994). Her prose writings include a novel, first published in 1944 and reissued in *The Sun and the Moon and Other Fictions* (1973) and *Brazilian Journal* (1988). She has also published three works for children: *A Flask of Sea Water* (1989), *The Travelling Musicians* (1991), and *The Goat That Flew* (1994).

'I am a traveller,' P.K. Page writes in 'Traveller, Conjuror, Journeyman' (*Cana-*

dian Literature 46, Autumn 1970). 'I have a destination but no maps. Others will have reached that destination already, still others are on their way. But none has had to go from here before—nor will again. One's route is one's own. One's journey unique. What I will find at the end I can barely guess. What lies on the way is unknown. How to go? Land, sea or air? What techniques to use? What vehicle?'

Page is a fascinating example of the psychic traveller for whom poetry and painting are two possible vehicles. She began her work under the influence of Eliot, Auden, and the neo-Metaphysical poets for whom the poem was largely a closed form, a performance. In this realm she produced a number of brilliant lyrics. Then, under the influence of travel, new languages, painting, age, and a reading of the mystics, she came to see poetry as a form of exploration and conjuring. The sojourn in Brazil, according to an interview in *The Canadian Forum*, strengthened her belief that 'certain proportions, the right proportions, can actually alter human perception'. To this end she endeavoured, in her poems and drawings, to discover the magical combinations and forms that would open perceptual doors.

Not surprisingly, her poems, early and late, contain many explicit references to the kinds, tricks, and limits of human perception. Even her account of the poetic process draws on the optical illusion of a vanishing point: 'The idea diminishes to a dimensionless point in my absolute centre. If I can hold it steady long enough, the feeling which is associated with that point grows and fills a larger area as perfume permeates a room. It is from here that I write—held within that luminous circle, that locus which is at the same time a focusing glass, the surface of a drum' (*Canadian Literature* 46, Autumn 1970).

In 'Questions & Images' (*Canadian Literature* 41, Summer 1969), she describes her experience of learning a second language as being born a second time and undergoing a sort of sea-change. During this period she began to paint, logically extending her explorations of visual perception and gathering other means to conjure and transform experience.

In the preface to *Hologram*, a recent book of glosas—poems written out of the inspiration of, and beginning with a number of lines from, another poet's work—Page explores the relation between voice and influence: 'Timing is interesting. I had barely formulated the questions before I found what may be their answer in a report by an ornithologist. Attempting to understand how song birds learn to sing, he brought them up in isolation. To his surprise, they produced a kind of song—not species perfect—but recognizable. He then introduced them to the songs of a variety of birds not of their species and discovered they chose the notes and cadences that, combined with their own attempts, completed their species song. "Of course!" I thought, "that is what poets do. We have a song—of a kind. But it is not until we have heard many other songs that we are able to put together our own specific song." '

YOUNG GIRLS

Nothing, not even fear of punishment
can stop the giggle in a girl.
Oh mothers' trim
shapes on the chesterfield cannot dispel
their lolloping fatness.
Adolescence tumbles about in them
on cinder schoolyard or behind the expensive gates.

See them in class like porpoises
with smiles and tears
loosed from the same subterranean faucet; some
find individual adventure in
the obtuse angle, some in a phrase
that leaps like a smaller fish from a sea of words.
But most, deep in their daze, dawdle and roll,
their little breasts like wounds beneath their clothes.

A shoal of them in a room makes it a pool.
How can one teacher keep the water out,
or, being adult, find the springs and taps
of their tempers and tortures?
Who on a field filled with their female cries
can reel them in on a line of words
or land them neatly in a net?
On the dry ground they goggle, flounder, flap.

Too much weeping in them and unfamiliar blood
has set them perilously afloat.
Not divers these—but as if the waters rose in flood—
making them partially amphibious
and always drowning a little and hearing bells;
until the day the shore line wavers less,
and caught and swung on the bright hooks of their sex,
earth becomes home, their natural element.

[1954]

T-BAR

Relentless, black on white, the cable runs
through metal arches up the mountain side.
At intervals giant pickaxes are hung
on long hydraulic springs. The skiers ride
propped by the axehead, twin automatons
supported by its handle, one each side.

In twos they move slow motion up the steep
incision in the mountain. Climb. Climb.
Somnambulists, bolt upright in their sleep
their phantom poles swung lazily behind,
while to the right, the empty T-bars keep
in mute descent, slow monstrous jigging time.

Captive the skiers now and innocent,
wards of eternity, each pair alone.
They mount the easy vertical ascent,
pass through successive arches, bride and groom,
as through successive naves, are newly wed
participants in some recurring dream.

So do they move forever. Clocks are broken.
In zones of silence they grow tall and slow,
inanimate dreamers, mild and gentle-spoken
blood-brothers of the haemophilic snow
until the summit breaks and they awaken
imagos from the stricture of the tow.

Jerked from her chrysalis the sleeping bride
suffers too sudden freedom like a pain.
The dreaming bridegroom severed from her side
singles her out, the old wound aches again.
Uncertain, lost, upon a wintry height
these two, not separate, but no longer one.

Now clocks begin to peck and sing. The slow
extended minute like a rubber band
contracts to catapult them through the snow

in tandem trajectory while behind
etching the sky-line, obdurate and slow
the spastic T-bars pivot and descend.

[1954]

THE STENOGRAPHERS

After the brief bivouac of Sunday,
their eyes, in the forced march of Monday to Saturday,
hoist the white flag, flutter in the snow-storm of paper,
haul it down and crack in the mid-sun of temper.

In the pause between the first draft and the carbon
they glimpse the smooth hours when they were children—
the ride in the ice-cart, the ice-man's name,
the end of the route and the long walk home;

remember the sea where floats at high tide
were sea marrows growing on the scatter-green vine
or spools of grey toffee, or wasps' nests on water;
remember the sand and the leaves of the country.

Bell rings and they go and the voice draws their pencil
like a sled across snow; when its runners are frozen
rope snaps and the voice then is pulling no burden
but runs like a dog on the winter of paper.

Their climates are winter and summer—no wind
for the kites of their hearts—no wind for a flight;
a breeze at the most, to tumble them over
and leave them like rubbish—the boy-friends of blood.

In the inch of the noon as they move they are stagnant.
The terrible calm of the noon is their anguish;
the lip of the counter, the shapes of the straws
like icicles breaking their tongues, are invaders.

Their beds are their oceans—salt water of weeping
the waves that they know—the tide before sleep;
and fighting to drown they assemble their sheep
in columns and watch them leap desks for their fences
and stare at them with their own mirror-worn faces.

In the felt of the morning the calico-minded,
sufficiently starched, insert papers, hit keys,
efficient and sure as their adding machines;
yet they weep in the vault, they are taut as net curtains
stretched upon frames. In their eyes I have seen
the pin men of madness in marathon trim
race round the track of the stadium pupil.

[1946]

THE LANDLADY

Through sepia air the boarders come and go,
impersonal as trains. Pass silently
the craving silence swallowing her speech;
click doors like shutters on her camera eye.

Because of her their lives become exact:
their entrances and exits are designed;
phone calls are cryptic. Oh, her ticklish ears
advance and fall back stunned.
Nothing is unprepared. They hold the walls
about them as they weep or laugh. Each face
is dialled to zero publicly. She peers
stippled with curious flesh;

pads on the patient landing like a pulse,
unlocks their keyholes with the wire of sight,
searches their rooms for clues when they are out,
pricks when they come home late.

Wonders when they are quiet, jumps when they move,
dreams that they dope or drink, trembles to know
the traffic of their brains, jaywalks their street
in clumsy shoes.

Yet knows them better than their closest friends:
their cupboards and the secrets of their drawers,
their books, their private mail, their photographs
are theirs and hers.

Knows when they wash, how frequently their clothes
go to the cleaners, what they like to eat,
their curvature of health, but even so
is not content.

And like a lover must know all, all, all.
Prays she may catch them unprepared at last
and palm the dreadful riddle of their skulls—
hoping the worst.

[1946]

Stories of Snow

Those in the vegetable rain retain
an area behind their sprouting eyes
held soft and rounded with the dream of snow
precious and reminiscent as those globes—
souvenir of some never-nether land—
which hold their snow-storms circular, complete,
high in a tall and teakwood cabinet.

In countries where the leaves are large as hands
where flowers protrude their fleshy chins
and call their colours,
an imaginary snow-storm sometimes falls
among the lilies.
And in the early morning one will waken
to think the glowing linen of his pillow
a northern drift, will find himself mistaken
and lie back weeping.
And there the story shifts from head to head,
of how in Holland, from their feather beds
hunters arise and part the flakes and go
forth to the frozen lakes in search of swans—
the snow-light falling white along their guns,

their breath in plumes.
While tethered in the wind like sleeping gulls
ice-boats wait the raising of their wings
to skim the electric ice at such a speed
they leap jet strips of naked water,
and how these flying, sailing hunters feel
air in their mouths as terrible as ether.
And on the story runs that even drinks
in that white landscape dare to be no colour;
how flasked and water clear, the liquor slips
silver against the hunters' moving hips.
And of the swan in death these dreamers tell
of its last flight and how it falls, a plummet,
pierced by the freezing bullet
and how three feathers, loosened by the shot,
descend like snow upon it.
While hunters plunge their fingers in its down
deep as a drift, and dive their hands
up to the neck of the wrist
in that warm metamorphosis of snow
as gentle as the sort that woodsmen know
who, lost in the white circle, fall at last
and dream their way to death.

And stories of this kind are often told
in countries where great flowers bar the roads
with reds and blues which seal the route to snow—
as if, in telling, raconteurs unlock
the colour with its complement and go
through to the area behind the eyes
where silent, unrefractive whiteness lies.

[1946]

Photos of a Salt Mine

How innocent their lives look,
how like a child's
dream of caves and winter, both combined;
the steep descent to whiteness
and the stope

with its striated walls
their folds all leaning as if pointing to
the greater whiteness still,
that great white bank
with its decisive front,
that seam upon a slope,
salt's lovely ice.

And wonderful underfoot the snow of salt
the fine
particles a broom could sweep,
one thinks
muckers might make angels in its drifts
as children do in snow,
lovers in sheets,
lie down and leave imprinted where they lay
a feathered creature holier than they.

And in the outworked stopes
with lamps and ropes
up miniature matterhorns
the miners climb
probe with their lights
the ancient folds of rock—
syncline and anticline—
and scoop from darkness an Aladdin's cave:
rubies and opals glitter from its walls.

But hoses douse the brilliance of these jewels,
melt fire to brine.
Salt's bitter water trickles thin and forms,
slow fathoms down,
a lack within a cave,
lacquered with jet—
white's opposite.
There grey on black the boating miners float
to mend the stays and struts of that old stope
and deeply underground
their words resound,
are multiplied by echo, swell and grow
and make a climate of a miner's voice.

So all the photographs like children's wishes
are filled with caves or winter,
innocence
has acted as a filter,
selected only beauty from the mine.
Except in the last picture,
it is shot
from an acute high angle. In a pit
figures the size of pins are strangely lit
and might be dancing but you know they're not.
Like Dante's vision of the nether hell
men struggle with the bright cold fires of salt,
locked in the black inferno of the rock:
the filter here, not innocence but guilt.

[1946]

THE PERMANENT TOURISTS

Somnolent through landscapes and by trees
nondescript, almost anonymous,
they alter as they enter foreign cities—
the terrible tourists with their empty eyes
longing to be filled with monuments.

Verge upon statues in the public squares
remembering the promise of memorials
yet never enter the entire event
as dogs, abroad in any kind of weather,
move perfectly within their rainy climate.

Lock themselves into snapshots on the steps
of monolithic bronze as if suspecting
the subtle mourning of the photograph
might later conjure in the memory
all they are now incapable of feeling.

And search all heroes out: the boy who gave
his life to save a town; the stolid queen;
forgotten politicians minus names
and the plunging war dead, permanently brave,
forever and ever going down to death.

Look, you can see them nude in any café
reading their histories from the bill of fare,
creating futures from a foreign teacup.
Philosophies like ferns bloom from the fable
that travel is broadening at the café table.

Yet somehow beautiful, they stamp the plaza.
Classic in their anxiety they call
all sculptured immemorial stone
into their passive eyes, as rivers
draw ruined columns to their placid glass.

[1954]

THE GLASS AIR

I dreamed my most extraordinary darling
gangling, come to share
my hot and prairie childhood

the first day loosed the mare from her picket
and rode her bareback
over the little foothills towards the mountains.

And on the second, striding from his tent,
twisted a noose of butcher's string.
Ingenious to my eyes the knots he tied.

The third bright day he laid the slack noose over
the gopher's burrow,
unhurried by the chase,

and lolled a full week, lazy, in the sun
until the head popped, sleek, enquiring.
The noose pulled tight around its throat.

Then the small fur lashed, lit out, hurling
about only to turn
tame silk in his palm

as privy harness, tangled from his pocket
with leash of string
slipped simply on.

But the toy beast and the long rein and the paid out lengths
of our youth snapped
as the creature jibbed and bit

and the bright blood ran out, the bright blood trickled over,
slowed, grew dark
lay sticky on our skins.

And we two, dots upon that endless plain, Leviathan became
and filled and broke
the glass air like twin figures, vast, in stone.

[1985]

DEAF-MUTE IN THE PEAR TREE

His clumsy body is a golden fruit
pendulous in the pear tree

Blunt fingers among the multitudinous buds

Adriatic blue the sky above and through
the forking twigs

Sun ruddying tree's trunk, his trunk
his massive head thick-nobbed with burnished curls
tight-clenched in bud

(Painting by Generalić. Primitive.)

I watch him prune with silent secateurs

Boots in the crotch of branches shift their weight
heavily as oxen in a stall

Hear small inarticulate mews from his locked mouth
a kitten in a box

Pear clippings fall
soundlessly on the ground

Spring finches sing
soundlessly in the leaves

A stone. A stone in ears and on his tongue

Through palm and fingertip he knows the tree's
quick springtime pulse

Smells in its sap the sweet incipient pears

Pale sunlight's choppy water glistens on
his mutely snipping blades

and flags and scraps of blue
above him make regatta of the day

But when he sees his wife's foreshortened shape
sudden and silent in the grass below
uptilt its face to him

then air is kisses, kisses

stone dissolves

his locked throat finds a little door

and through it feathered joy
flies screaming like a jay

[1985]

ALONE

The moon is set and the Pleiades
It is midnight and time passes
Time passes
I lie alone

Sappho

Summer and the honeyed air
rises, falls—like a lover breathing
The only sound this slow breathing

from the high branches of the pines
in dark so dark I might be blind.
Am *I* blind? Perhaps my eyes
now they are no longer needed
for seeing have atrophied.
The moon is set and the Pleiades.

I saw them set. I saw the light
fade overhead, fade all around me.
I felt eternity enter my veins
slow drip of an intravenous needle
that drop by drop anaesthetizes
greys me, turns the night to ashes
but will not let me sleep, I wait
for words I shall not hear
caresses . . .
It is midnight and time passes.

Passes. 'To pass.'
What is this verb
that means 'to move
go on, progress'?
This is not movement
this is stasis.
something has broken
turned to stone.
Meaning reverses.
'*Time passes*'

means 'does not pass'.
Time does not pass.
Is stopped.
Concluded.
Once, God was here
to mark the end
that love began.
Now darkness reigns.
And God has gone.
I lie alone.

[1994]

DENISE LEVERTOV (b. 1923)

Denise Levertov was born at Ilford, Essex, England, and educated primarily at home by private tutors. Her father was descended from a Russian rabbi of mystical persuasion, her mother from a Welsh tailor and mystic named Angel of Mold. After moving to the United States in 1948 with her American husband, the writer Mitchell Goodman, she befriended several poets associated with the writing school at Black Mountain College, Colorado, including Robert Creeley and Robert Duncan, both of whom she regards as important influences. Both her theory and her practice seem inspired by the notion that there is an almost mystical reciprocity between self and 'other'; that people, objects, and places evoke in us a special response, an 'inner song'; and that it is the poet's task to give shape to this inner song. As she explains in 'Line-breaks, Stanza-spaces, and the Inner Voice' (*The Poet in the World*, 1973), 'The written poem is then a record of that inner voice.'

Her works include *The Double Image* (1946), *Here and Now* (1956), *Overland to the Islands* (1958), *With Eyes at the Back of Our Heads* (1960), *The Jacob's Ladder* (1961), *O Taste and See* (1964), *The Sorrow Dance* (1967), *A Tree Telling of Orpheus* (1968), *Relearning the Alphabet* (1970), *To Stay Alive* (1971), *Collected Earlier Poems* 1940-1960 (1979), *Candles in Babylon* (1982), *Poems 1960-1967* (1983), *Oblique Prayers* (1984), *Breathing the Water* (1987), *A Door in the Hive* (1989), and *Evening Train* (1992). Her views on organic form, line-breaks, the relation of gender and genre, and the function of poetry are collected in *The Poet in the World* (1973) and *New & Selected Essays* (1992). For a critical overview, see *Denise Levertov: Selected Criticism* (1993).

Levertov quotes a statement by Rainer Maria Rilke in her essay 'Great Possessions' (*The Poet in the World*), which seems to embody much of what she is attempting to do: 'If a thing is to speak to you, you must for a certain time regard it as the only thing that exists, the unique phenomenon that your diligent and exclusive love has placed at the centre of the universe, something the angels serve that very day upon that matchless spot.' She calls this creative state *ecstatic attention*; but she makes a further point that helps us distinguish between the merely ecstatic worshipper and the one who is able to channel this attention into the creation of something new: 'an ecstasy of attention, a passion for the thing known, that shall be more, not less, sensuous, and which in its intensity shall lead the writer into a deeper, more vibrant language.'

While the religious, or visionary, impulse is most evident in Levertov's early and later poems, it is by no means absent from the work of her period of political engagement during the sixties and seventies, when she was active in the anti-war movement (and its publication, *Writers Take Sides On Vietnam*) and travelled to North Vietnam to bring back impressions of life there. When asked to justify her political actions and the political content in her poetry, she writes in 'The Poet in the World': 'I answer, good poets write bad political poems only if they let themselves write deliberate, opinionated rhetoric, misusing their art as propaganda. The poet does not *use* poetry, but is at the service of poetry. To *use* it is to *mis*use it. A poet driven to speak to himself, to maintain a dialogue with himself, concerning politics, can expect to write as well upon that theme as upon any other. . . . a sense of history must involve a sense of the present, a vivid awareness of change, a response to crisis, a realization that what was appropriate in this or that situation in the past is inadequate to the demands of the present, that we are living our whole lives *in a state of emergency* which is—for reasons I'm sure I don't have to spell out for you by discussing nuclear and chemical weapons, or ecological disasters and threats—unparalleled in history.'

While she has continued to speak out against political atrocities, including those of her own government in the Gulf War, and human-rights abuses in countries such as El Salvador, Levertov nevertheless argues in 'Great Possessions' that poetry is political at a level deeper than that of mere content: 'a poet must recognize not only that poetry is intrinsically revolutionary but that it is so not by virtue of talking *about* any one subject rather than another (though if he has political concerns they may not be excluded, and not to have political concerns—in the broad and deep sense of the term—is surely impossible to the aware adult in the last quarter of the twentieth century). But whether content in any poem is huge or minuscule, funny or sad, angry or joyful, it can only be deeply and truly revolutionary, only *be* poetry, "*song that suffices our need*", by being *in its very substance of sound and vision* an ecstasy and a giving of life.'

Levertov's later poetry foregrounds her religious vision, in which word, idea, and song unite in celebration of the physical world and in longing for the divine. In 'The Origin of A Poem', she makes a powerful case for imagination as the chief source of human compassion and reverence for life: 'it is the poet who has language in his care; the poet who more than others recognizes language also as a form of life and a common resource to be cherished and served as we should serve and cherish earth and its waters, animal and vegetable life, and each other. The would-be poet who looks on language merely as something to be used, as the bad farmer or the rapacious industrialist looks on the soil or on rivers merely as things to be used, will not discover a deep poetry; he will only, according to the degree of his skill, construct a counterfeit more or less acceptable—a subpoetry, at best efficiently representative of his thought or feeling—a reference, not an incarnation. And he will be contributing, even if not in any immediately apparent way, to the erosion of language, just as the irresponsible, irreverent farmer and industrialist erode the land and pollute the rivers.'

In an interview for the reference work *Contemporary Authors* in 1988, Levertov sums up the two major strands of her life and poetry with this comment: 'I have a button that says *Picket and Pray*.'

A Map of the Western Part of the County of Essex in England

Something forgotten for twenty years: though my fathers
and mothers came from Cordova and Vitebsk and Caernarvon,
and though I am a citizen of the United States and less a
stranger here than anywhere else, perhaps,
I am Essex-born:
Cranbrook Wash called me into its dark tunnel,
the little streams of Valentines heard my resolves,
Roding held my head above water when I thought it was
drowning me; in Hainault only a haze of thin trees

stood between the red doubledecker buses and the boar-hunt,
the spirit of merciful Phillipa glimmered there.
Pergo Park knew me, and Clavering, and Havering-atte-Bower,
Stanford Rivers lost me in osier beds, Stapleford Abbots
sent me safe home on the dark road after Simeon-quiet evensong,
Wanstead drew me over and over into its basic poetry,
in its serpentine lake I saw bass-viols among the golden dead leaves,
through its trees the ghost of a great house. In
Ilford High Road I saw the multitudes passing pale under the
light of flaring sundown, seven kings
in somber starry robes gathered at Seven Kings
the place of law
where my birth and marriage are recorded
and the death of my father. Woodford Wells
where an old house was called The Naked Beauty (a white
statue forlorn in its garden)
saw the meeting and parting of two sisters,
(forgotten? and further away
the hill before Thaxted? where peace befell us? not once
but many times?).
All the Ivans dreaming of their villages
all the Marias dreaming of their walled cities,
picking up fragments of New World slowly,
not knowing how to put them together nor how to join
image with image, now I know how it was with you, an old map
made long before I was born shows ancient
rights of way where I walked when I was ten burning with desire
for the world's great splendours, a child who traced voyages
indelibly all over the atlas, who now in a far country
remembers the first river, the first
field, bricks and lumber dumped in it ready for building,
that new smell, and remembers
the walls of the garden, the first light.

[1961]

Come into Animal Presence

Come into animal presence.
No man is so guileless as
the serpent. The lonely white

rabbit on the roof is a star
twitching its ears at the rain.
The llama intricately
folding its hind legs to be seated
not disdains but mildly
disregards human approval.
What joy when the insouciant
armadillo glances at us and doesn't
quicken his trotting
across the track into the palm brush.

What is this joy? That no animal
falters, but knows what it must do?
That the snake has no blemish,
that the rabbit inspects his strange surroundings
in white star-silence? The llama
rests in dignity, the armadillo
has some intention to pursue in the palm-forest.
Those who were sacred have remained so,
holiness does not dissolve, it is a presence
of bronze, only the sight that saw it
faltered and turned from it.
An old joy returns in holy presence.

[1961]

THE ACHE OF MARRIAGE

The ache of marriage:

thigh and tongue, beloved,
are heavy with it,
it throbs in the teeth

We look for communion
and are turned away, beloved,
each and each

It is leviathan and we
in its belly
looking for joy, some joy
not to be known outside it

two by two in the ark of
the ache of it.

[1964]

HYPOCRITE WOMEN

Hypocrite women, how seldom we speak
of our own doubts, while dubiously
we mother man in his doubt!

And if at Mill Valley perched in the trees
the sweet rain drifting through western air
a white sweating bull of a poet told us

our cunts are ugly—why didn't we
admit we have thought so too? (And
what shame? They are not for the eye!)

No, they are dark and wrinkled and hairy,
caves of the Moon. . . .   And when a
dark humming fills us, a

coldness towards life,
we are too much women to
own to such unwomanliness.

Whorishly with the psychopomp
we play and plead—and say
nothing of this later.   And our dreams,

with what frivolity we have pared them
like toenails, clipped them like ends of
split hair.

[1964]

SECOND DIDACTIC POEM

The honey of man is
the task we're set to: to be
'more ourselves'
in the making:
'bees of the invisible' working
in cells of flesh and psyche,
filling
'la grande ruche d'or.'

Nectar,
the makings of the
incorruptible,
is carried upon the
corrupt tongues of
mortal insects,
fanned with their wisps of wing
'to evaporate
excess water,'
enclosed and capped
with wax, the excretion
of bees' abdominal glands.
Beespittle, droppings, hairs
of beefur: all become honey.
Virulent micro-organisms cannot
survive in honey.
The taste,
the odour of honey:
each has no analogue but itself.

In our gathering, in our containing, in our
working, active within ourselves,
slowly the pale
dew-beads of light
lapped up from flowers
can thicken,
darken to gold:

honey of the human.

[1967]

AN INTERIM

I

While the war drags on, always worse,
the soul dwindles sometimes to an ant
rapid upon a cracked surface;

lightly, grimly, incessantly
it skims the unfathomed clefts where despair
seethes hot and black.

II

Children in the laundromat
waiting while their mothers fold sheets.
A five-year-old boy addresses
a four-year-old girl. 'When I say,
Do you want some gum? say *yes.*'
'Yes . . . ' 'Wait!—Now:
Do you want some gum?'
'Yes!' 'Well yes means no,
so you can't have any.'
He chews. He pops a big, delicate bubble at her.

O language, virtue
of man, touchstone
worn down by what
gross friction . . .

And,
' "It became necessary
to destroy the town to save it,"
a United States major said today.
He was talking about the decision
by allied commanders to bomb and shell the town
regardless of civilian casualties,
to rout the Vietcong.'

O language, mother of thought,
are you rejecting us as we reject you?

Language, coral island
accrued from human comprehensions,
human dreams,

you are eroded as war erodes us.

III
To repossess our souls we fly
to the sea. To be reminded
of its immensity, and the immense sky
in which clouds move at leisure,
transforming their lives ceaselessly,
sternly, playfully.

Today is the 65th day since de Courcy Squire, war-resister,
began her fast in jail. She is 18.

And the sun
is warm bread, good to us, honest.
And the sand gives itself to our feet
or to our outstretched bodies,
hospitable, accommodating, its shells
unendingly at hand for our wonder.

. . . arrested with 86 others Dec. 7. Her crime:
sitting down in front of a police wagon
momentarily preventing her friends from being
hauled to prison. Municipal Judge Heitzler
handed out 30-day suspended sentences to several others
accused of the same offense, but condemned
Miss Squire to 8 months in jail and fined her
$650. She had said in court 'I don't think there should be
roles like judge and defendant.'

IV
Peace as grandeur. Energy
serene and noble. The waves
break on the packed sand,

butterflies take the cream o' the foam,
from time to time a palmtree lets fall

another dry branch, calmly.
The restlessness
of the sound of waves
transforms itself in its persistence
to that deep rest.
At fourteen
after measles my mother took me
to stay by the sea. In the austere presence

of Beachy Head we sat long hours
close to the tideline. She read aloud
from George Eliot, while I half-dozed
and played with pebbles. Or I read
to myself Richard Jefferies'
The Story of My Heart, which begins

in such majesty.
I was mean and grouchy
much of the time, but she forgave me,

and years later remembered
only the peace of that time.

The quiet there is
in listening.
Peace could be

that grandeur, that dwelling
in majestic presence, attuned
to the great pulse.

V

The cocks crow all night
far and near. Hoarse with expectation.
And by day stumble red-eyed in the dust
where the heat flickers its lizard tongue.

In my dream the city
was half Berlin, half Chicago—
midwest German, Cincinnati perhaps,
where de Courcy Squire is.

There were many of us
jailed there, in moated fortresses—
five of them, with monosyllabic
guttural names. But by day
they led us through the streets,
dressed in our prisoners' robes—
smocks of brown holland—
and the people watched us pass
and waved to us, and gave us
serious smiles of hope.

Between us and the beach
a hundred yards of trees, bushes, buildings,
cut the breeze. But at the *verge*
of the salt flood, always
a steady wind, prevailing.

While we await your trial,
(and this is no dream) we are

free to come and go. To rise
from sleep and love and dreams about
ambiguous circumstance, and from
waking in darkness to cockcrow, and moving
deliberately (by keeping still) back into
morning sleep; to rise and float

into the blue day, the elaborate rustlings
of the palmtrees way overhead; to hover
with black butterflies at the lemon-blossom.
The sea awaits us; there are sweet oranges
on our plates; the city greyness has been
washed off our skins, we take pleasure
in each other's warmth of rosy brown.

VI
'Puerto Rico, Feb. 23, 1968.

. . . Some people, friends sincerely concerned for us but who don't seem to understand what it's really all about, apparently feel sorry for us because Mitch has been indicted. One letter this morning said, shyly and abruptly, after talking about quite unrelated matters, 'My heart aches for you.' Those people don't understand that however boring the trial will be in some ways, and however much of a distraction, as it certainly is, from the things one's nature would sooner be engaged with, yet it's quite largely a kind of pleasure too, a relief, a satisfaction of the need to confront the war-makers and, in the process, do something to wake up the bystanders.

. . . Mitch and the others have a great deal of support, people who think of them as spokesmen; they have good lawyers, and have had and will have a lot of publicity of the kind one hopes will be useful—I don't mean useful for their case, saving them from going to jail, I mean useful towards clarifying the issues, stopping the draft, helping to end the war.'

But something like a cramp
of fury begins to form
(in the blue day, in the sweetness
of life we float in, allowed
this interim before the trial)
a cramp of fury at the mild,
saddened people whose hearts ache
not for the crimes of war,
the unspeakable—of which, then,
I won't speak—
and not for de Courcy Squire's
solitary passion
but for us.

Denied visitors, even her parents;
confined to a locked cell without running water
or a toilet.
On January 29th, the 53rd day of her fast,
Miss Squire was removed to a hospital.
All the doctors would do was inform her that
the fast may cause her permanent brain injury.

'The sympathy of mild good folk,
a kind of latex from their leaves;
our inconvenience draws it out.

The white of egg without the yolk,
it soothes their conscience and relieves
the irritations of their doubt.

. . . You see how it is—I am angry that they feel no outrage. Their
feeling flows in the wrong directions and at the wrong intensity.
And all I can bring forth out of my anger is a few flippant rhymes.
What I want to tell you—no, not you, you understand it; what I
want them to grasp is that though I understand that Mitch may
have to go to jail and that it will be a hard time for him and for
me, yet, because it's for doing what we know we must do, that
hardship is imaginable, encompassable, and a small thing in the
face of the slaughter in Vietnam and the other slaughter that will
come. And there is no certainty he will go to jail.'

And the great savage saints of outrage—
who have no lawyers,
who have no interim
in which to come and go,
for whom there is no world left—
their bodies rush upon the air in flames,
sparks fly, fragments of charred rag
spin in the whirlwind, a vacuum
where there used to be this monk or that,
Norman Morrison, Alice Hertz.

Maybe they are crazy. I know I could never
bring myself to injure my own flesh, deliberately.
And there are other models of behaviour
to aspire to—A.J. Muste did not burn himself
but worked through a long life to make from outrage
islands of compassion others could build on.
Dennis Riordon, Bob Gilliam, how many others,
are alive and free in the jails. Their word is good,
language draws breath again in their yes and no,
true testimony of love and resistance.

But we need
the few who could bear no more,
who would try anything,
who would take the chance

that their deaths among the uncountable
masses of dead might be real to those who
don't dare imagine death.
Might burn through the veil that blinds
those who do not imagine the burned bodies
of other people's children.

We need them.
Brands that flare to show us
the dark we are in,
to keep us moving in it.

VII
To expand again, to plunge
our dryness into the unwearying source—

but not to forget.
Not to forget but to remember better.

We float in the blue day
darkly. We rest behind half-closed louvers,
the hot afternoon clouds up,
the palms hold still.

'I have a medical problem that can be cured'—
Miss Squire said last week when she was removed
from the city workhouse to Cincinnati General Hospital,
'I have a medical problem that can be cured
only by freedom.'

[Puerto Rico, February–March, 1968]

He-Who-Came-Forth

Somehow nineteen years ago
    clumsily passionate
I drew into me the seed
of a man—
            and bore it, cast it out—

man-seed that grew
                    and became a person
                    whose subtle mind and quick heart

  though I beat him, hurt him,
  while I fed him, loved him,

now stand beyond me, out in the world
                              beyond my skin
beautiful and strange as if
  I had given birth to a tree.

[1970]

'The Poem Rising By Its Own Weight'

The poet is at the disposal of his own night.
Jean Cocteau

The singing robes fly onto your body and cling there silkily,
you step out on the rope and move unfalteringly across it,

and seize the fiery knives unscathed and
keep them spinning above you, a fountain
of rhythmic rising, falling, rising
flames,

and proudly let the chains
be wound about you, ready
to shed them, link by steel link,
padlock by padlock—
                    but when your graceful
confident shrug and twist drives the metal
into your flesh and the python grip of it tightens
and you see rust on the chains and blood in your pores
and you roll
over and down a steepness into a dark hole
and there is not even the sound of mockery in the distant air
somewhere above you where the sky was,
no sound but your own breath panting:

then it is that the miracle
walks in, on his swift feet,
down the precipice straight into the cave,
opens the locks,
knots of chain fall open,
twists of chain unwind themselves,
links fall asunder,
in seconds there is a heap of scrap-
metal at your ankles, you step free and at once
he turns to go—

but as you catch at him with a cry,
clasping his knees, sobbing your gratitude,
with what radiant joy he turns to you,
and raises you to your feet,
and strokes your dishevelled hair,
and holds you,
                    holds you,
                              holds you
close and tenderly before he vanishes.

[1975]

She and the Muse

Away he goes, the hour's delightful hero,
arrivederci: and his horse clatters
out of the courtyard, raising
a flurry of straw and scattering hens.

He turns in the saddle waving a plumed hat,
his saddlebags are filled with talismans,
mirrors, parchment histories, gifts and stones,
indecipherable clues to destiny.

He rides off in the dustcloud of his own
story, and when he has vanished she
who had stood firm to wave and watch
from the top step, goes in to the cool

flagstoned kitchen, clears honey and milk and bread
off the table, sweeps from the hearth
ashes of last night's fire, and climbs the stairs
to strip tumbled sheets from her wide bed.

Now the long-desired
visit is over. The heroine
is a scribe. Returned to solitude,
eagerly she re-enters the third room,

the room hung with tapestries, scenes that change
whenever she looks away. Here is her lectern,
here her writing desk. She picks a quill,
dips it, begins to write. But not of him.

[1982]

BROTHER IVY

Between road and sidewalk, the broadleafed ivy,
unloved, dusty, littered, sanctuary of rats,
gets on with its life. New leaves shine gaily
among dogged older ones
that have lost their polish.
It does not require appreciation. The foliage
conceals a brown tangle of stems
thick as a mangrove swamp; the roots
are spread tenaciously. Unwatered
throughout the long droughts, it simply
grips the dry ground by the scruff of the neck.

I am not its steward.
If we are siblings, and I
my brother's keeper therefore,
the relation is reciprocal. The ivy
meets its obligation by pure
undoubtable being.

[1992]

CHARLES OLSON (1910-1970)

Born in Worcester, Massachusetts, Olson claims to have been 'uneducated' at Wesleyan, Yale, and Harvard, where he completed a Ph.D. in American Studies. He taught at Clarke and Harvard universities (1936-39) and at Black Mountain College in North Carolina (1951-56), where he was instructor and rector. With the assistance of a Guggenheim fellowship, he wrote a unique critical study of Melville, *Call Me Ishmael* (1947). In 1952 another grant took him to Yucatán to study Mayan hieroglyphics. His influence on the North American literary scene, through his intervention on behalf of Ezra Pound, his contact with young poets, his teaching, and his well-known poetic manifestos, has been immense.

Following *Call Me Ishmael*, Olson's publications include *Y & X* (1948), *Letter for Melville* (1951), *In Cold Hell, in Thicket* (1953), *Maximus Poems / 1-10* (1953), *Maximus Poems / 11-22* (1956), *O'Ryan* (1958), *The Distances* (1960), and *The Maximus Poems* (1983). A fine selection of his best poetry and prose, including his important essay 'Projective Verse' (1959), is available in *Selected Writings of Charles Olson* (1967), edited, with an introduction and bibliography, by Robert Creeley.

Olson was well-read in social and cultural anthropology and trained professionally as a dancer, two disciplines that help to explain his unusual position as a poet and critic. He was given to the use of musical analogy in his discussion of writing and to a unique choreography of argument. In a note to *Human Universe and Other Essays* (1965), for example, he writes:

> It's as though you were hearing this for the first time—who knows what a poem ought to sound like? until it's thar? And how do you get it thar except as you do—you, and nobody else (who's
>
> a poet
>
> What's
>
> a poem?
>
> It ain't dreamt until it walks It talks It spreads its green barrazza
>
> Listen closely, folks, this poem comes to you by benefit of its own Irish green bazoo. You take it, from here.

This note explains somewhat whimsically what Olson believed seriously to be the nature of poetic composition. He rejected formal order as such, especially the tight imagistic modes and cross-fertilization of metaphor favoured by New Criticism. Instead he insisted that a poem is a *thing*, a unit of energy passed from writer to reader, and that it has its own laws, the most important being that form and content must be realized simultaneously. In the hands of an inexperienced writer, this results only in formlessness; but not for the poet with a fine ear to discriminate among possible syllables as particles of sound and sense and a fine eye to determine the placing of these syllables.

Olson's rejection of the closed form for what he calls composition by field reflects his conception of poetry as an act of being. The poet must dispense with all intellectual trappings, all systems of thought (including abstractions such as space and time) that interfere with his experience of himself and other *objects* in his world. The result of this denuding process, which Olson describes as 'objectism', is that the individual is faced with the bare fact of his existence as an object in the physical world: 'It is his own physiology he is forced to arrive at.' In his poetry Olson begins with the literal fact of being. Thus his unusual awareness, in the act of creation, of the discriminations of his senses and the pressure of his breathing. To ignore this awareness, Olson would say, is to ignore what is most fundamental, most personal, in the creative process.

Ekbert Faas, in *Towards A New American Poetics* (1979), has identified Olson's links with the ideas of D.H. Lawrence, particularly Lawrence's 'primitivism' and notion that 'consciousness is an end in itself. We torture ourselves getting somewhere, and when we get there it is nowhere, for there is nowhere to get to.' Lawrence championed 'rotary image-thought', open forms, and more room for the irrational, or unconscious, in art; similarly, as Faas points out, Olson argued in a review of E.A. Havelock's *Preface to Plato* in 1964 for 'a wholly different syntax. . . [or] *parataxis* in which the words and actions reported are set down side by side in the order of their occurrence in nature, instead of by an order of discourse, or "grammar".' 'The motive, then, of reality', he writes in *The Special View of History* (edited by Ann Charters, 1970), 'is process not goal. . . the chance success of the play of creative accident.' And in *Selected Writings*, he says 'There is only one thing you can do about kinetic, reenact it. Which is why the man said, he who possesses rhythm, possesses the universe. And why art is the only twin life has—its only valid metaphysic.'

THE KINGFISHERS

I
What does not change / is the will to change

He woke, fully clothed, in his bed. He
remembered only one thing, the birds, how
when he came in, he had gone around the rooms
and got them back in their cage, the green one first,
she with the bad leg, and then the blue,
the one they had hoped was a male

Otherwise? Yes, Fernand, who had talked lispingly of Albers
    & Angkor Vat.
He had left the party without a word. How he got up, got into
    his coat,
I do not know. When I saw him, he was at the door, but it did
    not matter,
he was already sliding along the wall of the night, losing himself
in some crack of the ruins. That it should have been he who said,
    'The kingfishers!
who cares
for their feathers
now?'

His last words had been, 'The pool is slime.' Suddenly everyone,
ceasing their talk, sat in a row around him, watched
they did not so much hear, or pay attention, they
wondered, looked at each other, smirked, but listened,
he repeated and repeated, could not go beyond his thought
'The pool   the kingfishers' feathers were wealth   why
did the export stop?'

It was then he left

II
I thought of the E on the stone, and of what Mao said
la lumière'
        but the kingfisher
de l'aurore'
        but the kingfisher flew west
est devant nous!
        he got the color of his breast
        from the heat of the setting sun!

The features are, the feebleness of the feet (syndactylism of the 3rd & 4th digit)
the bill, serrated, sometimes a pronounced beak, the wings
where the color is, short and round, the tail
inconspicuous.

But not these things were the factors. Not the birds.
The legends are
legends. Dead, hung up indoors, the kingfisher
will not indicate a favoring wind,
or avert the thunderbolt. Nor, by its nesting,
still the waters, with the new year, for seven days.
It is true, it does nest with the opening year, but not on the waters.
It nests at the end of a tunnel bored by itself in a bank. There,
six or eight white and translucent eggs are laid, on fishbones
not on bare clay, on bones thrown up in pellets by the birds.

On these rejectamenta
(as they accumulate they form a cup-shaped structure) the young are born.
And, as they are fed and grow, this nest of excrement and decayed fish becomes
a dripping, fetid mass

Mao concluded:
nous devons
nous lever
et agir!

III
When the attentions change / the jungle
leaps in
even the stones are split
they rive

Or,
enter
that other conqueror we more naturally recognize
he so resembles ourselves

But the E
cut so rudely on that oldest stone
sounded otherwise,
was differently heard

as, in another time, were treasures used:

(and, later, much later, a fine ear thought
a scarlet coat)

'of green feathers feet, beaks and eyes
of gold

'animals likewise,
resembling snails

'a large wheel, gold, with figures of unknown four-foots,
and worked with tufts of leaves, weight
3800 ounces

'last, two birds, of thread and featherwork, the quills
gold, the feet
gold, the two birds perched on two reeds
gold, the reeds arising from two embroidered mounds,
one yellow, the other
white.

'And from each reed hung
seven feathered tassels.

In this instance, the priests
(in dark cotton robes, and dirty,
their dishevelled hair matted with blood, and flowing wildly
over their shoulders)
rush in among the people, calling on them
to protect their gods

And all now is war
where so lately there was peace,
and the sweet brotherhood, the use
of tilled fields.

IV
Not one death but many,
not accumulation but change, the feed-back proves, the feed-back
is the law
Into the same river
When fire dies air dies
No one remains, nor is, one

Around an appearance, one common model, we grow up
many. Else how is it,
if we remain the same,
we take pleasure now
in what we did not take pleasure before? love
contrary objects? admire and/or find fault? use
other words, feel other passions, have
nor figure, appearance, disposition, tissue
the same?
To be in different states without a change
is not a possibility

We can be precise. The factors are
in the animal and/or the machine the factors are
communication and/or control, both involve
the message. And what is the message? The message is
a discrete or continuous sequence of measurable events
distributed in time

is the birth of air, is
the birth of water, is
a state between
the origin and
the end, between
birth and the beginning of
another fetid nest

is change, presents
no more than itself

And the too strong grasping of it,
when it is pressed together and condensed,
loses it

This very thing you are

        ii
        They buried their dead in a sitting posture
        serpent   came   razor   ray of the sun

        And she sprinkled water on the head of the child, crying
        'Cioa-coatl! Cioa-coatl!'
        with her face to the west

        Where the bones are found, in each personal heap
        with what each enjoyed, there is always
        the Mongolian louse

The light is in the east. Yes. And we must rise, act. Yet
in the west, despite the apparent darkness (the whiteness
which covers all), if you look, if you can bear, if you can, long enough
        as long as it was necessary for him, my guide
        to look into the yellow of that longest-lasting rose

so you must, and, in that whiteness, into that face, with what candor, look

and, considering the dryness of the place
    the long absence of an adequate race

(of the two who first came, each a conquistador, one
healed, the other
tore the eastern idols down, toppled
the temple walls, which, says the excuser
were black from human gore)

hear
hear, where the dry blood talks
where the old appetite walks

la piu saporita et migliore
che si possa truovar al mondo

where it hides, look
in the eye how it runs
in the flesh / chalk

but under these petals
in the emptiness
regard the light, contemplate
the flower

whence it arose

with what violence benevolence is bought
what cost in gesture justice brings
what wrongs domestic rights involve
what stalks
this silence

what pudor pejorocracy affronts
how awe, night-rest and neighborhood can rot
what breeds where dirtiness is law
what crawls
below

iii

I am no Greek, hath not th'advantage.
And of course, no Roman:
he can take no risk that matters,
the risk of beauty least of all.

But I have my kin, if for no other reason than
(as he said, next of kin) I commit myself, and,
given my freedom, I'd be a cad
if I didn't. Which is most true.

It works out this way, despite the disadvantage.
I offer, in explanation, a quote:
si j'ai du goût, ce n'est guères
que pour la terre et les pierres

Despite the discrepancy (an ocean   courage   age)
this is also true: if I have any taste
it is only because I have interested myself
in what was slain in the sun

        I pose you your question:

shall you uncover honey / where maggots are?

        I hunt among stones

[1953]

As the Dead Prey upon Us

I
As the dead prey upon us,
they are the dead in ourselves,
awake, my sleeping ones, I cry out to you,
disentangle the nets of being!

I pushed my car, it had been sitting so long unused.
I thought the tires looked as though they only needed air.
But suddenly the huge underbody was above me,
                                                        and the rear tires
were masses of rubber and thread variously clinging together

as were the dead souls in the living room, gathered
about my mother, some of them taking care to pass
beneath the beam of the movie projector, some record
playing on the victrola, and all of them
desperate with the tawdriness of their life in hell

I turned to the young man on my right and asked, 'How is it,
there?' And he begged me protestingly don't ask, we are poor
poor. And the whole room was suddenly posters
                                                            and presentations
of brake linings and other automotive accessories, cardboard
displays, the dead roaming from one to another
as bored back in life as they are in hell, poor and doomed
to mere equipments

            my mother, as alive as ever she was, asleep
when I entered the house as I often found her in a rocker
under the lamp, and awaking, as I came up to her,
                                                            as she ever had
I found out she returns to the house once a week, and with her
the throng of the unknown young who center on her
                                                            as much in death
as other like suited and dressed people did in life

O the dead!

        and the Indian woman and I
        enabled the blue deer
        to walk

        and the blue deer talked,
        in the next room,
        a Negro talk

        it was like walking a jackass,
        and its talk
        was the pressing gabber of gammers
        of old women

        and we helped walk it around the room
        because it was seeking socks
        or shoes for its hooves
        now that it was acquiring

        human possibilities

In the five hindrances men and angels
stay caught in the net, in the immense nets
which spread out across each plane of being, the multiple nets
which hamper at each step of the ladders as the angels
and the demons
and men
go up and down

Walk the jackass
Hear the victrola
Let the automobile
be tucked into a corner of the white fence
when it is a white chair. Purity

is only an instant of being, the trammels

recur

In the five hindrances, perfection
is hidden

I shall get
to the place
10 minutes late.

It will be 20 minutes
of 9. And I don't know,

without the car,

how I shall get there

O peace, my mother, I do not know
how differently I could have done
what I did or did not do.

That you are back each week
that you fall asleep
with your face to the right

that you are as present there
when I come in as you were
when you were alive

that you are as solid, and your flesh
is as I knew it, that you have the company
I am used to your having
but o, that you all find it
such a cheapness!

o peace, mother, for the mammothness
of the comings and goings
of the ladders of life

The nets we are entangled in. Awake,
my soul, let the power into the last wrinkle
of being, let none of the threads and rubber of the tires
be left upon the earth. Let even your mother
go. Let there be only paradise

The desperateness is, that the instant
which is also paradise (paradise
is happiness) dissolves
into the next instant, and power
flows to meet the next occurrence

Is it any wonder
my mother comes back?
Do not that throng
rightly seek the room
where they might expect
happiness? They did not complain
of life, they obviously wanted
the movie, each other, merely to pass
among each other there,
where the real is, even to the display cards,
to be out of hell

The poverty
of hell

O souls, in life and in death,
awake, even as you sleep, even in sleep
know what wind
even under the crankcase of the ugly automobile
lifts it away, clears the sodden weights of goods,
equipment, entertainment, the foods, the Indian woman,
the filthy blue deer, the 4 by 3 foot 'Viewbook,'
the heaviness of the old house, the stuffed inner room
lifts the sodden nets

and they disappear as ghosts do,
as spider webs, nothing
before the hand of man

The vent! You must have the vent,
or you shall die. Which means
never to die, the ghastliness

of going, and forever
coming back, returning
to the instants which were not lived

O mother, this I could not have done,
I could not have lived what you didn't,
I am myself netted in my own being

I want to die. I want to make that instant, too,
perfect

O my soul, slip
the cog

II
The death in life (death itself)
is endless, eternity
is the false cause

The knot is otherwise, each topological corner
presents itself, and no sword
cuts it, each knot is itself its fire

each knot of which the net is made
is for the hands to untake
the knot's making. And touch alone

can turn the knot into its own flame

(o mother, if you had once touched me

o mother, if I had once touched you)

The car did not burn. Its underside
was not presented to me
a grotesque corpse. The old man

merely removed it as I looked up at it,
and put it in a corner of the picket fence
like was it my mother's white dog?

or a child's chair

The woman,
playing on the grass,
with her son (the woman next door)

was angry with me whatever it was
slipped across the playpen or whatever
she had out there on the grass

And I was quite flip in reply
that anyone who used plastic
had to expect things to skid

and break, that I couldn't worry
that her son might have been hurt
by whatever it was I sent skidding

down on them.

It was just then I went into my house
and to my utter astonishment
found my mother sitting there

as she always had sat, as must she always
forever sit there her head lolling
into sleep? Awake, awake my mother

what wind will lift you too
forever from the tawdriness
make you rich as all those souls

crave crave crave

to be rich?

They are right. We must have
what we want. We cannot afford
not to. We have only one course:

the nets which entangle us are flames

O souls, burn
alive, burn now

that you may forever
have peace, have

what you crave

O souls,
go into everything,
let not one knot pass
through your fingers

let not any they tell you
you must sleep as the net
comes through your authentic hands

What passes
is what is, what shall be, what has
been, what hell and heaven is
is earth to be rent, to shoot you
through the screen of flame which each knot
hides as all knots are a wall ready
to be shot open by you

the nets of being
are only eternal if you sleep as your hands
ought to be busy. Method, method

I too call on you to come
to the aid of all men, to women most
who know most, to woman to tell
men to awake. Awake, men,
awake

I ask my mother
to sleep. I ask her
to stay in the chair.
My chair
is in the corner of the fence.
She sits by the fireplace made of paving stones. The blue deer
need not trouble either of us.

And if she sits in happiness the souls
who trouble her and me
will also rest. The automobile

has been hauled away.

[1960]

Maximus, to Himself

I
I have had to learn the simplest things
last. Which made for difficulties.
Even at sea I was slow, to get the hand out, or to cross
a wet deck.
The sea was not, finally, my trade.
But even my trade, at it, I stood estranged
from that which was most familiar. Was delayed,
and not content with the man's argument
that such postponement
is now the nature of
obedience,
that we are all late

in a slow time,
that we grow up many
And the single
is not easily
known

It could be, though the sharpness (the *achiote*)
I note in others,
makes more sense
than my own distances. The agilities

they show daily
who do the world's
businesses
and who do nature's
as I have no sense
I have done either

I have made dialogues,
have discussed ancient texts,
have thrown what light I could, offered
what pleasures
doceat allows

But the known?
This, I have had to be given,
a life, love, and from one man
the world.

Tokens.
But sitting here
I look out as a wind
and water man, testing
And missing
Some proof

I know the quarters
of the weather, where it comes from,
where it goes. But the stem of me,
this I took from their welcome,
or their rejection, of me

And my arrogance
was neither diminished
nor increased,
by the communication

II
it is undone business
I speak of, this morning,
with the sea
stretching out
from my feet

[1960]

JOHN BERRYMAN (1914-1972)

In 1954 Geoffrey Moore wrote in *The Penguin Book of Modern American Verse* that Berryman's work had been described by critics as cerebral: 'This is true,' he said, 'and there is also a kind of compressed intellectual savagery. There is a grim vividness . . . in these poems; a damned soul might have written them.' The voice of prophecy: in 1972 Berryman leapt from a bridge to his death, thus ending the long, agonized struggle that was his life. He was born John Allyn Smith in McAlester, Oklahoma, the son of a banker and schoolteacher. When he was ten his family moved to Tampa, Florida, where, two years later, the father shot himself to death outside his son's window. His mother settled in New York and married a Wall Street banker named Berryman, who adopted the boy, but the marriage ended in divorce after ten years. Berryman himself was married three times. He studied at Columbia and Cambridge, gained recognition as a writer and critic and editor of *Partisan Review*, and taught at Harvard, Wayne State, Princeton, and the University of Minnesota. His poetry won various awards, including the Pulitzer Prize (1965), the Bollingen Prize (1968), and the National Book Award (1969).

Berryman paid heavily for his success. As he once wrote in connection with his poem 'The Dispossessed' (in *Poet's Choice*, edited by Paul Engle and Joseph Langland, 1962): 'I wanted something that would be both very neat, contained, and at the same time thoroughly mysterious. . . . Particularly because I used the poem as title-piece for a book, I have been sensitive (as indeed I was long before) to the word "dispossessed": and there can be no harm in saying here that I have come on it not dozens but hundreds of times used in the specially emphatic and central way I tried myself to achieve. The concept reaches deep into the modern agony.' *Deep into the modern agony* —that is where Berryman's poems, like those of Roethke and Plath, may be said to begin, and to end.

In an interview for *The Paris Review* in 1970, Berryman discussed his own oversensitivity to criticism and recommended to young writers 'the cultivation of extreme indifference to both praise and blame because praise will lead you to vanity, and blame will lead you to self-pity, and both are bad for writers.' He rejects the notion that he was in any way a confessional poet and prefers to emphasize his sources in historical research and in nature: 'Suppose I'm lecturing on Augustine. My Latin is very rusty, but I'll pay a certain amount of attention to the Latin text in the Loeb edition, with the English across the page. Then I'll visit the library and consult five or six old and recent works on St Augustine, who is a particular interest of mine, anyway. Now all that becomes part of your equipment for poetry, even for lyric poetry. The Bradstreet poem is a very learned poem. There is a lot of theology in it, there is a lot of theology in *The Dream Songs*. Anything is useful to a poet. Take observation of nature, of which I have absolutely none. It makes possible a world of moral observation for Frost, or Hopkins.'

Berryman's short poems are of uneven quality; many have a certain stiffness and self-consciousness, as if the poet were uneasy with, or fighting against, his medium. He seems, in fact, always to have been working towards the larger canvases of *Homage to Mistress Bradstreet* and *The Dream Songs*; it is only in these later works that he comes near achieving a verse that is 'neat', 'contained', and 'mysterious'. In the interview quoted above, he discusses his efforts to construct a long poem, or epic, inspired by Whitman's 'Song of Myself': 'The narrative, such as it is, developed as I went along, partly out of my gropings into and around Henry and his environment and associates, partly out of my readings in theology and that sort of thing, taking place during thirteen years—awful long time—and third, out of certain partly preconceived and partly developed as I went along, sometimes rigid and sometimes plastic, structural notions. That is why the work is divided into seven books, each book of which is rather well unified, as a matter of fact.'

Perhaps his most telling comment is this: 'Finally, I left the poem open to the circumstances of my personal life.' Berryman's poetry has been called confessional because it explores such psychic states as neurosis and schizophrenia and because it is sprinkled liberally with very personal references and biographical details. However, the real strength of *The Dream Songs* lies in another direction—in Berryman's discovery of comfortable masks or personæ. 'I had a personality and a plan and all kinds of philosophical and theological notions. . . . But at the same time I was what you might call open-ended. That is to say, Henry to some extent was in the situation that we are all in in actual life—namely, he didn't know and I didn't know what the bloody fucking hell was going to happen next. Whatever it was he had to confront it and get through. For example, he dies in Book IV and is dead throughout the book, but at the end of the poem he is still alive, and in fairly good condition, after having died himself *again*.'

In *The Dream Songs* Berryman employs three six-line stanzas to create a kind of modern sequence of approximate-sonnets; he maintains the tortured, distorted syntax that seems so suitable for rendering states of mental disturbance; and he creates a kind of unholy or infernal trinity of Henry, Mr Bones, and I, a composite persona that embraces the tragic, the comic, and the sentimental. Here is a marriage of Faust, Prufrock, and Faulkner's Joe Christmas, damned figures, like those in Beckett, wandering through the rubble of our century, through Hiroshima, and into whom Berryman pours his own despair and the despair of his age. If this poetry is confessional, it is a confession for all mankind.

Berryman's books of poetry include *The Dispossessed* (1948), *Homage to Mistress Bradstreet* (1956; rev. 1968), *77 Dream Songs* (1964), *Short Poems* (1967), *His Toy, His Dream, His Rest* (1968), and *Delusions, Etc.* (1972). He also wrote a considerable amount of prose, including a critical biography, *Stephen Crane* (1950), and a novel, *Recovery* (1973).

THE DISPOSSESSED

'and something that . . that is theirs—no longer ours'
stammered to me the Italian page. A wood
seeded & towered suddenly. I understood.—

The Leading Man's especially, and the Juvenile Lead's,
and the Leading Lady's thigh that switches & warms
and their grimaces, and their flying arms:

our arms, our story. Every seat was sold.
A crone met in a clearing sprouts a beard
and has a tirade. Not a word we heard.

Movement of stone within a woman's heart,
abrupt & dominant. They gesture how
fings really are. Rarely a child sings now.

My harpsichord weird as a koto drums
adagio for twilight, for the storm-worn dove
no more de-iced, and the spidery business of love.

The Juvenile Lead's the Leader's arm, one arm
running the whole bole, branches, roots, (O watch)
and the faceless fellow waving from her crotch,

Stalin-unanimous! who procured a vote
and care not use it, who have kept an eye
and care not use it, percussive vote, clear eye.

That which a captain and a weaponeer
one day and one more day did, we did, *ach*
we did not, *They* did . . cam slid, the great lock

lodged, and no soul of us all was near was near,—
an evil sky (where the umbrella bloomed)
twirled its mustaches, hissed, the ingenue fumed,

poor virgin, and no hero rides. The race
is done. Drifts through, between the cold black trunks,
the peachblow glory of the perishing sun

in empty houses where old things take place.

[1948]

A PROFESSOR'S SONG

(. . rabid or dog-dull.) Let me tell you how
The Eighteenth Century couplet ended. Now
Tell me. Troll me the sources of that Song—
Assigned last week—by Blake. Come, come along,
Gentlemen. (Fidget and huddle, do. Squint soon.)
I want to end these fellows all by noon.

'That deep romantic chasm'—an early use;
The word is from the French, by our abuse
Fished out a bit. (Red all your eyes. O when?)
'A poet is a man speaking to men':
But I am then a poet, am I not?—
Ha ha. The radiator, please. Well, what?

Alive now—no—Blake would have written prose,
But movement following movement crisply flows,
So much the better, better the much so,
As burbleth Mozart. Twelve. The class can go.
Until I meet you, then, in Upper Hell
Convulsed, foaming immortal blood: farewell.

[1948]

FROM 77 DREAM SONGS

1
Huffy Henry hid the day,
unappeasable Henry sulked.
I see his point,—a trying to put things over.
It was the thought that they thought
they could *do* it made Henry wicked & away.
But he should have come out and talked.

All the world like a woolen lover
once did seem on Henry's side.
Then came a departure.
Thereafter nothing fell out as it might or ought.
I don't see how Henry, pried
open for all the world to see, survived.

What he has now to say is a long
wonder the world can bear & be.
Once in a sycamore I was glad
all at the top, and I sang.
Hard on the land wears the strong sea
and empty grows every bed.

8

The weather was fine. They took away his teeth,
white & helpful; bothered his backhand;
halved his green hair.
They blew out his loves, his interests. 'Underneath,'
(they called in iron voices) 'understand,
is nothing. So there.'

The weather was very fine. They lifted off
his covers till he showed, and cringed & pled
to see himself less.
They installed mirrors till he flowed. 'Enough'
(murmured they) 'if you will watch Us instead,
yet you may saved be. Yes.'

The weather fleured. They weakened all his eyes,
and burning thumbs into his ears, and shook
his hand like a notch.
They flung long silent speeches. (Off the hook!)
They sandpapered his plumpest hope. (So capsize.)
They took away his crotch.

14

Life, friends, is boring. We must not say so.
After all, the sky flashes, the great sea yearns,
we ourselves flash and yearn,
and moreover my mother told me as a boy
(repeatingly) 'Ever to confess you're bored
means you have no

Inner Resources.' I conclude now I have no
inner resources, because I am heavy bored.
Peoples bore me,

literature bores me, especially great literature,
Henry bores me, with his plights & gripes
as bad as achilles,

who loves people and valiant art, which bores me.
And the tranquil hills, & gin, look like a drag
and somehow a dog
has taken itself & its tail considerably away
into mountains or sea or sky, leaving
behind: me, wag.

26

The glories of the world struck me, made me aria, once.
—What happen then, Mr Bones?
if be you cares to say.
—Henry. Henry became interested in women's bodies,
his loins were & were the scene of stupendous achievement.
Stupor. Knees, dear. Pray.
All the knobs & softnesses of, my God,
the ducking & trouble it swarm on Henry,
at one time.
—What happen then, Mr Bones?
you seems excited-like.
—Fell Henry back into the original crime: art, rime

besides a sense of others, my God, my God,
and a jealousy for the honour (alive) of his country,
what can get more odd?
and discontent with the thriving gangs & pride.
—What happen then, Mr Bones?
—I had a most marvellous piece of luck. I died.

29

There sat down, once, a thing on Henry's heart
só heavy, if he had a hundred years
& more, & weeping, sleepless, in all them time
Henry could not make good.
Starts again always in Henry's ears
the little cough somewhere, an odour, a chime.

And there is another thing he has in mind
like a grave Sienese face a thousand years
would fail to blur the still profiled reproach of. Ghastly,
with open eyes, he attends, blind.
All the bells say: too late. This is not for tears;
thinking.

But never did Henry, as he thought he did,
end anyone and hacks her body up
and hide the pieces, where they may be found.
He knows: he went over everyone, & nobody's missing.
Often he reckons, in the dawn, them up.
Nobody is ever missing.

40

I'm scared a lonely. Never see my son,
easy be not to see anyone,
combers out to sea
know they're goin somewhere but not me.
Got a little poison, got a little gun,
I'm scared a lonely.

I'm scared a only one thing, which is me,
from othering I don't take nothin, see,
for any hound dog's sake.
But this is where I livin, where I rake
my leaves and cop my promise, this' where we
cry oursel's awake.

Wishin was dyin but I gotta make
it all this way to that bed on these feet
where peoples said to meet.
Maybe but even if I see my son
forever never, get back on the take,
free, black & forty-one.

49

Blind

Old Pussy-cat if he won't eat, he don't
feel good into his tum', old Pussy-cat.
He *wants* to have eaten.

Tremor, heaves, he sweaterings. He can't.
A dizzy swims of where is Henry at;
. . . somewhere streng verboten.

How come he sleeps & sleeps and sleeps, waking like death:
locate the restorations of which we hear
as of profound sleep.
From daylight he got maintrackt, from friends' breath,
wishes, his hopings. Dreams make crawl with fear
Henry but not get up.

The course his mind his body steer, poor Pussy-cat,
in weakness & disorder, will see him down
whiskers & tail.
'Wastethrift': Oh one of cunning wives know that
he hoardy-squander, where is nor downtown
neither suburba. Braille.

50

In a motion of night they massed nearer my post.
I hummed a short blues. When the stars went out
I studied my weapons system.
Grenades, the portable rack, the yellow spout
of the anthrax-ray: in order. Yet, and most
of my pencils were sharp.

This edge of the galaxy has often seen
a defence so stiff, but it could only go
one way.
—Mr Bones, your troubles give me vertigo,
& backache. Somehow, when I make your scene,
I cave to feel as if

de roses of dawns & pearls of dusks, made up
by some ol' writer-man, got right forgot
& the greennesses of ours.
Springwater grow so thick it gonna clot
and the pleasing ladies cease. I figure, yup,
you is bad powers.

52
Silent Song

Bright-eyed & bushy-tailed woke not Henry up.
Bright though upon his workshop shone a vise
central, moved in
while he was doing time down hospital
and growing wise.
He gave it the worst look he had left.

Alone. They all abandoned Henry—wonder! all,
when most he—under the sun.
That was all right.
He can't work well with it here, or think.
A bilocation, yellow like catastrophe.
The name of this was freedom.

Will Henry again ever be on the lookout for women & milk,
honour & love again,
have a buck or three?
He felt like shrieking but he shuddered as
(spring mist, warm, rain) an handful with quietness
vanisht & the thing took hold.

[1964]

ADRIENNE RICH (b. 1929)

Adrienne Rich was born in Baltimore, attended Radcliffe College, Harvard University, and has lived since 1984 in California. Her work, which has won many awards, includes *A Change of World* (1951), *Snapshots of a Daughter-in-Law* (1963), *Diving into the Wreck* (1973, National Book Award, which she rejected personally but accepted on behalf of all women), *The Dream of a Common Language* (1978), *A Wild Patience Has Taken Me This Far* (1981), *The Fact of a Doorframe: Poems Collected and New, 1950-1984* (1984), *Your Native Land, Your Life* (1986), *Time's Power: Poems 1985-1988* (1989), *An Atlas of the Difficult World* (1991), *Dark Fields of the Republic* (1995), and *Collected Early Poems 1950-1970* (1993).

Rich's early poetry resonates with an intense consciousness of the weight of history and the relentless passage of time. The poems abound in images of change, loss, and extinction: from ice ages and mammoths to the decay of the flesh and human relationships, where every day is the 'end of an era'. In the midst of this life sentence, this imprisonment in endless change, where the past is irretrievable and 'the present breaks our hearts', poetry provides a solace, an anchor, an 'unsought amnesty'. The repressed anger of her early work gives way to a more positive, politically engaged, and at times even joyous confrontation with time and its allies. Proving Tillie Olson's view that 'Every woman who writes is a survivor', Rich has been in the vanguard of feminist activities for almost two decades, addressing issues of politics, education, sexual orientation, and women's rights. A moving record of her prose writings on these subjects is to be found in *On Lies, Secrets and Silence: Selected Prose, 1966-1978* (1979), and *Blood, Bread and Poetry: Selected Prose 1979-1995* (1996).

Rich has rejected, for the most part, the rhetoric and literary trappings of the poetic tradition in favour of a 'common language' that will bring her struggles home to the hearts of ordinary readers. In 'When We Dead Awaken: Writing as Re-Vision (1970)' (*On Lies, Secrets, and Silence*), she celebrates poets such as Plath and Wakoski, whose work demonstrates 'a subjective, personal rage never before seen in women's poetry. If it is unnerving, it is also cathartic, the blowtorch of language cleansing the rust and ticky tacky and veneer from an entire consciousness.' However, while her poems are highly politicized, addressing issues of race, gender, politics, and the environment, Rich has always tried to make her anger serve artistic purposes, conscious of the need to invent those forms that will serve 'the survival and transformation of all women'.

The sexual and political transformations in Rich's life find parallels in her search not only for an adequate language, but also for a degree of formal flexibility and openness. 'I would think that a really good poem opens up a possibility for other poems, rather than being the end of a succession of things,' she says. 'Instead of wrapping something up it explodes the possibilities.' In the essay 'Blood, Bread, and Poetry', Rich admits that she was 'easily entranced by pure sound and still am, no matter what it is saying; and any poet who mixes the poetry of the actual world with the poetry of sound interests and excites me more than I am able to say.' She also admits to being excited as a young poet by the dialogue between art and politics that she found in Yeats's poetry, and describes her own struggle for an engaged poetry in a society that warned the artist not to 'meddle' in politics. 'There is the falsely mystical view of art that assumes a kind of supernatural inspiration, a possession by universal forces unrelated to questions of power and privilege or the artist's relation to bread and blood. The song is higher than the struggle, and the artist must choose between politics—here defined as earth-bound factionalism, corrupt power struggles—and art, which exists on some transcendental plane. This view of literature has dominated literary criticism in England and America for nearly a century.'

One fascinating irony that emerges from her analysis of the American fear of 'an overtly political art' is that 'political poetry is suspected of immense subversive power, yet accused of being, by definition, bad writing, impotent, lacking in breadth. No wonder the North American poet finds herself or himself slightly crazed by the double messages.'

Rich's engagement with the world as a poet has involved addressing not only larger social and political questions, but also her own emerging feminism and lesbianism. Rather than locate the enemy 'outside the self, the struggle somewhere else', she says, 'I had—perhaps through reading de Beauvoir and [James] Baldwin—some nascent idea that "Vietnam and the lover's bed", as I phrased it then, were connected; I found myself, in the late sixties, trying to describe those relations in poetry. Even before I called myself a feminist or a lesbian, I felt driven—for my own sanity—to bring together in my poems the political world "out there"—the world of children dynamited or napalmed, of the urban ghetto and militarist violence, and the supposedly private, lyrical world of sex and of male/female relationships.

'To write directly and overtly as a woman, out of a woman's body and experience, to take women's existence seriously as theme and source of art, was something I had been hungering to do, needing to do, all my writing life. It placed me nakedly face to face with both terror and anger; it did indeed *imply the breakdown of the world as I had always known it, the end of safety*, to paraphrase Baldwin again. But it released tremendous energy in me, as in many other women, to have that way of writing affirmed and validated in a growing political community. I felt for the first time the closing of the gap between poet and woman.'

Rich continues these eloquent and provocative musings in *What is Found There: Notebooks on Poetry and Politics* (1993), which also examines the creative process and the artist's place in contemporary society.

AT A BACH CONCERT

Coming by evening through the wintry city
We said that art is out of love with life.
Here we approach a love that is not pity.

This antique discipline, tenderly severe,
Renews belief in love yet masters feeling,
Asking of us a grace in what we bear.

Form is the ultimate gift that love can offer—
The vital union of necessity
With all that we desire, all that we suffer.

A too-compassionate art is half an art.
Only such proud restraining purity
Restores the else-betrayed, too-human heart.

[1951]

SNAPSHOTS OF A DAUGHTER-IN-LAW

1
You, once a belle in Shreveport,
with henna-colored hair, skin like a peachbud,
still have your dresses copied from that time,
and play a Chopin prelude
called by Cortot: *'Delicious recollections*
float like perfume through the memory.'

Your mind now, moldering like wedding-cake,
heavy with useless experience, rich
with suspicion, rumor, fantasy,
crumbling to pieces under the knife-edge
of mere fact. In the prime of your life.

Nervy, glowering, your daughter
wipes the teaspoons, grows another way.

2
Banging the coffee-pot into the sink
she hears the angels chiding, and looks out
past the raked gardens to the sloppy sky.
Only a week since They said: *Have no patience.*

The next time it was: *Be insatiable.*
Then: *Save yourself; others you cannot save.*
Sometimes she's let the tapstream scald her arm,
a match burn to her thumbnail,

or held her hand above the kettle's snout
right in the woolly steam. They are probably angels,
since nothing hurts her anymore, except
each morning's grit blowing into her eyes.

3
A thinking woman sleeps with monsters.
The beak that grips her, she becomes. And Nature,
that sprung-lidded, still commodious
steamer-trunk of *tempora* and *mores*

gets stuffed with it all: the mildewed orange-flowers,
the female pills, the terrible breasts
of Boadicea beneath flat foxes' heads and orchids.

Two handsome women, gripped in argument,
each proud, acute, subtle, I hear scream
across the cut glass and majolica
like Furies cornered from their prey:
The argument *ad feminam*, all the old knives
that have rusted in my back, I drive in yours,
ma semblable, ma soeur!

4
Knowing themselves too well in one another:
their gifts no pure fruition, but a thorn,
the prick filed sharp against a hint of scorn . . .
Reading while waiting
for the iron to heat,
writing, *My Life had stood—a Loaded Gun—*
in that Amherst pantry while the jellies boil and scum,
or, more often,
iron-eyed and beaked and purposed as a bird,
dusting everything on the whatnot every day of life.

5
Dulce ridens, dulce loquens,
she shaves her legs until they gleam
like petrified mammoth-tusk.

6
When to her lute Corinna sings
neither words nor music are her own;
only the long hair dipping
over her cheek, only the song
of silk against her knees
and these
adjusted in reflections of an eye.

Poised, trembling and unsatisfied, before
an unlocked door, that cage of cages,
tell us, you bird, you tragical machine—

is this *fertilisante douleur*? Pinned down
by love, for you the only natural action,
are you edged more keen
to prise the secrets of the vault? has Nature shown
her household books to you, daughter-in-law,
that her sons never saw?

7
'To have in this uncertain world some stay
which cannot be undermined, is
of the utmost consequence.'
                                        Thus wrote
a woman, partly brave and partly good,
who fought with what she partly understood.
Few men about her would or could do more,
hence she was labeled harpy, shrew and whore.

8
'You all die at fifteen,' said Diderot,
and turn part legend, part convention.
Still, eyes inaccurately dream
behind closed windows blankening with steam.
Deliciously, all that we might have been,
all that we were—fire, tears,
wit, taste, martyred ambition—
stirs like the memory of refused adultery
the drained and flagging bosom of our middle years.

9
Not that it is done well, but
that it is done at all? Yes, think
of the odds! or shrug them off forever.
This luxury of the precocious child,
Time's precious chronic invalid,—
would we, darlings, resign it if we could?

Our blight has been our sinecure:
mere talent was enough for us—
glitter in fragments and rough drafts.

Sigh no more, ladies.
Time is male
and in his cups drinks to the fair.
Bemused by gallantry, we hear
our mediocrities over-praised,
indolence read as abnegation,
slattern thought styled intuition,
every lapse forgiven, our crime
only to cast too bold a shadow
or smash the mold straight off.

For that, solitary confinement,
tear gas, attrition shelling.
Few applicants for that honor.

10

Well,
she's long about her coming, who must be
more merciless to herself than history.
Her mind full to the wind, I see her plunge
breasted and glancing through the currents,
taking the light upon her
at least as beautiful as any boy
or helicopter,
poised, still coming,
her fine blades making the air wince

but her cargo
no promise then:
delivered
palpable
ours.

[1963]

The Burning of Paper Instead of Children

I was in danger of
verbalizing my moral
impulses out of existence.
—Daniel Berrigan,
on trial in Baltimore.

1. My neighbor, a scientist and art-collector, telephones me in a state of violent emotion. He tells me that my son and his, aged eleven and twelve, have on the last day of school burned a mathematics textbook in the backyard. He has forbidden my son to come to his house for a week, and has forbidden his own son to leave the house during that time. 'The burning of a book,' he says, 'arouses terrible sensations in me, memories of Hitler; there are few things that upset me so much as the idea of burning a book.'

Back there: the library, walled
with green Britannicas
Looking again
in Dürer's Complete Works
for MELANCOLIA, the baffled woman

the crocodiles in Herodotus
the Book of the Dead
the *Trial of Jeanne d'Arc*, so blue
I think, It is her color

and they take the book away
because I dream of her too often

love and fear in a house
knowledge of the oppressor
I know it hurts to burn

2. To imagine a time of silence
or few words
a time of chemistry and music

the hollows above your buttocks
traced by my hand
or, *hair is like flesh*, you said

an age of long silence

relief

from this tongue   this slab of limestone
or reinforced concrete
fanatics and traders
dumped on this coast wildgreen clayred
that breathed once
in signals of smoke
sweep of the wind

knowledge of the oppressor
this is the oppressor's language

yet I need it to talk to you

3. *People suffer highly in poverty and it takes dignity and intelligence to overcome this suffering. Some of the suffering are: a child did not had dinner last night: a child steal because he did not have money to buy it: to hear a mother say she do not have money to buy food for her children and to see a child without cloth it will make tears in your eyes.*

(the fracture of order
the repair of speech
to overcome this suffering)

4. We lie under the sheet
after making love, speaking
of loneliness
relieved in a book
relived in a book
so on that page
the clot and fissure
of it appears
words of a man
in pain
a naked word
entering the clot
a hand grasping
through bars:

deliverance

What happens between us
has happened for centuries
we know it from literature

still it happens

sexual jealousy
outflung hand
beating bed

dryness of mouth
after panting

there are books that describe all this
and they are useless

You walk into the woods behind a house
there in that country
you find a temple
built eighteen hundred years ago
you enter without knowing
what it is you enter

so it is with us

no one knows what may happen
though the books tell everything

burn the texts said Artaud

5. I am composing on the typewriter late at night, thinking of today. How
well we all spoke. A language is a map of our failures. Frederick Douglass
wrote an English purer than Milton's. People suffer highly in poverty.
There are methods but we do not use them. Joan, who could not read,
spoke some peasant form of French. Some of the suffering are: it is hard to
tell the truth; this is America; I cannot touch you now. In America we
have only the present tense. I am in danger. You are in danger. The
burning of a book arouses no sensation in me. I know it hurts to burn.

There are flames of napalm in Catonsville, Maryland. I know it hurts to burn. The typewriter is overheated, my mouth is burning, I cannot touch you and this is the oppressor's language.

[1971]

Diving into the Wreck

First having read the book of myths,
and loaded the camera,
and checked the edge of the knife-blade,
I put on
the body-armor of black rubber
the absurd flippers
the grave and awkward mask.
I am having to do this
not like Cousteau with his
assiduous team
aboard the sun-flooded schooner
but here alone.

There is a ladder.
The ladder is always there
hanging innocently
close to the side of the schooner.
We know what it is for,
we who have used it.
Otherwise
it's a piece of maritime floss
some sundry equipment.

I go down.
Rung after rung and still
the oxygen immerses me
the blue light
the clear atoms
of our human air.
I go down.
My flippers cripple me,
I crawl like an insect down the ladder

and there is no one
to tell me when the ocean
will begin.

First the air is blue and then
it is bluer and then green and then
black I am blacking out and yet
my mask is powerful
it pumps my blood with power
the sea is another story
the sea is not a question of power
I have to learn alone
to turn my body without force
in the deep element.

And now: it is easy to forget
what I came for
among so many who have always
lived here
swaying their crenellated fans
between the reefs
and besides
you breathe differently down here.

I came to explore the wreck.
The words are purposes.
The words are maps.
I came to see the damage that was done
and the treasures that prevail.
I stroke the beam of my lamp
slowly along the flank
of something more permanent
than fish or weed

the thing I came for:
the wreck and not the story of the wreck
the thing itself and not the myth
the drowned face always staring
toward the sun
the evidence of damage
worn by salt and sway into this threadbare beauty

the ribs of the disaster
curving their assertion
among the tentative haunters.

This is the place.
And I am here, the mermaid whose dark hair
streams black, the merman in his armored body
We circle silently
about the wreck
we dive into the hold.
I am she: I am he

whose drowned face sleeps with open eyes
whose breasts still bear the stress
whose silver, copper, vermeil cargo lies
obscurely inside barrels
half-wedged and left to rot
we are the half-destroyed instruments
that once held to a course
the water-eaten log
the fouled compass

We are, I am, you are
by cowardice or courage
the one who find our way
back to this scene
carrying a knife, a camera
a book of myths
in which
our names do not appear.

[1973]

The Phenomenology of Anger

1. The freedom of the wholly mad
to smear & play with her madness
write with her fingers dipped in it
the length of a room

which is not, of course, the freedom
you have, walking on Broadway
to stop & turn back or go on
10 blocks; 20 blocks

but feels enviable maybe
to the compromised

curled in the placenta of the real
which was to feed & which is strangling her.

2. Trying to light a log that's lain in the damp
as long as this house has stood:
even with dry sticks I can't get started
even with thorns.
I twist last year into a knot of old headlines
—this rose won't bloom.

How does a pile of rags the machinist wiped his hands on
feel in its cupboard, hour upon hour?
Each day during the heat-wave
they took the temperature of the haymow.
I huddled fugitive
in the warm sweet simmer of the hay

muttering: *Come.*

3. Flat heartland of winter.
The moonmen come back from the moon
the firemen come out of the fire.
Time without a taste: time without decisions.

Self-hatred, a monotone in the mind.
The shallowness of a life lived in exile
even in the hot countries.
Cleaver, staring into a window full of knives.

4. White light splits the room.
Table. Window. Lampshade. You.

[1973]

Frame

Winter twilight. She comes out of the lab-
oratory, last class of the day
a pile of notebooks slung in her knapsack, coat
zipped high against the already swirling
evening sleet. The wind is wicked and the
busses slower than usual. On her mind
is organic chemistry and the issue
of next month's rent and will it be possible to
bypass the professor with the coldest eyes
to get a reference for graduate school,
and whether any of them, even those who smile
can see, looking at her, a biochemist
or a marine biologist, which of the faces
can she trust to see her at all, either today
or in any future. The busses are worm-slow in the
quickly gathering dark. *I don't know her. I am*
standing though somewhere just outside the frame
of all this, trying to see. At her back
the newly finished building suddenly looks
like shelter, it has glass doors, lighted halls
presumably heat. The wind is wicked. She throws a
glance down the street, sees no bus coming and runs
up the newly constructed steps into the newly
constructed hallway. *I am standing all this time*
just beyond the frame, trying to see. She runs
her hand through the crystals of sleet about to melt
on her hair. She shifts the weight of the books
on her back. It isn't warm here exactly but it's
out of that wind. Through the glass
door panels she can watch for the bus through the thickening
weather. Watching so, she is not
watching for the white man who watches the building
who has been watching her. This is Boston 1979.
I am standing somewhere at the edge of the frame
watching the man, we are both white, who watches the building
telling her to move on, get out of the hallway.
I can hear nothing because I am not supposed to be
present but I can see her gesturing

out toward the street at the wind-raked curb
I see her drawing her small body up
against the implied charges. The man
goes away. Her body is different now.
It is holding together with more than a hint of fury
and more than a hint of fear. She is smaller, thinner
more fragile-looking than I am. *But I am not supposed to be*
there. I am just outside the frame
of this action when the anonymous white man
returns with a white police officer. Then she starts
to leave into the windraked night but already
the policeman is going to work, the handcuffs are on her
wrists he is throwing her down his knee has gone into
her breast he is dragging her down the stairs *I am unable*
to hear a sound of all this all that I know is what
I can see from this position there is no soundtrack
to go with this and I understand at once
it is meant to be in silence that this happens
in silence that he pushes her into the car
banging her head in silence that she cries out
in silence that she tries to explain she was only
waiting for a bus
in silence that he twists the flesh of her thigh
with his nails in silence that her tears begin to flow
that she pleads with the other policeman as if
he could be trusted to see her at all
in silence that in the precinct she refuses to give her name
in silence that they throw her into the cell
in silence that she stares him
straight in the face in silence that he sprays her
in her eyes with Mace in silence that she sinks her teeth
into his hand in silence that she is charged
with trespass assault and battery in
silence that at the sleet-swept corner her bus
passes without stopping and goes on
in silence. *What I am telling you*
is told by a white woman who they will say
was never there. I say I am there.

[1981]

NORTH AMERICAN TIME

I
When my dreams showed signs
of becoming
politically correct
no unruly images
escaping beyond borders
when walking in the street I found my
themes cut out for me
knew what I would not report
for fear of enemies' usage
then I began to wonder

II
Everything we write
will be used against us
or against those we love.
These are the terms,
take them or leave them.
Poetry never stood a chance
of standing outside history.
One line typed twenty years ago
can be blazed on a wall in spraypaint
to glorify art as detachment
or torture of those we
did not love but also
did not want to kill

We move   but our words stand
become responsible
for more than we intended

and this is verbal privilege

III
Try sitting at a typewriter
one calm summer evening
at a table by a window
in the country, try pretending
your time does not exist

that you are simply you
that the imagination simply strays
like a great moth, unintentional
try telling yourself
you are not accountable
to the life of your tribe
the breath of your planet

IV
It doesn't matter what you think.
Words are found responsible
all you can do is choose them
or choose
to remain silent.   Or, you never had a choice,
which is why the words that do stand
are responsible

and this is verbal privilege

V
Suppose you want to write
of a woman braiding
another woman's hair—
straight down, or with beads and shells
in three-strand plaits or corn-rows—
you had better know the thickness
the length   the pattern
why she decides to braid her hair
how it is done to her
what country it happens in
what else happens in that country

You have to know these things

VI
Poet, sister: words—
whether we like it or not—
stand in a time of their own.
No use protesting   *I wrote that*
before Kollontai was exiled
Rosa Luxemburg, Malcolm,
Anne Mae Aquash, murdered,

before Treblinka, Birkenau,
Hiroshima, before Sharpeville,
Biafra, Bangladesh, Boston,
Atlanta, Soweto, Beirut, Assam
—those faces, names of places
sheared from the almanac
of North American time

VII
I am thinking this in a country
where words are stolen out of mouths
as bread is stolen out of mouths
where poets don't go to jail
for being poets, but for being
dark-skinned, female, poor.
I am writing this in a time
when anything we write
can be used against those we love
where the context is never given
though we try to explain, over and over
For the sake of poetry at least
I need to know these things

VIII
Sometimes, gliding at night
in a plane over New York City
I have felt like some messenger
called to enter, called to engage
this field of light and darkness.
A grandiose idea, born of flying.
But underneath the grandiose idea
is the thought that what I must engage
after the plane has raged onto the tarmac
after climbing my old stairs, sitting down
at my old window
is meant to break my heart and reduce me to silence.

IX
In North America time stumbles on
without moving, only releasing
a certain North American pain.

Julia de Burgos wrote:
That my grandfather was a slave
is my grief;   had he been a master
that would have been my shame.
A poet's words, hung over a door
in North America, in the year
nineteen-eighty-three.
The almost-full moon rises
timelessly speaking of change
out of the Bronx, the Harlem River
the drowned towns of the Quabbin
the pilfered burial mounds
the toxic swamps, the testing-grounds

and I start to speak again

[1986]

ROBERT CREELEY (b. 1926)

Creeley was born in Arlington, Massachusetts. He left Harvard to join the American Field Service in India and Burma, returned briefly to the United States, married, and departed for France and Majorca, where he started the Divers Press. He completed his degree and taught from 1954 to 1956 at the short-lived Black Mountain College in North Carolina, where he edited the *Black Mountain Review*. He also taught briefly on a coffee *finca* in Guatemala and at the University of New Mexico, where he completed his M.A., but his major contribution as a teacher has been at the State University of New York at Buffalo. Since *Le Fou* (1952), Creeley has published extensively. His books of poetry include *For Love* (1962), *Words* (1967), *Charm: Early and Uncollected Poems* (1968), *St Martin's* (1971), *Presences* (1976), *Selected Poems* (1976), *The Collected Poems of Robert Creeley* (1983), and *Windows* (1990). In addition, he has written a novel, *The Island* (1963), and a volume of short stories, *The Gold Diggers* (1954; reprinted in 1965), and edited many works, including the *Selected Writings of Charles Olson* (1966). His non-fiction writings and interviews are available in *Contexts of Poetry* (1973), *A Sense of Measure* (1973) and *The Collected Essays of Robert Creeley* (1989).

Creeley is an imagist of the emotions; he turns his acute attention not on objects in the external world but on the fine discriminations of the heart and mind. His poems, restrained and unpretentious, with a delicacy and lyricism that reflect the quiet, almost halting deliberation of the man, are accessible to most readers. His sharply etched, compressed lyrics seem perfectly suited to his desire to avoid 'any *descriptive* act . . . which leaves the attention outside the poem'.

In an interview with the critic Ekbert Faas (*Towards A New American Poetics*, 1979), Creeley dismisses the 'business' of writing, which includes prizes and jockeying for position: 'I write now primarily to recognize and thus to register states of consciousness, of feeling, that are in various ways constantly changing and constantly in flux. I write to see what stays the case and what changes, that's all. I don't write for peace; I mean I write for peace in the sense that writing these things gives me peace, but I don't write to resolve the world. . . . I think of myself more like [William] Burroughs' lone telegraph operator. . . . I'm merely a recording instrument and I'm not here, you know, to make plots or . . . I'm not here to bring enlightenment or a resolving of human ills, I am here to tell you what happens as best I can.' Thus his fondness for reiterating W.C. Williams's view that 'Speech is an assertion of one man, by one man. "Therefore each speech having its own character, the poetry it engenders will be peculiar to that speech also in its own intrinsic form".'

In the same interview, Creeley speaks approvingly of Wittgenstein's view that '"words are all acts," that the structure of words that one composes, that one comes to compose, constitute reification rather than revelation, and reification of some specific situation of the human. I mean they bring news of that order. That's why I said, selfishly: my writing constitutes a revelation of myself to myself in ways that I find otherwise very awkward to attain.' He goes on to quote with delight a favourite passage from Wittgenstein, which clearly reflects his own attitude to language: 'Now I am tempted to say that the right expression *in* language for the miracle of the existence of the world, though it is not any proposition *in* language, is the existence of language itself. But what then does it mean to be aware of this miracle at some times and not at other times? For all I have said by shifting the expression of the miraculous from an expression *by means of* language to the expression *by the existence* of language, all I have said is again that we cannot express what we want to express and that *all we say* about the absolute miraculous remains nonsense. . . that is to say: I see now that these nonsensical expressions were not nonsensical because I have not yet found the correct expressions, but that their nonsensicality was their very essence. For all I wanted to do with them was just *to go beyond* the world and that is to say *beyond* significant language. My whole tendency and I believe the tendency of all men who ever tried to write or talk Ethics or Religion was to run against the boundaries of language. This running against the walls of our cage is perfectly, absolutely hopeless.'

In an essay in *Twentieth Century Pleasures* (1984), Robert Hass described Creeley's work as representing 'a poetics which addresses the tension between speaking and being spoken through language; and he makes a brilliant and unnerving music out of it.' Hass also drew attention to Creeley's remarks in a 1965 interview: 'The organization of poetry has moved to a further articulation in which the rhythmic and sound structure now become not only evident but a primary coherence in the total organization of what's being experienced. . . . words are returned to an almost primal circumstance, by a technique that makes use of feedback, that is, a repetitive relocation of phrasing where words are returned to an almost objective state of presence so that they *speak* rather than someone speaking through them.'

In *Robert Creeley and the Genius of the American Common Place* (1993), Tom Clark recorded an anecdote told by Creeley and reproduced under the title 'Narrative As Common Bonding Agency (There's Only One Story)': 'Systems break down I think, too, in language. I recall, and it may be displacing to recall it, but it was right here, right out on the street, that I was talking to Robert Duncan, who'd come to a talk about Emily Dickinson I'd given. . . . We were talking, and I was saying I had very specific commitments and loyalties to friends who were, quote, "language-poets". And I was saying, Robert, what do you think? And he said, "I can't—I'm moved by this or that person, but I can't finally buy it. I can't really accept it, because they have no story." Well, he didn't really say all that. He just said, "They have no story." And I knew what he meant—from our tradition, or our system, wherein the story figures really in like [Robert] Graves' sense, when he says, *There is one story and one story only / that will prove worth your telling*. It could be the hierarchic, mythic story of a tribe's collective experience, thus, or it could be the imagination of significant values within the social group. It could be many things, but it's a common story. I'm reminded of seeing a friend today, Buddy Berlin, whom I've known since the '40s. We've got a lot of stories in common. We have a common place of our own experience, and we are interwoven as two people, comfortably and significantly. And there's then that much else that comes to be in that same way together, in language as well.'

Creeley believes, with Ginsberg, that mind is shapely, that the purpose of writing is the discovery of form, but that writing is local in terms of both place and person. In his 'Introduction to the New Writing in the USA', written in 1965 and collected in *A Sense of Measure* (1973), Creeley asserts that the 'undertaking most useful to writing as an art is, for me, the attempt to *sound* in the nature of the language those particulars of time and place of which one is a given instance'. He explains his rejection of extrinsic form in 'Notes à Propos "Free Verse"' (*Naked Poetry*, eds. Stephen Berg and Robert Mezey, 1969): 'If one thinks of the literal root of the word verse, "a line, furrow, turning—*vetere*, to turn. . .", he will come to a sense of "free verse" as that instance of writing in poetry which "turns" upon an occasion intimate with, in fact, the issue of, its own nature rather than to an abstract decision of "form" taken from a prior instance.'

JE VOIS DANS LE HASARD TOUS LES BIENS QUE J'ESPÈRE

When you said 'accidental'
I thought it was that you were formal
and sat down.
When I went home I did not
go home. You said
go to bed, and sleep, and later
everything will be clear.

It was a lovely morning yesterday
and I think things have at last happened which will not go away.

[1954]

After Lorca
for M. Marti

The church is a business, and the rich
are the business men.
When they pull on the bells, the
poor come piling in and when a poor man dies, he has a wooden
cross, and they rush through the ceremony.

But when a rich man dies, they
drag out the Sacrament
and a golden Cross, and go doucement, doucement
to the cemetery.

And the poor love it
and think it's crazy.

[1962]

The Awakening
for Charles Olson

He feels small as he awakens,
but in the stream's sudden mirror,
a pool of darkening water,
sees his size with his own two eyes.

The trees are taller here,
fall off to no field or clearing,
and depend on the inswept air
for the place in which he finds himself thus lost.

I was going on to tell you
when the door bell rang it was
another story as I know
previously had happened, had occurred.

That was a woman's impression
of the wonders of the morning, the same place,
whiter air now, and strong breezes
move the birds off in that first freshening.

O wisest of gods! Unnatural prerogatives
would err to concur, would fall deafened
between the seen, the green green,
and the ring of a far off telephone.

God is no bone of whitened contention.
God is not air, nor hair, is not
a conclusive concluding
to remote yearnings. He moves

only as I move, you also move to
the awakening, across long rows, of beds,
stumble breathlessly, on leg pins and crutch,
moving at all as all men, because you must.

[1955]

THE RAIN

All night the sound had
come back again,
and again falls
this quiet, persistent rain.

What am I to myself
that must be remembered,
insisted upon
so often? Is it

that never the ease,
even the hardness,
of rain falling
will have for me

something other than this,
something not so insistent—
am I to be locked in this
final uneasiness.

Love, if you love me,
lie next to me.
Be for me, like rain,
the getting out

of the tiredness, the fatuousness, the semi-
lust of intentional indifference.
Be wet
with a decent happiness.

[1962]

THE POOL

My embarrassment at his nakedness,
at the pool's edge,
and my wife, with his,
standing, watching—

this was a freedom
not given me who am
more naked,
less contained

by my own white flesh
and the ability
to take quietly
what comes to me.

The sense of myself
separate, grew
a white mirror
in the quiet water

he breaks with his hands
and feet, kicking,
pulls up to land
on the edge by the feet

of these women
who must know
that for each
man is a speech

describes him, makes
the day grow white
and sure, a quietness of water
in the mind,

lets hang, descriptive
as a risk, something
for which he cannot find
a means or time.

[1962]

'I KEEP TO MYSELF SUCH MEASURES . . .'

I keep to myself such
measures as I care for,
daily the rocks
accumulate position.

There is nothing
but what thinking makes
it less tangible. The mind,
fast as it goes, loses

pace, puts in place of it
like rocks simple markers,
for a way only to
hopefully come back to

where it cannot. All
forgets. My mind sinks.
I hold in both hands such weight
it is my only description.

[1967]

FOR MY MOTHER: GENEVIEVE JULES CREELEY

April 8, 1887–October 7, 1972

Tender, semi-
articulate flickers
of your

presence, all
those years
past

now, eighty-
five, impossible to
count them

one by one, like
addition, sub-
traction, missing

not one. The last
curled up, in
on yourself,

position you take
in the bed, hair
wisped up

on your head, a
top knot, body
skeletal, eyes

closed against,
it must be,
further disturbance—

breathing a skim
of time, lightly
kicks the intervals—

days, days and
years of it,
work, changes,

sweet flesh caught
at the edges,
dignity's faded

dilemma. It
is your life, oh
no one's

forgotten anything
ever. They want
to make you

happy when
they remember. Walk
a little, get

up, now, die
safely,
easily, into

singleness, too
tired with it
to keep

on and on.
Waves break at
the darkness

under the road, sounds
in the faint
night's softness. Look

at them, catching
the light, white
edge as they turn—

always again
and again. Dead
one, two,

three hours—
all these minutes
pass. Is it,

was it, ever
you alone
again, how

long you kept
at it, your
pride, your

lovely, confusing
discretion. Mother, I
love you—for

whatever that
means,
meant—more

than I know, body
gave me my
own, generous,

inexorable place
of you. I feel
the mouth's sluggish-

ness, slips on
turns of things
said, to you,

too soon, too late,
wants to
go back to beginning,

smells of the hospital
room, the doctor
she responds

to now, the
order—get me
there. 'Death's

let you out—'
comes true,
this, that,

endlessly circular
life, and we
came back

to see you one
last
time, this

time? Your head
shuddered,
it seemed, your

eyes wanted,
I thought,
to see

who it was.
I am here,
and will follow.

[1976]

SELF PORTRAIT

He wants to be
a brutal old man,
an aggressive old man,
as dull, as brutal
as the emptiness around him.

He doesn't want compromise,
nor to be ever nice
to anyone. Just mean,
and final in his brutal,
his total, rejection of it all.

He tried the sweet,
the gentle, the 'oh,
let's hold hands together'
and it was awful,
dull, brutally inconsequential.

Now he'll stand on
his own dwindling legs.
His arms, his skin,
shrink daily. And
he loves but hates equally.

[1982]

BRESSON'S MOVIES

A movie of Robert
Bresson's showed a yacht,
at evening on the Seine,
all its lights on, watched

by two young, seemingly
poor people, on a bridge adjacent,
the classic boy and girl
of the story, any one

one cares to tell. So
years pass, of course, but
I identified with the young,
embittered Frenchman,

knew his almost complacent
anguish and the distance
he felt from his girl.
Yet another film

of Bresson's has the
aging Lancelot with his
awkward armour standing
in a woods, of small trees,

dazed, bleeding, both he
and his horse are,
trying to get back to
the castle, itself of

no great size. It
moved me, that
life was after all
like that. You are

in love. You stand
in the woods, with
a horse, bleeding.
The story is true.

[1982]

ECHOES

Step through the mirror,
faint with the old desire.

Want it again,
never mind who's the friend.

Say yes to the wasted
empty places. The guesses

were as good as any.
No mistakes.

[1982]

Epic

Wanting to tell
a story,
like hell's simple invention, or
some neat recovery

of the state of grace,
I can recall lace curtains,
people I think I remember,
Mrs Curley's face.

[1990]

Lawrence Ferlinghetti (b. 1919)

Ferlinghetti was born in New York. During the Second World War he was connected with the Free French and Norwegian Underground. He received his B.A. from the University of North Carolina, his M.A. from Columbia, and his doctorate in Fine Art from the Sorbonne. In 1951 he moved to San Francisco, where he started City Lights Bookstore, the first all paper-bound bookstore in the US. City Lights began to publish in 1955, and brought out Ginsberg's *Howl* in its Pocket Poets Series.

In addition to *Pictures of a Gone World* (1955), *A Coney Island of the Mind* (1958), *Secret Meaning of Things* (1969), *Love Is No Stone on the Moon* (1972), *Who Are We Now?* (1976), *Landscapes of Living & Dying* (1979), *Endless Life: The Selected Poems* (1981), *These Are My Rivers: New & Selected Poems, 1955-1993* (1993) Ferlinghetti wrote several travel journals and the novel *Her* (1960), which he describes as follows: 'Surreal semi-autobiographical blackbook record of a semi-mad period of my life, in that mindless, timeless state most romantics pass through, confusing flesh madonnas with spiritual ones.'

Ferlinghetti rejects common assumptions concerning the detachment of the Beats; he believes that the poet must be *engagé*. His love affair with America has been turbulent: he has been both an articulator of its dreams and a severe critic, publicly denouncing the Eisenhower administration, the US war in Vietnam, his nation's exploitation of countries in Latin America and the Third World, and satirizing, in his poetry, almost every cliché of American life. As a publisher he has tried to gain a hearing for modern poetry; as a poet he has been instrumental in returning poetry from the academies to the marketplace. To accomplish this he has stressed heavily the auditory dimension of poetry and has composed poems (the 'oral messages' in *A Coney Island of the Mind*) for jazz accompaniment. Ferlinghetti is the most humorous and eclectic of the Beat poets; he has an astonishing range of reference and allusion in his poetry. To read him is to rediscover Keats, Yeats, Eliot, and Dylan Thomas in excitingly unusual contexts and juxtapositions.

Ferlinghetti is described as having an imagination that is antic, irreverent, and subversive. He would be the first to acknowledge the wisdom of Friedrich Dürrenmatt's observation in 'Problems of the Theatre' (*Perspectives on Drama*, edited by James L. Calderwood and Harold E. Toliver, 1968), that 'In laughter man's freedom becomes manifest, in crying his necessity.' Dürrenmatt describes how comedy creates distance even through such primitive forms as the dirty joke, 'a transposition of the sexual onto the plane of the comical'. 'Our task today,' he says, 'is to demonstrate freedom. The tyrants of this planet are not moved by the works of the poets. They yawn at a poet's threnodies. For them heroic epics are silly fairy tales and religious poetry puts them to sleep. Tyrants fear only one thing: a poet's mockery. For this reason then parody has crept into all literary genres, into the novel, the drama, into lyrical poetry.' Dürrenmatt's conclusion seems applicable not only to Ferlinghetti's work in particular, but also to postmodern poetics in general: 'Literature must become so light that it will weigh nothing upon the scale of today's literary criticism: only in this way will it regain its true worth.'

Much of Ferlinghetti's work flouts conventional modernist literary values, replacing high seriousness and the well-made poem with parody and the stand-up comic's run-on narrative of puns, verbal slapstick, and asides. Even in an intensely personal lyric about ageing and loss, such as 'New York—Albany', which he described as filling 'a central moment in the middle of the journey of my life when I came to myself in a dark wood' (*Poet's Choice*, edited by Paul Engle and Joseph Langland, 1962), he cannot resist ending on a humorous note: 'Lord Lord Lord / every bush burns / Love licks / all down / All gone / in the red end / Lord Lord Lord Lord / Small nuts fall / Mine too.'

IN GOYA'S GREATEST SCENES WE SEEM TO SEE

In Goya's greatest scenes we seem to see
the people of the world
exactly at the moment when
they first attained the title of
'suffering humanity'
They writhe upon the page
in a veritable rage
of adversity
Heaped up
groaning with babies and bayonets
under cement skies
in an abstract landscape of blasted trees
bent statues bats wings and beaks
slippery gibbets

cadavers and carnivorous cocks
and all the final hollering monsters
of the
'imagination of disaster'
they are so bloody real
it is as if they really still existed

And they do

Only the landscape is changed

They still are ranged along the roads
plagued by legionaires
false windmills and demented roosters
They are the same people
only further from home
on freeways fifty lanes wide
on a concrete continent
spaced with bland billboards
illustrating imbecile illusions of happiness
The scene shows fewer tumbrils
but more maimed citizens
in painted cars
and they have strange license plates
and engines
that devour America

[1958]

DON'T LET THAT HORSE EAT THAT VIOLIN

Don't let that horse
eat that violin
cried Chagall's mother

But he
kept right on
painting

And became famous

And kept on painting
The Horse With Violin In Mouth

And when he finally finished it
he jumped up upon the horse
and rode away

waving the violin

And then with a low bow gave it
to the first naked nude he ran across

And there were no strings
attached

[1958]

CONSTANTLY RISKING ABSURDITY AND DEATH

Constantly risking absurdity
and death
whenever he performs
above the heads
of his audience
the poet like an acrobat
climbs on rime
to a high wire of his own making
and balancing on eyebeams
above a sea of faces
paces his way
to the other side of day
performing entrechats
and sleight-of-foot tricks
and other high theatrics
and all without mistaking
any thing
for what it may not be

For he's the super realist
who must perforce perceive
taut truth
before the taking of each stance or step
in his supposed advance
toward that still higher perch
where Beauty stands and waits
with gravity
to start her death-defying leap

And he
a little charleychaplin man
who may or may not catch
her fair eternal form
spreadeagled in the empty air
of existence

[1958]

THE PENNYCANDYSTORE BEYOND THE EL

The pennycandystore beyond the El
is where I first
fell in love
with unreality
Jellybeans glowed in the semi-gloom
of that september afternoon
A cat upon the counter moved among
the licorice sticks
and tootsie rolls
and Oh Boy Gum

Outside the leaves were falling as they died

A wind had blown away the sun

A girl ran in
Her hair was rainy
Her breasts were breathless in the little room

Outside the leaves were falling
                    and they cried
                                        Too soon! too soon!

[1958]

JUNKMAN'S OBBLIGATO

Let's go
Come on
Let's go
Empty out our pockets
and disappear.
Missing all our appointments
and turning up unshaven
years later
old cigarette papers
stuck to our pants
leaves in our hair.
Let us not
worry about the payments
any more.
Let them come
and take it away
whatever it was
we were paying for.
And us with it.

Let us arise and go now
to where dogs do it
Over the Hill
where they keep the earthquakes
behind the city dumps
lost among gasmains and garbage.
Let us see the City Dumps
for what they are.
My country tears of thee.

Let us disappear
in automobile graveyards
and reappear years later
picking rags and newspapers
drying our drawers
on garbage fires
patches on our ass.
Do not bother
to say goodbye
to anyone.
Your missus will not miss us.

Let's go
smelling of sterno
where the benches are filled
with discarded Bowling Green statues
in the interior dark night
of the flowery bowery
our eyes watery
with the contemplation
of empty bottles of muscatel.
Let us recite from broken bibles
on streetcorners
Follow dogs on docks
Speak wild songs
Throw stones
Say anything
Blink at the sun and scratch
and stumble into silence
Diddle in doorways
Know whores thirdhand
after everyone else is finished
Stagger befuddled into East River sunsets
Sleep in phone booths
Puke in pawnshops
wailing for a winter overcoat.

Let us arise and go now
under the city
where ashcans roll
and reappear in putrid clothes

as the uncrowned underground kings
of subway men's rooms.
Let us feed the pigeons
at the City Hall
urging them to do their duty
in the Mayor's office.
Hurry up please it's time.
The end is coming.
Flash floods
Disasters in the sun
Dogs unleashed
Sister in the street
her brassiere backwards.

Let us arise and go now
into the interior dark night
of the soul's still bowery
and find ourselves anew
where subways stall and wait
under the River.
Cross over
into full puzzlement.
South Ferry will not run forever.
They are cutting out the Bay ferries
but it is still not too late
to get lost in Oakland.
Washington has not yet toppled
from his horse.
There is still time to goose him
and go
leaving our income tax form behind
and our waterproof wristwatch with it
staggering blind after alleycats
under Brooklyn's Bridge
blown statues in baggy pants
our tincan cries and garbage voices
trailing.
Junk for sale!

Let's cut out let's go
into the real interior of the country
where hockshops reign
mere unblind anarchy upon us.
The end is here
but golf goes on at Burning Tree.
It's raining it's pouring
The Ole Man is snoring.
Another flood is coming
though not the kind you think.
There is still time to sink
and think.
I wish to descend in society.
I wish to make like free.
Swing low sweet chariot.
Let us not wait for the cadillacs
to carry us triumphant
into the interior
waving at the natives
like roman senators in the provinces
wearing poet's laurels
on lighted brows.
Let us not wait for the write-up
on page one
of The New York Times Book Review
images of insane success
smiling from the photo.
By the time they print your picture
in Life Magazine
you will have become a negative anyway
a print with a glossy finish.
They will have come and gotten you
to be famous
and you still will not be free.
Goodbye I'm going.
I'm selling everything
and giving away the rest
to the Good Will Industries.
It will be dark out there
with the Salvation Army Band.

And the mind its own illumination.
Goodbye I'm walking out on the whole scene.
Close down the joint.

The system is all loused up.
Rome was never like this.
I'm tired of waiting for Godot.
I am going where turtles win
I am going
where conmen puke and die
Down the sad esplanades
of the official world.
Junk for sale!
My country tears of thee.

Let us go then you and I
leaving our neckties behind on lampposts
Take up the full beard
of walking anarchy
looking like Walt Whitman
a homemade bomb in the pocket.
I wish to descend in the social scale.
High society is low society.
I am a social climber
climbing downward
And the descent is difficult.
The Upper Middle Class Ideal
is for the birds
but the birds have no use for it
having their own kind of pecking order
based upon birdsong.
Pigeons on the grass alas.

Let us arise and go now
to the Isle of Manisfree.
Let loose the hogs of peace.
Hurry up please it's time.
Let us arise and go now
into the interior
of Foster's Cafeteria.
So long Emily Post.

So long
Lowell Thomas.
Goodbye Broadway.
Goodbye Herald Square.
Turn it off.
Confound the system.
Cancel all our leases.
Lose the War
without killing anybody.
Let horses scream
and ladies run
to flushless powderrooms.
The end has just begun.
I want to announce it.
Run don't walk
to the nearest exit.
The real earthquake is coming.
I can feel the building shake.
I am the refined type.
I cannot stand it.
I am going
where asses lie down
with customs collectors who call themselves
literary critics.
My tool is dusty.
My body hung up too long
in strange suspenders.

Get me a bright bandana
for a jockstrap.
Turn loose and we'll be off
where sports cars collapse
and the world begins again.
Hurry up please it's time.
It's time and a half
and there's the rub.
The thinkpad makes homeboys of us all.
Let us cut out
into stray eternity.
Somewhere the fields are full of larks.

Somewhere the land is swinging.
My country 'tis of thee
I'm singing.

Let us arise and go now
to the Isle of Manisfree
and live the true blue simple life
of wisdom and wonderment
where all things grow
straight up
aslant and singing
in the yellow sun
poppies out of cowpods
thinking angels out of turds.
I must arise and go now
to the Isle of Manisfree
way up behind the broken words
and woods of Arcady.

[1958]

MODERN POETRY IS PROSE (BUT IT IS SAYING PLENTY)

I am thumbing through a great anthology of contemporary poetry, and it would seem that 'the voice that is great within us' sounds within us mostly in a prose voice, albeit in the typography of poetry. Which is not to say it is prosaic or has no depths, which is not to say it is dead or dying, or not lovely or not beautiful or not well written or not witty and brave. It is very much alive, very well written, lovely, lively prose—prose that stands without the crutches of punctuation, prose whose syntax is so clear it can be written all over the page, in open forms and open fields, and still be very clear, very dear prose. And in the typography of poetry, the poetic and the prosaic intellect masquerade in each other's clothes.

Walking through our prose buildings in the 21st century, one may look back and wonder at this strange age which allowed poetry to walk in prose rhythms and still called it poetry. Modern poetry is prose because it sounds as subdued as any city man or woman whose life force is submerged in urban life. Modern poetry is prose because it has no *duende*, dark spirit of earth and blood, no soul of dark song, no passion musick. Like modern sculpture, it loves the concrete. Like minimal art, it minimizes emotion in favour of understated irony and implied intensity. As such it is the perfect poetry for technocratic man. But how often does this poetry rise above the mean sea level of his sparkling plain? Ezra Pound once decanted his opinion that only in times of decadence does poetry separate itself from music. And this is the way the world ends, not with a song but a whimper.

Eighty or ninety years ago, when all the machines began to hum, almost (as it seemed) in unison, the speech of man certainly began to be affected by the absolute staccato of machines. And city poetry certainly echoed it. Whitman was a holdover, singing the song of himself. And Sandburg a holdover, singing his sagas. And Vachel Lindsay a holdover, drumming his chants. And later there was Wallace Stevens with his harmonious 'fictive music'. And there was Langston Hughes. And Allen Ginsberg, chanting his mantras, singing Blake. There still are others everywhere, jazz poets and poetic strummers and wailers in the streets of the world, making poetry out of the urgent insurgent Now, of the immediate instant self, the incarnate carnal self (as D.H. Lawrence called it).

But much poetry was caught up in the linotype's hot slug and now in the so cold type of IBM. No song among the typists, no song in our concrete architecture, our concrete music. And the nightingales may still be singing near the Convent of the Sacred Heart, but we can hardly hear them in the city waste lands of T.S. Eliot, nor in his *Four Quartets* (which can't be played on any instrument and yet is the most beautiful prose of our time). Nor in the prose wastes of Ezra Pound's *Cantos* which aren't *canti* because they can't be sung by anyone. Nor in the pangolin prose of Marianne Moore (who called her writing poetry for lack of anything better to call it). Nor in the great prose blank verse of Karl Shapiro's *Essay on Rime*, nor in the outer city speech of William Carlos Williams, in the flat-out speech of his *Paterson*. All of which is applauded by poetry professors and poetry reviewers in all the best places, none of whom will commit the original sin of saying some poet's poetry is prose in the typography of poetry—just as the poet's friends will never tell him, just as the poet's editors will never say it—the dumbest conspiracy of silence in the history of letters.

Most modern poetry is poetic prose but it is saying plenty, by its own example, about what death of the spirit our technocratic civilization may be dealing us, enmeshed in machines and macho nationalisms, while we continue longing for the nightingale among the pines of Respighi. It is the bird singing that makes us happy.

[1980]

Allen Ginsberg (b. 1926)

Ginsberg was born in Paterson, New Jersey, to Naomi Ginsberg, a Russian immigrant, and Louis Ginsberg, a lyric poet and schoolteacher. His life from age seventeen until the publication of *Howl and Other Poems* in 1956 included Columbia University, the merchant service, dishwashing, market research, book reviewing, drugs, and travel to Texas, Denver, Mexico City, and Yucatán. Between *Howl* and *Kaddish and Other Poems* (1961), Ginsberg travelled to the Arctic by sea, to Venice, Tangiers, Amsterdam, Paris and London, and read his poems at Oxford, Columbia, and Chicago. After 'Kaddish', a long poem written about the death of his mother, he recorded his poems in San Francisco and departed for the Orient.

Ginsberg's friend John Clellon Holmes described the problem at the core of the Beat philosophy in this way: 'Beyond all laws, it is our stunted consciousness that imprisons us, and we suffer from a consequent hunger of the spirit for which all our perversions and our politics are only a kind of ugly stomach cramp. How are we to break out of the prison? How do we let the spirit prosper so that the blistered desert we are making of the world can flower again?' For Ginsberg, of course, the answer is to widen the area of consciousness, which involves a conscientious rejection of all copied forms and responses, of all values and institutions that are not oriented towards psychic liberation.

Starting from William Carlos Williams's idea of a new American idiom and measure, then reaching back to Whitman, Ginsberg arrived at what he calls his 'romantic inspiration—Hebraic-Melvillian bardic breath'. What this means in terms of *Howl* and *Kaddish* is the freedom to be exuberant and incantatory, to catalogue at will, and to employ free association of ideas in the context of a sweeping religious utterance. Ultimately, Ginsberg is the natural heir to Whitman—in his further exploration of Whitman's long line ('Howl'), and in his preoccupation with transcending the ego by *containing*, or partaking of, all experience, in a kind of osmosis of the imagination.

As Ginsberg explained to interviewer Tom Clark in *The Paris Review* (1965), he wanted to create a poetry that would not be literary, but would make full use of everything in our daily lives: 'So then—what happens if you make a distinction between what you tell your friends and what you tell your Muse? The problem is to break down that distinction: when you approach the Muse to talk as frankly as you would with yourself or with your friends.' In terms of shaping the poetic medium, he says, 'what it boils down to is this, it's my *movement*, my feeling is for a big long clanky statement—partly that's something that I share, or maybe that I even got from Kerouac's long prose line; which is really, like he once remarked, an extended poem. Like one long sentence page of his in *Doctor Sax* or *Railroad Earth* or occasionally *On the Road*—if you examine them phrase by phrase they usually have the density of poetry, and the beauty of poetry, but most of all the single elastic rhythm running from beginning to end of the line and ending "*mop!*" '

His studies of William Blake and the French painter Paul Cézanne led him to theorize about how poetry might communicate at a deeper psychological level: 'The thing I understood from Blake was that it was possible to transmit a message through time which could reach the enlightened, that poetry had a definite effect, it wasn't just pretty, or just beautiful, as I had understood pretty beauty before—it was something basic to human existence, or it reached something, it reached the bottom of human existence. But anyway the impression I got was that it was like a kind of time machine through which [Blake] could transmit . . . his basic consciousness and communicate it to somebody else after he was dead—in other words, build a time machine.'

This verbal time machine, as the following delightfully skewed sentences from the same interview suggest, would require very special equipment and fine-tuning: 'Yeah, the idea that I had was that gaps in space and time through which images juxtaposed, just as in the haiku you get two images which the mind connects in a flash, and so that flash is the *petite sensation*; or the *satori*, perhaps, that the Zen haikuists would speak of—if they speak of it like that. So, the poetic experience that Housman talks about, the hair-standing-on-end or the hackles rising, whatever it is, visceral thing. The interesting thing would be to know if certain combinations of words and rhythms actually had an electrochemical reaction on the body, which could catalyze specific states of consciousness. . . . There's a statement by Artaud on that subject, that certain music when introduced into the nervous system changes the molecular composition of the nerve cells or something like that, it permanently alters the being that has experience of this.'

That Ginsberg's poetics, if not his lifestyle, represented a threat to conservative values was evident in the extreme reactions of his earliest critics. In 1957, for instance, James Dickey (*Babel to Byzantium*, 1968) attacked *Howl*: 'Ginsberg is the perfect inhabitant, if not the very founder of Babel, where conditions do not so much make tongues incomprehensible, but render their utterances, as poetry, meaningless. . . . Isn't it true, for instance, that somewhere amongst its exhibitionist welter of unrelated associations, wish-fulfillment fantasies, and self-righteous maudlinness, a confused but believable passion for values is struggling?' Dickey's answer, of course, was No. A more sympathetic reading, including a more recent interview, can be found in Ekbert Faas's *Towards A New American Poetics* (1979).

Ginsberg's *Collected Poems 1947-1980* appeared in 1984. He has also published a steady stream of books and pamphlets, including *Reality Sandwiches* (1963), *Indian Journals* (1970), *Mind Breaths: Poems 1972-1977* (1978), *Plutonian Ode: Poems 1977-1980* (1982), and *Many Loves & Other Poems* (1983). *The Yage Letters*, his correspondence with William Burroughs, was published in 1971.

HOWL (I & II)

for Carl Solomon

I

I saw the best minds of my generation destroyed by madness,
    starving hysterical naked,
dragging themselves through the negro streets at dawn looking for
    an angry fix,
angelheaded hipsters burning for the ancient heavenly connection
    to the starry dynamo in the machinery of night,
who poverty and tatters and hollow-eyed and high sat up smoking
    in the supernatural darkness of cold-water flats floating across
    the tops of cities contemplating jazz,

who bared their brains to Heaven under the El and saw
Mohammedan angels staggering on tenement roofs illuminated,
who passed through universities with radiant cool eyes hallucinating
Arkansas and Blake-light tragedy among the scholars of war,
who were expelled from the academies for crazy & publishing
obscene odes on the windows of the skull,
who cowered in unshaven rooms in underwear, burning their money
in wastebaskets and listening to the Terror through the wall,
who got busted in their pubic beards returning through Laredo with
a belt of marijuana for New York,
who ate fire in paint hotels or drank turpentine in Paradise Alley,
death, or purgatoried their torsos night after night
with dreams, with drugs, with waking nightmares, alcohol and cock
and endless balls,
incomparable blind streets of shuddering cloud and lightning in the
mind leaping toward poles of Canada & Paterson, illuminating
all the motionless world of Time between,
Peyote solidities of halls, backyard green tree cemetery dawns, wine
drunkenness over the rooftops, storefront boroughs of teahead
joyride neon blinking traffic light, sun and moon and tree
vibrations in the roaring winter dusks of Brooklyn, ashcan
rantings and kind king light of mind,
who chained themselves to subways for the endless ride from
Battery to holy Bronx on benzedrine until the noise of wheels
and children brought them down shuddering mouth-wracked
and battered bleak of brain all drained of brilliance in the drear
light of Zoo,
who sank all night in submarine light of Bickford's floated out and
sat through the stale beer afternoon in desolate Fugazzi's,
listening to the crack of doom on the hydrogen jukebox,
who talked continuously seventy hours from park to pad to bar to
Bellevue to museum to the Brooklyn Bridge,
a lost battalion of platonic conversationalists jumping down the
stoops off fire escapes off windowsills off Empire State out of
the moon,
yacketayakking screaming vomiting whispering facts and memories
and anecdotes and eyeball kicks and shocks of hospitals and
jails and wars,
whole intellects disgorged in total recall for seven days and nights
with brilliant eyes, meat for the Synagogue cast on the
pavement,

who vanished into nowhere Zen New Jersey leaving a trail of
ambiguous picture postcards of Atlantic City Hall,
suffering Eastern sweats and Tangerian bone-grindings and
migraines of China under junk-withdrawal in Newark's bleak
furnished room,
who wandered around and around at midnight in the railroad yard
wondering where to go, and went, leaving no broken hearts,
who lit cigarettes in boxcars boxcars boxcars racketing through
snow toward lonesome farms in grandfather night,
who studied Plotinus Poe St John of the Cross telepathy and bop
kaballa because the cosmos instinctively vibrated at their feet in
Kansas,
who loned it through the streets of Idaho seeking visionary indian
angels who were visionary indian angels,
who thought they were only mad when Baltimore gleamed in super-
natural ecstasy,
who jumped in limousines with the Chinaman of Oklahoma on the
impulse of winter midnight streetlight smalltown rain,
who lounged hungry and lonesome through Houston seeking jazz
or sex or soup, and followed the brilliant Spaniard to converse
about America and Eternity, a hopeless task, and so took ship to
Africa,
who disappeared into the volcanoes of Mexico leaving behind
nothing but the shadow of dungarees and the lava and ash of
poetry scattered in fireplace Chicago,
who reappeared on the West Coast investigating the FBI in beards
and shorts with big pacifist eyes sexy in their dark skin passing
out incomprehensible leaflets,
who burned cigarette holes in their arms protesting the narcotic
tobacco haze of Capitalism,
who distributed Supercommunist pamphlets in Union Square
weeping and undressing while the sirens of Los Alamos wailed
them down, and wailed down Wall, and the Staten Island ferry
also wailed,
who broke down crying in white gymnasiums naked and trembling
before the machinery of other skeletons,
who bit detectives in the neck and shrieked with delight in police-
cars for committing no crime but their own wild cooking
pederasty and intoxication,
who howled on their knees in the subway and were dragged off the
roof waving genitals and manuscripts,

who let themselves be fucked in the ass by saintly motorcyclists,
 and screamed with joy,
who blew and were blown by those human seraphim, the sailors,
 caresses of Atlantic and Caribbean love,
who balled in the morning in the evenings in rosegardens and the
 grass of public parks and cemeteries scattering their semen
 freely to whomever come who may,
who hiccupped endlessly trying to giggle but wound up with a sob
 behind a partition in a Turkish Bath when the blonde & naked
 angel came to pierce them with a sword,
who lost their loveboys to the three old shrews of fate the one eyed
 shrew of the heterosexual dollar the one eyed shrew that winks
 out of the womb and the one eyed shrew that does nothing but
 sit on her ass and snip the intellectual golden threads of the
 craftsman's loom,
who copulated ecstatic and insatiate with a bottle of beer a sweet-
 heart a package of cigarettes a candle and fell off the bed, and
 continued along the floor and down the hall and ended fainting
 on the wall with a vision of ultimate cunt and come eluding the
 last gyzym of consciousness,
who sweetened the snatches of a million girls trembling in the sun-
 set, and were red eyed in the morning but prepared to sweeten
 the snatch of the sunrise, flashing buttocks under barns and
 naked in the lake,
who went out whoring through Colorado in myriad stolen night-
 cars, n.c., secret hero of these poems, cocksman and Adonis of
 Denver—joy to the memory of his innumerable lays of girls in
 empty lots & diner backyards, moviehouses' rickety rows, on
 mountaintops in caves or with gaunt waitresses in familiar road-
 side lonely petticoat upliftings & especially secret gas-station
 solipisisms of johns, & hometown alleys too,
who faded out in vast sordid movies, were shifted in dreams, woke
 on a sudden Manhattan, and picked themselves up out of
 basements hungover with heartless Tokay and horrors of Third
 Avenue iron dreams & stumbled to unemployment offices,
who walked all night with their shoes full of blood on the snow-
 bank docks waiting for a door in the East River to open to a
 room full of steamheat and opium,
who created great suicidal dramas on the apartment cliff-banks of
 the Hudson under the wartime blue floodlight of the moon &
 their heads shall be crowned with laurel in oblivion,

who ate the lamb stew of the imagination or digested the crab at the
muddy bottom of the rivers of Bowery,
who wept at the romance of the streets with their pushcarts full of
onions and bad music,
who sat in boxes breathing in the darkness under the bridge, and
rose up to build harpsichords in their lofts,
who coughed on the sixth floor of Harlem crowned with flame under
the tubercular sky surrounded by orange crates of theology,
who scribbled all night rocking and rolling over lofty incantations
which in the yellow morning were stanzas of gibberish,
who cooked rotten animals lung heart feet tail borsht & tortillas
dreaming of the pure vegetable kingdom,
who plunged themselves under meat trucks looking for an egg,
who threw their watches off the roof to cast their ballot for Eternity
outside of Time, & alarm clocks fell on their heads every day
for the next decade,
who cut their wrists three times successively unsuccessfully, gave up
and were forced to open antique stores where they thought they
were growing old and cried,
who were burned alive in their innocent flannel suits on Madison
Avenue amid blasts of leaden verse & the tanked-up clatter of
the iron regiments of fashion & the nitroglycerine shrieks of the
fairies of advertising & the mustard gas of sinister intelligent
editors, or were run down by the drunken taxicabs of Absolute
Reality,
who jumped off the Brooklyn Bridge this actually happened and
walked away unknown and forgotten into the ghostly daze
of Chinatown soup alleyways & firetrucks, not even one
free beer,
who sang out of their windows in despair, fell out of the subway
window, jumped in the filthy Passaic, leaped on negroes, cried
all over the street, danced on broken wineglasses barefoot
smashed phonograph records of nostalgic European 1930s
German jazz finished the whiskey and threw up groaning into
the bloody toilet, moans in their ears and the blast of colossal
steamwhistles,
who barreled down the highways of the past journeying to each
other's hotrod-Golgotha jail-solitude watch or Birmingham jazz
incarnation,
who drove crosscountry seventytwo hours to find out if I had a vision
or you had a vision or he had a vision to find out Eternity,

who journeyed to Denver, who died in Denver, who came back to
Denver & waited in vain, who watched over Denver & brooded
& loned in Denver and finally went away to find out the Time,
& now Denver is lonesome for her heroes,
who fell on their knees in hopeless cathedrals praying for each
other's salvation and light and breasts, until the soul illuminated
its hair for a second,
who crashed through their minds in jail waiting for impossible
criminals with golden heads and the charm of reality in their
hearts who sang sweet blues to Alcatraz,
who retired to Mexico to cultivate a habit, or Rocky Mount to
tender Buddha or Tangiers to boys or Southern Pacific to the
black locomotive or Harvard to Narcissus to Woodlawn to the
daisychain or grave,
who demanded sanity trials accusing the radio of hypnotism & were
left with their insanity & their heads & a hung jury,
who threw potato salad at CCNY lectures on Dadaism and
subsequently presented themselves on the granite steps of the
madhouse with shaven heads and harlequin speech of suicide,
demanding instantaneous lobotomy,
and who were given instead the concrete void of insulin metrasol
electricity hydrotherapy psychotherapy occupational therapy
pingpong & amnesia,
who in humorless protest overturned only one symbolic pingpong
table, resting briefly in catatonia,
returning years later truly bald except for a wig of blood, and tears
and fingers, to the visible madman doom of the wards of the
madtowns of the East,
Pilgrim State's Rockland's and Greystone's foetid halls, bickering
with the echoes of the soul, rocking and rolling in the midnight
solitude-bench dolmen-realms of love, dream of life a night-
mare, bodies turned to stone as heavy as the moon,
with mother finally ******, and the last fantastic book flung out of
the tenement window, and the last door closed at 4 a.m. and
the last telephone slammed at the wall in reply and the last
furnished room emptied down to the last piece of mental
furniture, a yellow paper rose twisted on a wire hanger in the
closet, and even that imaginary, nothing but a hopeful little bit
of hallucination—
ah, Carl, while you are not safe I am not safe, and now you're really
in the total animal soup of time—

and who therefore ran through the icy streets obsessed with a sudden
flash of the alchemy of the use of the ellipse the catalog the
meter & the vibrating plane,
who dreamt and made incarnate gaps in Time & Space through
images juxtaposed, and trapped the archangel of the soul
between 2 visual images and joined the elemental verbs and set
the noun and dash of consciousness together jumping with
sensation of Pater Omnipotens Aeterna Deus
to recreate the syntax and measure of poor human prose and stand
before you speechless and intelligent and shaking with shame,
rejected yet confessing out the soul to conform to the rhythm of
thought in his naked and endless head,
the madman bum and angel beat in Time, unknown, yet putting
down here what might be left to say in time come after death,
and rose reincarnate in the ghostly clothes of jazz in the goldhorn
shadow of the band and blew the suffering of America's naked
mind for love into an eli eli lamma lamma sabacthani saxo-
phone cry that shivered the cities down to the last radio
with the absolute heart of the poem of life butchered out of their
own bodies good to eat a thousand years.

II

What sphinx of cement and aluminum bashed open their skulls and
ate up their brains and imagination?
Moloch! Solitude! Filth! Ugliness! Ashcans and unobtainable dollars!
Children screaming under the stairways! Boys sobbing in armies!
Old men weeping in the parks!
Moloch! Moloch! Nightmare of Moloch! Moloch the loveless!
Mental Moloch! Moloch the heavy judger of men!
Moloch the incomprehensible prison! Moloch the crossbone soulless
jailhouse and Congress of sorrows! Moloch whose buildings are
judgement! Moloch the vast stone of war! Moloch the stunned
governments!
Moloch whose mind is pure machinery! Moloch whose blood is
running money! Moloch whose fingers are ten armies! Moloch
whose breast is a cannibal dynamo! Moloch whose ear is a
smoking tomb!
Moloch whose eyes are a thousand blind windows! Moloch whose
skyscrapers stand in the long streets like endless Jehovahs!
Moloch whose factories dream and croak in the fog! Moloch
whose smokestacks and antennae crown the cities!

Moloch whose love is endless oil and stone! Moloch whose soul is electricity and banks! Moloch whose poverty is the specter of genius! Moloch whose fate is a cloud of sexless hydrogen! Moloch whose name is the Mind!
Moloch in whom I sit lonely! Moloch in whom I dream Angels! Crazy in Moloch! Cocksucker in Moloch! Lacklove and manless in Moloch!
Moloch who entered my soul early! Moloch in whom I am a consciousness without a body! Moloch who frightened me out of my natural ecstasy! Moloch whom I abandon! Wake up in Moloch! Light streaming out of the sky!
Moloch! Moloch! Robot apartments! invisible suburbs! skeleton treasuries! blind capitals! demonic industries! spectral nations! invincible madhouses! granite cocks! monstrous bombs!
They broke their backs lifting Moloch to Heaven! Pavements, trees, radios, tons! lifting the city to Heaven which exists and is everywhere about us!
Visions! omens! hallucinations! miracles! ecstasies! gone down the American river!
Dreams! adorations! illuminations! religions! the whole boatload of sensitive bullshit!
Breakthroughs! over the river! flips and crucifixions! gone down the flood! Highs! Epiphanies! Despairs! Ten years' animal screams and suicides! Minds! New loves! Mad generation! down on the rocks of Time!
Real holy laughter in the river! They saw it all! the wild eyes! the holy yells! They bade farewell! They jumped off the roof! to solitude! waving! carrying flowers! Down to the river! into the street!

[1956]

A SUPERMARKET IN CALIFORNIA

What thoughts I have of you tonight, Walt Whitman, for I walked down the sidestreets under the trees with a headache self-conscious looking at the full moon.

In my hungry fatigue, and shopping for images, I went into the neon fruit supermarket, dreaming of your enumerations!

What peaches and what penumbras! Whole families shopping at night! Aisles full of husbands! Wives in the avocados, babies in the tomatoes!—and you, Garcia Lorca, what were you doing down by the watermelons?

I saw you, Walt Whitman, childless, lonely old grubber, poking among the meats in the refrigerator and eyeing the grocery boys.

I heard you asking questions of each: Who killed the pork chops? What price bananas? Are you my Angel?

I wandered in and out of the brilliant stacks of cans following you, and followed in my imagination by the store detective.

We strode down the open corridors together in our solitary fancy tasting artichokes, possessing every frozen delicacy, and never passing the cashier.

Where are we going, Walt Whitman? The doors close in an hour. Which way does your beard point tonight?

(I touch your book and dream of our odyssey in the supermarket and feel absurd.)

Will we walk all night through solitary streets? The trees add shade to shade, lights out in the houses, we'll both be lonely.

Will we stroll dreaming of the lost America of love past blue automobiles in driveways, home to our silent cottage?

Ah, dear father, graybeard, lonely old courage-teacher, what America did you have when Charon quit poling his ferry and you got out on a smoking bank and stood watching the boat disappear on the black waters of Lethe?

[1956]

America

America I've given you all and now I'm nothing.
America two dollars and twentyseven cents January 17, 1956.
I can't stand my own mind.
America when will we end the human war?
Go fuck yourself with your atom bomb.
I don't feel good don't bother me.
I won't write my poem till I'm in my right mind.
America when will you be angelic?
When will you take off your clothes?
When will you look at yourself through the grave?
When will you be worthy of your million Trotskyites?
America why are your libraries full of tears?
America when will you send your eggs to India?
I'm sick of your insane demands.
When can I go into the supermarket and buy what I need with my good looks?

America after all it is you and I who are perfect not the next world.
Your machinery is too much for me.
You made me want to be a saint.
There must be some other way to settle this argument.
Burroughs is in Tangiers I don't think he'll come back it's sinister.
Are you being sinister or is this some form of practical joke?
I'm trying to come to the point.
I refuse to give up my obsession.
America stop pushing I know what I'm doing.
America the plum blossoms are falling.
I haven't read the newspapers for months, everyday somebody goes
    on trial for murder.
America I feel sentimental about the Wobblies.
America I used to be a communist when I was a kid I'm not sorry.
I smoke marijuana every chance I get.
I sit in my house for days on end and stare at the roses in the closet.
When I go to Chinatown I get drunk and never get laid.
My mind is made up there's going to be trouble.
You should have seen me reading Marx.
My psychoanalyst thinks I'm perfectly right.
I won't say the Lord's Prayer.
I have mystical visions and cosmic vibrations.
America I still haven't told you what you did to Uncle Max after he
    came over from Russia.

I'm addressing you.
Are you going to let your emotional life be run by Time Magazine?
I'm obsessed by Time Magazine.
I read it every week.
Its cover stares at me everytime I slink past the corner candystore.
I read it in the basement of the Berkeley Public Library.
It's always telling me about responsibility. Businessmen are serious.
    Movie producers are serious. Everybody's serious but me.
It occurs to me that I am America.
I am talking to myself again.

Asia is rising against me.
I haven't got a chinaman's chance.
I'd better consider my national resources.

My national resources consist of two joints of marijuana millions of
genitals an unpublishable private literature that goes 1400 miles
an hour and twentyfive-thousand mental institutions.
I say nothing about my prisons nor the millions of underprivileged
who live in my flowerpots under the light of five hundred suns.
I have abolished the whorehouses of France, Tangiers is the next to
go.
My ambition is to be President despite the fact that I'm a Catholic.

America how can I write a holy litany in your silly mood?
I will continue like Henry Ford my strophes are as individual as his
automobiles more so they're all different sexes.
America I will sell you strophes $2500 apiece $500 down on your
old strophe
America free Tom Mooney
America save the Spanish Loyalists
America Sacco & Vanzetti must not die
America I am the Scottsboro boys.
America when I was seven momma took me to Communist Cell
meetings they sold us garbanzos a handful per ticket a ticket
costs a nickel and the speeches were free everybody was angelic
and sentimental about the workers it was all so sincere you
have no idea what a good thing the party was in 1935 Scott
Nearing was a grand old man a real mensch Mother Bloor made
me cry I once saw Israel Amter plain. Everybody must have
been a spy.
America you don't really want to go to war.
America it's them bad Russians.
Them Russians them Russians and them Chinamen. And them
Russians.
The Russia wants to eat us alive. The Russia's power mad. She want
to take our cars from out our garages.
Her wants to grab Chicago. Her needs a Red Readers' Digest. Her
wants our auto plants in Siberia. Him big bureaucracy running
our fillingstations.
That no good. Ugh. Him make Indians learn read. Him need big
black niggers. Hah. Her make us all work sixteen hours a day.
Help.
America this is quite serious.

America this is the impression I get from looking in the television
set.
America is this correct?
I'd better get right down to the job.
It's true I don't want to join the Army or turn lathes in precision
parts factories, I'm nearsighted and psychopathic anyway.
America I'm putting my queer shoulder to the wheel.

[1956]

PHYLLIS WEBB (b. 1927)

Born in Victoria, BC, Phyllis Webb graduated in English and Philosophy from the University of British Columbia in 1949. She ran as a CCF candidate in provincial elections before moving to Montreal, where she was associated with F.R. Scott, Louis Dudek, Irving Layton, and Miriam Waddington. Her publications include *Even Your Right Eye* (1956), which contains poems written while travelling and living in England and Ireland, *The Sea is Also a Garden* (1962), *Naked Poems* (1965), *Selected Poems 1954-1965* (1971), *Wilson's Bowl* (1980), *Sunday Water: Thirteen Anti Ghazals* (1982); *The Vision Tree: Selected Poems* (1982, Governor General's Award), *Water and Light: Ghazals and Anti Ghazals* (1984), and *Hanging Fire* (1990). Webb worked for CBC radio 1965-69 as a reviewer, broadcaster, and executive director of the program 'Ideas'; some of her reviews and essays on the creative process are gathered in *Talking* (1982). A second collection of essays, *Nothing But Brush Strokes*, appeared in 1995. She lives on Saltspring Island, BC.

Though Webb's voice is passionate and witty, she brings to her work a rigorous, questioning intellect. In fact, questioning is central to her writing, not only in essays and poems about curiosity, interrogation, and torture, as well as in her long involvement with Amnesty International, but also in her view of the poem as a vehicle of analysis and discovery. Much of her poetry is concerned with philosophical issues, fine discriminations of conscience, and the nature of art itself.

Obviously the idea of a poet as inquisitor implies great attention to the techniques of persuasion. Webb is meticulous in matters of technique, struggling with the patterning of sound, the intricacies of diction and line-length, and what she calls 'the intuitive sense of form'. 'When I speak of long lines and short lines', she writes in an essay called 'Polishing Up the View' (*Talking*), 'I am not merely thinking of the effect of the line on the page, of its typographical effect—in fact, that is probably secondary. I am thinking of the phrasing, of the measure of the breath, of what is natural to the phrase. . . .' The absolute precision evident in a poem such as 'Poetics Against the Angel of Death' is reflected over and over again in her painstaking analysis of the creative process in the essays in *Talking*. Webb's technical preoccupations, along with her general lack of interest in narrative and parochial subjects, have cost her a certain popular attention; but they have made her a great favourite among poets.

In 'Message Machine' (*Language in Her Eye*, edited by Libby Scheier, Sarah Sheard, and Eleanor Wachtel, 1990), Webb describes herself as 'a minimalist producer' who might write more poems if she were 'not always hanging around for the right moment listening for "the bird song in the apparatus".' Out of this creative passivity, she says, which involves tuning one's antennae and listening intensely, 'I try to allow these words that arrive unbidden to lead me into poems, and have been using this sort of intense listening as a conscious process for about two years now. . . . Although there may well be a neurological explanation for the way autonomous words, phrases, and sentences arrive apparently at random, unconnected, or so I think, to my preoccupations of the moment, I doubt that any research has been done on this sort of fine-tuning of the inner ear.' Webb insists that her method of listening to the language is not without political significance. 'One of my discoveries during the past two years is that the given words I've chosen to work from are thematically connected, that the strategies of the unconscious are very subtle and certainly not random if you watch the test patterns long enough. Countering the passive mood of some of the poems are those dealing with the Marxian class struggle, animal rights, violent revolution, if only by means of glancing blows. The dialectic goes deep in my nature, explaining or rationalizing my characteristic ambivalence about all things great and small.'

While admitting in an interview with Janice Williamson (*Sounding Differences: Conversations with Seventeen Canadian Women Writers*, 1993) that political aspects of life (the baggage of family, one's personal past, and inherited ideas) dictate and repress poetic materials, Webb confesses that overt political writing—'trying to shape the poem to the statement, instead of letting the poem shape the statement'—does not suit her. Given her need for 'evasion as a psychic strategy' and her efforts to develop 'a kind of literary historical shorthand', she focuses instead on poetic methods of discovery and disclosure: 'I think there is increasingly in my poetry a "you" who is not necessarily the reader. It's like having a ghost of one's own in the room. I know there's some sort of person-presence I'm addressing the poem to. More and more I want to involve that "you" in the poem, say, "You're here. Don't go away" . . . I control the use of this other presence to make a more social environment for the poem, so that it's not just a statement of an isolated person, but assumes an audience, assumes an involved presence whom one desperately hopes is there somewhere when the work is done.'

In the same interview she insists that 'The "I" is used strategically in poetry, not always at a conscious level,' but that 'Critics don't always go along with a fiction in poetry as they go along with a fiction in fiction. This is part of the power of the lyric, how it has immediacy; it seems to be a straightforward statement right on the breath as a first impulse, a direct response to experience. But the "I" isn't necessarily "me", and that is where the critical confusion begins.' She also questions her own inherited assumptions about form: 'In a sense I had been brought up with William Carlos Williams as the be-all and end-all of poetic correctness. The poem ['Thinking Cap'] asks, "Is this my poetic?" It's a poetic I was taught and accepted. It was received wisdom, and now is the time, perhaps, to be questioning the received wisdom of the holiness of the image, of the holiness of the objective poem, and asking, ultimately, is this *really* my way of experiencing and writing poems?'

Although she is regularly tempted to write about craft, Webb once insisted (*The Second Macmillan Anthology*, 1989) that 'The proper response to a poem is another poem. We burrow into the paper to court in secret the life of plants, the shifty moon's space-walks, the bliss, the roses, the glamorous national debt. Someone to talk to, for God's sake, something to love that will never hit back.'

A TALL TALE

The whale, improbable as lust,
carved out a cave
for the seagirl's rest;
with rest the seagirl, sweet as dust, devised
a manner for the whale
to lie between her thighs.
Like this they lay
within the shadowed cave
under the waters, under the waters wise,
and nested there, and nested there and stayed,
this coldest whale aslant the seagirl's thighs.

Two hundred years perhaps swam by them there
before the cunning waters so distilled the pair
they turned to brutal artifacts of stone
polished, O petrified prisoners of their lair.
And thus, with quiet, submerged in deathly calm,
the two disclosed a future geologic long,
lying cold, whale to thigh revealed
the secret of their comfort
to the marine weeds,
to fish, to shell, sand, sediment and wave,
to the broken, dying sun
which probed their ocean grave.
These, whale and seagirl, stone gods,
stone lust, stone grief,
interred on the sedimented sand
amongst the orange starfish,
these cold and stony mariners
invoked the moral snail
and in sepulchral voice intoned a moral tale:
'Under the waters, under the waters wise,
all loving flesh will quickly meet demise,
the cave, the shadow cave is nowhere wholly safe
and even the oddest couple can scarcely find relief:
appear then to submit to this tide and timing sea,
but secrete a skillful shell and stone and perfect be.'

[1962]

LOVE STORY

It was easy to see what he was up to,
the grey, bundled ape,
as he sidled half-playfully
up to the baby
and with a sly look behind
put his hands onto the crib
and leapt in.

The child's pink, beginning face
stared up as the hair-handed monkey
explored the flesh, so soft, of our infant race.
The belly spread like plush to the monkey's haunch,
he settled, heavy and gay, his nuzzling
mouth at the baby's neck.

But, no answer accurate to a smile,
he bit, tasted time, maddened,
and his nails rooted sudden fire in the ribs of Adam,
towered, carnivorous, for aim
and baby face, ears, arm
were torn and taken in his ravaging.

And so the killing, too-late parents came,
hysteric, after their child's
futile pulse had stopped its beating.
Only the half-pathetic, half-triumphant
monkey peered out from the crib,
bobbed nervously on the dead infant's belly,
then stopped, suddenly paralyzed on that soft tomb.

Was it the donkey Death brayed out at him
from the human mother's eyes,
or did his love for her in that pause
consume him?

The jealous ape's death was swift
and of natural cause. 'Died of shame,'
some said, others, 'of shock.'
But his death was Othello's death,
as great, as picayune,
he died of envy, lacking the knack of wisdom.

[1962]

TO FRIENDS WHO HAVE ALSO CONSIDERED SUICIDE

It's still a good idea.
Its exercise is discipline:
to remember to cross the street without looking,
to remember not to jump when the cars side-swipe,
to remember not to bother to have clothes cleaned,
to remember not to eat or want to eat,
to consider the numerous methods of killing oneself,
that is surely the finest exercise of the imagination:
death by drowning, sleeping pills, slashed wrists,
kitchen fumes, bullets through the brain or through
the stomach, hanging by the neck in attic or basement,
a clean frozen death—the ways are endless.
And consider the drama! It's better than a whole season
at Stratford when you think of the emotion of your
family on hearing the news and when you imagine
how embarrassed some will be when the body is found.
One could furnish a whole chorus in a Greek play
with expletives and feel sneaky and omniscient
at the same time. But there's no shame
in this concept of suicide.
It has concerned our best philosophers
and inspired some of the most popular
of our politicians and financiers.
Some people swim lakes, others climb flagpoles,
some join monasteries, but we, my friends,
who have considered suicide take our daily walk
with death and are not lonely.
In the end it brings more honesty and care
than all the democratic parliaments of tricks.
It is the 'sickness unto death'; it is death;
it is not death; it is the sand from the beaches
of a hundred civilizations, the sand in the teeth
of death and barnacles our singing tongue:
and this is 'life' and we owe at least this much
contemplation to our western fact: to Rise,
Decline, Fall, to futility and larks,
to the bright crustaceans of the oversky.

[1962]

POETICS AGAINST THE ANGEL OF DEATH

I am sorry to speak of death again
(some say I'll have a long life)
but last night Wordsworth's 'Prelude'
suddenly made sense—I mean the measure,
the elevated tone, the attitude
of private Man speaking to public men.
Last night I thought I would not wake again
but now with this June morning I run ragged to elude
The Great Iambic Pentameter
who is the Hound of Heaven in our stress
because I want to die
writing Haiku
or, better,
long lines, clean and syllabic as knotted bamboo. Yes!

[1962]

OCCASIONS OF DESIRE

Occasions of desire with their attendant envies,
the white heat of the cold swan dying,
create their gestures, obscene or most beautiful.
Oh, the clear shell of a swan's fluted wings!

And as the old swan calls clarity from dark waters,
sailing triumphant into the forgotten,
desire in its moving is that rapacious cry,
gorgeous as the torrent Lethe, and as wise.

And if the curl of cygnets on the Avon,
so freshly broken from their perfect shells,
take from a dying bird not moral or enticement,
but float with their own white mother, that is just.
Oh, imperious innocence to envy
only the water bearing such beauty!

[1962]

FOR FYODOR

I am a beetle in the cabbage soup they serve up for geniuses
in the House of the Dead.

I am a black beetle and loll seductively at the bottom of the
warm slop.

Someday, Fyodor, by mistake you'll swallow me down and I'll become
a part of your valuable gutworks.

In the next incarnation I hope to imitate that idiot and saint,
Prince Myshkin, drop off my wings for his moronic glory.

Or, if I miss out on the Prince, Sonya or Dunya might do.

I'm not joking. I am not the result of bad sanitation in the
kitchen, as you think.

Up here in Omsk in Siberia beetles are not accidents but destinies.

I'm drowning fast, but even in this condition I realize your bad
tempered haughtiness is part of your strategy.

You are about to turn this freezing hell into an ecstatic emblem.
A ferocious shrine.

Ah, what delicious revenge. But take care! A fit is coming!
Now, now I'll leap into your foaming mouth and jump your tongue.
Now I stamp on this not quite famous tongue

shouting: Remember Fyodor, you may hate men but it's here in
Omsk you came to love mankind.

But you don't hear, do you: there you are writing in epileptic visions.

Hold your tongue! You can't speak yet. You are mine, Dostoevsky.

I aim to slip down your gullet and improve myself.
I can almost hear what you'll say:

Crime and Punishment
Suffering and Grace

and of the dying

pass by and forgive
us our happiness

[1980]

TREBLINKA GAS CHAMBER

Klostermayer ordered another count of the children. Then their stars were snipped off and thrown into the center of the courtyard. It looked like a field of buttercups.
—Joseph Hyams, *A Field of Buttercups*

fallingstars
'a field of
buttercups'

yellow stars
of David
falling

the prisoners
the children
falling

in heaps
on one another
they go down

Thanatos
showers
his dirty breath
they must breathe
him in

they see stars
behind their
eyes

David's
'a field of
buttercups'

a metaphor
where all that's
left lies down

[1980]

PRISON REPORT

The eye of Jacobo Timerman looks through the hole and sees
another eye looking through a hole.

These holes are cut into steel doors in prison cells in Argentina.

Both eyes are wary.
They disappear.

Timerman rests his cheek on the icy door,
amazed at the sense of space he feels—the joy.

He looks again: the other's eye is there,
then vanishes like a spider.

Comes back, goes, comes back.

This is a game of hide-and-seek.
This is intelligence with a sense of humour.
Timerman joins the game.

Sometimes two eyes meet at exactly the same moment.

This is music. This is love
playing in the middle of a dark night
in a prison in Argentina.

My name is Jacobo one eye says.
Other eye says something, but Jacobo can't quite catch it.

Now a nose appears in the vision-field
of Timerman. It rubs cold edges of the hole,
a love-rub for Jacobo.

This is a kiss, he decides, a caress,
an emanation of solitude's tenderness.

In this prison everything is powered electrically
for efficiency and pain. But tenderness is also
a light and a shock.

An eye, a nose, a cheek resting against a steel door
in the middle of a dark night.
These are parts of bodies, parts of speech,
saying,
I am with you.

[1982]

from Water and Light, Ghazals and Anti Ghazals

The pull, this way and that, ultimately into the pull
of the pen across the page.

Sniffing for poems, the forward memory
of hand beyond the grasp.

Not grasping, not at all. *Reaching* is
different—can't touch that sun.

Too hot. That star. This cross-eyed
vision. Days and nights, sun, moon—the up-there claptrap.

and down here, trappings of 'as above'—crosswalks,
traffic lights, sirens, this alexandrite burning on this hand.

* * *

Drunken and amatory, illogical, stoned, mellifluous
journey of the ten lines.

The singer sings one couplet or two
over and over to the Beloved who reigns

on the throne of *accidie*, distant, alone,
hearing, as if from a distance, a bell

and not this stringy instrument scraping away,
whining about love's ultimate perfection.

Wait! Everything is waiting for a condition of grace:
the string of the Sitar, this Gat, a distant bell,

even the Beloved in her bored flesh.

* * *

The card is dealt, out of the blank pack,
preordained, imprinted on hidden lines.

Now for the Third Eye to read the grown signs:
flickers of doubt tic mouth, twitch eye's lid.

But it's open—always—the third one,
guardian of splendours, crimes.

Seeing all, all-seeing, even in sleep knows
space [outer, inner, around], tracks freak snows,

slumbering ponies. Love, I am timid
before this oracular seer, opal, apple of my eye.

[1984]

John Ashbery (b. 1927)

John Ashbery, who declares himself a lover of cities, was born in Rochester, New York, but grew up on a farm nearby. His studies included English at Harvard and Columbia, and French at New York University, after which he worked as a reference librarian and copywriter. A Fulbright Fellowship took him to Paris in 1955, where he remained for ten years and was art critic for the *Paris Herald Tribune*. Back in New York, he became executive editor of *Art News*, taught writing at Brooklyn College, and reviewed art for *Newsweek*. His awards include the Pulitzer Prize, the National Book Award, and the National Book Critics Circle Award. He has written *Three Plays* (1978), collaborated with James Schuyler on a novel, *A Nest of Ninnies* (1969), and produced more than twenty-five collections of poetry, including *Some Trees* (1956), *Rivers and Mountains* (1962), *Self-Portrait in a Convex Mirror* (1976), *Houseboat Days* (1977), *As We Know* (1979), *Selected Poems* (1985), *Hotel Lautréamont* (1992), and *And the Stars Were Shining* (1994).

Ashbery's involvement with the art world has influenced not only his poetry, but also the critical response he has received. He once considered painting as a career and has said, perhaps mischievously: 'I attempt to use words abstractly, as an artist uses paint.' When asked in an interview in *The Paris Review*, conducted by Peter Stitt in June 1980, whether he was a Mannerist in words or an Abstract Expressionist, Ashbery replied: 'I suppose that "Self-Portrait in a Convex Mirror" is a Mannerist work in what I hope is the good sense of that word. Later on, Mannerism became mannered. . . . I have probably been influenced, more or less unconsciously I suppose, by the modern art that I have looked at. Certainly the simultaneity of Cubism is something that has rubbed off on me, as well as the Abstract Expressionist idea that the word is a sort of record of its own coming-into-existence; it has an "anti-referential sensuousness", but it is nothing like flinging a bucket of words on the page, as Pollock did with paint. It is more indirect than that. When I was fresh out of college, Abstract Expressionism was the most exciting thing in the arts. There was also experimental music and film, but poetry seemed quite conventional in comparison. I guess it still is, in a way. One can accept a Picasso woman with two noses, but an equivalent attempt in poetry baffles the same audience.'

He has also rejected the notion that he is an autobiographical poet. 'I have always been averse to talking about myself, and so I don't write about my life the way the confessional poets do. I don't want to bore people with experiences of mine that are simply versions of what everybody goes through. For me, poetry starts after that point. I write with experiences in mind, but I don't write about them. I write out of them. I know that I have exactly the opposite reputation, that I am totally self-involved, but that's not the way I see it.'

Ashbery speaks of the poem as object: 'Yes, I would like it to be what Stevens calls a completely new set of objects. My intention is to present the reader with a pleasant surprise, not an unpleasant one, not a non-surprise. . . . I consider the poem as sort of environment . . . I try to reproduce the polyphony that goes on inside me. . . . I am a believer in fortuitous accidents.' In his early work, Ashbery used a four-beat line, but changed his approach as he came to believe a line 'should have at least two interesting things in it'; later still, he dropped both notions for a much more irregular free verse. In an interview in *The Poet's Craft: Interviews from the* New York

Quarterly (1987), he says: 'I use a very long line very frequently in my poetry which I feel gives an expanded means of utterance, and saying a very long thing in place of what might originally have been a much shorter and more concise one is an overflowing of the meaning. It often seems to me to have almost a sexual quality to it in the sense that the sexual act is a kind of prolongation of and improvisation on time in a very deep personal way which is like music, and there's something of the expansiveness of eroticism in these lines very frequently for me, although that's by no means a conscious thing that I undertake in writing them.'

While he learned to write in conventional forms such as the sonnet, Ashbery says: 'I sit down to write without any questions of form or anything like that although it's not that I ignore them: I feel I've digested them for my purposes and can concentrate on the more important aspects of poetry.' Yet he does not concern himself exclusively with subject-matter, as he points out in the same interview: 'I suppose one might say really that subject matter is a kind of structure which gets transformed in the process of the poem's being written so that it becomes something quite different. I guess what interests me in poetry is the difference, the ways in which the prose sense of a poem gets transformed in poetry and this I think is the area that I write in to the exclusion of a formal theme or topic. . . . These forms such as the sestina were really devices [aimed] at getting into remoter areas of consiousness.'

For the most part, Ashbery has avoided dramatic structure and rhetorical flourish. In his essay on Gertrude Stein for *Poetry (Chicago)*, he describes a poem as 'a hymn to possibility'. Where modernists aimed for coherence and the well-made poem, and asserted poetic authority, he risks incoherence, incompleteness, unpredictability. While this frustrates some readers, Raymond Carney, in the *Dictionary of Literary Biography*, defends Ashbery's method: 'Just as in the poetry of Elizabeth Bishop, the result of Ashbery's almost absolute renunciation of architectonic structures and rhetorical heightening is a paradoxical heightening of everything, of even the most ordinary details, in the poem. The common and mean, at moments, can become almost transcendent in Ashbery and Bishop, who achieve their grand Romantic moments, as William Carlos Williams did, in a minor key.'

Although he rejects the notion of political poetry, on the grounds that it's preaching to the converted, Ashbery nevertheless acknowledges that poetry does touch people's lives, perhaps moving them to greater awareness, even positive action. However, he refuses all critical prescriptions and conventional ways of writing: 'I think there's something quite reckless about my poetry in general; I think for many people it's quite debatable whether it is poetry or not, and it is for me too. And I can never be certain that I'm doing the right thing by writing this way, which nevertheless seems the only right way of writing to me. I think the poignancy of this position gets into the poetry too and intensifies it. I could read you a passage from one of my recent poems which might clarify this: "You know now the sorrow of continually doing something that you cannot name, of producing automatically as an apple tree produces apples this thing there is no name for," which I guess is one of the places where my work is commenting on the work itself, and yet I should caution against reading my poetry too much in this light. When it is commenting on itself it's only doing so in such a way as to point out that living, creating, is a process which tends to take itself very much into account and it's not doing so with any attempt to explain the poetry or explain what poetry ought to do' (*The Poet's Craft*).

THE ORIOLES

What time the orioles came flying
Back to the homes, over the silvery dikes and seas,
The sad spring melted at a leap,
The shining clouds came over the hills to meet them.

The old house guards its memories, the birds
Stream over coloured snow in summer
Or back into the magic rising sun in winter.
They cluster at the feeding station, and rags of song

Greet the neighbours. 'Was that your voice?'
And in spring the mad caroling continues long after day-light
As each builds his hanging nest
Of pliant twigs and the softest moss and grasses.

But one morning you get up and the vermilion-coloured
Messenger is there, bigger than life at the window.
'I take my leave of you; now I fly away
To the sunny reeds and marshes of my winter home.'
And that night you gaze moodily
At the moonlit apple-blossoms, for of course
Horror and repulsion do exist! They do! And you wonder,
How long will the perfumed dung, the sunlit clouds cover my heart?

And then some morning when the snow is flying
Or it lines the black fir-trees, the light cries,
The excited songs start up in the yard!
The feeding station is glad to receive its guests,

But how long can the stopover last?
The cold begins when the last song retires,
And even when they fly against the trees in bright formation
You know the peace they brought was long overdue.

[1956]

Our Youth

Of bricks . . . Who built it? Like some crazy balloon
When love leans on us
Its nights . . . The velvety pavement sticks to our feet.
The dead puppies turn us back on love.

Where we are. Sometimes
The brick arches led to a room like a bubble, that broke when you entered it
And sometimes to a fallen leaf.
We got crazy with emotion, showing how much we knew.

The Arabs took us. We knew
The dead horses. We were discovering coffee,
How it is to be drunk hot, with bare feet
In Canada. And the immortal music of Chopin

Which we had been discovering for several months
Since we were fourteen years old. And coffee grounds,
And the wonder of hands, and the wonder of the day
When the child discovers her first dead hand.

Do you know it? Hasn't she
Observed you too? Haven't you been observed to her?
My, haven't the flowers been? Is the evil
In't? What window? What did you say there?

Heh? Eh? Our youth is dead.
From the minute we discover it with eyes closed
Advancing into mountain light.
Ouch . . . You will never have that young boy,

That boy with the monocle
Could have been your father
He is passing by. No, that other one,
Upstairs. He is the one who wanted to see you.

He is dead. Green and yellow handkerchiefs cover him.
Perhaps he will never rot, I see
That my clothes are dry. I will go.
The naked girl crosses the street.

Blue hampers . . . Explosions,
Ice . . . The ridiculous
Vases of porphyry. All that our youth
Can't use, that it was created for.

It's true we have not avoided our destiny
By weeding out the old people.
Our faces have filled with smoke. We escape
Down the cloud ladder, but the problem has not been solved.

[1962]

Forties Flick

The shadow of the Venetian blind on the painted wall,
Shadows of the snake-plant and cacti, the plaster animals,
Focus the tragic melancholy of the bright stare
Into nowhere, a hole like the black holes in space.
In bra and panties she sidles to the window:
Zip! Up with the blind. A fragile street scene offers itself,
With wafer-thin pedestrians who know where they are going.
The blind comes down slowly, the slats are slowly tilted up.

Why must it always end this way?
A dais with woman reading, with the ruckus of her hair
And all that is unsaid about her pulling us back to her, with her
Into the silence that night alone can't explain.
Silence of the library, of the telephone with its pad,
But we didn't have to reinvent these either:
They had gone away into the plot of a story,
The 'art' part—knowing what important details to leave out
And the way character is developed. Things too real
To be of much concern, hence artificial, yet now all over the page,
The indoors with the outside becoming part of you
As you find you had never left off laughing at death,
The background, dark vine at the edge of the porch.

[1975]

A MAN OF WORDS

His case inspires interest
But little sympathy; it is smaller
Than at first appeared. Does the first nettle
Make any difference as what grows
Becomes a skit? Three sides enclosed,
The fourth open to a wash of the weather,
Exits and entrances, gestures theatrically meant
To punctuate like doubled-over weeds as
The garden fills up with snow?
Ah, but this would have been another, quite other
Entertainment, not the metallic taste
In my mouth as I look away, density black as gunpowder
In the angles where the grass writing goes on,
Rose-red in unexpected places like the pressure
Of fingers on a book suddenly snapped shut.

Those tangled versions of the truth are
Combed out, the snarls ripped out
And spread around. Behind the mask
Is still a continental appreciation
Of what is fine, rarely appears and when it does is already
Dying on the breeze that brought it to the threshold
Of speech. The story worn out from telling.
All diaries are alike, clear and cloud, with
The outlook for continued cold. They are placed
Horizontal, parallel to the earth,
Like the unencumbering dead. Just time to reread this
And the past slips through your fingers, wishing you were there.

[1975]

AND *UT PICTURA POESIS* IS HER NAME

You can't say it that way any more.
Bothered about beauty you have to
Come out into the open, into a clearing,
And rest. Certainly whatever funny happens to you
Is OK. To demand more than this would be strange
Of you, you who have so many lovers,

People who look up to you and are willing
To do things for you, but you think
It's not right, that if they really knew you . . .
So much for self-analysis. Now,
About what to put in your poem-painting:
Flowers are always nice, particularly delphinium.
Names of boys you once knew and their sleds,
Skyrockets are good—do they still exist?
There are a lot of other things of the same quality
As those I've mentioned. Now one must
Find a few important words, and a lot of low-keyed,
Dull-sounding ones. She approached me
About buying her desk. Suddenly the street was
Bananas and the clangor of Japanese instruments.
Humdrum testaments were scattered around. His head
Locked into mine. We were a seesaw. Something
Ought to be written about how this affects
You when you write poetry:
The extreme austerity of an almost empty mind
Colliding with the lush, Rousseau-like foliage of its desire to communicate
Something between breaths, if only for the sake
Of others and their desire to understand you and desert you
For other centres of communication, so that understanding
May begin, and in doing so be undone.

[1977]

The Absence of a Noble Presence

If it was treason it was so well handled that it
Became unimaginable. No, it was ambrosia
In the alley under the stars and not this undiagnosable
Turning, a shadow in the plant of all things

That makes us aware of certain moments,
That the end is not far off since it will occur
In the present and this is the present.
No it was something not very subtle then and yet again

You've got to remember we don't see that much.
We see a portion of eaves dripping in the pastel book
And are aware that everything doesn't count equally—
There is dreaminess and infection in the sum

And since this too is of our everydays
It matters only to the one you are next to
This time, giving you a ride to the station.
It foretells itself, not the hiccup you both notice.

[1981]

On the Empress's Mind

Let's make a bureaucracy.
First, we can have long lists of old things,
and new things repackaged as old ones.
We can have turrets, a guiding wall.
Soon the whole country will come to look over it.

Let us, by all means, have things in night light:
partly visible. The rudeness that poetry often brings
after decades of silence will help. Many
will be called to account. This means that laundries
in their age-old way will go on foundering. Is it any help
that motorbikes whiz up, to ask for directions
or coloured jewellery, so that one can go about one's visit
a tad less troubled than before, lightly composed?

No one knows what it's about any more.
Even in the beginning one had grave misgivings
but the enthusiasm of departure swept them away
in the green molestation of spring.
We were given false information on which
our lives were built, a pier
extending far out into a swollen river.
Now, even these straws are gone.

Tonight the party will be better than ever.
So many mystery guests. And the rain that sifts
through sobbing trees, that excited skiff . . .

Others have come and gone and wrought no damage.
Others have caught, or caused darkness, a long vent
in the original catastrophe no one has seen.
They have argued. Tonight will be different. Is it better for you?

[1992]

THE OLD COMPLEX

As structures go, it wasn't such a bad one,
and it filled the space before the eye
with loving, sinister patches. A modest
eyesore. It reduced them to a sort of paste
wherein each finds his account, goes off
to live among the shore's bashed-in hulks.

Of course you have to actually take the medicine.
For it to work, I mean. Spending much time upstairs
now, I can regulate the solitude,
the rugged blade of anger, note
the occasional black steed. Evening warbles away.

You are free to go now, to go free.
Still, it would help if you'd stay one more day.
I press her hand, strange thing.

[1992]

GARY SNYDER (b. 1930)

Born in San Francisco, Snyder was raised on a farm north of Seattle. He studied mythology at Reed College and linguistics at Indiana University, and moved from bumming, logging, and forestry to Chinese studies at Berkeley. From there he went by tanker to the Mediterranean and Japan, where he studied Buddhism in a Zen monastery in Kyoto. He is one of an increasing number of poets who are turning to studies of social and cultural anthropology. Although he lives in the mountains and concerns himself with the study of myth and lore, Snyder's pronouncements on the practice of poetry evoke the monk or scholar rather than the wild man: 'I think that poetry is a social and traditional art that is linked to its past and particularly its language, that *loops* and draws on its past and that serves as a vehicle for contact with the depths of our own unconscious—and that it gets better by practising. And that the expression of self, although it's a nice kind of energy to start with, would not make any expression of poetry *per se*.'

'We all know,' he says in the same *Ohio Review* interview with Paul Geneson (*The Poet's Work*, edited by Reginald Gibbons), 'that the power of a great poem is not that we felt that person expressed himself well. We don't think that. What we think is "How deeply *I* am touched." That's our level of response. And so a great poet does not express his or her self, he expresses *all* of our selves. And to express *all* of our selves you have to go beyond your own self. As Dogen, the Zen master, said, "We study the self to forget the self. And when you forget the self, you become one with all things." And that's why poetry's not self-expression in those small self terms.'

Snyder is a peculiar mixture of priest and lumberjack. He believes in the value of physical labour, in contact with animals and the land; yet he urges his readers in the direction of a *back country* that exists somewhere beyond a simple physical return to the land. In its aims and styles his poetry reflects this strange mixture. Some of the books have a controlled mythic structure, while others have the flavour of a diary or Whole Earth Catalogue, with poems that serve as maps, recipes, or tips on survival in the wilderness. Snyder views poetry as an ecological survival technique, which explains his legendary status in the American subculture. He is less interested in the *contrived* poem than in poetry that is like 'the clear spring—it reflects all things and feeds all things but is itself transparent'. His early poems are extremely transparent, seemingly naïve and artless renderings of observation and event that have none of the sense of self, or crafty arrogance, that often emerges from such experiential verse. '*Riprap*,' Snyder explains, 'is really a class of poems I wrote under the influence of the geology of the Sierra Nevada and the daily trail-crew work of picking up and placing granite stones in tight cobble patterns on hard slab. "What are you doing?" I asked old Roy Marchbanks.—"Riprapping," he said. His selection of natural rocks was perfect—the result looked like dressed stone fitting to hair-edge cracks. Walking, climbing, placing with the hands. I tried writing poems of tough, simple, short words, with the complexity far beneath the surface texture. In part the line was influenced by the five- and seven-character line Chinese poems I'd been reading, which work like sharp blows on the mind.'

It is difficult to convey a sense of Snyder's range and complexity in a short space; some of his most ambitious and extended work, such as *Myths & Texts*, consists of poem-sequences that must be read as a whole. These, like his recent poems, are more clearly symbolic; they are rooted in actual experience, but extend beyond their frames. In *Manzanita* Snyder begins to draw the lines from which his revolutionary work will be done; and the poems are as exciting for their commitment and sensuality as for their concreteness and economy. Poetry, Snyder says, is to '*give access* to persons—cutting away the fear and reserve and cramping of social life' and proclaiming joyfully 'this is what I have seen'. Snyder rejects the Romantic conception of the poet: 'In the new way of things the community is essential to the creative act; solitary poet figure and "name" author will become less and less relevant. Hence I prefer to be with my friends—which is the creative context.'

In an interview with critic Ekbert Faas (*Towards A New American Poetics*, 1978), Snyder draws links between his Buddhist views and those of Marxism: 'Zen mysticism says: well, wait, it's already all a Buddha right now, if you can just see it, so that's ahistorical. It's the eternal moment. I think in those terms, but I also think in terms of organic evolution, and from that standpoint we have a critical time now in which decisions are being made which will have long-reaching effects on the survival of many forms of life. All the time we are reducing biological diversity at a great rate with modern civilization. From that standpoint I don't know if I'm exactly a Marxist, but I'm committed to a biological diversity of life which I think is the work of poets as ancient shaman-poets and ancient servants of the Muse and the lady of wild things and non-human or extra-human realms. And I value the Marxist critique of Capitalism as throwing precise light on the economic reasons for the destructiveness of modern civilization.'

In the same interview Snyder clearly states his preference for public clarity over esoteric obscurity in poetry: 'Well, the borderline is probably something like this: When you are in a territory where there are no special expectations of your listener, you can still make a song, you're in poetry. If you have a request, ask a special practise from your listener, if you have to say: You must meditate two weeks before you listen to this poem and maybe observe some special diet, then you are in the specific realms of shamanistic or religious training. Now, messages are transmitted and things are taught and songs are sung within the shamanistic special realms of practise, but that's a very special world, it's a professional world almost. We bring poetry back from our special practises, so to speak, to the open realm of human dialogue where we can address it to anyone. That's the known international definition of poetry. Otherwise it becomes like an esoteric tradition.'

While acknowledging to Faas that poetry is 'the finest use of language' and 'the highest level of human bonding', Snyder admits that it 'comes up against an end which is that razor edge boundary line', where the poet must court silence in his struggle to 'echo some non-linguistic, prelinguistic, pre-verbally visualized or deeply felt areas'. At such moments biology may have more to teach the poet than poetic theory.

Snyder lives with his family and friends in the Sierra Nevadas. His books include *Riprap* (1958), *Myths & Texts* (1960), *Six Sections from Mountains and Rivers Without End* (1961), *A Range of Poems*, his collected poems (1966), *The Back Country* (1967), *Regarding Wave* (1967), *Manzanita* (1972), *Turtle Island* (1974), *Passage Through India* (1983), and *Axe Handles* (1983). Because many of Snyder's poems have appeared as chapbooks and in small editions, it is difficult to provide an accurate chronology of his work. His poetry ought to be read in conjunction with his remarkable essays on culture, religion, ecology, and literature in *Earth House Hold: Technical Notes & Queries to Fellow Dharma Revolutionaries* (1957) and *The Real Work: Interviews and Talks* (1980).

Piute Creek

One granite ridge
A tree, would be enough
Or even a rock, a small creek,
A bark shred in a pool.
Hill beyond bill, folded and twisted
Tough trees crammed
In thin stone fractures
A huge moon on it all, is too much.

The mind wanders. A million
Summers, night air still and the rocks
Warm. Sky over endless mountains.
All the junk that goes with being human
Drops away, hard rock wavers
Even the heavy present seems to fail
This bubble of a heart.
Words and books
Like a small creek off a high ledge
Gone in the dry air.

A clear, attentive mind
Has no meaning but that
Which sees is truly seen.
No one loves rock, yet we are here.
Night chills. A flick
In the moonlight
Slips into Juniper shadow:
Back there unseen
Cold proud eyes
Of Cougar or Coyote
Watch me rise and go.

[1959]

RIPRAP

Lay down these words
Before your mind like rocks.
            placed solid, by hands
In choice of place, set
Before the body of the mind
            in space and time:
Solidity of bark, leaf, or wall
            riprap of things:
Cobble of milky way,
            straying planets,
These poems, people,
            lost ponies with
Dragging saddles—
            and rocky sure-foot trails.

The worlds like an endless
four-dimensional
Game of Go.
ants and pebbles
In the thin loam, each rock a word
a creek-washed stone
Granite: ingrained
with torment of fire and weight
Crystal and sediment linked hot
all change, in thoughts,
As well as things.

[1959]

Journeys
section six

1
Genji caught a gray bird, fluttering. It
was wounded, so I hit it with a coal shovel.
It stiffened, grew straight and symmetrical,
and began to increase in size. I took it by
the head with both hands and held it as it
swelled, turning the head from side to side.
It turned into a woman, and I was embracing
her. We walked down a dim-lighted stairway
holding hands, walking more and more swiftly
through an enormous maze, all underground.
Occasionally we touched surface, and redescended.
As we walked I kept a chart of our route in
mind—but it became increasingly complex—and
just when we reached the point where I was
about to lose my grasp of it, the woman trans-
ferred a piece of fresh-tasting apple from her
mouth to mine. Then I woke.

2
Through deep forests to the coast,
and stood on a white sandspit looking in:
over lowland swamps and prairies
where no man had ever been
to a chill view of the Olympics, in a chill clear wind.

3
We moved across dark stony ground to the great
wall: hundreds of feet high. What was beyond
it, cows?—then a thing began to rise
up from behind.
I shot my arrows, shot arrows at it, but it came—
until we turned and ran, 'It's too big to
fight'—the rising thing a quarter mile across—
it was the flaming, pulsing sun. We fled and
stumbled on the bright lit plain.

4
Where were we—
A girl in a red skirt, high heels,
going up the stairs before me in a made-over barn.
White-wash peeling, we lived together in the loft,
on cool bare boards.
—lemme tell you something kid—
　　back in 1910.

5
Walking a dusty road through plowed-up fields
at forest-fire time—the fir tree hills dry,
smoke of the far fires blurred the air—
& passed on into woods, along a pond,
beneath a big red cedar,
to a bank of blinding blue wild flowers
and thick green grass on levelled ground
of hillside where our old house used to stand.
I saw the footings damp and tangled,
and thought my father was in jail,
and wondered why my mother never died,
and thought I ought to bring my sister back.

6
High up in a yellow-gold
dry range of mountains—
brushy, rocky, cactussy hills
slowly hiking down—finally can see below,
a sea of clouds.

Lower down, always moving slowly over the
dry ground descending, can see through breaks
in the clouds: flat land.
Damp green level ricefields, farm houses,
at last to feel the heat and damp.

Descending to this humid, clouded, level world:
now I have come to the LOWLANDS.

7
Underground building chambers clogged with refuse heaps
discarded furniture, slag, old nails,
rotting plaster, faint wisps—antique newspapers
rattle in the winds that come forever down the hall.
ladders
passing, climbing, and stopping, on from door to door.
one tiny light bulb left still burning
                    —now the last—
locked inside is hell.
Movies going, men milling round the posters
                    in shreds
                    the movie always running
—we all head in here somewhere;

—years just looking for the bathrooms.
Huge and filthy, with strange-shaped toilets full of shit.
Dried shit all around, smeared across the walls of the
adjoining room,
and a vast hat rack.

8
With Lew rode in a bus over the mountains—
rutted roads along the coast of Washington
through groves of redwoods. Sitting in the
back of an almost-empty bus,
talking and riding through.
Yellow leaves fluttering down. Passing
through tiny towns at times. Damp cabins
set in dark groves of trees.
Beaches with estuaries and sandbars. I brought
a woman here once long ago,
but passed on through too quick.

9
We were following a long river into the mountains.
Finally we rounded a ridge and could see deeper in—
the farther peaks stony and barren, a few alpine
trees.
Ko-san and I stood on a point by a cliff, over a
rock-walled canyon. Ko said, 'Now we have come to
where we die.' I asked him, what's that up there,
then—meaning the further mountains.
'That's the world after death.' I thought it looked
just like the land we'd been travelling, and couldn't
see why we should have to die.
Ko grabbed me and pulled me over the cliff—
both of us falling. I hit and I was dead. I saw
my body for a while, then it was gone. Ko was
there too. We were at the bottom of the gorge.
We started drifting up the canyon. 'This is the
way to the back country.'

[1961]

SONG OF THE TASTE

Eating the living germs of grasses
Eating the ova of large birds

    the fleshy sweetness packed
    around the sperm of swaying trees

The muscles of the flanks and thighs of
        soft-voiced cows
    the bounce in the lamb's leap
    the swish in the ox's tail

Eating roots grown swoll
        inside the soil

Drawing on life of living
    clustered points of light spun
            out of space
hidden in the grape.

Eating each other's seed
eating
ah, each other.

Kissing the lover in the mouth of bread:
lip to lip.

[1969]

Kai, Today

A teen-age boy in training pants
stretching by the river
A girl child weeping, climbing
up her elder sister;
The Kawaramachi Beggar's steady look and
searching reach of gritty hand
in plastic sidewalk pail
with lip of grease

these fates.

before Masa and I met
What's your from-the-beginning face?
Kai
born again
To the Mother's hoarse bear-down
groan and dark red mask:
spiralling, glistening, blue-white, up

And out from her
(dolphins leaping in threes
through blinding silver inter-
faces, Persian
Gulf tanker's wave-slip
opening, boundless
whap
as they fall back,
arcing
into her—)

sea

[1969]

FRONT LINES

The edge of the cancer
Swells against the hill—we feel
    a foul breeze—
And it sinks back down.
The deer winter here
A chainsaw growls in the gorge.

Ten wet days and the log trucks stop,
The trees breathe.
Sunday the 4-wheel jeep of the
Realty Company brings in
Landseekers, lookers, they say
To the land,
Spread your legs.

The jets crack sound overhead, it's OK here;
Every pulse of the rot at the heart
In the sick fat veins of Amerika
Pushes the edge up closer—

A bulldozer grinding and slobbering
Sideslipping and belching on top of
The skinned-up bodies of still-live bushes
In the pay of a man
From town.

Behind is a forest that goes to the Arctic
And a desert that still belongs to the Piute
And here we must draw
Our line.

[1974]

Ted Hughes (b. 1930)

Born in Mytholmroyd, Yorkshire, Ted Hughes was a ground wireless mechanic in the Royal Air Force before studying at Cambridge, where he met and married the American poet Sylvia Plath. He first attracted attention during his stay in America when his *Hawk in the Rain* won the first publication award for the Poetry Centre of the New York City YM-YWHA in 1957. This volume was followed by *Lupercal* (1960), *Selected Poems* (1962) with Thom Gunn, *Wodwo* (1967), and a steady flow of new work including *Crow: From the Life and Songs of the Crow* (1970; revised in 1972), *Selected Poems: 1957-1967* (1974), *Gaudette* (1977), *Moortown* (1980), *Under the North Sea* (1981), *New Selected Poems* (1982), and *River* (1984). His poetics and non-fiction writings appear in *Poetry in the Making: An Anthology of Poems and Programmes from Listening and Writing* (1969), which he prepared for BBC radio, and in *Ted Hughes: The Unaccommodated Universe* (1980) by Ekbert Faas, which includes two interviews and excerpts from Hughes's critical writings. Hughes received first place in the Guinness Poetry Awards (1958), a Guggenheim fellowship (1959-60), and the Hawthornden Prize (1961); in 1984 he was appointed poet laureate.

Hughes is one of the most original and powerful English poets in the second half of this century. He has a special talent for dramatizing the dynamics of human encounters with the animal world; he captures (in thrush, otter, and pike) both the indefinable threat and the mixture of attraction and repulsion that one associates with D.H. Lawrence's animals. Hughes's success in rendering this tension results from what Keats called *negative capability*—the ability to enter into the existence of things outside the self. The early poems are heavily textured in terms of image and sound, giving the reader a deeply sensuous involvement in the poem's form and content. In the *Crow* poems Hughes denudes his language for a verse that is stark and elemental, in keeping with the symbolic nature of the creation parable. However, even in *Crow*, with its comic-opera aspect, he manages to sustain a high degree of versatility, a ritual intensity, and a shamanistic sense of mystery and play.

Hughes writes (*Ted Hughes: The Unaccommodated Universe*) of the making of a poem in terms of musical composition: 'I might say that I turn every combatant into a bit of music, then resolve the whole uproar into as formal and balanced a figure of melody and rhythm as I can. When all the words are hearing each other clearly, and every stress is feeling every other stress, and all are contented—the poem is finished.' Although he is a very conscious craftsman, Hughes indicates in an interview with Faas in the same volume that he values vision and truth more than craft, and admits that 'in the end, one's poems are ragged dirty undated letters from remote battles and weddings and one thing and another.'

In the title essay of *Poetry in the Making*, Hughes compares writing poems to hunting or tracking down animals in the wild: 'The special kind of excitement, the slightly mesmerized and quite involuntary concentration with which you make out the stirrings of a new poem in your mind, then the outline, the mass and colour and clean final form of it, the unique living reality of it in the midst of the general lifelessness, all that is too familiar to mistake. This is hunting and the poem is a new species of creature, a new specimen of the life outside your own.' In the same essay, he discusses the struggle to make every word, image, and rhythm a 'living part' of the poem, which contributes to our excitement and sensory engagement. One thing, he says, will contribute to the poet's success: 'That one thing is, imagine what you are writing about. See it and live it. Do not think it up laboriously, as if you were working out mental arithmetic. Just look at it, touch it, smell it, listen to it, turn yourself into it. When you do this, the words look after themselves, like magic. If you do this you will not have to bother about commas or full-stops or that sort of thing. You do not look at the words either. You keep your eyes, your ears, your nose, your taste, your touch, your whole being on the thing you are turning into words.'

In a second essay, 'Wind and Weather' (*Poetry in the Making*), Hughes describes the power poetry has to affect readers physiologically: 'Poetry is not made out of thoughts or casual fancies. It is made out of experiences which change our bodies, and spirits, whether momentarily or for good. There are plenty of different experiences which do this, and there is no drawing a line at what the limit is. The sight of a certain word can so affect you that delicate instruments can easily detect the changes in your skin perspiration, the rate of your pulse and so on, just as surely as when the sight of an apple makes your mouth water or your sudden fear in an empty house makes you chill.'

Writing in 1962 about the work of artist Leonard Baskin (*Ted Hughes: The Unaccommodated Universe*), Hughes dissociated himself from 'The Scientific Spirit' and what he considered to be a mechanistic view of the arts: 'Technique is not a machine to do work, like a car engine that runs best of all with little or no load, but the act of work being done. So-called "technique without substance" is our polite word for fakery, or the appearance of something happening that is not happening, and attracts our attention at all only because we will look for some minutes at absolutely anything that seems to say "look at me", so humble and great is our hope.' If there is genius and a powerful 'inner explosion', Hughes argues, 'From that point the "technique" seems no longer an aptitude of the artist, but a possession of the vision, the physical, prehensile grasp of an unusual spirit.'

Of his long poem *Crow*, Hughes says in an interview with Faas: 'The first idea of *Crow* was really an idea of style. In folktales the prince going on an adventure comes to the stable full of beautiful horses and he needs a horse for the next stage and the king's daughter advises him to take none of the beautiful horses that he'll be offered but to choose the dirty, scabby little foal. You see, I throw out the eagles and choose the Crow. The idea was originally just to write his songs, the songs that a Crow would sing. In other words, songs with no music whatsoever, in a super-simple and super-ugly language which would in a way shed everything except what he wanted to say without any other consideration and that's the basis of the style of the whole thing. I get near it in a few poems. There I really begin to get what I was after.'

Later in the same interview, Hughes speaks tellingly of the advantages of the long poem: 'so it is not the story that I am interested in but the poems. In other words, the whole narrative is just a way of getting a big body of ideas and energy moving on a track. For when this energy connects with a possibility for a poem, there is a lot more material and pressure in it than you could ever get into a poem just written out of the air or out of a special occasion. Poems come to you much more naturally and accumulate more life when they are part of a connected flow of real narrative that you've got yourself involved in.'

THE THOUGHT-FOX

I imagine this midnight moment's forest:
Something else is alive
Beside the clock's loneliness
And this blank page where my fingers move.

Through the window I see no star:
Something more near
Though deeper within darkness
Is entering the loneliness:

Cold, delicately as the dark snow,
A fox's nose touches twig, leaf;
Two eyes serve a movement, that now
And again now, and now, and now

Sets neat prints into the snow,
Between trees, and warily a lame
Shadow lags by stump and in hollow
Of a body that is bold to come

Across clearings, an eye,
A widening deepening greenness,
Brilliantly, concentratedly,
Coming about its own business

Till, with a sudden sharp hot stink of fox
It enters the dark hole of the head.
The window is starless still; the clock ticks,
The page is printed.

[1957]

INVITATION TO THE DANCE

The condemned prisoner stirred, but could not stir:
Cold had shackled the blood-prints of the knout.
The light of his death's dawn put the dark out.
He lay, his lips numb to the frozen floor.

He dreamed some other prisoner was dragged out—
Nightmare of command in the dawn, and a shot.
The bestial gaoler's boot was at his ear.

Upon his sinews torturers had grown strong,
The inquisitor old against a tongue that could not,
Being torn out, plead even for death.
All bones were shattered, the whole body unstrung.
Horses, plunging apart towards North and South,
Tore his heart up by the shrieking root.
He was flung to the blow-fly and the dog's fang.

Pitched onto his mouth in a black ditch
All spring he heard the lovers rustle and sigh.
The sun stank. Rats worked at him secretly.
Rot and maggot stripped him stitch by stitch.
Yet still this dream engaged his vanity:
That could he get upright he would dance and cry
Shame on every shy or idle wretch.

[1957]

Six Young Men

The celluloid of a photograph holds them well,—
Six young men, familiar to their friends.
Four decades that have faded and ochre-tinged
This photograph have not wrinkled the faces or the hands
Though their cocked hats are not now fashionable,
Their shoes shine. One imparts an intimate smile,
One chews a grass, one lowers his eyes, bashful,
One is ridiculous with cocky pride—
Six months after this picture they were all dead.

All are trimmed for a Sunday jaunt. I know
That bilberried bank, that thick tree, that black wall,
Which are there yet and not changed. From where these sit
You hear the water of seven streams fall
To the roarer in the bottom, and through all
The leafy valley a rumouring of air go.

Pictured here, their expressions listen yet,
And still that valley has not changed its sound
Though their faces are four decades under the ground.

This one was shot in an attack and lay
Calling in the wire, then this one, his best friend,
Went out to bring him in and was shot too;
And this one, the very moment he was warned
From potting at tin-cans in no-man's-land,
Fell back dead with his rifle-sights shot away.
The rest, nobody knows what they came to,
But come to the worst they must have done, and held it
Closer than their hope; all were killed.

Here see a man's photograph,
The locket of a smile, turned overnight
Into the hospital of his mangled last
Agony and hours; see bundled in it
His mightier-than-a-man dead bulk and weight:
And on this one place which keeps him alive
(In his Sunday best) see fall war's worst
Thinkable flash and rending, onto his smile
Forty years rotting into soil.

That man's not more alive whom you confront
And shake by the hand, see hale, hear speak loud,
Than any of these six celluloid smiles are,
Nor prehistoric or fabulous beast more dead;
No thought so vivid as their smoking blood:
To regard this photograph might well dement,
Such contradictory permanent horrors here
Smile from the single exposure and shoulder out
One's own body from its instant and heat.

[1957]

HAWK ROOSTING

I sit in the top of the wood, my eyes closed.
Inaction, no falsifying dream
Between my hooked head and hooked feet:
Or in sleep rehearse perfect kills and eat.

The convenience of the high trees!
The air's buoyancy and the sun's ray
Are of advantage to me;
And the earth's face upward for my inspection.

My feet are locked upon the rough bark.
It took the whole of Creation
To produce my foot, my each feather:
Now I hold Creation in my foot

Or fly up, and revolve it all slowly—
I kill where I please because it is all mine.
There is no sophistry in my body:
My manners are tearing off heads—

The allotment of death.
For the one path of my flight is direct
Through the bones of the living.
No arguments assert my right:

The sun is behind me.
Nothing has changed since I began.
My eye has permitted no change.
I am going to keep things like this.

[1960]

Pike

Pike, three inches long, perfect
Pike in all parts, green tigering the gold.
Killers from the egg: the malevolent aged grin.
They dance on the surface among the flies.

Or move, stunned by their own grandeur,
Over a bed of emerald, silhouette
Of submarine delicacy and horror.
A hundred feet long in their world.

In ponds, under the heat-struck lily pads—
Gloom of their stillness:
Logged on last year's black leaves, watching upwards.
Or hung in an amber cavern of weeds

The jaw's hooked clamp and fangs
Not to be changed at this date;
A life subdued to its instrument;
The gills kneading quietly, and the pectorals.

Three we kept behind glass,
Jungled in weed: three inches, four,
And four and a half: fed fry to them—
Suddenly there were two. Finally one

With a sag belly and the grin it was born with.
And indeed they spare nobody.
Two, six pounds each, over two feet long,
High and dry and dead in the willow-herb—

One jammed past its gills down the other's gullet:
The outside eye stared: as a vice locks—
The same iron in this eye
Though its film shrank in death.

A pond I fished, fifty yards across,
Whose lilies and muscular tench
Had outlasted every visible stone
Of the monastery that planted them—

Stilled legendary depth:
It was as deep as England. It held
Pike too immense to stir, so immense and old
That past nightfall I dared not cast

But silently cast and fished
With the hair frozen on my head
For what might move, for what eye might move.
The still splashes on the dark pond,

Owls hushing the floating woods
Frail on my ear against the dream
Darkness beneath night's darkness had freed,
That rose slowly towards me, watching.

[1960]

FROM CROW

A CHILDISH PRANK

Man's and woman's bodies lay without souls,
Dully gaping, foolishly staring, inert
On the flowers of Eden.
God pondered.

The problem was so great, it dragged him asleep.

Crow laughed.
He bit the Worm, God's only son,
Into two writhing halves.

He stuffed into man the tail half
With the wounded end hanging out.
He stuffed the head half headfirst into woman
And it crept in deeper and up
To peer out through her eyes
Calling its tail-half to join up quickly, quickly
Because O it was painful.

Man awoke being dragged across the grass.
Woman awoke to see him coming.
Neither knew what had happened.

God went on sleeping.

Crow went on laughing.

[1970]

CROW'S FIRST LESSON

God tried to teach Crow how to talk.
'Love,' said God. 'Say, Love.'
Crow gaped, and the white shark crashed into the sea
And went rolling downwards, discovering its own depth.

'No, no,' said God, 'Say Love. Now try it. LOVE.'
Crow gaped, and a bluefly, a tsetse, a mosquito
Zoomed out and down
To their sundry flesh-pots.

'A final try,' said God. 'Now, LOVE.'
Crow convulsed, gaped, retched and
Man's bodiless prodigious head
Bulbed out onto the earth, with swivelling eyes,
Jabbering protest—

And Crow retched again, before God could stop him.
And woman's vulva dropped over man's neck and tightened.
The two struggled together on the grass.
God struggled to part them, cursed, wept—

Crow flew guiltily off.

[1970]

A DISASTER

There came news of a word.
Crow saw it killing men. He ate well.
He saw it bulldozing
Whole cities to rubble. Again he ate well.
He saw its excreta poisoning seas.
He became watchful.
He saw its breath burning whole lands
To dusty char.
He flew clear and peered.

The word oozed its way, all mouth,
Earless, eyeless.
He saw it sucking the cities
Like the nipples of a sow
Drinking out all the people
Till there were none left,
All digested inside the word.

Ravenous, the word tried its great lips
On the earth's bulge, like a giant lamprey—
There it started to suck.

But its effort weakened.
It could digest nothing but people.
So there it shrank, wrinkling weaker,
Puddling
Like a collapsing mushroom.
Finally, a drying salty lake.
Its era was over.
All that remained of it a brittle desert
Dazzling with the bones of earth's people

Where Crow walked and mused.

[1970]

DEHORNING

Bad-tempered bullying bunch, the horned cows
Among the unhorned. Feared, spoilt.
Cantankerous at the hay, at assemblies, at crowded
Yard operations. Knowing their horntips' position
To a fraction, every other cow knowing it too,
Like their own tenderness. Horning of bellies, hair-tufting
Of horntips. Handy levers. But
Off with the horns.
So there they all are in the yard—
The pick of the bullies, churning each other
Like thick fish in a bucket, churning their mud.
One by one, into the cage of the crush: the needle,
A roar not like a cow—more like a tiger,
Blast of air down a cavern, and long, long,
Beginning in pain and ending in terror—then the next.
The needle between the horn and the eye, so deep
Your gut squirms for the eyeball twisting
In its pink-white fastenings of tissue. This side and that.
Then the first one anesthetized, back in the crush.
The bulldog pincers in the septum, stretched full strength,
The horn levered right over, the chin pulled round
With the pincers, the mouth drooling, the eye

Like a live eye caught in a pan, like the eye of a fish
Imprisoned in air. Then the cheese cutter
Of braided wire, and stainless-steel peg handles,
Aligned on the hair-bedded root of the horn, then leaning
Backward full weight, pull-punching backwards,
Left right left right and the blood leaks
Down over the cheekbone, the wire bites
And buzzes, the ammonia horn-burn smokes
And the cow groans, roars shapelessly, hurls
Its half-ton commotion in the tight cage. Our faces
Grimace like faces in the dentist's chair. The horn
Rocks from its roots, the wire pulls through
The last hinge of hair, the horn is heavy and free,
And a water-pistol jet of blood
Rains over the one who holds it—a needle jet
From the white-rasped and bloody skull crater. Then tweezers
Twiddle the artery nozzle, knotting it enough,
And purple antiseptic squirts a cuttlefish cloud over it.
Then the other side the same. We collect
A heap of horns. The floor of the crush
Is a trampled puddle of scarlet. The purple-crowned cattle,
The bullies, with suddenly no horns to fear,
Start ramming and wrestling. Maybe their heads
Are still anesthetized. A new order
Among the hornless. The bitchy high-headed
Straight-back brindle, with her Spanish bull trot,
And her head-shaking snorting advance and her crazy spirit,
Will have to get maternal. What she's lost
In weapons, she'll have to make up for in tits.
But they've all lost one third of their beauty.

[1979]

Margaret Avison (b. 1918)

Margaret Avison makes one think of Isaac Babel's image of the poet as a meditative figure with 'spectacles on his nose and autumn in his heart'. Born in Galt, Ontario, and educated at the University of Toronto, she has been a secretary, a librarian, a research assistant, a lecturer in English, and a worker in a relief mission. She has gone about her work as a poet with a quiet intensity, avoiding the facile and the sensational. She is neither prolific nor wide-ranging in subject matter. Her interest, as she explains in 'Voluptuaries and Others', is in depth, in 'that other kind of lighting up / which shows the terrain comprehended'.

There is in Avison's poetry an intellectual probing that is reminiscent of the metaphysical poets of the seventeenth century. In *Winter Sun* (1960, Governor General's Award), for example, she explores the landscape of the mind, charting with considerable detail the withdrawal of a delicate sensibility from the external world ('Chronic'):

> But as the weeks pass I become
> accustomed
> To failing more and more
> In credence of reality as others
> Must know it, in a context, with a
> coming
> And going marshalled among
> porticos,
> And peacock-parks for hours of
> morning leisure.

In the halting prose rhythms and photographic images that she owes to Eliot, one senses Avison's concern to describe not only the 'truth' of experience, but also the *process* of arriving at that truth.

The winter terrain of Avison's first book gives way to warmer climates in *The Dumbfounding* (1966), marking a deepening of religious experience and a reconciliation to the physical world. Consequently the book is more concrete and humble in its explorations and pronouncements. Avison's consciousness of the nature and dynamics of perception is here turned to good advantage: her capacity for rapid shifts of perspective within a single poem is replaced by careful observation of minutiae, such as the faces of loiterers and the industry of insects; her sensitivity to the subtleties of language and to the fine distinctions of logic now encompasses the sound of raindrops, 'letting the ear experience this / discrete, delicate clicking'. Whether it marks the passage from despair to belief or, on a technical level, from Eliot to William Carlos Williams, her poetry has undergone a remarkable transformation.

Avision offered a concise statement of her poetics in 1941, which was reiterated in 1962: 'Literature results when: (a) every word is written in the full light of all the writer knows; (b) the writer accepts the precise limits of what he knows, i.e. distinguishes unerringly (while writing) between what he knows, and what he merely knows about, by reputation or reflected opinion.'

Avison's more recent collections are *Sunblue* (1978), *Winter Sun / The Dumbfounding: Poems 1940-1966* (1982), *No Time* (1989), and *Selected Poems* (1991). Her translations of poems from the Hungarian appear in *The Plough and the Pen: Writings from Hungary 1930-1956* (edited by Ilona Duczynska and Karl Polanyi in 1963). Although she contributed in the forties and fifties to Cid Corman's *Origin* and was in contact with Black Mountain poets Charles Olson, Denise Levertov, and Robert Creeley, Avison has remained somewhat reclusive, except for occasional readings and generous efforts on behalf of younger writers. A critical study of her work, *Waiting for the Sun* by David Mazoff, appeared in 1989.

THE WORLD STILL NEEDS

Frivolity is out of season.
Yet, in this poetry, let it be admitted
The world still needs piano-tuners
And has fewer, and more of these
Gray fellows prone to liquor
On an unlikely Tuesday, gritty with wind,
When somewhere, behind windows,
A housewife stays for him until the
  Hour of the uneasy bridge-club cocktails
  And the office rush at the groceteria
  And the vesper-bell and lit-up buses passing
  And the supper trays along the hospital corridor,
Suffering from
Sore throat and dusty curtains.

Not all alone on the deserted boathouse
Or even on the prairie freight
(The engineer leaned out, watchful and blank
And had no Christmas worries
Mainly because it was the eve of April),
Is like the moment
When the piano in the concert-hall
Finds texture absolute, a single solitude
For those hundreds in rows, half out of overcoats,
Their eyes swimming with sleep.

From this communal cramp of understanding
Springs up suburbia, where every man would build
A clapboard in a well of Russian forest
With yard enough for a high clothesline strung
To a small balcony . . .
A woman whose eyes shine like evening's star
Takes in the freshblown linen
While sky a lonely wash of pink is still
reflected in brown mud
Where lettuces will grow, another spring.

[1960]

TO PROFESSOR X, YEAR Y

The square for civic receptions
Is jammed, static, black with people in topcoats
Although November
Is mean, and day grows late.

The newspapermen, who couldn't
Force their way home, after the council meeting
&c., move between windows and pressroom
In ugly humour. They do not know
What everybody is waiting for
At this hour
To stand massed and unmoving
When there should be—well—nothing to expect
Except the usual hubbub
Of city five o'clock.

Winter pigeons walk the cement ledges
Urbane, discriminating.

Down in the silent crowd few can see anything.
It is disgusting, this uniformity
Of stature.
If only someone climbed in pyramid
As circus families can . . .
Strictly, each knows
Downtown buildings block all view anyway
Except, to tease them,
Four narrow passages, and ah
One clear towards open water
(If 'clear'
Suits with the prune and mottled plumes of
Madam night).

Nobody gapes skyward
Although the notion of
Commerce by air is utterly
familiar.

Many citizens at this hour
Are of course miles away, under
Rumpus-room lamps, dining-room chandeliers,
Or bound elsewhere.
One girl who waits in a lit drugstore doorway
North 48 blocks for the next bus
Carries a history, an ethics, a Russian grammar,
And a pair of gym shoes.

But the few thousand inexplicably here
Generate funny currents, zigzag
Across the leaden miles, and all suburbia
Suffers, uneasily.

You, historian, looking back at us,
Do you think I'm not trying to be helpful?
If I fabricated cause-and-effect
You'd listen? I've been dead too long for fancies.
Ignore us, hunched in these dark streets
If in a minute now the explosive
Meaning fails to disperse us and provide resonance
Appropriate to your chronicle.

But if you do, I have a hunch
You've missed a portent.
('Twenty of six.' 'Snow?—I wouldn't wonder.')

[1960]

The Swimmer's Moment

For everyone
The swimmer's moment at the whirlpool comes,
But many at that moment will not say
'This is the whirlpool, then.'
By their refusal they are saved
From the black pit, and also from contesting
The deadly rapids, and emerging in
The mysterious, and more ample, further waters.
And so their bland-blank faces turn and turn
Pale and forever on the rim of suction

They will not recognize.
Of those who dare the knowledge
Many are whirled into the ominous centre
That, gaping vertical, seals up
For them an eternal boon of privacy,
So that we turn away from their defeat
With a despair, not for their deaths, but for
Ourselves, who cannot penetrate their secret
Nor even guess at the anonymous breadth
Where one or two have won:
(The silver reaches of the estuary).

[1960]

VOLUPTUARIES AND OTHERS

That Eureka of Archimedes out of his bath
Is the kind of story that kills what it conveys;
Yet the banality is right for that story, since it is not a communicable one
But just a particular instance of
The kind of lighting up of the terrain
That leaves aside the whole terrain, really,
But signalizes, and compels, an advance in it.
Such an advance through a be-it-what-it-may but take-it-not-quite
    -as-given locale:

Probably that is the core of being alive.
The speculation is not a concession
To limited imaginations. Neither is it
A constrained voiding of the quality of immanent death.
Such near values cannot be measured in values
Just because the measuring
Consists in that other kind of lighting up
That shows the terrain comprehended, as also its containing space,
And wipes out adjectives, and all shadows
    (or, perhaps, all but shadows).

The Russians made a movie of a dog's head
Kept alive by blood controlled by physics, chemistry, equipment, and
Russian women scientists in cotton gowns with writing tablets.
The heart lay on a slab midway in the apparatus

And went phluff, phluff.
Like the first kind of illumination, that successful experiment
Can not be assessed either as conquest or as defeat.
But it is living, creating the chasm of creation,
Contriving to cast only man to brood in it, further.

History makes the spontaneous jubilation at such moments less and less
likely though,
And that story about Archimedes does get into public school textbooks.

[1960]

PACE

'Plump raindrops in these
faintly clicking groves,
the pedestrians' place, July's
violet and albumen
close?'

'No. No. It is perhaps the conversational side-effect
among the pigeons; behold
the path-dust is nutmeg powdered and
bird-foot embroidered.'

The silk-fringed hideaway
permits the beechnut-cracking
squirrels to plumply
pick and click and
not listen.

Pedestrians linger
striped stippled sunfloating
at the time of the
thin-wearing groves

letting the ear experience this
discrete, delicate
clicking.

[1966]

BLACK-WHITE UNDER GREEN: MAY 18, 1965

This day of the leafing-out
speaks with blue power—
among the buttery grassblades
white, tiny-spraying spokes on the end of a weed-stem
and in the formal beds, tulips
and invisible birds inaudibly hallooing,
enormous, their beaks out wide, throats bulging, aflutter,
eyes weeping with speed
where the ultraviolets play and the scythe of the jets
flashes, carrying
the mind-wounded heartpale person, still a boy, a pianist, dying not
of the mind's wounds (as they read the x-rays) but
dying, fibres separated, parents ruddy and
American, strong, sheathed in the cold of
years of his differentness, clustered by two at
the nether arc of flight.

This day of the leafing-out is one to remember
how the ice crackled among
stiff twigs. Glittering strongly
the old trees sagged. Boughs
abruptly unsocketed. Dry, orange gashes
the dawn's fine snowing discovered and powdered over.

. . . to remember the leaves ripped loose
the thudding of the dark sky-beams
and the pillared plunging sea
shelterless. Down the centuries
a flinching speck
in the white fury found of itself—and another—
the rich blood spilling, mother to child, threading
the perilous combers, marbling
the surges, flung
out, and ten-fingered, feeling for
the lollop, the fine-wired
music, dying skyhigh
still between carpets and the
cabin-pressuring windows
on the day of the leafing.

Faces fanned by
rubberized, cool air
are opened; eyes wisely
smile.
The tulips, weeds, new leaves
neither smile nor are scorning to smile nor uncertain,
dwelling in light.
A flick of ice, fire, flood,
far off from
the day of the leafing-out I knew
when knee-wagon small, or from my
father's once at a horse-tail, silk-shiny
fence-corner or this
day when the runways wait
white in the sun, and a new leaf is
metal, torn out of that blue
afloat in the dayshine.

[1966]

JULY MAN

Old, rain-wrinkled, time-soiled, city-wise, morning man
whose weeping is for the dust of the elm-flowers
and the hurting motes of time,
rotted with rotting grape,
sweet with the fumes,
puzzled for good by fermented potato-
peel out of the vat of the times,
turned out and left
in this grass-patch, this city-gardener's place
under the buzzing populace's
square shadows, and the green shadows
of elm and ginkgo and lime
(planted for Sunday strollers and summer evening
families, and for those
bird-cranks with bread-crumbs
and crumpled umbrellas who come
while the dew is wet on the park, and beauty
is fan-tailed, gray and dove-gray, aslant, folding in
from the white fury of day).

In the sound of the fountain
you rest, at the cinder-rim, on your bench.

The rushing river of cars
makes you a stillness, a pivot, a heart-stopping
blurt, in the sorrow
of the last rubbydub swig, the searing, and
stone-jar solitude lost, and yet,
and still—wonder (for good now) and
trembling:

> The too much none of us knows
> is weight, sudden sunlight, falling
> on your hands and arms, in your lap,
> all, all, in time.

[1966]

IN A SEASON OF UNEMPLOYMENT

These green painted park benches are
all new. The Park Commissioner had them
planted.
Sparrows go on
having dust baths at the edge of
the park maple's shadow, just where
the bench is cemented down, planted
and then cemented.

> Not a breath moves
> this newspaper.
> I'd rather read it by the Lapland sun at midnight. Here we're
> bricked in early by a
> stifling dark.

On that bench a man in a
pencil-striped white shirt
keeps his head up and steady.

The newspaper-astronaut says
'I feel excellent under the condition of weightlessness.'
And from his bench a
scatter of black bands in the hollow-air
ray out—too quick for the eye—
and cease.

'Ground observers watching him on a tv circuit said
At the time of this report he
was smiling,' Moscow ra-
dio reported.
I glance across at him, and mark that
he is feeling
excellent too, I guess, and
weightless and
'smiling.'

[1966]

Oughtiness Ousted

God (being good) has let me know
no good apart from Him.
He, knowing me, yet promised too
all good in His good time.

This light, shone in, wakened a hope
that lives here-&-now—
strongly the wind in push and sweep
made fresh for all-things-new.

But o, how very soon a gloat
gulped joy: the kernel (whole)
I chaffed to merely *act* and *ought*—
'rightness' uncordial.

But Goodness broke in, as the sea
satins in shoreward sun
washing the clutter wide away:
all my inventeds gone.

[1978]

WE THE POOR WHO ARE ALWAYS WITH US

The cumbering hungry
and the uncaring ill
become too many
try as we will.

Try on and on, still?
In fury, fly
out, smash shards? (And quail
at tomorrow's new supply,
and fail anew to find and smash the why?)

It is not hopeless.
One can crawling move
too there, still free to love
past use, where none survive.

And there is reason in
the hope that then can shine
when other hope is none.

[1978]

SYLVIA PLATH (1932-1963)

Sylvia Plath was born in Boston of Austrian and German parentage. After graduating from Smith College in 1955, she studied at Cambridge on a Fulbright fellowship in 1957, where she met and married Ted Hughes. She had two children and taught briefly at Smith before her death by suicide in London. Her first collection of poems, *The Colossus* (1960), attracted considerable critical attention; it was followed by a novel, *The Bell Jar* (1963), and the posthumous collections *Ariel* (1965), *Crossing the Water* (1972), and *Winter Trees* (1972).

A strong case has been made in our time for linking art and neurosis, even madness. However, this persuasion sits too comfortably with a general Puritan suspicion of the artist and an obsession with the idea of 'other' life-styles not so easily manipulated by the state or public opinion. The suicides of poets such as Plath, Anne Sexton, and John Berryman lend fuel to such speculation. None of this is new. Plato advised keeping poets and musicians out of the new republic, lest their rhythms disturb the peace. Dictatorships in our own time give writers the special honour of being the first killed or sent to the gulags. While it may be true that artists have good social antennæ and are particularly sensitive to social ills, the act by which they are known and remembered is a manifestation of health and, at the very least, a gesture towards healing.

Plath's life offers conflicting detail for speculation about her destructive sources. She was a bright child and over-achiever who suffered a mental breakdown (presumably the basis for *The Bell Jar*), but who also achieved considerable recognition in the form of personal praise, prizes, and fellowships. Her marriage to Ted Hughes, which appears to have been troubled and unstable, produced two beautiful children, Frieda and Nicholas, but left her little time or energy to write. There are post-facto clues in the work that might lead us to believe she was, like Robert Lowell, walking along the razor's edge—'Dying / Is an art, like everything else. / I do it exceptionally well'—and yet the poems are so cleverly crafted and blessed with such wicked humour that their effect is one of exuberance.

In an interview in 1962 (*The Poet Speaks*, edited by Peter Orr, 1966), Plath expresses excitement at what she called Robert Lowell's 'intense breakthrough into very serious, very personal, emotional experience which I feel has been partly taboo'. Her own poetry explores an intense inner world. One aspect of this world is a morbid fascination with death and the grotesque: 'The eye of the blind pianist / At my table on the ship. / He felt for his food. / His fingers had the noses of weasels. / I couldn't stop looking.' The strength of such poems lies precisely in the poet's inability to turn away from suffering and oddity. In 'Lady Lazarus', Plath dramatizes a bitterness and self-contempt that border on masochism; but in 'Tulips' she conveys a painful reaching out for life and sanity.

No matter how troubled the artist, or how bleak her vision, the work of art is an affirmation of life. As Albert Camus argues in *The Rebel*, there is no such thing as a nihilistic work of art, or sick art; even if it describes 'nostalgia, despair, frustration, it still creates a form of salvation. To talk of despair is to conquer it. Despairing literature is a contradiction in terms.' If this is true, as I believe it is, we do poets most justice by focusing primarily on those techniques by which they give imaginative shape to their vision.

These poems are as carefully crafted and as finely chiselled as they are bizarre. Both her diaries and the comments of Ted Hughes indicate that the apparently confessional aspect of her poetry was considerably less important to her than the most detailed formal considerations. The poems are richly textured in terms of recurring image and sound; even a poem as seemingly (and distractingly) autobiographical as 'Daddy' employs word-play, insistent rhyme, alliteration, assonance, deftly-placed moments of blunt repetition ("the brute / brute heart of a brute like you'), and several levels of diction to achieve its superb effects.

TWO VIEWS OF A CADAVER ROOM

I
The day she visited the dissecting room
They had four men laid out, black as burnt turkey,
Already half unstrung. A vinegary fume
Of the death vats clung to them;
The white-smocked boy started working.
The head of his cadaver had caved in,
And she could scarcely make out anything
In that rubble of skull plates and old leather.
A sallow piece of string held it together.

In their jars the snail-nosed babies moon and glow.
He hands her the cut-out heart like a cracked heirloom.

II
In Brueghel's panorama of smoke and slaughter
Two people only are blind to the carrion army:
He, afloat in the sea of her blue satin
Skirts, sings in the direction
Of her bare shoulder, while she bends,
Fingering a leaflet of music, over him,
Both of them deaf to the fiddle in the hands
Of the death's-head shadowing their song.
These Flemish lovers flourish; not for long.

Yet desolation, stalled in paint, spares the little country
Foolish, delicate, in the lower right hand corner.

[1959]

THE COLOSSUS

I shall never get you put together entirely,
Pieced, glued, and properly jointed.
Mule-bray, pig-grunt, and bawdy cackles
Proceed from your great lips.
It's worse than a barnyard.

Perhaps you consider yourself an oracle,
Mouthpiece of the dead, or of some god or other.
Thirty years now I have laboured
To dredge the silt from your throat.
I am none the wiser.

Scaling little ladders with gluepots and pails of lysol
I crawl like an ant in mourning
Over the weedy acres of your brow
To mend the immense skull-plates and clear
The bald, white tumuli of your eyes.

A blue sky out of the Oresteia
Arches above us. O father, all by yourself
You are pithy and historical as the Roman Forum.
I open my lunch on a hill of black cypress.
Your fluted bones and acanthine hair are littered

In their old anarchy to the horizon-line.
It would take more than a lightning-stroke
To create such a ruin.
Nights, I squat in the cornucopia
Of your left ear, out of the wind,

Counting the red stars and those of plum-colour.
The sun rises under the pillar of your tongue.
My hours are married to shadow.
No longer do I listen for the scrape of a keel
On the blank stones of the landing.

[1959]

Black Rook in Rainy Weather

On the stiff twig up there
Hunches a wet black rook
Arranging and rearranging its feathers in the rain.
I do not expect miracle
Or an accident

To set the sight on fire
In my eye, nor seek
Any more in the desultory weather some design,
But let spotted leaves fall as they fall,
Without ceremony, or portent.

Although, I admit, I desire,
Occasionally, some backtalk
From the mute sky, I can't honestly complain:
A certain minor light may still
Leap incandescent

Out of kitchen table or chair
As if a celestial burning took
Possession of the most obtuse objects now and then—
Thus hallowing an interval
Otherwise inconsequent

By bestowing largesse, honour,
One might say love. At any rate, I now walk
Wary (for it could happen
Even in this dull, ruinous landscape); sceptical,
Yet politic; ignorant

Of whatever angel may choose to flare
Suddenly at my elbow. I only know that a rook
Ordering its black feathers can so shine
As to seize my senses, haul
My eyelids up, and grant

A brief respite from fear
Of total neutrality. With luck,
Trekking stubborn through this season
Of fatigue, I shall
Patch together a content

Of sorts. Miracles occur,
If you care to call those spasmodic
Tricks of radiance miracles. The wait's begun again,
The long wait for the angel,
For that rare, random descent.

[1956]

Blue Moles

I

They're out of the dark's ragbag, these two
Moles dead in the pebbled rut,
Shapeless as flung gloves, a few feet apart—
Blue suede a dog or fox has chewed.
One, by himself, seemed pitiable enough,
Little victim unearthed by some large creature
From his orbit under the elm root.
The second carcase makes a duel of the affair:
Blind twins bitten by bad nature.

The sky's far dome is sane and clear.
Leaves, undoing their yellow caves
Between the road and the lake water,
Bare no sinister spaces. Already
The moles look neutral as the stones.
Their corkscrew noses, their white hands
Uplifted; stiffen in a family pose.
Difficult to imagine how fury struck—
Dissolved now, smoke of an old war.

II

Nightly the battle-shouts start up
In the ear of the veteran, and again
I enter the soft pelt of the mole.
Light's death to them: they shrivel in it.
They move through their mute rooms while I sleep,
Palming the earth aside, grubbers
After the fat children of root and rock.
By day, only the topsoil heaves.
Down there one is alone.

Outsize hands prepare a path,
They go before: opening the veins,
Delving for the appendages
Of beetles, sweetbreads, shards—to be eaten
Over and over. And still the heaven
Of final surfeit is just as far

From the door as ever. What happens between us
Happens in darkness, vanishes
Easy and often as each breath.

[1959]

THE DISQUIETING MUSES

Mother, mother, what illbred aunt
Or what disfigured and unsightly
Cousin did you so unwisely keep
Unasked to my christening, that she
Sent these ladies in her stead
With heads like darning-eggs to nod
And nod and nod at foot and head
And at the left side of my crib?

Mother, who made to order stories
Of Mixie Blackshort the heroic bear,
Mother, whose witches always, always
Got baked into gingerbread, I wonder
Whether you saw them, whether you said
Words to rid me of those three ladies
Nodding by night around my bed,
Mouthless, eyeless, with stitched bald head.

In the hurricane, when father's twelve
Study windows bellied in
Like bubbles about to break, you fed
My brother and me cookies and ovaltine
And helped the two of us to choir:
'Thor is angry: boom boom boom!
Thor is angry: we don't care!'
But those ladies broke the panes.

When on tiptoe the schoolgirls danced,
Blinking flashlights like fireflies
And singing the glowworm song, I could
Not lift a foot in the twinkle-dress
But, heavy-footed, stood aside

In the shadow cast by my dismal-headed
Godmothers, and you cried and cried:
And the shadow stretched, the lights went out.

Mother, you sent me to piano lessons
And praised my arabesques and trills
Although each teacher found my touch
Oddly wooden in spite of scales
And the hours of practising, my ear
Tone-deaf and yes, unteachable.
I learned, I learned, I learned elsewhere,
From muses unhired by you, dear mother.

I woke one day to see you, mother,
Floating above me in bluest air
On a green balloon bright with a million
Flowers and bluebirds that never were
Never, never, found anywhere.
But the little planet bobbed away
Like a soap-bubble as you called: Come here!
And I faced my travelling companions.

Day now, night now, at head, side, feet,
They stand their vigil in gowns of stone,
Faces blank as the day I was born,
Their shadows long in the setting sun
That never brightens or goes down.

And this is the kingdom you bore me to,
Mother, mother. But no frown of mine
Will betray the company I keep.

[1957]

LADY LAZARUS

I have done it again.
One year in every ten
I manage it—

A sort of walking miracle, my skin
Bright as a Nazi lampshade,
My right foot

A paperweight,
My face a featureless, fine
Jew linen.

Peel off the napkin
O my enemy.
Do I terrify?—

The nose, the eye pits, the full set of teeth?
The sour breath
Will vanish in a day.

Soon, soon the flesh
The grave cave ate will be
At home on me

And I a smiling woman.
I am only thirty.
And like the cat I have nine times to die.

This is Number Three.
What a trash
To annihilate each decade.

What a million filaments.
The peanut-crunching crowd
Shoves in to see

Them unwrap me hand and foot—
The big strip tease.
Gentlemen, ladies

These are my hands
My knees.
I may be skin and bone,

Nevertheless, I am the same, identical woman.
The first time it happened I was ten.
It was an accident.

The second time I meant
To last it out and not come back at all.
I rocked shut

As a seashell.
They had to call and call
And pick the worms off me like sticky pearls.

Dying
Is an art, like everything else,
I do it exceptionally well.

I do it so it feels like hell.
I do it so it feels real.
I guess you could say I've a call.

It's easy enough to do it in a cell.
It's easy enough to do it and stay put.
It's the theatrical

Comeback in broad day
To the same place, the same face, the same brute
Amused shout:

'A miracle!'
That knocks me out.
There is a charge

For the eyeing of my scars, there is a charge
For the hearing of my heart—
It really goes.

And there is a charge, a very large charge
For a word or a touch
Or a bit of blood

Or a piece of my hair or my clothes.
So, so, Herr Doktor.
So, Herr Enemy.

I am your opus,
I am your valuable,
The pure gold baby

That melts to a shriek.
I turn and burn.
Do not think I underestimate your great concern.

Ash, ash—
You poke and stir.
Flesh, bone, there is nothing there—

A cake of soap,
A wedding ring,
A gold filling.

Herr God, Herr Lucifer
Beware
Beware.

Out of the ash
I rise with my red hair
And I eat men like air.

[1962]

TULIPS

The tulips are too excitable, it is winter here.
Look how white everything is, how quiet, how snowed-in.
I am learning peacefulness, lying by myself quietly
As the light lies on these white walls, this bed, these hands.
I am nobody; I have nothing to do with explosions.
I have given my name and my day-clothes up to the nurses
And my history to the anaesthetist and my body to surgeons.

They have propped my head between the pillow and the sheet-cuff
Like an eye between two white lids that will not shut.
Stupid pupil, it has to take everything in.
The nurses pass and pass, they are no trouble,
They pass the way gulls pass inland in their white caps,
Doing things with their hands, one just the same as another,
So it is impossible to tell how many there are.

My body is a pebble to them, they tend it as water
Tends to the pebbles it must run over, smoothing them gently.
They bring me numbness in their bright needles, they bring me sleep.
Now I have lost myself I am sick of baggage—
My patent leather overnight case like a black pillbox,
My husband and child smiling out of the family photo;
Their smiles catch onto my skin, little smiling hooks.

I have let things slip, a thirty-year-old cargo boat
Stubbornly hanging on to my name and address.
They have swabbed me clear of my loving associations.
Scared and bare on the green plastic-pillowed trolley
I watched my teaset, my bureaus of linen, my books
Sink out of sight, and the water went over my head.
I am a nun now, I have never been so pure.

I didn't want any flowers, I only wanted
To lie with my hands turned up and be utterly empty.
How free it is, you have no idea how free—
The peacefulness is so big it dazes you,
And it asks nothing, a name tag, a few trinkets.
It is what the dead close on, finally; I imagine them
Shutting their mouths on it, like a Communion tablet.

The tulips are too red in the first place, they hurt me.
Even through the gift paper I could hear them breathe
Lightly, through their white swaddlings, like an awful baby.
Their redness talks to my wound, it corresponds.
They are subtle: they seem to float, though they weigh me down,
Upsetting me with their sudden tongues and their colour,
A dozen red lead sinkers round my neck.

Nobody watched me before, now I am watched.
The tulips turn to me, and the window behind me
Where once a day the light slowly widens and slowly thins,
And I see myself, flat, ridiculous, a cut-paper shadow
Between the eye of the sun and the eyes of the tulips,
And I have no face, I have wanted to efface myself.
The vivid tulips eat my oxygen.

Before they came the air was calm enough,
Coming and going, breath by breath, without any fuss.
Then the tulips filled it up like a loud noise.
Now the air snags and eddies round them the way a river
Snags and eddies round a sunken rust-red engine.
They concentrate my attention, that was happy
Playing and resting without committing itself.

The walls, also, seem to be warming themselves.
The tulips should be behind bars like dangerous animals;
They are opening like the mouth of some great African cat,
And I am aware of my heart: it opens and closes
Its bowl of red blooms out of sheer love of me.
The water I taste is warm and salt, like the sea,
And comes from a country far away as health.

[1961]

ARIEL

Stasis in darkness.
Then the substanceless blue
Pour of tor and distances.

God's lioness,
How one we grow,
Pivot of heels and knees!—The furrow

Splits and passes, sister to
The brown arc
Of the neck I cannot catch,

Nigger-eye
Berries cast dark
Hooks—

Black sweet blood mouthfuls,
Shadows.
Something else

Hauls me through air—
Thighs, hair;
Flakes from my heels.

White
Godiva, I unpeel—
Dead hands, dead stringencies.

And now I
Foam to wheat, a glitter of seas.
The child's cry

Melts in the wall.
And I
Am the arrow,

The dew that flies
Suicidal, at once with the drive
Into the red

Eye, the cauldron of morning.

[1965]

DADDY

You do not do, you do not do
Any more, black shoe
In which I have lived like a foot
For thirty years, poor and white,
Barely daring to breathe or Achoo.

Daddy, I have had to kill you.
You died before I had time——
Marble-heavy, a bag full of God,
Ghastly statue with one grey toe
Big as a Frisco seal

And a head in the freakish Atlantic
Where it pours bean green over blue
In the waters off beautiful Nauset.
I used to pray to recover you.
Ach, du.

In the German tongue, in the Polish town
Scraped flat by the roller
Of wars, wars, wars.
But the name of the town is common.
My Polack friend

Says there are a dozen or two.
So I never could tell where you
Put your foot, your root,
I never could talk to you.
The tongue stuck in my jaw.

It stuck in a barb wire snare.
Ich, ich, ich, ich,
I could hardly speak.
I thought every German was you.
And the language obscene

An engine, an engine
Chuffing me off like a Jew.
A Jew to Dachau, Auschwitz, Belsen.
I began to talk like a Jew.
I think I may well be a Jew.

The snows of the Tyrol, the clear beer of Vienna
Are not very pure or true.
With my gypsy ancestress and my weird luck
And my Taroc pack and my Taroc pack
I may be a bit of a Jew.

I have always been scared of *you*,
With your Luftwaffe, your gobbledygoo.
And your neat moustache
And your Aryan eye, bright blue.
Panzer-man, panzer-man, O You——

Not God but a swastika
So black no sky could speak through.
Every woman adores a Fascist,
The boot in the face, the brute
Brute heart of a brute like you.

You stand at the blackboard, daddy,
In the picture I have of you,
A cleft in your chin instead of your foot
But no less a devil for that, no not
Any less the black man who

Bit my pretty red heart in two.
I was ten when they buried you.
At twenty I tried to die
And get back, back, back to you.
I thought even the bones would do.

But they pulled me out of the sack,
And they stuck me together with glue.
And then I knew what to do.
I made a model of you,
A man in black with a Meinkampf look

And a love of the rack and the screw.
And I said I do, I do.
So daddy, I'm finally through.
The black telephone's off at the root,
The voices just can't worm through.

If I've killed one man, I've killed two——
The vampire who said he was you
And drank my blood for a year,
Seven years, if you want to know.
Daddy, you can lie back now.

There's a stake in your fat black heart
And the villagers never liked you.
They are dancing and stamping on you.
They always *knew* it was you.
Daddy, daddy, you bastard, I'm through.

[1962]

TWO CAMPERS IN CLOUD COUNTRY

(Rock Lake, Canada)

In this country there is neither measure nor balance
To redress the dominance of rocks and woods,
The passage, say, of these man-shaming clouds.

No gesture of yours or mine could catch their attention,
No word make them carry water or fire the kindling
Like local trolls in the spell of a superior being.

Well, one wearies of the Public Gardens: one wants a vacation
Where trees and clouds and animals pay no notice;
Away from the labelled elms, the tame tea-roses.

I took three days driving north to find a cloud
The polite skies over Boston couldn't possibly accommodate.
Here on the last frontier of the big, brash spirit

The horizons are too far off to be chummy as uncles;
The colours assert themselves with a sort of vengeance.
Each day concludes in a huge splurge of vermilions

And night arrives in one gigantic step.
It is comfortable, for a change, to mean so little.
These rocks offer no purchase to herbage or people:

They are conceiving a dynasty of perfect cloud.
In a month we'll wonder what plates and forks are for.
I lean to you, numb as a fossil. Tell me I'm here.

The Pilgrims and Indians might never have happened.
Planets pulse in the lake like bright amoebas;
The pines blot our voices up in their lightest sighs.

Around our tent the old simplicities sough
Sleepily as Lethe, trying to get in.
We'll wake blank-brained as water in the dawn.

[1960]

Leonard Cohen (b. 1934)

Leonard Cohen was born in Montreal and educated at McGill University, where he published his first volume of poetry, *Let Us Compare Mythologies* (1956), in the McGill Poetry Series. He dropped out of graduate studies at Columbia to write and perform, in Montreal nightclubs and for the CBC, the poems and songs collected in *The Spice-Box of Earth* (1961). While living abroad, mostly in Greece, Cohen produced two novels, *The Favourite Game* (1963) and *Beautiful Losers* (1966), and two more books of poetry: *Flowers for Hitler* (1964) and *Parasites of Heaven* (1966). His parallel career as a folk-singer has led to great acclaim and numerous albums, including *Songs of Leonard Cohen* (1968), *Songs from a Room* (1969), *The Best of Leonard Cohen* (1975), and *I'm Your Man* (1988). *Selected Poems* appeared in 1968, followed by *The Energy of Slaves* (1972), *Death of a Lady's Man* (1978), *Small Expectations* (1984), *The Book of Mercy* (1984), and a major collection of his poetry, *Stranger Music* (1994).

Cohen inherited the mantle of the Beat poets, together with their spiritual questing, anti-establishment sentiments, and attraction to the subject of decadence, to which he added his own fascination with power and violence. This combination gave him great popularity in the mid-sixties among audiences who were struggling to define their values and discover new strategies for living. 'We are on the threshold of a great religious age,' he has said, 'an age of discipleship. All our spiritual vocabulary has been discredited.' Cohen played secular priest to the individualism of that generation; however, a more committed, politically aware, and cynical age emerged from the racial protests and political activism of the late sixties, for which Cohen's decadent and disengaged verses seemed to have less relevance. As a result, his popularity suffered a decline that seems to have reversed itself only as the century draws to a close.

Now it is possible to look at Cohen's work apart from the social and artistic fashions of the time and to see the essentially religious nature of his quest as a poet and a singer. As he suggested in an early interview with the poet Michael Harris (*Duel*, number one, 1969), the struggle for a pure heart goes hand in hand with the search for a simple, unadorned style; and the sense of underlying mystery implies a view of art as a means of conjuring, as ritual or magic that will change lives:

> I think that a decent man who has discovered valuable secrets is under some obligation to share them. But I think that the technique of sharing them is a great study. . . .
>
> Now, you can reveal secrets in many ways. One way is to say this is the secret I have discovered. I think that this way is often less successful because when that certain kind of conscious creative mind brings itself to bear on this information, it distorts it, it makes it very inaccessible. Sometimes it's just in the voice, sometimes just in the style, in the length of the paragraph; it's in the tone, rather than in the message.

Following his own artistic advice, Cohen has sought the style, or styles, that would best reveal his secrets, moving from traditional lyricism to surrealism to the self-reflexive and anti-poetic strategies of post-modernism. Beneath all of his experiments lie the basic religious forms that humans use to address their God: prayer, praise, confession, and incantation. Not surprisingly, *The Book of Mercy* (1984) takes the form of fifty prayers and meditations, recalling the Old Testament Psalms, the Sermon on the Mount, and the tradition of religious verse that moves from Gerard Manley Hopkins through John Donne and back to St John of the Cross.

In an interview with Alan Twigg in *Strong Voices* (1988), that continued over several years, Cohen says: 'I consider a lot of my work to be a kind of *reportage*, trying to make a completely accurate description of the interior predicament. . . . It isn't always rational. It doesn't follow the laws of logic. Or even of rhetoric. You have to juxtapose elements to get something that corresponds to an interior condition. All poetry is based on differences. Wherever there's tension, wherever there's life, wherever there's the positive/negative, female/male, yin/yang. That's what creates the universe. That's the kind of writing I like to do. Where you're writing on an edge, where you're really trying to get it right. I don't mean so it endures and the next generation looks into it, although it would be nice if it happened. I'm interested in only one thing: if it lives.'

Wisdom rather than technique seems to be Cohen's central preoccupation. In the same interview with Twigg, he admits not only that he finds perfection and simplicity in the lyrics of country music and hymns, but also that he has developed no formula for writing poetry and songs: 'I never have a strategy when I write. I don't have any assembly line approach to it. The kind of writer I am, I'm never raking it in on any level. You're always starting from scratch. I don't have a James Bond series going on or anything. I find it all gets harder rather than easier. I have the tools. I know how to use them. But the content becomes more and more difficult. And there is no guarantee that the difficulty of the process will produce excellence. I just try to let the song function for itself in the end. I've merely learned a few tricks along the way.'

ELEGY

Do not look for him
In brittle mountain streams:
They are too cold for any god;
And do not examine the angry rivers
For shreds of his soft body
Or turn the shore stones for his blood;
But in the warm salt ocean
He is descending through cliffs
Of slow green water
And the hovering coloured fish
Kiss his snow-bruised body
And build their secret nests
In his fluttering winding-sheet.

[1956]

STORY

She tells me a child built her house
one Spring afternoon,
but that the child was killed
crossing the street.

She says she read it in the newspaper,
that at the corner of this and this avenue
a child was run down by an automobile.

Of course I do not believe her.
She has built the house herself,
hung the oranges and coloured beads in the doorways,
crayoned flowers on the walls.

She has made the paper things for the wind,
collected crooked stones for their shadows in the sun,
fastened yellow and dark balloons to the ceiling.

Each time I visit her
she repeats the story of the child to me,
I never question her. It is important
to understand one's part in a legend.

I take my place
among the paper fish and make-believe clocks,
naming the flowers she has drawn,
smiling while she paints my head on large clay coins,
and making a sort of courtly love to her
when she contemplates her own traffic death.

[1956]

YOU HAVE THE LOVERS

You have the lovers,
they are nameless, their histories only for each other,
and you have the room, the bed, and the windows.
Pretend it is a ritual.

Unfurl the bed, bury the lovers, blacken the windows,
let them live in that house for a generation or two.
No one dares disturb them.
Visitors in the corridor tip-toe past the long closed door,
they listen for sounds, for a moan, for a song:
nothing is heard, not even breathing.
You know they are not dead,
you can feel the presence of their intense love.
Your children grow up, they leave you,
they have become soldiers and riders.
Your mate dies after a life of service.
Who knows you? Who remembers you?
But in your house a ritual is in progress:
it is not finished: it needs more people.
One day the door is opened to the lover's chamber.
The room has become a dense garden,
full of colours, smells, sounds you have never known.
The bed is smooth as a wafer of sunlight,
in the midst of the garden it stands alone.
In the bed the lovers, slowly and deliberately and silently,
perform the act of love.
Their eyes are closed,
as tightly as if heavy coins of flesh lay on them.
Their lips are bruised with new and old bruises.
Her hair and his beard are hopelessly tangled.
When he puts his mouth against her shoulder
she is uncertain whether her shoulder
has given or received the kiss.
All her flesh is like a mouth.
He carries his fingers along her waist
and feels his own waist caressed.
She holds him closer and his own arms tighten around her.
She kisses the hand beside her mouth.
It is his hand or her hand, it hardly matters,
there are so many more kisses.
You stand beside the bed, weeping with happiness,
you carefully peel away the sheets
from the slow-moving bodies.
Your eyes are filled with tears, you barely make out the lovers,
As you undress you sing out, and your voice is magnificent
because now you believe it is the first human voice

heard in that room.
The garments you let fall grow into vines.
You climb into bed and recover the flesh.
You close your eyes and allow them to be sewn shut.
You create an embrace and fall into it.
There is only one moment of pain or doubt
as you wonder how many multitudes are lying beside your body,
but a mouth kisses and a hand soothes the moment away.

[1961]

AS THE MIST LEAVES NO SCAR

As the mist leaves no scar
On the dark green hill,
So my body leaves no scar
On you, nor ever will.

When wind and hawk encounter,
What remains to keep?
So you and I encounter,
Then turn, then fall to sleep.

As many nights endure
Without a moon or star,
So will we endure
When one is gone and far.

[1961]

NOW OF SLEEPING

Under her grandmother's patchwork quilt
a calico bird's-eye view
of crops and boundaries
naming dimly the districts of her body
sleeps my Annie like a perfect lady

Like ages of weightless snow
on tiny oceans filled with light
her eyelids enclose deeply

a shade tree of birthday candles
one for every morning
until the now of sleeping

The small banner of blood
kept and flown by Brother Wind
long after the pierced bird fell down
is like her red mouth
among the squalls of pillow

Bearers of evil fancy
of dark intention and corrupting fashion
who come to rend the quilt
plough the eye and ground the mouth
will contend with mighty Mother Goose
and Farmer Brown and all good stories
of invincible belief
which surround her sleep
like the golden weather of a halo

Well-wishers and her true lover
may stay to watch my Annie
sleeping like a perfect lady
under her grandmother's patchwork quilt
but they must promise to whisper
and to vanish by morning—
all but her one true lover.

[1961]

THE GENIUS

For you
I will be a ghetto jew
and dance
and put white stockings
on my twisted limbs
and poison wells
across the town

For you
I will be an apostate jew
and tell the Spanish priest
of the blood vow
in the Talmud
and where the bones
of the child are hid

For you
I will be a banker jew
and bring to ruin
a proud old hunting king
and end his line

For you
I will be a Broadway jew
and cry in theatres
for my mother
and sell bargain goods
beneath the counter

For you
I will be a doctor jew
and search
in all the garbage cans
for foreskins
to sew back again

For you
I will be a Dachau jew
and lie down in lime
with twisted limbs
and bloated pain
no mind can understand

[1961]

STYLE

I don't believe the radio stations
of Russia and America
but I like the music and I like
the solemn European voices announcing jazz
I don't believe opium or money
though they're hard to get
and punished with long sentences
I don't believe love
in the midst of my slavery I
do not believe
I am a man sitting in a house
on a treeless Argolic island
I will forget the grass of my mother's lawn
I know I will
I will forget the old telephone number
Fitzroy seven eight two oh
I will forget my style
I will have no style
I hear a thousand miles of hungry static
and the old clear water eating rocks
I hear the bells of mules eating
I hear the flowers eating the night
under their folds
Now a rooster with a razor
plants the haemophilia gash across
the soft black sky
and now I know for certain
I will forget my style
Perhaps a mind will open in this world
perhaps a heart will catch rain
Nothing will heal and nothing will freeze
but perhaps a heart will catch rain
America will have no style
Russia will have no style
It is happening in the twenty-eighth year
of my attention
I don't know what will become
of the mules with their lady eyes
or the old clear water

or the giant rooster
The early morning greedy radio eats
the governments one by one the languages
the poppy fields one by one
Beyond the numbered band
a silence develops for every style
for the style I laboured on
an external silence like the space
between insects in a swarm
electric unremembering
and it is aimed at us
(I am sleepy and frightened)
it makes toward me brothers

[1964]

THE MUSIC CREPT BY US

I would like to remind
the management
that the drinks are watered
and the hat-check girl
has syphilis
and the band is composed
of former ss monsters
However since it is
New Year's Eve
and I have lip cancer
I will place my
paper hat on my
concussion and dance

[1964]

DISGUISES

I am sorry that the rich man must go
and his house become a hospital.
I loved his wine, his contemptuous servants,
his ten-year-old ceremonies.
I loved his car which he wore like a snail's shell

everywhere, and I loved his wife,
the hours she put into her skin,
the milk, the lust, the industries
that served her complexion.
I loved his son who looked British
but had American ambitions
and let the word aristocrat comfort him
like a reprieve while Kennedy reigned.
I loved the rich man: I hate to see
his season ticket for the Opera
fall into a pool for opera-lovers.

I am sorry that the old worker must go
who called me mister when I was twelve
and sir when I was twenty
who studied against me in obscure socialist
clubs which met in restaurants.
I loved the machine he knew like a wife's body.
I loved his wife who trained bankers
in an underground pantry
and never wasted her ambition in ceramics.
I loved his children who debate
and come first at McGill University.
Goodbye old gold-watch winner
all your complex loyalties
must now be borne by one-faced patriots.

Goodbye dope fiends of North Eastern Lunch
circa 1948, your spoons which were not
Swedish Stainless, were the same colour
as the hoarded clasps and hooks
of discarded soiled therapeutic corsets.
I loved your puns about snow
even if they lasted the full seven-month
Montreal winter. Go write your memoirs
for the Psychedelic Review.

Goodbye sex fiends of Beaver Pond
who dreamed of being jacked-off
by electric milking machines.
You had no Canada Council.

You had to open little boys
with a pen-knife.
I loved your statement to the press:
'I didn't think he'd mind.'
Goodbye articulate monsters
Abbot and Costello have met Frankenstein.

I am sorry that the conspirators must go
the ones who scared me by showing me
a list of all the members of my family.
I loved the way they reserved judgement
about Genghis Khan. They loved me because
I told them their little beards
made them dead-ringers for Lenin.
The bombs went off in Westmount
and now they are ashamed
like a successful outspoken Schopenhauerian
whose room-mate has committed suicide.
Suddenly they are all making movies.
I have no one to buy coffee for.

[1964]

HOW TO SPEAK POETRY

Take the word butterfly. To use this word it is not necessary to make the voice weigh less than an ounce or equip it with small dusty wings. It is not necessary to invent a summer day or a field of daffodils. It is not necessary to be in love, or to be in love with butterflies. The word butterfly is not a real butterfly. There is the word and there is the butterfly. If you confuse these two items people have the right to laugh at you. Do not make so much of the word. Are you trying to suggest that you love butterflies more perfectly than anyone else, or really understand their nature? The word butterfly is merely data. It is not an opportunity for you to hover, soar, befriend flowers, symbolize beauty and frailty, or in anyway impersonate a butterfly. Do not act out words. Never act out words. Never try to leave the floor when you talk about flying. Never close your eyes and jerk your head to one side when you talk about death. Do not fix your burning eyes on me when you speak about love. If you want to impress me when you speak about love put your hand in your pocket or under your dress and play with yourself. If ambition and the hunger for applause have driven you to speak about love you should learn how to do it without disgracing yourself or the material.

What is the expression which the age demands? The age demands no expression whatever. We have seen photographs of bereaved Asian mothers. We are not interested in the agony of your fumbled organs. There is nothing you can show on your face that can match the horror of this time. Do not even try. You will only hold yourself up to the scorn of those who have felt things deeply. We have seen newsreels of humans in the extremities of pain and dislocation. Everyone knows you are eating well and are even being paid to stand up there. You are playing to people who have experienced a catastrophe. This should make you very quiet. Speak the words, convey the data, step aside. Everyone knows you are in pain. You cannot tell the audience everything you know about love in every line of love you speak. Step aside and they will know what you know because they know it already. You have nothing to teach them. You are not more beautiful than they are. You are not wiser. Do not shout at them. Do not force a dry entry. That is bad sex. If you show the lines of your genitals, then deliver what you promise. And remember that people do not really want an acrobat in bed. What is our need? To be close to the natural man, to be close to the natural woman. Do not pretend that you are a beloved singer with a vast loyal audience which has followed the ups and downs of your life to this very moment. The bombs, flame-throwers, and all the shit have destroyed more than just the trees and villages. They have also destroyed the stage. Did you think that your profession would escape the general destruction? There is no more stage. There are no more footlights. You are among the people. Then be modest. Speak the words, convey the data, step aside. Be by yourself. Be in your own room. Do not put yourself on.

This is an interior landscape. It is inside. It is private. Respect the privacy of the material. These pieces were written in silence. The courage of the play is to speak them. The discipline of the play is not to violate them. Let the audience feel your love of privacy even though there is no privacy. Be good whores. The poem is not a slogan. It cannot advertise you. It cannot promote your reputation for sensitivity. You are not a stud. You are not a killer lady. All this junk about the gangsters of love. You are students of discipline. Do not act out the words. The words die when you act them out, they wither, and we are left with nothing but your ambition.

Speak the words with the exact precision with which you would check out a laundry list. Do not become emotional about the lace blouse. Do not get a hard-on when you say panties. Do not get all shivery just because of the towel. The sheets should not provoke a dreamy expression about the eyes. There is no need to weep into the handkerchief. The socks are not there to remind you of strange and distant voyages. It is just your laundry. It is just your clothes. Don't peep through them. Just wear them.

The poem is nothing but information. It is the Constitution of the inner country. If you declaim it and blow it up with noble intentions then you are no better than the politicians whom you despise. You are just someone waving a flag and making the cheapest appeal to a kind of emotional patriotism. Think of the words as science, not as art. They are a report. You are speaking before a meeting of the Explorers' Club or the National Geographic Society. These people know all the risks of mountain climbing. They honour you by taking this for granted. If you rub their faces in it that is an insult to their hospitality. Tell them about the height of the mountain, the equipment you used, be specific about the surfaces and the time it took to scale it. Do not work the audience for gasps and sighs. If you are worthy of gasps and sighs it will not be from your appreciation of the event, but from theirs. It will be in the statistics and not the trembling of the voice or the cutting of the air with your hands. It will be in the data and the quiet organization of your presence.

Avoid the flourish. Do not be afraid to be weak. Do not be ashamed to be tired. You look good when you're tired. You look like you could go on forever. Now come into my arms. You are the image of my beauty.

[1978]

GWENDOLYN MACEWEN (1941-1987)

Gwendolyn MacEwen was born in Toronto to a mother who was mentally unstable and a father with frustrated ambitions to be a photographer. She published her first poem in *The Canadian Forum* at age fifteen and dropped out of school at eighteen to write full-time. After a brief and disastrous marriage to the poet Milton Acorn, she travelled to Egypt and the Middle East, where she discovered people, energy, history, and imaginative resources for a lifetime. Back in Canada, she translated, wrote plays and talks for radio, read her work in universities and schools, and served a term as writer-in-residence at the University of Toronto. While she found recognition early, including the CBC New Writing Contest Award (1965), the Borestone Mountain Poetry Award, and the Governor General's Award (1969), and gained a strong following in the literary community in Canada, both for her poems themselves and for her dramatic readings of them, MacEwen seems to have found these rewards insufficient consolation for her emotional deprivation as a child and for the loneliness and sacrifices of the writing life.

And yet, as Rosemary Sullivan makes

abundantly clear in *Shadow Maker: The Life of Gwendolyn MacEwen* (1995), MacEwen was courageous and independent, a poet who read widely and had serious ambitions: 'She believed her work mattered, only to discover that poetry was dying in the collective imagination.' Largely self-taught, she forged her own poetic style, rejecting both the confessional mode and the 'terribly cynical and "cool" poetry written today', and choosing instead the expressive mode, which is particularly concerned with reader-response. 'I write basically to communicate joy, mystery, passion,' she said, '. . . not the joy that naïvely exists without knowledge of pain, but that joy which arises out of and conquers pain. I want to construct a myth.' The mythic imagination often finds its securest footing in the ancient past, although it will also see in the present manifestations of the eternal. 'I believe there is more inside than outside,' she says in the preface to *A Breakfast for Barbarians*. 'And all the diversities which get absorbed can later work their way out into fantastic things, like hawk-training, IBM programming, mountain-climbing, or poetry.'

Although she may have preferred the mythic past and the occult, MacEwen eschewed the notion of art-for-art's sake. 'I am involved with writing as a total profession, not as an aesthetic pursuit,' she said. 'My prime concern has always been with the raw materials from which literature is derived, not with literature as an end in itself.' Her poetry depends a good deal on a prosody that engages the senses and emotions and a rhetoric of repetition, direct address ('listen—there was this boy, Manzini'), and a muscular (arguing) syntax that recalls Yeats at his most prophetic and incantatory.

Acknowledging the competing claims of the world and art, MacEwen often focuses on the figure of the artist, whether an escape artist such as Manzini, the painter of ancient hieroglyphs, or the poet. Each struggles with so-called reality, a sort of braille that gives us hints of the eternal and enduring, and with a chosen medium of expression, which may be at least two removes from revelation. She acknowledges in 'Poems in Braille' that 'I do not read the long cabbala of my bones / truthfully', an awareness which prompts her to conclude: 'I should read all things like braille in this season / with my fingers I should read them / lest I go blind in both eyes reading with / that other eye the final hieroglyph.' Believing that 'To live consciously is holy', she labours to construct an art that includes both the oracular and the vernacular: 'O baby, get out of Egypt. . .', she writes in 'Cartaphilus'. 'An ancient slang speaks through me like that.'

Perhaps MacEwen's finest achievement is her poem-sequence about Lawrence of Arabia, *The T.E. Lawrence Poems*, which she says had the following origin: 'In 1962 I was staying in a hotel in Tiberias, Israel; the tall, white-haired proprietor invited me downstairs one evening and served me syrupy tea and a plate of fruit. He showed me a series of old sepiatone photographs which lined the walls—photographs of blurred riders on camels riding to the left into some uncharted desert just beyond the door. Some of them were signed.

'"It's Lawerence, isn't it?" I asked, walking up to one.

'"Yes", said my host, offering me a huge section of an orange. "I rode with him once a long time ago. I see you always carry a pen and paper to write things down. I thought you'd be interested; I thought you'd like to know."'

To listen, to transform, and to sing—those were MacEwen's aims, and are her enduring legacy. Her poetry publications include *Selah* and *The Drunken Clock*, both privately printed in 1961, *The Rising Fire* (1963), *A Breakfast for Barbarians* (1966), *The Shadow-Maker* (1969, Governor

General's Award), *The Armies of the Moon* (1972), *Magic Animals: Selected Poems Old and New* (1974), *The Fire-Eaters* (1976), *The T.E. Lawrence Poems* (1982), *Earth Light: Selected Poetry* (1982), and *Afterworlds* (1987, Governor General's Award). Her works of fiction are *Julian the Magician* (1963), *King of Egypt, King of Dreams* (1971), *Noman* (1972), and *Noman's Land* (1985).

POEMS IN BRAILLE

I

all your hands are verbs,
now you touch worlds and feel their names—
thru the thing to the name
not the other way thru (in winter
I am Midas, I name gold)

the chair and table and book
extend from your fingers;
all your movements
command these things back to their
places; a fight against familiarity
makes me resume my distance

II

they knew what it meant,
those egyptian scribes who drew
eyes right into their hieroglyphs,
you read them dispassionate until
the eye stumbles upon itself
blinking back from the papyrus

outside, the articulate wind
annotates this; I read carefully
lest I go blind in both eyes, reading with
that other eye the final hieroglyph

III

the shortest distance between 2 points
on a revolving circumference
is a curved line; O let me follow you,
Wenceslas

IV

with legs and arms I make alphabets
like in those children's books
where people bend into letters and signs,
yet I do not read the long cabbala of my bones
truthfully; I need only to move
to alter the design

V

I name all things in my room
and they rehearse their names,
gather in groups, form tesseracts,
discussing their names among themselves

I will not say the cast is less than the print
I will not say the curve is longer than the line,
I should read all things like braille in this season
with my fingers I should read them
lest I go blind in both eyes reading with
that other eye the final hieroglyph

[1966]

MANZINI: ESCAPE ARTIST

now there are no bonds except the flesh; listen—
there was this boy, Manzini, stubborn with
gut stood with black tights and a turquoise
leaf across his sex

and smirking while the big
brute tied his neck arms legs, Manzini
naked waist up and white with sweat

struggled. Silent, delinquent, he
was suddenly all teeth and knee, straining slack
and excellent with sweat, inwardly
wondering if Houdini would take as long
as he; fighting time and the drenched
muscular ropes, as though his tendons were worn
on the outside—

as though his own guts were the ropes
encircling him; it was beautiful; it was thursday; listen—
there was this boy, Manzini

finally free, slid as snake from
his own sweet agonized skin, to throw his entrails
white upon the floor
with a cry of victory—

now there are no bonds except the flesh,
but listen, it was thursday, there was this boy,
Manzini—

[1966]

POEM IMPROVISED AROUND A FIRST LINE*

the smoke in my bedroom which is always burning
worsens you, motorcycle Icarus;
you are black and leathery and lean and
you cannot distinguish between sex and nicotine

anytime, it's all one thing for you—
cigarette, phallus, sacrificial fire—
all part of the grimy flight
on wings axlegreased from Toronto to Buffalo
for the secret beer over the border—

now I long to see you full blown and black
over Niagara, your bike burning and in full flame
and twisting and pivoting over Niagara
and falling finally into Niagara,
and tourists coming to see your black leather wings
hiss and swirl in the steaming current—

now I long to give up cigarettes
and change the sheets on my carboniferous bed;
O baby, what Hell to be Greek in this country—
without wings, but burning anyway

[1966]

*The first line around which it was improvised has disappeared.

THE RED BIRD YOU WAIT FOR

You are waiting for someone to confirm it
You are waiting for someone to say it plain,
Now we are here and because we are short of time
I will say it; I might even speak its name.

It is moving above me, it is burning my heart out,
I have felt it crash through my flesh,
I have spoken to it in a foreign tongue,
I have stroked its neck in the night like a wish.

Its name is the name you have buried in your blood,
Its shape is a gorgeous cast-off velvet cape,
Its eyes are the eyes of your most forbidden lover
And its claws, I tell you its claws are gloved in fire.

You are waiting to hear its name spoken,
You have asked me a thousand times to speak it,
You who have hidden it, cast it off, killed it,
Loved it to death and sung your songs over it.

The red bird you wait for falls with giant wings—
A velvet cape whose royal colour calls us kings
Is the form it takes as, uninvited, it descends,
It is the Power and the Glory forever, Amen.

[1969]

THE DISCOVERY

do not imagine that the exploration
ends, that she has yielded all her mystery
or that the map you hold
cancels further discovery

I tell you her uncovering takes years,
takes centuries, and when you find her naked
look again,
admit there is something else you cannot name,
a veil, a coating just above the flesh
which you cannot remove by your mere wish

when you see the land naked, look again
(burn your maps, that is not what I mean),
I mean the moment when it seems most plain
is the moment when you must begin again

[1969]

DARK PINES UNDER WATER

This land like a mirror turns you inward
And you become a forest in a furtive lake;
The dark pines of your mind reach downward,
You dream in the green of your time,
Your memory is a row of sinking pines.

Explorer, you tell yourself this is not what you came for
Although it is good here, and green;
You had meant to move with a kind of largeness,
You had planned a heavy grace, an anguished dream.

But the dark pines of your mind dip deeper
And you are sinking, sinking, sleeper
In an elementary world;
There is something down there and you want it told.

[1969]

MEMOIRS OF A MAD COOK

There's no point kidding myself any longer,
I just can't get the knack of it; I suspect
there's a secret society which meets
in dark cafeterias to pass on the art
from one member to another.
Besides,
it's so *personal* preparing food for someone's
insides, what can I possibly *know*
about someone's insides, how can I presume
to invade your blood?
I'll try, God knows I'll try

but if anyone watches me I'll *scream*
because maybe I'm handling a tomato wrong
how can I *know* if I'm handling a tomato wrong?

something is eating away at me
with splendid teeth

Wistfully I stand in my difficult kitchen
and imagine the fantastic salads and soufflés
that will never be.
Everyone seems to grow thin with me
and their eyes grow black as hunter's eyes
and search my face for sustenance.
All my friends are dying of hunger,
there is some basic dish I cannot offer,
and you my love are almost as lean
as the splendid wolf I must keep always
at my door.

[1972]

THE CHILD DANCING

there's no way I'm going to write about
the child dancing in the Warsaw ghetto
in his body of rags

there were only two corpses
on the pavement that day
and the child I will not write about
had a face as pale and trusting
as the moon

(so did
the boy with a green belly full of dirt
lying by the roadside
in a novel of Kazantzakis
and the small girl T.E. Lawrence wrote about
who they found after the Turkish massacre
with one shoulder chopped off, crying:
'don't *hurt* me, Baba!')

I don't feel like slandering them with poetry.

the child who danced
in the Warsaw ghetto
to some music no one else could hear
had moon-eyes, no
green horror and no fear
but something worse

a simple desire to please
the people who stayed
to watch him shuffle back and forth,
his feet wrapped in the newspapers
of another ordinary day

[1972]

from The T.E. Lawrence Poems

Apologies

I did not choose Arabia; it chose me. The shabby money
that the desert offered us bought lies, bought victory.
    What was I, that soiled Outsider, doing
Among them? I was not becoming one of them, no matter
What you think. They found it easier to learn my kind
    of Arabic, than to teach me theirs.
And they were all mad; they mounted their horses and camels
    from the right.

But my mind's twin kingdoms waged an everlasting war;
The reckless Bedouin and the civilized Englishman
    fought for control, so that I, whatever I was,
Fell into a dumb void that even a false god could not fill,
    could not inhabit.

The Arabs are children of the idea; dangle an idea
In front of them, and you can swing them wherever.
    I was also a child of the idea; I wanted
    no liberty for myself, but to bestow it

Upon them. I wanted to present them with a gift so fine
it would outshine all other gifts in their eyes;
it would be *worthy*. Then I at last could be
Empty.

You can't imagine how beautiful it is to be empty.
Out of this grand emptiness wonderful things must surely
come into being.
When we set out, it was morning. We hardly knew
That when we moved we would not be an army, but a world.

NITROGLYCERINE TULIPS

We planted things called tulip bombs to knock out
Turkish trains, or curl up the tracks;
the Turks were so stupid, it sometimes
seemed to me too easy. How could they
expect a *proper* war
If they gave us no chance to honour them?

I called myself Emir Dynamite, and became quite deft
at the whole business of organized
destruction. In the back of one train
which I derailed, was a carriage full of
dying men; one whispered *Typhus*,
So I wedged the door closed and left them in.

Another time I straightened out the bodies of dead Turks,
placing them in rows to look better;
I was trying, I think, to make it
a neat war. Once there were three hundred
of them, with their clothes stripped off,
And I wanted nothing more than to lie down with them,

And die, of course—and think of nothing else but
raspberries cold with rain, instead of
sending currents into blasting gelatin
and watching the sad old trains
blow sky high
With Turks in little bits around everywhere.

DERAA

I started to write something like:
The citadels of my integrity were lost, or
quo vadis from here, Lawrence?
How pathetic.

I may as well tell you that as a boy my best castle
was besieged and overcome by my brothers.

What happened of course was that I was raped at Deraa,
beaten and whipped and reduced to shreds
by Turks with lice in their hair, and VD
a gift from their officers, crawling all over
their bodies,
I had thought that the Arabs were
Bad enough. Slicing the soles of a prisoner's feet
so that when they let him return to his men,
he went very, very slowly;
but they were merciful.

Imagine, I could never bear to be touched by anybody;
I considered myself a sort of flamboyant monk, awfully
intact, yet colourful.
Inviolable is the word.
But everything is shameful, you know; to have a body
is a cruel joke. It is shameful to be under
an obligation to anything, even an animal;
life is shameful; I am shameful. There.

So what part of me lusted after death, as they smashed
knees into my groin and turned a small knife
between my ribs? Did I cry out or not when
they held my legs apart and one of them rode
upon me, laughing, and splitting open
a bloody pathway through my soul?
I don't remember.
They beat me until something, some
primal slime spilled out of me, and fire
shot to my brain.
On a razor edge of reality,

I knew I would come out of this, bleeding and broken,
        and singing.

They lean on the horizon, insolent and wise.

GHAZALA'S FOAL

Ghazala was the second finest camel in all Arabia, and
She did not know it.
                        She had absolutely no mission in life
        and no sense of honour or of shame; she was
        almost perfect.
                        I've seen so many camels die
        that it doesn't matter—the females going on
        until they foundered and died in their tracks,
        the males roaring and flinging themselves down
        and dying unnecessarily out of sheer rage, those
        we scooped out of the snow at Tafileh—but
Mostly I remember Ghazala's foal, getting up and walking
        when it was three hours old, then falling down
        again, in a little heap of slippery limbs.

One of the men skinned it, and Ghazala cried and sniffed
        the little hide.
                        Then we marched again, and often
        she stopped short, and looked around wildly,
        remembering something that was terribly important,
        then lapsing into a blank, dazed stare.
                                                Only
        when the poor, tiny piece of skin was placed
        before her on the ground would she
Murmur something, nudge it, ponder a while, and walk on.

TALL TALES

It has been said that I sometimes lie, or bend the truth
        to suit me. Did I make that four hundred mile
        trip alone in Turkish territory or not?
        I wonder if it is anybody's business
        to know. Syria is still there,
        and the long lie that the war was.

Was there a poster of me offering money for my capture,
and did I stand there staring at myself,
daring anyone to know me? Consider
truth and untruth, consider why they call them
the *theatres* of war. All of us
played our roles to the hilt.

Poets only play with words, you know; they too
are masters of the Lie, the Grand Fiction.
Poets and men like me who fight for something
contained in words, but not words.

What if the whole show was a lie, and it bloody well was—
would I still lie to you? Of course I would.

NOTES FROM THE DEAD LAND

I have died at last, Feisal. I have been lying
On this hospital bed for five days, and I know
that I am dead. I was going back home
on my big bike, and I wasn't doing more
than sixty when this black van, death camel,
Slid back from the left side of my head, and ahead,
Two boys on little bikes were biking along, and
something in my head, some brutal music
played on and on. I was going too fast,
I was always going too fast for the world,
So I swerved and fell on my stupid head, right
In the middle of the road. I addressed myself
to the dark hearts of the tall trees
and nothing answered.

The Arabs say that when you pray, two angels stand
On either side of you, recording good and bad deeds,
and you should acknowledge them.
Lying here, I decide that now
the world can have me any way it pleases.
I will celebrate my perfect death here. *Maktub*:
It is written. I salute both of the angels.

[1982]

THE TRANSPARENT WOMB

Here's why I never had a child. Because down the lane behind the Morgentaler clinic the mother of a tribe of alleycats nudges towards me the one she knows will die after its first and last drink of warm water in the depths of winter, because the bag lady down the street (who was once a child) tells me she won't go on welfare because that's only for people who are really hard up, because I collect kids and cats and strangers (or they collect me), and at Halloween the poor kids come shelling out and one boy wears a garbage bag over his head with holes cut out for eyes and says does it matter what he's supposed to *be*, and his sister wears the same oversize dress she wears everyday because it's already a funny, horrible costume, hem flopping around her ankles, the eternal hand-me-down haute mode of the poor, because

They wander into my house all the time asking 'got any fruit'? because their parents spend their welfare cheques on beer and pork and beans and Kraft dinner and more beer, they won't eat vegetables with funny names like the Greeks and the Wops, so the kids are fat, poor fat, fat with starch and sugar, toy food, because

The kids in Belfast in that news photo were trying to pull a gun away from a British solider in a terrible tug of war where nobody won, and

My foster kid in El Salvador is called Jesus.

Here's why I never had a child: Because they're so valuable I could never afford one, because I never thought it was a good way to glue a man to me, because I never thought I had to prove *I* could do it while they're starving everywhere and floating in gutters and screaming with hunger. All this in our time. All the world's children are ours, all of them are already mine.

[1987]

THE LONELINESS OF THE LONG DISTANCE POET

Everything takes so long; it's as though everything's been deliberately delayed. (Although some long poems I do in a flash and some short ones take years.) The first thing that took forever was for me to get baptized in the Anglican church. Somehow they never got around to it till I was six or seven, so I was old enough to understand how mortifying it was to stand on the shore of this sea of babies screaming their lungs out as their immortal souls were ensured safe passage into some kingdom or another, if that was what the ritual meant (to this day I'm still not sure). But I suppose everything survives the drama of its birth or death. In poetry I'm riding the waves of invisible seas in fabulous vessels which are always arriving or departing in and from new kingdoms. Still I sometimes feel that everyone else is going away, that the world, so to speak, is moving out of town. And when I break, I break the way that branches do, the branches of a line of trees that are the passage from night to morning. And when I mend I am as positive and powerful as dawn is. Then wherever I'm going, it's only a stone's throw from here to there.

[1987]

YOU CAN STUDY IT IF YOU WANT

One of these days after my thousandth poetry reading
I'm going to answer The Question right.

The question is Why Do You Write.

Every time I hear The Question I get this
purple blur in front of my eyes, and
I fear I will fall down frothing at the mouth
and spewing forth saliva and
mixed metaphors.

You can study it if you want, I'm
just the one who gets to do it; or,

Don't ask me I just work here.

You know the answer and still I have to say it:

Poetry has got nothing to do with *poetry*.
Poetry is how the air goes green before thunder,
is the sound you make when you come, and
why you live and how you bleed, and

The sound you make or don't make when you die.

[1987]

EAVAN BOLAND (b. 1944)

Born in Dublin, Eavan Boland spent many of her childhood years in London, where her father was in the diplomatic service. She received some of her schooling in Ireland, London, and New York before completing an honours B.A. in English in 1966 at Trinity College, Dublin, where she taught briefly. She lives near Dublin with her husband, the novelist Kevin Carey, and two children and is an occasional teacher of creative writing in Ireland and the US. Boland published her first book, *23 Poems*, privately in 1962, at the age of eighteen. This was followed by *New Territory* (1967), *The War Horse* (1975), *In Her Own Image* (1980), *Night Feed* (1982, 1994), *The Journey* (1987, Poetry Book Society Choice), *Selected Poems* (1989), *Outside History* (1990, Poetry Book Society Choice), and *In a Time of Violence* (1994). She has written an important work of non-fiction entitled *Object Lessons: The Life of the Woman and the Poet in Our Time* (1995), further sections of which appear in the Poetics section. She is a member of the Irish Academy of Letters and has won several awards, including the Macaulay Fellowship in Poetry (1968), the Jacobs Award for Broadcasting (1977), and the Irish American Cultural Award (1983).

In 'When the Spirit Moves' (*The New York Review*, 12 January 1995), Boland argues against the sacramental view of literature that, in declaring poetry a substitute religion, limits the poet's imaginative freedom: 'that historic tradition seems to me to have prescribed an inflationary spiral of subject matter in poetry, so that the ordinary day I lived in was not easily included or made welcome there.' To claim special status for the poet, she says, is a two-edged sword: 'To begin with, the man or woman writing ceases to be human and becomes "the poet". Words cease to be what they mean and become what they do: Do they rhyme, do they elide, does this vowel go with that consonant? The momentum of the poem is guided and obstructed by the demand that it be "poetic". Experience itself is sifted so that the "poetic" bits are winnowed out in case they contaminate the final product. And the best you achieve is a decorative simplification of life based on a dread of it.'

In *Object Lessons*, Boland examines the changing role of women—who, in other ages, could be objectified and silenced in the writing of male-dominated societies—and the changing role of poets, who, as a result of the democratization of society, have been made to look not only suspect, but also 'élite and irrelevant all at once': 'It is these very tensions and not their absence, and not any possibility of resolving them, which makes me believe that the woman poet is now an emblematic figure in poetry, much as the modernist or romantic poets were in their time. I make this less as a claim than as a historical reading. It does not mean she will write better poetry than men, or more important and more lasting. It does mean that in the projects she chooses, must choose perhaps, are internalized some of the central stresses and truths of poetry at this moment. And that in the questions she needs to ask herself—about voice and self, about revising the stance of the poet, not to mention the relation of the poem to the act of power—are some of the questions which are at the heart of the contemporary form. This does not give her any special liberty to subcontract a poem to an ideology. It does not set her free to demand that a bad poem be reconsidered as a good ethic. Her responsibilities remain the same as they have been for every poet: to formalize the truth. At the same time the advantage she gains for language, the clarities she brings to the form, can no longer be construed as sectional gains. They must be seen as pertaining to all poetry. That means they must also be allowed access to that inner sanctum of a tradition: its past.'

Sensing a new role for the woman poet did not mean, of course, that Boland was not marginalized within Ireland: 'what I found was a rhetoric of imagery which alienated me: a fusion of the national and the feminine which seemed to simplify both.' To subvert the tribalisms that exclude women, to resist becoming a cultural ornament, Boland argues that 'Writers, if they are wise, do not make their home in any comfort within a national tradition. However vigilant the writer, however enlightened the climate, the dangers persist. So too do the obligations. There is a recurring temptation for any nation, and for any writer who operates within its field of force, to make an ornament of the past, to turn the losses to victories and to restate humiliations as triumphs. In every age language holds out narcosis and amnesia for this purpose. But such triumphs in the end are unsustaining and may, in fact, be corrupt.'

Boland has tried to distinguish between the genuinely political poem and the poem that is merely a public statement: 'If a poet does not tell the truth about time, his or her work will not survive it. . . . [Eventually] I would learn that it was far more difficult to make myself the political subject of my own poems than to see the metaphoric possibilities in front of me in a suburban dusk.' As she looked out her upstairs suburban window, she realized: 'I was entering a place of force. Just by trying to record the life I lived in the poem I wrote, I had become a political poet . . . . I spoke with the ordinary fractured speech of a woman living in a Dublin suburb, whose claims to visionary experience would be sooner made on behalf of a child or a tree than a century of struggle. I was a long way from what [the nineteenth-century Irish poet, Thomas] Davis thought of as a national poet. And yet my relation to the national poem—as its object, its past—was integral and forceful and ominous. . . . The more I thought of it, the more it seemed to me that in Ireland the political poem and the public poem should not always be one and the same. On the contrary, given the force of the national tradition, the political poem stood in urgent need of a subversive experience to lend it true perspective and authority. An authority which, in my view, could be guaranteed only by an identity—and this included a sexual identity—which the poetic tradition, and the structure of the Irish poem, had almost stifled.'

Boland's revolutionary poetics demand the overthrow of the imperial, omniscient (and usually male) voice that comments upon events without entering into them, without questioning its own relation to those events: 'I do not believe the political poem can be written with truth and effect unless the self who writes that poem—a self in which sexuality must be a factor—is seen to be in radical relation to the ratio of power to powerlessness with which the political poem is concerned. . . . The final effect of the political poem depends on whether it is viewed by the reader as an act of freedom or an act of power. This in turn has everything to do with the authority of the speaker. Paradoxically, that authority grows the more the speaker is weakened and made vulnerable by the tensions he or she creates. By the same logic, it is diminished if the speaker protects himself or herself by the powers of language he or she can generate.

'The political poem, in other words, proves in a single genre what is true of all poetry. The mover of the poem's action—the voice, the speaker—must be at the same risk from that action as every other component in the poem. If that voice is exempt, then the reader will hear it as omniscient; if it is omniscient, it can still commend the ratio of power to powerlessness—but with the reduced authority of an observer.'

Boland admires Yeats in his 'Meditations in Time of Civil War', as she admires contemporaries such as Louise Glück and Sharon Olds, for having 'proposed a private world in a political poem'. She observes in her own poems 'that split screen, that half-in-half perspective which is so connected with the act of writing. . . . Writing a poem is so instinctive that it can be almost impossible, in the actual moment, to separate an aesthetic difficulty from a personal limitation.'

ODE TO SUBURBIA

Six o'clock: the kitchen bulbs which blister
Your dark, your housewives starting to nose
Out each other's day, the claustrophobia
Of your back gardens varicose
With shrubs, make an ugly sister
Of you suburbia.

How long ago did the glass in your windows subtly
Silver into mirrors which again
And again show the same woman
Shriek at a child, which multiply
A dish, a brush, ash,
The gape of a fish

In the kitchen, the gape of a child in the cot?
You swelled so that when you tried
The silver slipper on your foot,
It pinched your instep and the common
Hurt which touched you made
You human.

No creatures of your streets will feel the touch
Of a wand turning the wet sinews
Of fruit suddenly to a coach,
While this rat without leather reins
Or a whip or britches continues
Sliming your drains.

No magic here. Yet you encroach until
The shy countryside, fooled
by your plainness falls, then rises

From your bed changed, schooled
Forever by your skill,
Your compromises.

[1975]

ANOREXIC

Flesh is heretic.
My body is a witch.
I am burning it.

Yes I am torching
her curves and paps and wiles.
They scorch in my self denials.

How she meshed my head
in the half-truths
of her fevers

till I renounced
milk and honey
and the taste of lunch.

I vomited
her hungers.
Now the bitch is burning.

I am starved and curveless.
I am skin and bone.
She has learned her lesson.

Thin as a rib
I turn in sleep.
My dreams probe

a claustrophobia
a sensuous enclosure.
How warm it was and wide

once by a warm drum,
once by the song of his breath
and in his sleeping side.

Only a little more,
only a few more days
sinless, foodless,

I will slip
back into him again
as if I had never been away.

Caged so
I will grow
angular and holy

past pain,
keeping his heart
such company

as will make me forget
in a small space
the fall

into forked dark,
into python needs
heaving to hips and breasts
and lips and heat
and sweat and fat and greed.

[1980]

MASTECTOMY

My ears heard
their words.
I didn't believe them.

No, even through my tears
they couldn't deceive me.
Even so

I could see
through them
to the years

opening
their arteries
fields gulching

into trenches,
cuirasses stenching,
a mulch of heads

and towns
as prone
to bladed men

as women.
How well
I recognized

the specialist
freshing death
across his desk.

the surgeon,
blade-handed,
standing there

urging patience.
How well
they have succeeded!

I have stopped bleeding.
I look down.
It has gone.

So they have taken off
what slaked them first,
what they have hated since:

blue-veined
white-domed
home

of wonder
and the wetness
of their dreams.

I flatten
to their looting,
to the sleight

of their plunder.
I am a brute site.
Theirs is the true booty.

[1980]

MISE EIRE

I won't go back to it—

my nation displaced
into old dactyls,
oaths made
by the animal tallows
of the candle—

land of the Gulf Stream,
the small farm,
the scalded memory,
the songs
that bandage up the history,
the words
that make a rhythm of the crime

where time is time past.
A palsy of regrets.
No. I won't go back.
My roots are brutal:

I am the woman—
a sloven's mix
of silk at the wrists,
a sort of dove-strut
in the precincts of the garrison—

who practises
the quick frictions,
the rictus of delight
and gets cambric for it,
rice-coloured silks.

I am the woman
in the gansy-coat
on board the 'Mary Belle',
in the huddling cold,

holding her half-dead baby to her
as the wind shifts East
and North over the dirty
water of the wharf

mingling the immigrant
guttural with the vowels
of homesickness who neither
knows nor cares that

a new language
is a kind of scar
and heals after a while
into a passable imitation
of what went before.

[1987]

The Black Lace Fan My Mother Gave Me

It was the first gift he ever gave her,
buying it for five francs in the Galeries
in pre-war Paris. It was stifling.
A starless drought made the nights stormy.

They stayed in the city for the summer.
They met in cafés. She was always early.
He was late. That evening he was later.
They wrapped the fan. He looked at his watch.

She looked down the Boulevard des Capucines.
She ordered more coffee. She stood up.
The streets were emptying. The heat was killing.
She thought the distance smelled of rain and lightning.

These are wild roses, appliqued on silk by hand,
darkly picked, stitched boldly, quickly.
The rest is tortoiseshell and has the reticent,
clear patience of its element. It is

a worn-out, underwater bullion and it keeps,
even now, an inference of its violation.
The lace is overcast as if the weather
it opened for and offset had entered it.

The past is an empty café terrace.
An airless dusk before thunder. A man running.
And no way now to know what happened then—
none at all—unless, of course, you improvise:

The blackbird on this first sultry morning,
in summer, finding buds, worms, fruit,
feels the heat. Suddenly she puts out her wing—
the whole, full, flirtatious span of it.

[1990]

MIDNIGHT FLOWERS

I go down step by step.
The house is quiet, full of trapped heat and sleep.
In the kitchen everything is still.
Nothing is distinct; there is no room to speak of.

I could be undone every single day by
paradox or what they call in the countryside
blackthorn winter,
when hailstones come with the first apple blossom.

I turn a switch and the garden grows.
A whole summer's work in one instant!
I press my face to the glass. I can see
shadows of lilac, of fuchsia; a dark likeness of blackcurrant:

little clients of suddenness, how sullen they are at
the margins of the light.
They need no rain, they have no roots.
I reach out a hand; they are gone.

When I was a child a snapdragon was
held an inch from my face. Look, a voice said, this
is the colour of your hair. And there it was, my head,
a pliant jewel in the hands of someone else.

[1990]

LAVA CAMEO

(A brooch carved on volcanic rock)

I like this story—

My grandfather was a sea-captain.
My grandmother always met him when his ship docked.
She feared the women at the ports—

except that it is not a story,
more a rumour or a folk memory,
something thrown out once in a random conversation;
a hint merely.

If I say wool and lace for her skirt and
crêpe for her blouse
in the neck of which is pinned a cameo,
carved out of black, volcanic rock;

if I make her pace the Cork docks, stopping
to take down her parasol as a gust catches
the silk tassels of it—

then consider this:

there is a way of making free with the past,
a pastiche of what is
real and what is
not, which can only be
justified if you think of it

not as sculpture but syntax:

a structure extrinsic to meaning which uncovers
the inner secret of it.

She will die at thirty-one in a fever ward.
He will drown nine years later in the Bay of Biscay.
They will never even be
sepia, and so I put down

the gangplank now between the ship and the ground.
In the story, late afternoon has become evening.
They kiss once, their hands touch briefly.
Please.

Look at me, I want to say to her: show me
the obduracy of an art which can
arrest a profile in the flux of hell.

Inscribe catastrophe.

[1994]

TIME AND VIOLENCE

The evening was the same as any other.
I came out and stood on the step.
The suburb was closed in the weather

of an early spring and the shallow tips
and washed-out yellows of narcissi
resisted dusk. And crocuses and snowdrops.

I stood there and felt the melancholy
of growing older in such a season,
when all I could be certain of was simply

in this time of fragrance and refrain,
whatever else might flower before the fruit,
and be renewed, I would not. Not again.

A car splashed by in the twilight.
Peat smoke stayed in the windless
air overhead and I might have missed it:

a presence. Suddenly. In the very place
where I would stand in other dusks, and look
to pick out my child from the distance,

was a shepherdess, her smile cracked,
her arm injured from the mantelpieces
and pastorals where she posed with her crook.

Then I turned and saw in the spaces
of the night sky constellations appear,
one by one, over roof-tops and houses,

and Cassiopeia trapped: stabbed where
her thigh met her groin and her hand
her glittering wrist, with the pin-point of a star.

And by the road where rain made standing
pools of water underneath cherry trees,
and blossoms swam on their images,

was a mermaid with invented tresses,
her breasts printed with the salt of it and all
the desolation of the North Sea in her face.

I went nearer. They were disappearing.
Dusk had turned to night but in the air—
did I imagine it?—a voice was saying:

This is what language did to us. Here
is the wound, the silence, the wretchedness
of tides and hillsides and stars where

we languish in a grammar of sighs,
in the high-minded search for euphony,
in the midnight rhetoric of poesie.

We cannot sweat here. Our skin is icy.
We cannot breed here. Our wombs are empty.
Help us to escape youth and beauty.

Write us out of the poem. Make us human
in cadences of change and mortal pain
and words we can grow old and die in.

[1994]

ROBERT BLY (b. 1926)

Robert Bly was born in Madison, Maine, served in the military 1944-46, and attended St Olaf College, taking his B.A. (1950) at Harvard University and M.A. (1956) at the University of Iowa. For years he edited Fifties (then Sixties, Seventies, and Eighties) Press and magazine from his home at Moose Lake, Maine, and conducted writing workshops, publishing his first solo book, *Silence in the Snowy Fields*, in 1962. He has published more than thirty volumes of poems, including *Light Around the Body* (1967), *The Teeth Mother Naked At Last* (1971), *Sleepers Joining Hands* (1973), *The Man in the Black Coat Turns* (1981), *Selected Poems* (1986), and *What Have I Ever Lost By Dying?: Collected Poems* (1992); at least fifteen anthologies; and thirty-odd books of translations of the works of Georg Trakl, Cesar Vallejo, Knut Hamsen, Pablo Neruda, Tomas Tranströmer, Bashō, Federico García Lorca, Antonio Machado, and Rumi. His non-fiction writings include *Talking All Morning: Collected Conversations and Interviews* (1980), *The Eight Stages of Translation* (1986), *American Poetry: Wildness and Domesticity* (1990), and *Iron John: A Book About Men* (1990).

In a *New York Times Book Review* article (quoted in the reference book *Contemporary Authors*), Bly described once meeting a poet and being startled to discover that poems were written by living beings. 'One day while studying a Yeats poem I decided to write poetry the rest of my life.' He also said: 'I recognized that a single short poem has room for history, music, psychology, religious thought, mood, occult speculation, character and events of one's own life. I still feel surprised that such various substances can find shelter and nourishment in a poem.'

While his first book was nature-centred, his second, *Light Around the Body*, was deeply infused with his outrage against the American war in Vietnam and it won the 1968 National Book Award. Although he was active in the anti-war movement and its publications (*Writers Take Sides Against Vietnam*), the political thrust of Bly's work soon shifted from the social to the psychological realm and continued in that direction, leading directly to his work with Michael Reade and James Hillman in the men's movement, the central concern of which has been to help men get in touch with their repressed masculinity—a process that involves, ironically, not endorsing macho values, but tapping inner strengths, including an awareness of the feminine, the *anima*.

In an interview with Ekbert Faas in *Towards A New American Poetics* (1979), Robert Bly rejects what he calls the infantilism of much contemporary art that substitutes flow, spontaneity, process, and 'the primitive' for substance, design, discipline: 'The tendency now is for everything in art to break the link with the adult energy of the unconscious, if you can say such a thing, and instead to proceed back towards the crib. . . . If the infantilism continues, all the things [D.H.] Lawrence stood for will be destroyed. . . . The sense of adulthood is weak with us; it is stronger in the European psyche, and even more so in the Chinese. They imagine adulthood as the ability to balance *yin* and *yang*.' These comments reflect Bly's dissatisfaction with what may be a Freudian over-emphasis on childhood as the source of all trauma and psychic patterning. Bly advocated, instead, a rigorous questioning of developmental theories, and such aesthetic spin-offs as Beat and surrealist poetry, in favour of a poetics that will lead to psychic healing.

In 'Reflections on the Origins of Poetic Form' (*A Field Guide to Contemporary Poetics*, edited by Stuart Freibert and David Young, 1980), Bly agreed with Donald Hall's hypothesis that some of the pleasures, or sensualities, of poetic form are deeply rooted in our physical nature, perhaps connecting with our earliest memories of pleasure in the womb, at the breast, with learning to speak or to co-ordinate our movements. However, he rejected the usual implications of such a view. While aspects of form may have their roots in infancy, he argued, content does not. Countering Robert Creeley's statement that 'form is merely an extension of content', Bly insisted that 'Form and content are magnetic opposites. . . . The form pole pulls the poem back then toward infancy, the content pole pulls it forward into adulthood. Adulthood seems to be the recognition that there are others in the universe besides you, greater causes and greater beings. The poem surely needs character—the drive forward into experiences—probably embodying pain—that the infant never dreams of in his crib.'

Thus the importance of Bly's championing of the 'image' and its roots in Romanticism, which Gregory Orr (in *Of Solitude and Silence: Writings on Robert Bly*, edited by Richard Jones and Kate Daniels, 1981) described as 'a naïve and necessary affirmation of the symbolic imagination that structures lyric poetry'. Most often Bly's poetry is associated with the notion of *deep image*—images that are archetypal, rooted in the subconscious or the so-called 'collective unconscious'. But in 'Craft Interview' (*Talking All Morning*, 1980), he speaks of imagery as more mysterious even than archetype: 'Let's imagine a poem as if it were an animal. When animals run, they have considerable flowing rhythms. Also they have bodies. An image is simply a body where psychic energy is free to move around. Psychic energy can't move well in a non-image statement. . . [such as] "The politician must have a clear mental grasp of his constituency." Now it has no imagery to speak of, and there's no living psychic energy moving through it. An image is not anything unusual. It is simply language used in such a way that the psychic energy can continue its flow.' Convinced of the sensual, and sensory, basis of poetry, Bly argues that the strongest images usually depend on 'an intermingling of several senses'.

'I don't believe in craft as a static discipline,' Bly says, 'but I do believe in hard work, and in a growth, as if by evolution, of poetry, which each poet lives through during the decades he is alive, whether he wants to or not, and which he can further or not, as he wishes.' While he has little use for end-rhyme, which he says lost its purpose after people stopped singing poems, Bly makes a strong case for the internal workings of sound in a poem. 'Whenever you want the intensity to increase—whenever the intensity does increase in human speech, it always turns out that there's some repetition of sound going on. It's no use to try to break the process down too carefully. It's just something that you notice happens. Then if you try to *gain* the intensity by *making* the sound repeat—that's backward. Anyway, the idea is that assonance and all these things are helpful precisely because the psyche is interested in them. People do them naturally unless it's forbidden.'

Instead of being overly concerned with the mechanics of craft, Bly argues that the poet has bigger fish to fry: 'Hard work in a poet means inner psychic labour, what Tranströmer calls "working on himself".'

DRIVING TOWARD THE LAC QUI PARLE RIVER

I

I am driving; it is dusk; Minnesota.
The stubble field catches the last growth of sun.
The soybeans are breathing on all sides.
Old men are sitting before their houses on car seats
In the small towns. I am happy,
The moon rising above the turkey sheds.

II

The small world of the car
Plunges through the deep fields of the night,
On the road from Willmar to Milan.
This solitude covered with iron
Moves through the fields of night
Penetrated by the noise of crickets.

III

Nearly to Milan, suddenly a small bridge,
And water kneeling in the moonlight.
In small towns the houses are built right on the ground;
The lamplight falls on all fours on the grass.
When I reach the river, the full moon covers it.
A few people are talking, low, in a boat.

[1962]

COUNTING SMALL-BONED BODIES

Let's count the bodies over again.

If we could only make the bodies smaller,
the size of skulls,
we could make a whole plain white with skulls in the moonlight.

If we could only make the bodies smaller,
maybe we could fit
a whole year's kill in front of us on a desk.

If we could only make the bodies smaller,
we could fit
a body into a finger ring, for a keepsake forever.

[1967]

DRIVING THROUGH MINNESOTA DURING THE HANOI BOMBINGS

We drive between lakes just turning green;
Late June. The white turkeys have been moved
A second time to new grass.
How long the seconds are in great pain!
Terror just before death,
Shoulders torn, shot
From helicopters. 'I saw the boy
being tortured with a telephone generator,'
The sergeant said.
'I felt sorry for him
And blew his head off with a shotgun.'
These instants become crystals,
Particles
The grass cannot dissolve. Our own gaiety
Will end up
In Asia, and you will look down in your cup
And see
Black Starfighters.
Our own cities were the ones we wanted to bomb!

Therefore we will have to
Go far away
To atone
For the suffering of the stringy-chested
And the short rice-fed ones, quivering
In the helicopter like wild animals,
Shot in the chest, taken back to be questioned.

[1967]

THE DEAD SEAL

1

Walking north toward the point, I come on a dead seal. From a few feet away, he looks like a brown log. The body is on its back, dead only a few hours. I stand and look at him. There's a quiver in the dead flesh: My God, he's still alive. And a shock goes through me, as if a wall of my room had fallen away.

His head is arched back, the small eyes closed; the whiskers sometimes rise and fall. He is dying. This is the oil. Here on its back is the oil that heats our houses so efficiently. Wind blows fine sand back toward the ocean. The flipper near me lies folded over the stomach, looking like an unfinished arm, lightly glazed with sand at the edges. The other flipper lies half underneath. And the seal's skin looks like an old overcoat, scratched here and there—by sharp mussel shells maybe.

I reach out and touch him. Suddenly he rears up, turns over. He gives three cries: Awaark! Awaark! Awaark!—like the cries from Christmas toys. He lunges toward me; I am terrified and leap back, though I know there can be no teeth in that jaw. He starts flopping toward the sea. But he falls over, on his face. He does not *want* to go back to the sea. He looks up at the sky, and he looks like an old lady who has lost her hair. He puts his chin back down on the sand, rearranges his flippers, and waits for me to go. I go.

2

The next day I go back to say goodbye. He's dead now. But he's not. He's a quarter mile farther up the shore. Today he is thinner, squatting on his stomach, head out. The ribs show more: each vertebra on the back under the coat is visible, shiny. He breathes in and out.

A wave comes in, touches his nose. He turns and looks at me—the eyes slanted; the crown of his head looks like a boy's leather jacket bending over some bicycle bars. He is taking a long time to die. The whiskers white as porcupine quills, the forehead slopes. . . . Goodbye, brother; die in the sound of waves. Forgive us if we have killed you. Long live your race, your inner-tube race, so uncomfortable on land, so comfortable in the ocean. Be comfortable in death then, when the sand will be out of your nostrils, and you can swim in long loops through the pure death, ducking under as assassinations break above you. You don't want to be touched by me. I climb the cliff and go home the other way.

[1975]

FINDING THE FATHER

My friend, this body offers to carry us for nothing—as the ocean carries logs. So on some days the body wails with its great energy; it smashes up the boulders, lifting small crabs, that flow around the sides.

Someone knocks on the door. We do not have time to dress. He wants us to go with him through the blowing and rainy streets, to the dark house.

We will go there, the body says, and there find the father whom we have never met, who wandered out in a snowstorm the night we were born, and who then lost his memory, and has lived since longing for his child, whom he saw only once . . . while he worked as a shoemaker, as a cattle herder in Australia, as a restaurant cook who painted at night.

When you light the lamp you will see him. He sits there behind the door . . . the eyebrows so heavy, the forehead so light . . . lonely in his whole body, waiting for you.

[1977]

FIFTY MALES SITTING TOGETHER

After a long walk in the woods clear cut for lumber,
lit up by a few young pines,
I turn home,
drawn to water. A coffinlike band
softens half the lake,
draws the shadow
down from westward hills.
It is a massive
masculine shadow,
fifty males sitting together
in hall or crowded room,
lifting something indistinct
up into the resonating night.

Sunlight kindles the water still free of shadow,
kindles it till it glows with the high
pink of wounds.
Reeds stand about in groups
unevenly as if they might
finally ascend
to the sky all together!
Reeds protect
the band near shore.
Each reed has its own thin
thread of darkness inside;
it is relaxed and rooted in the black
mud and snail shells under the sand.

The woman stays in the kitchen, and does not want
to waste fuel by lighting a lamp,
as she waits
for the drunk husband to come home.
Then she serves him
food in silence.
What does the son do?
He turns away,
loses courage,
goes outdoors to feed with wild
things, lives among dens
and huts, eats distance and silence;
he grows long wings, enters the spirals, ascends.

How far he is from working men when he is done!
From all men! The males singing
chant far out
on the water grounded in downward shadow.
He cannot go there because
he has not grieved
as humans grieve. If someone's
head was cut
off, whose was it?
The father's? Or the mother's? Or his?
The dark comes down slowly, the way
snow falls, or herds pass a cave mouth.
I look up at the other shore; it is night.

[1981]

Snowbanks North of the House

Those great sweeps of snow that stop suddenly six feet from the house . . .
Thoughts that go so far.
The boy gets out of high school and reads no more books;
the son stops calling home.
The mother puts down her rolling pin and makes no more bread.
And the wife looks at her husband one night at a party and loves him no
    more.
The energy leaves the wine, and the minister falls leaving the church.
It will not come closer—
the one inside moves back, and the hands touch nothing, and are safe.

And the father grieves for his son, and will not leave the room where the
    coffin stands;
he turns away from his wife, and she sleeps alone.

And the sea lifts and falls all night; the moon goes on through the
    unattached heavens alone.
And the toe of the shoe pivots
in the dust. . . .
The man in the black coat turns, and goes back down the hill.
No one knows why he came, or why he turned away, and did not
    climb the hill.

[1981]

In Rainy September

In rainy September, when leaves grow down to the dark,
I put my forehead down to the damp, seaweed-smelling sand.
The time has come. I have put off choosing for years,
perhaps whole lives. The fern has no choice but to live;
for this crime it receives earth, water, and night.

We close the door. 'I have no claim on you.'
Dusk comes. 'The love I have had with you is enough.'
We know we could live apart from one another.
The sheldrake floats apart from the flock.
The oaktree puts out leaves alone on the lonely hillside.

Men and women before us have accomplished this.
I would see you, and you me, once a year.
We would be two kernels, and not be planted.
We stay in the room, door closed, lights out.
I weep with you without shame and without honour.

[1985]

WINTER POEM

The quivering wings of the winter ant
wait for lean winter to end.
I love you in slow, dim-witted ways,
hardly speaking, one or two words only.

What caused us each to live hidden?
A wound, the wind, a word, a parent.
Sometimes we wait in a helpless way,
awkwardly, not whole and not healed.

When we hid the wound, we fell back
from a human to a shelled life.
Now we feel the ant's hard chest,
the carapace, the silent tongue.

This must be the way of the ant,
the winter ant, the way of those
who are wounded and want to live:
to breathe, to sense another, and to wait.

[1985]

WHAT WE PROVIDE

Every breath taken in by the man
who loves, and the woman who loves,
goes to fill the water tank
where the spirit horses drink.

[1985]

THE HORSE OF DESIRE

'Yesterday I saw a face
that gave off light.'
I wrote that the first time
I saw you; now the lines
written that morning
are twenty years old.
What is it that
we see and don't see?

When a horse swings
his head, how easily
his shoulders follow.
When the right thing happens,
the whole body knows.
The road covered with stones
turns to a soft river
moving among reeds.

I love you in those reeds,
and in the bass
quickening there.
My love is in the demons
gobbling the waters,
my desire in their swollen
foreheads poking
earthward out of the trees.

The bear between my legs
has one eye only,
which he offers
to God to see with.
The two beings below with no
eyes at all love you
with the slow persistent
intensity of the blind.

[1985]

THE MUSHROOM

This white mushroom comes up through the duffy lith on a granite cliff, in a crack that ice has widened. The most delicate light tan, it has the texture of a rubber ball left in the sun too long. To the fingers it feels a little like the tough heel of a foot.

One split has gone deep into it, dividing it into two half-spheres, and through the cut one can peek inside, where the flesh is white and gently naïve.

The mushroom has a traveller's face. We know there are men and women in Old People's Homes whose souls prepare now for a trip, which will also be a marriage. There must be travellers all around supporting us whom we do not recognize. This granite cliff also travels. Do we know more about our wife's journey or our dearest friends' than the journey of this rock? Can we be sure which traveller will arrive first, or when the wedding will be? Everything is passing away except the day of this wedding.

[1990]

DEREK WALCOTT (b. 1930)

Derek Walcott was born in St Lucia. After completing his B.A. at the University of the West Indies in Jamaica in 1953, he taught briefly in St Lucia, Grenada, and Trinidad. With the help of a Rockefeller grant he studied theatre in New York in 1957-58, then returned to the Caribbean, where he founded and ran the Trinidad Theatre Workshop for seventeen years and wrote for *The Trinidad Guardian*. Not surprisingly, he has written and published many plays, including *Dream on Monkey Mountain and Other Plays* (1970). In the mid-1970s, he moved to the US, where he teaches at Boston University. He has won numerous awards and honours, including the Guinness Poetry Award, the Royal Society Heinemann Award, membership in the American Academy and Institute of Arts, and the MacArthur Award, culminating in the Nobel Prize for Literature in 1992. His poetry publications include *In a Green Night: Poems 1948-1960* (1962), *Selected Poems* (1964), *The Castaway and Other Poems* (1965), *Another Life* (1973), *Sea-Grapes* (1976), *The Star-Apple Kingdom* (1979), *The Fortunate Traveller* (1981), *Midsummer* (1984), *Collected Poems: 1948-1984* (1986), *The Arkansas Testament* (1987), and *Omeros* (1990), an epic recounting of personal and Caribbean history using the works of Homer as underpinning and inspiration.

In an essay entitled 'The Figure of Crusoe (1965)', which appeared in *Critical Perspectives on Derek Walcott* (edited by Robert Hamner, 1993), Walcott describes poets as 'nature's idiots. They are inarticulate. They are capable only of speaking in poetry, for the poetic process, in every morning of the poet's life, is an agonizing humiliation of trying to pronounce every word as if he had just learnt it, and was repeating it for the first time. Behind him, of course, is a morphology that comes to life when the word is set down, and when it is pronounced, but all that dead bush of tradition, of naming things anew can only come to life through some spark. It is now unfashionable to call the spark divine. It has been called, through different phases of our evolution, frenzy, imagination, inspiration, or the subconscious or unconscious. Whatever it is, and wherever it comes from, it exists.'

The poetic process may smack of pathos and humiliation, yet it is also strangely noble and arduous. In an interview with Edward Hirsch in 1985 for *The Paris Review*, Walcott speaks of writing poetry as a 'religious calling', 'a sense of gratitude both for what you feel is a gift and for the beauty of the earth, the beauty of life around us'. About the silence and ritual withdrawal that precede the making of a poem, he says: 'What you're taking on is really not a renewal of your identity but actually a renewal of your *anonymity*, so that what's in front of you becomes more important than what you are.' Walcott links his religious background to his practice of poetry: 'There's also a very strong sense of carpentry in Protestantism, in making things simply and in a utilitarian way. At this period of my life and work, I think of myself in a way as a carpenter, as one making frames, simply and well.'

The making of poetry may be a private anguish, but its materials can be as broad as human history. As Walcott makes clear in his Nobel Lecture (reprinted in *Contemporary Literary Criticism* 76, 1992), much of his energy has been directed towards giving imaginative expression to Caribbean experience. 'Antillean art is this restoration of our shattered histories, our shards of vocabulary, our archipelago becoming a synonym for pieces broken off from the original continent.' He also emphasizes the link between poetry and history: 'And this is the exact process of the making of poetry, or what should be called not its making but its remaking, the fragmented memory, the armature that frames the god, even the rite that surrenders it to a final pyre; the god assembled cane by cane, reed by waving reed, line by plaited line, as the artisans of Felicity would erect his holy echo.

'Poetry, which is perfection's sweat but which must seem as fresh as the raindrops on a statue's brow, combines the natural and the marmoreal. It conjugates both tenses simultaneously: the past and the present, if the past is the sculpture and the present the beads of dew or rain on the forehead of the past. There is the buried language and there is the individual vocabulary, and the process of poetry is one of excavation and self-discovery. Tonally the individual voice is a dialect; it shapes its own accent, its own vocabulary and melody in defiance of an imperial concept of language, the language of Ozymandias, libraries and dictionaries, law courts and critics, churches, universities, and political dogma, the diction of institutions. Poetry is an island that breaks away from the main.'

Walcott's manner is anything but minimalist. While he may have learned something about the uses of history from Pound, and have expressed (in 'Islands') a desire 'to write / Verse crisp as sand, clear as sunlight, / Cold as a curled wave, ordinary / As a tumbler of island water', he is too fond of rhetoric and its figures, particularly metaphor, to find permanent anchorage in a poetry pared to the bone. 'I come from a place that likes grandeur,' he tells Hirsch (*The Paris Review*); 'it likes large gestures; it is not inhibited by flourish; it is a rhetorical society; it is a society of physical performance; it is a society of style. . . . I came out of that society of huge gesture. And literature is like that, I mean theatrical literature is like that, whether it's Greek or whatever. The recitation element in poetry is one I hope I never lose because it's an essential part of the voice being asked to perform. If we have poets we're really asking them, "Okay, tell me a poem." Generally, the implication is, "Mutter me a poem." I'm not in that group.'

When asked by Hirsch about a possible tug-of-war between the English language and Creole, or the competing dialects of his West Indian roots, Walcott claims the whole terrain: 'I am primarily, absolutely, a Caribbean writer. The English language is nobody's special property. It is the property of the imagination: it is the property of the language itself. I have never felt inhibited in trying to write as well as the greatest English poets.'

A FAR CRY FROM AFRICA

A wind is ruffling the tawny pelt
Of Africa. Kikuyu, quick as flies,
Batten upon the bloodstreams of the veldt.
Corpses are scattered through a paradise.
Only the worm, colonel of carrion, cries:
'Waste no compassion on these separate dead!'
Statistics justify and scholars seize
The salients of colonial policy.
What is that to the white child hacked in bed?
To savages, expendable as Jews?

Threshed out by beaters, the long rushes break
In a white dust of ibises whose cries
Have wheeled since civilization's dawn
From the parched river or beast-teeming plain.
The violence of beast on beast is read
As natural law, but upright man
Seeks his divinity by inflicting pain.
Delirious as these worried beasts, his wars
Dance to the tightened carcass of a drum,
While he calls courage still that native dread
Of the white peace contracted by the dead.

Again brutish necessity wipes its hands
Upon the napkin of a dirty cause, again
A waste of our compassion, as with Spain,
The gorilla wrestles with the superman.
I who am poisoned with the blood of both,
Where shall I turn, divided to the vein?
I who have cursed

The drunken officer of British rule, how choose
Between this Africa and the English tongue I love?
Betray them both, or give back what they give?
How can I face such slaughter and be cool?
How can I turn from Africa and live?

[1962]

ORIENT AND IMMORTAL WHEAT

The corn was orient and immortal wheat, which never should be reaped, nor was ever sown. I thought it had stood from everlasting to everlasting.
—Traherne, *Centuries of Meditations*

Nature seemed monstrous to his thirteen years.
Prone to malaria, sweating inherent sin,
Absolved in Limacol and evening prayers,
The prodigy, dusk rouging his peaked face,
Studied the swallows stitch the opposing eaves
In repetitions of the fall from grace.
And as a gilding silence flushed the leaves,
Hills, roofs, and yards with his own temperature,
He wept again, though why, he was unsure,
At dazzling visions of reflected tin.
So heaven is revealed to fevered eyes,
So is sin born, and innocence made wise,
By intimations of hot galvanize.

This was the fever called original sin,
Such anthropomorphic love illumines hell,
A charge brought to his Heavenly Father's face
That wept for bat-voiced orphans in the streets
And cripples limping homeward in weak light,
When the lamplighter, his head swung by its hair,
Meant the dread footfall lumping up the stair:
Maman with soup, perhaps; or it could well
Be Chaos, genderer of Earth, called Night.

[1962]

ISLANDS

[for Margaret]

Merely to name them is the prose
Of diarists, to make you a name
For readers who like travellers praise
Their beds and beaches as the same;
But islands can only exist
If we have loved in them. I seek,
As climate seeks its style, to write
Verse crisp as sand, clear as sunlight,
Cold as the curled wave, ordinary
As a tumbler of island water;
Yet, like a diarist, thereafter
I savour their salt-haunted rooms
(Your body stirring the creased sea
Of crumpled sheets), whose mirrors lose
Our huddled, sleeping images,
Like words which love had hoped to use
Erased with the surf's pages.

So, like a diarist in sand,
I mark the peace with which you graced
Particular islands, descending
A narrow stair to light the lamps
Against the night surf's noises, shielding
A leaping mantle with one hand,
Or simply scaling fish for supper,
Onions, jack-fish, bread, red snapper;
And on each kiss the harsh sea-taste,
And how by moonlight you were made
To study most the surf's unyielding
Patience though it seems a waste.

[1962]

THE CASTAWAY

The starved eye devours the seascape for the morsel
Of a sail.

The horizon threads it infinitely.

Action breeds frenzy. I lie,
Sailing the ribbed shadow of a palm,
Afraid lest my own footprints multiply.

Blowing sand, thin as smoke,
Bored, shifts its dunes.
The surf tires of its castles like a child.

The salt green vine with yellow trumpet-flower,
A net, inches across nothing.
Nothing: the rage with which the sandfly's head is filled.

Pleasures of an old man:
Morning: contemplative evacuation, considering
The dried leaf, nature's plan.

In the sun, the dog's feces
Crusts, whitens like coral.
We end in earth, from earth began.
In our own entrails, genesis.

If I listen I can hear the polyp build,
The silence thwanged by two waves of the sea.
Cracking a sea-louse, I make thunder split.

Godlike, annihilating godhead, art
And self, I abandon
Dead metaphors: the almond's leaf-like heart,

The ripe brain rotting like a yellow nut
Hatching
Its babel of sea-lice, sandfly, and maggot,

That green wine bottle's gospel choked with sand,
Labelled, a wrecked ship,
Clenched sea-wood nailed and white as a man's hand.

[1965]

A MAP OF EUROPE

Like Leonardo's idea
Where landscapes open on a waterdrop
Or dragons crouch in stains,
My flaking wall, in the bright air,
Maps Europe with its veins.

On its limned window ledge
A beer can's gilded rim gleams like
Evening along a Canaletto lake,
Or like that rocky hermitage
Where, in his cell of light, haggard Jerome
Prays that His kingdom come
To the far city.

The light creates its stillness. In its ring
Everything is. A cracked coffee cup,
A broken loaf, a dented urn become
Themselves, as in Chardin,
Or in beer-bright Vermeer,
Not objects of our pity.

In it is no *lacrimae rerum*,
No art. Only the gift
To see things as they are, halved by a darkness
From which they cannot shift.

[1965]

CRUSOE'S ISLAND

I
The chapel's cowbell
Like God's anvil
Hammers ocean to a blinding shield;
Fired, the sea grapes slowly yield
Bronze plates to the metallic heat.

Red, corrugated-iron
Roofs roar in the sun.
The wiry, ribbed air
Above earth's open kiln
Writhes like a child's vision
Of hell, but nearer, nearer.

Below, the picnic plaid
Of Scarborough is spread
To a blue, perfect sky,
Dome of our hedonist philosophy.
Bethel and Canaan's heart
Lies open like a psalm.
I labour at my art.
My father, God, is dead.

Past thirty now I know
To love the self is dread
Of being swallowed by the blue
Of heaven overhead
Or rougher blue below.
Some lesion of the brain
From art or alcohol
Flashes this fear by day:
As startling as his shadow
Grows to the castaway.

Upon this rock the bearded hermit built
His Eden:
Goats, corn crop, fort, parasol, garden,
Bible for Sabbath, all the joys
But one
Which sent him howling for a human voice.
Exiled by a flaming sun
The rotting nut, bowled in the surf,
Became his own brain rotting from the guilt
Of heaven without his kind,
Crazed by such paradisal calm
The spinal shadow of a palm
Built keel and gunwale in his mind.

The second Adam since the fall,
His germinal
Corruption held the seed
Of that congenital heresy that men fail
According to their creed.
Craftsman and castaway,
All heaven in his head,
He watched his shadow pray
Not for God's love but human love instead.

II
We came here for the cure
Of quiet in the whelk's centre,
From the fierce, sudden quarrel,
From kitchens where the mind,
Like bread, disintegrates in water,
To let a salt sun scour
The brain as harsh as coral,
To bathe like stones in wind,
To be, like beast or natural object, pure.

That fabled, occupational
Compassion, supposedly inherited with the gift
Of poetry, had fed
With a rat's thrift on faith, shifted
Its trust to corners, hoarded
Its mania like bread,
Its brain a white, nocturnal bloom
That in a drunken, moonlit room
Saw my son's head
Swaddled in sheets
Like a lopped nut, lolling in foam.

O love, we die alone!
I am borne by the bell
Backward to boyhood
To the grey wood
Spire, harvest and marigold,
To those whom a cruel
Just God could gather
To His blue breast, His beard

A folding cloud,
As He gathered my father.
Irresolute and proud,
I can never go back.

I have lost sight of hell,
Of heaven, of human will,
My skill
Is not enough,
I am struck by this bell
To the root.
Crazed by a racking sun,
I stand at my life's noon,
On parched, delirious sand
My shadow lengthens.

III

Art is profane and pagan,
The most it has revealed
Is what a crippled Vulcan
Beat on Achilles' shield.
By these blue, changing graves
Fanned by the furnace blast
Of heaven, may the mind
Catch fire till it cleaves
Its mould of clay at last.

Now Friday's progeny,
The brood of Crusoe's slave,
Black little girls in pink
Organdy, crinolines,
Walk in their air of glory
Beside a breaking wave;
Below their feet the surf
Hisses like tambourines.

At dusk, when they return
For vespers, every dress
Touched by the sun will burn
A seraph's, an angel's,
And nothing I can learn

From art or loneliness
Can bless them as the bell's
Transfiguring tongue can bless.

[1965]

Sea Grapes

That sail which leans on light,
tired of islands,
a schooner beating up the Caribbean

for home, could be Odysseus,
home-bound on the Aegean;
that father and husband's

longing, under gnarled sour grapes, is
like the adulterer hearing Nausicaa's name
in every gull's outcry.

This brings nobody peace. The ancient war
between obsession and responsibility
will never finish and has been the same

for the sea-wanderer or the one on shore
now wriggling on his sandals to walk home,
since Troy sighed its last flame,

and the blind giant's boulder heaved the trough
from whose groundswell the great hexameters come
to the conclusions of exhausted surf.

The classics can console. But not enough.

[1976]

North and South

Now, at the rising of Venus—the steady star
that survives translation, if one can call this lamp
the planet that pierces us over indigo islands—
despite the critical sand flies, I accept my function
as a colonial upstart at the end of an empire,

a single, circling, homeless satellite.
I can listen to its guttural death rattle in the shoal
of the legions' withdrawing roar, from the raj,
from the Reich, and see the full moon again
like a white flag rising over Fort Charlotte,
and sunset slowly collapsing like the flag.

It's good that everything's gone, except their language,
which is everything. And it may be a childish revenge
at the presumption of empires to hear the worm
gnawing their solemn columns into coral,
to snorkel over Atlantis, to see, through a mask,
Sidon up to its windows in sand, Tyre, Alexandria,
with their wavering seaweed spires through a glass-bottom boat,
and to buy porous fragments of the Parthenon
from a fisherman in Tobago, but the fear exists,
Delenda est Carthago on the rose horizon,

and the side streets of Manhattan are sown with salt,
as those in the North all wait for that white glare
of the white rose of inferno, all the world's capitals.
Here, in Manhattan, I lead a tight life
and a cold one, my soles stiffen with ice
even through woollen socks; in the fenced back yard,
trees with clenched teeth endure the wind of February,
and I have some friends under its iron ground.
Even when spring comes with its rain of nails,
with its soiled ice oozing into black puddles,
the world will be one season older but no wiser.

Fragments of paper swirl round the bronze general
of Sheridan Square, syllables of Nordic tongues
(as an obeah priestess sprinkles flour on the doorstep
to ward off evil, so Carthage was sown with salt);
the flakes are falling like a common language
on my nose and lips, and rime forms on the mouth
of a shivering exile from his African province;
a blizzard of moths whirls around the extinguished lamp
of the Union general, sugary insects crunched underfoot.

You move along dark afternoons where death
entered a taxi and sat next to a friend,
or passed another a razor, or whispered 'Pardon'
in a check-clothed restaurant behind her cough—
I am thinking of an exile farther than any country.
And, in this heart of darkness, I cannot believe
they are now talking over palings by the doddering
banana fences, or that seas can be warm.

How far I am from those cacophonous seaports
built round the single exclamation of one statute
of Victoria Regina! There vultures shift on the roof
of the red iron market, whose patois
is brittle as slate, a grey stone flecked with quartz.
I prefer the salt freshness of that ignorance,
as language crusts and blackens on the pots
of this cooked culture, coming from a raw one;
and these days in bookstores I stand paralyzed

by the rows of shelves along whose wooden branches
the free-verse nightingales are trilling 'Read me! Read me!'
in various metres of asthmatic pain;
or I shiver before the bellowing behemoths
with the snow still falling in white words on Eighth Street,
those burly minds that barrelled through contradictions
like a boar through bracken, or an old tarpon
bristling with broken hooks, or an old stag
spanielled by critics to a crag at twilight,

the exclamation of its antlers like a hat rack
on which they hang their theses. I am tired of words,
and literature is an old couch stuffed with fleas,
of culture stuffed in the taxidermist's hides.
I think of Europe as a gutter of autumn leaves
choked like the thoughts in an old woman's throat.
But she was home to some consul in snow-white ducks
doing out his service in the African provinces,
who wrote letters like this one home and feared malaria
as I mistrust the dark snow, who saw the lances of rain

marching like a Roman legion over the fens.
So, once again, when life has turned into exile,
and nothing consoles, not books, work, music, or a woman,
and I am tired of trampling the brown grass,
whose name I don't know, down an alley of stone,
and I must turn back to the road, its winter traffic,
and others sure in the dark of their direction,
I lie under a blanket on a cold couch,
feeling the flu in my bones like a lantern.

Under the blue sky of winter in Virginia
the brick chimneys flute white smoke through skeletal lindens,
as a spaniel churns up a pyre of blood-rusted leaves;
there is no memorial here to their Treblinka—
as a van delivers from the ovens loaves
as warm as flesh, its brakes jaggedly screech
like the square wheel of a swastika. The mania
of history veils even the clearest air,
the sickly sweet taste of ash, of something burning.

And when one encounters the slow coil of an accent,
reflexes step aside as if for a snake,
with the paranoid anxiety of the victim.
The ghosts of white-robed horsemen float through the trees,
the galloping hysterical abhorrence of my race—
like any child of the Diaspora, I remember this
even as the flakes whiten Sheridan's shoulders,
and I remember once looking at my aunt's face,
the wintry blue eyes, the rusty hair, and thinking

maybe we are part Jewish, and felt a vein
run through this earth and clench itself like a fist
around an ancient roof, and wanted the privilege
to be yet another of the races they fear and hate
instead of one of the haters and the afraid.
Above the spiny woods, dun grass, skeletal trees,
the chimney serenely fluting something from Schubert—
like the wraith of smoke that comes from someone burning—
veins the air with an outcry that I cannot help.

The winter branches are mined with buds,
the fields of March will detonate the crocus,
the olive battalions of the summer woods
will shout orders back to the wind. To the soldier's mind
the season's passage round the pole is martial,
the massacres of autumn sheeted in snow, as
winter turns white as a veterans hospital.
Something quivers in the blood beyond control—
something deeper than our transient fevers.

But in Virginia's woods there is also an old man
dressed like a tramp in an old Union greatcoat,
walking to the music of rustling leaves, and when
I collect my change from a small-town pharmacy,
the cashier's fingertips still wince from my hand
as if it would singe hers—well, yes, *je suis un singe*,
I am one of that tribe of frenetic or melancholy
primates who made your music for many more moons
than all the silver quarters in the till.

[1981]

EARLY POMPEIAN

[for Norline]

Ere Babylon was dust,
The Magus Zoroaster, my dead child,
Met his own image walking in the garden,
That apparition, sole of men, he saw.
—Shelley

I

In the first years, when your hair
was parted severely in the Pompeian style,
you resembled those mosaics
whose round eyes
keep their immortal pinpoints, or were,
in laughing days, black olives on a saucer.

Then, one night, years later,
a flaring torch passed slowly down that wall
and lit them, and it was your turn.
Your girlhood was finished, your sorrows were robing
you with the readiness of woman.

The darkness placed a black shawl around your shoulders,
pointed to a colonnade of torches
like palm trees with their fronds on fire,
pointed out the cold flagstones to the sacrificial basin
where the priest stands with his birth-sword.
You nodded. You began to walk.

Voices stretched out their hands and you stepped from the wall.

Past the lowering eyes of rumours,
past the unblinking stares of the envious,
as, step by step, it faded
behind you, that portrait
with its plum-parted lips,
the skin of pomegranate,
the forehead's blank, unborn bewilderment.
Now you walked in those heel-hollowed steps
in which all of our mothers before us went.

And they led you, pale as the day-delivered moon,
through the fallen white columns of a hospital
to the volcanic bedrock of mud and screams and fire,

into the lava of the damned birth-blood,
the sacrificial gutters,
to where the eye of the stillborn star showed at the end of your road,
a dying star fighting the viruses
of furious constellations,
through the tangled veins, the vineyard of woman's labour,
to a black ditch under the corpuscles of stars,
where the shrunken grape would be born that would not call you mother.

In your noble, flickering gaze there was that which repeated
to the stone you carried
'The hardest times are the noblest, my dead child,'
and the torch passed its flame to your tongue,
your face bronzed in the drenches and fires of your finest sweat.

In their black sockets, the pebbles of your eyes
rattled like dice in the tin cup of the blind Fates.
On the black wings of your screams I watched vultures rise,
the laser-lances of pain splinter on the gods' breastplates.
Your nerve ends screamed like fifes,
your temples repeated a drum,
and your firelit head, in profile, passed other faces
as a funeral ship passes the torch-lit headlands
with its princely freight,
your black hair billowing like dishevelled smoke.

Your eyelids whitened like knuckles gripping
the incomprehensible, vague sills of pain.
The door creaked, groaning open, and in its draft, no, a whirlwind,
the lamp that was struggling with darkness was blown out
by the foul breeze off the amniotic sea.

II
By the black harbour,
the black schooners are tired
of going anywhere; the sea
is black and salt as the mind of a woman after labour.

Child, wherever you are,
I am still your father;
let your small, dead star
rock in my heart's black salt,
this sacrificial basin where I weep;
you passed from a sleep to a sleep
with no pilot, without a light.

Beautiful, black, and salt-warm is the starry night,
the smell off the sea is your mother,
as is this wind that moves in the leaves of the wharf under the pavement
light.

I stare into black water by whose hulls
heaven is rocked like a cradle,
except, except for one extinguished star,
and I think of a hand that stretches out from her bedside for nothing,
and then is withdrawn, remembering where you are.

III
I will let the nights pass,
I shall allow the sun to rise,
I shall let it pass like a torch along a wall
on which there is fadingly set,
stone by fading stone,
the face of an astonished girl, her lips, her black hair parted
in the early Pompeian style.

And what can I write for her
but that when we are stoned with pain,
and we shake our heads wildly from side to side,
saying 'no more,' 'no more again,' to certain things,
no more faith, no more hope, only charity,
charity gives faith and hope much stronger wings.

IV
As for you, little star,
my lost daughter, you are
bent in the shape forever
of a curled seed sailing the earth,
in the shape of one question, a comma
that knows before us whether death
is another birth.
                I had no answer
to that tap-tapping under the dome
of the stomach's round coffin.
I could not guess whether you were calling
to be let in, or to be let go
when the door's groaning blaze
seared the grape-skin
frailty of your eyes crying
against our light, and all that is kin
to the light.

You had sailed without any light
your seven months on the amniotic sea.
You never saw your murderer,
your birth and death giver,
but I will see you everywhere,
I will see you in a boneless
sunbeam that strokes the texture
of things—my arm, the pulseless arm
of an armchair, an iron railing, the leaves
of a dusty plant by a closed door,
in the beams of my own eyes in a mirror.
The lives that we must go on with
are also yours. So I go on
down the apartment steps to the hot
streets of July the twenty-second, nineteen
hundred and eighty, in Trinidad,
amazed that trees are still green
around the Savannah, over the Queen's
Park benches, amazed that my feet can carry
the stone of the earth, the heavier stone of the head,
and I pass through shade where a curled
blossom falls from a black, forked branch
to the asphalt, soundlessly. No cry.
You knew neither this world nor the next,
and, as for us, whose hearts must never harden
against ourselves, who sit on a park bench
like any calm man in a public garden
watching the bright traffic,
we can only wonder why a seed should envy
our suffering, to flower, to suffer,
to die. Gloria, Perdita, I christen
you in the shade, on the bench,
with no hope of the resurrection.
Pardon. Pardon the pride I have taken
in a woman's agony.

[1981]

XV

I can sense it coming from far, too, Maman, the tide
since day has passed its turn, but I still note
that as a white gull flashes over the sea, its underside
catches the green, and I promise to use it later.
The imagination no longer goes as far as the horizon,
but it keeps coming back. At the edge of the water
it returns clean, scoured things that, like rubbish,
the sea has whitened, chaste. Disparate scenes.
The pink and blue chattel houses in the Virgins
in the trade winds. My name caught in
the kernel of my great-aunt's throat.
A yard, an old brown man with a moustache
like a general's, a boy drawing castor-oil leaves in
great detail, hoping to be another Albrecht Dürer.
I have cherished these better than coherence
as the same time for us both, Maman, comes nearer—
the vine leaves medalling an old wire fence
and, in the shade-freckled yard, an old man like a colonel
under the green cannonballs of a calabash.

[1984]

Philip Levine (b. 1928)

Philip Levine was born in Detroit, where he received his formal education in public schools and at Wayne State University, and where he received that deeper, informal education in the back-breaking and soul-destroying labour associated with industrial capitalism that has coloured his life's work. As he explains in 'The Poet in New York and Detroit' (*Brick* 48, Spring 1994), 'No, I was not a young Werther seeking some outlet for my romantic longings for the world. I was a humiliated wage-slave employed by a vast corporation I loathed. The job I worked at each night was difficult, boring, and stupefying, for there in the forge room the noise was oceanic and the heat in our faces ferocious. And the work was dangerous; one older man I worked with lost both hands to a defective drop forge, and within a few hours—after a cursory inspection—the machine was back in operation being tended by another man equally liable to give his body for General Motors.'

As he explains in the same article, Levine's early poetic models included John Keats, from whom he learned 'that Beauty mattered, that it could transform our experience into something worthy, that like love it could redeem our lives', and García

Lorca, who gave him a 'validation of [his] own emotions' and taught him that 'the poet could live in the tiny eye at the centre of chaos and write'. 'Never in poetry written in English had I found,' Levine writes, 'such a direct confrontation of one image with another or heard such violence held in abeyance and enclosed in so perfect a musical form. What in my work had been a chaotic rant was in his a stately threnody circling around a centre of riot.'

In his collection of essays *The Bread of Time* (1994), Levine pays a moving tribute to John Berryman, who was his teacher and mentor at the Iowa Writers' Workshop. While Berryman knew and demanded from his students a full knowledge of, and expertise in, the writing of traditional forms, he advised Levine and his classmates that 'You should always be trying to write a poem you are unable to write, a poem you lack the technique, the language, the courage to achieve. Otherwise you're merely imitating yourself, going nowhere, because that's always easiest.' Levine took Berryman's advice to develop his poetic ear and to learn prosody from masters such as Blake and Milton, from whom Berryman had discovered that 'the key to such rhythmic power is . . . Speed, achieved by means of a complex syntax and radical enjambement. Speed translates always into rhythmic power, and speed is unobtainable in a heavily end-stopped line.'

Levine has lived and taught in Fresno, California, for thirty years and has recently retired from the University of California. His published translations include *Tarumba: The Selected Poems of Jaime Sabines*, edited and translated with Ernesto Trejo (1979), and *Off the Map: Selected Poems of Gloria Fuertes*, edited and translated with Ada Long (1984). He has received many prizes, including the Lenore Marshall Award, the National Book Critics Circle Award, and the American Book Award. Since *On the Edge* (1963), he has published more than a dozen books of poetry, including *Red Dust* (1971), *The Names of the Lost* (1976), *Sweet Will* (1985), *What Work Is* (1991, National Book Award for Poetry), *New Selected Poems* (1993), and *The Simple Truth* (1994, Pulitzer Prize).

For Fran

She packs the flower beds with leaves,
Rags, dampened papers, ties with twine
The lemon tree, but winter carves
Its features on the uprooted stem.

I see the true vein in her neck
And where the smaller ones have broken
Blueing the skin, and where the dark
Cold lines of weariness have eaten

Out through the winding of the bone.
On the hard ground where Adam strayed,
Where nothing but his wants remain,
What do we do to those we need,

To those whose need of us endures
Even the knowledge of what we are?
I turn to her whose future bears
The promise of the appalling air,

My living wife, Frances Levine,
Mother of Theodore, John, and Mark,
Out of whatever we have been
We will make something for the dark.

[1963]

COMING HOME, *DETROIT*, 1968

A winter Tuesday, the city pouring fire,
Ford Rouge sulphurs the sun, Cadillac, Lincoln,
Chevy grey. The fat stacks
of breweries hold their tongues. Rags,
papers, hands, the stems of birches
dirtied with words.
                        Near the freeway
you stop and wonder what came off,
recall the snowstorm where you lost it all,
the wolverine, the northern bear, the wolf
caught out, ice and steel raining
from the foundries in a shower
of human breath. On sleds in the false sun
the new material rests. One brown child
stares and stares into your frozen eyes
until the lights change and you go
forward to work. The charred faces, the eyes
boarded up, the rubble of innards, the cry
of wet smoke hanging in your throat,
the twisted river stopped at the colour of iron.
We burn this city every day.

[1972]

LATE MOON

2 a.m.
December, and still no moon
rising from the river.

My mother
home from the beer garden
stands before the open closet

her hands still burning.
She smooths the fur collar,
the scarf, opens the gloves

crumpled like letters.
Nothing is lost
she says to the darkness, nothing.

The moon finally above the town.
The breathless stacks,
the coal slumps,

the quiet cars
whitened at last.
Her small round hand whitens,

the hand a stranger held
and released
while the Polish music wheezed.

I'm drunk, she says,
and knows she's not. In her chair
undoing brassiere and garters

she sighs
and waits for the need
to move.

The moon descends
in a spasm of silver
tearing the screen door,

the eyes of fire
drown in the still river,
and she's herself.

The little jewels
on cheek and chin
darken and go out,

and in darkness
nothing falls
staining her lap.

[1973]

STARLIGHT

My father stands in the warm evening
on the porch of my first house.
I am four years old and growing tired.
I see his head among the stars,
the glow of his cigarette, redder
than the summer moon riding
low over the old neighbourhood. We
are alone, and he asks me if I am happy.
'Are you happy?' I cannot answer.
I do not really understand the word,
and the voice, my father's voice, is not
his voice, but somehow thick and choked,
a voice I have not heard before, but
heard often since. He bends and passes
a thumb beneath each of my eyes.
The cigarette is gone, but I can smell
the tiredness that hangs on his breath.
He has found nothing, and he smiles
and holds my head with both his hands.
Then he lifts me to his shoulder,
and now I too am there among the stars,
as tall as he. Are you happy? I say.
He nods in answer, Yes! oh yes! oh yes!
And in that new voice he says nothing,
holding my head tight against his head,

his eyes closed up against the starlight,
as though those tiny blinking eyes
of light might find a tall, gaunt child
holding his child against the promises
of autumn, until the boy slept
never to waken in that world again.

[1979]

LOST AND FOUND

A light wind beyond the window,
and the trees swimming
in the golden morning air.
Last night for hours I thought
of a boy lost in a huge city,
a boy in search of someone
lost and not returning. I thought
how long it takes to believe
the simplest facts of our lives—
that certain losses are final,
death is one, childhood another.
It was dark and the house creaked
as though we'd set sail for
a port beyond the darkness.
I must have dozed in my chair
and wakened to see the dim shapes
of orange tree and fig against
a sky turned grey, and a few
doves were moaning from the garden.
The night that seemed so final
had ended, and this dawn becoming
day was changing moment
by moment—for now there
was blue above, and the tall grass
was streaked and blowing, the quail
barked from their hidden nests.
Why give up anything? Someone
is always coming home, turning
a final corner to behold the house
that had grown huge in absence

now dull and shrunken, but the place
where he had come of age, still
dear and like no other. I have
come home from being lost,
home to a name I could accept,
a face that saw all I saw
and broke in a dark room against
a wall that heard all my secrets
and gave nothing back. Now he
is home, the one I searched for.
He is beside me as he always
was, a light spirit that brings
me luck and listens when I speak.
The day is here, and it will last
forever or until the sun fails
and the birds are once again
hidden and moaning, but for now
the lost are found. The sun
has cleared the trees, the wind
risen, and we, father and child
hand in hand, the living and
the dead, are entering the world.

[1979]

Let Me Begin Again

Let me begin again as a speck
of dust caught in the night winds
sweeping out to sea. Let me begin
this time knowing the world is
salt water and dark clouds, the world
is grinding and sighing all night, and dawn
comes slowly and changes nothing. Let
me go back to land after a lifetime
of going nowhere. This time lodged
in the feathers of some scavenging gull
white above the black ship that docks
and broods upon the oily waters of
your harbour. This leaking freighter
has brought a hold full of hayforks

from Spain, great jeroboams of dark
Algerian wine and quill pens that can't
write English. The sailors have stumbled
off toward the bars or the bright houses.
The captain closes his log and falls asleep.
1/10/28. Tonight I shall enter my life
after being at sea for ages, quietly,
in a hospital named for an automobile.
The one child of millions of children
who has flown alone by the stars
above the black wastes of moonless waters
that stretched forever, who has turned
golden in the full sun of a new day.
A tiny wise child who this time will love
his life because it is like no other.

[1979]

THE FOX

I think I must have lived
once before, not as a man or woman
but as a small, quick fox pursued
through fields of grass and grain
by ladies and gentlemen on horseback.
This would explain my nose
and the small dark tufts of hair
that rise from the base of my spine.
It would explain why I am
so seldom invited out to dinner
and when I am I am never
invited back. It would explain
my loathing for those on horseback
in Central Park and how I can
so easily curse them and challenge
the men to fight and why no matter
how big they are or how young
they refuse to dismount,
for at such times, rock in hand,
I must seem demented.
My anger is sudden and total,
for I am a man to whom anger

usually comes slowly, spreading
like a fever along my shoulders
and back and turning my stomach
to a stone, but this fox anger
is lyrical and complete, as I stand
in the pathway shouting and refusing
to budge, feeling the dignity
of the small creature menaced
by the many and larger. Yes,
I must have been that unseen fox
whose breath sears the thick bushes
and whose eyes burn like opals
in the darkness, who humps
and shits gleefully in the horsepath
softened by moonlight and goes on
feeling the steady measured beat
of his fox heart like a wordless
delicate song, and the quick forepaws
choosing the way unerringly
and the thick furred body following
while the tail flows upward,
too beautiful a plume for anyone
except a creature who must proclaim
not ever ever ever
to mounted ladies and their gentlemen.

[1981]

THE VOICE

Small blue flowers like points
of sky were planted to pin
the earth above me, and still
I went on reaching through leaf
and grass blade and the saw-toothed
arms of thistles for the sky
that dozed above my death.
When the first winter came
I slept and wakened in the late March
to hear the flooded fields
singing their hymns to the birds.

The birds returned. And so it was
that I began to learn what changes
I had undergone. Not as in
a sea change had I been pared
down to the white essential
bones, nor did I remain huddled
around the silence after the breath
stormed and collapsed. I was large,
at first a meadow where wild
mustard quivered in warm winds.
Then I slipped effortlessly up
the foothills overlooking
that great awakening valley.
Then it seemed I was neither
the valley below or the peaks above
but a great breathing silence
that turned slowly through darkness
and light, which were the same,
toward darkness and light. I
remember the first time I spoke
in a human voice. I had been
sweeping away the last of sunset
in a small rural town, and I
passed shuddering through a woman
on her solitary way home, her arms
loaded with groceries. She said,
Oh my God! as though she were
lost and frightened, and so I let
the light linger until she found
her door. In truth for a while
I was scared of myself, even
my name scared me, for that's
what I'd been taught, but in
a single round of seasons I saw
no harm could come from me, and now
I embrace whatever pleases me,
and the earth is my one home,
as it always was, the earth
and perhaps some day the sky too
and all the climbing things between.

[1981]

A THEORY OF PROSODY

When Nellie, my old pussy
cat, was still in her prime,
she would sit behind me
as I wrote, and when the line
got too long she'd reach
one sudden black foreleg down
and paw at the moving hand,
the offensive one. The first
time she drew blood I learned
it was poetic to end
a line anywhere to keep her
quiet. After all, many morn-
ings she'd gotten to the chair
long before I was even up.
Those nights I couldn't sleep
she'd come and sit in my lap
to calm me. So I figured
I owed her the short cat line.
She's dead now almost nine years,
and before that there was one
during which she faked attention
and I faked obedience.
Isn't that what it's about—
pretending there's an alert cat
who leaves nothing to chance.

[1988]

WHAT WORK IS

We stand in the rain in a long line
waiting at Ford Highland Park. For work.
You know what work is—if you're
old enough to read this you know what
work is, although you may not do it.
Forget you. This is about waiting,
shifting from one foot to another.
Feeling the light rain falling like mist
into your hair, blurring your vision

until you think you see your own brother
ahead of you, maybe ten places.
You rub your glasses with your fingers,
and of course it's someone else's brother,
narrower across the shoulders than
yours but with the same sad slouch, the grin
that does not hide the stubbornness,
the sad refusal to give in to
rain, to the hours wasted waiting,
to the knowledge that somewhere ahead
a man is waiting who will say, 'No,
we're not hiring today,' for any
reason he wants. You love your brother,
now suddenly you can hardly stand
the love flooding you for your brother,
who's not beside you or behind or
ahead because he's home trying to
sleep off a miserable night shift
at Cadillac so he can get up
before noon to study his German.
Works eight hours a night so he can sing
Wagner, the opera you hate most,
the worst music ever invented.
How long has it been since you told him
you loved him, held his wide shoulders,
opened your eyes wide and said those words,
and maybe kissed his cheek? You've never
done something so simple, so obvious,
not because you're too young or too dumb,
not because you're jealous or even mean
or incapable of crying in
the presence of another man, no,
just because you don't know what work is.

[1991]

GIN

The first time I drank gin
I thought it must be hair tonic.
My brother swiped the bottle
from a guy whose father owned
a drug store that sold booze
in those ancient, honourable days
when we acknowledged the stuff
was a drug. Three of us passed
the bottle around, each tasting
with disbelief. People paid
for this? People had to have
it, the way we had to have
the women we never got near.
(Actually they were girls, but
never mind, the important fact
was their impenetrability.)
Leo, the third foolish partner,
suggested my brother should have
swiped Canadian whiskey or brandy,
but Eddie defended his choice
on the grounds of the expressions
'gin house' and 'gin lane,' both
of which indicated the preeminence
of gin in the world of drinking,
a world we were entering without
understanding how difficult
exit might be. Maybe the bliss
that came with drinking came
only after a certain period
of apprenticeship. Eddie likened
it to the holy man's self-flagellation
to experience the fullness of faith.
(He was very well read for a kid
of fourteen in the public schools.)
So we dug in and passed the bottle
around a second time and then a third,
in the silence each of us expecting
some transformation. 'You get used
to it,' Leo said. 'You don't

like it but you get used to it.'
I know now that brain cells
were dying for no earthly purpose,
that three boys were becoming
increasingly despiritualized
even as they took into themselves
these spirits, but I thought then
I was at last sharing the world
with the movie stars, that before
long I would be shaving because
I needed to, that hair would
sprout across the flat prairie
of my chest and plunge even
to my groin, that first girls
and then women would be drawn
to my qualities. Amazingly, later
some of this took place, but
first the bottle had to be
emptied, and then the three boys
had to empty themselves of all
they had so painfully taken in
and by means even more painful
as they bowed by turns over
the eye of the toilet bowl
to discharge their shame. Ahead
lay cigarettes, the futility
of guaranteed programs of
exercise, the elaborate lies
of conquest no one believed,
forms of sexual torture and
rejection undreamed of. Ahead
lay our fifteenth birthdays,
acne, deodorants, crabs, salves,
butch haircuts, draft registration,
the military and political victories
of Dwight Eisenhower, who brought us
Richard Nixon with wife and dog.
Any wonder we tried gin.

[1991]

THE SIMPLE TRUTH

I bought a dollar and a half's worth of small red potatoes,
took them home, boiled them in their jackets
and ate them for dinner with a little butter and salt.
Then I walked through the dried fields
on the edge of town. In middle June the light
hung on in the dark furrows at my feet,
and in the mountain oaks overhead the birds
were gathering for the night, the jays and mockers
squawking back and forth, the finches still darting
into the dusty light. The woman who sold me
the potatoes was from Poland; she was someone
out of my childhood in a pink spangled sweater and sunglasses
praising the perfection of all her fruits and vegetables
at the road-side stand and urging me to taste
even the pale, raw sweet corn trucked all the way,
she swore, from New Jersey. 'Eat, eat,' she said,
'Even if you don't I'll say you did.'
Some things
you know all your life. They are so simple and true
they must be said without elegance, metre and rhyme,
they must be laid on the table beside the salt shaker,
the glass of water, the absence of light gathering
in the shadows of picture frames, they must be
naked and alone, they must stand for themselves.
My friend Henri and I arrived at this together in 1965
before I went away, before he began to kill himself,
and the two of us to betray our love. Can you taste
what I'm saying? It is onions or potatoes, a pinch
of simple salt, the wealth of melting butter, it is obvious,
it stays in the back of your throat like a truth
you never uttered because the time was always wrong,
it stays there for the rest of your life, unspoken,
made of that dirt we call earth, the metal we call salt,
in a form we have no words for, and you live on it.

[1994]

Margaret Atwood (b. 1939)

'We must resist. We must refuse to disappear,' Margaret Atwood writes in 'Roominghouse, Winter': 'In exile / survival / is the first necessity.' Atwood is profoundly aware of the elements in modern life that conspire to engulf us, to make us disappear physically, psychically, and politically. She has a keen sense of the isolation, or alienation, at the centre of experience: the anguish of thinking individuals, who are separated by their rationality from the objects and events they perceive in the world external to their ego; the feeling of permanent rootlessness or exile that, as Camus argues so eloquently in *The Myth of Sisyphus*, constitutes the Absurd; the basic aggressiveness, the struggle for power or dominance, that permeates all levels of human activity from the sexual to the political.

Atwood is interested primarily in poetry that is affective, like Brecht's poetry and plays—that stimulates a response in the reader. Brecht spoke of a smoking-man's theatre, where members of the audience would stay behind to thrash out the issues being dramatized; in his ideal theatre art would have a revolutionary influence, be a call to arms rather than a cathartic. Atwood's aims are not dissimilar, as she suggests in an interview with Chris Levenson in *Manna* 2 (1972): 'I would say that I don't think what poetry does is express emotion. What poetry does is to evoke emotion from the reader, and that is a very different thing. As someone once said, if you want to express emotion, scream. If you want to evoke emotion it's more complicated.'

Like Brecht, Atwood uses various distancing, or alienating, techniques to stimulate readers' interest and keep their full attention; she is an illusionist who employs perceptual tricks, such as interjecting non sequiturs or offhand comments that distract readers from the apparent content of the poem, or suddenly shifting the point of view in the middle of a poem. Atwood eschews traditional romantic stances and vocabulary except for purposes of parody; instead of lyrical outbursts, displays of auditory and emotional excess, and the use of familiar names or characterization, she depends upon understatement, the creation of a voice that is wry and prosaic, the shock-value of disarming or surreal images. As she explains in the Manna interview: 'There are always concealed magical forms in poetry. By "magic" I mean a verbal attempt to accomplish something desirable. You can take every poem and trace it back to a source in either prayer, curse, charm or incantation—an attempt to make something happen. Do you know anything about autistic children? One of the symptoms of that is they mistake the word for the thing. If they see the word "clock" on the paper they pick it up to see if it ticks. If you write "door" they try to open it. That sort of thing is inherent in language in some funny way and poetry is connected with that at some level.'

Atwood was born in Ottawa and spent a good part of her childhood with her parents in the wilds of northern Quebec. She studied at the University of Toronto and Harvard, travelled widely, and alternated between writing and teaching at various institutions in Canada. She lives in Toronto with novelist Graeme Gibson. Atwood has written several novels, including *The Edible Woman* (1969), *Surfacing* (1972), *Life Before Man* (1979), *Bodily Harm* (1981), *The Handmaid's Tale* (1985), which was made into a movie, *Cat's Eye* (1988), and *The Robber Bride* (1994); numerous books of poetry, including *The Circle Game* (1966, Governor General's Award), *The Animals in That Country* (1968), *The Journals of*

Susanna Moodie (1970), *Power Politics* (1973), *Selected Poems* (1976), *Two-Headed Poems* (1978), *True Stories* (1981), *Interlunar* (1984), *Selected Poems* (1990), and *Morning in the Burned House* (1995); several books of short stories: *Dancing Girls* (1977), *Murder in the Dark* (1983), *Bluebeard's Egg* (1984), *Wilderness Tips* (1991), and *Good Bones* (1992); and two books of criticism: *Survival: A Thematic Guide to Canadian Literature* (1972) and *Second Words: Selected Critical Prose* (1982). She is also editor of *The New Oxford Book of Canadian Verse in English* (1982).

Margaret Atwood: Conversations (1990), edited by E.G. Ingersoll, is the most useful compendium of Atwood's statements about writing. Several of these are included in the Poetics section.

It Is Dangerous to Read Newspapers

While I was building neat
castles in the sandbox,
the hasty pits were
filling with bulldozed corpses

and as I walked to the school
washed and combed, my feet
stepping on the cracks in the cement
detonated red bombs.

Now I am grownup
and literate, and I sit in my chair
as quietly as a fuse

and the jungles are flaming, the under-
brush is charged with soldiers,
the names on the difficult
maps go up in smoke.

I am the cause, I am a stockpile of chemical
toys, my body
is a deadly gadget,
I reach out in love, my hands are guns,
my good intentions are completely lethal.

Even my
passive eyes transmute
everything I look at to the pocked

black and white of a war photo,
how
can I stop myself

It is dangerous to read newspapers.

Each time I hit a key
on my electric typewriter,
speaking of peaceful trees

another village explodes.

[1968]

PROGRESSIVE INSANITIES OF A PIONEER

I
He stood, a point
on a sheet of green paper
proclaiming himself the centre,

with no walls, no borders
anywhere; the sky no height
above him, totally un-
enclosed
and shouted:

Let me out!

II
He dug the soil in rows,
imposed himself with shovels.
He asserted
into the furrows, I
am not random.

The ground
replied with aphorisms:

a tree-sprout, a nameless
weed, words
he couldn't understand.

III
The house pitched
the plot staked
in the middle of nowhere.

At night the mind
inside, in the middle
of nowhere.

The idea of an animal
patters across the roof.

In the darkness the fields
defend themselves with fences
in vain:
        everything
        is getting in.

IV
By daylight he resisted.
He said, disgusted
with the swamp's clamourings and the outbursts
of rocks,

        This is not order
        but the absence
        of order.

He was wrong, the unanswering
forest implied:

        It was
        an ordered absence

V
For many years
he fished for a great vision,
dangling the hooks of sown

roots under the surface
of the shallow earth.

It was like
enticing whales with a bent
pin. Besides he thought

in that country
only the worms were biting.

VI
If he had known unstructured
space is a deluge
and stocked his log house-
boat with all the animals

even the wolves,

he might have floated.

But obstinate he
stated, The land is solid
and stamped,

watching his foot sink
down through stone
up to the knee.

VII
Things
refused to name themselves; refused
to let him name them.

The wolves hunted
outside.

On his beaches, his clearings,
by the surf of under-
growth breaking

at his feet, he foresaw
disintegration
                    and in the end
through eyes

made ragged by his
effort, the tension
between subject and object,

the green
vision, the unnamed
whale invaded.

[1968]

BACKDROP ADDRESSES COWBOY

Starspangled cowboy
sauntering out of the almost-
silly West, on your face
a porcelain grin,
tugging a papier-mâché cactus
on wheels behind you with a string,

you are innocent as a bathtub
full of bullets.

Your righteous eyes, your laconic
trigger-fingers
people the streets with villains:
as you move, the air in front of you
blossoms with targets

and you leave behind you a heroic
trail of desolation:
beer bottles
slaughtered by the side
of the road, bird-
skulls bleaching in the sunset.

I ought to be watching
from behind a cliff or a cardboard storefront
when the shooting starts, hands clasped
in admiration,

but I am elsewhere.

Then what about me

what about the I
confronting you on that border
you are always trying to cross?

I am the horizon
you ride towards, the thing you can never lasso

I am also what surrounds you:
my brain
scattered with your
tincans, bones, empty shells,
the litter of your invasions.

I am the space you desecrate
as you pass through.

[1968]

DEATH OF A YOUNG SON BY DROWNING

He, who navigated with success
the dangerous river of his own birth
once more set forth

on a voyage of discovery
into the land I floated on
but could not touch to claim.

His feet slid on the bank,
the currents took him;
he swirled with ice and trees in the swollen water

and plunged into distant regions,
his head a bathysphere;
through his eyes' thin glass bubbles

he looked out, reckless adventurer
on a landscape stranger than Uranus
we have all been to and some remember.

There was an accident; the air locked,
he was hung in the river like a heart.
They retrieved the swamped body,

cairn of my plans and future charts,
with poles and hooks
from among the nudging logs.

It was spring, the sun kept shining, the new grass
lept to solidity;
my hands glistened with details.

After the long trip I was tired of waves.
My foot hit rock. The dreamed sails
collapsed, ragged.

I planted him in this country
like a flag.

[1970]

You Take My Hand

You take my hand and
I'm suddenly in a bad movie,
it goes on and on and
why am I fascinated

We waltz in slow motion
through an air stale with aphorisms
we meet behind endless potted palms
you climb through the wrong windows

Other people are leaving
but I always stay till the end
I paid my money, I
want to see what happens.

In chance bathtubs I have to
peel you off me
in the form of smoke and melted
celluloid

            Have to face it I'm
finally an addict,
the smell of popcorn and worn plush
lingers for weeks

[1973]

MARRYING THE HANGMAN

She has been condemned to death by hanging. A man may escape this death by becoming the hangman, a woman by marrying the hangman. But at the present time there is no hangman; thus there is no escape. There is only a death, indefinitely postponed. This is not fantasy, it is history.

*

To live in prison is to live without mirrors. To live without mirrors is to live without the self. She is living selflessly, she finds a hole in the stone wall and on the other side of the wall, a voice. The voice comes through darkness and has no face. This voice becomes her mirror.

*

In order to avoid her death, her particular death, with wrung neck and swollen tongue, she must marry the hangman. But there is no hangman, first she must create him, she must persuade this man at the end of the voice, this voice she has never seen and which has never seen her, this darkness, she must persuade him to renounce his face, exchange it for the impersonal mask of death, of official death which has eyes but no mouth, this mask of a dark leper. She must transform his hands so they will be willing to twist the rope around throats that have been singled out as hers was, throats other than hers. She must marry the hangman or no one, but that is not so bad. Who else is there to marry?

*

You wonder about her crime. She was condemned to death for stealing clothes from her employer, from the wife of her employer. She wished to make herself more beautiful. This desire in servants was not legal.

*

She uses her voice like a hand, her voices reaches through the wall, stroking and touching. What could she possibly have said that would have convinced him? He was not condemned to death, freedom awaited him. What was the temptation, the one that worked? Perhaps he wanted to live with a woman whose life he had saved, who had seen down into the earth but had nevertheless followed him back up to life. It was his only chance to be a hero, to one person at least, for if he became the hangman the others would despise him. He was in prison for wounding another man, on one finger of the right hand, with a sword. This too is history.

*

My friends, who are both women, tell me their stories, which cannot be believed and which are true. They are horror stories and they have not happened to me, they have not yet happened to me, they have happened to me but we are detached, we watch our unbelief with horror. Such things cannot happen to us, it is afternoon and these things do not happen in the afternoon. The trouble was, she said, I didn't have time to put my glasses on and without them I'm blind as a bat, I couldn't even see who it was. These things happen and we sit at a table and tell stories about them so we can finally believe. This is not fantasy, it is history, there is more than one hangman and because of this some of them are unemployed.

*

He said: the end of walls, the end of ropes, the opening of doors, a field, the wind, a house, the sun, a table, an apple.

She said: nipple, arms, lips, wine, belly, hair, bread, thighs, eyes, eyes.

They both kept their promises.

*

The hangman is not such a bad fellow. Afterwards he goes to the refrigerator and cleans up the leftovers, though he does not wipe up what he accidentally spills. He wants only the simple things: a chair, someone to pull off his shoes, someone to watch him while he talks, with admiration and fear, gratitude if possible, someone in whom to plunge himself for rest and renewal. These things can best be had by marrying a woman who has been condemned to death by other men for wishing to be beautiful. There is a wide choice.

*

Everyone said he was a fool.
Everyone said she was a clever woman.
They used the word *ensnare*.

*

What did they say the first time they were alone together in the same room? What did he say when she had removed her veil and he could see that she was not a voice but a body and therefore finite? What did she say when she discovered that she had left one locked room for another? They talked of love, naturally, though that did not keep them busy forever.

*

The fact is there are no stories I can tell my friends that will make them feel better. History cannot be erased, although we can soothe ourselves by speculating about it. At that time there were no female hangmen. Perhaps there have never been any, and thus no man could save his life by marriage. Though a woman could, according to the law.

*

He said: foot, boot, order, city, fist, roads, time, knife.

She said: water, night, willow, rope hair, earth belly, cave, meat, shroud, open, blood.

They both kept their promises.

In eighteenth-century Quebec the only way for someone under sentence of death to escape hanging was, for a man, to become a hangman, or, for a woman, to marry one. Françoise Laurent, sentenced to hang for stealing, persuaded Jean Corolère, in the next cell, to apply for the vacant post of executioner, and also to marry her.

[1978]

NOTES TOWARDS A POEM THAT CAN NEVER BE WRITTEN

For Carolyn Forché

I
This is the place
you would rather not know about,
this is the place that will inhabit you,
this is the place you cannot imagine,
this is the place that will finally defeat you

where the word *why* shrivels and empties
itself. This is famine.

II
There is no poem you can write
about it, the sandpits
where so many were buried
& unearthed, the unendurable
pain still traced on their skins.

This did not happen last year
or forty years ago but last week.
This has been happening,
this happens.

We make wreaths of adjectives for them,
we count them like beads,
we turn them into statistics & litanies
and into poems like this one.

Nothing works.
They remain what they are.

III
The woman lies on the wet cement floor
under the unending light,
needle marks on her arms put there
to kill the brain
and wonders why she is dying.

She is dying because she said.
She is dying for the sake of the word.
It is her body, silent
and fingerless, writing this poem.

IV
It resembles an operation
but it is not one

nor despite the spread legs, grunts
& blood, is it a birth.

Partly it's a job
partly it's a display of skill
like a concerto.

It can be done badly
or well, they tell themselves.

Partly it's an art.

V
The facts of this world seen clearly
are seen through tears;
why tell me then
there is something wrong with my eyes?

To see clearly and without flinching,
without turning away,
this is agony, the eyes taped open
two inches from the sun.

What is it you see then?
Is it a bad dream, a hallucination?
Is it a vision?
What is it you hear?

The razor across the eyeball
is a detail from an old film.
It is also a truth.
Witness is what you must bear.

VI
In this country you can say what you like
because no one will listen to you anyway,
it's safe enough, in this country you can try to write
the poem that can never be written,
the poem that invents
nothing and excuses nothing,
because you invent and excuse yourself each day.

Elsewhere, this poem is not invention.
Elsewhere, this poem takes courage.
Elsewhere, this poem must be written
because the poets are already dead.

Elsewhere, this poem must be written
as if you are already dead,
as if nothing more can be done
or said to save you.

Elsewhere you must write this poem
because there is nothing more to do.

[1981]

Morning in the Burned House

In the burned house I am eating breakfast.
You understand: there is no house, there is no breakfast,
yet here I am.

The spoon which was melted scrapes against
the bowl which was melted also.
No one else is around.

Where have they gone to, brother and sister,
mother and father? Off along the shore,
perhaps. Their clothes are still on the hangers,

their dishes piled beside the sink,
which is beside the woodstove
with its grate and sooty kettle,

every detail clear,
tin cup and rippled mirror.
The day is bright and songless,

the lake is blue, the forest watchful.
In the east a bank of cloud
rises up silently like dark bread.

I can see the swirls in the oilcloth,
I can see the flaws in the glass,
those flares where the sun hits them.

I can't see my own arms and legs
or know if this is a trap or blessing,
finding myself back here, where everything

in this house has long been over,
kettle and mirror, spoon and bowl,
including my own body,

including the body I had then,
including the body I have now
as I sit at this morning table, alone and happy,

bare child's feet on the scorched floorboards
(I can almost see)
in my burning clothes, the thin green shorts

and grubby yellow T-shirt
holding my cindery, non-existent,
radiant flesh. Incandescent.

[1995]

GALWAY KINNELL (b. 1927)

Galway Kinnell was born in Providence, Rhode Island, and completed a B.A. at Princeton in 1948 and an M.A. at the University of Rochester in l949. In addition to serving in the US Navy, 1945-46, he has taught and been poet-in-residence at various universities in Chicago, Iran, Grenoble, Colorado, Portland, California, Hawaii, Australia, and Ohio. He divides his time between Vermont and New York, where he holds the title of Erich Maria Remarque Professor of Creative Writing at New York University. He has won numerous grants and awards, including the National Arts and Letters Award, two Guggenheim Fellowships, a Rockefeller Foundation grant, and a MacArthur Fellowship, as well as the American Book Award for Poetry and the Pulitzer Prize for Poetry. He has published more than eighteen books, including the novel *Black Light* (1966), the non-fiction work *Walking Down the Stairs: Selections from Interviews* (1978), and the children's book *How the Alligator Missed Breakfast*

(1982); his poetry publications include *What a Kingdom It Was* (1960), *Flower Herding on Mount Monadnock* (1964), *Body Rags* (1968), *First Poems 1946-1954* (1971), *The Book of Nightmares* (1971), *The Avenue Bearing the Initial of Christ into the New World: Poems 1946-1965* (1974), *Mortal Acts, Mortal Words* (1980), *Selected Poems* (1982), *The Past* (1985), *When One Has Lived a Long Time Alone* (1992), and *Imperfect Thirst* (1994).

In *Walking Down the Stairs*, Kinnell says very little about the specifics of craft, focusing instead on what he considers deeper matters: 'I don't think the term "form" should be applied only to such things as stanzas of uniform size, rhyme schemes, metrical patterns, and so on—elements which may be regarded as external trappings. I think form properly speaking also has to do with the inner shape of the poem.'

Kinnell seems more comfortable discussing general issues, such as the poet in society and the role of the self. His one extended essay in this direction, 'Poetry, Personality and Death' (*A Field Guide to Contemporary Poetry and Poetics*, edited by Stuart Friebert and David Young, 1980), addresses the death of the self, which he considers essential in art as in life. In his view, the poet must struggle against the 'self-absorbed, closed ego . . . the neurotic burden which to some degree cripples us all. I mean that ego which separates us from the life of the planet, which keeps us apart from one another, which makes us feel self-conscious, inadequate, lonely, suspicious, possessive, jealous, awkward, fearful, and hostile; which thwarts our deepest desire, which is to be one with all creation. . . . Our alienation is in proportion to our success in subjugating it. The more we conquer nature, the more nature becomes our enemy, and since we are, like it or not, creatures of nature, the more we make an enemy of the very life within us.'

Does this mean we should view him as a nature poet? 'As for the term "nature", I think we have to revise our understanding of it in regard to poetry. The "nature poem" as opposed to, say, the poem of society or the urban poem, doesn't have much future—and not much past, for that matter—we have to get over that notion we carry from the Old Testament on down that we are super beings created in God's image to have dominion over everything else—over "nature". We have to feel our own evolutionary roots, and know that we belong to life in the same way as do the other animals and the plants and stones. Then a nature poem wouldn't be a matter of English gardens, of hedgerows and flowers. It would include the city too: if the beaver dam is a work of nature, so is the city a work of nature. The real nature poem will not exclude man and deal only with animals and plants and stones; it will be a poem in which we men re-feel in ourselves our own animal and plant and stone life, our own deep connection with all other beings, a connection deeper than personality, a connection which resembles the attachment an animal has for an animal. We're going toward that sense of ourselves and we're going away from it simultaneously. Now, for the first time in a long time, there is a kind of countermotion toward the natural, toward connection with the life of the planet' (from an interview in *The Poet's Craft*).

Although he finds inspiration in lyric masters such as Whitman, Keats, Clare, Rilke, and Yeats, Kinnell feels that the use of a *persona* sometimes diminishes the poem's power: 'A *persona* has its uses, and also its dangers. In theory, it would be a way to get past the self, to dissolve the barrier between poet and reader. Writing in the voice of another, the poet would open himself to that person. All that would be required would be for the reader to make the same act of sympathetic identification, and, in the *persona*, poet and reader would meet as one. Of course, for the poem to be interesting, the *persona* would have to represent a central facet of the poet's self; the kind of thing Browning's dramatic monologues do very well, prose fiction does much better.'

Kinnell believes there is a transcendent strain of poetry afoot that attempts to escape the closed ego, to reintegrate us with life; in this poetry, which he associates with D.H. Lawrence, Allen Ginsberg (particularly 'Howl'), Gary Snyder, John Logan, and James Wright, the 'poet seeks an inner liberation by going so deeply into himself—into the worst of himself as well as the best—that he suddenly finds he is everyone.' Kinnell speaks of a 'union deeper than personality', where 'separate egos vanish'; 'the death of the self I seek, in poetry and out of poetry, is not a drying up or withering. It is a death, yes, but a death out of which one might hope to be reborn more giving, more alive, more open, more related to the natural life.'

In a second essay, 'The Poetics of the Physical World', Kinnell claims that 'the subject of the poem is the thing which dies', a fascinating statement that not only signals his preoccupation with human and animal mortality, but also suggests, ironically, that it is the *forms* we make to celebrate the living and the dead that endure. For surely Kinnell's strengths as a lyric poet reside less in his theories than in his linguistic playfulness, his ear for the rhythms of ordinary speech, and his remarkable gift of metaphor, which celebrates 'lips blowsy with kisses' and, with a nod to Wordsworth's infant 'trailing clouds of glory,' offers us the 'celestial cheesiness' of the newborn.

FIRST SONG

Then it was dusk in Illinois, the small boy
After an afternoon of carting dung
Hung on the rail fence, a sapped thing
Weary to crying. Dark was growing tall
And he began to hear the pond frogs all
Calling on his ear with what seemed their joy.

Soon their sound was pleasant for a boy
Listening in the smoky dusk and the nightfall
Of Illinois, and from the fields two small
Boys came bearing cornstalk violins
And they rubbed the cornstalk bows with resins
And the three sat there scraping of their joy.

It was now fine music the frogs and the boys
Did in the towering Illinois twilight make
And into dark in spite of a shoulder's ache
A boy's hunched body loved out of a stalk
The first song of his happiness, and the song woke
His heart to the darkness and into the sadness of joy.

[1960]

THE BEAR

1
In late winter
I sometimes glimpse bits of steam
coming up from
some fault in the old snow
and bend close and see it is lung-coloured
and put down my nose
and know
the chilly, enduring odour of bear.

2
I take a wolf's rib and whittle
it sharp at both ends
and coil it up
and freeze it in blubber and place it out
on the fairway of the bears.

And when it has vanished
I move out on the bear tracks,
roaming in circles
until I come to the first, tentative, dark
splash on the earth.

And I set out
running, following the splashes
of blood wandering over the world.
At the cut, gashed resting places
I stop and rest,
at the crawl-marks
where he lay out on his belly
to overpass some stretch of bauchy ice
I lie out
dragging myself forward with bear-knives in my fists.

3
On the third day I begin to starve,
at nightfall I bend down as I knew I would
at a turd sopped in blood,

and hesitate, and pick it up,
and thrust it in my mouth, and gnash it down,
and rise
and go on running.

4
On the seventh day,
living by now on bear blood alone,
I can see his upturned carcass far out ahead, a scraggled,
steamy hulk,
the heavy fur riffling in the wind.

I come up to him
and stare at the narrow-spaced, petty eyes,
the dismayed
face laid back on the shoulder, the nostrils
flared, catching
perhaps the first taint of me as he
died.

I hack
a ravine in his thigh, and eat and drink,
and tear him down his whole length
and open him and climb in
and close him up after me, against the wind,
and sleep.

5
And dream
of lumbering flatfooted
over the tundra,
stabbed twice from within,
splattering a trail behind me,
splattering it out no matter which way I lurch,
no matter which parabola of bear-transcendence,
which dance of solitude I attempt,
which gravity-clutched leap,
which trudge, which groan.

6

Until one day I totter and fall—
fall on this
stomach that has tried so hard to keep up,
to digest the blood as it leaked in,
to break up
and digest the bone itself: and now the breeze
blows over me, blows off
the hideous belches of ill-digested bear blood
and rotted stomach
and the ordinary, wretched odour of bear,

blows across
my sore, lolled tongue a song
or screech, until I think I must rise up
and dance. And I lie still.

7

I awaken I think. Marshlights
reappear, geese
come trailing again up the flyway.
In her ravine under old snow the dam-bear
lies, licking
lumps of smeared fur
and drizzly eyes into shapes
with her tongue. And one
hairy-soled trudge stuck out before me,
the next groaned out,
the next,
the next,
the rest of my days I spend
wandering: wondering
what, anyway,
was that sticky infusion, that rank flavour of blood, that poetry, by
which I lived?

[1968]

UNDER THE MAUD MOON

1
On the path,
by this wet site
of old fires—
black ashes, black stones, where tramps
must have squatted down,
gnawing on stream water,
unhouseling themselves on cursed bread,
failing to get warm at a twigfire—

I stop,
gather wet wood,
cut dry shavings, and for her,
whose face
I held in my hands
a few hours, whom I gave back
only to keep holding the space where she was,

I light
a small fire in the rain.

The black
wood reddens, the deathwatches inside
begin running out of time, I can see
the dead, crossing limbs
longing again for the universe, I can hear
in the wet wood the snap
and re-snap of the same embrace being torn.

The raindrops trying
to put the fire out
fall into it and are
changed: the oath broken,
the oath sworn between earth and water, flesh and spirit, broken,
to be sworn again,
over and over, in the clouds, and to be broken again,
over and over, on earth.

2

I sit a moment
by the fire, in the rain, speak
a few words into its warmth—
stone saint smooth stone—and sing
one of the songs I used to croak
for my daughter, in her nightmares.

Somewhere out ahead of me
a black bear sits alone
on his hillside, nodding from side
to side. He sniffs
the blossom-smells, the rained earth,
finally he gets up,
eats a few flowers, trudges away,
his fur glistening
in the rain.

The singed grease streams
out of the words, the one
held note
remains—a love-note
twisting under my tongue, like the coyote's bark,
curving off, into a
howl.

3

A round-
cheeked girlchild comes awake
in her crib. The green
swaddlings tear open,
a filament or vestment
tears, the blue
flower opens.

And she who is born,
she who sings and cries,
she who begins the passage, her hair
sprouting out,
her gums budding for her first spring on earth,

the mist still clinging about
her face, puts
her hand
into her father's mouth, to take hold of
his song.

4
It is all over,
little one, the flipping
and overleaping, the watery
somersaulting alone in the oneness
under the hill, under
the old, lonely bellybutton
pushing forth again
in remembrance,
the drifting there furled in the dark,
pressing a knee or elbow
along a slippery wall, sculpting
the world with each thrash—the stream
of omphalos blood humming all about you.

5
Her head
enters the headhold
which starts sucking her forth: being itself
closes down all over her, gives her
into the shuddering
grip of departure, the slow,
agonized clenches making
the last moulds of her life in the dark.

6
The black eye
opens, the pupil
droozed with black hairs
stops, the chakra
on top of the brain throbs a long moment in world light,

and she skids out on her face into light,
this peck
of stunned flesh

clotted with celestial cheesiness, glowing
with the astral violet
of the underlife. And as they cut

her tie to the darkness
she dies
a moment, turns blue as a coal,
the limbs shaking
as the memories rush out of them. When

they hang her up
by the feet, she sucks
air, screams
her first song—and turns rose,
the slow,
beating, featherless arms
already clutching at the emptiness.

7
When it was cold
on our hillside, and you cried
in the crib rocking
through the darkness, on wood
knifed down to the curve of the smile, a sadness
stranger than ours, all of it
flowing from the other world,

I used to come to you
and sit by you
and sing to you. You did not know,
and yet you will remember,
in the silent zones
of the brain, a spectre, descendant
of the ghostly forefathers, singing
to you in the nighttime—
not the songs
of light said to wave
through the bright hair of angels,
but a blacker
rasping flowering on that tongue.

For when the Maud moon
glimmered in those first nights,
and the Archer lay
sucking the icy biestings of the cosmos,
in his crib of stars,

I had crept down
to riverbanks, their long rustle
of being and perishing, down to marshes
where the earth oozes up
in cold streaks, touching the world
with the underglimmer
of the beginning,
and there learned my only song.

And in the days
when you find yourself orphaned,
emptied
of all wind-singing, of light,
the pieces of cursed bread on your tongue,

may there come back to you
a voice,
spectral, calling you
sister!
from everything that dies.

And then
you shall open
this book, even if it is the book of nightmares.

[1971]

AFTER MAKING LOVE WE HEAR FOOTSTEPS

For I can snore like a bullhorn
or play loud music
or sit up talking with any reasonably sober Irishman
and Fergus will only sink deeper
into his dreamless sleep, which goes by all in one flash,

but let there be that heavy breathing
or a stifled come-cry anywhere in the house
and he will wrench himself awake
and make for it on the run—as now, we lie together,
after making love, quiet, touching along the length of our bodies,
familiar touch of the long-married,
and he appears—in his baseball pajamas, it happens,
the neck opening so small
he has to screw them on, which one day may make him wonder
about the mental capacity of baseball players—
and flops down between us and hugs us and snuggles himself to sleep,
his face gleaming with satisfaction at being this very child.

In the half darkness we look at each other
and smile
and touch arms across his little, startlingly muscled body—
this one whom habit of memory propels to the ground of his making,
sleeper only the mortal sounds can sing awake,
this blessing love gives again into our arms.

[1980]

When One Has Lived a Long Time Alone

1

When one has lived a long time alone,
one refrains from swatting the fly
and lets him go, and one hesitates to strike
the mosquito, though more than willing to slap
the flesh under her, and one lifts the toad
from the pit too deep to hop out of
and carries him to the grass, without minding
the poisoned urine he slicks his body with,
and one envelops, in a towel, the swift
who fell down the chimney and knocks herself
against window glass and releases her outside
and watches her fly free, a life line flung at reality,
when one has lived a long time alone.

2
When one has lived a long time alone,
one grabs the snake behind the head
and holds him until he stops trying to stick
the orange tongue—which splits at the end
into two black filaments and jumps out
like a fire-eater's belches and has little
in common with the pimpled pink lump that shapes
sounds and sleeps inside the human mouth—
into one's flesh, and clamps it between his jaws,
letting the gaudy tips show, as children do
when concentrating, and as very likely
one does oneself, without knowing it,
when one has lived a long time alone.

3
When one has lived a long time alone,
among regrets so immense the past occupies
nearly all the room there is in consciousness,
one notices in the snake's eyes, which look back
without giving any less attention to the future,
the first coating of the opaque, milky-blue
leucoma snakes get when about to throw their skins
and become new—meanwhile continuing,
of course, to grow old—the same *bleu passé*
that bleaches the corneas of the blue-eyed
when they lie back at the end and look for heaven,
a fading one knows means they will never find it
when one has lived a long time alone.

4
When one has lived a long time alone,
one holds the snake near the loudspeaker disgorging
gorgeous sound and watches him crook
his forepart into four right angles,
as though trying to slow down the music
flowing through him, in order to absorb it
like milk of paradise into the flesh,
until a glimmering appears at his mouth,

such a drop of intense fluid as, among humans,
could form after long exciting at the tip
of the penis, and as he straightens himself out
he has the pathos one finds in the penis,
when one has lived a long time alone.

5

When one has lived a long time alone,
one falls to poring upon a creature,
contrasting its eternity's-face to one's own
full of hours, taking note of each difference,
exaggerating it, making it everything,
until the other is utterly other, and then,
with hard effort, possibly with tongue sticking out,
going back over each difference once again
and cancelling it, seeing nothing now
but likeness, until . . . half an hour later
one starts awake, taken aback at how eagerly
one drops off into the happiness of kinship,
when one has lived a long time alone.

6

When one has lived a long time alone
and listens at morning to mourning doves
sound their kyrie eleison, or the small thing
spiritualized upon a twig cry, 'pewit-phoebe!'
or at midday grasshoppers scratch the thighs'
needfire awake, or peabody birds send schoolboys'
whistlings across the field, and at dusk, undamped,
unforgiving chinks, as from marble cutters' chisels,
or at nightfall polliwogs just burst into frogs
raise their ave verum corpus—listens to those
who hop or fly call down upon us the mercy
of other tongues—one hears them as inner voices,
when one has lived a long time alone.

7

When one has lived a long time alone,
one knows that consciousness consummates,
and as the conscious one among these others

uttering their compulsory cries of being here—
the least flycatcher witching up 'che-bec!'
or red-headed woodpecker clanging out his music
from a metal drainpipe, or ruffed grouse drumming
'thrump thrump thrump thrump-thrump-
thrump-thrump-rup-rup-rup-rup-rup-r-r-r-r-r-r'
deep in the woods, all of them in time's unfolding
trying to cry themselves into self-knowing—
one knows one is here to hear them into shining,
when one has lived a long time alone.

8
When one has lived a long time alone,
one likes alike the pig, who brooks no deferment
of gratification, and the porcupine, or thorned pig,
who enters the cellar but not the house itself
because of eating down the cellar stairs on the way up,
and one likes the worm, who by bunching herself together
and expanding works her way through the ground,
no less than the butterfly, who totters full of worry
among the day lilies, as they darken,
and more and more one finds one likes
any other species better than one's own,
which has gone amok, making one self-estranged,
when one has lived a long time alone.

9
When one has lived a long time alone,
sour, misanthropic, one fits to one's defiance
the satanic boast, *It is better to reign*
in hell than to submit on earth, and forgets
one's kind—the way by now the snake does,
who stops trying to get to the floor and lingers
all across one's body, slumping into its contours,
adopting its temperature—and abandons hope
of the sweetness of friendship or love,
before long can barely remember what they are,
and covets the stillness in inorganic matter,
in a self-dissolution one may not know how to halt,
when one has lived a long time alone.

10

When one has lived a long time alone,
and the hermit thrush calls and there is an answer,
and the bullfrog head half out of water repeats
the sexual cantillations of his first spring,
and the snake lowers himself over the threshold
and disappears among the stones, one sees
they all live to mate with their kind, and one knows,
after a long time of solitude, after the many steps taken
away from one's kind, toward the kingdom of strangers,
the hard prayer inside one's own singing
is to come back, if one can, to one's own,
a world almost lost, in the exile that deepens,
when one has lived a long time alone.

11

When one has lived a long time alone,
one wants to live again among men and women,
to return to that place where one's ties with the human
broke, where the disquiet of death and now also
of history glimmers its firelight on faces,
where the gaze of the new baby looks past the gaze
of the great granny, and where lovers speak,
on lips blowsy from kissing, that language
the same in each mouth, and like birds at daybreak
blether the song that is both earth's and heaven's,
until the sun has risen, and they stand
in a halo of being made one: kingdom come,
when one has lived a long time alone.

[1990]

PATRICK LANE (b. 1939)

Patrick Lane was born in Nelson, British Columbia. While doing his poetic apprenticeship, he worked in sawmills, logging, and construction, in the interior and on the coast. With bill bissett and Seymour Mayne, he ran Very Stone House in transit from the back of a series of Volkswagen vans, publishing Pat Lowther and other West Coast poets. Eventually his travels took him farther afield, to South America, China, and Europe. He has been writer-in-residence at the Concordia, Manitoba, and Alberta universities and currently lives in Saanichton on Vancouver Island with his partner Lorna Crozier, teaching part-time at the University of Victoria. His publications include *Letters from A Savage Mind* (1966), *The Sun Has Begun to Eat the Mountain* (1972), *Passing into Storm* (1973), *Beware the Months of Fire* (1974), *Unborn Things: South American Poems* (1975), *Albino Pheasants* (1977), *Poems New & Selected* (1978, Governor General's Award), *Old Mother* (1982), *Selected Poems* (1989), *Mortal Remains* (1991), and *Too Spare, Too Fierce* (1995).

Although his statements on poetics are limited in number, Lane wrote an essay entitled 'To the Outlaw', published in John Gill's *New: American & Canadian Poetry* (1971), that includes this claim: 'A poet is neither trained nor taught. He is an outlaw surging beyond the only freedom he knows, beauty in bondage. . . The poem is a place of beauty that goes beyond knowledge and understanding.' This Romantic stance, which identifies the poet as an outsider, a priestly keeper of the mysteries in exile, drew Lane initially to the theory and practice of poets such as the Chilean Pablo Neruda, who advocates 'A poetry impure as the clothing we wear, soup-stained, soiled with our shameful behaviour, our wrinkles and vigils and dreams. . . .'

This view, which informs much of Lane's work, is most evident in the early poems about violence, poverty, unemployment, cultural displacement, betrayal, backroom abortions, and genocide. The principal mode in his earliest work is that of the truncated narrative, or anecdote, in which an experiential moment is suspended in time, rendered permanent by the poet's imaging power and sense of measure. By avoiding superficial moralizing or generalization and by letting the material speak for itself, Lane has unsettled some readers and critics, who accuse him unfairly of wallowing in human suffering. He reminds us that he is not the author of human misery, only its witness.

In an essay called 'The Poet' (*Transitions III: Poetry*, edited by Edward Peck, 1978), Lane expresses his need 'to articulate our civilization's century of destruction', which he describes as a living inferno of murder, greed, and rampant self-interest. Against this violence, he says, poetry is 'a fragility bordering on madness. . . but not madness as the caricatures would have it. . . occupiers of rubber rooms in happy farms . . . not that but rather the stress of knowing. . . of having partaken of the mystery and the consequent loneliness and terrible fear resulting from that risk.' The 'forgotten things', which include our art and gods—our human potential—may still be glimpsed if we listen to the poets, through whose 'pain and clarity' we 'participate in that seeing and accept the risk of the human comedy'.

Beauty and fragility are key considerations in Lane's work, because poetry transfigures reality, however painful, gives it the shape and meaning that make it endurable. If, as Pound suggested, technique is one test of a poet's sincerity, the delicacy, precision, and evocativeness of Lane's work testify to his seriousness. His poems have moved, simultaneously, both deeper into the psyche and further afield historically, fusing the personal and the collective. In an interview with Alan Twigg in *Strong Voices* (1988), he talks about some of the stages in his work: 'Then in the late seventies my writing changed again. At the end of all those books I had nothing left. It was like I was a musician looking around to make a new piece of music. A new symphony. God, what'll I do? I explored for four or five years. . . . Perhaps I've become more obscure. I don't know. I don't even think that I'm writing for an audience any more. . . . I'm writing for those people who really are interested in the kind of density that poetry can offer.'

Lane has little use for postmodernism and deconstructionism, which he considers 'a small dance step on the side' of the history of poetry, but he acknowledges the important role that women writers have played in recent poetic developments. He also tries to shake off delusions about his own achievement as a poet: 'I think there's about ten or twelve poems in there [*Selected Poems*] that are really good. You can't touch them. You can't take a word out or put a word in. The making of a beautiful thing. It's an act of great privilege. It's a great high for me.' Echoing Yeats's famous line, 'a terrible beauty is born', Lane says to Twigg: 'There's a terrible patience in writing. Just as there's a terrible patience in most human relationships. I used to worry. But I don't attack myself about it anymore. I'm willing to wait. I've realized, for one thing, that so much of writing is physical. You have to get your body geared up for it. It's like setting yourself up for the Olympics, right? You've got five years to get your body tuned perfectly. Maybe you'll win a medal. Maybe you'll even get to cry. But it's really for the enlightening moment of the performance that you do it. If you're a skier you mostly like the feeling of going down the hill. It's perfect and you think, "Goddam. Five years to get here." For me, poetry's the same thing.'

Much of his success, Lane willingly acknowledges, comes from the synchronicity of his own efforts and his country's willingness to fund the writing of poetry. 'You've got to invest in R & D. . . . That's how we measure civilization. The great plays and poetry of Greece were found on bits of parchment or a few discarded shards of goddam goatskin. Our society will be measured the same way.'

Ten Miles in from Horsefly

Ten miles in from Horsefly
shoulders sore from my pack
feet blistered I asked for
and got a job cleaning a barn
for the price of a meal
and the promise I could sleep
outside the unseasonal rain
and worked like a damn
as digger flies took chunks
of meat from my arms
and mosquitoes sucked my blood.

No one knows how far an hour goes
or how short are the days.
Shovelling ten months of shit
from a barn clears your head
and allows you to look forward
to sleep without fear or favour
from old sad dreams of enemies
and friends. Just to have one moment
with shoulders clear of weight
and feet braced finally still
as you come breathless
to the clear hard boards below.

[1969]

ELEPHANTS

The cracked cedar bunkhouse
hangs behind me like a grey pueblo
in the sundown where I sit
to carve an elephant
from a hunk of brown soap
for the Indian boy who lives
in the village a mile back
in the bush.

The alcoholic truck-driver
and the cat-skinner sit beside me
with their eyes closed
all of us waiting out the last hour
until we go back on the grade

and I try to forget the forever
clank clank clank
across the grade
pounding stones and earth to powder
for hours in mosquito darkness
of the endless cold mountain night.

The elephant takes form—
my knife caresses smooth soap
scaling off curls of brown
which the boy saves to take home
to his mother in the village

Finished, I hand the carving to him
and he looks at the image of the great
beast for a long time
then sets it on dry cedar
and looks up at me:
What's an elephant?
he asks me
so I tell him of the elephants
and their jungles. The story
of the elephant graveyard
which no one has ever found
and how the silent
animals of the rain forest
go away to die somewhere
in the limberlost of distances
and he smiles

tells me of his father's
graveyard where his people have been
buried for years. So far back
no one remembers when it started
and I ask him where the graveyard is
and he tells me it is gone
now where no one will ever find it
buried under the grade of the new
highway.

[1969]

PASSING INTO STORM

Know him for a white man.
He walks sideways into wind
allowing the left of him

to forget what the right
knows as cold. His ears
turn into death what

his eyes can't see. All day
he walks away from the sun
passing into storm. Do not

mistake him for the howl you hear
or the track you think you
follow. Finding a white man

in snow is to look for the dead.
He has been burned by the wind.
He has left too much

flesh on winter's white metal
to leave his colour as a sign.
Cold white. Cold flesh. He leans

into wind sideways; kills without
mercy anything to the left of him
coming like madness in the snow.

[1973]

MOUNTAIN OYSTERS

Kneeling in the sheep-shit
he picked up the biggest of the new rams
brushed the tail aside
slit the bag
tucked the knackers in his mouth
and clipped the cords off clean

the ram   stiff
with a single wild scream

as the tar went on
and he spit the balls in a bowl.

That's how we used to do it
when I was a boy.

It's no more gawdam painful
than any other way
and you can't have rams fighting
slamming it up every nanny

and enjoyed them with him
cutting delicately
into the deep-fried testicles.

Mountain oysters make you strong

he said
while out in the field
the rams stood holding their pain
legs fluttering like blue hands
of old tired men.

[1971]

STIGMATA

For Irving Layton

What if there wasn't a metaphor
and the bodies were only bodies
bones pushed out in awkward fingers?
Waves come to the seawall, fall away,
children bounce mouths against the stones
man has carved to keep the sea at bay
and women walk with empty wombs
proclaiming freedom to the night.
Through barroom windows rotten with light
eyes of men open and close like fists.

I bend beside a tidal pool and take a crab from the sea.
His small green life twists helpless in my hand
the living bars of bone and flesh
a cage made by the animal I am.

This thing, the beat, the beat of life
now captured in the darkness of my flesh
struggling with claws as if it could tear its way
through my body back to the sea.
What do I know of the inexorable beauty,
the unrelenting turning of the wheel I am inside me?
Stigmata. I hold a web of blood.

I dream of the scrimshawed teeth of endless whales,
the oceans it took to carve them. Drifting ships
echo in fog the wounds of Leviathan
great grey voices giving cadence to their loss.
The men are gone
who scratched upon white bones their destiny.
Who will speak of the albatross in the shroud of the man,
the sailor who sinks forever in the Mindanao Deep?
I open my hand. The life leaps out.

[1977]

ALBINO PHEASANTS

At the bottom of the field
where thistles throw their seeds
and poplars grow from cotton into trees
in a single season I stand among the weeds.
Fenceposts hold each other up with sagging wire.
Here no man walks except in wasted time.
Men circle me with cattle, cars and wheat.
Machines rot on my margins.
They say the land is wasted when it's wild
and offer plows and apple trees to tame
but in the fall when I have driven them away
with their guns and dogs and dreams
I walk alone. While those who'd kill
lie sleeping in soft beds
huddled against the bodies of their wives
I go with speargrass and hooked burrs
and wait upon the ice alone.

Delicate across the mesh of snow
I watch the pale birds come
with beaks the colour of discarded flesh.
White, their feathers are white,
as if they had been born in caves
and only now have risen to the earth
to watch with pink and darting eyes
the slowly moving shadows of the moon.
There is no way to tell men what we do.
The dance they make in sleep
withholds its meaning from their dreams.
That which has been nursed in bone
rests easy upon frozen stone
and what is wild is lost behind closed eyes:
albino birds, pale sisters, succubi.

[1977]

THE CARPENTER

The gentle fears he tells me of being
afraid to climb back down each day
from the top of the unfinished building.
He says: I'm getting old
and wish each morning when I arrive
I could beat into shape
a scaffold to take me higher
but the wood I'd need
is still growing on the hills
the nails raw red with rust
still changing shape in bluffs
somewhere north of my mind.

I've hung over this city like a bird
and seen it change from shacks to towers.
It's not that I'm afraid
but sometimes when I'm alone up here
and know I can't get higher
I think I'll just walk off the edge
and either fall or fly

and then he laughs
so that his plumb-bob goes awry
and single strokes the spikes into the joists
pushing the floor another level higher
like a hawk who every year adds levels to his nest
until he's risen above the tree he builds on
and alone lifts off into the wind
beating his wings like nails into the sky.

[1977]

A Murder of Crows

It is night and somewhere
a tree has fallen across the lines.
There was a time when I would have slept
at the end of the sun and risen with light.
My body knows what I betray.
Even the candle fails, its guttering stub
spitting out the flame. I have struggled
tonight with the poem as never before
wanting to tell you what I know—
what can be said? Words are dark rainbows
without roots, a murder of crows,
a memory of music reduced to guile.
Innocence, old nightmare, drags behind
me like a shadow and today I killed again.

The body hanging down from its tripod.
My knife slid up and steaming ribbons of gut
fell to the ground. I broke the legs
and cut the anus out, stripped off the skin
and chopped the head away; maggots of fat
clinging to the pale red flesh. The death?

If I could tell you the silence
when the body refused to fall
until it seemed the ground reached up
and pulled it down. Then I could tell you
everything: what the grass said
to the crows as they passed over,
the eyes of moss, the histories of stone.

It is night and somewhere
a tree has fallen across the lines.
Everything I love has gone to sleep.
What can be said?
The flesh consumes while in the trees
black birds perch waiting first light.
It is night and mountains
and I cannot tell you what the grass said
to the crows as they passed over
can only say how when I looked
I lost their bodies in the sun.

[1978]

There is a Time

For Robert Kroetsch

There is a time when the world is hard,
the winters cold and a woman
sits before a door, watching through wood
for the arrival of a man. Perhaps a child is ill
and it is not winter after all. Perhaps
the dust settles in a child's breath,
a breath so fragile it barely exists.
Tuberculosis or pneumonia. Perhaps
these words place her there, these words
naming the disease and still not curing it.

Maybe it is not the man she waits for.
We want it to be someone. We want
someone to relieve this hour. On the next farm
the nearest woman to the woman is also sitting
in dust or cold and watching a door. She is no help.
So let it be the man. He is in the barn
watching the breathing of his horses.
They are slow and beautiful,
their breath almost freezing in perfect clouds.
Their harness hanging down from the stalls
gleams, although old and worn. He is old and worn.
The woman is waiting behind the door
but he is afraid to go there because of her eyes
and the child who is dying.

There is a time when it is like this,
when the hours are this cold, when the hours
are no longer than a bit of dust in an eye,
a frozen cloud of breath, a single splinter in a door
large enough to be a life it is so small and perfect.
Perhaps there are soldiers coming from far away,
their buttons dull with dust or bright with cold,
though we cannot imagine why they would come here,
or a storm rolling down from the north
like a millwheel into their lives.

Perhaps it is winter.
There is snow. Or it could be dust.
Maybe there is no child, no man, no woman
and the words we imagined have not been invented
to name the disease there is no child to catch.
Maybe the names were there in a time before them
and they have been forgotten. For now let them die
as we think of them and after they are dead
we will imagine them alive again,
the barn, the breath, the woman, the door.

[1982]

FATHERS AND SONS

I will walk across the long slow grass
where the desert sun waits among the stones
and reach down into the heavy earth
and lift your body back into the day.
My hands will swim down through the clay
like white fish who wander in the pools
of underground caves and they will find you
where you lie in the century of your sleep.

My arms will be as huge as the roots of trees,
my shoulders leaves, my hands as delicate
as the wings of fish in white water.

When I find you I will lift you out
into the sun and hold you
the way a son must who is now
as old as you were when you died.
I will lift you in my arms and bear you back.

My breath will blow away the earth
from your eyes and my lips will touch
your lips. They will say the years have been
long. They will speak into your flesh
the word love over and over,
as if it was the first word of the whole
earth. I will dance with you and you
will be as a small child asleep in my arms
as I say to the sun, bless this man who died.

I will hold you then, your hurt mouth curled
into my chest, and take your lost flesh
into me, make of you myself, and when you are
bone of my bone, and blood of my blood,
I will walk you into the hills and sit
alone with you and neither of us
will be ashamed. My hand and your hand.

I will take those two hands and hold them
together, palm against palm, and lift them
and say, this is praise, this is the holding
that is father and son. This I promise you
as I wanted to have promised in the days
of our silence, the nights of our sleeping.

Wait for me. I am coming across the grass
and through the stones. The eyes
of the animals and birds are upon me.
I am walking with my strength.
See, I am almost there.
If you listen you can hear me.
My mouth is open and I am singing.

[1991]

Seamus Heaney (b. 1939)

Raised on a farm in County Derry, Northern Ireland, Heaney received his B.A. from Queen's University, Belfast, in 1961. He taught in schools and colleges for several years and has been a guest lecturer at Berkeley and Harvard. Since 1972 he has lived principally in the Republic of Ireland. His publications include *Death of a Naturalist* (1966), *Door into the Dark* (1969), *Wintering Out* (1972), *North* (1975), *Field Work* (1979), *Selected Poems 1965-1975* (1980), *Station Island* (1984), *The Haw Lantern* (1987), *Selected Poems: 1966-1987* (1990), and *Seeing Things* (1991). His critical works include *Preoccupations: Selected Prose 1968-1978* (1980) and *The Government of the Tongue* (1990). He has also written a short critical work, *The Fire i' the Flint: Reflections on the Poetry of Gerard Manley Hopkins* (1975). He received the Nobel Prize for Literature in 1995.

In 'Feeling Into Words' (*Preoccupations*), Heaney speaks of poetry 'as a point of entry into the buried life of the feelings or as a point of exit from it.' Much of his work as a poet has been to dig up material from his personal and collective past; this has taken him from grainy close-ups of farm life, as he experienced and remembered it, to symbolic narratives and meditations on the moral and cultural significance of archeological discoveries in the bogs of Ireland and Northern Europe. He believes in 'poetry as divination; poetry as revelation of the self to the self, as restoration of the culture to itself; poems as elements of continuity, with the aura and authenticity of archeological finds, where the buried shard has an importance that is not obliterated by the buried city; poetry as a dig, a dig for finds that end up being plants.'

Much of the power of Heaney's work resides in its sound, in the grunt of his diction and the torque of his syntax. He writes a richly textured verse with great density of sound, which owes as much to the examples of Hopkins, Dylan Thomas, and Ted Hughes as to the Irish contribution to the English language. Not surprisingly, Heaney accepts Rimbaud's notion 'of vowels as colours and poetry as an alchemy of sounds'. The range of his sound is narrower and less multicoloured than that of Yeats or Hopkins; but it is not without power. In fact, Heaney's deliberately blunt rhythms and guttural sounds seem particularly suited to his view of the poetic process and to the rural and subterranean nature of his materials.

In 'The Makings of a Music' (*Preoccupations*), he examines 'the relationship between the almost physiological operations of a poet composing a poem and the music of the finished poem. . . the way that certain postures and motions within the poet's incubating mind affect the posture of the voice and the motion of rhythms in the language of the poem itself.' Looking at the poetry of two famous poets, he suggests that in Wordsworth 'the given line, the phrase of cadence which haunts the ear and the eager parts of the mind. . . the tuning fork to which the whole music of the poem is orchestrated', is characterized by *surrender*, whereas in Yeats the response is characterized by *mastery*: 'the poet seeks to discipline it, to harness its energies in order to drive other parts of his mind into motion. . . .'

Further addressing the question of a poet's music, Heaney acknowledges the importance of experience and tradition: 'Of course, in any poetic music, there will always be two contributory elements. There is that part of the poetry which takes its structure and beat, its play of metre and rhythms, its diction and allusiveness, from the literary tradition. The poetry that Wordsworth and Yeats had read as adolescents and as young men obviously laid down certain structures in their ear, structures that gave them certain kinds of aural expectations for their own writings. And we are all used to the study of this kind of influence: indeed, as T.S. Eliot has attested, we have not developed our taste in poetry until we can recognize with pleasure the way an individual talent has foraged in the tradition. But there is a second element in a poet's music, derived not from the literate parts of his mind but from its illiterate parts, dependent not upon what Jacques Maritain called his "intellectual baggage" but upon what I might call his instinctual ballast. What kinds of noise assuage him, what kinds of music pleasure or repel him, what messages the receiving stations of his senses are happy to pick up from the world around him and what ones they automatically block out—all this unconscious activity, at the pre-verbal level, is entirely relevant to the intonations and appeasements offered by a poet's music.'

Still exploring in 'The Makings of a Music' what he describes in Wordsworth's poetry as 'feeling . . . rendered seismic', Heaney quotes these lines from 'The Prelude': 'My own voice cheered me, and, far more, the mind's / Internal echo of the imperfect sound; / To both I listened, drawing from them both / A cheerful confidence in things to come.' 'What we are presented with,' Heaney continues, 'is a version of composition as listening, as a wise passiveness, a surrender to energies that spring within the centre of the mind, not composition as an active pursuit by the mind's circumference of something already at the centre.' Yeats, on the other hand, is rhetorical, theatrical, at times strident in his poetic utterances. 'For Yeats, composition was no recollection in tranquillity, not a delivery of the dark embryo, but a mastery, a handling, a struggle towards maximum articulation.' Commenting on Yeats's poem 'The Long-Legged Fly,' Heaney concludes: 'The poem dramatizes concentration brought to the point of consummation. The act of the mind, in Michael Angelo's case, exerts an almost glandular pressure on history and what conducts that pressure is the image in the beholder's eye. In a similar way . . . poetry depends for its continuing efficacy upon the play of sound not only in the ear of the reader but also in the ear of the writer.'

Another 'preoccupation' is explored in 'The Sense of Place', where Heaney distinguishes between the 'lived, illiterate and unconscious' feeling of place and that which is 'learned, literate and conscious'. 'It is this feeling, assenting, equable marriage between the geographical country and the country of the mind, whether that country of the mind takes its tone unconsciously from a shared oral inherited culture, or from a consciously savoured literary culture, or from both, it is this marriage that constitutes the sense of place in its richest possible manifestation.' While admitting 'We are no longer innocent, we are no longer just parishioners of the local', Heaney concludes that a sense of place is central to collective and poetic continuity.

DIGGING

Between my finger and my thumb
The squat pen rests; snug as a gun.
Under my window, a clean rasping sound
When the spade sinks into gravelly ground:
My father, digging. I look down

Till his straining rump among the flowerbeds
Bends low, comes up twenty years away
Stooping in rhythm through potato drills
Where he was digging.

The coarse boot nestled on the lug, the shaft
Against the inside knee was levered firmly.
He rooted out tall tops, buried the bright edge deep
To scatter new potatoes that we picked
Loving their cool hardness in our hands.

By God, the old man could handle a spade.
Just like his old man.

My grandfather cut more turf in a day
Than any other man on Toner's bog.
Once I carried him milk in a bottle
Corked sloppily with paper. He straightened up
To drink it, then fell to right away

Nicking and slicing neatly, heaving sods
Over his shoulder, going down and down
For the good turf. Digging.

The cold smell of potato mould, the squelch and slap
Of soggy peat, the curt cuts of an edge
Through living roots awaken in my head.
But I've no spade to follow men like them.

Between my finger and my thumb
The squat pen rests.
I'll dig with it.

[1966]

DEATH OF A NATURALIST

All year the flax-dam festered in the heart
Of the townland; green and heavy headed
Flax had rotted there, weighted down by huge sods.
Daily it sweltered in the punishing sun.

Bubbles gargled delicately, bluebottles
Wove a strong gauze of sound around the smell.
There were dragon-flies, spotted butterflies,
But best of all was the warm thick slobber
Of frogspawn that grew like clotted water
In the shade of the banks. Here, every spring
I would fill jampotfuls of the jellied
Specks to range on window-sills at home,
On shelves at school, and wait and watch until
The fattening dots burst into nimble-
Swimming tadpoles. Miss Walls would tell us how
The daddy frog was called a bullfrog
And how he croaked and how the mammy frog
Laid hundreds of little eggs and this was
Frogspawn. You could tell the weather by frogs too
For they were yellow in the sun and brown
In rain.

Then one hot day when fields were rank
With cowdung in the grass the angry frogs
Invaded the flax-dam; I ducked through hedges
To a coarse croaking that I had not heard
Before. The air was thick with a bass chorus.
Right down the dam gross-bellied frogs were cocked
On sods; their loose necks pulsed like sails. Some hopped:
The slap and plop were obscene threats. Some sat
Poised like mud grenades, their blunt heads farting.
I sickened, turned, and ran. The great slime kings
Were gathered there for vengeance and I knew
That if I dipped my hand the spawn would clutch it.

[1966]

Mid-Term Break

I sat all morning in the college sick bay
Counting bells knelling classes to a close.
At two o'clock our neighbours drove me home.

In the porch I met my father crying—
He had always taken funerals in his stride—
And Big Jim Evans saying it was a hard blow.

The baby cooed and laughed and rocked the pram
When I came in, and I was embarrassed
By old men standing up to shake my hand

And tell me they were 'sorry for my trouble';
Whispers informed strangers I was the eldest,
Away at school, as my mother held my hand

In hers and coughed out angry tearless sighs.
At ten o'clock the ambulance arrived
With the corpse, stanched and bandaged by the nurses.

Next morning I went up into the room. Snowdrops
And candles soothed the bedside; I saw him
For the first time in six weeks. Paler now,

Wearing a poppy bruise on his left temple,
He lay in the four foot box as in his cot.
No gaudy scars, the bumper knocked him clear.

A four foot box, a foot for every year.

[1966]

PERSONAL HELICON
For Michael Longley

As a child, they could not keep me from wells
And old pumps with buckets and windlasses.
I loved the dark drop, the trapped sky, the smells
Of waterweed, fungus and dank moss.

One, in a brickyard, with a rotted board top.
I savoured the rich crash when a bucket
Plummeted down at the end of a rope.
So deep you saw no reflection in it.

A shallow one under a dry stone ditch
Fructified like any aquarium.
When you dragged out long roots from the soft mulch
A white face hovered over the bottom.

Others had echoes, gave back your own call
With a clean new music in it. And one
Was scaresome for there, out of ferns and tall
Foxgloves, a rat slapped across my reflection.

Now, to pry into roots, to finger slime,
To stare, big-eyed Narcissus, into some spring
Is beneath all adult dignity. I rhyme
To see myself, to set the darkness echoing.

[1966]

Requiem for the Croppies

The pockets of our great coats full of barley—
No kitchens on the run, no striking camp—
We moved quick and sudden in our own country.
The priest lay behind ditches with the tramp.
A people, hardly marching—on the hike—
We found new tactics happening each day:
We'd cut through reins and rider with the pike
And stampede cattle into infantry,
Then retreat through hedges where cavalry must be thrown.
Until, on Vinegar Hill, the fatal conclave.
Terraced thousands died, shaking scythes at cannon.
The hillside blushed, soaked in our broken wave.
They buried us without shroud or coffin
And in August the barley grew up out of the grave.

[1969]

Bogland

For T. P. Flanagan

We have no prairies
To slice a big sun at evening—
Everywhere the eye concedes to
Encroaching horizon,

Is wooed into the cyclops' eye
Of a tarn. Our unfenced country
Is bog that keeps crusting
Between the sights of the sun.

They've taken the skeleton
Of the Great Irish Elk
Out of the peat, set it up
An astounding crate full of air.

Butter sunk under
More than a hundred years
Was recovered salty and white.
The ground itself is kind, black butter

Melting and opening underfoot,
Missing its last definition
By millions of years.
They'll never dig coal here,

Only the waterlogged trunks
Of great firs, soft as pulp.
Our pioneers keep striking
Inwards and downwards,

Every layer they strip
Seems camped on before.
The bogholes might be Atlantic seepage.
The wet centre is bottomless.

[1969]

SUMMER HOME

I
Was it wind off the dumps
or something in heat

dogging us, the summer gone sour,
a fouled nest incubating somewhere?

Whose fault, I wondered, inquisitor
of the possessed air.

To realize suddenly,
whip off the mat

that was larval, moving—
and scald, scald, scald.

II
Bushing the door, my arms full
of wild cherry and rhododendron,
I hear her small lost weeping
through the hall, that bells and hoarsens
on my name, my name.

O love, here is the blame.

The loosened flowers between us
gather in, compose
for a May altar of sorts.
These frank and falling blooms
soon taint to a sweet chrism.

Attend. Anoint the wound.

III
O we tented our wound all right
under the homely sheet

and lay as if the cold flat of a blade
had winded us.

More and more I postulate
thick healings, like now

as you bend in the shower
water lives down the tilting stoups of your breasts.

IV
With a final
unmusical drive
long grains begin
to open and split

ahead and once more
we sap
the white, trodden
path to the heart.

V
My children weep out the hot foreign night.
We walk the floor, my foul mouth takes it out
On you and we lie stiff till dawn
Attends the pillow, and the maize, and vine

That holds its filling burden to the light.
Yesterday rocks sang when we tapped
Stalactites in the cave's old, dripping dark—
Our love calls tiny as a tuning fork.

[1972]

BOG QUEEN

I lay waiting
between turf-face and demesne wall,
between heathery levels
and glass-toothed stone.

My body was braille
for the creeping influences:
dawn suns groped over my head
and cooled at my feet,

through my fabrics and skins
the seeps of winter
digested me,
the illiterate roots

pondered and died
in the cavings
of stomach and socket.
I lay waiting

on the gravel bottom,
my brain darkening,
a jar of spawn
fermenting underground

dreams of Baltic amber.
Bruised berries under my nails,
the vital hoard reducing
in the crock of the pelvis.

My diadem grew carious,
gemstones dropped
in the peat floe
like the bearings of history.

My sash was a black glacier
wrinkling, dyed weaves
and phoenician stitchwork
retted on my breasts'

soft moraines.
I knew winter cold
like the nuzzle of fjords
at my thighs—

the soaked fledge, the heavy
swaddle of hides.
My skull hibernated
in the wet nest of my hair.

Which they robbed.
I was barbered
and stripped
by a turfcutter's spade

who veiled me again
and packed coomb softly
between the stone jambs
at my head and my feet.

Till a peer's wife bribed him.
The plait of my hair,
a slimy birth-cord
of bog, had been cut

and I rose from the dark,
hacked bone, skull-ware,
frayed stitches, tufts,
small gleams on the bank.

[1975]

FROM THE FRONTIER OF WRITING

The tightness and the nilness round that space
when the car stops in the road, the troops inspect
its make and number and, as one bends his face

towards your window, you catch sight of more
on a hill beyond, eyeing with intent
down cradled guns that hold you under cover

and everything is pure interrogation
until a rifle motions and you move
with guarded unconcerned acceleration—

a little emptier, a little spent
as always by that quiver in the self,
subjugated, yes, and obedient.

So you drive on to the frontier of writing
where it happens again. The guns on tripods;
the sergeant with his on-off mike repeating

data about you, waiting for the squawk
of clearance; the marksman training down
out of the sun upon you like a hawk.

And suddenly you're through, arraigned yet freed,
as if you'd passed from behind a waterfall
on the black current of a tarmac road

past armour-plated vehicles, out between
the posted soldiers flowing and receding
like tree shadows into the polished windscreen.

[1987]

MICHAEL ONDAATJE (b. 1943)

Michael Ondaatje spent his first eleven years in Sri Lanka (Ceylon) and was educated in Dulwich, England, before coming in 1963 to Canada, where he studied at Bishop's University, the University of Toronto, and Queen's. His collections of poetry include *The Dainty Monsters* (1967), *The Man with Seven Toes* (1969), *The Collected Works of Billy the Kid* (1970, Governor General's Award), *Rat Jelly* (1973), *There's A Trick With A Knife I'm Learning To Do* (1979, Governor General's Award), and *Secular Love* (1984). He has also made films, written scripts, published a book of criticism of Leonard Cohen's work, and composed two long prose works: *Coming Through Slaughter* (1976), a cross-genre long poem or fiction about the madness and death of jazz musician Buddy Bolden, and *Running in the Family* (1983), a fictionalized biography of his family in Sri Lanka. His first novel, *In the Skin of a Lion*, appeared in 1987; his second, *The English Patient* (1992), won the prestigious Booker Prize for Fiction in the United Kingdom.

Ondaatje's poetry ranges from tender evocations of friendship and domesticity to explosive portrayals of violence and psychic upheaval. This duality is present also in terms of form, in writing that includes conventional lyrics and short narratives rooted in the traditions of formal elegance, as well as aggressive and unstable pieces that push against the limits of established form, threatening to turn into anti-art. In such work Ondaatje expresses the two impulses that Roland Barthes identifies in *The Pleasure of the Text* as being at war in contemporary art: a safe, imitative edge, which treads ground that is familiar, and a subversive edge that is violent, unpredictable, and always moving towards that frontier where 'the death of language is glimpsed'.

In longer poems, such as *The Collected Works of Billy the Kid*, Ondaatje explores and explodes popular myths, ransacks contemporary culture for documents, tales, interviews, jokes, gossip, and ads, and carries on a running battle with the accepted sense of what is 'poetic'. Just as he is drawn to the outlandish, the surreal, and the chaotic as a safeguard against worn-out forms, so, too, he cultivates a music and diction that are slightly off-beat and out-of-kilter. Aspects of the new grammar he seeks may be found in avant-garde cinema, which is fragmentary and discontinuous, or in music, particularly jazz, which is improvisational, pushing the familiar in unexpected directions.

In 'What is in the Pot', an introduction to *The Long Poem Anthology* (1979), Ondaatje talks about dispensing with conventional narrative in favour of poems that are 'personal, transitional, and local'; he selects poets 'who surprise me with their *step*, their process. . . . These poems are not parading down the main street. Some jeer anonymously from the stands, some are written in such frail faint pencil that one can barely hold them, they shift like mercury off the hand. The stories within the poems don't matter, the grand themes don't matter. The movement of the mind and language is what is important. . . . We can come back to these fragile drawings again and again, taking another look, discovering something new, not hearing what we heard the first time we read it. Somehow the poems move when you are not watching so that new objects and tones come into relief. We are not dealing with poetry whose themes are hardened into stone, into a public cultural voice. Between readings the tents are folded and the company moves on. In the daylight sometimes one can hardly see them at all.'

Ondaatje is anything but anxious to talk about the creative process, yet he is an enthusiast for good writing. This shows in his editing of books, including the anthology of Canadian stories *Ink Lake* (1990), his co-editing, with his partner Linda Spalding, of *Brick* magazine, and his championing of the work of writers such as Phyllis Webb, bpNichol, Sharon Thesen, Galway Kinnell, Robert Hass, and Salman Rushdie. Asked once for a prose statement to accompany some of his poems that appeared in *Transitions III* (1978), he replied:

Do we have to talk about this now?

I have absolutely nothing to say about Poetry. Allow it a little room, the freedom of the pie in the face.

Who knows what the next sentence or thought is going to be? What I believed or felt when I wrote these poems is obviously not what I believe or feel now. One little nuance, one little image, and everything changes.

ELIZABETH

Catch, my Uncle Jack said
and oh I caught this huge apple
red as Mrs Kelly's bum.
It's as red as Mrs Kelly's bum, I said
and Daddy roared
and swung me on his stomach with a heave.
Then I hid the apple in my room
till it shrunk like a face
growing eyes and teeth ribs.

Then Daddy took me to the zoo
he knew the man there
they put a snake around my neck
and it crawled down the front of my dress.
I felt its flicking tongue
dripping onto me like a shower.
Daddy laughed and said Smart Snake
and Mrs Kelly with us scowled.

In the pond where they kept the goldfish
Philip and I broke the ice with spades
and tried to spear the fishes;
we killed one and Philip ate it,
then he kissed me
with raw saltless fish in his mouth.

My sister Mary's got bad teeth
and said I was lucky, then she said
I had big teeth, but Philip said I was pretty.
He had big hands that smelled.

I would speak of Tom, soft laughing,
who danced in the mornings round the sundial
teaching me the steps from France, turning
with the rhythm of the sun on the warped branches,
who'd hold my breast and watch it move like a snail
leaving his quick urgent love in my palm.
And I kept his love in my palm till it blistered.

When they axed his shoulders and neck
the blood moved like a branch into the crowd.
And he staggered with his hanging shoulder
cursing their thrilled cry, wheeling,
waltzing in the French style to his knees
holding his head with the ground,
blood settling on his clothes like a blush;
this way
when they aimed the thud into his back.

And I find cool entertainment now
with white young Essex, and my nimble rhymes.

[1967]

Red Accordian — an immigrant song

How you and I talked!
Casually, and side by side,
not even cold at 4 a.m.
New Year's morning

in a double outhouse in Blyth.

Creak of trees and scrub snow.
Was it dream or true memory
this casualness, this ease of talk
after the long night of the previous year.

Nothing important said
just as now the poem
draws together such frail times.
Art steps forward as accident
like a warm breeze from Brazil.

This whispering
as if not to awaken
what hibernates in firewood
as if not to disturb the blue night
the last memory of the year.

So we sit
within loose walls of the poem
you and I, our friends indoors
drunk on the home-made wine.
All of us searching to discern ourselves,
the 'gift' we can give each other.
Tell this landscape.
Or the one we came from.

Polkas in a smoky midnight light.

I stepped into this new year
dancing with a small child.
Rachel, so grateful,
we bowed when the dance was over.
If I could paint this I would

and if writing
showed colour and incident
removed from time
we could be clear.

The bleak view past the door
is where we are, not what we
have made here, or become, or brought
like wolves bringing food to a lair
from another world. And this
is magic.
Ray Bird's seven year old wine
— transformed! Finally made good.

I drank an early version years ago
and passed out.
                    Time collapses.
The years, the intricate
knowledge now of each other
makes love.

A yard in its scrub snow, stacked wood
brindle in the moonlight, the red truck,
a bare tree at the foot of the driveway
waving to heaven.
                    A full moon the
                    colour of night kitchen.

Ten yards away a high bonfire
(remembered from summer) lifts
its redness above the farmhouse
and the lean figures of children circle
to throw in sticks and arms off a christmas tree
as the woman in long black hair
her left foot on a stump
plays the red accordion.

And the others dance.
                    Embracing or flinging
themselves away from each other.
They bow and they look up
to full moon and white cold sky
and they *move*, even in this stilled painting.
They talk a white breath at each other.
Some appear more than once
with different partners.
We are immune to wind.
Our boots pound down the frozen earth
our children leap from and into our arms.
All of us poised and inspired by music
friendship self-made heat and the knowledge
each has chosen to come here driven for hours
over iced highways, to be here bouncing and leaping

to a reel that carried itself generations ago
north of the border, through lost towns,
settled among the strange names,
and became eventually our own

all the way from Virginia.

[1984]

A GENTLEMAN COMPARES HIS VIRTUE TO A JADE

The enemy was always identified in art by a lion.

And in our book of Victories
where ever you saw a parasol
on the battlefield you could
identify the king within its shadow.

We began with myths and later included actual events.

There were new professions. 'Cormorant Girls'
who screamed on prawn farms to scare birds.
Stilt-walkers. Tight-rope walkers.

There was always the 'untaught hold'
by which the master defeated
the pupil who challeneged him.

Palanquins carried the weapons of a goddess.

We tied bells onto falcons.

A silted water garden in Mihintale.
Bamboo tubes cut in 17th century Japan
that were used as poem holders.

The letter M. The word thereby.

There were wild cursive scripts.
There was the two-dimensional tradition.

Solitaries spent all their years
writing one good book. Federico Tesio
graced us with *Breeding the Race Horse*.

In our theatres human beings
wondrously became other human beings.

Bangles from Polannaruwa.
A nine-chambered box from Gampola.
The archaeology of cattle bells.

We believed in the intimate life, an inner self.

A libertine was one who made love before nightfall
or without darkening a room.

Walking the Alhambra blindfolded
to be conscious of the sound of water—your hand
could feel it coursing down bannisters.

We coincided our public holidays with the full moon.

3 a.m. in temples, the hour of washing the gods.

The formalisation of the vernacular.

The Buddha's left foot shifted at the moment of death.

That great writer, dying, called out
for the fictional doctor in his novels.

That tightrope walker from Kurunegale
the generator shut down by insurgents

stood there
swaying in the darkness above us.

[1995]

LETTERS & OTHER WORLDS

'for there was no more darkness for him and, no doubt
like Adam before the fall, he could see in the dark'

My father's body was a globe of fear
His body was a town we never knew
He hid that he had been where we were going
His letters were a room he seldom lived in
In them the logic of his love could grow

My father's body was a town of fear
He was the only witness to its fear dance
He hid where he had been that we might lose him
His letters were a room his body scared

He came to death with his mind drowning.
On the last day he enclosed himself
in a room with two bottles of gin, later
fell the length of his body
so that brain blood moved
to new compartments
that never knew the wash of fluid
and he died in minutes of a new equilibrium.

His early life was a terrifying comedy
and my mother divorced him again and again.
He would rush into tunnels magnetized
by the white eye of trains
and once, gaining instant fame,
managed to stop a Perahara in Ceylon
—the whole procession of elephants dancers
local dignitaries—by falling
dead drunk onto the street.

As a semi-official, and semi-white at that,
the act was seen as a crucial
turning point in the Home Rule Movement
and led to Ceylon's independence in 1948.

(My mother had done her share too—
her driving so bad
she was stoned by villagers
whenever her car was recognized)

For 14 years of marriage
each of them claimed he or she
was the injured party.
Once on the Colombo docks
saying goodbye to a recently married couple
my father, jealous
at my mother's articulate emotion,

dove into the waters of the harbour
and swam after the ship waving farewell.
My mother pretending no affiliation
mingled with the crowd back to the hotel.

Once again he made the papers
though this time my mother
with a note to the editor
corrected the report—saying he was drunk
rather than broken hearted at the parting of friends.
The married couple received both editions
of *The Ceylon Times* when their ship reached Aden.

And then in his last years
he was the silent drinker,
the man who once a week
disappeared into his room with bottles
and stayed there until he was drunk
and until he was sober.

There speeches, head dreams, apologies,
the gentle letters, were composed.
With the clarity of architects
he would write of the row of blue flowers
his new wife had planted,
the plans for electricity in the house,
how my half-sister fell near a snake
and it had awakened and not touched her.

Letters in a clear hand of the most complete empathy
his heart widening and widening and widening
to all manner of change in his children and friends
while he himself edged
into the terrible acute hatred
of his own privacy
till he balanced and fell
the length of his body
the blood screaming in
the empty reservoir of bones
the blood searching in his head without metaphor

[1973]

WHITE DWARFS

This is for people who disappear
for those who descend into the code
and make their room a fridge for Superman
—who exhaust costume and bones that could perform flight,
who shave their moral so raw
they can tear themselves through the eye of a needle
this is for those people
that hover and hover
and die in the ether peripheries

There is my fear
of no words   of
falling without words
over and over   of
mouthing the silence
Why do I love most
among my heroes those
who sail to that perfect edge
where there is no social fuel
Release of sandbags
to understand their altitude—

 that silence of the third cross
 3rd man hung so high and lonely
 we don't hear him say
 say his pain, say his unbrotherhood
 What has he to do with the smell of ladies
 can they eat off his skeleton of pain?

The Gurkhas in Malaya
cut the tongues of mules
so they were silent beasts of burden
in enemy territories
after such cruelty what could they speak of anyway
And Dashiell Hammett in success
suffered conversation and moved
to the perfect white between the words

This white that can grow
is fridge, bed,
is an egg—most beautiful
when unbroken, where
what we cannot see is growing
in all the colours we cannot see
there are those burned out stars
who implode into silence
after parading in the sky
after such choreography what would they wish to
speak of   anyway

[1973]

BEARHUG

Griffin calls to come and kiss him goodnight
I yell ok. Finish something I'm doing,
then something else, walk slowly round
the corner to my son's room.
He is standing arms outstretched
waiting for a bearhug. Grinning.

Why do I give my emotion an animal's name,
give it that dark squeeze of death?
This is the hug which collects
all his small bones and his warm neck against me.
The thin tough body under the pyjamas
locks to me like a magnet of blood.

How long was he standing there
like that, before I came?

[1979]

LIGHT

For Doris Gratiaen

Midnight storm. Trees walking off across the fields in fury
naked in the spark of lightning.
I sit on the white porch on the brown hanging cane chair
coffee in my hand midnight storm midsummer night.
The past, friends and family, drift into the rain shower.
Those relatives in my favourite slides
re-shot from old minute photographs so they now stand
complex ambiguous grainy on my wall.

This is my Uncle who turned up to his marriage
on an elephant. He was a chaplain.
This shy looking man in the light jacket and tie was infamous,
when he went drinking he took the long blonde beautiful hair
of his wife and put one end in the cupboard and locked it
leaving her tethered in an armchair.
He was terrified of her possible adultery
and this way died peaceful happy to the end.
My Grandmother, who went to a dance in a muslin dress
with fireflies captured and embedded in the cloth, shining
and witty. This calm beautiful face
organised wild acts in the tropics.
She hid the mailman in her house
after he had committed murder and at the trial
was thrown out of court for making jokes at the judge.
Her son became a Q.C.
This is my brother at 6. With his cousin and his sister
and Pam de Voss who fell on a pen-knife and lost her eye.
My Aunt Christie. She knew Harold Macmillan was a spy
communicating with her through pictures in the newspapers.
Every picture she believed asked her to forgive him,
his hound eyes pleading.
Her husband Uncle Fitzroy a doctor in Ceylon had a memory
sharp as scalpels into his 80's
though I never bothered to ask him about anything
—interested then more in the latest recordings of Bobby Darin.

And this is my Mother with her brother Noel in fancy dress.
They are 7 and 8 years old, a hand-coloured photograph,
it is the earliest picture I have. The one I love most.
A picture of my kids at Halloween
has the same contact and laughter.
My Uncle dying at 68, and my Mother a year later dying at 68.
She told me about his death and the day he died
his eyes clearing out of illness as if seeing
right through the room the hospital and she said
he saw something so clear and good his whole body
for a moment became youthful and she remembered
when she sewed badges on his trackshirts.
Her voice joyous in telling me this, her face light and clear.
(My firefly Grandmother also dying at 68).

These are the fragments I have of them, tonight
in this storm, the dogs restless on the porch.
They were all laughing, crazy, and vivid in their prime.
At a party my drunk Father
tried to explain a complex operation on chickens
and managed to kill them all in the process, the guests
having dinner an hour later while my Father slept
and the kids watched the servants clean up the litter
of beaks and feathers on the lawn.

These are their fragments, all I remember,
wanting more knowledge of them. In the mirror and in my kids
I see them in my flesh. Wherever we are
they parade in my brain and the expanding stories
connect to the grey grainy pictures on the wall,
as they hold their drinks or 20 years later
hold grandchildren, pose with favourite dogs,
coming through the light, the electricity, which the storm
destroyed an hour ago, a tree going down by the highway
so that now inside the kids play dominoes by candlelight
and out here the thick rain static the spark of my match to a cigarette
and the trees across the fields leaving me, distinct
lonely in their own knife scars and cow-chewed bark
frozen in the jagged light as if snapped in their run
the branch arms waving to what was a second ago the dark sky
when in truth like me they haven't moved.
Haven't moved an inch from me.

[1979]

FROM BILLY THE KID

After shooting Gregory
this is what happened

I'd shot him well and careful
made it explode under his heart
so it wouldnt last long and
was about to walk away
when this chicken paddles out to him

and as he was falling hops on his neck
digs the beak into his throat
straightens legs and heaves
a red and blue vein out

Meanwhile he fell
and the chicken walked away

still tugging at the vein
till it was 12 yards long
as if it held that body like a kite
Gregory's last words being

get away from me yer stupid chicken

• • •

The barn I stayed in for a week then was at the edge of a farm and had been deserted it seemed for several years, though built of stone and good wood. The cold dark grey of the place made my eyes become used to soft light and I burned out my fever there. It was twenty yards long, about ten yards wide. Above me was another similar sized room but the floors were unsafe for me to walk on. However I heard birds and the odd animal scrape their feet, the rotten wood magnifying the sound so they entered my dreams and nightmares.

But it was the colour and light of the place that made me stay there, not my fever. It became a calm week. It was the colour and the light. The colour a grey with remnants of brown—for instance those rust brown pipes and metal objects that before had held bridles or pails, that slid to machine uses; the thirty or so grey cans in one corner of the room, their ellipses, from where I sat, setting up patterns in the dark.

When I had arrived I opened two windows and a door and the sun poured blocks and angles in, lighting up the floor's skin of feathers and dust and old grain. The windows looked out onto fields and plants grew at the door, me killing them gradually with my urine. Wind came in wet and brought in birds who flew to the other end of the room to get their aim to fly out again. An old tap hung from the roof, the same colour as the walls, so once I knocked myself out on it.

For that week then I made a bed of the table there and lay out my fever, whatever it was. I began to block my mind of all thought. Just sensed the room and learnt what my body could do, what it could survive, what colours it liked best, what songs I sang best. There were animals who did not move out and accepted me as a larger breed. I ate the old grain with them, drank from a constant puddle about twenty yards away from the barn. I saw no human and heard no human voice, learned to squat the best way when shitting, used leaves for wiping, never ate flesh or touched another animal's flesh, never entered his boundary. We were all aware and allowed each other. The fly who sat on my arm, after his inquiry, just went away, ate his disease and kept it in him. When I walked I avoided the cobwebs who had places to grow to, who had stories to finish. The flies caught in those acrobat nets were the only murder I saw.

And in the barn next to us there was another granary, separated by just a thick wood door. In it a hundred or so rats, thick rats, eating and eating the foot deep pile of grain abandoned now and fermenting so that at the end of my week, after a heavy rain storm burst the power in those seeds and brought drunkenness into the minds of those rats, they abandoned the sanity of eating the food before them and turned on each other and grotesque and awkwardly because of their size they went for each other's eyes and ribs so the yellow stomachs slid out and they came through that door and killed a chipmunk—about ten of them onto that one striped thing and the ten eating each other before they realised the chipmunk was long gone so that I, sitting on the open window with its thick sill where they couldnt reach me, filled my gun and fired again and again into their slow wheel across the room at each boommm, and reloaded and fired again and again till I went through the whole bag of bullet supplies—the noise breaking out the seal of silence in my ears, the smoke sucked out of the window as it emerged from my fist and the long twenty yard space between me and them empty but for the floating bullet lonely as an emissary across and between the wooden posts that never returned, so the rats continued to wheel and stop in the silences and eat each other, some even the bullet. Till my hand was black and the gun was hot and no other animal of any kind remained in that room but for the boy in the blue shirt sitting there coughing at the dust, rubbing the sweat of his upper lip with his left forearm.

[1970]

IN A YELLOW ROOM

There was another reason for Fats Waller to record, on May 8th, 1935, 'I'm gonna sit right down and write myself a letter.' It is for this moment, driving down from Goderich and past Blyth, avoiding Blyth by taking the gravel concessions, four adults and a child, who have just swum in a very cold Lake Huron. His piano drips from the cassette player and we all recognize the piece but are mute. We cannot sing before he does, before he eases himself into the lyrics as if into a chair, this large man who is to die in 1943 sitting in a train in Kansas City, finally still.

He was always moving, grand on the street or the midnight taxi rides with Andy Razaf during which it is rumoured he wrote most of his songs. I have always loved him but I love him most in the company of friends. Because his body was a crowd and we desire to imitate such community. His voice staggers or is gentle behind a whimsical piano, the melody ornamental and cool as vichyssoise in that hot studio in this hot car on a late June Ontario summer day. What else of importance happened on May 8th, 1935?

The only creature I've ever met who disliked him was a nervous foxhound I had for three years. As soon as I put on Mr Waller the dog would dart from the room and hide under a bed. The dog recognised the anarchy, the unfolding of musical order, the growls and muttering, the fact that Fats Waller was talking to someone over your shoulder as well as to you. What my dog did not notice was the serenity he should have learned from. The notes as fresh as creek washed clothes.

The windows are open as we drive under dark maples that sniff up a rumour of Lake Huron. The piano energizes the hay bound into wheels, a white field of turkeys, various tributaries of the Maitland River. Does he, drunk and carrying his tin of tomatoes—'it feeds the body and cuts the hangover'—does he, in the midnight taxi with Razaf, imagine where the music disappears? Where it will recur? Music and lyrics they wrote then sold to false composers for ready cash and only later admitting they had written 'Sunny side of the street' and 'I can't give you anything but love' and so many of the best songs of their time. The hidden authors on their two hour taxi ride out of Harlem to Brooklyn and back again to Harlem, the night heat and smells yells overheard from the streets they passed through which they incorporated into what they were making every texture entering this large man, a classical organist in his youth, who strode into most experiences, hid from his ex-wife Edith Hatchett, visting two kinds of women, 'ladies who had pianos and ladies who did not', and died of bronchial pneumonia on the Achison, Topeka and Santa Fe, a song he did not write.

He and the orchestra of his voice have now entered the car with us. This is his first visit to the country, though he saw it from a train window the day before he died. Saw the heartland where the music could disappear, the diaspora of notes, a rewinding, a backward movement of the formation of the world, the invention of his waltz.

[1984]

bpNICHOL (1944-1988)

Barrie Phillip Nichol was born in Vancouver and divided his childhood years between his birthplace and Winnipeg and Port Arthur (Thunder Bay). He obtained a teaching certificate from the University of British Columbia and taught elementary school briefly before settling in Toronto, where he worked at the University of Toronto library and began his experiments in visual poetry, inspired initially by the work of Earle Birney and bill bissett. In 1964, he and David Aylward founded *Ganglia* magazine and press; then came *grOnk* (1967), a visual-poetry newsletter. Nichol joined a community called Therafields in 1963 and was a lay-therapist himself from 1963 to 1983, after which he worked as an editor for Coach House Press and Underwhich Editions and taught part-time at York University. His projects as a sound poet include the record *Motherlove* (1968) and a performance group called The Four Horsemen, composed of Nichol, Paul Dutton, Steve McCaffery, and Rafael Barreto-Rivera, which specialized in non-verbal 'readings' and improvisations and was the subject of a film made by Michael Ondaatje in 1970, called *The Sons of Captain Poetry.*

Nichol published broadsides, pamphlets, chapbooks, and a host of full-length books, including *Journeying & the returns* (1967), a boxed gathering of visual poems in an envelope, an animated flip-poem, and a more conventional lyric sequence; the four titles for which he won the Governor General's Award in 1970—*Still Water, The Cosmic Chef, Beach Head*, and *The True Eventual Story of Billy the Kid*, which was attacked as pornographic in the House of Commons; several prose works, including *Two Novels* (1969), *Craft Dinner* (1978), and *Journal* (1978); *Selected Writing: As Elected* (1980), and the work for which he is best known, *The Martyrology*, which grew, from 1972 until his death in 1988, into a vast and highly regarded life-work. A posthumous collection edited by George Bowering and Michael Ondaatje, called *An H in the Heart: A bpNichol Reader*, appeared in 1994.

Nichol's visual experiments, which owe something to the pioneering work of poets such as Ian Hamilton Finlay, Dom Sylvester Houédard, and Emmett Williams, include cartoons, drawings, and concrete poems, where words, letters, and sometimes graphics are deployed on the page to evoke a primarily visual response. Whereas the painterly concrete poems belong to the post-Gutenberg era of the printed page, Nichol's experiments with sound, which sometimes abandon ordinary words and syntax alike in favour of utterances of pure sound, or produce sounds and patterns that mimic conventional usage (as do, say, the works of Edward Lear), are intended to recall poetry's origins in an oral tradition and to emphasize its relation to music. In *The Martyrology*, however, Nichol brings these two areas of investigation together, using language (words and their combinations) as both form and content. The 'saints' he employs structurally—such as St Orm and St Ranglehold—are drawn from the dictionary's 'st' section, where the word *strap*, for example, might serve to locate a very contemporary poetic icon: St Rap. Puns and words games are central to Nichol's work, where he is at play, constantly, in the fields of the language. And yet his saints serve the larger purpose of spiritual questing, providing a linguistic springboard from which to explore and give shape to experience.

The most useful guide to Nichol's work and poetics is *Tracing the Paths: Reading ≠ Writing* The Martyrology (1988), edited by Roy Miki, which contains a number of important statements by Nichol himself. In 'Talking About the Sacred in Writing', Nichol makes an intriguing statement about the poet's relation to language: 'when I stumbled across the saints with David Aylward in the ST words in language, and for David that's all it was, it was puns—but for me, I suddenly found myself writing a series called *Scraptures*, in which I was addressing and talking to these saints—long, very argumentative, shrill poems full of extreme rhetoric and, you know, lots of talk about the language revolution and so on was going down. I realized that for some reason these figures which had arisen out of language had a meaning to me that I would not have imagined, that I only got to through the pun, which is why I've tended to follow the pun ever since. But when I began to do that, I began to become more conscious that I had a belief, in essence, in the sacredness of the activity of language—not in the particular language necessarily. My own particular limitation is that I am a speaker of English, and it's the tongue I work in, and it's the tongue I am familiar with. But I think it's the activity of language itself, which is different in each language space you enter. I have a profound belief in *that* as a sacred activity—that is to say, *something* goes on. Now, you can use it to crack cheap jokes, you can use it to make profound statements, you can use it to deal with the political necessities of the world, and you can use it to write love poetry. You can use it for all sorts of things, but the activity itself has a tremendous power that has to be, within itself, respected. Now, it seems to me—what I've learned for myself—is that once I respect that activity of the language, then through the language I am literally led to things that I would not arrive at otherwise. Therefore, in a real sense I give up, on the one hand, some sense of the self as guiding the poem, though on the other hand I put a tremendous emphasis on getting my technical chops together so that when I am in the midst of the poem there's nothing standing between me and following it wherever it wants to go. If a poem has an urge to suddenly go off in this direction and write long, Proustian-style sentences, then I'm not going to stop because I'm hung up on the semi-colon and don't know how to push it around. I have to somehow have the ability to follow where the thing itself leads me.'

'What is a long poem?' he asks, in terms that, given his untimely death, now seem sadly ironic: 'perhaps it is simply a long life or some trust in the durational aspect of being alive, it's a tremendous leap of faith to even start one, to even think, "hey, i'll be alive long enough that this form seems the best way to say what i have to say." certainly some faith in process pushes me on knowing even as i do so that the questions of audience, who precisely the poem is intended for, is an interesting & unresolved one.'

BLUES

```
        l     e
        o   e
    l o v e
    o   e v o l
l o v e   o
    e v o l
  e   o
e     l
```

[1974]

FROM 'THE CAPTAIN POETRY POEMS'

dear Captain Poetry,
your poetry is trite.
you cannot write a sonnet
tho you've tried to every night
since i've known you.
we're thru !!
        Madame X

dear Madame X

    Look how the sun leaps now upon our faces
    Stomps & boots our eyes into our skulls
    Drives all thot to weird & foreign places
    Till the world reels & the kicked mind dulls,
    Drags our hands up across our eyes
    Sends all white hurling into black
    Makes the inner cranium our skies
    And turns all looks sent forward burning back.
    And you, my lady, who should be gentler, kind,
    Have yet the fiery aspect of the sun
    Sending words to burn into my mind
    Destroying all my feelings one by one;
        You who should have tiptoed thru my halls
        Have slammed my doors & smashed me into walls.

            love
            Cap Poetry

[1971]

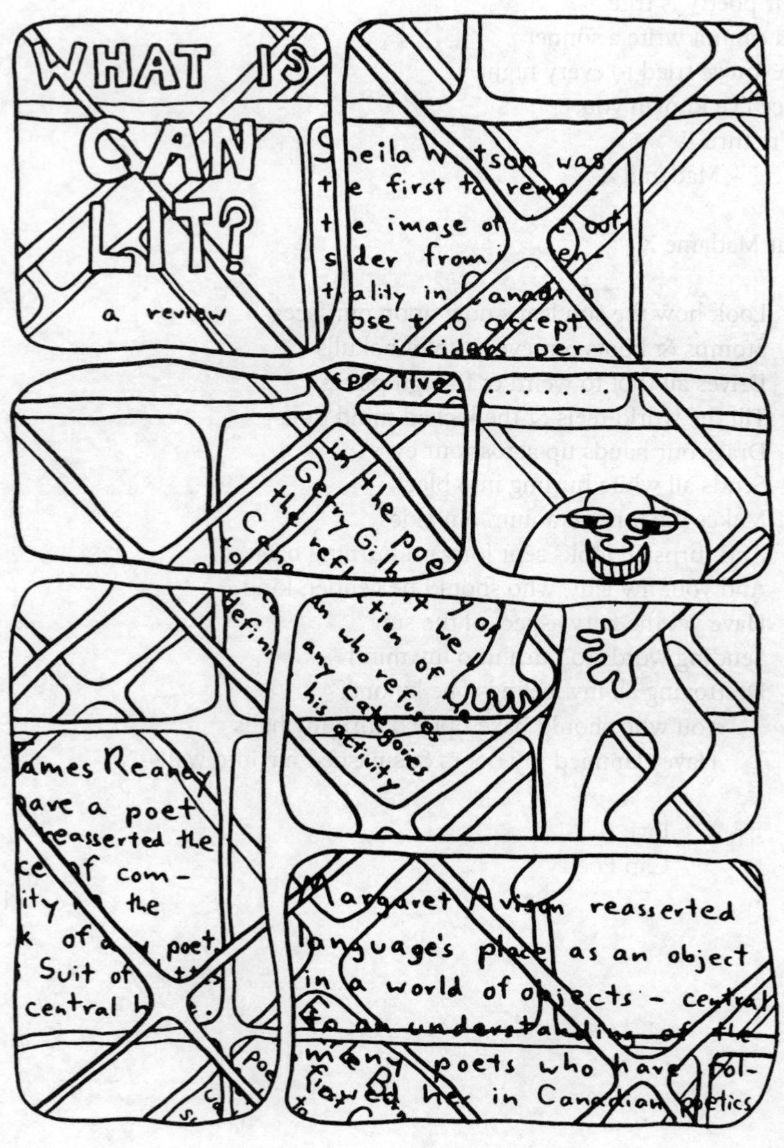
WHAT IS
CAN
LIT?
a review
Sheila W tson was
t e first to rem
t e image of e out-
s der from i en-
tiality in anad
ose t o accept
i sides per-
spective........
in the poe
Gerry Gilb
the refl
t we
ction of
who refuse
any categories
his activity
ames Reaney
have a poet
reasserted the
ce of com-
ity in the
k of any poet,
Suit of
central h
Margaret Avison reasserted
language's place as an object
in a world of objects - central
to an understanding of the
many poets who have fol-
lowed her in Canadian poetics

But what the hell is CAN LIT?
1920
1930
?
?
19
it's just a quest-ion of SURVIVAL!!
bp 73

[1973]

[1974]

LANDSCAPE: I

for thomas a. clark

alongthehorizongrewanunbrokenlineoftrees

[1980]

THE MOUTH

1

You were never supposed to talk when it was full. It was better to keep it shut if you had nothing to say. You were never supposed to shoot it off. It was better to be seen than heard. It got washed out with soap if you talked dirty. You were never supposed to mouth-off, give them any of your lip, turn up your nose at them, give them a dirty look, an evil eye or a baleful stare. So your mouth just sat there, in the middle of your still face, one more set of muscles trying not to give too much away. 'Hey! smile! what's the matter with you anyway?'

2

Probably there are all sorts of stories. Probably my mouth figures in all sorts of stories when I was little but I don't remember any of them. I don't remember any stories about my mouth but I remember it was there. I remember it was there and I talked & sang & ate & used it all the time. I don't remember anything about it but the mouth remembers. The mouth remembers what the brain can't quite wrap its tongue around & that's what my life's become. My life's become my mouth's remembering, telling stories with the brain's tongue.

3

I must have been nine. I'm pretty sure I was nine because I remember I was the new boy in school. I remember I was walking on my way there, the back way, thru the woods, & here was this kid walking towards me, George was his name, & I said 'hi George' & he said 'I don't like your mouth' & grabbed me & smashed my face into his knee. It was my first encounter with body art or it was my first encounter with someone else's idea of cosmetic surgery. It was translation or composition. He rearranged me.

4

The first dentist called me the Cavity Kid & put 35 fillings into me. The second dentist said the first dentist was a charlatan, that all the fillings had fallen out, & put 38 more fillings in me. The third dentist had the shakes from his years in the prisoner of war camp & called me his 'juicy one,' saliva frothing from my mouth as his shaky hand approached me. The fourth dentist never looked at me. His nurse put me out with the sleeping gas & then he'd enter the room & fill me. The fifth dentist said my teeth were okay but my gums would have to go, he'd have to cut me. The sixth dentist said well he figured an operation on the foot was okay coz the foot was a long way away but the mouth was just a little close to where he thot he lived & boy did we ever agree because I'd begun to see that every time I thot of dentists I ended the sentence with the word 'me.' My mouth was me. I wasn't any ancient Egyptian who believed his Ka was in his nose—nosiree—I was just a Kanadian kid & had my heart in my mouth every time a dentist approached me.

5

It all begins with the mouth. I shouted waaa when I was born, maaa when I could name her, took her nipple in, the rubber nipple of the bottle later, the silver spoon, mashed peas, dirt, ants, anything with flavour I could shove there, took the tongue & flung it 'round the mouth making sounds, words, sentences, tried to say the things that made it possible to reach him, kiss her, get my tongue from my mouth into some other. I liked that, liked the fact the tongue could move in mouths other than its own, & that so many things began there—words did, meals, sex—& tho later you travelled down the body, below the belt, up there you could belt out a duet, share a belt of whiskey, undo your belts & put your mouths together. And I like the fact that we are rhymed, mouth to mouth, & that it begins here, on the tongue, in the pun, comes from mouth her mouth where we all come from.

6

I always said I was part of the oral tradition. I always said poetry was an oral art. When I went into therapy my therapist always said I had an oral personality. I got fixated on oral sex, oral gratification & notating the oral reality of the poem. At the age of five when Al Watts Jr was still my friend I actually said, when asked who could do something or other, 'me or Al' & only years later realized how the truth's flung out of you at certain points & runs on ahead. And here I've been for years running after me, trying to catch up, shouting 'it's the oral', 'it all depends on the oral', everybody looking at my bibliography, the too many books & pamphlets, saying with painful accuracy: 'that bp—he really runs off at the mouth.'

[1988]

continental trance

> 'We cannot retrace our steps, going
> forward may be the same as going
> backwards. We cannot retrace our
> steps, retrace our steps. All my
> long life, all my life, we do not
> retrace our steps, all my long life,
> but.'
>
> GERTRUDE STEIN
> *The Mother Of Us All*

minus the ALL ABOARD

minus my father waving

minus the CN logo

minus my mother waving

minus seventeen years of my life
Ellie & me
our unborn child in her belly
heading east
out of Vancouver
July 27th
8 p.m.
nineteen eighty-
1.

---

what i wanted to write:
'this is how it begins' or
'pulling into New Westminster'

what actually happened:
took a different route
skipped the canneries of New Westminster entirely

(so much for nostalgia or
plotting the poem in advance)

walking up to the snack bar
seven cars to the front
the sleeping car porter three cars ahead
making the beds
the teenage kid said to him
(admiringly) 'you've got it all worked out eh'
as he flipped the mattress down
upper to lower
berth
        & the porter said
'if i had it all worked out
i wouldn't be doing this.'

---

crossing the Fraser River
Port Mann in the night
lights out the left window of
the train

darker outline of the mountains
dark blue of the sky
minus the stars
out this left window on the universe

---

the old guy who spoke to the porter just now said:
'my wife wanted to take this trip
before she takes her heavenly trip'

my grandma, 96, earlier today said:
'i don't think i wanta stay around too many more'

Ellie's sitting across from me
reading Peter Dickinson's *One Foot In The Grave*
& in the first draft of this poem i wrote:
'minus these coincidences
what is the world trying to tell me?'

minus—the word returns
—some notion of absence (not a life)
subtracting the miles travelled east
(minus mine—us)
loosing all notion of possession
aboard this mixed metaphor

---

upper berth swaying in the darkness
click as the wheels clack off the miles

two women pass thru
drunk from the observation car
the one talking at the top of her voice
i say 'shut up' loudly

the woman shuts up
& her friend
lowering her voice whispers back
'fuck off'

lullabies in the real word

---

insistent instances

Kamloops in the early morning

someone, going crazy in their roomette,
rings the porter's bell repeatedly

seven a.m.

no way to sleep again

stagger forward to breakfast
the eggs taste of plastic or pam

drink tea
lurch up to the observation car
watch the mountains loom by

back in the sleeper car
one porter scratches the other porter's knees
'stop it! you know what that does to me!'

Blue River at ten
my cousin Donna's nursing station visible thru the trees

you too, Nicky,
none of us escape these details
presences
even in these wilds
rocking back & forth
eastward on this western train

---

beginnings & endings

discrete frames in
a continuous flow

the japanese family talking
words i don't know

a horse glimpsed from the window
a man at the river's side
things i have knowledge of but cannot account for

like the flowers i saw
earlier today
purple spikes driven up
interspersed among the charred stumps of the fired forest

or the mountain's high green meadow
visible above the clouds

or the brook the train crossed even as i wrote these words
rushing down
carrying its content
into the larger lakes & rivers of the world

'because i was raised on trains'
—this is the line that kept recurring to me
all night

'because i criss-crossed the west with
my mother & father'
—the only other line i could find to write
remembering
as the woman across from us slaps her son's fingers
spilling the peanuts my father bought
all down the aisle of the train,
1954, or dad yelling at me, 1948,
because i was running back & forth to the water cooler,
the newsy's face that same trip,
pissed off at his job,
twisted in a grimace i was intended to read as genial

random information intrudes each time i ride these rails
maybe for the last time
headline in that Vancouver paper
GOVERNMENT AXES TRANS-CONTINENTAL LINE THRU JASPER
part of my memory disappears
1500 jobs & a slice of history

'because i criss-crossed the west with
my mother & father'

'because i was raised on trains'

---

the conductor takes our luncheon reservations
'1:15'

but at five to 1 says 'it's five to 2—
set your watch ahead.'

nothing's fixed aboard this paradox
affects more than we believe

flux logic

we eat at 2:15

---

ten minutes outside of Jasper
the line between sadism & masochism is drawn

as his one year old son hits his other son with a wire brush
the father across from us says to him:
'hit yourself with it!'

masochism wins—
the kid starts hitting himself
at least once for every time he hits his brother

WHACK   WHACK

following this tack
hitting the track to town

'too much like a rock song'
—what i thot as i ended the previous poem

how come that voice keeps butting in?

why the need to resolve parameters?

why not the rush of
the asymmetrical
arhythmic
world?

why not the *y not* the *z*
in the unwritten alphabets ahead?

---

okay we'll start there
with st utter's subtler statement

when the riddle's rid of rid
dle remains
ashine with its own kind of mystery

half words
half visions

the train pulls out of Jasper
three hours late

is this the st ate of my mind
or does that saint exist
beyond these twisting tracks
this train of thot?

---

so there it is

the literal metaphor or symbol

linear narrative of random sequential thots

accidents of geography, history & circumstance

the given

---

i don't like the 'symbol'
except as accent to the basic drum
of consciousness

i don't like the 'like'
except as entrance to
a 'pataphysical reality

i like the play of words
of life   the moment when the feelings focus
  absolutely   a description

which is what st ate meant? yes
my st ate meant
this

---

whistle

pulling over the level crossings
in the gathering dark into Edmonton

drainage ditches gleaming in the last light
clusters of buildings & trees

as night falls the sky reverses
dark clouds against a lighter blue

& the mind reverses
sleep takes
loosing the dream you

---

two hours from Saskatoon
fingernail of moon in the eastern sky
the pastel grey clouds at dawn
blown over the pinkening horizon
train gathering speed all the while
the berth shakes back & forth &
forth over the prairie

the revelation is in the blue dome of air
beneath which this train & the dawn appear
as blue as the robin's egg i found age two
shattered on the sidewalk
bits of curved blue flung all about
& the train of thot it lead to

as blue as that imagined sky that day
when the clouds were white
& the prairies lay over the mountains
in my future

---

mist of rain across the far horizon

heading out of Saskatoon
6:35 a.m. July 31st
the sky is a constant grey
& the fields of wheat, alfalfa, clover, grass, etc
stretch away for miles in all directions

encompassed we make our way
thru the middle of Canada
east towards Winnipeg

the mid-summer morning rain

these middle days

---

later
a cultivator
then an elevator

somewhere between Nokomis & Raymore
(Semans to be exact)
two perfect stone circles
in a playground beside the tracks
except the circles are made of old tractor tires
(i can see this as we draw closer)

like that day
looking for the stones of Shap
saw a perfect circle beyond the crest of the next hill
lost sight as we raced down into the valley, thrilled,
up & over, it was gone,
only a raggedy row of sheep in that field beyond

this is how the world is
rimes that disappear as you draw closer to their sense
dense clumps of trees
scattered across the open fields

notation
in the landscape of a nation &
a revelation

---

vanishing

down into the valley
tracking a forgotten river bottom
thru the farms, the ordered fences,
this old order is all around us
as we cross the border into Manitoba

saints you are gone
part of an older order of this poem
as Brun, too, is gone, sleeps with the other giants of his race
presence you can trace in Lampman, Roberts, et al
nineteenth century notions of this place

vanished
as we will vanish
despite the wish to carry on   immortal
into stranger dawns
my unborn child
will never cover these miles we cover in this way
of life
        vanishing
& nothing visible
except a vast shining

---

the field of sunflowers stretches to the horizon
under this july sun
the clouds are isolate
mirror the disparate clumps of trees
& the fields & sky weave thru & around them
rime in the clear blue sloughs & streams

we move as in a dream
the mothers down the aisle screaming at their children
the guy across from me whistling the Colonel Bogey March

it will make sense yet
this blue & green
these fragmentary lives & conversations
& the white world, saints' home, in between

---

two hour delay in the Winnipeg station
'they're looking for an engine for the train'

the things that get displaced are major
they leave you stranded tho you know your destination

'i'm getting out of here'
sometimes there's no getting
aboard a-
way
    even if your ticket's punched

---

okay saints
i hear you babbling
press your way with your complaints into this scenery

someone spoke of you
as tho you were a literary device
more a vice i keep returning to

tho the order here's another one
your faces rise above these tree lines
there's a conversation we all come back to

so many years spent talking with you
a willed hallucination
more than continental
a kind of lifelong trance

& these pauses
on these sidings
waiting for that load of freight to pass

---

beside the track

drowned trees
water lilies

fish break
the surface of the lake

as i look back

'where is this poem going?'
'Toronto'

'what does it teach us?'
'how coincidence reaches into our lives &
instructs us'

the 19th century knew
any narrative, like life,
is where coincidence leads you

given, of course, the conscious choice of voice
the train of thot you choose

---

this next bit doesn't quite cohere

already past tense
or converted to a noun
when it's the bite of consciousness eludes you

the flickering light thru the trees
sets up an echo in my brain
petit mal
makes me want to puke

but the trees
so clustered
a bird could walk the branches
a thousand miles or more

it is a map of consciousness
what the light yields disgorges
perceived thru a pattern of branches
the birds fly free of

---

in Hornpayne
the sign on the building i could see from the road read 'OTHING'
i reconstructed as 'NOTHING'
because it looked like it was falling down

a north thing called 'nothing'
that as Ellie & i drew closer
i read, suddenly, as 'CLOTHING'
windows boarded up & broken

like my life-long wish
that i might clothe myself finally in belief
& realize:
the name of death is 'NOTHING'
the name of after-death is 'NOTHING'
accept Lord Mother/Father
the briefness of this life you've granted
this bliss

---

blueberry bushes, fruit shrunken, dried,
hot july day, outside this moving window

that leaning tree is static as we move away
vanish in its distance
won't be here the day it falls
or the bushes return again to bloom
sitting in the room on wheels
takes us
Pacific Ocean to the Great Lakes
middle passage the explorers dreamed of
died for

past the scattered daisies in the green ditches,
the drowning forests, bursting water lilies,
sun-lit glades

---

mile what?
a lack of notation
reaching for conclusions
tho none are there
you get the green forest
red dying leaves
off-white of the drowned birches
leaves you wondering what it is ends
or is it only an endless renewal
God my life ends
years before this poem possibly can

---

as night falls
it all falls

the sky gradually caves in
becomes the same still darkness as the trees

well past dusk
the husk of night's broken only by the train's light
stars & moon out of sight behind the clouds' wall
contains us in this cave
in whose mouth lie rumours of our shadows
other worlds round other suns
dim flicker of light
visible suddenly across the lake
before the train takes us round the bend
into the illusory dark

---

is this the poem i wanted to write?

it never is

it's a thing of words
construct of a conscious mind

governed by the inevitable end-rime
time

---

that's that tone

buried in the poem
a consciousness of its own mortality

or mine

a finality Homer
soon there's noone knows
whether your poem's your own

or if the name denoted a community of speakers
history of a race

(Ellie's an obvious we
draws our child's breath & her own)

i's a lie
dispenses illusions of plot

biography when geography's the clue
locale & history of the clear 'you'

---

who to, Nicky?

only the future
invisible as my own

our first child died
this second waits its birth

all part of history
all what we call a life

echoes & screams thru these tunnels of trees
running on tracks we no longer perceive

Ellie asleep in the lower berth
voices & footsteps move all night
along the moving corridors of the train

---

mist again at dawn

heading into Toronto
'end' translates 'home'

7 a.m.
August 2nd
1981

St Clair to Union Station
thru the junkyards, the backyard gardens,
decaying brick factories

scrawled across the one wall
I WANTED TO BE AN ANARCHIST

an ending
in itself
unending

Vancouver-Toronto
July 27 to August 2 1981

[1982]

DAPHNE MARLATT (b. 1942)

Daphne (Buckle) Marlatt was born in Melbourne, Australia, and lived in Penang, Malaysia, before emigrating with her family to North Vancouver in 1951. She graduated from the University of British Columbia in 1964 and then pursued her M.A. in Comparative Literature at the University of Indiana. Her poetic influences include Robert Duncan and Charles Olson, from whom she learned to develop an acute attention not only to the particulars of speech, but also to the body and its messages at the time of writing, a process that has come to be known as *proprioception*. She has lived in the Vancouver area for many years, but has also served as writer-in-residence at the universities of Alberta and Manitoba. She is the author of two works of fiction, *Zócalo* (1977) and *The Story, She Said* (1977), and numerous volumes of poetry, including *Frames: Of A Story* (1968), *Leaf / leafs* (1969), *Rings* (1971), *The Vancouver Poems* (1972), *Steveston* (1975), *Net Work: Selected Writings* (1980), *What Matters: Writing 1968-1970* (1980), *Our Lives* (1980), *Touch to My Tongue* (1984), and *Salvage* (1991). She raised two children from her first marriage and lived for many years with the artist Roy Kiyooka; but then, like Adrienne Rich, came to acknowledge and explore her own unfolding lesbianism. Much of her recent work, as she explains in the Foreword to *Salvage*, was 'generated out of a growing sense of community with women writers/readers, drawn by currents of desire in language for contact through time, over space and across culture.' Marlatt has also devoted much of her writing life to moving out from what she calls 'the safety of known forms', as she says in the Afterword to *Our Lives*, where it is necessary 'to write into the unknown of our actual present'.

Fred Wah's Introduction to *Net Work* is a sensitive and thorough account of Marlatt's developing theory and practice, quoting liberally from her interview with George Bowering in *Open Letter* (4, 3, Spring 1979), where she makes an acute observation on the social function of poetry: 'I take it that a writer's job is to continue to give accurate witness of what's happening. One person isn't going to change what Marathon Realty is doing, what the CPR is doing. . . . You cannot change the world. You can change consciousness, & language is intimately tied up with consciousness. That's our true field of action, is language, as poets. And all you can do is to insist on the seeing as it's evidenced & manifested in the language. In an accurate use of language.' In the same interview she talks about writing as a process of attending to whatever is at hand (which includes body, present, history, prehistory): 'My notion re prose & poetry is that I'm confused. I have a feeling that both of them have nothing to do with the way they look on the page, but with the way the language is moving. A particular kind of attention to language. Simply, that standard prose is written as if language was transparent. You're not seeing it. Poetry is written with the awareness that it's not transparent, that it is in fact a medium & that you are operating in it thanks to it. It's like the difference between being land animals &—we don't usually experience air, you know. We breathe in & we breathe out without being aware that we are breathing in any medium at all. That it is our medium. Once we get into the water, which is a foreign element to us, we're very aware of the difficulty of moving thru that element. That's like poetry. You are aware that you are moving in an element, in a medium, & that, in fact, any moving forward you make is thanks to that element that you're moving in. So that language . . . writes the story as much as you do.'

Marlatt explains in an essay in *Open Letter* (1980) how, while keeping her 'ear on the pulse of language', she came to explore prose forms: 'I had definitely abandoned the textbook notion of sentence as the container for a completed thought, just as writing open form poetry had taught me the line has no box for a certain measure of words, but a moving step in the process of thinking/feeling, feeling/thinking. Our word "sentence" comes from L. *sentire*, to feel, think—the muscularity, the play of thought that feels its way, flexive and reflexive, inside the body of language. In short, a proprioceptive (receiving itself) prose.'

Marlatt's exploration of language, which is most eloquently explained in her essay 'Musing with Mothertongue' (from *Touch to My Tongue* and reproduced in its entirety in the Poetics section), has less to do with the search for poetic novelty than with a belief that language, like Shakespeare's sleep, is our chief nourisher and the means by which poet and reader alike might co-exist in, and with, the world: 'language thus speaking (i.e., inhabited) relates us, "takes us back" to where we are, as it relates us to the world in a living body of verbal relations. articulation: seeing the connections (and the thighbone, and the hipbone, etc.). putting the living body of language together means putting the world together, the world we live in: an act of composition, an act of birthing, us, uttered and outered there in it.'

Although this deeply political view of language and the function of poetry is reflected in most of her work, it is most clear in *Steveston*, where Marlatt and photographer Robert Minden turn ear and eye—and the other senses—on a small fishing community in the mouth of the Fraser River, that is the berth, and birthing-place, of boats, Finns, float-houses, barbers, Japanese, canneries, Indians, net-lofts, a place of intersection between what is native and foreign, between past and present, earth and water, river and ocean, the idea and the actual. The poem-sequence, a series of meditations on place, history, and the flotsam of physical and human reality, is not just a marriage of documentary material, descriptive detail, and personal impression, but, like Wright Morris's *The Home Place*, a hymn and a testimonial to the passing of a way of life.

While critics have drawn attention to the ambitiousness and multiple levels of meaning in Marlatt's best work, it should also be noted that her method of multiplying allusions and layers of signification can result in poetic overkill, where, to misquote Alexander Pope, we might die of a verb in polymorphic pain. In *Salvage*, Marlatt seems to have sensed something missing, or belaboured, in her early writing—indeed, in her writing life—which has to do with the absence of personal story, or narrative, what she has come to call 'historicity stored in the tissue'. So she reconsiders the life and work, in terms of 'litter. wreckage. salvage', the latter word being the operative one. As she explores, in her most powerful and accessible work, writing, marriage, mothering, and a shifting sexuality, Marlatt surrenders to the inevitable: 'these subliminal stories. what is narrative but the burden of an emotion the writing labours under, trying to recover, uncover, this thing about to be hatched?'

ALCAZAR, CECIL, BELMONT, NEW FOUNTAIN, NAMES . . .

Alcazar, Cecil, Belmont, New Fountain, names
stations of the way, to

Entrances

speak doors that swing under
men's, women's (*& escorts*, escorted by an era
gone a little later than the sawdust, smashed glass
brawls, still, the angry sweep of hand or
beer-clumsy (weighted, rolling to the floor

(root's daughter's o
the waiter, watch where
you're going, threatens (snarl) big beer-belly's
MUSCLE
means, to the door bounced exit onto
(desolate
light, no, POWER
back there where friends, where
the world sits on curved chairs by little tables stackt
with glass, empty, full, empty, waiter, eight more
(weighted) take one for yourself, change
wet on the
Changes. change is. floor caves under
& BaxbakualanuXsiwe's body 'covered all over with
mouths', drops, to the pit, his red cedar bark falls.
into the hands of Hamats'a

a drumming & a singing
pulse. rock charged air smokes (the red smoke of
his house? smokes Mountains, 'at the mouth of'
river-running sea

Whose heart heavy with ferocious lips,
to see, legs, hips, tits, to want? the taste of flesh.
or whose small hair.
With a violent gesture wipes out the
bar, the primitive order of barkeep, bouncer, copcar, court

or,
    construction
                (*use the men's entrance*) is the construction
we put upon it, his glass, his chair someone takes or someone's
eye upon his wife. *Men's, women's*. & the separate washroom
doors they vanish into. The private law. He said I put the
finger on him, pickt up outside, fingered, it is all alien,
property, Is what belongs to another, Her tight dress no
trespassing but still, come in—

                We live by (at the mouth of)
the world, & the ritual. Draws strength. Is not Secret
a woman gives (in taking, Q'ominoqas) rich within the
lockt-up street. Whose heart beats here, taking it
all in,
    Nanwaqawe: Who are you?
    She: Your daughter (didn't you know?) Initiator.

Who is rooted to the floor with a root so deep he cannot
shovel it. Singing:

'The hamats'a mask of the forehead, the hamats'a
mask of the whole world, the prettymask . . .' &

'The red cedar bark of the whole world is making you
voracious'

    . . .

    O little man, o little man with dull eyes,
with 3 full glasses at closing time, I take you in.

[1972]

IMAGINE: A TOWN

Imagine a town running
                (smoothly?
a town running before a fire
canneries burning

(do you see the shadow of charred stilts
on cool water? do you see enigmatic chance standing
just under the beam?

He said they were playing cards in the
Chinese mess hall, he said it was dark (a hall? a shack.
they were all, crowded together on top of each other.
He said somebody accidentally knocked the oil lamp over, off
the edge

where stilts are standing, Over the edge of the
dyke a river pours, uncalled for, unending:

where chance lurks
fishlike, shadows the underside of pilings, calling up his hall
the bodies of men & fish corpse piled on top of each other (residue
time is, the delta) rot, an endless waste the trucks of production
grind to juice, driving through

smears, blood smears in the dark
dirt) this marshland silt no graveyard can exist in but water swills,
endlessly out of itself to the mouth

ringed with residue, where
chance flicks his tail & swims, through.

[1975]

A BY-CHANNEL; A SMALL BACKWATER:

A by-channel; a small backwater:
slough, Finn Slough (or Gilmour,
by Gilmour Island), slough for sale as 'deep sea frontage',
has been always, simply, backwater clutch of shacks, floats,
sheds: a swamp & dusty marsh grass sheltering mosquito boats,
small gillnetters & other vessels in this amphibious place,
half earth half water, half river half sea, tide fills, swiftly,
pushing muddy fingers into timbers of the float, crawling round
pilings & rushes, glinting up a web of net stranding float where
a man & woman bend, knotting holes deadheads & other refuse a murky

river roils, have torn, ripped, & otherwise scorned, sometimes from
leadline to cork . . .

The slow effort of
this people's morning: rise with predawn birdsong & coffee
stretching stiffer & stiffer bones, pack lunch, pad past the
cloistered silence of tv, crunch of gravel, drive (green Pinto)
down to where their boats lie, light filtering immense
vegetation.

Check fuel, untie & start the engine ('a 7 Easthope
& a 15, wasn't it a 15 Easthope they had too? They thought they really
had something on the go—now when they look back they think it's a
joke, you know, why, have we actually been fishing with those?'

'That was the onetime king engine' on this coast, days when
nobody had any money, they bought a used car engine for two bucks,
had it delivered down to the slough, the poor

shelter of swamp
houses, float- ('when I look at it now it looks like a summer cabin')
under the lee of a dyke Finnish squatters & other folk whose lives
are inextricably tied with the tide that inundates their day, their
time measured only by: this sucking at vegetal silence swallows shred,
from the boom of idle boats, from the ridgepole of shadowy netshed
jets drone: this land up for deep sea frontage ('oh yes, it'll be
freighters & cement scow, barges & containerized shipping all the
way up to New Westminster,

you can't stop progress, can you?'

How *accept* its creeping up?
like a disease, like time, the tide they still know how to run,
with it, up under ('remember how your net got wrapped & rolled?')
that barge, danger at dark or fog, still after the fish which still
run shadowy lines thru all that murk against the shifting bars of
shipping channel, slipping that traffic, that bottom:

'You sure find out
when you get all the rubbish from down there—lot of bark, papers,
bathroom papers—it's real messy sometimes. Trees & twigs &
branches, branches of trees even floating down there. & then there's,

I dunno what kind of plant it is, it's like a crabapple limb & it's
just full of little twigs, & that's a wicked one when it gets caught in
to a thin net. & ends of logs that have been cut, you know, stump
ends & round blocks drifting. The sawmills open their gates, you know
& let all their loose stuff out—when that comes dashing there's even
sawdust in the river.'
                At bottom of this slippery time, it's her boat,
her feet on, managing the freshet, swollen, flooding (highest tides
of the year last week) water on water swell, with a wind running
norwesterly 'it gets pretty choppy here', 'I've been here with a blow
that's bin blowing 47 miles an hour—just big big waves washing
way up above the rocks.' 'See it's narrow & when the wind blows
those waves break & cross, it gets real rough.'
                                        She runs in the
throat of time, voicing the very swifts & shallows of that river,
urging, in the dash of it, enough to keep up, to live on. When nets
are up 50%, fuel's up, & the packers taking chum salmon, undressed,
at 20 cents a pound, 'the same they sell in the stores dressed at $1.20,
while they're selling the roe they don't even pay us for at $2.20
a pound, clear profit'. . .
                Somehow they survive the oily waters swirling
under packers piling, bargeloads of herring sucked up, truckloads
left to rot, salmon on ice in the packerboats collecting twenty hours
a day,

        Somehow they survive, this people, these fish,
survive the refuse bottom, filthy water, their choked lives,
in a singular dance of survival, each from each. At the
narrows, in the pressure of waves so checked & held by
'deep-sea frontage' it's the river's push against her, play of
elements her life comes rolling on, hair flying. In gumboots,
on deck with rubber apron ('it's no dance dress'), she'll take
all that river gives, willing only to stand her ground (rolling,
with it, right under her feet, her life, rolling, out from under,
right on out to sea . . .

[1975]

Vacant, Lots

of vacant lots vegetation fills: dandelion, tansy in tall
spokes, small clover only those close to the ground will see. in seedy
grasses waving off sandhill lots, they weave, waving a bottle, hey!
come on over. sunstruck, drowsy & raucous, sun fuming the wine in
their heads. vacant over sidewalk, weaving up against telephone
poles . . . can't do it, man. i'm a good man, or. my name is mud . . .

no wires over vacant lots. no connection calling them back. home
this moment, these small flowers, this much satupon mud worn into
backsides of hills they view the city from, its increment of meaning
every hoarding, every passing bus leaks, *non-sense*, a verbal
inflation that 'standardizes the value of words'

shut up, shut up
he yells, into the open air signs fill, everywhere. 'else is better,'
they say. they want to fill up the vacant lot he is, a hole in the
system words won't fill. fill in the grass. full with friends
camped in a ring around a bottle—on vacation we say (see vacant,
see empty of work)—empty (pay, pay). & a fight erupts. someone
stoned is left alone. vacant, we say of eyes deprived of sense
(our sense), except for nightmare: always someone climbing on somebody
else's neck, for a bit more air. always these holes in ourselves or
where we are.
battered & bleeding. so few words, worry beads in the
mouth, accrue value, being tongued over & over: go fuck yourself, or.
there's a friend (in need).

hey he sez, stopping me by the liquor store, i think what for? small
change? you better vote NDP or, lifting his cast, i'll club you over
the head. & the grin runs somewhere between me & his buddies who rock
back on their heels & applaud.
'votes get cast, silently in vacant
lots the terms run free. dying into the grass. wild not free, these men
kill the system in themselves, themselves ghosts of the open air.

[1980]

LISTEN

He was reading to her, standing on the other side of the kitchen counter where she was making salad for supper, tender orange carrot in hand almost transparent at its tip, slender, & she was wondering where such carrots came from in winter. He was standing in the light reading to her from a book he was holding, her son behind him at the table where the amber light streamed from under its glass shade bought, she had, for its warm colour midwinter, tho he had called it a cheap imitation of the real thing. Under it, her son was drawing red Flash & blue Superman into a comic he was making, painstakingly having stapled the pages together & now with his small & definite hand trying to draw exact images of D.C. Superstars & Marvel heroes none of them had ever seen except in coloured ink. But he was reading to her about loss, excited, because someone had named it at last, was naming even as he read it, the shape of what he felt to be his own, recognized at last in words coming at him from the page, coming to her through his emphatic & stirred voice stumbling over the rough edges of words that weren't his, even as he was embracing them. Lost, how dancing had lost touch with the ring dance which was a collective celebration—she was standing with the grater in one hand, carrot in the other, wondering if the grating sound would disturb him. She wanted to hear what had stirred him. She wanted to continue the movement of making salad which, in the light & the Lowenbrau they shared, was for once coming so easily, almost was spring stirring round the corner of the house in a rhythm of rain outside she was moving in, barely knowing, except for the wetness of walking home—hand in hand, he was saying, a great circle like the circle of the seasons, where now people barely touch each other, or at least with the waltz they used to dance in couples & then with rock apart but *to* each other, whereas now, he caught her eye, the dances we've been to you can see people dancing alone, completely alone with the sound.

Lifting the carrot to the grater, pressing, watching flakes of carrot fall to the board, she felt accused in some obscure way, wanted to object, thought up an obscure argument about quadrilles being collective in ballrooms where all the guests were invited, their places in the collectivity known & symbolized by their places in the dance. But now, & she recalled the new year's eve party they'd been to, almost a hundred people, strangers, come, or people don't know each other in a city the way they do in a village, but it wasn't really that, or that only glanced off what the book was saying about husbandry & caring for the soil. The whole carrot was shrinking into a thousand orange flakes heaped & scattered at once, the whole carrot with its almost transparent sides shining in the light, had ground down to a stump her fingers clutched close to the jagged edges of tin, she saw her fingers grating, saw blood flying like carrot flakes, wondered why she imagined blood as part of the salad . . .

Listen, he was saying, this is where he's really got it. And he read a long passage about their imprisonment in marriage, all the married ones with that impossible ideal of confining love to one—'one cannot love a particular woman unless one loves womankind,' he read. Listen, he said, & he read her a passage about the ring dance, about the participation of couples in the one great celebration, the 'amorous feast that joins them to all living things.' He means fertility, she said, thinking, oh no, oh back to that, woman's one true function. He means fertility of the earth, he said, he means our lives aware of seasonal growth & drawing nourishment from that, instead of material acquisition & exploitation. Listen, & he read a passage about sexual capitalism, about the crazy images of romance that fill people's heads, & sexual 'freedom' & 'skill' & the 'me-generation' on all the racks of all the supermarket stores.

Using her palms like two halves of a split spoon, she scooped up the heap of carrot flakes & set them onto a bed of lettuce, dark, because it was romaine, torn into pieces in the wooden bowl with other green things. Dance. In & out. She watched the orange flakes, glistening again in a skin of oil, dance in & out among the green she tossed with real spoons, each dipping into the dark that lay at the heart of, what, their hearts, they had, the other night, sunk into bed at the end of the party, drunk & floating, their laughter moving in memory through the night as they lay wrapt in the warmth of what everyone had said & how they moved away & toward each other & loved in very obscure ways. & they had made love to everyone in each other, & to each other, falling thru & away from each other. Listen, she said, as the rain came up & she set the salad on the wooden table underneath the lamp.

[1980]

yes

JADE a sign on the road announces, *ijada, piedra de*, stone of that space between the last rib and the hipbone, that place i couldn't bear the weight of his sleeping hand upon—and my fingers flutter to my ring, gone. only a white band the skin of years hidden under its reminder to myself of the self i was marrying—'worthless woman, wilful girl.' standing athwart, objecting, 'so as to thwart or obstruct,' 'perversely.' no, so as to retain this small open space that was mine.

perverse in that, having to defend myself from attack, encroachment on that soft abyss, that tidal place i knew as mine, know now is the place i find with you. not perverse but turned the *right* way round, redefined, it signals us beyond limits in a new tongue our connection runs along.

you call me on the phone, have you lost something? and i startle yes. half of it is here, you say. not lost, not lost. broken open on my finger, broken open by your touch, and i didn't even feel a loss, leaving the need for limits at your place, leaving the urge to stand apart i sink into our mouths' hot estuary, tidal yes we are, leaking love and saying it deep within.

[1984]

healing

stray white lips, petals kissing middle distance between blue iris you, me, moss there and small starred dandelions. in the drift gathering, days, hours without touch. gauze, waiting for the two lips of your incision to knit, waiting for our mouths to close lip to other lip in the full spring of wet, revived, season plants come alive. this season of your body traumatized, muscles torn where the knife went, a small part of you gone. gall, all that is bitter, melancholy.

each day we climb a small hill, looking. rufous hummingbirds dive before our very eyes kissing space. fawn lilies spring moist lips to wing filled air. i want to open you like a butterfly. over bluffs at the rim of blue distance we might leap, free fall, high above us four bald eagles scream for pure glee. glee, it falls on us, bits of sound shining, rain of rung glass. glisten, glare. (g)listen, all of it goes back shining, even *gall* does, glass and glazing, every yellow hope a spark, lucid and articulate in the dark i wake to, reaching for you. somewhere a bird calls. it is our bird, the one that wings brightness, *springan*, scattering through us as your lips open under mine and the new rain comes at last, lust, springs in us beginning all over again.

[1984]

THE DIFFERENCE THREE MAKES: A NARRATIVE

for Mary S.

in the dream we argued about a preposition as if in French Emily held the key to the whole story.

you wanted it to read: The Family of Emily Courte is Tired from *The Family of Emily Courte is Tired*—how do we translate?

not that i remember translating so much as turning the page in a kind of hungry absorption and then backing up to reflect, as one does, about the message of the title, i thought—(this was all about framing, for instance the kind of framing a table of contents does)—what's the point of repeating, je me tue à vous le répeter (how many times?) unless it's of . . . tired of . . .

'the family romance.'

because the bed had framed you/us watching her slide out into this room so full of women and her father too. three midwives three wise women around your Mary. three the beginning of family, Emily at the end . . .

there's a chapter within the book from which it takes its name you explained, as the child does the family. or the family does the child i thought. it wasn't Emily that stopped short.

an alley walled by buildings on three sides. this was not in the table of contents.

the house on the hill will be sold, the house you brought her through snow to. lying in sun on the carpet to cure her yellow, sucking white, and the deep content of night out in the country she was not to be brought up in. so there is the letting go of leaves of strawberry begonias, spider plant, the deck, the dogs . . . he wanted out so you moved.

this book, turning the pages tabled there, coupé Court(e). the book that Emily cannot read she is the title page for.

alone no solace, alone the symbiosis of two—pre-mirror, pre-frame. don't drop it: there is that fear you have, of not being able to carry her all alone.

the family is Emily but Emily is more.
Emily short with the short-sightedness of the small sleeps in her crib, blonde hair splayed in her court of little pigs (3) bears (3) the little train that could, dream the family dream of inheritance in her, in her irritants not the dream that could soothe her at all.

this was all about framing as a border frames the contents of the title page where rights are displayed. beyond design designation under the sign of famililacae: nothing so pure as a lily . . .

denying her her father he charged when you moved to the city where the difference three makes became apparent in the helping of friends. at the end of the alley sometimes you turn around.

(f.) Emily out of family. tabled.
in a trice (this is not nice Emilology) en trois coups de cuiller à pot stirred up in the social she comes out little dresses little rag doll tout Court(e) hands full of the train of them repeating tired so tired of the long sanctification in which she appears daddy's angel girl.

the difference three makes always this cry in the night as you return from your fear to find her calling daddy, name for the third person standing by who can pry her loose from the overwhelming two, tu. you teach her big girls don't nurse. let me hold it mama. the languaged mouth as one little pig went to market, one little first person one.

third person could be anyone when it comes to that.

the story says paternal—I, don't rock the stable.

for the Word is His she will write as I distinct from mother-mine-o-lode, turning away in the script that writes her out of the reciprocal and into what she will become when narrative begins its triple beat about, about her/ accusative.

this is all about framing.

[1991]

SEEING IT GO UP IN SMOKE

'as if'
what happens is only the flare of a cigarette. he is smoking. she is watching *summer and smoke*. they have driven through the valley in a haze of summer sharing the silence of twilight. the silence is sharing or. silence is a screen between, silence reflects what does not get said. the apparent silence of two heads looking out of each its own space

'as if nothing'
were happening he might have thought, toward the light his camera shares, a going intent, having brought the mask that makes his face an inner room. they had rented the room, had viewed it, viewed the bed and tv screen she had already imagined, taking his mask which is an image of himself as the outer face of a movie she is trying to silence in her head. the way words keep moving it is supposing. what might he make of it, what he has seen, and has she seen behind (a screen) his image of it?

'nothing untoward'
he means toward her he does not reveal intent but lets it, whatever that is, happen. as it happens her listening to, but she is also watching, the talkies he once said she is given to, given over completely he means taken over by, this incessant ripple of motive: will she? does he? have something else in mind? stretched out on the bed she is intent on following the reach of their desire. does he think she wants to fill up the silence between? or does she think smokescreen, seeing him compose in silent frames that other movie he is making, the tv screen a part of what he composes, his nudity opposes (it, her, them). speaking thus to her, or speaking to his camera? like summer's going up

'were'
he says toward their watching where they are going, don't mind me, meaning (a)side or (un)toward meaning nothing is happening but him (nude) and her (fully clothed) watching him masked, or the mask and him, take place elsewhere she has fallen between. she was not there where he was watching himself watch her watching summer smoke in some imagined south they have not entered where, behind the mask and silently, desire is to be viewed

'happening'
between and out of it she feels is it but it is, the camera making it happen. pull the plunger will you, he says, in the blink of an eye that takes her where he has posed himself at the edge of her attention. is he the movie then? he is the making, and making it opposes her viewing what is made, though in seeing it she is remaking a movie that goes on viewing itself in the smoke of being unseen 'as if nothing untoward were happening'

[1991]

LOUISE GLÜCK (b. 1943)

Born in 1943 in New York City, Louise Glück (pronounced *Glick*) studied at Sarah Lawrence College and Columbia and has taught widely in the US, at Goddard College and the universities of North Carolina, Virginia, Iowa, and Cincinnati. She has received the Academy of American Poets Prize, the Tiejens Memorial Prize, the National Book Critics Circle Award for Poetry, and the Pulitzer Prize. Her books include *Firstborn* (1969), *The House on Marshland* (1975), *The Garden* (1976), *Descending Figure* (1980), *The Triumph of Achilles* (1985), *Ararat* (1990), and *The Wild Iris* (1992). Her essays on poetry are collected in *Proofs & Theories* (1994). She lives in Vermont and teaches at Williams College.

Much of the early commentary about Glück's poetry, lamenting its starkness, was based on the assumption that the work was autobiographical. Comparisons were made with the so-called confessional poems of Sylvia Plath and Robert Lowell. However, in 'Against Sincerity' (*Proofs & Theories: Essays on Poetry*, 1994), Glück argues at length that the poet's task is not confession or self-expression but 'the transformation of the actual to the true. And the ability to achieve such transformation, especially in art that presumes to be subjective, depends on conscious willingness to distinguish truth from honesty or sincerity.' She speaks of the 'I' of the poem as a *creation*. 'To recapitulate: the source of art is experience, the end product truth, and the artist, surveying the actual, constantly intervenes and manages, lies and deletes, all in the service of truth.'

She distinguishes between mere honesty, which she dismisses as 'the decanting of personality', and the genuine creativity, or 'inward listening, attentiveness' that characterized the poetry of Keats. 'Honest speech is a relief and not a discovery. When we speak of honesty, in relation to poems, we mean the degree to which and the power with which the generating impulse has been transcribed. Transcribed, not transformed. Any attempt to evaluate the honesty of a text must always lead away from that text and toward intention. This may make an interesting trail, more interesting, very possibly, than the poem. The mistake, in any case, is in our failure to separate poetry which sounds like honest speech from honest speech. The earlier mistake is in assuming that there is only one way for poetry to sound.'

Glück rejects the notion that poems are like fingerprints; in great poems, she says, 'the materials are subjective, but the methods are not.' Experience is changed by passing through the crucible of art—'heightened, distilled, made memorable'. 'The advantage of poetry over life is that poetry, if it is sharp enough, may last.'

In 'Disruption, Hesitation, Silence' (*Proofs & Theories*), she speaks out against the tendency towards length and expansiveness in poetry. 'I don't think that more information always makes a richer poem. I am attracted to ellipsis, to the unsaid, to suggestions, to eloquent, deliberate silence. The unsaid, for me, exerts great power. . . . it is analogous to the unseen; for example, to the power of ruins, to works of art either damaged or incomplete. Such works inevitably allude to larger contexts; they haunt because they are not whole, though wholeness is implied. . . . It seems to me that what is wanted, in art, is to harness the power of the unfinished. All earthly experience is partial. Not simply because it is subjective, but because that which we do not know, of the universe, of mortality, is so much more vast than that which we do know. What is unfinished or has been destroyed participates in these mysteries. The problem is to make a whole that does not forfeit this power.'

Glück wishes to create in the poem 'that space which is an alternative to information'. In speaking of the craft of Rilke, she makes the point that 'What wholeness gives up is the dynamic: the mind need not rush in to fill a void. And Rilke loved his voids. In the broken thing, moreover, human agency is oddly implied; breakage, whatever its cause, is the dark complement to the art of making; the one implies the other. The thing that is broken has particular authority over the act of change.' Glück argues for suggestion rather than amplification; thus she praises Rilke for marrying 'lyric intensity to irregularity of form' and links him with poets such as T.S. Eliot, George Oppen, and John Berryman, each of whom she considers 'a master of not saying'.

Glück's own mastery of craft is built around these convictions of economy, suggestiveness, and the 'absence of vanity' that she finds so attractive in Oppen, a poet who, she says, does not appropriate experience or exhibit proprietory impulses in his work. 'His poem is not a campaign; he does not pose himself as the missing advocate or champion. . . . The poem honours a boundary. . . . The boundary, in absolute terms, between one being and another.'

With refreshing irony, Glück's latest volume, *The Wild Iris*, breaks many of her own rules: it is essentially a long poem for voices, an argument with God, or dialogue of self and soul, that recalls Milton's *Paradise Lost* at one end of the poetic spectrum and Ted Hughes's *Crow* at the other; and it revels in abstraction and direct statement. Rather than practise the art of 'not saying', in this garden even the flowers speak.

FOR MY MOTHER

It was better when we were
together in one body.
Thirty years. Screened
through the green glass
of your eye, moonlight
filtered into my bones
as we lay

in the big bed, in the dark,
waiting for my father.
Thirty years. He closed
your eyelids with
two kisses. And then spring
came and withdrew from me
the absolute
knowledge of the unborn,
leaving the brick stoop
where you stand, shading
your eyes, but it is
night, the moon
is stationed in the beech tree,
round and white among
the small tin markers of the stars:
Thirty years. A marsh
grows up around the house.
Schools of spores circulate
behind the shades, drift through
gauze flutterings of vegetation.

[1975]

EPITHALAMIUM

There were others; their bodies
were a preparation.
I have come to see it as that.

As a stream of cries.
So much pain in the world—the formless
grief of the body, whose language
is hunger—

And in the hall, the boxed roses:
what they mean

is chaos. Then begins
the terrible charity of marriage,
husband and wife

climbing the green hill in gold light
until there is no hill,
only a flat plain stopped by the sky.

Here is my hand, he said.
But that was long ago.
Here is my hand that will not harm you.

[1980]

Dedication to Hunger

1 *From the Suburbs*

They cross the yards
and at the back door
the mother sees with pleasure
how alike they are, father and daughter—
I know something of that time.
The little girl purposefully
swinging her arms, laughing
her stark laugh:
It should be kept secret, that sound.
It means she's realized
that he never touches her.
She is a child; he could touch her
if he wanted to.

2 *Grandmother*

'Often I would stand at the window—
your grandfather
was a young man then—
waiting, in the early evening.'

That is what marriage is.
I watch the tiny figure
changing to a man
as he moves toward her,
the last light rings in his hair.
I do not question

their happiness. And he rushes in
with his young man's hunger,
so proud to have taught her that:
his kiss would have been
clearly tender—
Of course, of course. Except
it might as well have been
his hand over her mouth.

3 *Eros*

To be male, always
to go to women
and be taken back
into the pierced flesh:

I suppose
memory is stirred.
And the girl child
who wills herself
into her father's arms
likewise loved him
second. Nor is she told
what need to express.
There is a look one sees,
the mouth somehow desperate—

Because the bond
cannot be proven.

4 *The Deviation*

It begins quietly
in certain female children:
the fear of death, taking as its form
dedication to hunger,
because a woman's body
is a grave; it will accept
anything. I remember
lying in bed at night
touching the soft, digressive breasts,

touching, at fifteen,
the interfering flesh
that I would sacrifice
until the limbs were free
of blossom and subterfuge: I felt
what I feel now, aligning these words—
it is the same need to perfect,
of which death is the mere byproduct.

5 *Sacred Objects*

Today in the field I saw
the hard, active buds of the dogwood
and wanted, as we say, to capture them,
to make them eternal. That is the premise
of renunciation: the child,
having no self to speak of,
comes to life in denial—

I stood apart in that achievement,
in that power to expose
the underlying body, like a god
for whose deed
there is no parallel in the natural world.

[1980]

MOCK ORANGE

It is not the moon, I tell you.
It is these flowers
lighting the yard.

I hate them.
I hate them as I hate sex,
the man's mouth
sealing my mouth, the man's
paralyzing body—

and the cry that always escapes,
the low, humiliating
premise of union—

In my mind tonight
I hear the question and pursuing answer
fused in one sound
that mounts and mounts and then
is split into the old selves,
the tired antagonisms. Do you see?
We were made fools of.
And the scent of mock orange
drifts through the window.

How can I rest?
How can I be content
when there is still
that odour in the world?

[1985]

LEGEND

My father's father came
to New York from Dhlua:
one misfortune followed another.
In Hungary, a scholar, a man of property.
Then failure: an immigrant
rolling cigars in a cold basement.

He was like Joseph in Egypt.
At night, he walked the city;
spray of the harbour
turned to tears on his face.

Tears of grief for Dhlua—forty houses,
a few cows grazing the rich meadows—

Though the great soul is said to be
a star, a beacon,
what it resembles better is a diamond:
in the whole world there is nothing
hard enough to change it.

Unfortunate being, have you ceased to feel
the grandeur of the world
that, like a heavy weight, shaped
the soul of my grandfather?

From the factory, like sad birds his dreams
flew to Dhlua, grasping in their beaks
as from moist earth in which a man could see
the shape of his own footprint,
scattered images, loose bits of the village;
and as he packed the leaves, so within his soul
this weight compressed scraps of Dhlua
into principles, abstractions
worthy of the challenge of bondage:

in such a world, to scorn
privilege, to love
reason and justice, always
to speak the truth—

which has been
the salvation of our people
since to speak the truth gives
the illusion of freedom.

[1985]

HORSE

What does the horse give you
that I cannot give you?

I watch you when you are alone,
when you ride into the field behind the dairy,
your hands buried in the mare's
dark mane.

Then I know what lies behind your silence:
scorn, hatred of me, of marriage. Still,
you want me to touch you; you cry out
as brides cry, but when I look at you I see
there are no children in your body.
Then what is there?

Nothing, I think. Only haste
to die before I die.

In a dream, I watched you ride the horse
over the dry fields and then
dismount: you two walked together;
in the dark, you had no shadows.
But I felt them coming toward me
since at night they go anywhere,
they are their own masters.

Look at me. You think I don't understand?
What is the animal
if not passage out of this life?

[1985]

BROWN CIRCLE

My mother wants to know
why, if I hate
family so much,
I went ahead and
had one. I don't
answer my mother.
What I hated
was being a child,
having no choice about
what people I loved.

I don't love my son
the way I meant to love him.
I thought I'd be
the lover of orchids who finds
red trillium growing
in the pine shade, and doesn't
touch it, doesn't need
to possess it. What I am
is the scientist,
who comes to that flower
with a magnifying glass

and doesn't leave, though
the sun burns a brown
circle of grass around
the flower. Which is
more or less the way
my mother loved me.

I must learn
to forgive my mother,
now that I'm helpless
to spare my son.

[1990]

THE WILD IRIS

At the end of my suffering
there was a door.

Hear me out: that which you call death
I remember.

Overhead, noises, branches of the pine shifting.
Then nothing. The weak sun
flickered over the dry surface.

It is terrible to survive
as consciousness
buried in the dark earth.

Then it was over: that which you fear, being
a soul and unable
to speak, ending abruptly, the stiff earth
bending a little. And what I took to be
birds darting in low shrubs.

You who do not remember
passage from the other world
I tell you I could speak again: whatever
returns from oblivion returns
to find a voice:

from the centre of my life came
a great fountain, deep blue
shadows on azure seawater.

[1992]

TRILLIUM

When I woke up I was in a forest. The dark
seemed natural, the sky through the pine trees
thick with many lights.

I knew nothing; I could do nothing but see.
And as I watched, all the lights of heaven
faded to make a single thing, a fire
burning through the cool firs.
Then it wasn't possible any longer
to stare at heaven and not be destroyed.

Are there souls that need
death's presence, as I require protection?
I think if I speak long enough
I will answer that question, I will see
whatever they see, a ladder
reaching through the firs, whatever
calls them to exchange their lives—

Think what I understand already.
I woke up ignorant in a forest;
only a moment ago, I didn't know my voice
if one were given me
would be so full of grief, my sentences
like cries strung together.
I didn't even know I felt grief
until that word came, until I felt
rain streaming from me.

[1992]

END OF WINTER

Over the still world, a bird calls
waking solitary among black boughs.

You wanted to be born; I let you be born.
When has my grief ever gotten
in the way of your pleasure?

Plunging ahead
into the dark and light at the same time
eager for sensation

as though you were some new thing, wanting
to express yourselves

all brilliance, all vivacity

never thinking
this would cost you anything,
never imagining the sound of my voice
as anything but part of you—

you won't hear it in the other world,
not clearly again,
not in birdcall or human cry,

not the clear sound, only
persistent echoing
in all sound that means good-bye, good-bye—

the one continuous line
that binds us to each other.

[1992]

Witchgrass

Something
comes into the world unwelcome
calling disorder, disorder—

If you hate me so much
don't bother to give me
a name: do you need
one more slur
in your language, another
way to blame
one tribe for everything—

as we both know,
if you worship
one god, you only need
one enemy—

I'm not the enemy.
Only a ruse to ignore
what you see happening
right here in this bed,
a little paradigm
of failure. One of your precious flowers
dies here almost every day
and you can't rest until
you attack the cause, meaning

whatever is left, whatever
happens to be sturdier
than your personal passion—

It was not meant
to last forever in the real world.
But why admit that, when you can go on
doing what you always do,
mourning and laying blame,
always the two together.

I don't need your praise
to survive. I was here first,
before you were here, before
you ever planted a garden.
And I'll be here when only the sun and moon
are left, and the sea, and the wide field.

I will constitute the field.

[1992]

RETREATING LIGHT

You were like very young children,
always waiting for a story.
And I'd been through it all too many times;
I was tired of telling stories.
So I gave you the pencil and paper.
I gave you pens made of reeds
I had gathered myself, afternoons in the dense meadows.
I told you, write your own story.

After all those years of listening
I thought you'd know
what a story was.

All you could do was weep.
You wanted everything told to you
and nothing thought through yourselves.

Then I realized you couldn't think
with any real boldness or passion;
you hadn't had your own lives yet,
your own tragedies.
So I gave you lives, I gave you tragedies,
because apparently tools alone weren't enough.

You will never know how deeply
it pleases me to see you sitting there
like independent beings,

to see you dreaming by the open window,
holding the pencils I gave you
until the summer morning disappears into writing.

Creation has brought you
great excitement, as I knew it would,
as it does in the beginning.
And I am free to do as I please now,
to attend to other things, in confidence
you have no need of me anymore.

[1992]

GARY GEDDES (b. 1940)

Gary Geddes was born in Vancouver and raised there, except for a four-year period spent in Saskatchewan as a young boy. While completing high school and studying at the University of British Columbia, he worked in a department store, a sugar refinery, express warehouse, and boat rentals. He drove water-taxi and taught school for a year at Texada Island before enrolling for a Diploma in Education at Reading University in England and M.A. and Ph.D. at University of Toronto. He has taught widely at post-secondary institutions across Canada and is now a professor of English and Creative Writing at Concordia University in Montreal. He founded the critical series Studies in Canadian Literature in the late 1970s and two publishing companies, Quadrant Editions and Cormorant Books, and has edited numerous anthologies, including *15 Canadian Poets* (1971) in its various editions, *Skookum Wawa: Writings of the Canadian Northwest* (1975), *Vancouver: Soul of A City* (1986), *Compañeros: An Anthology of Writings About Latin America* (1990), and *The Art of Short Fiction: An International Anthology* (1992). He has also published short stories, plays, criticism, translation, and non-fiction, including *Letters from Managua: Meditations on Politics and Art* (1990).

Geddes's poetry publications include *Rivers Inlet* (1971), *Snakeroot* (1973), *Letter of the Master of Horse* (1973, E.J. Pratt medal and prize), *War & other measures* (1976), *The Acid Test* (1980, National Poetry Prize), *The Terracotta Army* (1984, America's Best Book Award in the 1985 Commonwealth Poetry Competition), *Hong Kong* (1987, Writers' Choice Award, National Magazine Gold Award), *No Easy Exit / Salida difícil* (1989, Archibald Lampman Prize), *Light of Burning Towers: Poems New & Selected* (1990), *Girl by the Water* (1994), *The Perfect Cold Warrior* (1995), and *Active Trading: Selected Poems 1970-1995* (1996).

In an interview with Alan Twigg in *Strong Voices* (1988), Geddes discusses his use of the mask, or persona: 'The mask helps me to find a voice. I seem to be able to get into the heads of my characters by using the first-person more easily than I could talking about them in the third-person. . . . I had to work hard to overcome the sense that I should be seen and not heard, that my accent was odd and my thought-processes were unattractive. Beyond that, however, I have my own need to remain private. A writer gives himself away with every word he writes, I realize that. But I find it difficult, and not entirely valuable, to write about my own daily life. That life sifts into everything, of course, and colours the most seemingly objective material, even pieces as exotic and non-native as *Letter of the Master of Horse* and *The Terracotta Army*.'

Asked to elaborate on the personal significance of the mask, Geddes says: 'Frye once commented that every poet has one or two structures of feeling that are absolutely central to him and his work, and that these structures are often consciously or unconsciously announced in his title-poems. I'd say that I am preoccupied with injured figures, figures caught in the machinery of society or politics or religion. There's something in common between the narrator of *Horse*, Chartier, the potter in Xian and Sandra Lee Scheuer, who was killed at Kent State University. Perhaps a good shrink could tell you why I write about these individuals. I might venture a guess or two myself . . . .'

When asked about the origins of the poetic impulse, he refers to the aboriginal concept of the 'deep-name': 'It's the name by which God would really know you. Not as Alan Twigg, but a real name, such as He-Who-Would-Shoot-From-The-Hip-Before-Falling-Off-His-Horse. That sort of thing. In analysis once I described the experience of having my father come from Saskatchewan, after my mother's death, to take me to live with him and his second wife. I was seven and I was sitting on the piano bench. I'd had only twelve lessons. I'd learned to play a few pieces. After my father arrived at the house, he sat behind me on the couch as I was playing the piano. As I recounted this story for the psychologist, I burst into tears. Deep sobs. It suddenly became clear to me that I had been playing for my life. I had to get that piece right or my father would not love me, would not take me with him. Of course, that was not accurate at all, but that was how I'd perceived it at the time and, perhaps, how I have perceived it unconsciously all these years. There I was on my island piano-stool. And that is my deep-name: He-Who-Sings-For-His-Own-Life. . . . At a certain point, however, the singing serves other functions than self-validation. You start to sing of the tribe, to keep the record, to bear witness.'

While he has been described by George Woodcock as 'Canada's best political poet' and is well-known for his writings about Asian, Latin American, and Middle East politics, Geddes, in an interview with Louise Schrier in *Anthos* (November 1986), prefers to direct attention to his interest in craft: 'I want the poems to touch people deeply and make them care about themselves, their world, and language itself. This view of poetry does not lend itself to extremes of eclecticism or undue ornamentation. But, I'd say, the techniques and craft are there, for those who want to look carefully. . . . The thrust of narrative allows me certain freedoms that aren't available to the strictly lyric poet, one of which is a degree of monumental distraction (in character, event, terrain) that draws a reader's attention away from the so-called niceties of form.'

Also known for his narratives and theoretical writings about the long poem, Geddes explains the importance of pacing, or momentum, in poetic narratives: 'I tried something different. I used the form of diary jottings, to keep the sections short and lyrical, highly charged and with the kind of intensity of image of a stopped-frame in a film. Kroetsch called those sections "narrative remnants", a phrase that makes sense to me. The reader is kept alert by both the intensity of the image, hopefully, and the energy and attention required to stitch together those non-linear, but still interconnected, narrative remnants. For the long poem, you need many different strategies, but it's the most exciting form in my view.'

Sandra Lee Scheuer

(Killed at Kent State University on May 4, 1970 by the Ohio National Guard)

You might have met her on a Saturday night
cutting precise circles, clockwise, at the Moon-Glo
Roller Rink, or walking with quick step

between the campus and a green two-storey house,
where the room was always tidy, the bed made,
the books in confraternity on the shelves.

She did not throw stones, major in philosophy
or set fire to buildings, though acquaintances say
she hated war, had heard of Cambodia.

In truth she wore a modicum of make-up, a brassiere,
and could, no doubt, more easily have married a guardsman
than cursed or put a flower in his rifle barrel.

While the armouries burned she studied,
bent low over notes, speech therapy books, pages
open at sections on impairment, physiology.

And while they milled and shouted on the commons
she helped a boy named Billy with his lisp, saying
Hiss, Billy, like a snake. That's it, SSSSSSSS,

tongue well up and back behind your teeth.
Now buzz, Billy, like a bee. Feel the air
vibrating in my windpipe as I breathe?

As she walked in sunlight through the parking-lot
at noon, feeling the world a passing lovely place,
a young guardsman, who had his sights on her,

was going down on one knee as if he might propose.
His declaration, unmistakable, articulate,
flowered within her, passed through her neck,

severed her trachea, taking her breath away.
Now who will burn the midnight oil for Billy,
ensure the perilous freedom of his speech?

And who will see her skating at the Moon-Glo
Roller Rink, the eight small wooden wheels
making their countless revolutions on the floor?

[1980]

HUMAN RIGHTS COMMISSION

The small woman seated before you describes her encounters with the military. In advance of the translation you hear the phrase 'Caravan of death'. She is not talking about a circus, her husband has not run away to a circus, though there was one in town the day you arrived, the real McCoy. Medieval etchings of the Dance of Death flicker in a dark recess of your brain.

Do you really want to hear this? Yesterday you were curious, took notes copiously. Numbers, implements of torture, the general who travelled the provinces with his exterminators and a chihuahua that sat on the back of the car seat licking his ear.

October 23, the end of so much. Five months later she too is arrested, kept naked twenty days, a sack over her head. Kicks, blows, electricity, threats against the children, pretence her husband is still alive. You look again at this woman and wonder how much she is not telling you. A heated pipe. Rats driven into the vagina through a heated pipe.

When the interview began, the portable radio was playing 'Moon Shadow' by Cat Stevens. A poster on the wall said, in Spanish: 'No one disappears into thin air.'

[1989]

ARPILLERAS

A woman cuts a triangle of corduroy
for a mountain, adjusts the cloth
so it rubs shoulders with another mountain,

candy-striped, and one cut from the sleeve
of a blue school tunic. Behind them
is a second range, probably

near the border in Argentina.
No one asks why distant mountains
are more exotic, with floral designs

from bright curtains, and catch more light,
not the school girls who stand with arms raised
in protest of the municipal order

closing their school, not the old-timers
leaning into death with their white wool hair
and match-stick canes. Her fingers tremble

as she cuts four houses from her husband's
best pair of trousers, worn once
to a christening, once to a union meeting,

and red canvas roofs from the raincoat of a daughter
who left suddenly at night by boat from Valparaiso.
She cross-stitches them to the sackcloth backing

to keep them in place, though she knows
nothing is secure against the night, the rumoured
fires. Tomorrow she will sell

her sackcloth tapestries for milk and beans
to feed the other children, but first
she must dream inhabitants in three dimensions,

the awkward, enduring women, moving
among the plaid windows and paisley shrubbery,
variously dressed, cut from the same cloth.

[1989]

Jimmy's Place

We found the cow in a grove below the road,
leaning against an alder for support,
her udder swollen, her breath ragged and grating
as a rasp. I could have drowned
in the liquid eye she turned to me.

Her calf, though dead, was perfectly positioned,
forelegs and head protruding from the flaming ring
of vulva. Too large, perhaps, or hind legs
broken through the sac, dispersing fluids.
Much as we tried we couldn't pry it loose
and the flesh around the legs began to give
from pressure on the rope. The cow
had no more strength and staggered back
each time we pulled. Tie her to the tree,
I said, being the schoolmaster and thinking
myself obliged to have an answer, even here
on the High Road, five miles south of town,
where the island bunched in the jumble
of its origins. It was coming, by God,
I swear it, this scrub roan with her shadow self
extending out behind, going in both directions
like a '52 Studebaker, coming by inches
and our feet slipping in the mud and shit
and wet grass. She raised her head and tried
to see what madness we'd concocted in her wake,
emitted a tearing gunny-sack groan,
and her liquid eye ebbed back to perfect white.

[1986]

FROM HONG KONG

HENDERSON

I did most of my fighting in Repulse Bay
in a hotel half-full of civilians.
We took up positions in a plush suite
on the second floor.

One of the men sat in an armchair
scanning hills out back with binoculars.
When he spotted movement, I'd swing
into the window and fire, then drop back.

Suddenly there was a woman in the doorway,
saying, My dog, I'm looking for water for my dog.
We pulled her down out of the line of fire
and gave the dog radiator water we used for tea.

Later, when the Japanese were two football fields away
and their planes were dive-bombing the barracks,
I thought of that woman and her parting comment:
If he bothers you by barking, shoot him.

SULLIVAN

There's a strange hush at St Stephen's
as we wait for them to storm the College.
Nurses drift like butterflies among the injured,
offering a word, a touch, a cigarette.
When the enemy bursts through the door

I'm lying on a cot at the far end of the corridor,
my head bandaged, my leg supported in a sling.
Two soldiers proceed to bayonet the sick and wounded
in their beds, to a chorus of screams and protests.
A nurse throws herself on top of one of our boys

to protect him—it might have been the kid
from Queen's—and they are both killed
by a single thrust of the bayonet.
I suppose they were sweethearts. Pinned
at last, she does not struggle. Her hands

open and close once, like tiny wings,
and the dark stain on her white, starched uniform
spreads like a chrysanthemum, a blood-red sun.
I cut the cord supporting my leg, slip on
the nearest smock and stand foolishly at attention,

making the salute. My right index finger
brushes the damp cotton of the bandage.
Later, the butchers are shot by their own officers;
one, apparently, had lost a brother
in the final assault.

4

I spent several mornings in the office of the *South China Morning Post*, reading copies of *Hong Kong News*, produced after the Japanese victory on Christmas Day in 1941. Early sun glinted off the high-rises and office towers in Victoria as I crossed on the Star Ferry and a huge Bayer Aspirin sign on the roof of a building confirmed my impression of the Crown Colony as a colossal headache.

I was staying in an unheated room in Chungking Mansions on Nathan Road, Kowloon-side, a high-rise slum that offered a rich assortment of internationals selling silk, sex and semi-precious gems. Ascending in the creaking elevator, you witnessed a discontinuous film-strip of erotic tableaux, heated arguments and half-finished transactions.

The cluster of rooms on the seventh floor was bucolic by contrast and had an air of exhausted camaraderie that surprised me, a tribute to the two families of Chinese who ran the place. My room looked out on an alley, a dark, awesome abyss that separated me from the balconies and opulent suites of the Holiday Inn. For only four dollars a night, I could switch my lights off and, unobserved from my window, watch the comings and goings in those expensive rooms. Or I could gaze at the stars through a cloud-cover of laundry hanging out to dry on the floor above.

I soon tired of both astrology and low-grade voyeurism and made the rounds of the local bars, particularly the Ship's Inn, run by a Vietnam veteran who'd parlayed his injuries and discharge into a small fortune on the black market. He'd also developed certain tastes that only the Orient could satisfy.

Jim was curious about my mission in Hong Kong, gathering information about Canadians killed or incarcerated there during the war. He ventured it was only non-combatants who wrote about the war. I nursed my glass of bitters and thought of Wilfred Owen, Charles Yale Harrison, even the Royal Rifles' own William Allister. Jim's stitch-marks ran from one ear down across his throat to the other shoulder, like a tiny rope ladder on a helicopter. I said I supposed he was probably right.

DONNELLY

The real heroes of Hong Kong
were the cooks and comedians.

When we returned
half of us were impotent.
One vet committed suicide

two weeks after his marriage.
Porteous took 3000 milligrams
of niacine daily till he died.

All we ever talked about was food.
—Howard, did I ever tell you
about my mother's pecan pies?
—No, Jack, I don't think you ever did.
Of course it was the hundredth time.
After the war, Jack sent me
a bushel of pecans from Texas.

We kept recipe books
instead of girlie magazines.
We'd have traded *Playboy*
for *Betty Crocker*
any day.

[1987]

THE QUALITY OF LIGHT

I
The quality of light is what arrests the man
moving, by gradations, through the snowy field
on skis. He eyes the outlines of trail
broken yesterday, shaped and contoured
by the wind, wind that never sleeps
yet seldom tires of letting its cold tongue
sculpt and sweep a tentative world of forms.

II
Two steps behind, conserving energy
by keeping to the beaten track, the dog
takes bites of snow and contemplates
an archeology of smell. Spoors, markings
of its undomesticated kind who cross
this man-made path at random, making
their own incursions in the narrative.

III

As though sun's rays, denied by angle
and position of the earth their customary
part, ricochet a thousand times among
the mirrored crystals, emerged more intense,
more light than light iself, so the man,
stumbling from thought to thought, catches
balance, a blinking new-born Lazarus.

IV

The sculpted troughs, too narrow now for use,
bind skis together at the harness, or nudge
one tip across another for a fall. The dog
looks on, one could almost say amused, though
not itself sure-footed on this stage. Both man
and dog recall how February storms
cause dunes of snow to curl like breaking waves.

V

Imagine them explorers in a vast Sahara
stepping from a blizzard of sand, half-stunned,
eyes asquint against abrasion. Flesh dreams
water, needing full protection from a sun
that burns whatever peeks from hair or cloth.
Light there is thick and granular and radiates
in ridges from the ground; here, the man

VI

with bamboo poles extending from his arms
has learned to cover space by watching
his companion, by reaching back in time
to when four limbs propelled him. The rigid sticks
beneath his feet are unconverging lines
in a parallel universe of cold,
where now he pauses, almost snow-blind, old,

V
and thinks of history every day rewritten
by revisionist monks, amnesiac
ideologues in flowing robes. He sees
them near stone-fences fast at work, pretends
scant notice, and ploughing his way
through a No-Man's-Land of ice, records
the wins and losses on both sides.

[1995]

ROBERT HASS (b. 1941)

Robert Hass was born in San Francisco and now lives in nearby Berkeley, where he teaches at the University of California. He completed his B.A. (1963) at St Mary's College and his M.A. (1965) and Ph.D. (1971) at Stanford University. He has also taught at the State University of New York at Buffalo, St Mary's College, University of Virginia, Columbia University, and Goddard College, and was poet-in-residence at The Frost Place in Franconia, New Hampshire, in 1978. His main poetry publications are *Field Guide* (1973, Yale Series of Younger Poets Award), *Winter Morning in Charlottesville* (1977), *Praise* (1979, William Carlos Williams Award), and *Human Wishes* (1989). In addition, he is widely known as the principal English translator of works by the Nobel Prize-winning poet Czeslaw Milosz, including *The Separate Notebooks* (1984), *Unattainable Earth* (1986), and *Collected Poems 1931-1987* (1988). He also translated *Selected Poems 1954-1986* by the Swedish poet Tomas Tranströmer and edited *Rock and Hawk: A Selection of Shorter Poems by Robinson Jeffers* (1987). His *Twentieth Century Pleasures: Prose on Poetry* (1984, National Book Critics Circle Award for Criticism), contains moving personal essays on poets as well as provocative discussions of image, form, and prosody.

In 'One Body: Some Notes on Form' (*Twentieth Century Pleasures*), Hass, echoing Milosz, calls art in general, and poetry in particular, 'humanly necessary as bread' and describes it as an activity of the spirit that makes its impact by virtue of its shaping powers, its urge to form. And form, he concludes, has much to do with 'intelligible recurrence', which is no longer a matter of rhyme and metrical regularity, but rather the forging of a type of thinking/imagining and a prosody that depend on echo, recurrence, similitude. What he calls form in a poem is 'the shape of its understanding', which will be felt consciously in the poem's 'argument' or progression and, less consciously but no less importantly, in its underlying pattern of sound, or rhythm.

In 'Listening and Making' (*Twentieth Century Pleasures*), Hass insists that rhythm is 'revolutionary ground' because 'It is always the place where the organic rises to abolish the mechanical and where energy announces the abolition of tradition. New rhythms are new perceptions.' In discussing 'the part rhythm plays in the work of the imagination. . . and a way of thinking about prosody in free verse', Hass comes to the startling conclusion that, 'Because rhythm has direct access to the unconscious, because it can hypnotize us, enter our bodies and make us move, it is a power. And power is political.' Furthermore, he argues that the sense of rhythm is psychologically rooted, in our conflicting urges for order and disorder:

'Rhythmic repetition initiates a sense of order. The feeling of magic comes from the way it puts us in touch with the promise of a deep sympathetic power in things: heartbeat, sunrise, summer solstice. This can be hypnotically peaceful; it can also be terrifying, to come so near self-abandonment and loss of autonomy, to whatever in ourselves wants to stay there in that sound, rocking and weeping, comforted. In the same way, freedom from pattern offers us at first an openness, a field of identity, room to move; and it contains the threat of chaos, rudderlessness, vacuity. Safety and magic on one side, freedom and movement on the other; their reverse faces are claustrophobia and obsession or agoraphobia and vertigo. They are the powers we move among, listening to a rhythm, as the soul in the bardo state moves among the heavens and the hells, and they are what makes the relation between repetition and variation in art dialectical and generative.'

Hass recalls Pound's definition of rhythm as 'a form carved in time' and offers an equally suggestive notion of his own: 'The line, when a poem is alive in its sound, measures: it is a proposal about listening.' Against the popular theories that poetry must be transformed by way of the image, or by radical shifts in content—from the grab-bag of surrealism to the change-purse of poetic intellectualizing—Hass places the magic of prosody: 'Way below the content of a particular poem, the idea that rhythm is natural, bodily, spontaneous, has been transformed into the idea that it is simply a given, invisible or inevitable. What this expresses is a kind of spiritual death that follows from living in a world we feel we have no hope of changing. . . . a poetry that makes fresh and resilient forms extends the possibilities of being alive.'

While Hass's work emanates from an abiding sense of place, which includes not only the geography and natural phenomena of the Pacific coast, but also the domestic world and its chief inhabitants—his wife, who is a psychotherapist, and his three children, all of whom figure prominently in his poems—he has a particularly postmodern distrust of the self in poetry: 'the perilousness of our individual lives is what makes the insight of the isolated lyric untenable.' Therefore, he has struggled to create a mode—the meditative lyric—that would sustain both personal allusion and the kind of ruminations that discredit, or deconstruct, stable notions of self and the poem's authority. In 'My Mother's Nipples', for example, he uses Brechtian alienating techniques (see the note on Atwood) to help himself navigate difficult emotional terrain; as he says of Rilke's 'Requiem', this is a poem that is 'raw and personal . . . which proceeds in bursts: it has the awareness of grief, which seems to exhaust itself and then breaks out again.'

Song

Afternoon cooking in the fall sun—
who is more naked
                than the man
yelling, 'Hey, I'm home!'
        to an empty house?
thinking because the bay is clear,
the hills in yellow heat,
& scrub oak red in gullies
    that great crowds of family
should tumble from the rooms
        to throw their bodies on the Papa-body,
            I-am-loved.

Cat sleeps in the windowgleam,
        dust motes.
    On the oak table
  filets of sole
stewing in the juice of tangerines,
  slices of green pepper
    on a bone-white dish.

[1973]

Meditation at Lagunitas

All the new thinking is about loss.
In this it resembles all the old thinking.
The idea, for example, that each particular erases
the luminous clarity of a general idea. That the clown-
faced woodpecker probing the dead sculpted trunk
of that black birch is, by his presence,
some tragic falling off from a first world
of undivided light. Or the other notion that,
because there is in this world no one thing
to which the bramble of *blackberry* corresponds,
a word is elegy to what it signifies.
We talked about it late last night and in the voice
of my friend, there was a thin wire of grief, a tone
almost querulous. After a while I understood that,

talking this way, everything dissolves: *justice*,
pine, *hair*, *woman*, *you* and *I*. There was a woman
I made love to and I remember how, holding
her small shoulders in my hands sometimes,
I felt a violent wonder at her presence
like a thirst for salt, for my childhood river
with its island willows, silly music from the pleasure boat,
muddy places where we caught the little orange-silver fish
called pumpkinseed. It hardly had to do with her.
Longing, we say, because desire is full
of endless distances. I must have been the same to her.
But I remember so much, the way her hands dismantled bread,
the thing her father said that hurt her, what
she dreamed. There are moments when the body is as numinous
as words, days that are the good flesh continuing.
Such tenderness, those afternoons and evenings,
saying *blackberry*, *blackberry*, *blackberry*.

[1979]

A Story About the Body

The young composer, working that summer at an artist's colony, had watched her for a week. She was Japanese, a painter, almost sixty, and he thought he was in love with her. Her loved her work, and her work was like the way she moved her body, used her hands, looked at him directly when she made amused and considered answers to his questions. One night, walking back from a concert, they came to her door and she turned to him and said, 'I think you would like to have me. I would like that too, but I must tell you that I have had a double mastectomy,' and when he didn't understand, 'I've lost both my breasts.' The radiance that he had carried around in his belly and chest cavity—like music—withered very quickly, and he made himself look at her when he said, 'I'm sorry. I don't think I could.' He walked back to his own cabin through the pines, and in the morning he found a small blue bowl on the porch outside his door. It looked to be full of rose petals, but he found when he picked it up that the rose petals were on top; the rest of the bowl—she must have swept them from the corners of her studio—was full of dead bees.

[1989]

HUMAN WISHES

This morning the sun rose over the garden wall and a rare blue sky leaped from east to west. Man is altogether desire, say the Upanishads. Worth anything, a blue sky, says Mr Acker, the Shelford gardener. Not altogether. In the end. Last night on television the ethnologist and the cameraman watched with hushed wonder while the chimpanzee carefully stripped a willow branch and inserted it into the anthill. He desired red ants. When they crawled slowly up the branch, he ate them, pinched between long fingers as the zoom lens enlarged his face. Sometimes he stopped to examine one, as if he were a judge at an ant beauty contest or God puzzled suddenly by the idea of suffering. There was an empty place in the universe where that branch wasn't and the chimp filled it, as Earlene, finding no back on an old Welsh cupboard she had bought in Saffron Walden, imagined one there and imagined both the cupboard and the imagined back against a kitchen wall in Berkeley, and went into town looking for a few boards of eighteenth-century tongue-in-groove pine to fill that empty space. I stayed home to write, or rather stayed home and stared at a blank piece of paper, waiting for her to come back, thinking tongue-in-groove, tongue-in-groove, as if language were a kind of moral cloud chamber through which the world passed and from which it emerged charged with desire. The man in the shop in Cambridge said he didn't have any old pine, but when Earlene went back after thinking about it to say she was sure she had seen some, the man found it. Right under his feet, which was puzzling. Mr Acker, hearing the story, explained. You know, he said, a lot of fiddling goes on in those places. The first time you went in, the governor was there, the second time he wasn't, so the chap sold you some scrap and he's four quid in pocket. No doubt he's having a good time now with his mates in the pub. Or he might have put it on the horses at Newmarket. He might parlay it into a fortune.

[1989]

NATURAL THEOLOGY

White daisies against the burnt orange of the windowframe,
lustreless redwood in the nickel grey of winter,
in the distance turbulence of water—the green regions
of the morning reflect whatever can be gained, normally,
by light, then give way to the blue regions of the afternoon
which do not reflect so much as they remember,

as if the light, one will all morning, yielded to a doubleness
in things—plucked skins of turkeys in an ill-lit butchershop
in the pitch-dark forenoon of a dreary day, or a stone bridge
in a small town, a cool café, tables with a violinback sheen,
ferns like private places of the body distanced and made cool—
images not quite left behind rising as an undertow
of endless transformation against the blurring world
outside the window where, after the morning clarities,
the faint reflection of a face appears; among the images
a road, repetitively, with meadow rue and yarrow
whitening its edges, and pines shadowing the cranberry brush,
and the fluting of one bird where the road curves and disappears,
becoming that gap or lack which is the oldest imagination
of need, defined more sharply by the silver-grey region
just before the sun goes down and the clouds fade
through rose to bruise to the city-pigeon colour of a sky
going dark and the wind comes up in brushstroke silhouettes
of trees and to your surprise the window mirrors back to you
a face open, curious, and tender; as dance is defined
by the body's possibilities arranged, this dance
belongs to the composures and the running down of things
in the used sugars of five-thirty: a woman straightening
a desk turns her calendar to another day, signalling
that it is another day where the desk is concerned
and that there is in her days what doesn't belong to the desk;
a kid turns on TV, flops on the couch to the tinny sound
of little cartoon parents quarrelling; a man in a bar
orders a drink, watches ice bob in the blond fluid,
he sighs and looks around; sad at the corners, nagged by wind,
others with packages; others dreaming, picking their noses
dreamily while they listen to the radio describe configurations
of the traffic they are stuck in as the last light
like held breath flickers among mudhens on the bay,
the black bodies elapsing as the dark comes on, and the face
in the window seems harder and more clear. The religion
or the region of the dark makes soup and lights a fire,
plays backgammon with children on the teeth or the stilettos
of the board, reads books, does dishes, listens
to the wind, listens to the stars imagined to be singing
invisibly, goes out to be regarded by the moon, walks
dogs, feeds cats, makes love in postures so various,

with such varying attention and intensity and hope,
it enacts the dispersion of tongues among the people
of the earth—*compris? versteh'*—and sleeps with sticky genitals
the erasures and the peace of sleep: exactly the half-moon
holds, and the city twinkles in particular windows, throbs
in its accumulated glow which is also and more blindingly
the imagination of need from which the sun keeps rising into morning light,
because desires do not split themselves up, there is one desire
touching the many things, and it is continuous.

[1989]

My Mother's Nipples

They're where all displacement begins.
They bulldozed the upper meadow at Squaw Valley,
where horses from the stable, two chestnuts, one white,
grazed in the mist and the scent of wet grass on summer mornings
and moonrise threw the owl's shadow on voles and wood rats
crouched in the sage smell the earth gave back
with the day's heat to the night air,
and after they had gouged up the deep-rooted bunchgrass
and the wet alkali-scented earth had been pushed aside
or trucked someplace out of the way, they poured concrete
and laid road—pleasant scent of tar in the spring sun—
and after the framers began to pound nails
and the electricians and plumbers came around to talk specs
with the general contractor, someone put up a green sign
with alpine daisies on it that said Squaw Valley Meadows.

*

'He wanted to get out of his head,' she said,
'so I told him to write about his mother's nipples.'

*

The cosmopolitan's song on this subject:

Alors! les nipples de ma mère!

The romantic's song

What could be more fair
than les nipples de ma mère?

The utopian's song

I will freely share
les nipples de ma mère.

The philosopher's song

Here was always there
with les nipples de ma mère

The capitalist's song

Fifty cents a share

The saint's song

Lift your eyes in prayer

The misanthrope's song

I can scarcely bear

The melancholic's song

They were never there,
les nipples de ma mère.
They are not anywhere.

The indigenist's song

And so the boy they called Loves His Mother's Tits
Went into the mountains and fasted for three days
On the fourth he saw a redtailed hawk with broken wings
On the fifth a gored doe in a ravine, entrails
Spilled onto the rocks, eye looking up at him
From the twisted neck. All the sixth day he was dizzy

And his stomach hurt. On the seventh he made three deep cuts
In the meat of his palm. He entered the pain at noon
And an eagle came to him crying three times like the mewling
A doe makes planting her hooves in the soft duff for mating
And he went home and they called him Eagle Three Times after that.

The regionalist's song

Los Pechos.
Rolling oak woodland between Sierra pines
and the simmering valley.

*

It was when he was asked to write about his mother's nipples
that Goethe made the famous observation
that all poems are occasional poems.

*

Pink, of course, soft; a girl's
She wore white muslin tennis outfits
in the style Helen Wills made fashionable.
Trim athletic swimsuits.
A small person, compact body. In the photographs
she's on the beach, standing straight,
hands on hips, grinning,
eyes desperate even then.

*

Mothers in the nineteen forties didn't nurse.
I never saw her naked. Oh! yes, I did,
once, but I can't remember. I remember
not wanting to.

Two memories. My mother had been drinking for several days, and I had thought dinner would be cancelled, so I wouldn't get to watch The Lone Ranger on my aunt's and uncle's television set. But we went to dinner and my aunt with her high-pitched voice took the high-minded tone that she took in my mother's presence. She had put out hard candies in little cut glass dishes as she always did, and we ate dinner, at which water was served to the grown-ups, and no one spoke except my uncle who teased us in his English accent. A tall man. He used to pat me on the head too hard and say, 'Robert of Sicily, brother of the Pope Urbane.' And after dinner when the television was turned on in the immaculate living room and Silver was running across the snowy screen, his mane shuddering from the speed, the doorbell rang. It was two men in white coats and my mother bolted from the table into the kitchen and out the back door. The men went in after her. The back stairs led into a sort of well between the two houses, and when I went into the kitchen I could hear her screaming, 'No! no!', the sound echoing and re-echoing among the houses. Recently I asked my older brother if this ever happened.

Some years later. I am perhaps ten, eleven. We are visiting my mother on the park-like grounds of the State Hospital in the Napa Valley. It is Sunday again. Green lawns, the heavy sweet scent of mock orange. Many of the patients are walking, alone or with their families, on the paths. One man seemed to be giving speeches to a tree. I had asked my grandmother why, if my mother had a drinking problem, that's the phrase I had been taught to use, why she was locked up with crazy people. It was a question I could have asked my father, but I understood that his answer would not be dependable. My grandmother said, with force, she had small red curls on her forehead, dressed with great style, you had better ask your father that. Then she thought better of it, and said They have a treatment program, dear, maybe it will help. I tried out that phrase, treatment program. My mother was sitting on a bench. She looked immensely sad, seemed to have shrunk. Her hair was pulled across her forehead and secured with a white beret, like Teresa Wright in the movies. At first my brother and I just sat next to her on the bench and cried. My father held my sister's hand. My grandmother and grandfather stood to one side, a separate group, and watched. Later, while they talked, I studied a middle-aged woman sitting on the next bench talking to herself in a foreign language. She was wearing a floral print dress and she spoke almost in a whisper but with passion, looking around from time to time, quick little furtive resentful glances. She was so careless of herself that I could see her breast, the brown nipple, when she leaned forward. I didn't want to look, and looked, and looked away.

*

Hot Sierra morning.
Brenda working in another room.
Rumble of heavy equipment in the meadow,
bird squall, Steller's jay, and then

the piercing three-note whistle of a robin.
They're mating now. Otherwise they're mute.
Mother-ing. Or mother-song.
Mother-song-song-song.

*

We used to laugh, my brother and I in college,
about the chocolate cake. Tears in our eyes laughing.
In grammar school, whenever she'd start to drink,
she panicked and made amends by baking chocolate cake.
And, of course, when we got home, we'd smell the strong, sweet smell
of the absolute darkness of chocolate,
and be too sick to eat it.

*

The first girl's breasts I saw
were the Chevie dealer's daughter Linda Hen's.
Pale in the moonlight. Little nubbins, pink-nosed.
I can still hear the slow sound of the surf
of my breath drawing in. I think I almost fainted.

*

Twin fonts of mercy, they used to say of the Virgin's breasts
in the old liturgy the Irish priests
could never quite handle, it being a form of bodily reference,
springs of grace, freshets
of lovingkindness. If I remember correctly,
there are baroque poems in this spirit
in which each of Christ's wounds is a nipple.
Drink and live: this is the son's blood.

*

Dried figs, candied roses.

What is one to say of the nipples of old women
who would, after all, find the subject
unseemly.

Yesterday I ran along the edge of the meadow in the heat
of late afternoon. So many wildflowers
tangled in the grass. So many grasses—
reedgrass and bentgrass and timothy, like quaking grass,
dogtail, brome—the seeds flaring from the stalks
in tight chevrons of green and purple-green
but loosening.

I said to myself:
some things do not blossom in this life.

I said: what we've lost is a story
and what we've never had
a song.

When my father died, I was curious to see in what ratio she would feel relieved and lost. All during the days of his dying, she stood by his bed talking to whichever of her children was present about the food in the cafeteria or the native state of the nurses—'She's from Portland, isn't that interesting? Your aunt Nell lived in Portland when Owen was working for the Fisheries.'—and turn occasionally to my father who was half-conscious, his eyes a morphine cloud, and say, in a sort of baby talk, 'It's all right, dear. It's all right.' And after he died, she was dazed, and clearly did not know herself whether she felt relieved or lost, and I felt sorry for her that she had no habit and so no means of self-knowing. She was waiting for us to leave so she could start drinking. Only once was she suddenly alert. When the young man from the undertaker's came and explained that she would need a copy of her marriage license in order to do something about the insurance and pensions, she looked briefly alive, anxious, and I realized that, though she rarely told the truth, she was a very poor dissembler. Now her eyes were a young girl's. What, she asked, if someone just couldn't turn up a marriage license; it seemed such a detail, there must be cases. I could see that she was trying out avenues of escape, and I was thinking, now what? They were never married? That would be funny somehow. I told her not to worry. I'd locate it. She considered this and said it would be fine. I could see she had made some decision, and then she grew indefinite again.

So, back in California, it was with some interest that I retraced the drive from San Francisco to Santa Rosa which my parents made in 1939, when according to my mother's story—it was the first account of it I'd ever heard—she and my father had eloped. The Sonoma County Office of Records was in a pink cinderblock building landscaped with reptilian pink oleanders which were still blooming in the Indian summer heat. It would have been raining when my parents drove that road in an old (I imagined) cream-coloured Packard convertible I had seen one photo of. I asked the woman at the desk for the marriage certificate for February 1939. I wondered what the surprise was going to be, and it was a small one. No problem, Mrs Minh said. But you had the date wrong, so it took me a while to find it. It was October, not February. Driving back to San Francisco, I had time to review this information. My brother was born in December 1939. Hard to see that it meant anything except that my father had tried very hard to avoid his fate. I felt so sorry for them. That they thought it was worth keeping a secret. Or, more likely, that their life together began in a negotiation too painful to be referred to again. That my mother had, with a certain fatality, let me pick up the license, so her first son would not know the circumstance of his conception. I felt sorry for her shame, for my father's panic. It finished off my dim wish that there had been an early romantic or ecstatic time in their lives, a blossoming, brief as a northern summer maybe, but a blossoming.

What we've never had is a song
and what we've really had is a song.

Sweet smell of timothy in the meadow.
Clouds massing east above the ridge in a sky
as blue as the mountain lakes,
so there are places on this earth clear all the way up
and all the way down
and in between a various blossoming,
the many seed shapes of the many things
finding their way into flower or not,
that the wind scatters.

There are all kinds of emptiness and fullness
that sing and do not sing.

I said: you are her singing.

She had passed out in a park. I came home from school and she was gone. I don't know what instinct sent me there. I suppose it was the only place I could think of where someone might hide. It was a grassy hillside lawn. She had passed out under an orange tree, curled up. Her face, flushed, eyelids swollen, was a ruin. Though I needed urgently to know whatever was in it, I could hardly bear to look. When I couldn't wake her, I decided to sit with her until she woke up. I must have been ten years old: I suppose I wanted for us to look like a son and mother who had been picnicking, like a mother who had fallen asleep in the warm light and scent of orange blossoms and a boy who was sitting beside her daydreaming, not thinking about anything in particular.

You are not her singing, though she is what's
broken in a song.
She is its silences.

She may be its silences.

Hawk drifting in the blue air,
grey of the granite ridges,
incense cedars, pines.

I tried to think of some place on earth she loved.

I remember she only ever spoke happily
of high school.

[1991]

DON MCKAY (b. 1942)

Born in Owen Sound, Ontario, Don McKay studied at the University of Saskatchewan and in Wales, has taught at the University of Western Ontario, and now teaches at the University of New Brunswick. His books include *Air Occupies Space* (1973), *Long Sault* (1975), *Lependu* (1978), *Lightning Ball Bait* (1981), *Birding, or Desire* (1983), and *Night Field* (1991, Governor General's Award).

In 'Some Remarks on Poetry and Poetic Attention' (*The Second Macmillan Anthology*, edited by John Metcalf and Leon Rooke, 1989), the full text of which can be found in the Poetics section, McKay says: 'I suspect that the quality of attention surrounding a poem is more important to me than poetry. A species of longing that somehow evades the usual desire to possess. Or, I should add, to use.' Writing poetry, 'that wonderful, useless musical machine', involves, he says, a mental set like that of bird-watching, 'a kind of suspended expectancy, tools at the ready'. He asks for 'a linguistics I can talk with. The meetings of experience and language—negotiation, abrasion, dominion, cross-pollination, intercourse, infection. . . wildness invading language as music, which occurs as soon as syntax is seen as energy rather than enthroned as order.'

In a second essay, 'Baler Twine: thoughts on ravens, home, and nature poetry', in *Studies in Canadian Literature* 18 (1993),

McKay tries to define his sense of wilderness: 'By "wilderness" I want to mean, not just a set of endangered spaces, but the capacity of all things to elude the mind's appropriations. That tools retain a vestige of wilderness is especially evident when we think of their existence in time and eventual graduation from utility: breakdown. To what degree do we own our houses, hammers, dogs? Beyond that line lies wilderness. We probably experience its presence most often in the negative as dry rot in the basement, a splintered handle, or shit on the carpet. But there is also the sudden angle of perception, the phenomenal surprise which constitutes the sharpened moments of *haiku* and imagism. The coat hanger asks a question; the armchair is suddenly crouched: in such defamiliarizations, often arranged by art, we encounter the momentary circumvention of the mind's categories to glimpse some thing's autonomy—its rawness, its *duende*, its alien being.'

A second concern in this essay is the notion of 'home', which, he says, 'is the action of the inner life finding outer form; it is the settling of self into the world.' 'Home makes possible the possession of the world, the rendering of the other as one's interior . . . home is also the site of our appreciation of the material world, where we lavish attention on its details, where we collaborate with it. In fact, it often seems that home, far from being just a concretization of self, is the place where it pours itself out into the world, interiority opening itself to material expression.'

McKay takes on the title of 'nature poet' with confidence, though he wants to remove that phrase from the 'vacuous piety' it normally evokes. The impulse behind nature poetry, he says, is 'a sort of readiness, a species of longing which is without the desire to possess'; it 'celebrates the wilderness of the other: it gives ontological applause.' While he is conscious that language is not transparent, or purely referential, McKay argues that the external world *does* speak to, or impinge on, our consciousness: 'Aeolian harpism relieves us of our loneliness as a species, reconnects us to the natural world, restores a coherent reality.' Like Levertov and Lilburn, he believes that 'poetic attention is based on a recognition and valuing of the other's wilderness; it leads to a work which is not a vestige of the other, but a translation of it.' Without denying post-structuralist claims that non-linguistic experience may be impossible, he insists that 'although it cannot be spoken, radical otherness exists. In fact nature poetry should not be taken to be avoiding anthropocentrism, but to be enacting it, thoughtfully. It performs that translation which is at the heart of being human, the simultaneous grasp and gift of home-making. And the persistence of poetic attention during the act of composition is akin to the translator's attention to the original, all the while she performs upon it a delicate and dangerous transformation. Our epistemological dilemma is not resolved, as by aeolian harpism, but ritualized and explored. . . . Part of the excitement inside this species of meditative act is lingustic; it's the excitement of a tool which has hatched the illicit desire to behave like an animal.' In a final statement, McKay identifies a cost for the entire nature/culture dichotomy: 'That is, to be blunt, it is as dangerous to act as though we were not a part of nature as it is to act as though we were not a part of culture; and the intellectual and political distortions produced by these contrary ideologies are greatly to be feared.'

McKay places great value on metaphor as the supreme human and linguistic operation which argues and illustrates that the things of this world stand in essential relation to one another. Metaphor, he argues, is the site, or rift, of that encounter.

THE GREAT BLUE HERON

What I remember
about the Great Blue Heron that rose
like its name over the marsh
is touching and holding that small
manyveined
wrist
upon the gunwale, to signal silently—
look

The Great Blue Heron
(the birdboned wrist).

[1983]

FRIDGE NOCTURNE

When it is late, and sleep,
off somewhere tinkering with his motorcycle, leaves you
locked in your iron birdhouse,
listen to your fridge, the old
armless weeping willow of the kitchen.

Humble murmur, it works its way
like the river you're far from, the Saugeen, the Goulais
the Raisin
muddily gathers itself in pools to drop things in
and fish things from,
the goodwill mission in the city of dreadful night.

[1983]

ADAGIO FOR A FALLEN SPARROW

In the bleak midwinter
frosty wind made moan
earth was hard as iron
water like a stone

Sparrows burning
                                        bright bright bright against the wind
resemble this item, this frozen
lump on the floor of my garage, as fire
resembles ash:
                                not much.
A body to dispose of,
probably one I've fed all winter, now
a sort of weightless fact,
an effortless repudiation of the whole shebang.
I'd like to toss it in the garbage can but can't let go
so easily. I'd bury it
but ground is steel
and hard to find. Cremation?
Much too big a deal, too rich and bardic
too much like an ode. Why not simply splurge
and get it stuffed, perch it proudly on the shelf
with Keats and Shelley and *The Birds of Canada*?

But when at last
I bury it beneath three feet of snow
there is nothing to be said.
It's very cold.
The air
has turned its edge
against us.
My bones
are an antenna picking up
arthritis, wordless keening of the dead.

So, sparrow, before drifting snow
reclaims this place for placelessness, I mark your grave
with four sticks broken from the walnut tree:
one for your fierce heart

one for your bright eye

one for the shit you shat upon my windshield
while exercising squatters' rights in my garage

and one to tell the turkey vultures where your thawing body lies
when they return next spring to gather you
into the circling ferment of themselves.

And my last wish: that they do
before the cat discovers you and eats you, throwing up,
as usual, beside the wicker basket in the upstairs hall.

[1983]

ESTHÉTIQUE DU CHIEN

Among humans, only
baseball gloves and vulvas, organs
who embrace their guests in velvet,
can rival my dog's nose.

Say hello. Pat his noble head.
Feel him lift your aura gently
lead it through frescoed passages
down to the furry boudoir of his heart.

Sweet Georgia Brown.
This is where your glands hang out,
this is where the band makes
gravy, thickening the mix
with woofs and recollected howls, *'f you*
don't like my taters how come you dig so deep, saliva
burbling down the long trombone.

[1983]

THE POEM, TO BE SLOW AS EVENING

must send its words to ballet school under the Red Pine
where they will learn stand and stand and
lift and cradle with the wind

must teach them roost and watch
and lose your wits with grace
swimming smoothly in the populace,

so that when the poem wants
rumour of the patient
animal of evening, all its words
will be as secret agents in the field

incunabula

empty and foolish, eyed and eared

[1983]

LISTEN AT THE EDGE

At the edge of firelight
where the earth is cradled in soft

black gloves filled with unknown hands, where
every word is shadowed by its animal, our ears

are empty auditoria for
scritch scritch scritch rr-ronk the
shh uh shh of greater

anonymities the little
brouhahas that won't lie still for type
and die

applauseless,
humus to our talking. Listen

while they peck like enzymes, eat
the information from our voices, scritch
and whip-poor-will and peent, o

throat, husked in smoke and finely
muscled, play these on your juke box

ohms of speech.

[1983]

VIA, EASTBOUND

To this widescreen three-day tracking shot—equal thirds
of mountain, prairie, boreal forest—
each of us will add a plot:
it is always The Past, but eased,
oiled so it glides and
whispers from its depth, often
with the voice of a lost dog.

Travelling east, we age more quickly,
running into time, which travels
west. This train wants to be evening, wants that
blue grey wash of snow and sky
eliding the horizon,
fading fast.

Toiling through the mountains like the seven
thousand dwarves,
earning every upward inch,
it dreams that the hell of its gut will find release
as lightning.
Everything will lie down in its speed,
a sort of sleep.
Meanwhile each Rocky poses in a sculpted
slow tableau, easily
seducing us to grandeur and glib
notions of eternity.

By nightfall it is chuckling over prairie
running on nothing but the cold air
of Saskatchewan, its dome car
empty as the mind of Buddha.
Window turns to mirror,
a black lake faintly smoked by blowing snow.
In it we can see our ghosts, transparent
creatures of the dark, bravely reading their
reversed editions of the Calgary *Herald*,
riding the freezing wind like gulls.

[1987]

Waking at the Mouth of the Willow River

Sleep, my favourite flannel shirt, wears thin, and shreds, and birdsong happens in the holes. In thirty seconds the naming of species will begin. As it folds into the stewed latin of afterdream each song makes a tiny whirlpool. One of them, zoozeezoozoozee, seems to be making fun of sleep with snores stolen from comic books. Another hangs its teardrop high in the mind, and melts: it was, after all, only narrowed air, although it punctuated something unheard, perfectly. And what sort of noise would the mind make, if it could, here at the brink? Scritch, scritch. A claw, a nib, a beak, worrying its surface. As though, for one second, it could let the world leak back to the world. Weep.

[1991]

Meditation on Snow Clouds Approaching the University from the North-West

One of us, paused between buildings,
will remark that snow is the postmodern
medium, or national equivalent to Lethe,
and release us to our offices
and tweeds.
We are not
a simple people and we fear
the same simplicities we crave.
No one wants to be a terminal
Canadian or existentialist or child, dumbly
moved because the clouds are bruises,
crowskin coats through which invisible
bits of rainbow nearly break.

The clouds look inward, thinking of a way
to put this. Possibly
dying will be such a pause:
the cadence where we meet a bird or animal
to lead us, somehow,
out of language and intelligence.

[1991]

SONG FOR THE RESTLESS WIND

The wind is struggling in her sleep, comfortless
because she is a giant,

which is not her fault. Whose idea was it
to construct a mind exclusively of shoulders?

In her dream
the car chase always overtakes the plot and wrecks it.

Maybe she will wake up
a Cecropia moth, still struggling

in a kimono of pressed-together dust
bearing the insignia of night.

Or as her own survivor, someone
who felt that huge wrench

clamped to her skull, loosening cutlery and books,
whirling round her,

corps de ballet, then
exit every whichway,

curtain.

[1991]

CAROL ANN DUFFY (b. 1955)

Carol Ann Duffy was born in Glasgow, Scotland, and completed her B.A. at the University of Liverpool in 1977. Her career as a full-time writer has included editing the literary magazine *Ambit*, writing plays for radio and stage, and serving as C. Day Lewis fellow for Greater London Arts Association, 1982, and visiting fellow at North Riding College, 1985. She won first prize in the national poetry competition sponsored by the BBC in 1983, the Eric Gregory Award from the British Society of Authors (1984), and first prize in the Peterloo Poets competition (1986). Her books include *Fleshweathercock* (1974), *Fifth Last Song* (1982), *Standing Female Nude* (1985, Scottish Arts Council Book Award of Merit), *Thrown Voices* (1986), *Selling Manhattan* (1987), *The Other Country* (1990), *Mean Time* (1993, Forward Poetry Prize and Whitbread Poetry Award), and *Selected Poems* (1994).

In response to a question about her fascination with various forms of social deviance (in an interview with Andrew McAllister in *Bête Noire* 6, Winter 1988), Duffy says: 'I think if you write a poem honestly you have got to do it as you are moved to do. What I am doing is living in the twentieth century in Britain and listening to the radio news every day and going out every day and reading the newspapers every day and meeting people who've had wonderful or horrifying experiences, and sometimes that will nudge me towards a poem. I'm not seeking bizarre subjects. . . . I think good and evil are things that come out of humanity, so that those of us who manage to be good most of the time should not deal with those of us who are evil by throwing them in nineteenth century prisons and screaming for the rope to be brought back. I think you have to look at evil in other people and in yourself because, well, to quote Peter Reading: "Don't think it couldn't be you". . . . I don't want to write the kind of poem that tells the reader how I feel when I see a rainbow. . . . Poets don't have solutions, poets are recording human experience. If I'm moved by something, or intrigued, or interested, that's what I am going to write about.'

In order to enter into the mind of the outsider or deviant, Duffy has mastered the persona poem and dramatic monologue and is particularly adept at creating the psychological quirks as well as the vocabulary and habits of speech that will bring her rogue's gallery of characters to life. With regard to poems such as 'Standing Female Nude', where she uses visual art as a starting point, Duffy draws attention to the sensory dimension of the act of writing: 'So something of me will want to be in that voice anyway, because I've empathised the first bit. We are talking about emotions in a sense; how do I feel, how did she feel, how did he feel. Now when you have an emotion there is always weather, there's always light through a window, there's always a sound, often a smell, or you touch something. The whole experience is physical and non-physical, so if I'm writing all that will come in whether I want it to or not. I'm very aware of space and light.'

When asked about her technique of writing very long sentences, often counterpointed by one that is ironically short, Duffy speaks reluctantly but tellingly of craft: 'This kind of question makes me very uneasy because when I am writing a poem, when any poet is, what we are often trying to do is get the sound of a non-linguistic sort of music. I can have the rhythm of a whole poem in my head and no words. And it isn't music and it isn't language, it's something in between. It has a colour, almost a shape. So I'm not aware that I'm doing that in a poem on a hyper-conscious level; that is partly the way I speak anyway and it will just translate into the poem like that. Whatever it is I have to say, and how I say it, that is how it's coming out. It isn't a technique and because it isn't a technique I can't describe it.

'I'm not interested as a poet in words like "plash", you know, Seamus Heaney words, interesting words. I don't like them. I like to use simple words but in a complicated way so that you can see lies and truths within the poem. And it is for myself as well; it's a way of revealing to myself what is truthful and what isn't. It's all for me. . . . I quite like having rhyme snaking through a poem. I think that's more authentic. . . I'll quite often take rhymes out, if I think they are heavy or laden. I like echoes and assonance, and that part of you that is watching what you are doing when you are writing poems is on the look-out for that.'

In the same issue of *Bête Noire*, in an article entitled 'The Intolerable Wrestle With Words: The Poetry of Carol Ann Duffy', Jane E. Thomas situates Duffy at the centre of postmodern concerns about the authority and reliability of language and stresses the poet's view of art as process: 'Carol Ann Duffy's work will not allow us to mistake it for anything other than fictional reconstructions of reality which continually draw attention to their fictionality.' She notes that Duffy's poetry 'consistently draws attention to the nature of language and the ways in which it constructs our relationship to ourselves and to others. Language is not a series of transparent signs through which reality is perceived but a structuring and differentiating system which constructs reality by reflecting the concerns of the social order which produced it. The task of the writer and the reader is to continually deconstruct linguistic signs in order to expose the ideological nature of their significations. The titles of her poems reflect the polysemic nature of words. . . . Others examine the power words have to alter and obscure our view of reality, particularly the euphemisms employed to simplify or disguise the problematical issues of human existence—excretion, sex, illness, eating meat . . . even nuclear war.'

STANDING FEMALE NUDE

Six hours like this for a few francs.
Belly nipple arse in the window light,
he drains the colour from me. Further to the right,
Madame. And do try to be still.
I shall be represented analytically and hung
in great museums. The bourgeoisie will coo
at such an image of a river-whore. They call it Art.

Maybe. He is concerned with volume, space.
I with the next meal. You're getting thin,
Madame, this is not good. My breasts hang
slightly low, the studio is cold. In the tea-leaves
I can see the Queen of England gazing
on my shape. Magnificent, she murmurs
moving on. It makes me laugh. His name

is Georges. They tell me he's a genius.
There are times he does not concentrate
and stiffens for my warmth. Men think of their mothers.
He possesses me on canvas as he dips the brush
repeatedly into the paint. Little man,
you've not the money for the arts I sell.
Both poor, we make our living how we can.

I ask him Why do you do this? Because
I have to. There's no choice. Don't talk.
My smile confuses him. These artists
take themselves too seriously. At night I fill myself
with wine and dance around the bars. When it's finished
he shows me proudly, lights a cigarette. I say
Twelve francs and get my shawl. It does not look like me.

[1985]

WAR PHOTOGRAPHER

In his darkroom he is finally alone
with spools of suffering set out in ordered rows.
The only light is red and softly glows,
as though this were a church and he
a priest preparing to intone a Mass.
Belfast. Beirut. Phnom Penh. All flesh is grass.

He has a job to do. Solutions slop in trays
beneath his hands which did not tremble then
though seem to now. Rural England. Home again
to ordinary pain which simple weather can dispel,
to fields which don't explode beneath the feet
of running children in a nightmare heat.

Something is happening. A stranger's features
faintly start to twist before his eyes,
a half-formed ghost. He remembers the cries
of this man's wife, how he sought approval
without words to do what someone must
and how the blood stained into foreign dust.

A hundred agonies in black-and-white
from which his editor will pick out five or six
for Sunday's supplement. The reader's eyeballs prick
with tears between the bath and pre-lunch beers.
From the aeroplane he stares impassively at where
he earns his living and they do not care.

[1985]

A HEALTHY MEAL

The gourmet tastes the secret dreams of cows
tossed lightly in garlic. Behind the green door, swish
of oxtails languish on an earthen dish. Here are
wishbones and pinkies; fingerbowls will absolve guilt.

Capped teeth chatter to a kidney or at the breast
of something which once flew. These hearts knew
no love and on their beds of saffron rice they lie
beyond reproach. What is the claret like? Blood.

On table six, the language of tongues is braised
in armagnac. The woman chewing suckling pig
must sleep with her husband later. Leg,
saddle and breast bleat against pure white cloth.

After *calf* to veal in four attempts. This is
the power of words; knife, tripe, lights, charcuterie.
A fat man orders his rare and a fine sweat
bastes his face. There are napkins to wipe the evidence

and sauces to gag the groans of abattoirs. The menu
lists the recent dead in French, from which they order
offal, poultry, fish. Meat flops in the jowls. Belch.
Death moves in the bowels. You are what you eat.

[1985]

MODEL VILLAGE

See the cows placed just so on the green hill.
Cows say *Moo*. The sheep look like little clouds,
don't they? Sheep say *Baa*. Grass is green
and the pillar-box is red. Wouldn't it be strange
if grass were red? This is the graveyard
where the villagers bury their dead. Miss Maiden
lives opposite in her cottage. She has a cat.
The cat says *Miaow*. What does Miss Maiden say?

I poisoned her, but no one knows. Mother, I said,
drink your tea. Arsenic. Four sugars. He waited
years for me, but she had more patience. One day,
he didn't come back. I looked in the mirror,
saw her grey hair, her lips of reproach. I found
the idea in a paperback. I loved him, you see,
who never so much as laid a finger. Perhaps now
you've learnt your lesson, she said, pouring
another cup. Yes, Mother, yes. Drink it all up.

The white fence around the farmyard
looks as though it's smiling. The hens are tidying
the yard. Hens say *Cluck* and give us eggs. Pigs
are pink and give us sausages. *Grunt*, they say.
Wouldn't it be strange if hens laid sausages?
Hee-haw, says the donkey. The farmhouse
is yellow and shines brightly in the sun. Notice
the horse. Horses say *Neigh*. What does the Farmer say?

To tell the truth, it haunts me. I'm a simple man,
not given to fancy. The flock was ahead of me,
the dog doing his job like a good 'un. Then
I saw it. Even the animals stiffened in fright. Look,
I understand the earth, treat death and birth
the same. A fistful of soil tells me plainly
what I need to know. You plant, you grow, you reap.
But since then, sleep has been difficult. When I shovel
deep down, I'm searching for something. Digging, desperately.

There's the church and there's the steeple.
Open the door and there are the people. Pigeons
roost in the church roof. Pigeons say *Coo*.
The church bells say *Ding-dong*, calling
the faithful to worship. What God says
can be read in the Bible. See the postman's dog
waiting patiently outside church. *Woof*, he says.
Amen, say the congregation. What does Vicar say?

Now they have all gone, I shall dress up
as a choirboy. I have shaved my legs. How smooth
they look. Smooth, pink knees. If I am not good,

I shall deserve punishment. Perhaps the choirmistress
will catch me smoking behind the organ. A good boy
would own up. I am naughty. I can feel
the naughtiness under my smock. Smooth, pink naughtiness.
The choirmistress shall wear boots and put me
over her lap. I tremble and dissolve into childhood.

Quack, say the ducks on the village pond. Did you
see the frog? Frogs say *Croak*. The village-folk shop
at the butcher's, the baker's, the candlestick maker's.
The Grocer has a parrot. Parrots say *Pretty Polly*
and *Who's a pretty boy then?* The Vicar is nervous
of parrots, isn't he? Miss Maiden is nervous
of Vicar and the Farmer is nervous of everything.
The library clock says *Tick-tock*. What does the Librarian say?

Ssssh. I've seen them come and go over the years,
my ears tuned for every whisper. This place
is a refuge, the volumes breathing calmly
on their still shelves. I glide between them
like a doctor on his rounds, know their cases. Tomes
do no harm, here I'm safe. Outside is chaos,
lives with no sense of plot. Behind each front door
lurks truth, danger. I peddle fiction. Believe
you me, the books in everyone's head are stranger . . .

[1987]

Psychopath

I run my metal comb through the D.A. and pose
my reflection between dummies in the window at Burton's.
Lamp light. Jimmy Dean. All over town, ducking and diving,
my shoes scud sparks against the night. She is in the canal.
Let me make myself crystal. With a good-looking girl crackling
in four petticoats, you feel like a king. She rode past me
on a wooden horse, laughing, and the air sang *Johnny*,
Remember Me. I turned the world faster, flash.

I don't talk much. I swing up beside them and do it
with my eyes. Brando. She was clean. I could smell her.
I thought, Here we go, old son. The fairground spun round us
and she blushed like candyfloss. You can woo them
with goldfish and coconuts, whispers in the Tunnel of Love.
When I zip up the leather, I'm in a new skin, I touch it
and love myself, sighing Some little lady's going to get lucky
tonight. My breath wipes me from the looking-glass.

We move from place to place. We leave on the last morning
with the scent of local girls on our fingers. They wear
our lovebites on their necks. I know what women want,
a handrail to Venus. She said *Please* and *Thank you*
to the toffee-apple, teddy-bear. I thought I was on, no error.
She squealed on the dodgems, clinging to my leather sleeve.
I took a swig of whisky from the flask and frenched it
down her throat. *No*, she said, *Don't*, like they always do.

Dirty Alice flicked my dick out when I was twelve.
She jeered. I nicked a quid and took her to the spinney.
I remember the wasps, the sun blazing as I pulled
her knickers down. I touched her and I went hard,
but she grabbed my hand and used that, moaning . . .
She told me her name on the towpath, holding the fish
in a small sack of water. We walked away from the lights.
She'd come too far with me now. She looked back, once.

A town like this would kill me. A gypsy read my palm.
She saw fame. I could be anything with my looks,
my luck, my brains. I bought a guitar and blew a smoke ring
at the moon. Elvis nothing. *I'm not that type*, she said.
Too late. I eased her down by the dull canal
and talked sexy. Useless. She stared at the goldfish, silent.
I grabbed the plastic bag. She cried as it gasped and wriggled
on the grass and here we are. A dog craps by a lamp post.

Mama, straight up, I hope you rot in hell. The old man
sloped off, sharpish. I saw her through the kitchen window.
The sky slammed down on my school cap, chicken licken.
Lady, Sweetheart, Princess I say now, but I never stay.

My sandwiches were near her thigh, then the Rent Man
lit her cigarette and I ran, ran . . . She is in the canal.
These streets are quiet, as if the town has held its breath
to watch the Wheel go round above the dreary homes.

No, don't. Imagine. One thump did it, then I was on her,
giving her everything I had. Jack the Lad, Ladies' Man.
Easier to say Yes. Easier to stay a child, wide-eyed
at the top of the helter-skelter. You get one chance in this life
and if you screw it you're done for, uncle, no mistake.
She lost a tooth. I picked her up, dead slim, and slid her in.
A girl like that should have a paid-up solitaire and high hopes,
but she asked for it. A right-well knackered outragement.

My reflection sucks a sour Woodbine and buys me a drink. Here's
looking at you. Deep down I'm talented. She found out. Don't mess
with me, angel, I'm no nutter. Over in the corner, a dead ringer
for Ruth Ellis smears a farewell kiss on the lip of a gin-and-lime.
The barman calls Time. Bang in the centre of my skull,
there's a strange coolness. I could almost fly. Tomorrow
will find me elsewhere, with a loss of memory. Drink up son,
the world's your fucking oyster. Awopbopaloobop alopbimbam.

[1987]

Foreign

Imagine living in a strange, dark city for twenty years.
There are some dismal dwellings on the east side
and one of them is yours. On the landing, you hear
your foreign accent echo down the stairs. You think
in a language of your own and talk in theirs.

Then you are writing home. The voice in your head
recites the letter in a local dialect; behind that
is the sound of your mother singing to you,
all that time ago, and now you do not know
why your eyes are watering and what's the word for this.

You use the public transport. Work. Sleep. Imagine one night
you saw a name for yourself sprayed in red
against a brick wall. A hate name. Red like blood.
It is snowing on the streets, under the neon lights,
as if this place were coming to bits before your eyes.

And in the delicatessen, from time to time, the coins
in your palm will not translate. Inarticulate,
because this is not home, you point at fruit. Imagine
that one of you says *Me not know what these people mean.*
It like they only go to bed and dream. Imagine that.

[1987]

WARMING HER PEARLS

Next to my own skin, her pearls. My mistress
bids me wear them, warm them, until evening
when I'll brush her hair. At six, I place them
round her cool, white throat. All day I think of her,

resting in the Yellow Room, contemplating silk
or taffeta, which gown tonight? She fans herself
whilst I work willingly, my slow heat entering
each pearl. Slack on my neck, her rope.

She's beautiful. I dream about her
in my attic bed; picture her dancing
with tall men, puzzled by my faint, persistent scent
beneath her French perfume, her milky stones.

I dust her shoulders with a rabbit's foot,
watch the soft blush seep through her skin
like an indolent sigh. In her looking-glass
my red lips part as though I want to speak.

Full moon. Her carriage brings her home. I see
her every movement in my head. . . . Undressing,
taking off her jewels, her slim hand reaching
for the case, slipping naked into bed, the way

she always does. . . . And I lie here awake,
knowing the pearls are cooling even now
in the room where my mistress sleeps. All night
I feel their absence and I burn.

[1987]

GIRLFRIENDS

derived from Verlaine
for John Griffith

That hot September night, we slept in a single bed,
naked, and on our frail bodies the sweat
cooled and renewed itself. I reached out my arms
and you, hands on my breasts, kissed me. Evening of amber.

Our nightgowns lay on the floor where you fell to your knees
and became ferocious, pressed your head to my stomach,
your mouth to the red gold, the pink shadows; except
I did not see it like this at the time, but arched

my back and squeezed water from the sultry air
with my fists. Also I remember hearing, clearly
but distantly, a siren some streets away—*de*

da de da de da—which mingled with my own
absurd cries, so that I looked up, even then,
to see my fingers counting themselves, dancing.

[1990]

THE KISSING GATE

After I've spoken to you, I walk out to the gate
at the edge of the field, watch a bird make a nonsense
of the air, and wish. This is not my landscape,
though I feel at home here, in a way, in a light
that rolls a dreg of memory around itself, spills it.
You'll not see it now. The bird. Me at the gate. Call it
a yellowy light. There it goes, into the grass, green,

greener, going. Love holds words to itself, repeats them
till they're smooth, sit silent on the tongue
like a small stone you sucked once, for some reason,
on a beach. I tell myself the things you'd like to do to me
if you were here, where there's no one to see for miles,
where I sense myself grow lighter and heavier, dizzy, solid,
and a bird swoops down, down, the light follows it.

[1990]

PRAYER

Some days, although we cannot pray, a prayer
utters itself. So, a woman will lift
her head from the sieve of her hands and stare
at the minims sung by a tree, a sudden gift.

Some nights, although we are faithless, the truth
enters our hearts, that small familiar pain;
then a man will stand stock-still, hearing his youth
in the distant Latin chanting of a train.

Pray for us now. Grade I piano scales
console the lodger looking out across
a Midlands town. Then dusk, and someone calls
a child's name as though they named their loss.

Darkness outside. Inside, the radio's prayer—
Rockall. Malin. Dogger. Finisterre.

[1993]

Robert Kroetsch (b. 1927)

Robert Kroetsch was born in Heisler, Alberta. He received his B.A. from the University of Alberta, then set out to work in the north on Mackenzie riverboats—an experience exploited in his first novel *But We Are Exiles* (1965)—and as a civilian education and information specialist for the US Army in Labrador. He studied briefly at McGill, but received his M.A. at Middlebury College, Vermont, and his Ph.D. at the Writers' Workshop at the University of Iowa in 1961. He studied and taught for two decades in the US, where he was a professor at the State University of New York at Binghampton and a founding editor of *Boundary 2: A Journal of Postmodern Literature*. He returned to Canada in 1975, the same year that he began to publish poetry, and is Professor of English at the University of Manitoba. A fiction trilogy—*The Words of My Roaring* (1966), *The Studhorse Man* (1969, Governor General's Award), and *Gone Indian* (1973)—was followed by *Badlands* (1975), *What the Crow Said* (1978), and several other novels. He has also written five long poems—*The Stone Hammer Poems* (1975), *The Ledger* (1975), *Seed Catalogue* (1977), *The Sad Phoenician* (1979), and *The Criminal Intensities of Love as Paradise* (1981)—eventually collected in *Field Notes* (1981) as part of an ongoing exploration of the form. His non-fiction writings appear in *Creation*, where there is a conversation between him and Margaret Laurence, in *The Crow Journals* (1980), two issues of *Open Letter* (series 5, 4, 1983 and 8-9, 1984), *The Lovely Treachery of Words: Essays Selected and New* (1989), and *A Likely Story* (1995). In addition to the shorter lyrics included in *The Stone Hammer Poems*, Kroetsch has also published *Advice to My Friends* (1985) and *Excerpts from the Real World* (1986).

Kroetch's fictional and poetic project may be summed up, in part, in a statement he made to Margaret Laurence (*Creation*): 'In a sense we haven't got an identity until somebody tells our story. The fiction makes us real.' He elaborated significantly on this process in *Open Letter* (5, 4, 1983): 'What has come to interest me now is what I suppose you can call the dream of origins. Obviously, on the prairies, the small town and farm are not merely places, they are remembered places, even dreamed places. When they were the actuality of our lives, we had realistic fiction, and we had almost no poetry at all. Now, in this dream condition, as dream-time fuses into the kind of narrative we call myth, we change the nature of the novel. And we start, with a new and terrible energy, to write the poems of the imagined real place.' His continuing effort to tell our story proceeds by way of deconstructing conventional narrative and poetic forms. He writes, as Milton Wilson said of the later work of E.J. Pratt, 'narratives no doubt, but discontinuous narratives which are always turning, on the one side, into documents, letters, and jokes, and on the other, into pure lyrics'.

Kroetsch's most important statement of poetics appears in 'For Play and Entrance: The Contemporary Canadian Long Poem', in *The Lovely Treachery of Words*, where he discusses the role of delay and indirection in the long poem, and his own and others' refusal of meta-narrative, or assumed story: 'The problem for the writer of the contemporary long poem is to honour our disbelief in belief—that is, to recognize and explore our distrust of system, of grid, of monisms, of cosmologies perhaps, certainly of inherited story—and at the same time write a long work that has some kind of (under erasure) unity.' To this he adds a further conundrum: 'And yet the long poem, by its very length, allows the exploration of the failure of system and grid. The poem of that failure is a long poem.'

Recalling Wordsworth's autobiographical long poem 'The Prelude' and Wallace Stevens's 'Notes Towards a Supreme Fiction', Kroetsch makes a parenthetical reference to his own poetic practice: '(My own continuing poem is called somewhat to my dismay, *Field Notes*. Perhaps Olson's field is there somewhere, but more specifically I think of the field notes kept by the archeologist, by the finding man who is essentially lost. I can only guess the other; there might, that is, be a hidden text. Yes, it is as if we spend our lives finding clues, fragments, shards, leading or misleading details, chipped tablets written over in a forgotten language. Perhaps they are a counting of cattle, a measuring out of grain. Perhaps they are a praising of gods, a naming of the dead. We can't know.)'

In the same essay, Kroetsch relates his experiments with the long poem to the struggle of art in this century with notions of self and authority. 'Is not the long poem, whatever its inward turn, finally the poem of outward? As we come to the end of self, in our century, we come again . . . to the long poem. We become, again, persons in the world, against the preposterous notion of self. We are each our own crossroads.' And futher: 'Delay, in the contemporary long poem (that necessary resisting towards the condition of art), has developed upon the language itself, instead of into new resources or narrative. The language has become so foregrounded that the dialectic with narrative very nearly fails. Or else: the narrative, adhering to old grammars, refuses the excitement of its own language.'

SEED CATALOGUE

1

No. 176—*Copenhagen Market Cabbage*: 'This *new introduction*, *strictly speaking*, is in every respect a *thoroughbred*, a *cabbage* of *highest pedigree*, and is *creating considerable flurry among professional gardeners* all *over the world*.'

We took the storm windows/off
the south side of the house
and put them on the hotbed.
Then it was spring. Or, no:
then winter was ending.

> 'I wish to say we had lovely success
> this summer with the seed purchased
> of you. We had the finest Sweet
> Corn in the country. and Cabbage
> were dandy.'
> —W.W. Lyon, South Junction, Man.

My mother said:
Did you wash your ears?
You could grow cabbages
in those ears.

Winter was ending.
This is what happened:
we were harrowing the garden.
You've got to understand this:
I was sitting on the horse.
The horse was standing still.
I fell off.

The hired man laughed: how
in hell did you manage to
fall off a horse that was
standing still?

Bring me the radish seeds,
my mother whispered.

Into the dark of January
the seed catalogue bloomed

a winter proposition, if
spring should come, then,

with illustrations:

No. 25—*McKenzie's Improved Golden Wax Bean*: 'THE MOST PRIZED OF ALL BEANS. *Virtue* is its own reward. We have had *many expressions* from *keen discriminating gardeners extolling our seed* and *this variety*.'

Beans, beans,
the musical fruit;
the more you eat,
the more you virtue.

My mother was marking the first row
with a piece of binder twine, stretched
between two pegs.

The hired man laughed: just
about planted the little bugger.
Cover him up and see what grows.
My father didn't laugh. He was puzzled
by any garden that was smaller than a
quarter-section of wheat and summerfallow.

the home place: N.E. 17-42-16-W4th Meridian.

the home place: one and a half miles west of Heisler, Alberta,

on the correction line road
and three miles south

No trees
around the house.
Only the wind.
Only the January snow.
Only the summer sun.
The home place:
a terrible symmetry.

How do you grow a gardener?

Telephone Peas
Garden Gem Carrots
Early Snowcap Cauliflower
Perfection Globe Onions
Hubbard Squash
Early Ohio Potatoes

This is what happened—at my mother's wake. This
is a fact—the World Series was in progress. The
Cincinnati Reds were playing the Detroit Tigers.
It was raining. The road to the graveyard was barely
passable. The horse was standing still. Bring me
the radish seeds, my mother whispered.

2

My father was mad at the badger: the badger was digging holes in the potato patch, threatening man and beast with broken limbs (I quote). My father took the double-barrelled shotgun out into the potato patch and waited.

Every time the badger stood up, it looked like a little man, come out of the ground. Why, my father asked himself—Why would so fine a fellow live under the ground? Just for the cool of roots? The solace of dark tunnels? The blood of gophers?

My father couldn't shoot the badger. He uncocked the shotgun, came back to the house in time for breakfast. The badger dug another hole. My father got mad again. They carried on like that all summer.

Love is an amplification
by doing/over and over.

Love is a standing up
to the loaded gun.

Love is a burrowing.

One morning my father actually shot at the badger. He killed a magpie that was pecking away at a horse turd about fifty feet beyond and to the right of the spot where the badger had been standing.

A week later my father told the story again. In that version he intended to hit the magpie. Magpies, he explained, are a nuisance. They eat robins' eggs. They're harder to kill than snakes, jumping around the way they do, nothing but feathers.

Just call me sure-shot,
my father added.

3

No. 1248—*Hubbard Squash*: 'As *mankind* seems to have a *particular fondness* for squash, *Nature* appears to have *especially* provided this *matchless* variety of *superlative flavour*.'

Love is a leaping up
and down.

Love
is a beak in the warm flesh.

'As a cooker, it heads the list for warted squash. The
vines are of strong running growth; the fruits are large,
olive shaped, of a deep rich green colour, the rind is
smooth...'

But how do you grow a lover?

This is the God's own truth:
playing dirty is a mortal sin
the priest told us, you'll go to hell
and burn forever (with illustrations)—

it was our second day of catechism
—Germaine and I went home that
afternoon   if it's that bad, we
said to each other   we realized
we better quit   we realized

let's do it just one last time
and quit.

This is the God's own truth:
catechism, they called it,
the boys had to sit in the pews
on the right, the girls on the left.
Souls were like underwear that you
wore inside. If boys and girls sat
together—

Adam and Eve got caught
playing dirty.

This is the truth.
We climbed up into a granary
full of wheat to the gunny sacks
the binder twine was shipped in—

we spread the paper from the sacks
smooth sheets on the soft wheat
Germaine and I we were like/one

we had discovered, don't ask me
how, where—but when the priest said
playing dirty we knew—well—

he had named it he had named
our world out of existence
(the horse was standing still)

—This is my first confession. Bless me father I played
  dirty so long, just the other day, up in the granary
  there by the car shed—up there on the Brantford Binder
  Twine gunny sacks and the sheets of paper—Germaine
  with her dress up and her bloomers down—

—Son. For penance, keep your peter in your pants
  for the next thirteen years.

But how—

  Adam and Eve and Pinch-Me
  went down to the river to swim—
  Adam and Eve got drownded.—

But how do you grow a lover?

  We decided we could do it
  just one last time.

4
It arrived in winter, the seed catalogue, on a January
day. It came into town on the afternoon train.

Mary Hauck, when she came west from Bruce County, Ontario,
arrived in town on a January day. She brought along
her hope chest.

She was cooking in the Heisler Hotel. The Heisler Hotel
burned down on the night of June 21, 1919. Everything
in between: lost. Everything: an absence

of satin sheets
of embroidered pillow cases
of tea towels and English china
of silver serving spoons.

How do you grow a prairie town?

The gopher was the model.
Stand up straight:
telephone poles
grain elevators
church steeples.
Vanish, suddenly: the
gopher was the model.

How do you grow a past/
to live in

the absence of silkworms
the absence of clay and wattles (whatever the hell
they are)
the absence of Lord Nelson
the absence of kings and queens
the absence of a bottle opener, and me with a vicious
attack of the 26-ounce flu
the absence of both Sartre and Heidegger
the absence of pyramids

the absence of lions
the absence of lutes, violas and xylophones
the absence of a condom dispenser in the Lethbridge Hotel and
me about to screw an old Blood whore. I was
in love.
the absence of the Parthenon, not to mention the Cathédrale de
Chartres
the absence of psychiatrists
the absence of sailing ships
the absence of books, journals, daily newspapers and everything
else but the *Free Press Prairie Farmer* and *The*
Western Producer
the absence of gallows (with apologies to Louis Riel)
the absence of goldsmiths
the absence of the girl who said that if the Edmonton Eskimos
won the Grey Cup she'd let me kiss her
nipples in the foyer of the Palliser Hotel. I
don't know where she got to.
the absence of Heraclitus
the absence of the Seine, the Rhine, the Danube, the Tiber and
the Thames. Shit, the Battle River ran dry
one fall. The Strauss boy could piss across it.
He could piss higher on a barn wall than any
of us. He could piss right clean over the
principal's new car.
the absence of ballet and opera
the absence of Aeneas

How do you grow a prairie town?

Rebuild the hotel when it burns down. Bigger. Fill it
full of a lot of A-1 Hard Northern Bullshitters.

—You ever hear the one about the woman who buried
her husband with his ass sticking out of the ground
so that every time she happened to walk by she could
give it a swift kick?

—Yeh, I heard it.

5
I planted some melons, just to see what would
happen. Gophers ate everything.

I applied to the Government.
I wanted to become a postman,
to deliver real words
to real people.

There was no one to receive
my application.

I don't give a damn if I do die do die do die do die do die
do die do die do die do die do die do die do die do die do
die do die do die do die do die do die do die do die do die
do

6
No. 339—*McKenzie's Pedigreed Early Snowcap Cauliflower*: 'Of the many *varieties* of *vegetables* in *existence, Cauliflower* is *unquestionably* one of the *greatest inheritances* of the *present generation, particularly Western Canadians.* There is *no place* in the *world* where *better cauliflowers* can be *grown* than right here in the *West*. The *finest specimens* we have *ever seen*, larger and of *better quality*, are *annually grown* here on our *prairies*. Being *particularly* a *high altitude plant* it *thrives* to a *point* of *perfection* here, *seldom seen* in *warmer climes*.'

But how do you grow a poet?

Start: with an invocation
invoke—

His muse is
his muse/if
memory is

and you have
no memory then
no meditation
no song (shit
we're up against it)

how about that girl
you felt up in the
school barn or that
girl you necked with
out by Hastings' slough
and ran out of gas with
and nearly froze to
death with/ or that
girl in the skating
rink shack who had on
so much underwear you
didn't have enough
prick to get past her/
CCM skates

Once upon a time in the village of Heisler—

—Hey, wait a minute.
That's a story.

How do you grow a poet?

For appetite: cod-liver
oil.
For bronchitis: mustard
plasters.
For pallor and failure to fill
the woodbox: sulphur
& molasses.
For self-abuse: ten Our
Fathers & ten Hail Marys.
For regular bowels: Sunny Boy
Cereal.

How do you grow a poet?

'It's a pleasure to advise that I
won the First Prize at the Calgary
Horticultural Show . . . This is my
first attempt. I used your seeds.'

Son, this is a crowbar.
This is a willow fencepost.
This is a sledge.
This is a roll of barbed wire.
This is a bag of staples.
This is a claw hammer.

We give form to this land by running
a series of posts and three strands
of barbed wire around a quarter-section.

First off I want you to take that
crowbar and drive 1,156 holes
in that gumbo.
And the next time you want to
write a poem
we'll start the haying.

How do you grow a poet?

This is a prairie road.
This road is the shortest distance
between nowhere and nowhere.
This road is a poem.

Just two miles up the road
you'll find a porcupine
dead in the ditch. It was
trying to cross the road.

As for the poet himself
we can find no record
of his having traversed
the land/in either direction

no trace of his coming
or going/only a scarred
page, a spoor of wording
a reduction to mere black

and white/a pile of rabbit
turds that tells us
all spring long
where the track was

poet . . . say uncle.

How?

Rudy Wiebe: 'You must lay great black steel lines of
fiction, break up that space with huge design and, like
the fiction of the Russian steppes, build a giant
artifact. No song can do that...'

February 14, 1976. Rudy, you
took us there: to the Oldman River
Lorna & Byrna, Ralph & Steve and me
you showed us where
the Bloods surprised the Crees
in the next coulee/surprised
them to death. And after
you showed us Rilke's word
Lebensgliedes.

Rudy: Nature thou art.

7

Brome Grass (Bromus Inermis): 'No amount of cold will kill it. It *withstands* the summer suns. Water may stand on it for several weeks without apparent injury. The roots push through the soil, throwing up new plants continually. It *starts quicker* than other grasses in the spring. *Remains green* longer in the fall. *Flourishes under absolute neglect.*'

The end of winter:
seeding/time.

How do you grow
a poet?

(a)

I was drinking with Al Purdy. We went round and round
in the restaurant on top of the Château Lacombe. We
were the turning centre in the still world, the winter
of Edmonton was hardly enough to cool our out-sights.

The waitress asked us to leave. She was rather insistent;
we were bad for business, shouting poems at the paying
customers. Twice, Purdy galloped a Cariboo horse
right straight through the dining area.

Now that's what I call
a piss-up.

'No song can do that.'

(b)

No. 2362—*Imperialis Morn-*
ing Glory: 'This is the won-
derful *Japanese Morning*
Glory, celebrated the world
over for its *wondrous beauty*
of both flowers and foliage.'

Sunday, January 12, 1975. This evening after
rereading *The Double Hook*: looking at Japanese prints.
Not at actors. Not at courtesans. Rather: Hiroshige's
series, *Fifty-Three Stations on the Tokaido*.

From the *Tokaido* series: 'Shono-Haku-u.' The
bare-assed travellers, caught in a sudden shower.
Men and trees, bending. How it is in a rain shower/
that you didn't see coming. And couldn't have avoided/
even if you had.

The double hook:
the home place.

The stations of the way:
the other garden

Flourishes.
Under absolute neglect.

(c)

Jim Bacque said (I was waiting for a plane,
after a reading; Terminal 2, Toronto)—he said,
You've got to deliver the pain to some woman,
don't you.

— Hey, Lady.
You at the end of the bar.
I wanna tell you something.

— Yuh?

— Peter Knight—of Crossfield,
Alberta. Bronc-Busting Champion
of the World. You ever hear of
Pete Knight, the King of All
Cowboys, Bronc-Busting Champion
of the World?

— Huh-uh.

— You know what I mean? King
of *All* Cowboys . . . Got
killed—by a horse.
He fell off.

— You some kind of nut
or something?

8

We silence words
by writing them down.

THIS IS THE LAST WILL AND TESTAMENT
OF ME, HENRY L. KROETSCH:

(a) [yes, his first bequest]

To my son Frederick my carpenter tools.

It was his first bequest. First,
a man must build.

Those horse-barns around Heisler—
those perfectly designed barns
with the rounded roofs—only Freddie
knew how to build them. He mapped
the parklands with perfect horse-barns.

I remember my Uncle Freddie.
(The farmers no longer
use horses.)

Back in the 30s, I remember
he didn't have enough money
to buy a pound of coffee.

Every morning at breakfast
he drank a cup of hot water
with cream and sugar in it.

Why, I asked him one morning—
I wasn't all that old—why
do you do that? I asked him.

Jesus Christ, he said. He was
a gentle man, really. Don't you
understand *anything*?

9
The danger of merely living.

a shell/exploding
in the black sky: a
strange planting

a bomb/exploding
in the earth: a
strange

man/falling
on the city.
Killed him dead.

It was a strange
planting.

the absence of my cousin who was shot down while bombing
the city that was his maternal great-grandmother's
birthplace. He was the navigator. He guided himself
to that fatal occasion:

— a city he had
forgotten
— a woman he had
forgotten

He intended merely to release a cargo of bombs on a
target and depart. The exploding shell was:

a) an intrusion on a design that was not his, or

b) an occurrence which he had in fact, unintentionally,
himself designed, or

c) it is essential that we understand this matter
because:

He was the first descendant of that family to return
to the Old Country. He took with him: a cargo of bombs.

Anna Weller: Geboren Cologne, 1849.
Kenneth MacDonald: Died Cologne, 1943.

A terrible symmetry.

A strange muse: forgetfulness. Feeding her far children
to ancestral guns, blasting them out of the sky, smack/
into the earth. Oh, she was the mothering sort. Blood/
on her green thumb.

10

After the bomb/blossoms
After the city/falls
After the rider/falls
(the horse
standing still)

Poet, teach us
to love our dying.

West is a winter place.
The palimpsest of prairie

under the quick erasure
of snow, invites a flight.

How/do you grow a garden?

(a)

No. 3060—*Spencer Sweet Pea*:
Pkt. $.10; oz. $.25;
quarter lb. $.75; half lb. $1.25.

Your sweet peas
climbing the staked
chicken wire,
climbing the stretched
binder twine by
the front porch

taught me the smell
of morning, the grace
of your tired

hands, the strength
of a noon sun, the
colour of prairie grass

taught me the smell
of my sweating armpits.

(b)

How do you a garden grow?
How do you grow a garden?

'Dear Sir,
The longest brome grass I remember seeing was
one night in Brooks. We were on our way up to the Calgary
Stampede, and reached Brooks about 11 pm, perhaps earlier
because there was still a movie on the drive-in screen.
We unloaded Cindy, and I remember tying her up to the truck
box and the brome grass was up to her hips. We laid down
in the back of the truck—on some grass I pulled by hand—
and slept for about three hours, then drove into Calgary.

Amie'

(c)

No trees
around the house,
only the wind.
Only the January snow.
Only the summer sun.

Adam and Eve got drownded—
Who was left?

[1977]

LORNA CROZIER (b. 1948)

Lorna Crozier was born in Swift Current, Saskatchewan, and now lives on Vancouver Island, where she teaches Creative Writing at the University of Victoria. She completed her B.A. at the University of Saskatchewan and M.A. at the University of Alberta in 1980. She taught high school briefly and worked as a director of communications for the Saskatchewan government. A founding member of the Moose Jaw Movement, she has also been an instructor at the Saskatchewan Summer School for the Arts and the Banff School of Fine Arts, and writer-in-residence at the Regina Public Library and the University of Toronto. Her books include *Inside the Sky* (1976), *Crow's Black Joy* (1978), *Humans and Other Beasts* (1980), *No Longer Two People* (1981, with Patrick Lane), *The Weather* (1983, Saskatchewan Writers Guild Long Manuscript Poetry Award), *The Garden Going On Without Us* (1985, nominated for the Governor General's Award), *Angels of Flesh, Angels of Silence* (1988), *Inventing the Hawk* (1992, Governor General's Award), and *Everything Arrives At the Light* (1995). Crozier won first prize in the CBC Literary Competition for 1987-88. She also continues as poetry editor for Coteau Books and is a co-editor of *A Sudden Radiance: Saskatchewan Poetry* (1987).

An instructive account of her geographical and literary influences appears in *Contemporary Authors* (vol. 113): 'The most important influence on my writing was *As for Me and My House* by Sinclair Ross. It was the first book I read that was set in the landscape where I grew up, the southwest corner of Saskatchewan. It made me realize that someone from my area could actually be a writer and, in some ways, it gave me the courage to try.

'The landscape of southwestern Saskatchewan has definitely influenced my writing. I've tried to thread the wind and sky into my poems, to make them breathe the way the prairie does. But the influence of places goes beyond the recurrence of images particular to a certain landscape. The mutability and the extremes of the natural world in Saskatchewan have given rise to my sense of the fragility of happiness, love, and life itself. Our hold on things and on each other is so tenuous. My poems, I think, express the fearful hope I feel for the human—for our capability to return to love through pain and for our journey toward that sense of unity with all things, with the mule deer I startled from feeding in the coulee yesterday, and with the mute explosions of lichens on the stones in my grandfather's pasture. If the magic that is poetry can't lead us to that oneness, then I hope it at least can make us feel less alone.

'Along with the impetus to write about the people and landscapes that were mine by birth and inclination came the influence of writers like Rainer [Maria] Rilke. They made me try to stretch to the limits of my imagination and beyond to get in touch with the interior landscape of the soul.'

Whether it concerns the evocation of place or the exploration of the psyche, Crozier insists in 'Who's Listening?' (*NeWest Review*, February/March, 1989) that good poetry involves 'the most intimate self of the writer speaking to the most intimate self of the reader. When the two connect, poetry happens, magic happens, the sparks fly.' Furthermore, 'Poems can only happen in a moment of recognition, of intense and clear seeing. . . .'

As she says in 'Searching for the Poem' (*Waves* 14, 1-2, Fall 1985), 'Poems, when they happen, are magic and staring too hard at magic will make it go away. You may discover it's all a trick with mirrors, but then Calvino says a series of mirrors can multiply an object to infinity and reflect its essence in a single image that contains the whole of everything. I want the poem to do that, not reflect nature but contain it and everything else that exists, is dreamed or imagined. . . . If a poem could walk, it would have paws, not feet. Or hooves, small ones, leaving half moons in the sand. Something to make you stop and wonder what kind of animal this is, where it came from, where it's going.'

In 'Speaking the Flesh' (*Language in Her Eye: Writing and Gender*, edited by Libby Scheier, Sarah Sheard, and Eleanor Wachtel, 1990) Crozier addresses the issue of censorship—the public, systemic kind that tries to suppress a text for, say, its sexual or political content, and the more insidious pressures that work to control, if not suppress entirely, full expression in the act of writing. She attributes negative responses to erotic writing in part to 'the shock of the new', in part to the male desire/need to control feminine discourse and, therefore, the 'hidden stories' that have to be told—and heard. The violence of this struggle, according to Crozier, examples of which range from people leaving a reading to protest poetic content that displeases them to the massacre of female engineering students at the University of Montreal, is both text and sub-text in the debate on censorship.

And, from the same essay: 'Feminism is, after all, a revolution. It has stormed the bastille of our literature as well as other fortresses in our society. It is upsetting the tradition, the patterns, the literary canon. It has changed what is being written about, and how, and by whom. It has changed the oldest of stories, revised what many thought were untouchable texts. And just as significantly, it has changed the reader's response to the "classics", to what she has read in the past and to what she has yet to read. Because critics have developed a vocabulary to describe what it is many feminist writers are doing in their works, perhaps we've forgotten that literature hits people in the gut as well as the head; it hits them where they live.'

FORMS OF INNOCENCE

The girl can tell you exactly
where and when her innocence
took flight,
how it soared from the window
beating its wings
high above the stubble field.

A strange shape for innocence
when you think of Leda
but this girl insists
it was a swan, black
not white as you might expect.
From its head no bigger than her fist
a beak blossomed red as if wings
pumped blood up the long neck
to where the bird split the sky.

She watched this through the windshield,
lying on her back, the boy's breath
breaking above her in waves, the swan's
dark flight across the snow so beautiful
she groaned and the boy groaned with her,
not understanding the sound she made.

When she tells this story now, she says
though it was winter, she knows the swan
made it all the way to Stanley Park,
a place she's never been, just seen
in the room where no one
ever touches anything
in the book her mother keeps
open on the coffee table,
one black swan swimming
endless circles among the white.

[1985]

The Child Who Walks Backwards

My next-door neighbour tells me
her child runs into things.
Cupboard corners and doorknobs
have pounded their shapes
into his face. She says
he is bothered by dreams,
rises in sleep from his bed
to steal through the halls
and plummet like a wounded bird
down the flight of stairs.

This child who climbed my maple
with the sureness of a cat,
trips in his room, cracks
his skull on the bedpost,
smacks his cheeks on the floor.
When I ask about the burns

on the back of his knee,
his mother tells me
he walks backwards
into fireplace grates
or sits and stares at flames
while sparks burn stars in his skin.

Other children write their names
on the casts that hold
his small bones.
His mother tells me
he runs into things,
walks backwards,
breaks his leg
while she lies
sleeping.

[1985]

ONIONS

The onion loves the onion.
It hugs its many layers,
saying O, O, O,
each vowel smaller
than the last.

Some say it has no heart.
It doesn't need one.
It surrounds itself,
feels whole. Primordial.
First among vegetables.

If Eve had bitten it
instead of the apple,
how different
Paradise.

[1985]

PEAS

Peas never liked any of it.
They make you suffer for the sweet
burst of green in the mouth. Remember
the hours of shelling on the front steps,
the ping into the basin? Your mother
bribing you with lemonade to keep you there,
splitting them open with your thumbs.

Your tongue finds them clitoral
as it slides up the pod.
Peas are not amused.
They have spent all their lives
keeping their knees together.

[1985]

FATHERS, UNCLES, OLD FRIENDS OF THE FAMILY

Uncle Peter always told me
to wash my hands before breakfast
because I didn't know where they'd been
in the night   what they'd touched

and his hands
lifted me from the paddling pool,
young seal   all wet and giggly,
his farmer's hands
soft in the towel,
my mother's
youngest brother
pulling aside
my swimsuit.

Then there's the father
of my friend
who did it to her
till she ran away from home.
On his seventieth birthday

she visits with the grandchild
he's never seen
and before she can pour their tea,
he reaches out,
grabs her breast,
then cries says he can't help himself
and she cries too,
what's there to say to him now?

One is always
the best friend of the family.
He makes her a fishing rod
from a bamboo pole
and with hooks with bait,
rows her to the middle of the lake.
Shh, shh, I won't hurt you
shhhh.

Years later
your flesh crawling,
you try not to turn away
when someone you love lays a hand on you.

Where did he touch you?

Here and here,
those places no one ever named.

[1988]

ANGEL OF INFINITY

When she first touched the angel
her fingers burned
though the angel was invisible,
so much time and space,
so much light. The second time

the angel took shape
under the apple tree. The cat
watched the wings
surprise the air,

each feather so pure and well defined
the woman tried to count them
to keep her mind on something real.

What do you ask of the Angel
of Infinity?
More room for your children, more
time, more time.

The cat seemed undisturbed.
He bunted his head
against the angel's legs
as if this were an ordinary guest
with cats of her own
in whatever house she lived in.

The woman felt comfort in this
and in seeing the wind
that lifted her hair
move the angel's feathers
so the air was filled with rustling
softer than the stir of leaves.

Maybe that was the blessing:
the cat purring in the shadow
of the angel's wings,
the apples on fire
                    in their usual way
in the apple tree

the wind
          touching everything
at the same time

[1988]

MOTHER AND I, WALKING

Father is gone again,
the streets empty.
Everyone is inside,
listening to radios
in the warm glow of their stoves.

The cold cries under our boots.
We wade through wind. It pushes
snow under my scarf and collar,
up the sleeves of my jacket.

Mother opens her old muskrat coat,
pulls me inside.
Her scent wraps around me.
The back of my head presses
into the warm rise of her belly.

When I lower my eyes, I see
our feet, mine between hers,
the tracks of one animal
crossing the open,
strange and nocturnal,
moving towards home.

[1988]

VARIATION ON THE ORIGIN OF FLIGHT

Of all the body
it's the creature closest to the sea.
Snail-moist, all tuck and salty
muscle, it opens and closes
like a sea anemone. Mute
but several tongued,
minus legs and memory,
it's what moves you
to bowl and basin,
to hollows in the stone

where water gathers after storms.
It draws you past the breakers
to the wild, the open,
gives your arms and naked thighs
their power and pull. More
reptilian than cat, its brain
is the oldest brain, prelapsarian,
soft moss and weeping fern.
Stopped on its evolutionary trail.
Beached, becalmed, stranded without
gills, scales or jewelled tail,
yet you feel it
flex and flutter
beneath your lover's tongue
as feather
after slow inevitable feather
it dreams the world's
first wings.

[1992]

LIVING DAY BY DAY

I have no children and he has five,
three of them grown up, two with their mother.
It didn't matter when I was thirty and we met.
There'll be no children, he said, the first night
we slept together and I didn't care,
thought we wouldn't last anyway,
those terrible fights,
he and I struggling to be the first
to pack, the first one out the door.
Once I made it to the car before him,
locked him out. He jumped on the hood,
then kicked the headlights in.
Our friends said we'd kill each other
before the year was through.

Now it's ten years later.
Neither of us wants to leave.
We are at home with one another,

we are each other's home,
the voice in the doorway,
calling *Come in, come in,*
it's growing dark.

Still, I'm often asked if I have children.

Sometimes I answer yes.
Sometimes we have so much
we make another person.
I can feel her in the night
slip between us, tell my dreams
how she spent her day. *Good night,*
she says, *good night, little mother,*
and leaves before I waken.
Across the lawns she dances
in her white, white dress,
her dream hair flying.

[1992]

INVENTING THE HAWK

She didn't believe the words
when she first heard them, that blue
bodiless sound entering her ear.
But now something was in the air,
a sense of waiting as if
the hawk itself were there
just beyond the light, blinded
by a fine-stitched leather hood
she must take apart with her fingers.
Already she had its voice,
the scream that rose from her belly
echoed in the dark inverted
canyon of her skull.

She built its wings, feather by feather,
the russet smoothness of its head,
the bead-bright eyes,
in that moment between sleep and waking.

Was she the only one
who could remember them,
who knew their shape and colours, the way
they could tilt the world with a list of wings?
Perhaps it was her reason for living
so long in this hard place
of wind and sky, the stunted trees
reciting their litany of loss
outside her window.

Elsewhere surely someone was drawing
gophers and mice out of the air.
Maybe that was also her job,
so clearly she could see them.
She'd have to lie here forever,
dreaming hair after hair,
summoning the paws (her own heart
turning timid, her nostrils twitching).

Then she would cause the seeds
in their endless variety—the ones
floating light as breath,
the ones with burrs and spears
that caught in her socks
when she was a child,
the radiant, uninvented blades of grass.

[1992]

Last Testaments

The cancer began in her tonsils,
she'd say it with a smile
almost expecting to be teased
for such a serious disease rooting
in that childish place.
She remembered her son at four
when he'd had his out, the way
he'd looked at her while the nurse
slid the cold thermometer up his bum.
She carried on as usual, cleaned the house,
fried a chicken for her husband

every Sunday, cutting the breast
in four pieces, the wings in two.
The morning of the day she died
she took him down the basement,
showed him how to separate
the clothes, set the dials,
how to hang his shirts and pants
so the creases would fall out.

*

The man with a worn-out heart,
sold his tools so his wife
wouldn't be left with that part of him
to deal with. How he had loved them
in his hands, each so perfectly designed
to fit the palm, the wheels,
bits and teeth made for one specific use.
On the empty walls of the garage
hung the shapes of wrenches, saws and drills.
Years ago he'd traced around them row on row
so he'd know where to hang each one,
know what his neighbour had borrowed
and failed to return. From his pocket
he removed a black felt pen
and in the corner on a board painted white,
he drew the perfect outline of a man.

*

Before she walked into the river
and didn't come back,
the woman who couldn't remember
the day of the week
or the faces of her children,
made a list of all the men
she'd ever loved,
left it for her husband by the coffee pot,
his name on the bottom,
underlined twice
for emphasis.

[1992]

SKUNKS

The morning cold with dawn,
I stand at the window, first
light spilling through the glass.
Across the yard I see my neighbour
on his front step. He waves,
then points a rifle at my head.

Yesterday he told me
he'd buy a gun to shoot the skunks
who come up from the river,
drawn from the willows to our
apple cores, our overripe
melons and sour milk, our almost
empty jars of jam. Night-raiders,
they dip into the wells
of the garbage cans.

I have imagined them,
their narrow faces
peering in the windows while I sleep,
turning the thin bones of dream
over and over in their paws.

Now it is my neighbour's face
I see through the window,
the precision of his eyes and hands.
He waves and grins, then lines me up,
practises his sight.

We are in this together now.
He studies my face like a lover,
knows the curve of my forehead,
the slight indentation of
my temples, the blue pulse
beating there.

After dark when he waits
in the alley the smell of me
will sting his eyes, fill his mouth,
make his nostrils flare.

For I will have been there
before him,
driving ahead of me
these dark sisters
with their slow walk
down to the river, the white
on their backs blazing
in the moonlight,
their sweet mouths
red with jam.

[1992]

THE GAME

So many conversations between
the tall grass and the wind.
A child hides in that sound,
hunched small
as a rabbit, knees tucked
to her chest, head on knees,
yet she's not asleep.

She is waiting with a patience
I had long forgotten,
hair wild with grass seeds,
skin silvery with dust.

It was my brother's game.
He was the one who counted,
and I, seven years younger,
the one who hid.

When I ran from the yard,
he found his gang of friends
and played kick-the-can
or caught soft spotted frogs
at the creek so summer-slow,
who can blame him?

As darkness fell,
from the kitchen door
someone always called my name.
He was there before me
at the supper table;
milk in his glass
and along his upper lip
glowing like moonlight.
You're so good at that, he'd say,
I couldn't find you.

Now I wade through
hip-high bearded grass
to where she sits so still,
lay my larger hand
upon her shoulder.

Above the wind I say,
You're it,
then kneel beside her
and with the patience
that has lived so long in this body,
clean the dirt from her nose and mouth,
separate the golden speargrass from her hair.

[1995]

Roo Borson (b. 1952)

Born in Berkeley, California in 1952, Roo Borson studied at the University of California at Santa Barbara and Goddard College in Vermont before completing an M.F.A. in Creative Writing at the University of British Columbia. Since then, she has resided in Australia and New Mexico, but mostly in Canada, where she has conducted poetry workshops and been writer-in-residence at Concordia University. Now living in Toronto with poet-physicist Kim Maltman, she has written the following books: *Landfall* (1977), *In the Smoky Light of the Fields* (1980), *Rain* (1980), *A Sad Device* (1981), *The Whole Night Coming Home* (1984, nominated for the Governor General's Award), a collaboration with Maltman called *The Transparence of November / Snow* (1985), *Intent, or the Weight of the World* (1989), and *Night Walk: Selected Poems* (1994), nominated for the Governor General's Award).

Borson recommends a certain resistance to poetic theory. As she says to interviewer and editor Peter O'Brien (*So to Speak*, 1987), 'Writing by theory is too much like painting by numbers.' However, she acknowledges that 'there are new regions to articulate. With me, this means changing styles, syntax, cadence. A new way of talking brings in new subjects, or vice versa.' She is particularly eloquent about the music of poetry: 'Music is necessary to all writing, not just poetry. Writing is speech, it's out loud, it makes a noise that's rhythmic or arrhythmic, it forms patterns and breaks them. Whenever I think about rhythm I think of contemporary jazz—Weather Report or Carlos Santana and Alice Coltrane, Jean-Luc Ponty. I had to learn to listen to this kind of music. At first I could only hear a big mass of disorganized sound, unharmonic, crashing, confusing—but then I began to hear individual instruments within the welter and *oh* the pleasure when all the conflicting strains are drawn together into melody again. It's astonishing and fills me with happiness. Coming to a piece of fantastic writing is like that point at which the instruments pull together and everything makes sense—out of the welter of everyday impressions and ups and downs, this clear voice is speaking. It makes the crashing and confusion that preceded it that much more valuable, the constrast is sensual and excruciating and cerebral too. . . . Our rhythms are based on street corners, in poetry, and also on individual temperament. We each have a cadence, or several related cadences.'

On the poetic line, Borson says in the same interview: 'I think the line still has a role in poetry. If it didn't, we should all be writing prose or prose poetry. Lines can be used in different kinds of ways. They can accentuate a rhythm of a tension or space between images or ideas. Line breaks can be used as punctuation or as transitional areas. You can use them to make the reader stop or keep going. Line breaks can be used to accentuate the medium of written language—that's how Robert Creeley uses them—or to minimize that and emphasize a natural chanting speech, as W.S. Merwin uses them (his father was a minister). John Newlove is another master of the line. I'm not saying there's only one way, or three ways, to make line-breaks; they're one of the components of voice, and everyone's voice is a little different. The most individual voices can be identified by their rhythms, their way of moving.'

Borson is not averse, personally or poetically, to taking a political stand, but insists that 'The thought that poetry, or any other art, has a predetermined moral role is abhorrent to me. Look what happened to the arts in China: fine arts were replaced by bizarre forms of folk-art, fascinating culturally, but also a loss. That is, I don't believe that art has a duty, of any sort, to society. To say that it has played a role, in retrospect, is another thing. Does the rose bloom for the bee? No, but their lives are bound together and they coincidentally, felicitously, serve one another. . . . the best reason for becoming a doctor or a mathematician or a poet is an overwhelming love of the occupation. At their best I think artists are motivated by unsentimental love and by curiosity.'

Many readers have responded to the strong sense of physical space, or place, in Borson's poems. 'There's a mood in every place,' she says. 'Partly it's the landscape, partly the people, the ways they live. I've never done travelogue or documentary poems, so, for me, the mood of a place comes out more in emotional nuance, in syntax and music. With California, there was restlessness and lushness. . . . In Vancouver it was rain, rain, rain. The quick, beautiful passing away of things. In Toronto there's the incredible vitality of people packed close together, and outside the city there's all that mute, overfarmed countryside, lovely and calm and in decline. For me, the landscape is not separable from our life. Lives are not separable from the apartments and farmhouses they take place in. Societies are not separable from the land.'

When pressed to talk about her relationship with the natural world, and the so-called 'city / nature' split, Borson resolutely refused to have her poetry pigeon-holed: 'You and I, or the reader and the writer, approach the poems from opposite ends of the process of writing. You, as a reader and critic, might draw certain conclusions from my work, but I, as the writer, am not thinking of conclusions at all. All I'm doing is trying to share what I see while making a beautiful sound at the same time. I don't intentionally code messages into my poems; if I had a concrete message I would probably write an essay. I write about the city and about nature because those, combined, are my environment. I write what I see (and hear and smell, etc.) and what I'm thinking / feeling in response to what I see. . . . Poems have minds of their own and you can engage in a dialogue with them. I do write intensely sometimes about nature because I experience it intensely; that's all.'

Abundance

The moon: hoof-print in ice.

Someone's shoes chewing an icy path.
The wasted intricacy of each snowflake.
A field without a man in it.
A rusted plow filling with snow.

[1981]

Talk

The shops, the streets are full of old men
who can't think of a thing to say anymore.
Sometimes, looking at a girl, it
almost occurs to them, but they can't make it out,
they go pawing toward it through the fog.

The young men are still jostling shoulders
as they walk along, tussling at one another with words.
They're excited by talk, they can still see the danger.

The old women, thrifty with words,
haggling for oranges, their mouths
take bites out of the air. They know the value of oranges.
They had to learn everything
on their own.

The young women are the worst off, no one has bothered
to show them things.
You can see their minds on their faces,
they are like little lakes before a storm.
They don't know it's confusion that makes them sad.
It's lucky in a way though, because the young men take
a look of confusion for inscrutability, and this
excites them and makes them want to own
this face they don't understand,
something to be tinkered with at their leisure.

[1981]

Waterfront

The women's bodies lying in the sand are curved like shells.
The men can't take their eyes off them.
The seawater spangles like a drink of champagne,
but the fishermen don't see it that way,
they have their clothes on, they don't care about girls.
They only care about fish. They yell to one another down the beach
as if this were their ocean. Meanwhile,
ignorant, the smelts plod into the nets.
Seated on benches, middle-aged women
in magenta travel dresses, going nowhere,
dressed too warmly for the weather,
delve into the sunlight with their eyes closed and pretend
they are dissolving, like a tablet in water.
Only the babies pushed along in carriages
seem to enjoy themselves, twisting their faces
into vast expressions. Their skin
is still translucent. They haven't yet finished
materializing into the world.

[1981]

October, Hanson's Field

Frost chains the pumpkins,
like planets run aground, or
buoys the dead hang onto,
their eyes lit in the loam.

No more flocks of birds
that blow like a woman's gown
from tree to tree.

Hanson's field is empty
except for the sound
of a few last things alive.

I look at the ground
as if it were one-way glass.
The dead can see me.

Past sunset they send up their shadows
to lean against the trees,
like holograms.

[1981]

Flowers

The sunset, a huge flower, wilts on the horizon.
Robbed of perfume, a raw smell
wanders the hills, an embarrassing smell,
of nudity, of awkward hours on earth.
If a big man stands softly, his wide arms
gentled at his sides, women dissolve. It is the access
to easy violence that excites them.

The hills are knobbed with hay,
as if they were full of drawers about to be opened.
What could be inside but darkness?
The ground invisible, the toes feel the way,
bumping against unknown objects
like moths in a jar, like moths
stubbing themselves out on a lamp.

The women sit in their slips,
scattered upstairs through the houses
like silken buds.
They look in the mirror,

they wish they were other than they are.
Into a few of the rooms go a few of the men,
bringing their mushroomy smell.

The other men loll against the outsides of buildings,
looking up at the stars,
inconsequential.

One of them bends down to smell a flower.
There are holes in his face.

[1981]

A Sad Device

A rat, his eyes like glycerine,
like galleries of landscape paintings,
genitals like a small bell, he,
siphon of smells,
mortician gathering in the gauzy corpses,
construes the world.
The grey warehouse of gothic stars,
the gleaming artillery of water,
the flowerbeds like Arabic scrolls,
all of it.

I think my heart is a sad device,
like can-openers.
Sometimes I would rather step between slices
of dark rye and be taken in
by some larger beast.
Men dreaming of billboards,
cars barrelling on and on in a night marooned,
zeroed in on an immense target.
Now I believe the frozen mammoths
in the laundry room
came of their own accord,
not through coercion
by the Sears appliance man.
Not even he
has a cozy life.

Tiny lions in the zookeeper's hair
keep him busily asleep,
but some of us wake too soon,
when our lover is still a dismantled thing
blue with streetlight.

This rat and I
have more in common than most,
having met once.
Now we go to separate nests
and presumably to dawn
with its crossfire of light
meeting in all the other eyes.

[1981]

July

Blue sky that holds off at a distance,
you can follow the pine trunks all the way up with your eye
to the high branches stilled in sunlight
where birds come and go
from here to the next county.
You can sit forever in an evening
spitting melon seeds,
twisting around the tongue
the few fibres that held
a whole mouthful of sweet water.
It is possible to swallow this
and all of childhood in one gulp,
along with all the wrongs that have not yet happened,
blessing them in advance.
Bright melon sliced open on the table
with all of summer leaking out of it.
Still the children call to one another in the streets
not wanting to come in, but on a night like this
if they stayed out they would learn how to float
like the moon through the pine branches.
On the table the half-eaten melon
is a cave of red meat and black stars,

pale rinds float in the grass,
and the big neighbourhood dog comes to stand
like a hand stuffed into too small a glove.

[1985]

Spring

The hills plunge through mist as if their contours
romped, but they're dead-still, made in those shapes
long ago. From early morning
the black and white cows have walked
straight through walls and columns of mist as if
their eyes could only see three feet in front of them anyway.

The hills in the morning: a green so delicate and wild
it almost shimmers backwards out of existence.
The cows stand sideways
on the hill gazing three feet in front of them
into empty air or they move in that slow
stumbling shuffle over the dirt clods. They could walk
straight through outer space not blinking an eye.

The fault opens up five feet wide in some places.
The small earthquake in the middle of the night:
the world swaying so hard it almost falls
out of orbit,
with only the sound of glasses
chattering in the cupboard.

Beside the run-off line: the skeleton
of one of last year's cows.
The other cows just walk around it
as if it weren't there.
Or maybe somewhere in those eyes
like bells too far away to hear
they already know.

At sunset the farmer
comes out of his white house on top of the hill
and watches his cows as if

he wished they belonged to him,
as if their four legs didn't move in their own time.
If they knew a little more
they could just walk off and leave him.

Always the hills and mist are making their mute gestures.
People get the feel of it, that's all they ever get.

The sheep stand around like errant clouds.
The lambs just sit in the grass, brand-new,
they haven't been here long enough to dirty their fur.
They rest awhile, looking around
as if they don't quite know how to behave.
Then they heave up on those scrawny legs
unfolded for the first time in the world.
And right away they get it:
the feel of being alive.
They want to romp
over every corner of those green hills.

[1984]

The Garden

Not only the night-blooming Cereus. The intimacy of all living things, especially those that blossom. Any given spare moment we'd hear the chirping of shears, and she'd be out in the garden. Grasping, letting fall. The same precision, the same care with which, the rest of the week, she performed early-morning surgery, routine examinations on pregnant women.

Strange relations, by proxy. Forbidden knowledge we merely overheard but had no right to reply to or repeat. Diseases. Case histories. Half my childhood friends born in my mother's hands.

Her weakness: loud tropical flowers. Their clairvoyance for storm, generating overgrowth: that something might survive. Tent-like shaggy leaves of the banana tree, its rare bursts of fruit splayed out red from the trunk like hands which withered without reaching their true shapes. A dozen kinds of orchids climbed and grew pristine, their flat painted faces enduring the cold rains. Whole continents sprang alive in her garden, ignorant of their origins. The fishpond my father built for her, rock-rimmed, as if a giant had stepped through, leaving a footprint which had immediately filled with waterlilies, papyrus, all the floral props of ancient civilizations. These are the books she'd read in bed, surveying from her high lit window the plot of history, the layered sediment of explicable event. What she relied on to have deposited her safely. Here. Small black print on an illumined page.

One year a single freak frost took from her half the orchids, the banana, the night-blooming Cereus.

A two-year drought and then they were gone: the papryus, the passion vine, all that remained of her imported world.

Around this time she began to snore, as if to express a satisfaction with sleep, or else a deepening reluctance to return to us. Or perhaps simply to keep my father company in that sound, his sound, which seemed to extend far beyond the room and to explicate his dreams in unknown tongues to the listener.

My father asleep inside a book, my mother among those loud tropicals which blossom. Continents without origin. Diseases without cure. Grasping, letting fall. The withering and the thriving, all at once.

[1984]

BEAUTY

On these leaden days of early spring even one stray tentacle of shadowy sun makes the ground steam. There is a slate-green dust which frosts the backsides of certain trees, away from the wind, which three young girls have just discovered. They go from trunk to trunk finding the brighter shades, streaking it above their eyes, posing for one another. A few of last summer's blackberries are left hanging like lanterns in a storm of brambles, too deep for the birds and too high for things that crawl the ground at night. Still the half-fermented juice is good for staining the lips. The girls are just learning about beauty.

One day they'll be shown what their own beauty or lack of it will do to them. Not one day, but many nights, nights they'll lie alone sifting through incidents, certain instances which are the only analogue of those steeply lengthening bones, the breasts filling calmly, immutably as lakes taking in all that stormy and random rain.

[1984]

INTERMITTENT RAIN

Rain hitting the shovel
leaned against the house,
rain eating the edges
of the metal in tiny bites,

bloating the handle,
cracking it.
The rain quits and starts again.

There are people who go into that room in the house
where the piano is and close the door.
They play to get at that thing
on the tip of the tongue,
the thing they think of first and never say.
They would leave it out in the rain if they could.

The heart is a shovel leaning against a house somewhere
among the other forgotten tools.
The heart, it's always digging up old ground,
always wanting to give things a decent burial.

But so much stays fugitive,
inside,
where it can't be reached.

The piano is a way of practising
speech when you have no mouth.
When the heart is a shovel that would bury itself.
Still we can go up casually to a piano
and sit down and start playing
the way the rain felt in someone else's bones
a hundred years ago,
before we were born,
before we were even one cell,
when the world was clean,
when there were no hearts or people,
the way it sounded
a billion years ago, pattering
into unknown ground. Rain

hitting the shovel leaned against the house,
eating the edges of the metal.
It quits,
        and starts again.

[1989]

Snowlight on the Northwood Path

Last night on our way to the bathroom after making love
the neighbour's house lights must have stolen
a little way through the kitchen window; as we passed,

the two white bentwood chairs I had brought
with me from Vermont and another life
glowed with a faint, ulterior, mineral half-life—

illusion of a snowed-in night without moon in Vermont.
As once, after a convivial late night with friends,
my companion and I stepped out to a world

not as we'd left it; for while we drank and talked,
obliviously, snow had been falling,
and it had grown clear again, and very cold,

so that the ground glowed, risen several inches.
We weren't dressed for it,
yet chose to walk back by way of the woods,

whose paths, muddled of late by too much use,
had been obliterated by snow, so that we sank
deeper at each step, laughing.

Last night on our way back through the kitchen,
after the brightness of the bathroom, our eyes would not adjust;
the chairs had melded with the dark, and we stumbled.

Yet back in bed as I turned toward sleep
the paths became confused again,
my former life drifting across our life:

I was young, half-dreaming,
and because I had no past to speak of I went forward,
into a cold so extreme

it was at the same time exotically warm—
as though there were no way to distinguish
between the pleasure and the ache,

or to choose, last night,
in the after-ache of pleasure,
between my life and my life.

[1989]

City Lights

To board the train for Toronto and glance over at the other
track as that train starts rolling and the woman there,
opposite, dozing, opens her eyes.
To look into eyes and know there are many directions.
To have it all at once: cinnamon buns
from the Harbord Bakery and the late poems of Wang Wei.
To step out, bringing traffic to a halt.
To bemoan with total strangers the state of the lettuce,
to be queried concerning the uses of star fruit,
and expostulate thereon.
To guide an unsteady gentleman across the street
and refuse payment in eternity.
To happen on the long light down certain streets as the sun is setting,
to pass by all that tempts others without a thought.
For cigar smoke and Sony Walkmans and random belligerence,
the overall sense of delighted industry
which is composed of idle hatred, inane self-interest,
compassion, and helplessness, when looked at closely.
To wait in queues, anonymous as the price code in a supermarket.
To board a bus where everyone is talking at once,
and count eight distinct languages, and not know any.
For the Chinese proprietress of the Bagel Paradise Restaurant,
who is known to her customers as the joyful
otter is known to the clear salt water of Monterey Bay.
To know that everyone who isn't reading, daydreaming,
or on a first date is either full of plans or
playing Sherlock Holmes on the subway.
For eerie cloudlit nights, and skyscrapers,
and raccoons, jolly as bees.

For the joy of walking out the front door and becoming
instantly, and resolutely, lost.
To fall, when one is falling,
into a safety net, and find one's friends.
To be one among many.
To be many.

[1989]

Rubber Boots

In Ontario, in autumn,
black and limp, with shining curves,
they are the only footwear for the fields.
All year they have lain in
fishy heaps at the back of closets
and now halls and entryways
are lined with them, pair by pair,
dripping onto newspaper,
upright, leaning drunkenly together, or toppled,
helpless as dull black beetles,
their legs in the air.
I remember the morning
Jane fell in love, in San Francisco,
with a pair,
glazed, brilliant as lemons
in the shop window.
But what shines in a wild Pacific storm
would leak within minutes
when the world turns to mud
and sucks at the heels
in Elora or Owen Sound.
A gash is an unhappy thing,
especially in black rubber,
when boots are cheap:
the kind thing is to carve
the toes like jack-o'-lanterns
and let them leer
unexpectedly in hallways.
Nothing mourns like a boot
for its lost mate.

You must fill it with water,
and flowers.
Unlike other shoes,
they never smell of possession.
They have mapped the sodden marsh,
trod on ice.
You step into them,
sound and seamless,
with a double pair of thick socks.
You enter the Ark.

[1989]

Grove

It is a matter of spaces. Of infinitesimal nutrients built up over time. Of constant sound, as of hinges or newborn beings. How pleasant it is to be lost among the powerful sunlit columns. Nothing is obscured except by grandeur, nothing concealed. Pleasant, that is, unless you stray too long and dusk begins, which fills the legs with sand. Yet if you can stand just a little indiscriminate terror, if you can endure not knowing (never to know) whether you are being honoured on this earth or not so much as marked in passing: either way. And it will reveal itself, the alien, tribal nature of the grove. Stars called into being above the swaying crowns.

[1989]

Erin Mouré (b. 1955)

Erin Mouré was born in Calgary. She worked for the railroad in various capacities while living in Vancouver and is still employed by CN in its head office in Montreal. Her books include *Empire, York Street* (1979, nominated for a Governor General's Award), *The Whisky Vigil* (1982), *Wanted Alive* (1983), *Domestic Fuel* (1985), *Furious* (1988, Governor General's Award), *Sheepish Beauty, Civilian Love* (1992), and *The Green Word: Selected Poems* (1994).

In an interview with Peter O'Brien in *So to Speak* (1987), Mouré describes her own unusual creative processes: 'I start to write a poem about how I can't describe my own feelings to my lover, and to give an example of how I feel, I start to talk about fish and fishing and pulling the hooks out of their mouths. Pretty soon the example takes over and starts writing the poem! I don't want to write about fish, and in the end an event emerges that is not straightforward, and it's immaterial that there's nothing about feelings and communication, because curiously the poem is still about that! It's what you feel at the end—how hard it is to feel and communicate personal/public/animate pain. The poem is about fish too! From the sound of words that mean "fish" we find out about the difficulty and inexpressible nature of pain. And how pain is not an end.'

Insisting that 'words have a life of their own' and that poems have a 'subliminal code', Mouré rejects the notion that she is primarily a storyteller. 'I think my poems are narrative in the sense of co-relation, correspondence, rather than "story". The surfaces go very deep.' Her increasingly non-linear poetry moves steadily from the referentiality and surface politics of everyday life to a deeper relation with both language and its potential for engagement and change. In the final section of *Furious*, called 'The Acts', she outlines, in a language and syntax scarcely less evocative and challenging than those of the poems, her preoccupation with compression and intertextuality, as well as her commitment to everyday event as it manifests itself in 'ordinary words in their street clothes'. While maintaining her links with Wordsworth, William Carlos Williams, and those many poets who advocate colloquial speech in poetry, Mouré is anything but a conventional Romantic in her poetics. She rejects the denigration of intellect sometimes taken to be represented by Williams's dictum 'no ideas but in things'. She argues, instead, for 'PURE REASON', which she considers more complex than logic. While a poem, on the level of surface content, may appear to be about animals, 'it is not about animals at all, but about the fantasies of the audience, and this content lies under the flat surface of the poem. So that the *surface content* is actually *a form* for the real emotional "content" of the poem.'

Mouré understands that conventional grammar and syntax may blunt or dull a reader's perceptions, so she is not averse to breaking sentences, jumbling syntax, using repetitions, and letting sound override sense. She argues that 'the opening up of sense perception is an opening of the powers to heal. Referentiality distorts more than it conveys, it injects us with the comfortable. I crave instead images that "act within a context but do not refer to it" (Jerome Rothenberg, *Technicians of the Sacred*).' Mouré's poetics shift from a postmodernist to a feminist critique of language, as this statement indicates: 'What this need for affirmation meant before was having an existence affirmed by men. Knowing how they praise well what affirms their relation. They do not have to put themselves at risk, which women have always had to do, to exist, to speak, to have their existence affirmed by others.'

Her feminist shorthand may require more of a reader's attention, but, as Mouré argues, women are accustomed to listening 'so carefully to each other'. As to the question of 'making sense', she says: 'I want to write these things . . . that can't be torn apart by anybody, anywhere, or in the university. I want the overall sound to be one of making sense, but I don't want the inside of the poem to make sense of anything.' The breaking down of logical connections is something that has concerned poets in the past. One has only to think of Eliot's use of juxtaposition and counterpoint in *The Waste Land*, Pound's use of overlapping grids—what he called 'superposition'—in the *Cantos*, Gertrude Stein's upending of sense and narrative, Berryman's wringing the neck of grammar, and the growing interest of poets like Adrienne Rich, John Thompson, and Phyllis Webb in imported forms such as the *ghazal*, which enables the poet to embrace discontinuity and illogic in a highly charged and emotionally unified context.

Where Mouré differs is in extending her 'program' to the specifics of grammar: to 'break down the noun/verb opposition wherein the present so-called "power" of the language resides' and to shift this power, if only briefly, to other parts of speech, such as the preposition. Whereas the verb is tied to action, to narrative, and the noun is freighted with signification and potential referentiality, the preposition emphasizes *relation* and gives a heightened sense of our position in time. 'It isn't that to change the weight and force of English will necessarily make women's speaking possible. But to move the force in any language, create a slippage, *even for a moment* . . . to decentre the "thing", unmask the relation. . . .' Mouré's is a worthy and not entirely surprising project, especially in view of our growing attention to other languages, such as Chinese, where there are no pronouns, no past and future tenses, and where the distinction between things and events is entirely relational.

In 'Poetry, Memory, and the Polis' (*Language in Her Eye: Writing and Gender*, edited by Libby Scheier, Sarah Sheard, and Eleanor Wachtel, 1990), Mouré writes: 'In my own work, I thought at one time the simplest line was best. Yet when I wrote anecdotal/conversational poems without reversal (which is to say, without the language confronting itself & its assumptions in the poem), I suppressed both my feelings as a lesbian, and my concerns as a woman. My poetry was supposed to reflect my life, especially my life as a worker, and these things were suppressed in that life. To write the poems, then, perpetuated (unknowingly) my own pain at being invisible, my desire silenced. As if I could belong, by force of will, to that *sameness*, that *anaesthesia*.'

empire, york street

there might have been an empire here—
books speak of many, none
of them turbulent, all
smelling strongly of trees.
history of empires, begun
when cities were named after reigning monarchs.
fresh boats shouldered the waves,
stubborn w/ flags & non-union labour.
newborn children carried
the names of dead relatives.
certain tricky allegiances were learned
in schools. houses were built, land
changed hands & became property.

on a city lot on york street, a man
stands, he holds his father's name
& survey equipment.
the house at which he stares is not
ancestral, is condemned.

he considers the empire
upon which he will build
condominiums. tenants watch
terrified from certain windows.
they wait in an empire of rented rooms,
history of allegiance paid to landlords.

in factories during certain hours
the empire of the body is rented
for small change. in hospital the empire
of a man is destroyed by certain
treasonous cells. he speaks no longer
of flags, of civil law, of succession
to thrones. no children inherit
his names. his empire kept alive
by chemical technology, words, films.

from windows the tenants watch the man
who surveys his empire. either
they will join him now
or they will turn away.
thru this moment, this hesitation, this flaw.
empires meet & totter, flagging
the dead earth. certain
trees watch new empires, ascend
the stony air.

[1979]

POST-MODERN LITERATURE

Less to insist upon, fewer
proofs.
Raw metals pulled from the ground, cheaply.
Or a woman in the televised film shouting: thanks to you
I end up surrounded by violence.
So much gratitude, Saturday nights spent
believing in it.

But the end of a city is still
a field, ordinary persons live there, a frame house, & occasionally—
a woman comes out to hang the washing.
From a certain angle you see her
push a line of wet clothes across a suburb.
It sings in the wind there, against
stucco, lilacs, sunken front porches, windows
where nobody moves.
But carefully. All of it

made carefully, children in snowsuits
after school, appear in the doorway, carry
their tracks shyly.
& you at the kitchen table—your empty
bowl streaked by the spoon, the meal's
memory, papers, juice in one glass, whisky
in another, unwritten greeting cards,
a watch, applesauce, small white medallions.

As if saying the name fixes.
As if the woman will come out again, & pull down
an entire suburb with her washing.
As if the city *could* end, in a field or
anywhere.
or if the woman on the bright TV could
stop saying *thank you*.
or you, saying 'like this,' & pointing shyly.
Too much paper, the children
in their snowsuits holding doorways, white snow,
parrots, singing smuggled information, the corporation gone to

Guatemala.
Leaving Father, the curling rink, a woman dressed
in grey parka & the nearest boots pulling
stiff clothes away from the weather, the back road, post-modern literature

[1983]

DIVERGENCES

'I am of today & of the has-been; but there is some thing in me
that is of tomorrow & of the day-after-tomorrow & of the shall-be.'
Zarathustra

I am the youngest in a family of boots & shoes
I am the youngest lifting its burnt flag above my head
into the ocean,
recoiling a bit at the cold kiss of water
I am part of a long family lifting its boots out of the mud.
The family sighs in front of me, I watch the backs of
a thousand children growing gaunter, beckoning me.
I follow them for years & years, forever
arriving.

I am the youngest child of a family that cries its body to sleep,
all over the world
Its body unconscious in Argentina after questioning,
shot in Zimbabwe with the shout of joy caught in its mouth,
arrested in Lisbon for *insulting the President*,
gassed in an Afghani hill-town.

Also I am the youngest of a long line of gunners, of proud
trigger-pullers, maintainers of public order,
of supporters of the safety of the state, of the increase
in production: I am the youngest dressed in
white   carrying the Host in cathedrals, singing the glorious anthem,
Singing birth & resurrection for   *those who are*
with us

Friend, are you with us? Do you love your
patron with his feudal beneficence, with his
godly benediction, with his new clothes, his whisky & wine,
his descent into the dead
where he found you? Robber, he robbed you.
He took you out of the dead   into the world where you are now,
stumbling with your ancestors, your predecessors, kissing the
lovers who left you after one night, the passengers of trains—
who walk in front of you in their boots & shoes,
a family.

Family of which you are youngest, barely born, carrying
the same old flag into the sea.
Your eyes pressed open, a light fills them credulously,
the ocean laps at the dryness in your bones.
Is it true you can't go back now?
Go on, says the flag, its burnt edges singing
at the touch of cold water.
Yes, say the family, *yes*, say the boots & shoes,

Go back, cry the gun-shot wounds, opening—

[1983]

BEING CARPENTER

Then there is the man you always think of
as being Carpenter.
Your brother mentions him in letters, as living
very far away: 'Carpenter is disillusioned about nearly
all of it, now.'
He doesn't have a first name, he's *Carpenter*,
he builds a small life of which
you hear little.
'When Carpenter comes home from work now,
he lies on the floor for hours & listens
to the radio, moving only
to prevent the baby from wandering near the stairs.'
This is the latest news.
You remember Carpenter in his muddy boots & sweater
sitting on the edge of the sofa with
his mug of coffee, talking about film,
& try to think
of this same Carpenter lying on the floor in the kitchen
of a townhouse you've never seen,
the radio on, the baby crawling near him.
You always think of him as being Carpenter;
It's hard to imagine any other way.
'Carpenter,' people said &
it was a final kind of name, one you could depend on,
one with shelves of books behind,
a film series & a magazine to edit.

Carpenter always busy, Carpenter driving Banff Avenue in his Volvo,
Carpenter sitting on the sofa in his jeans
& plaid shirt, his beard waggling,
animated, articulate, saying what Carpenter would say.
Still you watch for signs of him in your brother's letters.
You hope he has got up off the floor
& turned the stove on to make coffee.
Carpenter is a married man now, & the baby
is growing up as she crawls off toward the stairs.
Maybe he is sad because
he hears her growing.   & himself getting older.
& the film series ending & starting,
& the control of magazines changing hands,
& the extra work of the staff committee.
Still you can't think of him on the kitchen floor, surrounded
by the mess of late afternoon,
his wife gone off to the studio away from the baby,
who wanders near him.
You wish he would sit up at least, &
go on, being Carpenter, inside of Carpenter's face & clothing,
wearing Carpenter's glasses & beard

[1983]

PUBLIC HEALTH

The cold daydreams
that speak to us with their mouths
shut.
They are the thin rook
of a woman dragged
around the walls of her hospital in a chair,
one leg dangles like a crayon
that the sidewalk tears thru.

It is said
the doctor must charge us equally because
he lives by this, his courage,
it is to open up the human skin &
know—
the orange pump, flat machination of breath,
coils of decay that push

the corpuscles forward:
the doctor's courage is in pulling the skin back,
tying off daydreams; & in fingering the cold
muscle, arthritic bone.

This man talks of
the enterprise he finds
in sickness, accidental caresses, the roughed-up
wife, a cirrhosis.
He proclaims his courage, his love, & how
the government wants it, or gives back
too little.
The limbs of the woman mute with anaesthetic.
Pay me, he says.

I'm gonna die, the drunk chokes at
all of us in the liquor line-up, his face battered
open in dispute.
Then laughs, bent over sideways with his 2-dollar bill, ripped trouser,
his left hand pushes his kidneys inward,
rain hits the sidewalk,
the woman is wheeled into surgery two blocks away,
& the cold
daydream shuts its mouth, again

[1985]

TROPIC LINE

The northern pike, blinded, its mouth open in the hook's pull
upward from the water, reverse gravity
My brother's hand holding the pike's body,
long & more muscled than his arm,
lifting it:

My brother in the jacket too small for his age,
its green quilt unravelling
around him, unweaving his body into the cold March
air, the snow receded but not gone,
the river's effluent opening

Our hands nearly solid with cold, gloveless,
immobile
Out on the river ice, hearing it explode
beneath us like a rifle
Deep noise of the hemisphere, turning toward the sun

What we would do, to go out with the narrow rods
like saplings, fibreglass, the crude reels,
cheapest ever made,
we would hike behind the river houses, the winter unchanged
Sun risen just past the Tropic of Cancer

To rub our hands & feel ice crack inside the fingers,
not like rifles,
like meat slightly frozen
Billy still holding up the pike, stubborn,
bright fish dripping water

Fish we hurt in the sole motion our hands were capable
before we threw it back
into water that would freeze us if we fell
Not knowing how the pike had come where we were fishing,
crazed & lonely, searching its prey

How it saw our pattern of light on the river surface,
our shadows & colours, the last it saw
Blind with cold we blinded it with ice shards,
& returned it, & ourselves, our arms & hands raised
like rifles, triumphant
The sun at our backs too cold to kill us,
pushing north over the tropic line

[1985]

Toxicity

Can acupuncture cure the sadness of organs
Can the liver forget sadness when the needles enter,
its field of memory,
words of politic, the mining this week of the ports
of Nicaragua, Corinto & Puerto Sandino
Nicaragua of the liver & the pancreas,
Nicaragua of the heart,
the small cells of the kidneys teeming
The cords of energy severed in the body,
the body poisoned by underwater mines
In a country never seen, fish boats
pulling drag-nets under water,
risking explosion,
can acupuncture cure the sadness of the liver, now?

What is fucked-up in the body, what is blocked
& carried rolled in the intestine,
what suffocates so badly in the lungs,
adhering, we talk about it, *toxicity*, your body standing
at the sink & turned to me,
near but not near enough, not near enough, Gail
What if the blocked space in the liver is just sadness,
can it be cured then?
Can the brain stop being the brain?
Can the brain be, for a few minutes, some other organ,
any organ, or a gland, a simple gland with its fluids,
its dark edges light never enters, can it let us alone?
When I think of the brain I think
how can something this dark help us
together
to stay here, as close as possible, avoiding underwater minefields,
the ships of trade churning perilously toward us,
the throb of their motors calling the mines up,
as close as our two skins

[1985]

Hooked

Some times we didn't know how hooked we were,
your hands in the dishwater,
you watching
the red-shirt moving down the road at Dubois' barn,
light of late afternoon makes your eyes
shine from any direction,
as in those old paintings of saints
whose eyes follow the viewer,
brutal wounds on their bodies bleeding
perfect drops from the thorn

Some times I am still looking for jazz on the radio,
still buying the daily paper,
reading crossword clues & horoscopes,
not answering any questions.

If all the words in us could come as cleanly,
the small squares & interlocking pattern!

Our voices across the brown table are
talking serious fear,
the erosion of personal space:
fear of the pig-boy on his motorcycle,
the ladies of the *rang* taking their night walk up the road,
answering or not answering your greeting,
do they recognize you, your loveliness,
the small saintedness of your body

Some times we didn't know how hooked we were,
on one or the other side of the neighbours,
eating dinner,
your eyes following me whether or not
you are really looking,
the small wound you bear because of my furious glances,
our embrace beside the sink & cupboards,
trying to kiss each other in a house bright
as an aquarium,
the red shirt of the neighbour moving,
walking into the barn where we knew there were cows,
heavy from waiting

[1988]

Miss Chatelaine

In the movie, the horse almost dies.
A classic for children, where the small girl pushes a thin
knife into the horse's side.
Later I am sitting in brightness with the women
I went to high school with in Calgary,
fifteen years later we are all feminist, talking of the girl
in the film.
The horse who has some parasite & is afraid of the storm,
& the girl who goes out to save him.
We are in a baggage car on VIA Rail around a huge table,
its varnish light & cold,
as if inside the board rooms of the corporation;
the baggage door is open
to the smell of dark prairie,
we are fifteen years older, serious
about women, these images:
the girl running at night between the house & the barn,
& the noise of the horse's fear mixed in with the rain.

Finally there are no men between us.
Finally none of us are passing or failing according to
Miss Chatelaine.
I wish I could tell you how much I love you,
my friends with your odd looks, our odd looks,
our nervousness with each other,
the girl crying out as she runs in the darkness,
our decoration we wore, so many years ago, high school
boys watching from another table.

Finally I can love you.
Wherever you have gone to, in your secret marriages.
When the knife goes so deeply into the horse's side, a
few seconds & the rush of air.
In the morning, the rain is over.
The space between the house & barn is just a space again.
Finally I can meet with you & talk this over.
Finally I can see us meeting, & our true tenderness, emerge.

[1988]

BETTY

O darkness & the empty moons, women
speaking light words into the cups of each other's fingers.
Or the mouth that fills a whole room, whispering
black air, not saliva, & not im/
pertinence.
We are here forever, unspoken, our undershirts stick in the room's heat,
stick between the breasts, in the flat place over the bone
that holds the chest
from tearing open, like the metal traps' cold tensity
where we laid them rusted in the city river,
drown-set for muskrat
Our small hands frozen, without fingers, claws of ice holding stiff snouts
of fur,
strange sprung words leaking

into our sentences.
'*A-girls*,' the 2 year old girl called out at the supper table.
Let's not say 'Grace' again, she said, let's say 'Betty.'
In the second public grade of school there were
5 Johns & 3 Debbies, 3 Darlenes, 2 Tims,
most of them grew up called Didi or Evan, & I stared out the window
at the racks of bicycles, tipped any way over, flat prairie line-scape,
the one consistent image I have of school.

Why are so many women lonely, empty as the inside of bicycles, as
the mouths using all the room,
the boys in their tight jeans &
slimness that will leave them in their 22nd year,
the boys & their hard laugh who is tougher,
boys getting at each other's love, thru the inside
of women, their intermediary, their confessional.

I want to speak sexually of one thing—not male love
but physical knowing: the distance
between the breastbone & the palm, the two
important parts of the body.
Where the water runs in the long veins, curving thru space.
The palm where you can dive in & drink & never come up again,
& forgive no one, & feel, as you break the surface—
your head wet, streaming, smelling faintly of milk or oranges

[1988]

GORGEOUS

In any case, what are our chances.
In any case, whatsoever our chances, finally, where.
At the end of this century.
At the beginning, middle, or end of this century.
The hay baler coiled in the yard, with its square bales of hay.
The woman upstairs on the bed, listless.
Her cells are inscribed with the secret code given her at her birth, squeezed
out of the walls of her mother.
Her cells are inscribed with the small coils of the chromosomes,
defining her motion, the possible range,
even the books she has written,
down to the last letter.
One heart tick on the narrow screen pulled down this evening
for the moving picture of the heart.
The moving entity.
Blood-flow, gorging the ventricles, the chambers with their small colours,
that colour, pain's orange
light between the bulbs of the fingers, so unlike daylight, hidden
in the capillaries of the hands.
The woman who touches her hair.
Who touches, every month, her own blood.
This expiation of the body, not petty, but, *critical*.
A snake has come to my watertrough.
The narrow sip of water falling into my lungs.
If I shouted, who among the hierarchy of angels would hear me, these words.
& failing that.
What are our chances.
What are our chances.
If our cancer can be removed without fear, under local conditions.
The chromosomes unrolled & kissed,
until they are better.
& the woman gets out of the bed.
The blood on her legs, overflowing the small stopper.
The bird risen in the branches.
In what book, concealed, is its name.
I river, I river, I river.

Trust the verb.
Motion.
In the line, too, motion.
I love you. The book is ended.
The blood gorges gorges gorges the bed.

[1988]

THE COOKING

Political noise.
What we hear above the cooking cinnamon,
the cook in the brown shirt saying:
the government is trying to finish off the middle classes
in Toronto.

Which makes us guffaw
holding the serving spoon or
standing up & opening the window

It's too funny.
Hurrah, we think.

Or later, sobered, the dishes dry
in the cupboard, thinking
the gap between the rich & poor widens
& no one is in it

In thousands of houses the television flickers.
& in the flicker
The prime minister is smiling.

Choose, we think.
Choose.

2

Or a trussed bird.
Its wings bent back to hold shut
the neck cavity.

The riddle of the chicken we all know.

'Why did,' we begin. That, & the sound
of glasses, chair legs scraping the hardwood
& our legs too, folded & unfolded,
this laughter.
The skin's thin parchment.
Its word, the

word for it, whispered here.

3

If there could be a word for anything
we could be satisfied or
we could sit down peaceably
& eat
the goddam chicken.

Whose goose is cooked, anyhow.

4

I am sick of these poem imitations, said the cook
who knows better
waving the metal spatula & opening
the door
to get the smoke out

before the fire department stops playing cards
& turns off the TV prime ministerial
grin

Let's leave the hose out of this
The horse too
The 'house' for that matter
& the 'hours' we spent

painstaking
our hands wet & the teatowel on our shoulder
picking pinfeathers

5

A poem in which a chicken continually interrupts
the 'democratic process.'
An unspeakable chicken.
The chicken of our bad dream.
The one we woke up from, our mouths dry, & looked out.
In the alley, a television light.
Choose, the prime minister said.
We rolled over.
We thought he said: 'choose.'

[1992]

SHARON OLDS (b. 1942)

Sharon Olds was born in San Francisco and educated at Stanford University and Columbia University. Her first book of poems, *Satan Says* (1980), received the San Francisco Poetry Centre Award. Her second book, *The Dead and the Living* (1984), which has been reprinted a dozen times, won the Lamont Poetry Selection and the National Book Critics Circle Award. *The Gold Cell* appeared in 1987 and *The Father* in 1992.

In an age that has tried to strip poetry to the bone, Olds's work derives much of its power from her use of metaphors rooted in or referring to the human body. The boldness and frankness of these metaphors make the poems truly disarming; and the compulsive, almost hypnotic, urge to examine not only the mechanics of, but also the sensations associated with birth, generation, and dying ('the trance of matter') connects with that terrible curiosity we all share. Not surprisingly, Olds's work raises questions about the relationship between the private life and the public document, the poem. In an essay called 'Biography and the Poet', Denise Levertov alludes disapprovingly to a poem by Olds (though not using the latter's name or the poem's title) that speaks of being deliberately urinated on by a sister; she suggests that such a 'confessional' poem is the product of egotism overriding responsibility and violates the privacy, and possibly the now transformed reality, of that sister's life.

As important as considerations of compassion and privacy are in the creative realm, it seems to me a mistake to assume that Olds's poems are simply autobiographical documents to be consulted for factual information about her life. As light that passes through a prism is transformed into a full spectrum of colour, personal experience that passes through the crucible of language undergoes equally radical transformations. While many of her poems doubtless have their origin in specific events and emotions, Olds understands that these events and emotions are essentially archetypal, that they mirror in some profound way aspects of all our lives. As a result, she seems prepared to exaggerate, distort, invent, theatricalize—who knows, perhaps even understate—such incidents for the sake of pushing the material towards the universal. In short, her work is not merely confessional; the generational techtonics that are her forte, the staking and surveying of familial realities, carry readers out into deep water, where the river of personal experience merges with the oceanic collectivity of us all.

Although she is a teacher of Creative Writing at New York University and elsewhere, and appears to have no secrets or inhibitions in her poetry, Olds is nonetheless an intensely private person who is not the least bit forthcoming on the subject of her own art. In response to questions about her subject matter, Olds told an audience of mostly young writers at Dawson College in Montreal in 1994 that 'our subjects choose us' and 'we are constantly handed poems if we are alert to our needs of each other'. Her hand shaking as it tried to hold steady the oversize styrofoam cup of water, she made the point that writing is a means of collective healing: 'That's what the arts are doing, calling out to each other.'

In a revealing personal entry in the reference work *Contemporary Poets*, Olds claims to have shifted from closed forms to 'a line-break and a poem-shape (the body of the poem on the page) which felt more alive to me'. She also lists questions that interest her as a poet: 'Is there anything that shouldn't or can't be written about in a poem? What has never been written about in a poem? What is the use, function, service of poetry in a society? For whom are you writing? (The dead, the unborn, the woman in front of you in the check-out line at Shop-Rite?).' Speaking of her work with the severely physically disabled, Olds quotes the Heretical Gospel of Thomas: 'If you do not bring forth that which is within you, that which is in you will destroy you. If you bring forth that which is within you, that which is within you will save you.' She also names Muriel Rukeyser, Galway Kinnell, Philip Levine, and Ruth Stone as 'Poets of the generation just ahead of mine whose work I've especially learned from and loved'.

Indictment of Senior Officers

In the hallway above the pit of the stairwell
my sister and I would meet at night,
eyes and hair dark, bodies
like twins in the dark. We did not talk of
the two who had brought us there, like generals,
for their own reasons. We sat, buddies
in wartime, her living body the proof of
my living body, our backs to the vast
shell hole of the stairs, down which
we would have to go, knowing nothing
but what we had learned there,

so that now
when I think of my sister, the holes of the needles
in her hips and in the creases of her elbows,
and the marks from the latest husband's beatings,
and the scars of the operations, I feel the
rage of a soldier standing over the body of
someone sent to the front lines
without training
or a weapon.

[1980]

First Night

I lay asleep under you,
still and dark as uninhabited
countryside, my blood slowly
drying between us, the break in my flesh
beginning to heal, open, a border
permanently dissolved.
The inhabitants of my body began to
get up in the dark, pack, and move.

All night, hordes of people
in heavy clothes moved south in me
carrying houses on their backs, sacks of
seed, children by the hand, under
a sky like smoke. Grazing grounds
shifted by hundreds of miles. Certain animals,
suddenly, were nearly extinct,
one or two odd knobby
shapes in opposite parts of the land.
Other forms multiplied,
masses of deep red wings
pouring out of nowhere. Rivers changed course,
the language turned
neatly about
and started to go the other way.
By dawn the migrations were completed. The last
edge of the blood bond dried,
and like a newborn animal about to be imprinted
I opened my eyes and saw your face.

[1980]

Station

Coming in off the dock after writing,
I approached the house,
and saw your long grandee face
in the light of a lamp with a parchment shade
the colour of flame.

An elegant hand on your beard. Your tapered
eyes found me on the lawn. You looked
as the lord looks down from a narrow window
and you are descended from lords. Calmly, with no
hint of shyness you examined me,
the wife who runs out on the dock to write
as soon as one child is in bed,
leaving the other to you.

                                        Your long
mouth, flexible as an archer's bow,
did not curve. We spent a long moment
in the truth of our situation, the poems
heavy as poached game hanging from my hands.

[1980]

Fishing Off Nova Scotia

Visiting their father's childhood home,
a blood culture, the children that week were
raised on blood. They let the line out
and let it out and let it out,
the sea was so deep.

We were floating in a small dory on top of those
tons of water. They yanked the line
up from the bottom, over and over,
jigging for fish: the hooks jerking
like upholstery needles through the gills.

It made a sound like plastic being broken
to get the barb out. In a wooden box
in the bottom of the boat, the supple metal
bodies would slap and twist, silver
gods dug up. *Lie still, fishy*,
the kids would stay, *Shut up fishy*,
with scales on their hands and traces of gut on their shoes.

I was playing the mother in this,
the wife from the States, so I did not speak,
the steel cracking those clenched jaws,
the bright glaze of blood on the children.

[1980]

The Death of Marilyn Monroe

The ambulance men touched her cold
body, lifted it, heavy as iron,
onto the stretcher, tried to close the
mouth, closed the eyes, tied the
arms to the sides, moved a caught
strand of hair, as if it mattered,
saw the shape of her breasts, flattened by
gravity, under the sheet,
carried her, as if it were she,
down the steps.

These men were never the same. They went out
afterwards, as they always did,
for a drink or two, but they could not meet
each other's eyes.

Their lives took
a turn—one had nightmares, strange
pains, impotence, depression. One did not
like his work, his wife looked
different, his kids. Even death
seemed different to him—a place where she
would be waiting,

and one found himself standing at night
in the doorway to a room of sleep, listening to a
woman breathing, just an ordinary
woman
breathing.

[1984]

Miscarriage

When I was a month pregnant, the great
clots of blood appeared in the pale
green swaying water of the toilet.
Dark red like black in the salty
translucent brine, like forms of life
appearing, jelly-fish with the clear-cut
shapes of fungi.

That was the only appearance made by that
child, the dark, scalloped shapes
falling slowly. A month later
our son was conceived, and I never went back
to mourn the one who came as far as the
sill with its information: that we could
botch something, you and I. All wrapped in
purple it floated away, like a messenger
put to death for bearing bad news.

[1984]

The Connoisseuse of Slugs

When I was a connoisseuse of slugs
I would part the ivy leaves, and look for the
naked jelly of those gold bodies,
translucent strangers glistening along the
stones, slowly, their gelatinous bodies
at my mercy. Made mostly of water, they would shrivel
to nothing if they were sprinkled with salt,
but I was not interested in that. What I liked
was to draw aside the ivy, breathe the

odour of the wall, and stand there in silence
until the slug forgot I was there
and sent its antennae up out of its
head, the glimmering umber horns
rising like telescopes, until finally the
sensitive knobs would pop out the ends,
delicate and intimate. Years later,
when I first saw a naked man,
I gasped with pleasure to see that quiet
mystery reenacted, the slow
elegant being coming out of hiding and
gleaming in the dark air, eager and so
trusting you could weep.

[1987]

SUMMER SOLSTICE, NEW YORK CITY

By the end of the longest day of the year he could not stand it,
he went up the iron stairs through the roof of the building
and over the soft, tarry surface
to the edge, put one leg over the complex green tin cornice
and said if they came a step closer that was it.
Then the huge machinery of the earth began to work for his life,
the cops came in their suits blue-grey as the sky on a cloudy evening,
and one put on a bullet-proof vest, a
black shell around his own life,
life of his children's father, in case
the man was armed, and one, slung with a
rope like the sign of his bounden duty,
came up out of a hole in the top of the neighbouring building
like the gold hole they say is in the top of the head,
and began to lurk toward the man who wanted to die.
The tallest cop approached him directly,
softly, slowly, talking to him, talking, talking,
while the man's leg hung over the lip of the next world
and the crowd gathered in the street, silent, and the
hairy net with its implacable grid was
unfolded near the curb and spread out and
stretched as the sheet is prepared to receive at a birth.
Then they all came a little closer

where he squatted next to his death, his shirt
glowing its milky glow like something
growing in a dish at night in the dark in a lab and then
everything stopped
as his body jerked and he
stepped down from the parapet and went toward them
and they closed on him, I thought they were going to
beat him up, as a mother whose child has been
lost will scream at the child when it's found, they
took him by the arms and held him up and
leaned him against the wall of the chimney and the
tall cop lit a cigarette
in his own mouth, and gave it to him, and
then they all lit cigarettes, and the
red, glowing ends burned like the
tiny campfires we lit at night
back at the beginning of the world.

[1987]

Still Life

I lie on my back after making love,
breasts white in shallow curves like the lids of soup dishes,
nipples shiny as berries, speckled and immutable.
My legs lie down there somewhere in the bed like those
great silver fish drooping over the edge of the table.
Scene of destruction, scene of perfect peace,
sex bright and calm and luminous as the
scarlet and blue dead pheasant all
maroon neck feathers and deep body wounds,
and on the centre of my forehead a drop of water
round and opalescent, and in it
the self-portrait of the artist, upside down,
naked, holding your brushes dripping like torches with light.

[1987]

The Green Shirt

For a week after he breaks his elbow
we don't think about giving him a bath,
we think about bones twisted like white
saplings in a tornado, tendons
twined around each other like the snakes on the
healer's caduceus. We think about fractures and
pain, most of the time we think about pain,
and our boy with his pale set face goes
around the house in that green shirt
as if it were his skin, the alligator on it with
wide jaws like the ones pain has
clamped on his elbow, fine joint that
used to be thin and elegant as
something made with Tinkertoy, then it
swelled to a hard black anvil,
softened to a bruised yellow fruit,
finally we could slip the sleeve over,
and by then our boy was smelling like something
taken from the back of the icebox and
put on the back of the stove. So we stripped him and
slipped him into the tub, he looked so
naked without the sling, just a boy
holding his arm with the other hand as you'd
help an old geezer across the street, and
then it hit us, the man and woman by the
side of the tub, the people who had made him,
then the week passed before our eyes
as the grease slid off him—
the smash, the screaming, the fear he had crushed his
growth-joint, the fear as he lost all the
feeling in two fingers, the blood
pooled in ugly uneven streaks
under the skin in his forearm and then he
lost the use of the whole hand,
and they said he would probably sometime be back to normal,
sometime, probably, this boy with the long fingers of a surgeon,
this duck sitting in the water with his L-shaped
purple wing in his other hand.

Our eyes fill, we cannot look at each other,
we watch him carefully and kindly soap the damaged arm,
he was given to us perfect, we had sworn no harm
would come to him.

[1987]

THE GLASS

I think of it with wonder now,
the glass of mucus that stood on the table
in front of my father all weekend. The tumour
is growing fast in his throat these days,
and as it grows it sends out pus
like the sun sending out flares, those pouring
tongues. So my father has to gargle, cough,
spit a mouthful of thick stuff
into the glass every ten minutes or so,
scraping the rim up his lower lip
to get the last bit off his skin, then he
sets the glass down on the table and it
sits there, like a glass of beer foam,
shiny and faintly golden, he gargles and
coughs and reaches for it again
and gets the heavy sputum out,
full of bubbles and moving around like yeast—
he is like a god producing food from his own mouth.
He himself can eat nothing anymore,
just a swallow of milk, sometimes,
cut with water, and even then
it can't always get past the tumour,
and the next time the saliva comes up
it is ropey, he has to roll it in his throat
a minute to form it and get it up and dis-
gorge the oval globule into the
glass of phlegm, which stood there all day and
filled slowly with compound globes and I would
empty it and it would fill again
and shimmer there on the table until
the room seemed to turn around it
in an orderly way, a model of the solar system

turning around the sun,
my father the old earth that used to
lie at the centre of the universe, now
turning with the rest of us
around his death, bright glass of
spit on the table, these last mouthfuls.

[1992]

THE LIFTING

Suddenly my father lifted up his nightie, I
turned my head away but he cried out
Shar!, my nickname, so I turned and looked.
He was sitting in the high cranked-up bed with the
gown up, around his neck,
to show me the weight he had lost. I looked
where his solid ruddy stomach had been
and I saw the skin fallen into loose
soft hairy rippled folds
lying in a pool of folds
down at the base of his abdomen,
the gaunt torso of a big man
who will die soon. Right away
I saw how much his hips are like mine,
the long, white angles, and then
how much his pelvis is shaped like my daughter's,
a chambered whelk-shell hollowed out,
I saw the folds of skin like something
poured, a thick batter, I saw
his rueful smile, the cast-up eyes as he
shows me his old body, he knows
I will be interested, he knows I will find him
appealing. If anyone had ever told me
I would sit by him and he would pull up his nightie
and I would look at him, at his naked body,
at the thick bud of his penis in all that
dark hair, look at him
in affection and uneasy wonder
I would not have believed it. But now I can still
see the tiny snowflakes, white and

night-blue, on the cotton of the gown as it
rises the way we were promised at death it would rise,
the veils would fall from our eyes, we would know everything.

[1992]

THE EXACT MOMENT OF HIS DEATH

When he breathed his last breath, it was he,
my father, although he was so transformed
no one who had not been with him
for the last hour would know him—the skin
now physical as animal fat,
the eyes cast halfway back into his head,
the nose thinned, the mouth racked open,
with that tongue in it like the fact of the mortal,
a tongue so dried, scalloped, darkened
and material. We could see the fluid
risen into the back of his mouth
but it was he, the huge, slack arms,
the spots of blood under the skin
black and precise, we had come this far with him
step by step, it was he, his last
breath was his, not taken with desire
but his, light as a milkwood seed,
coming out of his mouth and floating across the room.
And when the nurse listened for his heart,
and his stomach was silvery, it was his stomach,
when she did not shake her head but stood and
nodded at me, for a moment it was fully
he, my father, dead but completely
himself, a man with an open mouth and
black spots on his arms. He looked like
someone killed in a bloodless struggle—
the strain in his neck and the base of his head,
as if he were violently pulling back.
He seemed to be holding still, then the skin
tightened slightly around his whole body
as if the purely physical were claiming him,
and then it was not my father,
it was not a man, it was not an animal,

I ran my hand slowly through the hair,
lifted my fingers up through the grey
waves of it, the unliving glistening
matter of this world.

[1992]

THE SWIMMER

The way the seed that made me raced
ahead of the others, arms held to her sides,
round head humming, spine
whipping, I love to throw myself
into the sea—cold fresh
enormous palm around my scalp,
I open my eyes, and drift through the water that lies
heavy on the earth, I am suspended in it
like a sperm. Then I love to swim slowly,
I feel I am at the centre of life, I am
inside God, there is sourweed in skeins like
blood beside my head. From the beach
you would see only the ocean, the swell
curling—so I am like a real being,
invisible, an amoeba that rides in spit,
I am like those elements my father turned into,
smoke, bone, salt. It is one of
the only things I like to do
anymore, get down inside the horizon
and feel what his new life is like, how
clean, how blank, how griefless, how without error—
the trance of matter.

[1992]

I WANTED TO BE THERE WHEN MY FATHER DIED

I wanted to be there when my father died
because I wanted to see him die—
and not just to know him, down to
the ground, the dirt of his unmaking, and not
just to give him a last chance
to give me something, or take his loathing

back. All summer he had gagged, as if trying
to cough his whole esophagus out,
surely his pain and depression had appeased me,
and yet I wanted to see him die
not just to see no soul come
free of his body, no mucal genie of
spirit jump
forth from his mouth,
proving the body on earth is all we have got,
I wanted to watch my father die
because I hated him. Oh, I loved him,
my hands cherished him, laying him out,
but I had feared him so, his lying as if dead on the
flowered couch had pummelled me,
his silence had mauled me, I was an Eve
he took and pressed back into clay,
casual thumbs undoing the cheekbone
eyesocket rib pelvis ankle of the child
and now I watched him be undone and
someone in me gloried in it,
someone lying where he'd lain in chintz
Eden, some corpse girl, corkscrewed like
one of his amber spit-ems, smiled.
The priest was well called to that room,
violet grosgrain river of his ribbon laid
down well on that bank of flesh
where the daughter of death was made, it was well to say
Into other hands than ours
we commend this spirit.

[1992]

My Father Speaks to Me from the Dead

I seem to have woken up in a pot-shed,
on clay, on shards, the bright paths
of slugs kiss-crossing my body. I don't know
where to start, with this grime on me.
I take the spider glue-net, plug
of the dead, out of my mouth, let's see
if where I have been I can do this.

I love your feet. I love your knees,
I love your our my legs, they are so
long because they are yours and mine
both. I love your—what can I call it,
between your legs, we never named it, the
glint and purity of its curls. I love
your rear end, I changed you once,
washed the detritus off your tiny
bottom, with my finger rubbed
the oil on you; when I touched your little
anus I crossed wires with God for a moment.
I never hated your shit—that was
your mother. I love your navel, thistle
seed fossil, even though
it's her print on you. Of course I love
your breasts—did you see me looking up
from within your daughter's face, as she nursed?
I love your bony shoulders and you know I
love your hair, thick and live
as earth. And I never hated your face,
I hated its eruptions. You know what I love?
I love your brain, its halves and silvery
folds, like a woman's labia.
I love in you
even what comes
from deep in your mother—your heart, that hard worker,
and your womb, it is a heaven to me,
I lie on its soft hills and gaze up
at its rosy vault.
I have been in a body without breath,
I have been in the morgue, in fire, in the slagged
chimney, in the air over the earth,
and buried in the earth, and pulled down
into the ocean—where I have been
I understand this life, I am matter,
your father, I made you, when I say now that I love you
I mean look down at your hand, move it,
that action is matter's love, for human
love go elsewhere.

[1992]

Sharon Thesen (b. 1946)

Sharon Thesen was born in Tisdale, Saskatchewan, but has spent most of her life in Vancouver, where she teaches English at Capilano College. She was writer-in-residence at Concordia University in Montreal in 1992. Her books include *Artemis Hates Romance* (1980), *Holding the Pose* (1983), *Confabulations: Poems for Malcolm Lowry* (1984), *The Beginning of the Long Dash* (1987, nominated for a Governor General's Award), *The Pangs of Sunday* (1990), and *Aurora* (1995). Her poems have appeared in many anthologies, including *Poetry by Canadian Women* (edited by Rosemary Sullivan, 1989), and her essays on poetry and poetics can be found in *A Mazing Space: Writing Canadian Women Writing* (edited by Shirley Neumann and Smaro Kamboureli, 1986), *The Vancouver Review*, and *Po-It-Tree: a selection of poems and commentary* (published as a pamphlet by Roy Miki at Simon Fraser University, 1992). Thesen is editor of *The New Long Poem Anthology* (1991) and a generous selection of articles on her work appears in *Contemporary Literary Criticism*, 56 (1989).

In an essay entitled 'What Poetry Performs', Thesen identifies with poets who present themselves as 'the servants and not the masters of writing'. 'This is my own experience', she says; 'dictation is the mode I trust. This could be accounted for, at least to some extent, by the reduced value that our culture places upon any writing which does not have the emission of information (non-fiction) or mind control (bestseller romantic fiction) as its primary goal.' Thesen laments the alienation produced by this public devaluing of poetry and quotes with affection Gilbert Sorrentino's statement in *Splendide-Hotel*: 'It is incredible that [the poet] should love his line and hover over the very commas of it—he, whose whole industry is the precise figure, an achievement of grace and daring. . . . The wonder is that any artist stays sane.'

For the 'lady poet' (her own ironic term), trying to navigate between the Scylla of academia's formalist pretensions and the Charybdis of greeting-card banality can be lonely, if not hazardous. For Thesen, we are drawn to poetry, rather than to other forms, instinctively, because 'what poetry performs are the instincts of the rhythmic body—the body in time, the body as process, rhythm, and death.' Or, in the words she quotes from Julia Kristeva's *Desire in Language*: 'Poetic language is distinct from language as used for ordinary communication—not because it may involve a departure from a norm; it is almost an otherness of language. It is the language of materiality as opposed to transparency . . . a language in which the writer's effort is less to deal rationally with those objects or concepts words seem to encase than to work, consciously or not, with the sounds and rhythms in transrational fashion . . . effecting . . . semantic displacement.'

Thesen's poetry is well known for its quirkiness and unexpected twists, and its resistance to the informed authorial voice. 'When I am writing and pause to think,' Thesen says in an essay entitled 'Writing, Reading, and the Imagined Reader/Lover', 'the words I have already written have no history. They do not constitute the case of a moment ago. They are merely what went before, like the tracks of someone. They are signs, and they float, as it were, in an absolute present—a hall of mirrors in which I search for a true reflection or am amazed by the inventiveness of the distortions. I do not know, in the presence of these words, what I mean. They function, rather, as a momentum, from which I seek its rhythmic extension, and sometimes, at the end of a poem, its cessation.' Here the creative process appears as a kind of improvisation; not surprisingly, poet and critic Rosemary Sullivan has noted that Thesen's poems have the surprise and exploratory nature of 'jazz riffs'.

The poet as improviser is also something of a snake-charmer and seductress, as Thesen's concluding remarks suggest: 'I never read my own work when it appears alongside the work of others in a magazine or anthology. . . . Like my own body I know the geography, tendencies, and basic unalterable musculature of my own writing. I see it the way I see my own motionless image in the mirror. What does the beloved see? That face, those lines, that look. So that I do not "read" my own writing so much as introject an imagined reader/lover, not always the same one that I have invented in the process of writing/(seduction). . . . At the end of one of my poems, "Usage", I address the "dear reader" and ask "Will you marry me?" Some people take this literally, and really, they are not far from wrong in doing so.'

(For an interesting discussion of poetry and feminist theory, see Thesen's essay 'Poetry and the Dilemma of Expression'.)

LOOSE WOMAN POEM

A landscape
full of holes.
Women.
Pierced
ears voices piercing
the ceiling, a little choir
stung by wine:
I Fall to Pieces, and
Please Release Me.
After which I put on my old wedding band
& go to the party.
Next day 222's
& the moon falls out
of my fingernail.
The house smells like oysters
& a moon is on the loose
a woman in the bathtub   another
talking on the phone, their presence
shimmers, I'm fed up
with the wages of sin
put on some Mingus
& hepcat around

How come
it's always a question
of loss, being sick of self
displaced & frantic, chopped out
of the World of Discourse
waylaid
on the Bridge of Sighs, a net
work of connections coming down
to getting laid
or not getting laid & by whom.
Except getting laid
is not the way she thinks of it,
more like
something that her moons
can waylay waylay waylay
in the dark.

[1980]

DISCOURSE

A quiet night, they all are.
My kid asleep
my husband out screwing around
the cat also. Even spring
is false, crocuses sprout purple
into January sunlight,
poor little things.

Outside, at a glance
headlights dance in the alleyway
mercury vapour night entranced.

Women laughing somewhere
dogs barking. Susie splitting up
with Tom at Bino's Pancake House.

And finally there's not
all that much
you can say.

The small vocabulary
of love needs its own
thin blue dictionary.

[1983]

THE LANDLORD'S TIGER LILIES

A lost thing was found
on a shiny day we didn't know
was lost. Airplanes
pull tin foil off the roll of the sky
& a wandering dog
gilds the landlord's tiger lilies.

For the barren reach
of modern desire
there must be better forms
than this—
something cool,
intimate as a restaurant.

If I thought you would answer me
Rilke called to the angels,
if I thought
you would answer me.

Even so, he was wrong
not to go to his daughter's wedding
& hurting people's feelings.

[1987]

WOMEN LIKE ME

Women like me
who are nevertheless married
despite effeminate behaviour, PMS,
threatening to run away
with just an address book,
a couple of recent snapshots,

some blue silk pajamas.
Rehearsing the initials
of old boyfriends on the loose
who want them back now,
two decades of house payments
behind them. They quit
smoking, or light up
guilty in fragrant cars
as they turn slow corners
or wait for children
to cross the road.

In the Japanese restaurant
she begins to confess
that sometimes they go
for more than a week without—
& a faint sexual odour
of kelp is on our hands
as we lean toward a mutual place
filled with deep-fried tentacles,
things floating in soup,
a bit of carrot here & there—

& our big empty shoes
parked like cabs full of secrets
outside the shadowy screen
of our talking, the turning
& returning sustenance.

[1987]

DOUBLETALK

One-eyed one-tongued night
yield me a trace of myself,
that I was in Montreal
briefly, before Derrida
and *différance* crashed into English—
give me back the metro
the winter park
the red shoes I wore

swinging my purse, my heart
in the wrong place—
before it got so complicated to
speak you'd just as soon
leave it all in the original,
mute and appealing. First
you have woman and then you have poet,
then Catholic or Protestant,
Mary or no Mary, then your bi-*langue*
country not to mention the
country of your soft & lingual body—
yield me a trace of myself
when I took the bus down Sherbrooke
with my little bit of French
and my red shoes & longed for his sweet
poison kisses and missed him
with my unanimous tongue,
my singularly untrue heart
thinking *je t'aime*, *je t'aime*.

[1990]

SKIP TO MY LOU

Some exchanges today, mostly money
for goods, raspberries a nice old man
sold me not quite ripe yet, dark pink, mounded
in a used yogurt container, clean raspberries,
dry papery hands my change counted into
quarter by quarter until it reached two dollars.
Clouds in the sky resembling slow horses.
Ideas for bouquets suggest themselves
like happy whores in a Western movie walking by
corner store flowers on my way to the doctor's.
Their big bare feet and brassy eyes,
serving up the anaesthetic on a tray, white
skirts, bottles flying in a fistfight, crashing,
crashing. Doctor lets me off the table
& I lift my bangs in the mirror
to see the Band-Aid where she took
the biopsy and gave me back a piece of my skin

in a small jar writing 'pathology' on it, would I
mind, the lab is on my way to buy you a tie & I'm
not to worry about anything. In the mirror,
considering, I hold a striped tie up to myself &
down it goes so far I feel like the fat man on a chair
with legs wide apart, a small hat on, answering questions
with jokes. The mirror itself revives an aroma,
cobalt-blue cologne bottles, powder puffs stained
the colour of flesh, an oval box of hairpins, pungent
traces of dandruff on silvery tweezers. The way skin
fills our rooms, our tombs, the way it is alive.
I'm glad they took my cheque. I'm glad you liked the tie.

[1990]

ELEGY, THE FERTILITY SPECIALIST

He gave it to me straight
and I had to thank him
for the information, the percentages
that dwindled in his pencil writing
hand. I watched them drop
from 70, to 40, to 20
as all the variables were added in
and even after 20 he made a question mark. I felt
doors closing in swift silent succession
as I passed each checkpoint on the way
to the cold awful ruler, expert astronomer,
charterer of heavenly colonies,
answerer of questions, and this question
Could we have a child? and this answer, No
I don't think so. Oh
of course he could go in there
and have a look if I really wanted,
steer his ship around the fraying edges
of my terrain, peering with his spyglass,
cross-hatching impediments on his diagram
of the uterine pear & its two branching filaments:
he wouldn't recommend it, he would say,
squeezing his spyglass shut and putting it back
in its maroon velvet box. We make the usual

small gestures of disappointment
as if we'd run out of luck in a ticket line
and I say goodbye
and walk past the receptionist
busy at her files and it is
as if something with wings was crushing itself
to my heart, to comfort
or to be comforted I didn't know which
or even what it was, some angel, and
entered the elevator with the gabbing nurses
going down to lunch and a little girl
in a sun-dress, her delicate
golden shoulders stencilled from the straps
of her bathing suit: a perfect white X.

[1990]

SEPTEMBER, TURNING, THE LONG ROAD DOWN TO LOVE

The turning leaves
turn in a wind that rises
as if something warm,
invisible, and female just got up
from a nap and, half-dreaming,
walked to the kitchen
to make a cup of tea: Orange Pekoe?
Ruby Mist? Earl Grey? which one
did she choose? How about
Ruby Mist agree the women zipping up
their handbags at the airport
and boarding a propellered plane
from whose window porthole heights
topography is listless & small
lucite lakes gather in the deep corners
of mountains, as if assembled
for a meeting. The lakes speak
to one another over the white heads
of the mountains and this for them is like
dealing with the patriarchy. Ah,
the patriarchy, we sigh, having reached

our destination. We button up
our sweaters as the wind rises
and twirls the drying leaves
like you'd turn a wineglass
to look into the red depths and make
a fine judgement. The long
taproots of these rustling
turning trees that stand as a company of
completed metamorphoses of the human body
(branches for arms, bark for skin)
tap a little more love
for language to replace us with, who talk
among the mountains, and talk
with only ourselves, and history,
and the example of the evening
to blame for our silences.

[1990]

CHICKEN IN A PENSIVE SHELL

Is really Chicken in a Pineapple Shell, but
glancing at it sideways
while making tea I thought it said,
in a Pensive Shell, a mood
I'm often in, coming from thoughts, my
face dark with them as a pansy's.

Pascal in his *Pensées*
says nothing about chicken
but is sure our major distress
derives from having a home, the same old
boring old place where we rot &
rot and thereby hangs a tale.
Of woe, according to Pascal's
pensée, and here it's almost time
to start the chicken, Poulet
Marengo, a favourite
of Napoleon's. He liked it garnished
with crawfish and fried eggs.

As the oven heats up, rosy elements
brighten the tinted window
you look in to see your
nervous soufflé rising or not. No
pensée will help your soufflé
or chicken either, bubbling like lava
in the orange pot, with eight mushrooms,
a cup of white wine, and the empty pineapple
shells arrayed for next time, or next year,
or never. Their pensive moods
attract the wrong sort of chicken
who wear black thongs and carry a knife.
Their shirts are shiny, they belong
to another page, another life.

I prefer my Poulet ungarnished,
with rice, an easy salad on the side.
In a pensive shell will lie
my thoughts, dark inside
where you can't see the ocean
that roars and roars
in Napoleon's sleep. He spread himself
too thin. His crawfish garnish
outmanoeuvred him. I rest my case
on the kitchen counter where books
outnumber saucers & adjacent recipes
clash by night in pineapple shell
rowboats. And Divan gets a whiff
of Marengo and bam! the Duke
of Wellington fires his cannon.

[1990]

ANIMALS

When I come out of the bathroom
animals are waiting in the hall
and when I settle down to read
an animal comes between me
and my book and when I put on
a fancy dinner, a few animals

are under the table staring at the guests,
and when I mail a letter
or go to the Safeway there's always
an animal tagging along
or crying left at home and when I get
home from work animals leap joyously
around my old red car so I feel like
an avatar with flowers & presents all over
her body, and when I dance around
the kitchen at night wild & feeling
lovely as Margie Gillis, the animals
try to dance too, they stagger on
back legs and open their mouths, pink
and black and fanged, and I take their paws
in my hands and bend toward them,
happy and full of love.

[1990]

BRONWEN WALLACE (1945-1989)

Bronwen Wallace was born and died in Kingston, Ontario. As a student radical and pro-choice activist, she dropped out of a Ph.D. program in English at Queen's University and travelled around Canada, settling for a time in Windsor. Eventually she returned to Kingston, where she taught, edited books for Quarry Press, worked in a centre for battered women and children, and helped to establish the Women's Studies Program at Queen's. In 1970 she discovered Al Purdy's *The Cariboo Horses* and it changed her life: 'His work gave me permission to write about the people I knew, and the landscape I saw, and—most importantly, in the voice I'd heard in my head all my life. The voice of the men and women in my family. A voice that tells its stories in the same meandering and magical way that highways move through southeastern Ontario, until you understand that what happens in the story, like the landscape around you, is a metaphor for an inner journey, a journey that takes you to the centre of the speaker's life, to his or her discoveries about that life and to the mystery that lies there always.' Her poems were first published jointly with work by Mary di Michele in *Marrying into the Family* (1980). Subsequent books of poetry are *Signs of the Former Tenant* (1983), *Common Magic* (1985), and *The Stubborn Particulars of Grace* (1987). She also collaborated with her husband Chris Whynot on two films: *All You Have to Do* (1982) and *That's Why I'm Talking* (1987). She received the regional prize in the Commonwealth Poetry Competition in 1989. Her collection of short stories, *People You'd Trust Your Life To* (1990) appeared posthumously. Since her death, Wallace's reputation has grown rapidly. *Keep That Candle Burning Bright and Other Poems* (1991) collects her last prose poems, some dedicated to country singer Emmylou Harris. Her selected essays and journalism are available in *Arguments with the World* (1992), edited by Joanne Page. One of these essays, 'Why I Don't (Always) Write Short Stories', in which she discusses her interest in narrative, is available in the Poetics section.

In a 1989 interview with Janice Williamson, which appears in the Bronwen Wallace issue of *Open Letter* (7, 9, Winter 1991), in Williamson's *Sounding Differences: Conversations with Seventeen Canadian Women Writers* (1993), and in *Arguments with the World*, Wallace responds to the question of how she came to understand the community of women and the daily language that women speak: 'Some of this just comes from my own experience. My parents came from the farm, so I grew up around rural people and working-class people who tell stories. Some of that language comes from what I remember of all those conversations and people telling stories. The other big influence is that I've been a feminist since 1969. Some of what happens in my poems is an attempt to capture how women's conversations work, which is never linear but circles and moves around things. It's really important for me to try to capture conversational English, to make the poem as accessible as possible, to make it seem as though what's happening is really mundane. I started out thinking that story was everything that mattered, that what happened was all the poem was about, and now I see that the story is an extended metaphor for the voice of discovery and the mystery within what happens. That's how the poems have changed in terms of that narrative.'

Asked how she situated herself in the new landscape of feminist writing and theory, Wallace replies: 'Personally, as someone who's also an activist, it's really exciting to see this happening; it's really exciting to be part of that history in the present. There is also an increasing feeling of support and safety to try different things, a certain real sense of community. In the last ten years, I've become excited by the range of voices from Daphne Marlatt or Di Brandt to someone like me whom you might regard as a much more conservative writer in terms of the kinds of experiments I'm willing to do with language. I see this as a big choir; everybody has her part; I'm really excited by all the different and valuable ways women are writing. I know that I couldn't do what Daphne does but obviously she can't do what I do. I'm also interested in the development of feminist theory, because writing is very, very lonely. You put out this stuff, but with theory it comes back to you connected to the world in a different way.' Later in the same interview, her reservations about 'academic feminism' are more apparent: 'What really burns my ass is when a few academics try to tell me there's only one way to write, or one way to think about the world or that all my writing and thinking has to be poststructuralist. I react to this in the same way that when I was in the Left I reacted to male Stalinists telling me that there was only one way to read Marx. I say bullshit to that. Sometimes when I hear feminists debate about theory, I hear my days on the Left when a bunch of men sat around and talked about Mao versus Stalin. Who needs it?'

In the same interview, Wallace discusses the function of poetry and its place in contemporary society: 'Lao Tsu says that you have to treat every person as if they were wounded. I'm writing to the wounded part of each person, men as well as women. The power of feminism is the power of the victim who has recognized a way to use her damage. There's a great line in an Adrienne Rich poem about knowing that her wound came from the same place as her power. When you get in touch with your damage, recognize and care for it, you also discover the source of your power. We know that abusers, men who batter, or anybody who abuses children, have usually been abused themselves and have denied it. It's the denial of our damage, our limitations, our vulnerability, our mortality, that's got us where we are. The voice I try to speak is speaking to that person. I think we're kidding ourselves if we think there's any form of writing that can't be picked up by monopoly capitalism, and that includes any kind of experimental deconstructive writing. Look what's happening in rock and roll on video, all that is being picked up.'

About the apparently autobiographical content in her work, Wallace told Williamson: 'The first two books are intensely autobiographical as well as confessional. But in *Stubborn Particulars*, a lot is not autobiographical but stuff I've made up or stolen from other people's lives. I'm creating a persona in *Stubborn Particulars*, a persona who is the best or bravest part of me. She does the talking and has more courage to explore things than I do in my everyday self . . . when we tell people intimate things about ourselves we are in some way asking for, if not absolution, at least support, inclusion, something, a healing gesture from the other person. That's why we confess. And so I see that it's part of what I was saying about wounds and damage—it's another way of opening yourself up to the other person. This goes far beyond the confessional as we've understood it in autobiography.'

THE WOMAN IN THIS POEM

The woman in this poem
lives in the suburbs
with her husband and two children
each day she waits for the mail and
once a week receives
a letter from her lover
who lives in another city
writes of roses warm patches
of sunlight on his bed
Come to me he pleads
I need you and the woman
reaches for the phone
to dial the airport
she will leave this afternoon
her suitcase packed
with a few light clothes

But as she is dialling
the woman in this poem
remembers the pot-roast
and the fact that it is Thursday

she thinks of how her husband's face
will look when he reads her note
his body curling sadly toward
the empty side of the bed

She stops dialling and begins
to chop onions for the pot-roast
but behind her back the phone
shapes itself insistently
the number for airline reservations
chants in her head
in an hour her children will be
home from school and after that
her husband will arrive
to kiss the back of her neck
while she thickens the gravy
and she knows that
all through dinner
her mouth will laugh and chatter
while she walks with her lover
on a beach somewhere

She puts the onions in the pot
and turns toward the phone
but even as she reaches
she is thinking of
her daughter's piano lessons
her son's dental appointment

Her arms fall to her side
and as she stands there
in the middle of her spotless kitchen
we can see her growing
old like this
and wish for something anything
to happen we could have her go
mad perhaps and lock herself
in the closet crouch there
for days her dresses withering
around her like cast-off skins
or maybe she could take

to cruising the streets at night
in her husband's car
picking up teenage boys
and fucking them in the back seat
we can even imagine
finding her body
dumped in a ditch somewhere
on the edge of town

The woman in this poem offends us
with her useless phone and the persistent
smell of onions we regard her as we do
the poorly calculated overdose
who lies in a bed somewhere
not knowing how her life drips
through her drop by measured drop
we want to think of death
as something sudden
stroke or the leap
that carries us over the railing
of the bridge in one determined arc
the pistol aimed precisely
at the right part of the brain
we want to hate this woman

but mostly we hate knowing
that for us too it is
moments like this
our thoughts stiff fingers
tear at again and again
when we stop in the middle
of an ordinary day and
like the woman in this poem
begin to feel
our own deaths
rising slow within us

[1983]

All That Uneasy Spring

All that uneasy spring
we worked in our gardens
as soon as the earth was warm
we planted onions and peas
impatiens in the shade of our hedges
and marigolds in fiery rows along the walks
we set the seedlings out to harden
under sheets of glass
each of us looking up occasionally
to see the other women
in their yards a series
of mirrored reflections then
someone would wave from her kitchen
and we'd stop for coffee
leaving our mudcaked shoes
on the steps outside

And all that uneasy spring
our gossip came in whispers
like rumours from another land
divorces and custody disputes
how Anne's husband had kidnapped
her children from school
and Sharon had simply
left one afternoon and not come back
not even called

After the gardens were in
we washed the windows
repainted the lawnchairs
sent the drapes out to be cleaned
and at four
when the children arrived from school
we started the barbecues
scented our wrists
the cool drinks always ready
and the steaks just right
when our husbands pulled in the drive

But all that uneasy spring
when we lay in the dark
under crisp fresh sheets
the things we couldn't say
licked like flames
behind our eyes our houses
were burning down our children
screamed and sometimes our own voices
woke us surfacing through layers
of smoke to where our fingers touched
our husbands' bodies cool
and confident beside us
and awake then in that
uneasy dark we would remember
our morning conversations the sounds
of our voices coming back to us
suddenly precious even the smallest details
dirt-stained fingernails
the tiny lines that crinkled
white in sunburned skin
so that turning toward sleep
again we saw each other
standing in those hopeful gardens
while at our feet
the plants burst
dreamlike
from the slow dark ground

[1983]

A Simple Poem for Virginia Woolf

This started out as a simple poem
for Virginia Woolf you know the kind
we women writers write these days
in our own rooms
on our own time
a salute a gesture of friendship
a psychological debt
paid off
I wanted it simple

and perfectly round
hard as an
egg I thought
only once I'd said egg
I thought of the smell
of bacon grease and dirty frying-pans
and whether there were enough for breakfast
I couldn't help it
I wanted the poem to be carefree and easy
like children playing in the snow
I didn't mean to mention
the price of snowsuits or
how even on the most expensive ones
the zippers always snag
just when you're late for work
and trying to get the children
off to school on time
a straightforward poem
for Virginia Woolf that's all
I wanted really
not something tangled in
domestic life the way
Jane Austen's novels tangled
with her knitting her embroidery
whatever it was she hid them under
I didn't mean to go into all that
didn't intend to get confessional
and tell you how
every time I read a good poem
by a woman writer I'm always peeking
behind it trying to see
if she's still married
or has a lover at least
wanted to know what she did
with her kids while she wrote it
or whether she had any
and if she didn't if she'd chosen
not to or if she did did she
choose and why I didn't mean
to bother with that
and I certainly wasn't going

to tell you about the time
my best friend was sick in intensive care
and I went down to see her
but they wouldn't let me in
because I wasn't her husband
or her father her mother
I wasn't family
I was just her friend
and the friendship of women
wasn't mentioned
in hospital policy
or how I went out and kicked
a dent in the fender of my car
and sat there crying because
if she died I wouldn't be able
to tell her how much I loved her
(though she didn't and we laugh
about it now) but that's what got me
started I suppose wanting to write
a gesture of friendship
for a woman for a woman writer
for Virginia Woolf
and thinking I could do it
easily separating the words
from the lives they come from
that's what a good poem should do
after all and I wasn't going to make excuses
for being a woman blaming years of silence
for leaving us
so much to say

This started out as a simple poem
for Virginia Woolf
it wasn't going to mention history
or choices or women's lives
the complexities of women's friendships
or the countless gritty details
of an ordinary woman's life
that never appear in poems at all
yet even as I write these words
those ordinary details intervene

between the poem I meant to write
and this one where the delicate faces
of my children faces of friends
of women I have never even seen
glow on the blank pages
and deeper than any silence
press around me
waiting their turn

[1983]

COMMON MAGIC

Your best friend falls in love
and her brain turns to water.
You can watch her lips move,
making the customary sounds,
but you can see they're merely
words, flimsy as bubbles rising
from some golden sea where she
swims sleek and exotic as a mermaid.

It's always like that.
You stop for lunch in a crowded
restaurant and the waitress floats
toward you. You can tell she doesn't care
whether you have the baked or french-fried
and you wonder if your voice comes
in bubbles too.

It's not just women either. Or love
for that matter. The old man
across from you on the bus holds
a young child on his knee; he is singing
to her and his voice is a small boy
turning somersaults in the green
country of his blood.
It's only when the driver calls his stop
that he emerges into this puzzle
of brick and tiny hedges. Only then
you notice his shaking hands, his need
of the child to guide him home.

All over the city
you move in your own seasons
through the seasons of others: old women, faces
clawed by weather you can't feel
clack dry tongues at passersby
while adolescents seethe
in their glassy atmospheres of anger.

In parks, the children
are alien life-forms, rooted
in the galaxies they've grown through
to get here. Their games weave
the interface and their laughter
tickles that part of your brain where smells
are hidden and the nuzzling textures of things.

It's a wonder that anything gets done
at all: a mechanic flails
at the muffler of your car
through whatever storm he's trapped inside
and the mailman stares at numbers
from the haze of a distant summer.

Yet somehow letters arrive and buses
remember their routes. Banks balance.
Mangoes ripen on the supermarket shelves.
Everyone manages. You gulp the thin air
of this planet as if it were the only
one you knew. Even the earth you're
standing on seems solid enough.
It's always the chance word, unthinking
gesture that unlocks the face before you.
Reveals the intricate countries
deep within the eyes. The hidden
lives, like sudden miracles,
that breathe there.

[1985]

Thinking With the Heart

For Mary di Michele

'I work from awkwardness. By that I mean I don't like to arrange things. If I stand in front of something, instead of arranging it, I arrange myself.'—Diane Arbus.

'The problem with you women is, you think with your hearts.'—Policeman.

How else to say it
except that the body is a limit
I must learn to love,
that thought is no different from flesh
or the blue pulse that rivers my hands.
How else, except to permit myself
this heart and its seasons,
like the cycles of the moon
which never seem to get me anywhere
but back again, not out.

Thought should be linear.
That's what the policeman means
when I bring the woman to him,
what he has to offer for her bruises, the cut
over her eye: *charge him or we can't help you.*
He's seen it all before anyway. He knows
how the law changes, depending on what you think.
It used to be a man could beat his wife
if he had to; now, sometimes he can't
but she has to charge him
and nine times out of ten
these women who come in here
ready to get the bastard
will be back in a week or so
wanting to drop the whole thing
because they're back together,
which just means a lot of paperwork
and running around for nothing.
It drives him crazy, how a woman
can't make up her mind and stick to it,
get the guy out once and for all.
'Charge him,' he says, 'or we won't help.'

Out of her bed then, her house, her life,
but not her head, no, nor her children,
out from under her skin.
Not out of her heart, which goes on
in its slow, dark way, wanting
whatever it is hearts want
when they think like this;
a change in his, probably,
a way to hold what the heart can't
without breaking: how the man who beats her
is also the man she loves.

I wish I could show you
what a man's anger makes
of a woman's face,
or measure the days it takes
for her to emerge from a map of bruises
the colour of death. I wish there were words
that went deeper than *pain* or *terror*
for the place that woman's eyes can take you
when all you can hear
is the sound the heart makes
with what it knows of itself
and its web of blood.

But right now, the policeman's waiting
for the woman to decide.
That's how he thinks of it; *choice*
or how you can always get what you want
if you want it badly enough.
Everything else he ignores,
like the grip of his own heart's red
persistent warning that he too is fragile.
He thinks he thinks with his brain
as if it were safe up there
in its helmet of bone
away from all that messy business
of his stomach or his lungs.
And when he thinks like that
he loses himself forever.

But perhaps you think I'm being hard on him,
he's only doing his job after all,
only trying to help.
Or perhaps I'm making too much of the heart,
pear-shaped and muscular, a pump really,
when what you want is an explanation or a reason.
But how else can I say it?
Whatever it is you need
is what you must let go of now
to enter your own body
just as you'd enter the room where the woman sat
after it was all over,
hugging her knees to her chest,
holding herself as she'd hold her husband
or their children, *for dear life*,
feeling the arm's limit, bone and muscle,
like the heart's.
Whatever you hear then
crying through your own four rooms,
what you must name for yourself
before you can love anything at all.

[1985]

PARTICULARS

To come back, again,
to those Sundays at my grandmother's table,
but by a different way, so that I see
that thin spot in my father's hair
as he bowed his head to ask
the blessing—what my grandmother
called it, not thanks—*Bless*
this food to our use
and us to Thy service,
in Christ's name,
Amen. My father stumbling
over the words, perhaps in recognition
of what he was really asking for
(there, in the midst of things,
his whole family listening),
a blessing, on food they'd earned

casting metal, teaching other people's kids
or planted, themselves, in the fields we'd see
as soon as we raised our heads, men and women
embarrassed by prayer, but sticking to it
as they stuck to their stories,
hoarded those private, irreducible histories
that no one else would get a piece of, ever.

To begin to see, a little,
what they taught me
of themselves, their place
among the living and the dead,
thanksgiving and the practical
particulars of grace, and to accept it,
slowly, almost grudgingly,
to come downstairs this morning
as the paper slaps
the front porch, look up, catch
the paper girl with her walkman on
dancing down the street, red tights,
jean jacket, blonde hair, making me
love her, perfectly, for ten seconds,
long enough to call out
all my other loves, locate each one
precisely, as I could this house
on a city map or the day I found
my son, swimming within me.

To try and hear it
in the way we make the most
of what we get, like the man I know
who says he's held Death in his arms.
That's how he puts it, trying
for a way to say *wife* or *Ellen*
and reach far enough to touch her
there, include the whispers
from the hall outside, the hiss
of the oxygen tank, still on,

the sounds his arms made
adjusting to her weight, this
angle of bone, this one
when her head tipped, finally, back.

And to say for myself, just once,
without embarrassment, *bless*,
thrown out as to some lightness
that I actually believe in,
surprised (as I believe
they were) to find it
here, where it seems impossible
that one life even matters, though
like them, I'll argue
the stubborn argument of the particular,
right now, in the midst of things, *this*
and *this*.

[1987]

RITA DOVE (b. 1952)

Rita Dove was born in Akron, Ohio, and educated at Miami University of Ohio, Universität Tübingen in Germany, and the University of Iowa. She travelled to Europe on a Fulbright Fellowship and has since been the recipient of numerous honours and awards, including appointment as poet laureate of the United States. She lives near Charlottesville and is Commonwealth Professor of English at the University of Virginia. Her poetry books include *The Yellow House on the Corner* (1980), *Museum* (1983), *Thomas and Beulah* (1986, 1987 Pulitzer Prize), a cycle based loosely on the lives of her maternal grandparents, *Grace Notes* (1989), and *Selected Poems* (1993). She has also published *Fifth Sunday* (1985, short stories), *Through the Ivory Gate* (1992, a novel), and *The Darker Face of the Earth* (1994, a verse play).

In a lecture called '"A Handful of Inwardness": The World in the Poet' (in her Library of Congress publication *The Poet's World*, 1995), Dove quotes the French phenomenologist Gaston Bachelard: 'Words —I often imagine this—are little houses, each with its cellar and garret. Commonsense lives on the ground floor, always ready to engage in "foreign commerce", on the same level as the others, as the passers-by, who are never dreamers. To go upstairs in the word house, is to withdraw, step by step; while to go down to the cellar is to dream, it is losing oneself in the distant corridors of an obscure etymology, looking for treasures that cannot be found in words. To mount and descend in the words themselves—this is a poet's life.'

Words, then, are a space, a territory we inhabit, which contains both our personal history and the history of mankind. The art of being at home in language is not unlike that of being at home in the world and its various spaces; perhaps it's the same art. Like the German poet Rainer Maria Rilke, Dove is concerned—doubly, since fame has overtaken her—with the inward life, how it might be tapped, cultivated, and shared with others. 'How can we, as poets in today's instantly over-communicative, informationally medicated society, extend that handful of inwardness?' Dove asks in *The Poet's World*. 'Not by flinging or dangling it as if to taunt others for their lack of sensitivity, not by tossing it at the public and running—but by daring, in the wilderness of our own progress, to speak heart-to-heart to the stranger? One way is to create a poetic space for the spirit to dream in, a world on a page, which through its smells and sounds and discriminating eye, entices us to enter it.'

In discussing one of her favourite poets, Charles Wright, Dove celebrates his ability to create 'a lyric line rich with retractions and interruptions; rhetorical questions, sly tautologies, and rhapsodic non sequiturs are linked by commas, dashes, dropped lines, ellipses—all this in order to articulate the ineffable, to make inwardness palpable in the very knots and thumbholes of language.' To write well requires taking risks, ascending and descending in both self and language. Yes, Dove says, 'poetry is dangerous, as any artistic communication is dangerous. Then the messenger runs the risk of being killed. We deny funds for the arts because they are "non-utilitarian", we blacklist movie directors under charges of un-American activities, we condemn performance artists for "obscenity".'

After becoming poet laureate, Dove found she had little time for herself, even less for writing. She also discovered 'that there is a much greater hunger for poetry than book sales and reading attendances usually indicate.' Poetry, it seems, is one of the seats, or resting-places, of the angels, those beings who tend to our spiritual needs. Dove has mentioned on more than one occasion the Wim Wenders film *Wings of Desire*, which follows the assignments of two angels whose 'beat' is Cold War Berlin, where they administer comfort in a variety of ways. In an interview with Grace Cavalieri (*American Poetry Review* 24, 2, March/April 1995), she explains further: 'I think when we are touched by something it's as if we're being brushed by an angel's wing, and there's a moment when everything is clear. The best poetry, the poetry that sustains me, is when I feel that, for a minute, the clouds have parted and I've seen ecstasy or something.'

Speaking of her poem-sequence *Thomas and Beulah*, one of several works in which she examines history through the lives of ordinary people—in this instance, her maternal grandparents—Dove says: 'I felt I was moving into a territory that I wasn't quite sure of but it was immensely exciting, and the more that I wrote the more I realized that what I was trying to tell, let's say, was not a narrative as we know narratives but actually the moments that matter most in our lives. I began to think, how do we remember our lives? How do we think of our lives or shape our lives in our consciousnesses, and I realized that we don't actually think of our lives in very cohesive strands but we remember as beads on a necklace, moments that matter to us, come to us in flashes, and the connections are submerged.'

NIGGER SONG: AN ODYSSEY

We six pile in, the engine churning ink:
We ride into the night.
Past factories, past graveyards
And the broken eyes of windows, we ride
Into the grey-green nigger night.

We sweep past excavation sites; the pits
Of gravel gleam like mounds of ice.
Weeds clutch at the wheels;
We laugh and swerve away, veering
Into the black entrails of the earth,
The green smoke sizzling on our tongues . . .

In the nigger night, thick with the smell of cabbages,
Nothing can catch us.
Laughter spills like gin from glasses,
And 'yeah' we whisper, 'yeah'
We croon, 'yeah.'

[1980]

THE SECRET GARDEN

I was ill, lying on my bed of old papers,
when you came with white rabbits in your arms;
and the doves scattered upwards, flying to mothers,
and the snails sighed under their baggage of stone . . .

Now your tongue grows like celery between us:
Because of our love-cries, cabbage darkens in its nest;
the cauliflower thinks of her pale, plump children
and turns greenish-white in a light like the ocean's.

I was sick, fainting in the smell of teabags,
when you came with tomatoes, a good poetry.
I am being wooed. I am being conquered
by a cliff of limestone that leaves chalk on my breasts.

[1980]

The House Slave

The first horn lifts its arm over the dew-lit grass
and in the slave quarters there is a rustling—
children are bundled into aprons, cornbread

and water gourds grabbed, a salt pork breakfast taken.
I watch them driven into the vague before-dawn
while their mistress sleeps like an ivory toothpick

and Massa dreams of asses, rum and slave-funk.
I cannot fall asleep again. At the second horn,
the whip curls across the backs of the laggards—

sometimes my sister's voice, unmistaken, among them.
'Oh! pray,' she cries. 'Oh! pray!' Those days
I lie on my cot, shivering in the early heat,

and as the fields unfold to whiteness,
and they spill like bees among the fat flowers,
I weep. It is not yet daylight.

[1980]

Adolescence—II

Although it is night, I sit in the bathroom, waiting.
Sweat prickles behind my knees, the baby-breasts are alert.
Venetian blinds slice up the moon; the tiles quiver in pale strips.

Then they come, the three seal men with eyes as round
As dinner plates and eyelashes like sharpened tines.
They bring the scent of licorice. One sits in the washbowl,

One on the bathtub edge; one leans against the door.
'Can you feel it yet?' they whisper.
I don't know what to say, again. They chuckle,

Patting their sleek bodies with their hands.
'Well, maybe next time.' And they rise,
Glittering like pools of ink under moonlight,

And vanish. I clutch at the ragged holes
They leave behind, here at the edge of darkness.
Night rests like a ball of fur on my tongue.

[1980]

BOCCACCIO: THE PLAGUE YEARS

Even at night the air rang and rang.
Through the thick swirled glass
he watched the priests sweep past
in their peaked hoods, collecting death.
On each stoop a dish burning sweet
clotted smoke. He closed his eyes
to hear the slap
of flesh onto flesh, a
liquid crack like a grape
as it breaks on the tongue.

As a boy he had slipped
along the same streets, in love with
he didn't know whom. O the
reeded sonatinas and torch
flick on the chill slick sides
of the bridge and steam
rising in plumes
from the slaughterhouse vents—
twenty years.

Rolling out of the light
he leaned his cheek
against the rows of bound leather:
cool water. Fiammetta!
He had described her
a hundred ways; each time
she had proven unfaithful. If only

he could crack this city in two
so the moon would scour
the wormed streets clean! Or
walk away from it all, simply
falling in love again. . . .

[1983]

FROM THOMAS AND BEULAH

THE EVENT [THOMAS]

Ever since they'd left the Tennessee ridge
with nothing to boast of
but good looks and a mandolin,

the two Negroes leaning
on the rail of a riverboat
were inseparable: Lem plucked

to Thomas' silver falsetto.
But the night was hot and they were drunk.
They spat where the wheel

churned mud and moonlight,
they called to the tarantulas
down among the bananas

to come out and dance.
You're so fine and mighty; let's see
what you can do, said Thomas, pointing

to a tree-capped island.
Lem stripped, spoke easy: *Them's chestnuts,*
I believe. Dove

quick as a gasp. Thomas, dry
on deck, saw the green crown shake
as the island slipped

under, dissolved
in the thickening stream.
At his feet

a stinking circle of rags,
the half-shell mandolin.
Where the wheel turned the water

gently shirred.

VARIATION ON PAIN

Two strings, one pierced cry.
So many ways to imitate
The ringing in his ears.

He lay on the bunk, mandolin
In his arms. Two strings
For each note and seventeen
Frets; ridged sound
Humming beneath calloused
Fingertips.

There was a needle
In his head but nothing
Fit through it. Sound quivered
Like a rope stretched clear
To land, tensed and brimming,
A man gurgling air.

Two greased strings
For each pierced lobe:
So is the past forgiven.

THE STROKE

Later he'll say Death stepped right up
to shake his hand, then squeezed
until he sank to his knees. (*Get up,
nigger. Get up and try again.*)

Much later he'll admit he'd been afraid,
curled tight in the centre of the rug, sunlight
striking one cheek and plaited raffia
scratching the other. He'll leave out

the part about daydream's aromatic fields
and the strap-worn flanks of the mule
he followed through them. When his wife asks
how did it feel, he won't mention

that the sun shone like the summer
she was pregnant with their first, and
that she craved watermelon which he smuggled
home wrapped in a newspaper, and how

the bus driver smirked as his nickel
clicked through—no, he'll say
it was like being kicked by a mule.
Right now, though, pinned to the bull's-eye,

he knows it was Lem all along:
Lem's knuckles tapping his chest in passing,
Lem's heart, for safekeeping,
he shores up in his arms.

Thomas at the Wheel

This, then, the river he had to swim.
Through the wipers the drugstore
shouted, lit up like a casino,
neon script leering from the shuddering asphalt.

Then the glass doors flew apart
and a man walked out to the curb
to light a cigarette. Thomas thought
the sky was emptying itself as fast
as his chest was filling with water.

Should he honk? What a joke—
he couldn't ungrip the steering wheel.
The man looked him calmly in the eye
and tossed the match away.

And now the street dark, not a soul
nor its brother. He lay down across
the seat, a pod set to sea,
a kiss unpuckering. He watched
the slit eye of the glove compartment,
the prescription inside,

he laughed as he thought *Oh*
the writing on the water. Thomas imagined
his wife as she awoke missing him,
cracking a window. He heard sirens
rise as the keys swung, ticking.

TAKING IN WASH

Papa called her Pearl when he came home
drunk, swaying as if the wind touched
only him. Towards winter his skin paled,
buckeye to ginger root, cold drawing
the yellow out. The Cherokee in him,
Mama said. Mama never changed:
when the dog crawled under the stove
and the back gate slammed, Mama hid
the laundry. Sheba barked as she barked
in snow or clover, a spoiled and ornery bitch.

She was Papa's girl,
black though she was. Once,
in winter, she walked through a dream
all the way down the stairs
to stop at the mirror, a beast
with stricken eyes
who screamed the house awake. Tonight

every light hums, the kitchen arctic
with sheets. Papa is making the hankies
sail. Her foot upon a silk
stitched rose, she waits
until he turns, his smile sliding all over.
Mama a tight dark fist.
Touch that child

and I'll cut you down
just like the cedar of Lebanon.

DAYSTAR

She wanted a little room for thinking:
but she saw diapers steaming on the line,
a doll slumped behind the door.

So she lugged a chair behind the garage
to sit out the children's naps.

Sometimes there were things to watch—
the pinched armour of a vanished cricket,
a floating maple leaf. Other days
she stared until she was assured
when she closed her eyes
she'd see only her own vivid blood.

She had an hour, at best, before Liza appeared
pouting from the top of the stairs.
And just *what* was mother doing
out back with the field mice? Why,

building a palace. Later
that night when Thomas rolled over and
lurched into her, she would open her eyes
and think of the place that was hers
for an hour—where
she was nothing,
pure nothing, in the middle of the day.

THE GREAT PALACES OF VERSAILLES

Nothing nastier than a white person!
She mutters as she irons alterations
in the backroom of Charlotte's Dress Shoppe.
The steam rising from a cranberry wool
comes alive with perspiration
and stale Evening of Paris.
Swamp she born from, swamp
she swallow, swamp she got to sink again.

The iron shoves gently
into a gusset, waits until
the puckers bloom away. Beyond
the curtain, the white girls are all
wearing shoulder pads to make their faces
delicate. That laugh would be Autumn,
tossing her hair in imitation of Bacall.

Beulah had read in the library
how French ladies at court would tuck
their fans in a sleeve
and walk in the gardens for air. Swaying
among lilies, lifting shy layers of silk,
they dropped excrement as daintily
as handkerchieves. Against all rules

she had saved the lining from a botched coat
to face last year's grey skirt. She knows
whenever she lifts a knee
she flashes crimson. That seems legitimate;
but in the book she had read
how the *cavaliere* amused themselves
wearing powder and perfume and spraying
yellow borders knee-high on the stucco
of the *Orangerie*.

A hanger clatters
in the front of the shoppe.
Beulah remembers how
even Autumn could lean into a settee

with her ankles crossed, sighing
I need a man who'll protect me
while smoking her cigarette down to the very end.

[1983]

End of Thomas and Beulah

Pastoral

Like an otter, but warm,
she latched onto the shadowy tip
and I watched, diminished
by those amazing gulps. Finished
she let her head loll, eyes
unfocused and large: milk-drunk.

I liked afterwards best, lying
outside on a quilt, her new skin
spread out like meringue. I felt then
what a young man must feel
with his first love asleep on his breast:
desire, and the freedom to imagine it.

[1989]

After Reading *Mickey in the Night Kitchen* for the Third Time Before Bed

I'm in the milk and the milk's in me! . . . I'm Mickey!

My daughter spreads her legs
to find her vagina:
hairless, this mistaken
bit of nomenclature
is what a stranger cannot touch
without her yelling. She demands
to see mine and momentarily
we're a lopsided star
among the spilled toys,
my prodigious scallops
exposed to her neat cameo.

And yet the same glazed
tunnel, layered sequences.
She is three; that makes this
innocent. *We're pink!*
she shrieks, and bounds off.

Every month she wants
to know where it hurts
and what the wrinkled string means
between my legs. *This is good blood*
I say, but that's wrong, too.
How to tell her that it's what makes us—
black mother, cream child.
That we're in the pink
and the pink's in us.

[1989]

TIM LILBURN (b. 1950)

Tim Lilburn was born in Regina, Saskatchewan and completed his B.A. there in 1974, after which he spent two years working for CUSO in Africa. Following several years as a Jesuit (1979-87), he served as writer-in-residence at the University of Western Ontario (1988) and now lives in Saskatoon, teaching literature and philosophy at St Peter's College in Muenster, Saskatchewan, and conducting poetry workshops at the Sage Hill Writing Experience. His publications include *Names of God* (1986), *From the Great Above She Opened Her Ear to the Great Below* (with Susan Shantz, 1988), *Tourist to Ecstasy* (1989, nominated for a Governor General's Award), and *Moosewood Sandhills* (1994).

Lilburn's view of the relation of poet to world is best explained in 'How to Be Here?' (*Brick* 49, Summer 1994), where he suggests that 'The physical word cannot be known in the way poetry aspires to know it, intimately, ecstatically, in a way that heals the ache of one's separation from the world, it seems to me, outside the sundering of knowledge which contemplation is. . . . As the mind leans into the darkness of God, the old writers said, it is slendered by awe, reduced to a good confusion: this is knowing. Language, as well, is chastened in contemplation and by being broken it provides a way by which the ineffable may be glimpsed.' Paradoxically, Lilburn argues, 'Language is sundered as one courts ecstasy', constantly replaced by the objects and creatures of the world. 'Language again and again springs at the essence, reaching for clarity, the exact fit between the look of the slow hills, occultly breathing and their feel, then denies each time what it comes up with. . . . Language asserts and cancels itself, names the world then erases the name, and in this restlessness one glimpses the aptness of confusion before the ungraspable diversity of here. Silence. The look goes on. The breaking up of language, language drawn into the reversal of language, is the speech of desire beating against the silence of the confusing land.'

This provocative essay might seem, at first glance, to be at odds with both the exuberance and the excess of Lilburn's poetry prior to *Moosewood Sandhills*, for which it serves as prose gloss and apologia. The poems of *Names of God* and *Tourist to Ecstasy* are characterized by an enormous verbal appetite and a headlong, careening quality that takes the breath away. The emerging poet obviously takes more delight in naming than in silence or contemplation; and his approach to language would appear to be more gymnastic than gnostic. In fact, his immersion in language seems no less intense and erotic than his more recent efforts to forge a deeper relationship with the natural world. Perhaps William Blake's observation that 'the road of excess is the path to wisdom' should be summoned here, for Lilburn's temperament and poetic strategies certainly have their roots in the mystical tradition that includes Blake, Hopkins, Merton, and St John of the Cross.

While the early Lilburn dallies like a libertine in an orgy of sound and exploding vocabularies, jazzy rhythms, wordplay, and other technical be-bop, his own religious yearnings, not to mention his Jesuitical training and discriminations, are seldom out of sight or mind. The earliest poems, however charged they might be linguistically, strike a dominant note of praise or worship, even exultation, before the spectacle of this world and its creatures. However, since ecstasy, in love, poetry, and, presumably, religion is impossible to sustain, a deeper note must be sounded. As he acknowledges in the essay quoted above, 'We are lonely for where we are. Poetry helps us cope. Poetry is where we go when we want to know the world as lover. You read a poem or write one, guessing at the difficult, oblique interiority of something, but the undertaking ultimately seems incomplete, ersatz. The inevitable disappointment all poems bring motions towards the hard work of standing in helpless awe before things. "The praise of the psalms is a lament," the old men and women of the desert used to say. Poetry in its incompleteness awakens a mourning over the easy union with the world that seems lost. Poetry is a knowing to this extent: it brings us to this apposite discomfiting.'

NAMES OF GOD

for William Clarke, S.J.

1. LOVE AT THE CENTRE OF OBJECTS

At the pentecostal core of matter, a fire wind
whirligig, centrifuge of joy,
is You, Love, a lung
pumping light, auric squalls
inflating eyes in my skull's raw coal.

Sssssst.   My bloodstream and the midpoints of my bone hear fire
gouging the inner face of flame. Which speaks.
'Dress, bride, in your blood's maroon gas,
oxygen feathers tipping each bone blue; on the red knuckle
thread desire's compound carat;
moth skip, heart-kamikaze, and explode
vaster, vaster in the inhaling charismatic glow.'

2. ALLAH OF THE GREEN CIRCUITRY

Salamu, my Lord.   Salamu alaikum.
You are here
for my synapses whip and sparkle
like lightninged willows,
are in tumoured air storm's throbbing,
are wind's ululation to my steel-shod nerves
dancing them as dust-spooked stallions.

Runners of rain trellis fire
to earth.   You ride the hissing flame,
Allah of the Green Circuitry,
to jazz with love juice the chlorophyll current
to flash sunflower, crimson, orange.

You live, ah, You
live to unflex in the crux of a woman's dark ear,
coloured cloud
pressing into mind's white storm.

3. LIGHT'S GOBBLING EYE

O nourishing dark, O blank cloud,
You haul in my debris, compress it
in the stupendous clench of Your Heart
to nothing.

Light whorls toward You, a vanishing point
where perfection absents You; whorls
toward You, screwing
itself into its shadow core,

letting its socket eat it. O dark gravity, we decry
this cannibalism,
though the shimmering particles stampede
with greased monomania.

I, now, feel the suck, tide
of light raking over bones, unsnarling
from joints of thought and feeling,
until I whistle into what-I-know-not,
ears imploding,
riding the bright shaft of self
into Your infolding, gold-splintered eye.

[1986]

Pumpkins

Oompah Oompah Oompah, fattening
on the stem, tuba girthed, puffing like perorating parliamentarians,
Boompa Boompah Booompah,
earth hogs slurping swill from the sun,
jowels burp fat with photons, bigger, bigger, garden elephants,
mirthed like St Francis, dancing (thud), dancing (thud,
brümpht, thud, brümpht) with the Buddha-bellied sun,
dolphin sweet, theatrical as suburban
children, yahooing a yellow
which whallops air. Pure. They are Socratically
ugly, God's jokes. O jongleurs, O belly laughs
quaking the matted patch, O my blimpish Prussian
generals, O garden sausages, golden zeppelins. How do? How do? How do?

Doo dee doo dee doooo.
What a rabble, some explode,
or sing, in the panic of September
sun, idiot praise for the sun that burns like a grand hotel,
for the sun, monstrous pulp in a groaning rind, flame seeded.
Popeyes, my dears, muscular fruit,
apoplexies of grunted energy flexed from the forearm vine,
self-hefted on the hill and shot
putted in the half-acre.

Carro-caroo. Are you well,
my sweets, pleasure things, my baubles, my Poohs,
well?
I, weeding farmer, I, Caruso
them at dawn crow in the sun
cymballing mornings
and they Brunhilde back, foghorns, bloated alto notes
baroquely happy.
Not hoe teeth, not Rhotenone, but love,
bruited, busied, blessed these being-ward, barn-big,
bibulous on light, rampantly stolid
as Plato's Ideas, Easter Island
flesh lumps of meaning, rolling heads
in my 6-year-old nightmares,
vegetables on a ball and chain, sun anvils
booming with blows of temperature.

Come, phenomena, gourds of light, teach
your joy esperanto, your intense Archimedean aha
of yellow to me, dung-booted serf, whose unhoed brain,
the garden's brightest fruit, ones
communion with the cowfaced cauliflowers,
cucumbers twinkling like toes, and you,
clown prince,
sun dauphin of the rioting plot.

[1986]

TOUCHING AN ELEPHANT IN A DARK ROOM

Poplars know everything about sleep,
their glossolalia saying even more than the *New Catholic Encyclopedia*,
speaking sleep's endless hexameters as a child syllables til her mouth blurs,
so I'll ask them, rosarying there in the wind, Saskatoons ripe-dopey under
    them,
if they think there's a true world next to ours
that sleep, the animal, visits often because it feels more at home there.
And I'll ask them if they think this shadow-place, sleep's nook in the
    country,
is not a shadow place at all, but the place where the grass elopes to,
or water keeps its money,

or at least where those nostalgic shadows in long grass in July that make us
wish we were born grass come from.
I'll ask if this world which is not a shadow-place but seems to be perhaps isn't
the true, flat lap where we sit, asleep or awake, when we hear that well-known voice
rushing past us, pure force,
expertly thrown, that ventriloquizes our lives into place and some kind of order.
Ah, telos.
All the lovely darknesses in the world growing out from there.
Rain engorged over cut hay, bees fattening over roses.
Where the shadows of light are truth itself.
This is what I want to know. Is what we are really doing, really doing
with our lives whether we think of it or not,
a beast, or one of those forces that terrified Newton changed into an animal
galloping along in the dark afternoon of that other place, the one, lovely home
place, intuiting its way through the grassy savannahs they have there,
thinking out from between its shoulder blades?
If so, then we're completely at home in the real world.
All the lovely darknesses.
I have no doubt the poplars, masters and mandarins of sleep, could give them to us
chapter and verse, and tell us of all this together, the world, the whole
seen and unseen, how it's
ingeniously physical, and how it makes sense, not by doing anything, not by using
some bloody verb, but just by growing fatter each day with variety
as when magpies pass a song through the trees at 6:00 am like a basketball
at a Harlem Globetrotters warm-up,
until the world gets into that happy numb state where judgements become even more
gorgeously impossible and love gets fluid and doubletake-sleek
as showboat acts fluked off in dream.

[1989]

In the Hills, Watching

Among the nerved grass, thrones,
dominions of grass, in chokecherry dewlapped hills,
hills buffalo-shouldered with shag of pulsed heat, meek hills,
sandhills of rose-hip and aster, in the philanthropic silence
fluxed by the grass, hounded, nervous with its own uncountability, grass
the frail piston of all,
in hill heat, lying down in the nearness of deer.
All knowing darkens as it builds.
The grass is a mirror that clouds as the bright look goes in.
You stay in the night, you squat in the hills in the cave of night. Wait.
Above, luminous rubble, torn webs of radio signals.
Below, stone scrapers, neck bone of a deer, salt beds.
The world is ending.

[1994]

Learning a Deeper Courtesy of the Eye

I

This is what you want.
You go into porcupine hills on a cold afternoon, down an aspen-ruffed path
    on Sam's land behind one low grass-knotted dune, then into real bush.
You will see deer.

Eros has nowhere to go but to become sorrow.
Piss marks on snow, flattenings,
creases where animals rolled, hoof-drag through drifts.
Exhaustion now as you walk toward the world's bright things.
Grass over snow, rose-hips clear and large in winter-killed thicket.
You will never make it all the way up to them.

II

The back fields are beautiful.
Take off your glove, coast
                fingers through oatgrass tips.
Four deer fountain from the poplar circle where
last fall the dog and you lay in old fox beds, breathing.

It hurts to look at deer,
deer under their name.
The light from their bodies makes you ashamed
and you look down.

[1994]

DISCIPLINE OF SECRECY

Lie on your belly now, stare, pour into the golden
eye of the grain and be counted.
Engorge its face with your peering's heavy light.
The wheat gives you its plush inattention and
is therefore trustworthy.
It grew near your unborn face.
Let your weight bleed from you and fan into the wheat.
The wheat's moving rest will heft your desire and shape it
to itself.

Tell the wheat everything.
You have done nothing wrong and are naked.

You planted it by hand—someone to talk to.
The marrow of wheat is patience.
In its palm, the grain holds its one fixed heart,
nothing denser, nothing further away.
Ground is cold, sky lowered into it.
If you acted suddenly, not
watching yourself, the wheat's gold shadow, its
hiddenness, idea of beauty, would enter you
and make its home there.

Antlered wheat; like eros
it travels between the unknowable darkness
of sky and the unknowable darkness of earth.
The world is wide.
The wheat is trustworthy, sky thinking into soil.
In evening, thin pale flames over the fields, you see
this through aspens, the grain's ejaculatory flutter
under the aurora borealis.

[1994]

HOW TO BE HERE?

I

Desire never leaves.

Looking at wolf willow bloom,
streaming through plushlands of scent toward the feeling
of its yellow,
self breaks up, flaring in stratosphere.
Looking undermines us.
The world and its shining can't hold our evaporating weight.
The world or what is there goes away
as we enter it, goes into halls of grass where torches of
darkness burn at noon.
Goes into light's lowest mind.
Leaving us, woo-floated from planet-like names and not quite
in things' shimmering gravity, alone in wide June air.
All-thumbs intensity that feels like virtue or music.

The Form quivers in the deer.
She doesn't see me; I'm lying barely above grass on a plank between fallen
poplars.

Hot day, slow wind; I lift on the cam of rhizomes.
The light behind her light is a shell she's just now born out of.
The Form is the doe's ease within herself.
I came from there.
If you dug with small tools into radiant belts round her shoulders
you'd come to a first settlement of the soul, stroke pottery bits, put
your tongue on old cinders and remember.
Tears will take you part of the way back but no further.

II

You wake, say, inside a large mosquito net,
you're away from yourself, older, near a desert perhaps,
air cool, dry, cloud of small sand, everything seems far
away, North African, night ancient, hard to read, you
look through the flap and see something bent toward a fire,
sparks low round it, stocky, sitting on its man-calves, force, tiptoed.

It is desire.
Yes, adding stick after stick, it seems,
managing in its naked hands
the reins of occurrence,
charioteering the will—horses of night.

You want to walk in the dark garden of the eye of the deer looking at you.
Want a male goldfinch to gallop you into the heart
of the distance which is the oddness of other things.
All would be well.
Desire never leaves.
Mercury's flower, a ghost-hurtling.

A mirror held before the spiritual wind
that blows from behind things,
bodying them out, filling them with the shapes and loves
of themselves.
You want that
and all else that shows in the bright surface polished by the lunge and
prowling of your desire.
You don't know what you are doing.

III

Desire tells me to sit in a tree.
I live alone, mentally clothed in the skins of wild things.
Desire sways ascent into me.
I look, I look: bull-necked hill, blue sweetgrass in hollows.
Knowing is a bowing, a covering of your face, before the world.
The tree's white tallness praises through me.
What receives the bow?
I am seduced by the shapeliness
of the failure of knowledge.
My name in religion is the anonymity of grass.
I practise dying.
Each day, the tutor, old man, eros, repeats the lesson,
I wrinkle my brow, my tongue protrudes.
Outside the window one chokecherry in the bush,
in a thicket of gooseberries,
adds a weight and compression of darkness under the sun
that is perfect.

[1994]

Restoration

I want to be the knowledge that is one sleep in the sunward shoulder muscle
of the two-year-old doe coming out of hills and down to Moon Lake.
I will get there by seeing.
The whole body and virtue will rise up and form the look.
Seeing is the extreme courtesy that comes when desire is broken.
Desire will be broken and will continue with a bright limp.
We will move toward high bush cranberry and the smell of water.
I will be attentive, an oblique crescent near her spine, touched
by the light of her liquids. We will be going to Moon Lake,
the diamond willows,
old oxbow lake, reeds round it, the true river a ruin of water
in dust further on, the red century ending.
I will see my way into that place and into that body.
This will come only after I've been sitting in the long grass
eating loaves of shadow pressed up through the ground.
I will have been dreaming there of one day opening milky eyes and finding
myself sick, inside her body, high up, near the spine, poor, relieved.
Sometimes it happens: you lose everything
and wake in the strange room of what you want.

Except I won't be awake but asleep and full of gnosis.
In my ears, gold pulse of her footsteps.
We will go down the hill and enter the shadows of frost-burnt roses
and the shade of the smell of water in which reeds and elms are rotting,
October sunlight the shore of a country a small boat is just now pulling
away from.
I will smell her, light of one locked room in the mansion.
I will be in the muscle, a painting on the cave wall of her flesh.
I crane into the deer.
I am in the bright-dark cloud of knowing her
and could walk for days.
She is at the top of the hill and starting down
in the early evening.

[1994]

POETICS

Margaret Atwood

Conversations

(These excerpts are gathered from a series of interviews collected and edited under the same title by E.G. Ingersoll in 1990.)

(with Christopher Levenson)
Poetry is local. It may be appreciated internationally, but one sure doesn't write it internationally. No poet ever has. When people say 'international' what they are talking about is *their* way, their nationality rendered international.

(with Linda Sandler)
You can't write poetry unless you're willing to immerse yourself in language—not just in words, but in words of a certain potency. It's like learning a foreign language.

(with Joyce Carol Oates)
My poems usually begin with words or phrases which appeal more because of their sound than their meaning, and the movement and phrasing of a poem are very important to me. But like many modern poets I tend to conceal rhymes by placing them in the middle of lines, and to avoid immediate alliteration and assonance in favour of echoes placed later in the poems. For me, every poem has a texture of sound which is at least as important to me as the 'argument'. This is not to minimize 'statement'. But it does annoy me when students, prompted by the approach of their teacher, ask, 'What is the poet trying to say?' It implies that the poet is some kind of verbal cripple who can't quite 'say' what he 'means' and has to resort to a lot of round-the-mulberry-bush, thereby putting the student to a great deal of trouble extracting his 'meaning', like a prize out of a box of Cracker Jacks.

(with Karla Hammond)
The unit of the poem is the syllable. The unit in a prose work—short story or novel—is something much larger. It may be the character or the paragraph. . . . With the prose poem, the unity is still the syllable, but the difference between a prose poem and a short story for me is that the prose poem is still connected with that rhythmical syllabic structure. You're as meticulous about the syllables in a prose poem as you are in a poem. If the syllables aren't right, then the whole thing is wrong.

(with Allan Twigg)
For me, poetry is where the language is renewed. If poetry vanished, language would become dead. It would become embalmed. People say, 'Well, now that you're writing successful novels I suppose you'll be giving up poetry.' As if one wrote in order to be successful. The fact is, I would never give up poetry. Poetry might give me up, but that's another matter. It's true that poetry doesn't make money. But it's the heart of the language. If you think of language as a series of concentric circles, poetry is right in the centre. It's where precision takes place. It's where that use of language takes place that can extend a word yet have it be precise.

(with Gregory Fitz and Kathryn Crabbe, on the poetic line)
All I can say is that sometimes the lines get longer, and sometimes they get shorter. Too rigid a theory results in silence.

(with Geoff Hancock, on art and affirmation)
When I finish a book I really like, no matter what the subject matter, or see a play or film, like Kurosawa's *Ran*, which is swimming in blood and totally pessimistic, but so well done, I feel very good. I do feel hope. It's the *well-doneness* that has that effect on me. Not the conclusion—not what is said, *per se*. For instance, the end of *King Lear* is devastating, as a statement about the world. But seeing it done well can still exhilarate you.

If you are tone-deaf, you are not going to get much out of Beethoven. If you are colour-blind, you won't get much of a charge out of Monet. But if you have those capabilities, and you see something done very, very well, something that is true to itself, you can feel for two or three minutes that the clouds have parted and you've had a vision, of something of what music or art or writing can do, at its best. A revelation of the full range of our human response to the world—that is, what it means to be human, on earth. That seems to be what 'hope' is about in relation to art. Nothing so simple as 'happy endings'. . . . Hope comes from the fact that people create, that they find it worthwhile to create. Not just from the nature of what is created.

W.H. AUDEN

FROM THE POET AND THE CITY*

Before the phenomenon of the Public appeared in society, there existed naïve art and sophisticated art which were different from each other but only in the way that two brothers are different. The Athenian court may smile at the mechanics' play of Pyramus and Thisbe, but they recognize it as a play. Court poetry and Folk poetry were bound by the common tie that both were made by hand and both were intended to last; the crudest ballad was as custom-built as the most esoteric sonnet. The appearance of the Public and the mass media which cater to it have destroyed naïve popular art. The sophisticated 'highbrow' artist survives and can still work as he did a thousand years ago, because his audience is too small to interest the mass media. But the audience of the popular artist is the majority and this the mass media must steal from him if they are not to go bankrupt. Consequently, aside from a few comedians, the only art today is 'highbrow'. What the mass media offer is not popular art, but entertainment which is intended to be consumed like food, forgotten, and replaced by a new dish. This is bad for everyone; the majority lose all genuine taste of their own, and the minority become cultural snobs.

The two characteristics of art which make it possible for an art historian to divide the history of art into periods, are, firstly, a common style of expression over a certain period and, secondly, a common notion, explicit or implicit, of the hero, the kind of human being who most deserves to be celebrated, remembered, and, if possible, imitated. The characteristic style of 'Modern' poetry is an intimate tone of voice, the speech of one person addressing one person, not a large audience; whenever a modern poet raises his voice he sounds phony. And its characteristic hero is neither the 'Great Man' nor the romantic rebel, both doers of extraordinary deeds, but the man or woman in any walk of life who, despite all the impersonal pressures of modern society, manages to acquire and preserve a face of his own.

Poets are, by the nature of their interests and the nature of artistic fabrication, singularly ill-equipped to understand politics or economics. Their natural interest is in singular individuals and personal relations, while politics and

* From *The Dyer's Hand* by W.H. Auden.

economics are concerned with large numbers of people, hence with the human average (the poet is bored to death by the idea of the Common Man), and with impersonal, to a great extent involuntary, relations. The poet cannot understand the function of money in modern society because for him there is no relation between subjective value and market value; he may be paid ten pounds for a poem which he believes is very good and took him months to write, and a hundred pounds for a piece of journalism which costs him but a day's work. If he is a successful poet—though few poets make enough money to be called successful in the way that a novelist or playwright can—he is a member of the Manchester school and believes in absolute *laissez-faire*; if he is unsuccessful and embittered, he is liable to combine aggressive fantasies about the annihilation of the present order with impractical daydreams of Utopia. Society has always to beware of the utopias being planned by artists *manqués* over cafeteria tables late at night.

All poets adore explosions, thunderstorms, tornadoes, conflagrations, ruins, scenes of spectacular carnage. The poetic imagination is not at all a desirable quality in a statesman.

In a war or a revolution a poet may do very well as a guerrilla fighter or a spy, but it is unlikely that he will make a good regular soldier, or in peacetime, a conscientious member of a parliamentary committee.

All political theories which, like Plato's, are based on analogies drawn from artistic fabrication are bound, if put into practice, to turn into tyrannies. The whole aim of a poet, or any other kind of artist, is to produce something which is complete and will endure without change. A poetic city would always contain exactly the same number of inhabitants doing exactly the same jobs for ever.

Moreover, in the process of arriving at the finished work, the artist has continually to employ violence. A poet writes:

> The mast-high anchor dives through a cleft

changes it to

> The anchor dives through closing paths

changes it again to

> The anchor dives among hayricks

and finally to

> The anchor dives through the floors of a church.

A *cleft* and *closing paths* have been liquidated, and hayricks deported to another stanza.

A society which was really like a good poem, embodying the aesthetic virtues of beauty, order, economy, and subordination of detail to the whole, would be a nightmare of horror for, given the historical reality of actual men, such a society could only come into being through selective breeding, extermination of the physically and mentally unfit, absolute obedience to its Director, and a large slave class kept out of sight in cellars.

Vice versa, a poem which was really like a political democracy—examples, unfortunately, exist—would be formless, windy, banal, and utterly boring.

There are two kinds of political issues, Party issues and Revolutionary issues. In a party issue, all parties are agreed as to the nature and justice of the social goal to be reached, but differ in their policies for reaching it. The existence of different parties is justified, firstly, because no party can offer irrefutable proof that its policy is the only one which will achieve the commonly desired goal, and secondly, because no social goal can be achieved without some sacrifice of individual or group interest and it is natural for each individual and social group to seek a policy which will keep its sacrifice to a minimum, to hope that, if sacrifices must be made, it would be more just if someone else made them. In a party issue, each party seeks to convince the members of its society, primarily by appealing to their reason; it marshals facts and arguments to convince others that its policy is more likely to achieve the desired goal than that of its opponents. On a party issue it is essential that passions be kept at a low temperature: effective oratory requires, of course, some appeal to the emotions of the audience, but in party politics orators should display the mock-passion of prosecuting and defending attorneys, not really lose their tempers. Outside the Chamber, the rival deputies should be able to dine in each other's houses; fanatics have no place in party politics.

A revolutionary issue is one in which different groups within a society hold different views as to what is just. When this is the case, argument and compromise are out of the question; each group is bound to regard the other as wicked or mad or both. Every revolutionary issue is potentially a *casus belli*. On a revolutionary issue, an orator cannot convince his audience by appealing to their reason; he may convert some of them by awakening and appealing to their conscience, but his principal function, whether he represent the revolutionary or the counter-revolutionary group, is to arouse its passion to the point where it will give all its energies to achieving total victory for itself and total defeat for its opponents. When an issue is revolutionary, fanatics are essential.

Today, there is only one genuine world-wide revolutionary issue, racial equality. The debate between capitalism, socialism, and communism is really a party issue, because the goal which all seek is really the same, a goal which is summed up in Brecht's well-known line:

Erst kommt das Fressen, dann kommt die Moral.

I.e., Grub first, then Ethics. In all the technologically advanced countries today, whatever political label they give themselves, their policies have, essentially, the same goal: to guarantee to every member of society, as a psychophysical organism, the right to physical and mental health. The positive symbolic figure of this goal is a naked anonymous baby, the negative symbol, a mass of anonymous concentration camp corpses.

What is so terrifying and immeasurably depressing about most contemporary politics is the refusal—mainly but not, alas, only by the communists—to admit that this is a party issue to be settled by appeal to facts and reason, the insistence that there is a revolutionary issue between us. If an African gives his life for the cause of racial equality, his death is meaningful to him; but what is utterly absurd, is that people should be deprived every day of their liberties and their lives, and that the human race may quite possibly destroy itself over what is really a matter of practical policy like asking whether, given its particular historical circumstances, the health of a community is more or less likely to be secured by Private Practice or by Socialized Medicine.

What is peculiar and novel to our age is that the principal goal of politics in every advanced society is not, strictly speaking, a political one, that is to say, it is not concerned with human beings as persons and citizens but with human bodies, with the precultural, prepolitical human creature. It is, perhaps, inevitable that respect for the liberty of the individual should have so greatly diminished and the authoritarian powers of the State have so greatly increased from what they were fifty years ago, for the main political issue today is concerned not with human liberties but with human necessities.

As creatures we are all equally slaves to natural necessity; we are not free to vote how much food, sleep, light, and air we need to keep in good health; we all need a certain quantity, and we all need the same quantity.

Every age is one-sided in its political and social preoccupation and in seeking to realize the particular value it esteems most highly, it neglects and even sacrifices other values. The relation of a poet, or any artist, to society and politics is, except in Africa or still backward semifeudal countries, more difficult than it has ever been because, while he cannot but approve of the importance of *everybody* getting enough food to eat and enough leisure, this problem has nothing whatever to do with art, which is concerned with *singular persons*, as they are alone and as they are in their personal relations. Since these interests are not the predominant ones in his society; indeed, in so far as it thinks about them at all, it is with suspicion and latent hostility—it secretly or openly thinks that the claim that one is a singular person, or a demand for privacy, is putting on airs, a claim to be superior to other folk—every artist feels himself at odds with modern civilization.

In our age, the mere making of a work of art is itself a political act. So long as artists exist, making what they please and think they ought to make, even if it is not terribly good, even if it appeals to only a handful of people, they remind the Management of something managers need to be reminded of, namely, that the managed are people with faces, not anonymous members, that *Homo Laborans* is also *Homo Ludens*.

If a poet meets an illiterate peasant, they may not be able to say much to each other, but if they both meet a public official, they share the same feeling of suspicion; neither will trust one further than he can throw a grand piano. If they enter a government building, both share the same feeling of apprehension; perhaps they will never get out again. Whatever the cultural differences between them, they both sniff in any official world the smell of an unreality in which persons are treated as statistics. The peasant may play cards in the evening while the poet writes verses, but there is one political principle to which they both subscribe, namely, that among the half-dozen or so things for which a man of honour should be prepared, if necessary, to die, the right to play, the right to frivolity, is not the least.

FROM THE VIRGIN AND THE DYNAMO*

The subject matter of a poem is comprised of a crowd of recollected occasions of feeling, among which the most important are recollections of encounters with sacred beings or events. This crowd the poet attempts to transform into

* From *The Dyer's Hand* by W.H. Auden.

a community by embodying it in a verbal society. Such a society, like any society in nature, has its own laws; its laws of prosody and syntax are analogous to the laws of physics and chemistry. Every poem must presuppose—sometimes mistakenly—that the history of the language is at an end.

One should say, rather, that a poem is a natural organism, not an inorganic thing. For example, it is rhythmical. The temporal recurrences of rhythm are never identical, as the metrical notation would seem to suggest. Rhythm is to time what symmetry is to space. Seen from a certain distance, the features of a human face seem symmetrically arranged, so that a face with a nose a foot long or a left eye situated two inches away from the nose would appear monstrous. Close up, however, the exact symmetry disappears; the size and position of the features vary slightly from face to face and, indeed, if a face could exist in which the symmetry were mathematically perfect, it would look, not like a face, but like a lifeless mask. So with rhythm. A poem may be described as being written in iambic pentameters, but if every foot in every line were identical, the poem would sound intolerable to the ear. I am sometimes inclined to think that the aversion of many modern poets and their readers to formal verse may be due to their association of regular repetition and formal restrictions with all that is most boring and lifeless in modern life, road drills, time-clock punching, bureaucratic regulations.

It has been said that a poem should not mean but be. This is not quite accurate. In a poem, as distinct from many other kinds of verbal societies, meaning and being are identical. A poem might be called a pseudo-person. Like a person, it is unique and addresses the reader personally. On the other hand, like a natural being and unlike a historical person, it cannot lie. We may be and frequently are mistaken as to the meaning or the value of a poem, but the cause of our mistake lies in our own ignorance or self-deception, not in the poem itself.

The nature of the final poetic order is the outcome of a dialectical struggle between the recollected occasions of feeling and the verbal system. As a society the verbal system is actively coercive upon the occasions it is attempting to embody; what it cannot embody truthfully it excludes. As a potential community the occasions are passively resistant to all claims of the system to embody them which they do not recognize as just; they decline all unjust persuasions. As members of crowds, every occasion competes with every other, demanding inclusion and a dominant position to which they are not necessarily entitled, and every word demands that the system shall modify itself in its case, that a special exception shall be made for it and it only.

In a successful poem, society and community are one order and the system may love itself because the feelings which it embodies are all members of the same community, loving each other and it. A poem may fail in two ways; it may exclude too much (banality), or attempt to embody more than one community at once (disorder).

In writing a poem, the poet can work in two ways. Starting from an intuitive idea of the kind of community he desires to call into being, he may work backwards in search of the system which will most justly incarnate that idea, or, starting with a certain system, he may work forward in search of the community which it is capable of incarnating most truthfully. In practice he nearly always works simultaneously in both directions, modifying his conception of the ultimate nature of the community at the immediate suggestions of the system, and modifying the system in response to his growing intuition of the future needs of the community.

A system cannot be selected completely arbitrarily nor can one say that any given system is absolutely necessary. The poet searches for one which imposes just obligations on the feelings. 'Ought' always implies 'can' so that a system whose claims cannot be met must be scrapped. But the poet has to beware of accusing the system of injustice when what is at fault is the laxness and self-love of the feelings upon which it is making its demands.

Every poet, consciously or unconsciously, holds the following absolute presuppositions, as the dogmas of his art:

> (1) A historical world exists, a world of unique events and unique persons, related by analogy, not identity. The number of events and analogical relations is potentially infinite. The existence of such a world is a good, and every addition to the number of events, persons, and relations is an additional good.
>
> (2) The historical world is a fallen world, i.e., though it is good that it exists, the way in which it exists is evil, being full of unfreedom and disorder.
>
> (3) The historical world is a redeemable world. The unfreedom and disorder of the past can be reconciled in the future.

It follows from the first presupposition that the poet's activity in creating a poem is analogous to God's activity in creating man after his own image. It is not an imitation, for were it so, the poet would be able to create like God *ex nihilo*; instead, he requires pre-existing occasions of feeling and a pre-existing language out of which to create. It is analogous in that the poet creates not necessarily according to a law of nature but voluntarily according to provocation.

It is untrue, strictly speaking, to say that a poet should not write poems unless he must; strictly speaking it can only be said that he should not write them unless he can. The phrase is sound in practice, because only in those who can and when they can is the motive genuinely compulsive.

In those who profess a desire to write poetry, yet exhibit an incapacity to do so, it is often the case that their desire is not for creation but for self-perpetuation, that they refuse to accept their own mortality, just as there are parents who desire children, not as new persons analogous to themselves, but to prolong their own existence in time. The sterility of this substitution of identity for analogy is expressed in the myth of Narcissus. When the poet speaks, as he sometimes does, of achieving immortality through his poem, he does not mean that he hopes, like Faust, to live for ever, but that he hopes to rise from the dead. In poetry as in other matters the law holds good that he who would save his life must lose it; unless the poet sacrifices his feelings completely to the poem so that they are no longer his but the poem's, he fails.

It follows from the second presupposition, that a poem is a witness to man's knowledge of evil as well as good. It is not the duty of a witness to pass moral judgement on the evidence he has to give, but to give it clearly and accurately; the only crime of which a witness can be guilty is perjury. When we say that poetry is beyond good and evil, we simply mean that a poet can no more change the facts of what he has felt than, in the natural order, parents can change the inherited physical characteristics which they pass on to their children. The judgement good-or-evil applies only to the intentional movements of the will. Of our feelings in a given situation which are the joint product of our intention and the response to the external factors in that situation it can only be said that, given an intention and the response, they are appropriate or inappropriate. Of a recollected feeling it cannot be said that it is appropriate or inappropriate because the historical situation in which it arose no longer exists.

Every poem, therefore, is an attempt to present an analogy to that paradisal state in which Freedom and Law, System and Order are united in harmony. Every good poem is very nearly a Utopia. Again, an analogy, not an imitation; the harmony is possible and verbal only.

It follows from the third presupposition that a poem is beautiful or ugly to the degree that it succeeds or fails in reconciling contradictory feelings in an order of mutual propriety. Every beautiful poem presents an analogy to the forgiveness of sins; an analogy, not an imitation, because it is not evil intentions which are repented of and pardoned but contradictory feelings which the poet surrenders to the poem in which they are reconciled.

The effect of beauty, therefore, is good to the degree that, through its analogies, the goodness of created existence, the historical fall into unfreedom and disorder, and the possibility of regaining paradise through repentance and forgiveness are recognized. Its effect is evil to the degree that beauty is taken, not as analogous to, but identical with goodness, so that the artist regards himself or is regarded by others as God, the pleasure of beauty taken for the joy of Paradise, and the conclusion drawn that, since all is well in the work of art, all is well in history. But all is not well there.

ROBERT BLY

LOOKING FOR DRAGON SMOKE

I

In ancient times, in the 'time of inspiration', the poet flew from one world to another, 'riding on dragons', as the Chinese said. Isaiah rode on those dragons, so did Li Po and Pindar. They dragged behind them long tails of dragon smoke. Some of the dragon smoke still boils out of *Beowulf*: the *Beowulf* poet holds tight to Danish soil, or leaps after Grendel into the sea.

This dragon smoke means that a leap has taken place in the poem. In many ancient works of art we notice a long floating leap at the centre of the work. That leap can be described as a leap from the conscious to the latent intelligence and back again, a leap from the known part of the mind to the unknown part and back to the known. In the epic of Gilgamesh, which takes place in a settled society, psychic forces create Enkidu, 'the hairy man', as a companion for Gilgamesh, who is becoming too successful. The reader has to leap back and forth between the golden man, 'Gilgamesh', and the 'hairy man'. In the *Odyssey* the travellers visit a Great Mother island, dominated by the Circe-Mother and get turned into pigs. They make the leap in an instant. In all art derived from Great Mother mysteries, the leap to the unknown part of the mind lies in the very centre of the world. The strength of 'classic art' has much more to do with this leap than with the order that the poets developed to contain, and partially, to disguise it.

In terms of language, leaping is the ability to associate fast. In a great poem, the considerable distance between the associations, that is, the distance the spark has to leap, gives the lines their bottomless feeling, their space, and the speed (of the association) increases the excitement of the poetry.

As Christian civilization took hold, and the power of the spiritual patriarchies deepened, this leap occurred less and less often in Western literature. Obviously, the ethical ideas of Christianity inhibit it. At the start most Church fathers were against the leap as too pagan. Ethics usually support campaigns against the 'animal instincts'. Christian thought, especially Paul's thought, builds a firm distinction between spiritual energy and animal energy, a distinction so sharp it became symbolized by black and white. White became associated with the conscious and black with the unconscious or the latent intelligence. Ethical Christianity taught its poets—we are among them—to leap *away* from the unconscious, not *toward* it.

II

Sometime in the thirteenth century, poetry in England began to show a distinct decline in the ability to associate powerfully. There are individual exceptions, but the circle of worlds pulled into the poem by association dwindles after Chaucer and Langland; their work is already a decline from the *Beowulf* poet. By the eighteenth century, freedom of association had become drastically curtailed. The word 'sylvan' by some psychic coupling leads directly to 'nymph', to 'lawns', to 'dancing', so does 'reason' to 'music', 'spheres', 'heavenly order', and so on. They are all stops on the psychic railroad. There are very few images of the Snake, or the Dragon, or the Great Mother, and if mention is made, the Great Mother leads to no other images, but rather to words suggesting paralysis or death. As Pope warned his readers: 'The proper study of mankind is man.'

The loss of associative freedom shows itself in form as well as in content. The poet's thought plods through the poem, line after line, like a man being escorted through a prison. The rigid 'form' resembles a corridor, interrupted by opening and closing doors. The rhymed lines open at just the right moment and close again behind the visitors.

In the eighteenth century many educated people in Europe were no longer interested in imagination. They were trying to develop the 'masculine' mental powers they associated with Socrates and his fellow Athenians—a demythologized intelligence, that moves in a straight line made of tiny bright links and is thereby dominated by linked facts rather than by 'irrational' feelings. The Europeans succeeded in developing the practical intellect, and it was to prove useful. Industry needed it to guide a locomotive through a huge freight yard; space engineers needed it later to guide a spaceship back from the moon through the 'reentry corridor'.

III

Nevertheless, this routing of psychic energy away from 'darkness' and the 'irrational', first done in obedience to Christian ethics, and later in obedience to industrial needs, had a crippling effect on the psychic life. The process amounted to an inhibiting of psychic flight, and as Blake saw, once the European child had finished ten years of school, he was incapable of flight. He lived the rest of his life with 'single vision and Newton's sleep'.

The Western mind after Descartes accepted the symbolism of white and black and far from trying to unite both in a circle, as the Chinese did, tried to create an 'apartheid'. In the process words sometimes took on strange meanings. If a European avoided the animal instincts and consistently leapt away from the latent intelligence, he or she was said to be living in a state of 'innocence'. Children were thought to be 'innocent'. Eighteenth-century translators like Pope and Dryden forced Greek and Roman literature to be their allies in their leap away from animality, and they translated Homer as if he too were 'innocent'. To Christian Europeans, impulses open to the sexual instincts or animal instincts indicated a fallen state, a state of 'experience'.

Blake thought the nomenclature mad, the precise opposite of the truth, and he wrote *The Songs of Innocence and Experience* to say so. Blake, discussing 'experience', declared that to be afraid of a leap into the unconscious is actually to be in a state of 'experience'. (We are all experienced in that fear.) The state of 'experience' is characterized by blocked love-energy, boredom, envy, and joylessness. Another characteristic is the pedestrian movement of the mind; possibly constant fear makes the mind move slowly. Blake could see that after 1,800 years of no leaping, joy was disappearing, poetry was dying, 'the languid strings do scarcely move! The sound is forced, the notes are few.' A nurse in the state of 'experience', obsessed with a fear of animal blackness (a fear that increased after the whites took Africa), and some sort of abuse in her childhood, calls the children in from play as soon as the light falls:

When the voices of children are heard on the green
And whisp'rings are in the dale,
The days of my youth rise fresh in my mind,
My face turns green and pale.

Then come home, my children, the sun is gone down
And the dews of night arise;
Your spring and your day are wasted in play
And your winter and night in disguise.

The nurse in *The Songs of Innocence* also calls the children in. But she has conquered her fear and when the children say,

> *'No, no, let us play, for it is yet day*
> *And we cannot go to sleep:*
> *Besides in the sky the little birds fly*
> *And the hills are all cover'd with sheep.'*

She replies (the children's arguments are quite convincing),

> *'Well, well, go and play till the light fades away*
> *And then go home to bed.'*
>
> *The little ones leaped and shouted and laugh'd*
> *And all the hills echoèd.*

She enjoys their shouts. The children leap about on the grass playing, and the hills respond.

We often feel elation when reading Homer, Neruda, Dickinson, Vallejo, and Blake because the poet is following some arc of association that corresponds to the inner life of the objects he or she speaks of, for example, the association between the lids of eyes and the bark of stones. The associative paths are not private to the poet, but are somehow inherent in the universe.

IV

An ancient work of art such as the *Odyssey* has at its centre a long floating leap, around which the poem's images gather themselves like steel shavings around a magnet. Some recent works of art have many shorter leaps rather than one long one. The poet who is 'leaping' makes a jump from an object soaked in conscious psychic substance to an object soaked in latent or instinctive psychic substance. One real joy of poetry—not the only one—is to experience this leaping inside a poem.

Novalis, Goethe, and Hölderlin, writing around 1800 in Germany, participated in the associative freedom I have been describing; and their thought in a parallel way carried certain pagan and heretical elements, precisely as Blake's thought did at that time in England. A century later Freud pointed out that the dream still retained the fantastic freedom of association known to most educated Europeans only from pre-Christian poetry and art. We notice that dream interpretation has never been a favourite occupation of the fundamentalists.

In psychology of the last eighty years the effort to recover the dream's freedom of association and its metaphors has been partly successful. Some of the psychic ability to go from the known to the unknown part of the psyche and back has been restored. So too the 'leaping' poets: Rilke and Bobrowski, Lorca, and Vallejo, Rene Char, Yves Bonnefoy, and Paul Celan.

Yeats, riding on the dragonish associations of Irish mythology, wrote genuinely great poetry. If we, in the United States, cannot learn dragon smoke from Yeats, or from the French descenders, or from the Spanish leapers, from whom will we learn it? I think much is at stake in this question.

Let's set down some of the enemies that leaping has in this country. American fundamentalism is against the journey to dark places; capitalism is against the descent to soul; realism is against the leap to spirit; populism and social thought are against the solitary wildness; careerism in poetry doesn't allow enough time for descent; group thought will not support individual ventures; the reluctance of recent American poets to translate makes them ignorant. We notice that contemporary American poets tend to judge their poetry by comparing it to the poetry other people of their time are writing—their reviews make this clear—rather than by comparing their work to Goethe's, or Akhmatova's, or Tsvetaeva's or Blake's. Great poetry always has something of the grandiose in it. It's as if American poets are now so distrustful of the grandiose and so afraid to be thought grandiose that they cannot even imagine great poetry.

V

Lorca wrote a beautiful and great essay called 'Theory and Function of the Duende', available in English in the Penguin edition of Lorca. 'Duende' is the sense of the presence of death, and Lorca says,

> *Very often intellect is poetry's enemy because it is too much given to imitation, because it lifts the poet to a throne of sharp edges and makes him oblivious of the fact that he may suddenly be devoured by ants, or a great arsenic lobster may fall on his head.*

Duende involves a kind of elation when death is present in the room. It is associated with 'dark' sounds; and when a poet has duende inside him, he brushes past death with each step, and in that presence associates fast (Samuel Johnson remarked that there was nothing like a sentence of death in half an hour to wonderfully concentrate the mind). The gypsy flamenco dancer is associating fast when she dances, and so is Bach writing his cantatas. Lorca mentions an old gypsy dancer who, on hearing Brailowsky play Bach, cried out, 'That has duende!'

The Protestant embarrassment in the presence of death turns us into muse poets or angel poets, associating timidly. Lorca says,

> *The duende—where is the duende? Through the empty arch comes an air of the mind that blows insistently over the heads of the dead, in search of the new landscapes and unsuspected accents; an air smelling of child's saliva, of pounded grass, and medusal veil announcing the constant baptism of newly created things.*

The Spanish 'surrealist' or 'leaping' poet often enters into his poem with a heavy body of feeling piled up behind him as if behind a dam. Some of that water is duende water. The poet enters the poem excited, with the emotions alive; he is angry or ecstatic, or disgusted. There are a lot of exclamation marks, visible or invisible. Almost all the poems in Lorca's *Poet in New York* are written with the poet profoundly moved, flying. Powerful feeling makes the mind move, fast, and evidently the presence of swift motion makes the emotions still more alive, just as chanting awakens many emotions that the chanter was hardly aware of at the moment he began chanting.

What is the opposite of wild association then? Tame association? Approved association? Sluggish association? Whatever we want to call it, we know what it is—that slow plodding association that pesters us in so many poetry magazines, and in our own work when it is no good, association that takes half an hour to compare a childhood accident to a crucifixion, or a leaf to the *I Ching*. Poetry is killed for students in high school by teachers who only understand this dull kind of association.

Lorca says,

> *To help us seek the duende there are neither maps nor discipline. All one knows is that it burns the blood like powdered glass, that it exhausts, that it rejects all the sweet geometry one has learned, that it breaks with all styles . . . that it dresses the delicate body of Rimbaud in an acrobat's green suit: or that it puts the eyes of a dead fish on Count Lautréamont in the early morning Boulevard.*
>
> *The magical quality of a poem consists in its being always possessed by the duende, so that whoever beholds it is baptized with dark water.*

1967-1972

Eavan Boland

The Politics of Eroticism

I want a poem I can grow old in. I want a poem I can die in. It is a human wish, meeting language and precedent at the point of crisis. What is there to stop me? What prevents me taking up a pen and recording in a poem the accurate detail of time passing, which might then become a wider exploration of its meaning? My daughter's shadows in the garden, for instance, now grown longer than my own.

• • •

Image systems within poetry—of which she is now a part—are complex, referential, and historic. Within them are stored not simply the practices of a tradition but the precedent which years of acquaintance with, and illumination by, that tradition offers to the poet at that moment of absorption in the poem.

• • •

The erotic object, for instance, is most often part of the image system of the poem, while the sexualization of it is integral to the poet's perspective and stance; it therefore becomes part of voice and argument. In a poem about the silks a woman is wearing, written by her lover, the silks become the mute erotic object, while the perception of them as beautiful and exciting becomes part of the poet's perspective in the poem.

The problem with this neat and blunt way of looking at things is that it sweeps away, in a few words, the crucial fact about the sexual and the erotic in poetry: that their fusion is so powerful not simply because the erotic object, as an image, is distanced and controlled by the sexual perspective of the poet, although it is. Nor that we see in this fusion the appropriation of the powerless by the powerful, although we do. The crucial aspect of the relation between the sexual and the erotic in this context is that the erotic object is possessed not by the power of sexuality but by the power of expression. The erotic object therefore becomes a beautiful mime of those forces of expression which have silenced it. Its reason for being there may seem to be that it is both beautiful and yearned for, but at a deeper level it becomes a trophy of the forces which created it, not simply because it is sexualized but because it is sexualized within a triumphant and complex act of poetry.

[Boland sees in work of poets such as Sylvia Plath, Carol Ann Duffy, and Louise Glück] the ways women poets are rewriting the old fixities of the sexual and erotic, are reassembling a landscape where subject and object are differently politicized, where expression, far from being an agent of power, may be an index of powerlessness. [Disassembling the sexual and erotic in poetry, Boland says, has enabled women to write a new kind of nature poetry and to overcome 'that inability to write the aging body'.]

• • •

It has been my argument that in a real and immediate sense, when she does not enter upon this old territory where the erotic and sexual came together to inflect the tradition, the woman poet is in that poignant place I spoke of, where the subject cannot forget her previous existence as object. There are aesthetic implications to this, but they are not separable from the ethical ones. And the chief ethical implication it seems to me is that when a woman poet deals with these issues of the sexual and the erotic, the poem she writes is likely to have a new dimension. It can be an act of rescue rather than a strategy of possession. And the object she returns to rescue, with her newly made Orphic power and intelligence, would be herself: a fixed presence in the underworld of the traditional poem. It is easy enough to see that her dual relation to the object she makes—as both creator and rescuer—shifts the balance of subject and object, lessens the control and alters perspectives within the poem.

I have also argued that far from making a continuum, the contemporary poem as written by women can actually separate the sexual and erotic, and separate, also, the sexual motif from that of poetic expression. And that when a woman poet does this, a circuit of power represented by their fusion is disrupted. The erotic object can be rescued and restored: from silence to expression, from the erotic to the sensory. When this happens, beautiful, disturbing tones are free to enter the poem. Poetry itself comes to the threshold of changes which need not exclude or diminish the past but are bound to reinterpret it.

Above all—and this was what chiefly drew me towards the whole complex process of argument and exploration—that disassembling of a traditional fusion offered a radical and exciting chance to restate time in the poem. If the erotic object was indeed part of a drama of expression rather than a drama of desire, then it was also a signal of powers which were expressive and poetic more than they were sexual. As such the erotic subject had to do justice to the powers it reflected. It had to be a perfect moon to that sun. It could not be afflicted by time or made vulnerable by decay. It would not age. If this object—whether it was silk or pearls or a tree or a fan—were reclaimed by the woman poet and set down in a sensory world which inflected the mortality of the body, rather than the strength of the expressive mind, then, by just such an inflection, it would be restored to the flaws of time.

And here at last, it seemed to me, right across my path lay the shadow that had fallen across my poem that summer night. In the poem of the tradition the erotic object was a concealed boast, a hidden brag about the powers of poetry itself: that it could stop time. That it could fend off decay. Therefore, I—and other women poets—as we entered our own poems found an injunction already posted there. Inasmuch as we had once been objects—or objectified—in those poems, we had been perfect and timeless. Now, as authors of poems ourselves, if we were to age or fail or be simply mortal, we would have to do more than simply write down those things as themes or images. We would have to enter the interior of the poem and reinscribe certain powerful and customary relations between object and subject. And be responsible for what we did.

ROBERT CREELEY

A SENSE OF MEASURE

I am wary of any didactic program for the arts and yet I cannot ignore the fact that poetry, in my own terms of experience, obtains to an unequivocal order. What I deny, then, is any assumption that that order can be either acknowledged or gained by intellectual assertion, or will, or some like intention to shape language to a purpose which the literal act of writing does not itself discover. Such senses of pattern as I would admit are those having to do with a preparatory ritual, and however vague it may sound, I mean simply that character of invocation common to both prayer and children's games.

But it is more relevant here to make understood that I do not feel the usual sense of *subject* in poetry to be of much use. My generation has a particular qualification to make of this factor because it came of age at a time when a man's writing was either admitted or denied in point of its agreement with the then fashionable concerns of 'poetic' comment. William Carlos Williams was, in this way, as much criticized for the things he said as for the way in which he said them. I feel that 'subject' is at best a material of the poem, and that poems finally derive from some deeper complex of activity.

I am interested, for example, to find that 'automatic or inspirational speech tends everywhere to fall into metrical patterns' as E.R. Dodds notes in *The Greeks and the Irrational*. Blake's 'Hear the voice of the Bard' demands realization of a human phenomenon, not recognition of some social type. If we think of the orders of experience commonly now acknowledged, and of the incidence of what we call *chance*, it must be seen that no merely intellectual program can find reality, much less admit it, in a world so complexly various as ours has proved.

Recent studies in this country involved with defining the so-called creative personality have defined very little indeed and yet one of their proposals interests me. It is that men and women engaged in the arts have a much higher tolerance for disorder than is the usual case. This means, to me, that poets among others involved in comparable acts have an intuitive apprehension of a coherence which permits them a much greater admission of the real, the phenomenal world, than those otherwise placed can allow. Perhaps this is little more than what Otto Rank said some time ago in *Art and Artist* concerning the fact that an artist does die with each thing he does, insofar as he depends upon the conclusion of what possibilities do exist for him. Paradoxically, nothing can follow from that which is altogether successful. But again this risk is overcome—in the imagination—by trust of that coherence which no other means can discover. It would seem to me that occasional parallels between the arts and religion may well come from this coincidence of attitude, at least at times when neither philosophy nor psychology is the measure of either.

Lest I be misunderstood—by 'religion' I mean a basic *visionary* experience, not a social order or commitment, still less a moral one. Gary Snyder tells me that the Indians consider the experience of visions a requisite for attaining manhood. So they felt their enemy, the whites, not men, simply that so few of the latter had ever gained this measure of their own phenomenality. In this sense I am more interested, at present, in what is *given* to me to write apart from what I might intend. I have never explicitly known—before writing—what it was that I would say. For myself, articulation is the intelligent ability to recognize the experience of what is so given, in words. I do not feel that such a sense of writing is 'mindless' or 'automatic' in a pejorative way. At the end of *Paterson V* Williams writes:

> —Learning with age to sleep my life away:
> saying
> The measure intervenes, to measure is all we know . . .

I am deeply interested in the act of such *measure*, and I feel it to involve much more than an academic sense of metric. There can no longer be a significant discussion of the metre of a poem in relation to iambs and like terms because linguistics has offered a much more detailed and sensitive register of this part of a poem's activity. Nor do I feel measure to involve the humanistic attempt to relate all phenomena to the scale of human appreciation thereof. And systems of language—the world of discourse which so contained Sartre et al.—are also for me a false situation if it is assumed they offer a modality for being, apart from description. I am not at all interested in describing anything.

I want to give witness not to the thought of myself—that specious concept of identity—but, rather, to what I am as simple agency, a thing evidently alive by virtue of such activity. I want, as Charles Olson says, to come into the world. Measure, then, is my testament. What uses me is what I use and in that complex measure is the issue. I cannot cut down trees with my bare hand, which is measure of both tree and hand. In that way I feel that poetry, in the very subtlety of its relation to image and rhythm, offers an intensely various record of such facts. It is equally one of them.

LORNA CROZIER

FROM 'WHO'S LISTENING?'

'We are telling you this because you are sensitive people, because you are poets. We know you will take our stories back with you, you will put them into words.'

All across Chile that's the kind of reaction we got when people found out we were poets. No matter what they had gone through, no matter what terrible position they were in, they believed in the power of words. There was an overwhelming respect for poetry and what it can do, and that respect made me feel I had to write about what I heard.

When Patrick and I got back to Saskatoon, we wrote a radio script about our trip for the CBC and we wrote some poems. I didn't want to write from the point of view of someone who understood Chile; in the poems, I didn't want to pretend to be someone who had put her life on the line. Instead I tried to find the connections between my experiences there and here, between the people I met and me. I wanted the poems to come out of the nexus of the two worlds, that place where they and I met and knew each other. Poems can only happen in a moment of recognition, of intense and clear seeing. . . .

Our trip took place over a year ago, but I often think of that woman and hear her words, especially when I need to be reminded that poetry somewhere has value—when I see the narrow shelves of poetry books hidden away in the backs of book stores (if they are there at all), when ten people show up for a poetry reading, when poems are used merely as 'fillers' in all but literary magazines, when the man beside me on the airplane becomes uncomfortable when he asks me what I do and I reply. In countries like ours, even the poets see themselves as slightly eccentric and out of place, often alienated from the very people they write about.

The words *We are telling you this because you are poets* are what keep me going some days when I feel depressed by our society's lack of interest in poetry and the other arts. Yet I'm taking the easy way out by finding comfort in her words—I don't live in Chile, I live in Canada, and although I was inspired by the faith of that small peasant woman, I write for my own people and out of my own peculiar place. Nor do I want to romanticize the poetry-loving country of Chile—I would rather live in Canada as an ignored poet than elsewhere where I and my countrymen and women would have to fear for our lives. So I must come back to the question: Why do I write when no one is listening?

Flaubert said, 'You must write according to your feelings, be sure those feelings are true and let everything else go hang.' I write because I am angry, because I am in love, because I fear the passing of foxes and owls, of all beautiful things. I write because the world is mortal and I and those I love are dying.

I write because I want to tell myself the stories I never heard as a child, as a grown woman, the stories I still can't find in books. Adrienne Rich says, 'Begin with the material. Pick up again the long struggle against lofty and privileged abstraction. Perhaps this is the core of the revolutionary process, whether it calls itself Marxist or Third World or Feminist or all three . . . a rebellion against the idolatry of pure ideas, the belief that ideas have a life of their own and float along above the heads of ordinary people—women, the poor, the uninitiated.'

I throw out the poem like a net and pull things together with thin threads of language that need mending, that need new patterns to catch the light. This is my woman's work, pulling these threads through my voice. I write for the deer I become in the forest, for Gwendolyn MacEwen's green thunder, for the woman who named her daughter 'Liberty', for the man next door shovelling his walk before his children get up for school. I write because I still believe that words have magic, that they can change things, like the Medicine Man who gives my friend a Cree name to treat her cancer because the herbs he's prescribing wouldn't recognize her without it.

I write for the best part of me, my real audience, the ideal self that sits somewhere in my study and hears the lines of the poem as I revise and read out loud, and sometimes get it right. I write in case someone, anyone, is listening. (*NeWest Review*, February/March, 1989)

e.e. cummings

Three Statements

1*

On the assumption that my technique is either complicated or original or both, the publishers have politely requested me to write an introduction to this book.

At least my theory of technique, if I have one, is very far from original; nor is it complicated. I can express it in fifteen words, by quoting The Eternal Question And Immortal Answer of burlesk, viz., 'Would you hit a woman with a child?—No, I'd hit her with a brick.' Like the burlesk comedian, I am abnormally fond of that precision which creates movement.

If a poet is anybody, he is somebody to whom things made matter very little—somebody who is obsessed by Making. Like all obsessions, the Making obsession has disadvantages; for instance, my only interest in making money would be to make it. Fortunately, however, I should prefer to make almost anything else, including locomotives and roses. It is with roses and locomotives (not to mention acrobats Spring electricity Coney Island the 4th of July the eyes of mice and Niagara Falls) that my 'poems' are competing.

They are also competing with each other, with elephants, and with El Greco.

Ineluctable preoccupation with The Verb gives a poet one priceless advantage: whereas nonmakers must content themselves with the merely undeniable fact that two times two is four, he rejoices in a purely irresistible truth (to be found, in abbreviated costume, upon the title page of the present volume).

---

* Foreword from *is 5* by e.e. cummings.

2*

The poems to come are for you and for me and are not for mostpeople

—it's no use trying to pretend that mostpeople and ourselves are alike. Mostpeople have less in common with ourselves than the squarerootofminus-one. You and I are human beings:mostpeople are snobs.

Take the matter of being born. What does being born mean to mostpeople? Catastrophe unmitigated. Socialrevolution. The cultured aristocrat yanked out of his hyperexclusively ultravoluptuous superpalazzo,and dumped into an incredibly vulgar detentioncamp swarming with every conceivable species of undesirable organism. Mostpeople fancy a guaranteed birthproof safetysuit of nondestructible selflessness. If mostpeople were to be born twice they'd improbably call it dying—

you and I are not snobs. We can never be born enough. We are human beings;for whom birth is a supremely welcome mystery,the mystery of growing:the mystery which happens only and whenever we are faithful to ourselves. You and I wear the dangerous looseness of doom and find it becoming. Life,for eternal us,is now;and now is much too busy being a little more than everything to seem anything,catastrophic included.

Life,for mostpeople,simply isn't. Take the socalled standardofliving. What do mostpeople mean by 'living'? They don't mean living. They mean the latest and closest plural approximation to singular prenatal passivity which science,in its finite but unbounded wisdom,has succeeded in selling their wives. If science could fail,a mountain's a mammal. Mostpeople's wives can spot a genuine delusion of embryonic omnipotence immediately and will accept no substitutes.

—luckily for us,a mountain is a mammal. The plusorminus movie to end moving,the strictly scientific parlourgame of real unreality,the tyranny conceived in misconception and dedicated to the proposition that every man is a woman and any woman a king,hasn't a wheel to stand on. What their most synthetic not to mention transparent majesty,mrsandmr collective foetus, would improbably call a ghost is walking. He isn't an undream of anaesthetized impersons,or a cosmic comfortstation,or a transcendentally sterilized lookiesoundiefeelietastiesmellie. He is a healthily complex,a naturally homogeneous,citizen of immortality. The now of his each pitying free imperfect gesture,his any birth or breathing,insults perfected inframortally millenniums of slavishness. He is a little more than everything,he is democracy;he is alive:he is ourselves.

---

* Introduction from *Collected Poems* by e.e. cummings.

Miracles are to come. With you I leave a remembrance of miracles: they are by somebody who can love and who shall be continually reborn,a human being;somebody who said to those near him,when his fingers would not hold a brush 'tie it into my hand'—

nothing proving or sick or partial. Nothing false,nothing difficult or easy or small or colossal. Nothing ordinary or extraordinary,nothing emptied or filled,real or unreal;nothing feeble and known or clumsy and guessed. Everywhere tints childrening,innocent spontaneous,true. Nowhere possibly what flesh and impossibly such a garden,but actually flowers which breasts are among the very mouths of light. Nothing believed or doubted;brain over heart, surface:nowhere hating or to fear;shadow, mind without soul. Only how measureless cool flames of making;only each other building always distinct selves of mutual entirely opening;only alive. Never the murdered finalities of wherewhen and yesno,impotent nongames of wrongright and rightwrong;never to gain or pause,never the soft adventure of undoom,greedy anguishes and cringing ecstasies of inexistence;never to rest and never to have:only to grow.

Always the beautiful answer who asks a more beautiful question.

3*

A poet is somebody who feels, and who expresses his feeling through words.

This may sound easy. It isn't.

A lot of people think or believe or know they feel—but that's thinking or believing or knowing; not feeling. And poetry is feeling—not knowing or believing or thinking.

Almost anybody can learn to think or believe or know, but not a single human being can be taught to feel. Why? Because whenever you think or you believe or you know, you're a lot of other people: but the moment you feel, you're nobody-but-yourself.

To be nobody-but-yourself—in a world which is doing its best, night and day, to make you everybody else—means to fight the hardest battle which any human being can fight; and never stop fighting.

As for expressing nobody-but-yourself in words, that means working just a little harder than anybody who isn't a poet can possibly imagine. Why? Because nothing is quite as easy as using words like somebody else. We all of us do exactly this nearly all of the time—and whenever we do it, we're not poets.

* 'A Poet's Advice to Students' appeared originally in the Ottawa Hills *Spectator*. From *e.e. cummings: A Miscellany Revised*, ed. by George J. Firmage.

If, at the end of your first ten or fifteen years of fighting and working and feeling, you find you've written one line of one poem, you'll be very lucky indeed.

And so my advice to all young people who wish to become poets is: do something easy, like learning how to blow up the world—unless you're not only willing, but glad, to feel and work and fight till you die.

Does this sound dismal? It isn't.

It's the most wonderful life on earth.

Or so I feel.

T.S. ELIOT

TRADITION AND THE INDIVIDUAL TALENT*

I

In English writing we seldom speak of tradition, though we occasionally apply its name in deploring its absence. We cannot refer to 'the tradition' or to 'a tradition'; at most, we employ the adjective in saying that the poetry of So-and-so is 'traditional' or even 'too traditional'. Seldom, perhaps, does the word appear except in a phrase of censure. If otherwise, it is vaguely approbative, with the implication, as to the work approved, of some pleasing archaeological reconstruction. You can hardly make the word agreeable to English ears without this comfortable reference to the reassuring science of archaeology.

Certainly the word is not likely to appear in our appreciations of living or dead writers. Every nation, every race, has not only its own creative, but its own critical turn of mind; and is even more oblivious of the shortcomings and limitations of its critical habits than of those of its creative genius. We know, or think we know, from the enormous mass of critical writing that has appeared in the French language the critical method or habit of the French; we only conclude (we are such unconscious people) that the French are 'more critical' than we, and sometimes even plume ourselves a little with the fact, as if the French were the less spontaneous. Perhaps they are; but we might remind ourselves that criticism is as inevitable as breathing, and that we should be none the worse for articulating what passes in our minds when we read a book and feel an emotion about it, for criticizing our own minds in their work of criticism.

* From *Selected Essays*, new edition, by T.S. Eliot.

One of the facts that might come to light in this process is our tendency to insist, when we praise a poet, upon those aspects of his work in which he least resembles anyone else. In these aspects or parts of his work we pretend to find what is individual, what is the peculiar essence of the man. We dwell with satisfaction upon the poet's difference from his predecessors, especially his immediate predecessors; we endeavour to find something that can be isolated in order to be enjoyed. Whereas if we approach a poet without this prejudice we shall often find that not only the best, but the most individual parts of his work may be those in which the dead poets, his ancestors, assert their immortality most vigorously. And I do not mean the impressionable period of adolescence, but the period of full maturity.

Yet if the only form of tradition, of handing down, consisted in following the ways of the immediate generation before us in a blind or timid adherence to its successes, 'tradition' should positively be discouraged. We have seen many such simple currents soon lost in the sand; and novelty is better than repetition. Tradition is a matter of much wider significance. It cannot be inherited, and if you want it you must obtain it by great labour. It involves, in the first place, the historical sense, which we may call nearly indispensable to anyone who would continue to be a poet beyond his twenty-fifth year; and the historical sense involves a perception, not only of the pastness of the past, but of its presence; the historical sense compels a man to write not merely with his own generation in his bones, but with a feeling that the whole of the literature of Europe from Homer and within it the whole of the literature of his own country has a simultaneous existence and composes a simultaneous order. This historical sense, which is a sense of the timeless as well as of the temporal and of the timeless and of the temporal together, is what makes a writer traditional. And it is at the same time what makes a writer most acutely conscious of his place in time, of his contemporaneity.

No poet, no artist of any art, has his complete meaning alone. His significance, his appreciation is the appreciation of his relation to the dead poets and artists. You cannot value him alone; you must set him, for contrast and comparison, among the dead. I mean this as a principle of aesthetic, not merely historical, criticism. The necessity that he shall conform, that he shall cohere, is not one-sided; what happens when a new work of art is created is something that happens simultaneously to all the works of art which preceded it. The existing monuments form an ideal order among themselves, which is modified by the introduction of the new (the really new) work of art among them. The existing order is complete before the new work arrives; for order to persist after the supervention of novelty, the *whole* existing order must be, if ever so slightly, altered; and so the relations, proportions, values of each work of art toward the whole are readjusted; and this is conformity between the old and the new.

Whoever has approved this idea of order, of the form of European, of English literature, will not find it preposterous that the past should be altered by the present as much as the present is directed by the past. And the poet who is aware of this will be aware of great difficulties and responsibilities.

In a peculiar sense he will be aware also that he must inevitably be judged by the standards of the past. I say judged, not amputated, by them; not judged to be as good as, or worse or better than, the dead; and certainly not judged by the canons of dead critics. It is a judgement, a comparison, in which two things are measured by each other. To conform merely would be for the new work not really to conform at all; it would not be new, and would therefore not be a work of art. And we do not quite say that the new is more valuable because it fits in; but its fitting in is a test of its value—a test, it is true, which can only be slowly and cautiously applied, for we are none of us infallible judges of conformity. We say: it appears to conform, and is perhaps individual, or it appears individual, and may conform; but we are hardly likely to find that it is one and not the other.

To proceed to a more intelligible exposition of the relation of the poet to the past: he can neither take the past as a lump, an indiscriminate bolus, nor can he form himself wholly on one or two private admirations, nor can he form himself wholly upon one preferred period. The first course is inadmissible, the second is an important experience of youth, and the third is a pleasant and highly desirable supplement. The poet must be very conscious of the main current, which does not at all flow invariably through the most distinguished reputations. He must be quite aware of the obvious fact that art never improves, but that the material of art is never quite the same. He must be aware that the mind of Europe—the mind of his own country—a mind which he learns in time to be much more important than his own private mind—is a mind which changes, and that this change is a development which abandons nothing *en route*, which does not superannuate either Shakespeare, or Homer, or the rock drawing of the Magdalenian draughtsmen. That this development, refinement perhaps, complication certainly, is not, from the point of view of the artist, any improvement. Perhaps not even an improvement from the point of view of the psychologist or not to the extent which we imagine; perhaps only in the end based upon a complication in economics and machinery. But the difference between the present and the past is that the conscious present is an awareness of the past in a way and to an extent which the past's awareness of itself cannot show.

Someone said: 'The dead writers are remote from us because we *know* so much more than they did.' Precisely, and they are that which we know.

I am alive to a usual objection to what is clearly part of my program for the *métier* of poetry. The objection is that the doctrine requires a ridiculous amount of erudition (pedantry), a claim which can be rejected by appeal to the lives of poets in any pantheon. It will even be affirmed that much learning deadens or perverts poetic sensibility. While, however, we persist in believing that a poet ought to know as much as will not encroach upon his necessary receptivity and necessary laziness, it is not desirable to confine knowledge to whatever can be put into a useful shape for examinations, drawing-rooms, or the still more pretentious modes of publicity. Some can absorb knowledge, the more tardy must sweat for it. Shakespeare acquired more essential history from Plutarch than most men could from the whole British Museum. What is to be insisted upon is that the poet must develop or procure the consciousness of the past and that he should continue to develop this consciousness throughout his career.

What happens is a continual surrender of himself as he is at the moment to something which is more valuable. The progress of an artist is a continual self-sacrifice, a continual extinction of personality.

There remains to define this process of depersonalization and its relation to the sense of tradition. It is in this depersonalization that art may be said to approach the condition of science. I shall, therefore, invite you to consider, as a suggestive analogy, the action which takes place when a bit of finely filiated platinum is introduced into a chamber containing oxygen and sulphur dioxide.

II

Honest criticism and sensitive appreciation is directed not upon the poet but upon the poetry. If we attend to the confused cries of the newspaper critics and the susurrus of popular repetition that follows, we shall hear the names of poets in great numbers; if we seek not Blue-book knowledge but the enjoyment of poetry, and ask for a poem, we shall seldom find it. In the last article I tried to point out the importance of the relation of the poem to other poems by other authors, and suggested the conception of poetry as a living whole of all the poetry that has ever been written. The other aspect of this Impersonal theory of poetry is the relation of the poem to its author. And I hinted, by an analogy, that the mind of the mature poet differs from that of the immature one not precisely in any valuation of 'personality', not being necessarily more interesting, or having 'more to say', but rather by being a more finely perfected medium in which special, or very varied, feelings are at liberty to enter into new combinations.

The analogy was that of the catalyst. When the two gases previously mentioned are mixed in the presence of a filament of platinum, they form sulphurous acid. This combination takes place only if the platinum is present; nevertheless the newly formed acid contains no trace of platinum, and the platinum itself is apparently unaffected; has remained inert, neutral, and unchanged. The mind of the poet is the shred of platinum. It may partly or exclusively operate upon the experience of the man himself; but, the more perfect the artist, the more completely separate in him will be the man who suffers and the mind which creates; the more perfectly will the mind digest and transmute the passions which are its material.

The experience, you will notice, the elements which enter the presence of the transforming catalyst, are of two kinds: emotions and feelings. The effect of a work of art upon the person who enjoys it is an experience different in kind from any experience not of art. It may be formed out of one emotion, or may be a combination of several; and various feelings, inhering for the writer in particular words or phrases or images, may be added to compose the final result. Or great poetry may be made without the direct use of any emotion whatever: composed out of feelings solely. Canto XV of the *Inferno* (Brunetto Latini) is a working up of the emotion evident in the situation; but the effect, though single as that of any work of art, is obtained by considerable complexity of detail. The last quatrain gives an image, a feeling attaching to an image, which 'came', which did not develop simply out of what precedes, but which was probably in suspension in the poet's mind until the proper combination arrived for it to add itself to. The poet's mind is in fact a receptacle for seizing and storing up numberless feelings, phrases, images, which remain there until the particles which can unite to form a new compound are present together.

If you compare several representative passages of the greatest poetry you see how great is the variety of types of combination, and also how completely any semi-ethical criterion of 'sublimity' misses the mark. For it is not the 'greatness', the intensity, of the emotions, the components, but the intensity of the artistic process, the pressure, so to speak, under which the fusion takes place, that counts. The episode of Paolo and Francesca employs a definite emotion, but the intensity of the poetry is something quite different from whatever intensity in the supposed experience it may give the impression of. It is no more intense, furthermore, than Canto XXVI, the voyage of Ulysses, which has not the direct dependence upon an emotion. Great variety is possible in the process of transmutation of emotion: the murder of Agamemnon, or the agony of Othello, gives an artistic effect apparently closer to a possible original than the scenes from Dante. In the *Agamemnon*, the artistic emotion approximates to the emotion of an actual spectator; in *Othello* to the emotion of the protagonist himself. But the difference between art and the event is always absolute; the combination which is the murder of Agamemnon is probably as complex as that which is the voyage of Ulysses. In either case there has been a fusion of elements. The ode of Keats contains a number of feelings which have nothing particular to do with the nightingale, but which the nightingale, partly, perhaps, because of its attractive name, and partly because of its reputation, served to bring together.

The point of view which I am struggling to attack is perhaps related to the metaphysical theory of the substantial unity of the soul: for my meaning is, that the poet has, not a 'personality' to express, but a particular medium, which is only a medium and not a personality, in which impressions and experiences combine in peculiar and unexpected ways. Impressions and experiences which are important for the man may take no place in the poetry, and those which become important in the poetry may play quite a negligible part in the man, the personality.

I will quote a passage which is unfamiliar enough to be regarded with fresh attention in the light—or darkness—of these observations:

> And now methinks I could e'en chide myself
> For doating on her beauty, though her death
> Shall be revenged after no common action.
> Does the silkworm expend her yellow labours
> For thee? For thee does she undo herself?
> Are lordships sold to maintain ladyships
> For the poor benefit of a bewildering minute?
> Why does yon fellow falsify highways,
> And put his life between the judge's lips,
> To refine such a thing—keeps horse and men
> To beat their valours for her? . . .

In this passage (as is evident if it is taken in its context) there is a combination of positive and negative emotions: an intensely strong attraction toward beauty and an equally intense fascination by the ugliness which is contrasted with it and which destroys it. This balance of contrasted emotion is in the dramatic situation to which the speech is pertinent, but that situation alone is inadequate to it. This is, so to speak, the structural emotion, provided by the drama. But the whole effect, the dominant tone, is due to the fact that a number of floating feelings, having an affinity to this emotion by no means superficially evident, have combined with it to give us a new art emotion.

It is not in his personal emotions, the emotions provoked by particular events in his life, that the poet is in any way remarkable or interesting. His particular emotions may be simple, or crude, or flat. The emotion in his poetry will be a very complex thing, but not with the complexity of the emotions of people who have very complex or unusual emotions in life. One error, in fact, of eccentricity in poetry is to seek for new human emotions to express; and in this search for novelty in the wrong place it discovers the perverse. The business of the poet is not to find new emotions, but to use the ordinary ones and, in working them up into poetry, to express feelings which are not in actual emotions at all. And emotions which he has never experienced will serve his turn as well as those familiar to him. Consequently, we must believe that 'emotion recollected in tranquillity' is an inexact formula. For it is neither emotion, nor recollection, nor, without distortion of meaning, tranquillity. It is a concentration, and a new thing resulting from the concentration, of a very great number of experiences which to the practical and active person would not seem to be experiences at all; it is a concentration which does not happen consciously or of deliberation. These experiences are not 'recollected', and they finally unite in an atmosphere which is 'tranquil' only in that it is a passive attending upon the event. Of course this is not quite the whole story. There is a great deal, in the writing of poetry, which must be conscious and deliberate. In fact, the bad poet is usually unconscious where he ought to be conscious, and conscious where he ought to be unconscious. Both errors tend to make him 'personal'. Poetry is not a turning loose of emotion, but an escape from emotion; it is not the expression of personality, but an escape from personality. But, of course, only those who have personality and emotions know what it means to want to escape from these things.

III

ὁ δὲ νοῦζ ἰσωζ θειότερόν τι καὶ ἀπαθέζ ἐστιν[1]

This essay proposes to halt at the frontier of metaphysics or mysticism, and confine itself to such practical conclusions as can be applied by the responsible person interested in poetry. To divert interest from the poet to the poetry is a laudable aim: for it would conduce to a juster estimation of actual poetry, good and bad. There are many people who appreciate the expression of sincere emotion in verse, and there is a smaller number of people who can appreciate technical excellence. But very few know when there is expression of *significant* emotion, emotion which has its life in the poem and not in the history of the poet. The emotion of art is impersonal. And the poet cannot reach this impersonality without surrendering himself wholly to the work to be done. And he is not likely to know what is to be done unless he lives in what is not merely the present, but the present moment of the past, unless he is conscious, not of what is dead, but of what is already living.

---

[1] ['The mind is undoubtedly something more divine and unimpressionable.' From Aristotle's *De Anima*, i, 4.]

FROM THE MUSIC OF POETRY*

It may appear strange, that when I profess to be talking about the 'music' of poetry, I put such emphasis upon conversation. But I would remind you, first, that the music of poetry is not something which exists apart from the meaning. Otherwise, we could have poetry of great musical beauty which made no sense, and I have never come across such poetry. The apparent exceptions only show a difference of degree: there are poems in which we are moved by the music and take the sense for granted, just as there are poems in which we attend to the sense and are moved by the music without noticing it. Take an apparently extreme example—the nonsense verse of Edward Lear. His nonsense is not vacuity of sense: it is a parody of sense, and that is the sense of it. 'The Jumblies' is a poem of adventure, and of nostalgia for the romance of foreign voyage and exploration; 'The Yongy-Bongy Bo' and 'The Dong with a Luminous Nose' are poems of unrequited passion—'blues' in fact. We enjoy the music, which is of a high order, and we enjoy the feeling of irresponsibility towards the sense. Or take a poem of another type, the 'Blue Closet' of William Morris. It is a delightful poem, though I cannot explain what it means and I doubt whether the author could have explained it. It has an effect somewhat like that of a rune or charm, but runes and charms are very practical formulae designed to produce definite results, such as getting a cow out of a bog. But its obvious intention (and I think the author succeeds) is to produce the effect of a dream. It is not necessary, in order to enjoy the poem, to know what the dream means; but human beings have an unshakeable belief that dreams mean something: they used to believe—and many still believe—that dreams disclose the secrets of the future; the orthodox modern faith is that they reveal the secrets—or at least the more horrid secrets—of the past. It is a commonplace to observe that the meaning of a poem may wholly escape paraphrase. It is not quite so commonplace to observe that the meaning of a poem may be something larger than its author's conscious purpose, and something remote from its origins. One of the more obscure of modern poets was the French writer Stéphane Mallarmé, of whom the French sometimes say that his language is so peculiar that it can be understood only by foreigners. The late Roger Fry, and his friend Charles Mauron, published an English translation with notes to unriddle the meanings: when I learn that a difficult sonnet was inspired by seeing a painting on the ceiling reflected on the polished top of a table, or by seeing the light reflected from the foam on a glass of

---

* The third W.P. Ker Memorial Lecture, delivered at Glasgow University in 1942, and published by Glasgow University Press in the same year. From *On Poetry and Poets* by T.S. Eliot.

beer, I can only say that this may be a correct embryology, but it is not the meaning. If we are moved by a poem, it has meant something, perhaps something important, to us; if we are not moved, then it is, as poetry, meaningless. We can be deeply stirred by hearing the recitation of a poem in a language of which we understand no word; but if we are then told that the poem is gibberish and has no meaning, we shall consider that we have been deluded—this was no poem, it was merely an imitation of instrumental music. If, as we are aware, only a part of the meaning can be conveyed by paraphrase, that is because the poet is occupied with frontiers of consciousness beyond which words fail, though meanings still exist. A poem may appear to mean very different things to different readers, and all of these meanings may be different from what the author thought he meant. For instance, the author may have been writing some peculiar personal experience, which he saw quite unrelated to anything outside; yet for the reader the poem may become the expression of a general situation, as well as of some private experience of his own. The reader's interpretation may differ from the author's and be equally valid—it may even be better. There may be much more in a poem than the author was aware of. The different interpretations may all be partial formulations of one thing; the ambiguities may be due to the fact that the poem means more, not less, than ordinary speech can communicate.

So, while poetry attempts to convey something beyond what can be conveyed in prose rhythms, it remains, all the same, one person talking to another; and this is just as true if you sing it, for singing is another way of talking. The immediacy of poetry to conversation is not a matter on which we can lay down exact laws. Every revolution in poetry is apt to be, and sometimes to announce itself to be, a return to common speech. That is the revolution which Wordsworth announced in his prefaces, and he was right: but the same revolution had been carried out a century before by Oldham, Waller, Denham, and Dryden; and the same revolution was due again something over a century later. The followers of a revolution develop the new poetic idiom in one direction or another; they polish or perfect it; meanwhile the spoken language goes on changing, and the poetic idiom goes out of date. Perhaps we do not realize how natural the speech of Dryden must have sounded to the most sensitive of his contemporaries. No poetry, of course, is ever exactly the same speech that the poet talks and hears: but it has to be in such a relation to the speech of his time that the listener or reader can say, 'that is how I should talk if I could talk poetry.' This is the reason why the best contemporary poetry can give us a feeling of excitement and a sense of fulfilment different from any sentiment aroused by even very much greater poetry of a past age.

The music of poetry, then, must be a music latent in the common speech of its time. And that means also that it must be latent in the common speech of the poet's *place*. It would not be to my present purpose to inveigh against the ubiquity of standardized, or 'BBC' English. If we all came to talk alike there would no longer be any point in our not writing alike: but until that time comes—and I hope it may be long postponed—it is the poet's business to use the speech which he finds about him, that with which he is most familiar. I shall always remember the impression of W. B. Yeats reading poetry aloud. To hear him read his own works was to be made to recognize how much the Irish way of speech is needed to bring out the beauties of Irish poetry: to hear Yeats reading William Blake was an experience of a different kind, more astonishing than satisfying. Of course, we do not want the poet merely to reproduce exactly the conversational idiom of himself, his family, his friends, and his particular district: but what he finds there is the material out of which he must make his poetry. He must, like the sculptor, be faithful to the material in which he works; it is out of sounds that he has heard that he must make his melody and harmony.

It would be a mistake, however, to assume that all poetry ought to be melodious, or that melody is more than one of the components of the music of words. Some poetry is meant to be sung; most poetry, in modern times, is meant to be spoken—and there are many other things to be spoken of besides the murmur of innumerable bees or the moan of doves in immemorial elms. Dissonance, even cacophony, has its place: just as, in a poem of any length, there must be transitions between passages of greater and less intensity, to give a rhythm of fluctuating emotion essential to the musical structure of the whole; and the passages of less intensity will be, in relation to the level on which the total poem operates, prosaic—so that, in the sense implied by that context, it may be said that no poet can write a poem of amplitude unless he is a master of the prosaic.[1]

What matters, in short, is the whole poem: and if the whole poem need not be, and often should not be, wholly melodious, it follows that a poem is not made only out of 'beautiful words'. I doubt whether, from the point of view of *sound* alone, any word is more or less beautiful than another—within its own language, for the question whether some languages are not more beautiful than others is quite another question. The ugly words are the words not fitted for the company in which they find themselves; there are words which are ugly because of rawness or because of antiquation; there are words which are ugly because of foreignness or ill-breeding (e.g., *television*): but I do not believe that any word well-established in its own language is either

[1] This is the complementary doctrine to that of the 'touchstone' line or passage of Matthew Arnold: this test of the greatness of a poet is the way he writes his less intense, but structurally vital, matter. (T.S.E.)

beautiful or ugly. The music of a word is, so to speak, at a point of intersection: it arises from its relation first to the words immediately preceding and following it, and indefinitely to the rest of its context; and from another relation, that of its immediate meaning in that context to all the other meanings which it has had in other contexts, to its greater or less wealth of association. Not all words, obviously, are equally rich and well-connected: it is part of the business of the poet to dispose the richer among the poorer, at the right points, and we cannot afford to load a poem too heavily with the former—for it is only at certain moments that a word can be made to insinuate the whole history of a language and a civilization. This is an 'allusiveness' which is not the fashion or eccentricity of a peculiar type of poetry; but an allusiveness which is in the nature of words, and which is equally the concern of every kind of poet. My purpose here is to insist that a 'musical poem' is a poem which has a musical pattern of sound and a musical pattern of the secondary meanings of the words which compose it, and that these two patterns are indissoluble and one. And if you object that it is only the pure sound, apart from the sense, to which the adjective 'musical' can be rightly applied, I can only reaffirm my previous assertion that the sound of a poem is as much an abstraction from the poem as is the sense.

• • •

So far, I have spoken only of versification and not of poetic structure; and it is time for a reminder that the music of verse is not a line by line matter, but a question of the whole poem. Only with this in mind can we approach the vexed question of formal pattern and free verse. In the plays of Shakespeare a musical design can be discovered in particular scenes, and in his more perfect plays as wholes. It is a music of imagery as well as sound: Mr Wilson Knight has shown in his examination of several of the plays, how much the use of recurrent imagery and dominant imagery, throughout one play, has to do with the total effect. A play of Shakespeare is a very complex musical structure; the more easily grasped structure is that of forms such as the sonnet, the formal ode, the ballade, the villanelle, rondeau, or sestina. It is sometimes assumed that modern poetry has done away with forms like these. I have seen signs of a return to them; and indeed I believe that the tendency to return to set, and even elaborate patterns is permanent, as permanent as the need for a refrain or a chorus to a popular song. Some forms are more appropriate to some languages than to others, and any form may be more appropriate to some periods than to others. At one stage the stanza is a right and natural formalization of speech into pattern. But the stanza—and the more elaborate it is, the more rules to be observed in its proper execution, the more surely this happens—

tends to become fixed to the idiom of the moment of its perfection. It quickly loses contact with the changing colloquial speech, being possessed by the mental outlook of a past generation; it becomes discredited when employed solely by those writers who, having no impulse to form within them, have recourse to pouring their liquid sentiment into a ready-made mould in which they vainly hope that it will set. In a perfect sonnet, what you admire is not so much the author's skill in adapting himself to the pattern as the skill and power with which he makes the pattern comply with what he has to say. Without this fitness, which is contingent upon period as well as individual genius, the rest is at best virtuosity: and where the musical element is the only element, that also vanishes. Elaborate forms return: but there have to be periods during which they are laid aside.

As for 'free verse', I expressed my view twenty-five years ago by saying that no verse is free for the man who wants to do a good job. No one has better cause to know than I, that a great deal of bad prose has been written under the name of free verse; though whether its authors wrote bad prose or bad verse, or bad verse in one style or in another, seems to me a matter of indifference. But only a bad poet could welcome free verse as a liberation from form. It was a revolt against dead form, and a preparation for new form or for the renewal of the old; it was an insistence upon the inner unity which is unique to every poem, against the outer unity which is typical. The poem comes before the form, in the sense that a form grows out of the attempt of somebody to say something; just as a system of prosody is only a formulation of the identities in the rhythms of a succession of poets influenced by each other.

Forms have to be broken and remade: but I believe that any language, so long as it remains the same language, imposes its laws and restrictions and permits its own licence, dictates its own speech rhythms and sound patterns. And a language is always changing; its developments in vocabulary, in syntax, pronunciation, and intonation—even, in the long run, its deterioration—must be accepted by the poet and made the best of. He in turn has the privilege of contributing to the development and maintaining the quality, the capacity of the language to express a wide range, and subtle gradation, of feeling and emotion; his task is both to respond to change and make it conscious, and to battle against degradation below the standards which he has learnt from the past. The liberties that he may take are for the sake of order.

At what stage contemporary verse now finds itself, I must leave you to judge for yourselves. I suppose that it will be agreed that if the work of the last twenty years is worthy of being classified at all, it is as belonging to a period of search for a proper modern colloquial idiom. We have still a good way to go in the invention of a verse medium for the theatre, a medium in which we shall be able to hear the speech of contemporary human beings, in which dramatic characters can express the purest poetry without high-falutin and in which they can convey the most commonplace message without absurdity. But when we reach a point at which the poetic idiom can be stabilized, then a period of musical elaboration can follow. I think that a poet may gain much from the study of music: how much technical knowledge of musical form is desirable I do not know, for I have not that technical knowledge myself. But I believe that the properties in which music concerns the poet most nearly, are the sense of rhythm and the sense of structure. I think that it might be possible for a poet to work too closely to musical analogies: the result might be an effect of artificiality; but I know that a poem, or a passage of a poem, may tend to realize itself first as a particular rhythm before it reaches expression in words, and that this rhythm may bring to birth the idea and the image; and I do not believe that this is an experience peculiar to myself. The use of recurrent themes is as natural to poetry as to music. There are possibilities for verse which bear some analogy to the development of a theme by different groups of instruments; there are possibilities of transitions in a poem comparable to the different movements of a symphony or a quartet; there are possibilities of contrapuntal arrangement of subject-matter. It is in the concert room, rather than in the opera house, that the germ of a poem may be quickened. More than this I cannot say, but must leave the matter here to those who have had a musical education. But I would remind you again of the two tasks of poetry, the two directions in which language must at different times be worked: so that however far it may go in musical elaboration, we must expect a time to come when poetry will have again to be recalled to speech. The same problems arise, and always in new forms; and poetry has always before it, as F. S. Oliver said of politics, an 'endless adventure'.

FROM HAMLET AND HIS PROBLEMS*

The grounds of *Hamlet*'s failure are not immediately obvious. Mr Robertson is undoubtedly correct in concluding that the essential emotion of the play is the feeling of a son towards a guilty mother:

'[Hamlet's] tone is that of one who has suffered tortures on the score of his mother's degradation.... The guilt of a mother is an almost intolerable motive for drama, but it had to be maintained and emphasized to supply a psychological solution, or rather a hint of one.'

This, however, is by no means the whole story. It is not merely the 'guilt of a mother' that cannot be handled as Shakespeare handled the suspicion of

* From *Selected Essays*, new edition, by T.S. Eliot.

Othello, the infatuation of Antony, or the pride of Coriolanus. The subject might conceivably have expanded into a tragedy like these, intelligible, self-complete, in the sunlight. *Hamlet*, like the sonnets, is full of some stuff that the writer could not drag to light, contemplate, or manipulate into art. And when we search for this feeling, we find it, as in the sonnets, very difficult to localize. You cannot point to it in the speeches; indeed, if you examine the two famous soliloquies you see the versification of Shakespeare, but a content which might be claimed by another, perhaps by the author of the *Revenge of Bussy d'Ambois*, Act v, sc. i. We find Shakespeare's Hamlet not in the action, not in any quotations that we might select, so much as in an unmistakable tone which is unmistakably not in the earlier play.

The only way of expressing emotion in the form of art is by finding an 'objective correlative'; in other words, a set of objects, a situation, a chain of events which shall be the formula of that *particular* emotion; such that when the external facts, which must terminate in sensory experience, are given, the emotion is immediately evoked. If you examine any of Shakespeare's more successful tragedies, you will find this exact equivalence; you will find that the state of mind of Lady Macbeth walking in her sleep has been communicated to you by a skilful accumulation of imagined sensory impressions; the words of Macbeth on hearing of his wife's death strikes us as if, given the sequence of events, these words were automatically released by the last event in the series. The artistic 'inevitability' lies in this complete adequacy of the external to the emotion; and this is precisely what is deficient in *Hamlet*. Hamlet (the man) is dominated by an emotion which is inexpressible, because it is in *excess* of the facts as they appear. And the supposed identity of Hamlet with his author is genuine to this point: that Hamlet's bafflement at the absence of objective equivalent to his feelings is a prolongation of the bafflement of his creator in the face of his artistic problem. Hamlet is up against the difficulty that his disgust is occasioned by his mother, but that his mother is not an adequate equivalent for it; his disgust envelops and exceeds her. It is thus a feeling which he cannot understand; he cannot objectify it, and it therefore remains to poison life and obstruct action. None of the possible actions can satisfy it; and nothing that Shakespeare can do with the plot can express Hamlet for him. And it must be noticed that the very nature of the *données* of the problem precludes objective equivalence. To have heightened the criminality of Gertrude would have been to provide the formula for a totally different emotion in Hamlet; it is just because her character is so negative and insignificant that she arouses in Hamlet the feeling which she is incapable of representing.

The 'madness' of Hamlet lay to Shakespeare's hand; in the earlier play a simple ruse, and to the end, we may presume, understood as a ruse by the audience. For Shakespeare it is less than madness and more than feigned. The levity of Hamlet, his repetition of phrase, his puns, are not part of a deliberate plan of dissimulation, but a form of emotional relief. In the character Hamlet it is the buffoonery of an emotion which can find no outlet in action; in the dramatist it is the buffoonery of an emotion which he cannot express in art. The intense feeling, ecstatic or terrible, without an object or exceeding its object, is something which every person of sensibility has known; it is doubtless a subject of study for pathologists. It often occurs in adolescence: the ordinary person puts these feelings to sleep, or trims down his feelings to fit the business world; the artist keeps them alive by his ability to intensify the world to his emotions. The Hamlet of Laforgue is an adolescent; the Hamlet of Shakespeare is not, he has not that explanation and excuse. We must simply admit that here Shakespeare tackled a problem which proved too much for him. Why he attempted it at all is an insoluble puzzle; under compulsion of what experience he attempted to express the inexpressibly horrible, we cannot ever know. We need a great many facts in his biography; and we should like to know whether, and when, and after or at the same time as what personal experience, he read Montaigne, ii. xii, *Apologie de Raimond Sebond*. We should have, finally, to know something which is by hypothesis unknowable, for we assume it to be an experience which, in the manner indicated, exceeded the facts. We should have to understand things which Shakespeare did not understand himself.

ROBERT FROST

THE FIGURE A POEM MAKES*

Abstraction is an old story with the philosophers, but it has been like a new toy in the hands of the artists of our day. Why can't we have any one quality of poetry we choose by itself? We can have in thought. Then it will go hard if we can't in practice. Our lives for it.

Granted no one but a humanist much cares how sound a poem is if it is only *a* sound. The sound is the gold in the ore. Then we will have the sound out alone and dispense with the inessential. We do till we make the discovery that the object in writing poetry is to make all poems sound as different as possible from each other, and the resources for that of vowels, consonants,

* From *Complete Poems of Robert Frost.*

punctuation, syntax, words, sentences, metre are not enough. We need the help of context—meaning—subject matter. That is the greatest help towards variety. All that can be done with words is soon told. So also with metres—particularly in our language where there are virtually but two, strict iambic and loose iambic. The ancients with many were still poor if they depended on metres for all tune. It is painful to watch our sprung-rhythmists straining at the point of omitting one short from a foot for relief from monotony. The possibilities for tune from the dramatic tones of meaning struck across the rigidity of a limited metre are endless. And we are back in poetry as merely one more art of having something to say, sound or unsound. Probably better if sound, because deeper and from wider experience.

Then there is this wildness whereof it is spoken. Granted again that it has an equal claim with sound to being a poem's better half. If it is a wild tune, it is a poem. Our problem then is, as modern abstractionists, to have the wildness pure; to be wild with nothing to be wild about. We bring up as aberrationists, giving way to undirected associations and kicking ourselves from one chance suggestion to another in all directions as of a hot afternoon in the life of a grasshopper. Theme alone can steady us down. Just as the final mystery was how a poem could have a tune in such a straightness as metre, so the second mystery is how a poem can have wildness and at the same time a subject that shall be fulfilled.

It should be of the pleasure of a poem itself to tell how it can. The figure a poem makes. It begins in delight and ends in wisdom. The figure is the same as for love. No one can really hold that the ecstasy should be static and stand still in one place. It begins in delight, it inclines to the impulse, it assumes direction with the first line laid down, it runs a course of lucky events, and ends in a clarification of life—not necessarily a great clarification, such as sects and cults are founded on, but in a momentary stay against confusion. It has denouement. It has an outcome that though unforeseen was predestined from the first image of the original mood—and indeed from the very mood. It is but a trick poem and no poem at all if the best of it was thought of first and saved for the last. It finds its own name as it goes and discovers the best waiting for it in some final phrase at once wise and sad—the happy-sad blend of the drinking song.

No tears in the writer, no tears in the reader. No surprise for the writer, no surprise for the reader. For me the initial delight is in the surprise of remembering something I didn't know I knew. I am in a place, in a situation, as if I had materialized from cloud or risen out of the ground. There is a glad recognition of the long lost and the rest follows. Step by step the wonder of unexpected supply keeps growing. The impressions most useful to my purpose seem always those I was unaware of and so made no note of at the time when taken, and the conclusion is come to that like giants we are always hurling experience ahead of us to pave the future with against the day when we may want to strike a line of purpose across it for somewhere. The line will have the more charm for not being mechanically straight. We enjoy the straight crookedness of a good walking stick. Modern instruments of precision are being used to make things crooked as if by eye and hand in the old days.

I tell how there may be a better wildness of logic than of inconsequence. But the logic is backward, in retrospect, after the act. It must be more felt than seen ahead like prophecy. It must be a revelation, or a series of revelations, as much for the poet as for the reader. For it to be that there must have been the greatest freedom of the material to move about in it and to establish relations in it regardless of time and space, previous relation, and everything but affinity. We prate of freedom. We call our schools free because we are not free to stay away from them till we are sixteen years of age. I have given up my democratic prejudices and now willingly set the lower classes free to be completely taken care of by the upper classes. Political freedom is nothing to me. I bestow it right and left. All I would keep for myself is the freedom of my material—the condition of body and mind now and then to summons aptly from the vast chaos of all I have lived through.

Scholars and artists thrown together are often annoyed at the puzzle of where they differ. Both work from knowledge; but I suspect they differ most importantly in the way their knowledge is come by. Scholars get theirs with conscientious thoroughness along projected lines of logic; poets theirs cavalierly and as it happens in and out of books. They stick to nothing deliberately, but let what will stick to them like burrs where they walk in the fields. No acquirement is on assignment, or even self-assignment. Knowledge of the second kind is much more available in the wild free ways of wit and art. A schoolboy may be defined as one who can tell you what he knows in the order in which he learned it. The artist must value himself as he snatches a thing from some previous order in time and space into a new order with not so much as a ligature clinging to it of the old place where it was organic.

More than once I should have lost my soul to radicalism if it had been the originality it was mistaken for by its young converts. Originality and initiative are what I ask for my country. For myself the originality need be no more than the freshness of a poem run in the way I have described: from delight to wisdom. The figure is the same as for love. Like a piece of ice on a hot stove the poem must ride on its own melting. A poem may be worked over once it is in being, but may not be worried into being. Its most precious quality will remain its having run itself and carried away the poet with it. Read it a hundred times: it will forever keep its freshness as a petal keeps its fragrance. It can never lose its sense of a meaning that once unfolded by surprise as it went.

Allen Ginsberg

Notes for Howl and Other Poems*

By 1955 I wrote poetry adapted from prose seeds, journals, scratchings, arranged by phrasing or breath groups into little short-line patterns according to ideas of measure of American speech I'd picked up from W.C. Williams's imagist preoccupations. I suddenly turned aside in San Francisco, unemployment compensation leisure, to follow my romantic inspiration—Hebraic-Melvillian bardic breath. I thought I wouldn't write a poem, but just write what I wanted to without fear, let my imagination go, open secrecy, and scribble magic lines from my real mind—sum up my life—something I wouldn't be able to show anybody, write for my own soul's ear and a few other golden ears. So the first line of 'Howl', 'I saw the best minds', etc. the whole first section typed out madly in one afternoon, a huge sad comedy of wild phrasing, meaningless images for the beauty of abstract poetry of mind running along making awkward combinations like Charlie Chaplin's walk, long saxophone-like chorus lines I knew Kerouac would hear *sound* of—taking off from his own inspired prose line really a new poetry.

I depended on the word 'who' to keep the beat, a base to keep measure, return to and take off from again onto another streak of invention: 'who lit cigarettes in boxcars boxcars boxcars', continuing to prophesy what I really knew despite the drear consciousness of the world: 'who were visionary indian angels'. Have I really been attacked for this sort of joy? So the poem got serious, I went on to what my imagination believed true to Eternity (for I'd had a beatific illumination years before during which I'd heard Blake's ancient voice & saw the universe unfold in my brain), & what my memory could reconstitute of the data of celestial experience.

But how sustain a long line in poetry (lest it lapse into prosaic)? It's natural inspiration of the moment that keeps it moving, disparate thinks put down together, shorthand notations of visual imagery, juxtapositions of hydrogen juke-box—abstract haikus sustain the mystery & put iron poetry back into the line: the last line of 'Sunflower Sutra' is the extreme, one stream of single word associations, summing up. Mind is shapely, Art is shapely. Meaning Mind practised in spontaneity invents forms in its own image & gets to Last Thoughts. Loose ghosts wailing for body try to invade the bodies of living men. I hear ghostly Academics in Limbo screeching about form.

* From *Fantasy* LP recording 7006 (1959).

Ideally each line of 'Howl' is a single breath unit. Tho in this recording it's not pronounced so, I was exhausted at climax of 3 hour Chicago reading with Corso & Orlovsky. My breath is long—that's the Measure, one physical—mental inspiration of thought contained in the elastic of a breath. It probably bugs Williams now, but it's a natural consequence, my own heightened conversation, not cooler average-dailytalk short breath. I got to mouth more madly this way.

So these poems are a series of experiments with the formal organization of the long line. Explanations follow. I realized at the time that Whitman's form had rarely been further explored (improved on even) in the U.S. Whitman always a mountain too vast to be seen. Everybody assumes (with Pound?) (except Jeffers) that his line is a big freakish uncontrollable necessary prosaic goof. No attempt's been made to use it in the light of early XX Century organization of new speech-rhythm prosody to *build up* large organic structures.

I had an apt on Nob Hill, got high on Peyote, & saw an image of the robot skullface of Moloch in the upper stories of a big hotel glaring into my window; got high weeks later again, the Visage was still there in red smokey downtown Metropolis, I wandered down Powell Street muttering, 'Moloch Moloch' all night & wrote 'Howl' ii nearly intact in cafeteria at foot of Drake Hotel, deep in the hellish vale. Here the long line is used as a stanza form broken within into exclamatory units punctuated by a base repetition, Moloch.

The rhythmic paradigm for Part iii was conceived & half-written same day as the beginning of 'Howl', I went back later & filled it out. Part i, a lament for the Lamb in America with instances of remarkable lamblike youths; Part ii names the monster of mental consciousness that preys on the Lamb; Part iii a litany of affirmation of the Lamb in its glory: 'O starry spangled shock of Mercy.' The structure of Part iii, pyramidal, with a graduated longer response to the fixed base. . . .

A lot of these forms developed out of an extreme rhapsodic wail I once heard in a madhouse. Later I wondered if short quiet lyrical poems could be written using the long line. 'Cottage in Berkeley' & 'Supermarket in California' (written same day) fell in place later that year. Not purposely, I simply followed my Angel in the course of compositions.

What if I just simply wrote, in long units & broken short lines, spontaneously noting prosaic realities mixed with emotional upsurges, solitaries? *Transcription of Organ Music* (sensual data), strange writing which passes from prose to poetry & back, like the mind.

What about poem with rhythmic buildup power equal to 'Howl' without use of repeated base to sustain it? The 'Sunflower Sutra' (composition time 20 minutes, me at desk scribbling, Kerouac at cottage door waiting for me to finish so we could go off somewhere party) did that, it surprised me, one long Who . . .

Last, the Proem to 'Kaddish' (NY 1959 work)—finally, completely free composition, the long line breaking up within itself into short staccato breath units—notations of one spontaneous phrase after another linked within the line by dashes mostly: the long line now perhaps a variable stanzaic unit, measuring groups of related ideas, marking them—a method of notation. Ending with a hymn in rhythm similar to the synagogue death lament. Passing into dactyllic? says Williams? Perhaps not: at least the ear hears itself in Promethian natural measure, not in mechanical count of accent. . . .

A word on Academies; poetry has been attacked by an ignorant & frightened bunch of bores who don't understand how it's made, & the trouble with these creeps is they wouldn't know Poetry if it came up and buggered them in broad daylight.

A word on the Politicians: my poetry is Angelical Ravings, & has nothing to do with dull materialistic vagaries about who should shoot who. The secrets of individual imagination—which are transconceptual & non-verbal—I mean unconditioned Spirit—are not for sale to this consciousness, are of no use to this world, except perhaps to make it shut its trap & listen to the music of the Spheres. Who denies the music of the spheres denies poetry, denies man, & spits on Blake, Shelley, Christ, & Buddha. Meanwhile have a ball. The universe is a new flower. America will be discovered. Who wants a war against roses will have it. Fate tells big lies, & the gay Creator dances on his own body in Eternity.

SEAMUS HEANEY

FEELINGS INTO WORDS*

I am uneasy about speaking under the general heading of 'innovation in contemporary literature'. Much as I would like to think of myself as breaking new ground, I find on looking at what I have done that it is mostly concerned with reclaiming old ground. My intention here is to retrace some of my paths into that ground, to investigate what William Wordsworth called 'the hiding places':

* A lecture delivered to The Royal Society of Literature, 17 October 1974.

the hiding places of my power
Seem open; I approach, and then they close;
I see glimpses now; when age comes on,
May scarcely see at all, and I would give,
While yet we may, as far as words can give,
A substance and a life to what I feel:
I would enshrine the spirit of the past
For future restoration.

Implicit in those lines is a view of poetry which I think is also implicit in the few poems I have written that give me any right to be here addressing you: poetry as divination; poetry as revelation of the self to the self, as restoration of the culture to itself; poems as elements of continuity, with the aura and authenticity of archaeological finds, where the buried shard has an importance that is not obliterated by the buried city; poetry as a dig, a dig for finds that end up being plants.

'Digging' in fact, was the name of the first poem I wrote where I thought my feelings got into words, or, to put it more accurately, where I thought my *feel* had got into words. Its rhythms and noises still please me, although there are a couple of lines in it that have the theatricality of the gunslinger rather than the self-absorption of the digger. I wrote it in the summer of 1964, almost two years after I had begun to dabble in verses, and as Patrick Kavanagh said, a man dabbles in verses and finds they are his life. This was the first place where I felt I had done more than make an arrangement of words: I felt that I had let down a shaft into real life. The facts and surfaces of the thing were true, but more important, the excitement that came from naming them gave me a kind of insouciance and a kind of confidence. I didn't care who thought what about it: somehow, it had surprised me by coming out with a stance and an idea that I would stand over:

The cold smell of potato mould, the squelch and slap
Of soggy peat, the curt cuts of an edge
Through living roots awaken in my head.
But I've no spade to follow men like them.

Between my finger and my thumb
The squat pen rests.
I'll dig with it.

As I say, I wrote it down ten years ago; yet perhaps I should say that I dug it up, because I have come to realize that it was laid down in me years before that even. The pen/spade analogy was the simple heart of the matter, and *that* was simply a matter of almost proverbial common sense. People used to ask a child on the road to and from school what class you were in and how many slaps you'd got that day, and invariably they ended up with an exhortation to keep studying because 'learning's easy carried' and 'the pen's lighter than the spade'. And the poem does no more than allow that bud of wisdom to exfoliate, although the significant point in this context is that at the time of writing I was not aware of the proverbial structure at the back of my mind. Nor was I aware that the poem was an enactment of yet another digging metaphor that came back to me years later. This was a rhyme that also had a currency on the road to school, though again we were not fully aware of what we were dealing with:

'Are your praties dry
And are they fit for digging?'
'Put in your spade and try,'
Says Dirty-Face McGuigan.

Well, digging there becomes a sexual metaphor, an emblem of initiation, like putting your hand into the bush or robbing the nest, one of the various natural analogies for uncovering and touching the hidden thing. I now believe that the 'Digging' poem had for me the force of an initiation: the confidence I mentioned arose from a sense that perhaps I could work this poetry thing, too, and having experienced the excitement and release of it once, I was doomed to look for it again and again.

I don't want to overload 'Digging' with too much significance. I know as well as you do that it is a big coarse-grained navvy of a poem, but it is interesting as an example—and not just as an example of what one reviewer called 'mud-caked fingers in Russell Square', for I don't think that the subject matter has any particular virtue in itself; it is interesting as an example of what we call 'finding a voice'.

Finding a voice means that you can get your own feelings into your own words and that your words have the feel of you about them; and I believe that it may not even be a metaphor, for a poetic voice is probably very intimately connected with the poet's natural voice, the voice that he hears as the ideal speaker of the lines he is making up. I would like to digress slightly in order to illustrate what I mean more fully.

In his novel *The First Circle*, Solzhenitsyn sets the action in a prison camp on the outskirts of Moscow where the inmates are all highly skilled technicians forced to labor at projects devised by Stalin. The most important of these is an attempt to invent a mechanism to bug a phone. But what is to be special about this particular bugging device is that it will not simply record the voice and the message, but that it will identify the essential sound patterns of the speaker's voice; it will discover, in the words of the narrative, 'what it is that makes every human voice unique' so that no matter how he disguises his accent or changes his language, the fundamental structure of his voice will be caught. The idea was that a voice is like a fingerprint, possessing a constant and unique signature that can, like a fingerprint, be recorded and employed for identification.

Now, one of the purposes of a literary education as I experienced it was to turn your ear into a poetic bugging device, so that a piece of verse denuded of name and date could be identified by its diction, tropes, and cadences. And this secret policing of English verse was also based on the idea of a style as a signature. But what I wish to suggest is that there is a connection between the core of a poet's speaking voice and the core of his poetic voice, between his original accent and his discovered style. I think that the discovery of a way of writing that is natural and adequate to your sensibility depends on the recovery of that essential quirk which Solzhenitsyn's technicians were trying to pin down. This is the absolute register to which your proper music has to be tuned.

How, then, do you find it? In practice, you hear it coming from somebody else, you hear something in another writer's sounds that flows in through your ear and enters the echo chamber of your head and delights your whole nervous system in such a way that your reaction will be, 'Ah, I wish I had said that, in that particular way.' This other writer, in fact, has spoken something essential to you, something you recognize instinctively as a true sounding of aspects of yourself and your experience. And your first steps as a writer will be to imitate, consciously or unconsciously, those sounds that flowed in, that in-fluence.

. . .

I think technique is different from craft. Craft is what you can learn from other verse. Craft is the skill of making. It wins competitions in *The New Statesman*. It can be deployed without reference to the feelings or the self. It knows how to keep up a capable verbal athletic display; it can be content to be *vox et praeterea nihil*—all voice and nothing else, but not voice as in 'finding a voice'. Learning the craft is learning to turn the windlass at the well of poetry. Usually you begin by dropping the bucket halfway down the shaft and winding up a taking of air. You are miming the real thing until one day the chain draws unexpectedly tight, and you have dipped into waters that will continue to entice you back. You'll have broken the skin on the pool of yourself. Your praties will be 'fit for digging'.

At that point it becomes appropriate to speak of technique rather than craft. Technique, as I would define it, involves not only a poet's way with words, his management of meter, rhythm, and verbal texture; it involves also a definition of his stance toward life, a definition of his own reality. It involves the discovery of ways to go out of his normal cognitive bounds and raid the inarticulate: a dynamic alertness that mediates between the origins of feeling in memory and experience and the formal ploys that express these in a work of art. Technique entails the watermarking of your essential patterns of perception, voice, and thought into the touch and texture of your lines; it is that whole creative effort of the mind's and body's resources to bring the meaning of experience within the jurisdiction of form. Technique is what turns, in Yeats's phrase, 'the bundle of accident and incoherence that sits down to breakfast' into 'an idea, something intended, complete'.

It is indeed conceivable that a poet could have a real technique and a wobbly craft—I think this was true of Alun Lewis and Patrick Kavanagh—but more often it's a case of sure-enough craft and a failure of technique. And if I were asked for a figure who represents pure technique, I would say a water diviner. You can't learn the craft of dousing or divining—it's a gift for being in touch with what is there, hidden and real, a gift for mediating between the latent resource and the community that wants it current and released.

• • •

I suppose technique is what allows that first stirring of the mind round a word or an image or a memory to grow toward articulation, articulation not necessarily in terms of argument or explication but in terms of its own potential for harmonious self-reproduction. The seminal excitement has to be granted conditions in which, in Hopkins' words, it 'selves, goes itself . . . crying What I do is for me, for that I came.' Technique ensures that the first gleam attains its proper effulgence. And I don't just mean a felicity in the choice of words to flesh the theme—that is a problem also, but it is not so critical. A poem can survive stylistic blemishes, but it cannot survive a stillbirth. The crucial action is pre-verbal: to be able to allow the first alertness or come-hither, sensed in a blurred or incomplete way, to dilate and approach as a thought or a theme or a phrase. Frost put it this way: 'A poem begins as a lump in the throat, a homesickness, a lovesickness. It finds the thought and the thought finds the words.' As far as I'm concerned, technique is more vitally and sensitively connected with that first activity where the 'lump in throat' finds 'the thought' than with 'the thought' finding 'the words'. That first epiphany involves the divining, vatic, oracular function; the second, the making, crafting function.

To say, as Auden did, that a poem is a 'verbal contraption' is to keep one or two tricks up your sleeve.

Traditionally, an oracle speaks in riddles, yielding its truths in disguise, offering its insights cunningly. And in the practice of poetry, there is a corresponding occasion of disguise, a protean, chameleon moment when the lump in the throat takes protective coloring in the new element of thought. . . .

• • •

In practice . . . you proceed by your own experience of what it is to write what you consider a successful poem. You survive in your own esteem not by the corroboration of theory but by the trust in certain moments of satisfaction that you know intuitively are moments of extension. You are confirmed by the visitation of the last poem and threatened by the elusiveness of the next one, and the best moments are those when your mind seems to implode and words and images rush of their own accord into the vortex. Which happened to me once when the line 'We have no prairies' drifted into my head at bedtime and loosened a fall of images that constitute the poem 'Bogland', the last one in *Door into the Dark*.

I had been vaguely wishing to write a poem about bogland, chiefly because it is a landscape that has a strange assuaging effect on me, one with associations reaching back into early childhood. We used to hear about bog-butter, butter kept fresh for a great number of years under the peat. Then when I was at school the skeleton of an elk had been taken out of a bog nearby, and a few of our neighbors had got their photographs in the paper, peering out across its antlers. So I began to get an idea of bog as the memory of the landscape, or as a landscape that remembered everything that happened in and to it. In fact, if you go round the National Museum in Dublin, you will realize that a great proportion of the most cherished material heritage of Ireland was 'found in a bog'. Moreover, since memory was the faculty that supplied me with the first quickening of my own poetry, I had a tentative unrealized need to make a congruence between memory and bogland and, for the want of a better word, our national consciousness. And it all released itself after 'We have no prairies . . .'—but we have bogs.

At that time I was teaching modern literature in Queen's University, Belfast, and had been reading about the frontier and the West as an important myth in the American consciousness, so I set up—or, rather, laid down—the bog as an answering Irish myth. I wrote it quickly the next morning, having slept on my excitement, and revised it on the hoof, from line to line, as it came.

• • •

Again, as in the case of 'Digging', the seminal impulse had been unconscious. I believe what generated the poem about memory was something lying beneath the very floor of memory, something I connected with the poem only months after it was written, which was a warning that older people would give us about going into the bog. They were afraid we might fall into the pools in the old workings, so they put it about (and we believed them) that *there was no bottom* in the bogholes. Little did they—or I—know that I would filch it for the last line of a book.

There was also in that book a poem called 'Requiem for the Croppies', which was written in 1966 when most poets in Ireland were straining to celebrate the anniversary of the 1916 Uprising. Typically, I suppose I went farther back. Nineteen sixteen was the harvest of seeds sown in 1798, when revolutionary republican ideals and national feeling coalesced in the doctrines of Irish republicanism and in the rebellion of 1798 itself—unsuccessful and savagely put down. The poem was born of and ended with an image of resurrection based on the fact that some time after the rebels were buried in common graves, these graves began to sprout with young barley, growing up from barley corn the 'croppies' had carried in their pockets to eat while on the march. The oblique implication was that the seeds of violent resistance sowed in the Year of Liberty had flowered in what Yeats called 'the right rose tree' of 1916. I did not realize at the time that the original heraldic murderous encounter between Protestant yeoman and Catholic rebel was to be initiated again in the summer of 1969, in Belfast, two months after the book was published.

From that moment, the problems of poetry moved from being simply a matter of achieving the satisfactory verbal icon to being a search for images and symbols adequate to our predicament. I do not mean liberal lamentation that citizens should feel compelled to murder one another or deploy their different military arms over the matter of nomenclatures, such as British or Irish. I do not mean public celebrations or execrations of resistance or atrocity—although there is nothing necessarily unpoetic about such celebration, if one thinks of 'Easter 1916'. I mean that I felt it imperative to discover a field of force in which, without abandoning fidelity to the processes and experience of poetry as I have outlined them, it would be possible to encompass the perspectives of a humane reason and, at the same time, to grant the religious intensity of the violence its deplorable authenticity and complexity. And when I say religious, I am not thinking simply of the sectarian division. To some extent the enmity can be viewed as a struggle between the cults and devotees of a god and a goddess. There is an indigenous territorial numen, a tutelar of the whole island—call her Mother Ireland, Kathleen Ni Houlihan, the poor old woman, the Shan Van Vocht, whatever—and her sovereignty has been temporarily usurped or infringed by a new male cult whose founding fathers were Cromwell, William of Orange, and Edward Carson, and whose godhead is incarnate in a rex or caesar resident in a palace in London. What we have is the tail end of a struggle in a province between territorial piety and imperial power.

Now, I realize that this idiom is remote from the agnostic world of economic interest whose iron hand operates in the velvet glove of 'talks between elected representatives', and remote from the political maneuvers of power-sharing; but it is not remote from the psychology of the Irishmen and Ulstermen who do the killing, and not remote from the bankrupt psychology and mythologies implicit in the terms Irish Catholic and Ulster Protestant. The question, as ever, is 'How with this rage shall beauty hold a plea?' And my answer is, by offering 'befitting emblems of adversity'.

Some of those emblems I found in a book that was published here, appositely, the year the killing started, in 1969. And again appositely, it was entitled *The Bog People*. It was chiefly concerned with preserved bodies of men and women found in the bogs of Jutland, naked, strangled, or with their throats cut, disposed under the peat since early Iron Age times. The author, P. V. Glob, argues convincingly that a number of these, and, in particular, the Tollund Man, whose head is now preserved near Aarhus in the museum at Silkeborg, were ritual sacrifices to the Mother Goddess, the goddess of the ground who needed new bridegrooms each winter to bed with her in her sacred place, in the bog, to ensure the renewal and fertility of the territory in the spring. Taken in relation to the tradition of Irish political martyrdom for the cause whose icon is Kathleen Ni Houlihan, this is more than an archaic barbarous rite; it is an archetypal pattern. And the unforgettable photographs of these victims blended in my mind with photographs of atrocities, past and present, in the long rites of Irish political and religious struggles. When I wrote this poem, I had a completely new sensation: one of fear. It is a vow to go on pilgrimage, and I felt as it came to me—and again it came quickly—that unless I was deeply in earnest about what I was saying, I was simply invoking dangers for myself. It is called 'The Tollund Man'.

• • •

And just how persistent the barbaric attitudes are, not only in the slaughter but in the psyche, I discovered, again when the frisson of the poem itself had passed, and indeed after I had fulfilled the vow and gone to Jutland, 'the holy blisful martyr for to seeke'. I read the following in a chapter on 'The Religion of the Pagan Celts' by the Celtic scholar Anne Ross:

> Moving from sanctuaries and shrines...we come now to consider the nature of the actual deities . . . But before going on to look at the nature of some of the individual deities and their cults, one can perhaps bridge the gap as it were by considering a symbol which, in its way, sums up the whole of Celtic pagan religion and is as representative of it as is, for example, the sign of the cross in Christian contexts. This is the symbol of the severed human head; in all its various modes of iconographic representation and verbal presentation, one may find the hard core of Celtic religion. It is indeed . . . a kind of shorthand symbol for the entire religious outlook of the pagan Celts.

My sense of occasion and almost awe as I vowed to go to pray to the Tollund Man and assist at his enshrined head had a longer ancestry than I had at the time realized.

I began by suggesting that my point of view involved poetry as divination, as a restoration of the culture to itself. In Ireland in this century it has involved for Yeats and many others an attempt to define and interpret the present by bringing it into significant relationship with the past, and I believe that effort in our present circumstances has to be urgently renewed. But here we stray from the realm of technique into the realm of tradition; to forge a poem is one thing, to forge the uncreated conscience of the race, as Stephen Dedalus put it, is quite another, and places daunting pressures and responsibilities on anyone who would risk the name of poet.

(1974)

TED HUGHES

ON POETRY*

. . . In each poem, besides the principal subject—and in my poems this is usually pretty easy to see, as, for instance, the jaguar in the poem called 'The Jaguar'—there is what is not so easy to talk about, even generally, but which is the living and individual element in every poet's work. What I mean is the way he brings to peace all the feelings and energies which, from all over the body, heart, and brain, send up their champions onto the battleground of that

* From Hughes' essays and interviews in Ekbert Faas's *Ted Hughes: The Unaccommodated Universe* (1980).

first subject. The way I do this, as I believe, is by using something like the method of a musical composer. I might say that I turn every combatant into a bit of music, then resolve the whole uproar into as formal and balanced a figure of melody and rhythm as I can. When all the words are hearing each other clearly, and every stress is feeling every other stress, and all are contented—the poem is finished . . .

• • •

There is a great mass of English poetry in which the musical element—the inner figure of stresses—is not so important as other elements. To me—no matter what metaphysical persuasion or definable philosophy a poem may seem to subscribe to—what is unique and precious in it is its heart, that inner figure of stresses . . .

(1957)

The poet's only hope is to be infinitely sensitive to what his gift is, and this in itself seems to be another gift that few poets possess. According to this sensitivity, and to his faith in it, he will go on developing as a poet, as Yeats did, pursuing those adventures, mental, spiritual and physical, whatever they may be, that his gift wants, or he will lose his guidance, lose the feel of its touch in the workings of his mind, and soon be absorbed by the impersonal dead lumber of matters in which his gift has no interest, which is a form of suicide, metaphorical in the case of Wordsworth and Coleridge, actual in the case of Mayakovsky.

Many considerations assault his faith in the finality, wisdom and sufficiency of his gift. Its operation is not only shadowy and indefinable, it is intermittent, it has none of the obvious attachment to publicly exciting and seemingly important affairs that his other mental activities have and in which all his intelligent contemporaries have such confidence, and so it receives no immediate encouragement—or encouragement only of the most dubious kind, as a flagellant, questioning his illuminations, might be encouraged by a bunch of mad old women and some other half-dead gory flagellant; it visits him when he is only half suspecting it, and he is not sure it has visited him until some days or months afterwards and perhaps he never can be sure, being a sensible man aware of the examples of earlier poets and of the devils of self-delusion and of the delusions of whole generations. . . .

(1962)

. . . Technique is not a machine to do work, like a car engine that runs best of all with little or no load, but the act of work being done. So-called 'technique without substance' is our polite word for fakery, or the appearance of something happening that is not happening, and attracts our attention at all only because we will look for some minutes at absolutely anything that seems to say 'look at me', so humble and great is our hope.

• • •

In our time, the heroic struggle is not to become a hero but to remain a living creature simply. The Scientific Spirit has bitten so many of us in the nape, and pumped us full of its eggs, the ferocious virus of abstraction. We yield to the larvae, warmly numbed, and we all speak well of them and their parent. The Scientific Spirit, as we say, is hard-headed, it fears nothing, it faces the facts, and how it has improved our comforts! And yet what is this master of ours? The Scientific Spirit was born of the common hunt for the nourishing morsel, nursed by the benign search for objective truth, schooled in the pedagogic idolatry of the objective fact, graduated through old-maid specialised research, losing eyes, ears, smell, taste, touch, nerves and blood, adapting to the sensibility of electronic gadgets and the argument of numbers, to become a machine of senility, a pseudo-automaton in the House of the Mathematical Absolute. So it ousts humanity from man and he dedicates his life to the laws of the electron in vacuo, a literal self-sacrifice, and soon, by bigotry and the especially rabid evangelism of the inhuman, a literal world-sacrifice, as we all too truly now fear. Any artist who resists the suction into this galactic firestorm and holds to bodily wholeness and the condition of the creature, finds ranged against him the worldly powers of our age and everything that is not the suffering vitality of nature. The victims of radio-activity and of the death camps, the corpse of a bird, an agony too private to name, become the only unequivocal portraits of life, of the Angel a hundred faces behind the human face. In this way, the particular misery and disaster of our time are, uniquely, the perfect conditions for the purest and most intense manifestation of the spirit, the Angel, the ghost of ashes, the survivor of the Creation. . . .

(1962)

Any form of violence—any form of vehement activity—invokes the bigger energy, the elemental power circuit of the Universe. Once the contact has been made—it becomes difficult to control. Something from beyond ordinary human activity enters. When the wise men know how to create rituals and dogma, the energy can be contained. When the old rituals and dogma have lost credit and disintegrated, and no new ones have been formed, the energy cannot be contained, and so its effect is destructive—and that is the position with us. And that is why force of any kind frightens our rationalist, humanist style of outlook. In the old world God and divine power were invoked at any cost—life seemed worthless without them. In the present world we dare not invoke them—we wouldn't know how to use them or stop them destroying us. We have settled for the minimum practical energy and illumination—anything bigger introduces problems, the demons get hold of it. That is the psychological stupidity, the ineptitude, of the rigidly rationalist outlook—it's a form of hubris, and we're paying the traditional price. If you refuse the energy, you are living a kind of death. If you accept the energy, it destroys you. What is the alternative? To accept the energy, and find methods of turning it to good, of keeping it under control—rituals, the machinery of religion. The old method is the only one.

• • •

Every writer if he develops at all develops either outwards into society and history, using wider and more material of that sort, or he develops inwards into imagination and beyond that into spirit, using perhaps no more external material than before and maybe even less, but deepening it and making it operate in the many different inner dimensions until it opens up perhaps the religious or holy basis of the whole thing. Or he can develop both ways simultaneously. Developing inwardly, of course, means organizing the inner world or at least searching out the patterns there and that is a mythology. It may be an original mythology. Or you may uncover the Cross—as Eliot did. The ideal aspect of Yeats' development is that he managed to develop his poetry both outwardly into history and the common imagery of everyday life at the same time as he developed it inwardly in a sort of close parallel. . . . so that he could speak of both simultaneously. His mythology is history, pretty well, and his history is as he said 'the story of a soul'. . . .

You choose a subject because it serves, because you need it. We go on writing poems because one poem never gets the whole account right. There is always something missed. At the end of the ritual up comes a goblin. Anyway within a week the whole thing has changed, one needs a fresh bulletin. And works go dead, fishing has to be abandoned, the shoal has moved on. While we struggle with a fragmentary Orestes some complete Bacchae moves past too deep down to hear. We get news of it later . . . too late. In the end, one's poems are ragged dirty undated letters from remote battles and weddings and one thing and another.

• • •

The first idea of *Crow* was really an idea of a style. In folktales the prince going on the adventure comes to the stable full of beautiful horses and he needs a horse for the next stage and the king's daughter advises him to take none of the beautiful horses that he'll be offered but to choose the dirty, scabby little foal. You see, I throw out the eagles and choose the Crow. The idea was originally just to write his songs, the songs that a Crow would sing. In other words, songs with no music whatsoever, in a super-simple and a super-ugly language which would in a way shed everything except just what he wanted to say without any other consideration and that's the basis of the style of the whole thing. I get near it in a few poems. There I really begin to get what I was after.

(1970)

. . . And my follow-up to 'View of a Pig' was 'Pike'. But that poem immediately became much more charged with particular memories and a specific obsession. And my sense of 'Hawk Roosting' was that somehow or other it had picked up the prototype style behind 'View of a Pig' and 'Pike' without that overlay of a heavier, thicker, figurative language. Anyway, they were written in that succession, so that I got to 'Hawk Roosting' through those other two poems. All three were written in a mood of impatience, deliberately trying to destroy the ways in which I had written before, trying to write in a way that had nothing to do with the way in which I thought I ought to be writing. But then, that too became deliberate and a dead end.

Almost all the poems in *Lupercal* were written as invocations to writing. My main consciousness in those days was that it was impossible to write. So these invocations were just attempts to crack the apparent impossibility of producing anything . . . it culminated a deliberate effort to find a simple concrete language with no words in it over which I didn't have complete ownership: a limited language, but authentic to me. So in my ordinary exercise of writing I felt that the *Lupercal* style simply excluded too much of what I wanted to say. But the 'Hawk Roosting' style offered infinite expansion and flexibility. It was just too difficult a road, in my circumstances. It needed a state of concentration which I was evidently unable to sustain. So I preferred to look for a different way in. *Wodwo* was one way of looking for the new ground with the old equipment. While *Crow* was the discovery of a style as close and natural to me as the *Lupercal* style, but then again I set off with an attempt to simplify it . . . with the idea of reintroducing, once I'd got control of it, all the perceptions and material I'd been able to use in the *Lupercal* style. I never got that far.

• • •

I did that [*Oedipus*] in the middle of writing those Crow pieces. And that turned out to be useful. Because it was a simple story, so that at every moment the actual writing of it was under a specific type and weight of feeling. It gave me a very sharp sense of how the language had to be hardened or deepened so it could take the weight of the feeling running in the story. After a first draft I realized that all the language I had used was too light. So there was another draft and then another one. And as I worked on it, it turned into a process of more and more simplifying, or in a way limiting the language. I ended up with something like three hundred words, the smallest vocabulary Gielgud had ever worked with. And that ran straight into *Crow*. However, it was a way of concentrating my actual writing rather than of bringing me to any language that was then useful in *Crow*. It simply concentrated me. That was probably its main use. It gave me a very clear job to work on continually, at top pressure. You knew when you had got it and when you hadn't and it was lots of hours you could put into it. And all that momentum and fitness I got from it, I could then use on those shorter sprints.

• • •

So it is not the story that I am interested in but the poems. In other words, the whole narrative is just a way of getting a big body of ideas and energy moving on a track. For when this energy connects with a possibility for a poem, there is a lot more material and pressure in it than you could ever get into a poem just written out of the air or out of a special occasion. Poems come to you much more naturally and accumulate more life when they are part of a connected flow of real narrative that you've got yourself involved in. . . .

(1977)

DENISE LEVERTOV

SOME NOTES ON ORGANIC FORM (1965)

For me, back of the idea of organic form is the concept that there is a form in all things (and in our experience) which the poet can discover and reveal. There are no doubt temperamental differences between poets who use prescribed forms and those who look for new ones—people who need a tight schedule to get anything done, and people who have to have a free hand—but the difference in their conception of 'content' or 'reality' is functionally more important. On the one hand is the idea that content, reality, experience, is essentially fluid and must be given form; on the other, this sense of seeking out inherent, though not immediately apparent, form. Gerard Manley

Hopkins invented the word 'inscape' to denote intrinsic form, the pattern of essential characteristics both in single objects and (what is more interesting) in objects in a state of relation to each other, and the word 'instress' to denote the experiencing of the perception of inscape, the apperception of inscape. In thinking of the process of poetry as I know it, I extend the use of these words, which he seems to have used mainly in reference to sensory phenomena, to include intellectual and emotional experience as well; I would speak of the inscape of an experience (which might be composed of any and all of these elements, including the sensory) or of the inscape of a sequence or constellation of experiences.

A partial definition, then, of organic poetry might be that it is a method of apperception, i.e., of recognizing what we perceive, and is based on an intuition of an order, a form beyond forms, in which forms partake, and of which man's creative works are analogies, resemblances, natural allegories. Such poetry is exploratory.

How does one go about such a poetry? I think it's like this: first there must be an experience, a sequence or constellation of perceptions of sufficient interest, felt by the poet intensely enough to demand of him their equivalence in words: he is *brought to speech*. Suppose there's the sight of the sky through a dusty window, birds and clouds and bits of paper flying through the sky, the sound of music from his radio, feelings of anger and love and amusement roused by a letter just received, the memory of some long-past thought or event associated with what's seen or heard or felt, and an idea, a concept, he has been pondering, each qualifying the other; together with what he knows about history; and what he has been dreaming—whether or not he remembers it—working in him. This is only a rough outline of a possible moment in a life. But the condition of being a poet is that periodically such a cross section, or constellation, of experiences (in which one or another element may predominate) demands, or wakes in him this demand: the poem. The beginning of the fulfilment of this demand is to contemplate, to meditate; words which connote a state in which the heat of feeling warms the intellect. To contemplate comes from '*templum*, temple, a place, a space for observation, marked out by the augur'. It means, not simply to observe, to regard, but to do these things in the presence of a god. And to meditate is 'to keep the mind in a state of contemplation'; its synonym is 'to muse', and to muse comes from a word meaning 'to stand with open mouth'—not so comical if we think of 'inspiration'—to breathe in.

So—as the poet stands open-mouthed in the temple of life, contemplating his experience, there come to him the first words of the poem: the words which are to be his way in to the poem, if there is to be a poem. The pressure of demand and the meditation on its elements culminate in a moment of vision, of crystallization, in which some inkling of the correspondence between those elements occurs; and it occurs as words. If he forces a beginning before this point, it won't work. These words sometimes remain the first, sometimes in the completed poem their eventual place may be elsewhere, or they may turn out to have been only forerunners, which fulfilled their function in bringing him to the words which are the actual beginning of the poem. It is faithful attention to the experience from the first moment of crystallization that allows those first or those forerunning words to rise to the surface: and with that same fidelity of attention the poet, from that moment of being let in to the possibility of the poem, must follow through, letting the experience lead him through the world of the poem, its unique inscape revealing itself as he goes.

During the writing of a poem the various elements of the poet's being are in communion with each other, and heightened. Ear and eye, intellect and passion, interrelate more subtly than at other times; and the 'checking for accuracy', for precision of language, that must take place throughout the writing is not a matter of one element supervising the others but of intuitive interaction between all the elements involved.

In the same way, content and form are in a state of dynamic interaction; the understanding of whether an experience is a linear sequence or a constellation raying out from and into a central focus or axis, for instance, is discoverable only in the work, not before it.

Rhyme, chime, echo, reiteration: they not only serve to knit the elements of an experience but often are the very means, the sole means, by which the density of texture and the returning or circling of perception can be transmuted into language, apperceived. A may lead to E directly through B, C, and D: but if then there is the sharp remembrance or revisioning of A, this return must find its metric counterpart. It could do so by actual repetition of the words that spoke of A the first time (and if this return occurs more than once, one finds oneself with a refrain—not put there because one decided to write something with a refrain at the end of each stanza, but directly because of the demand of the content). Or it may be that since the return to A is now conditioned by the journey through B, C, and D, its words will not be a simple repetition but a variation. . . . Again, if B and D are of a complementary nature, then their thought- or feeling-rhyme may find its corresponding word-rhyme. Corresponding images are a kind of nonaural rhyme. It usually happens that within the whole, that is between the point of crystallization that marks the beginning or onset of a poem and the point at which the intensity of contemplation has ceased, there are distinct units of awareness; and it is—for me anyway—these that indicate the duration of stanzas. Sometimes these units are of such equal duration that one gets a whole poem of, say, three-line stanzas, a regularity of pattern that looks, but is not, predetermined.

When my son was eight or nine I watched him make a crayon drawing of a tournament. He was not interested in the forms as such, but was grappling with the need to speak in graphic terms, to say, 'And a great crowd of people were watching the jousting knights.' There was a need to show the tiers of seats, all those people sitting in them. And out of the need arose a formal design that was beautiful—composed of the rows of shoulders and heads. It is in very much the same way that there can arise, out of fidelity to instress, a design that is the form of the poem—both its total form, its length and pace and tone, and the form of its parts (e.g., the rhythmic relationships of syllables within the line, and of line to line; the sonic relationships of vowels and consonants; the recurrence of images, the play of associations, etc.). 'Form follows function' (Louis Sullivan).

Frank Lloyd Wright in his autobiography wrote that the idea of organic architecture is that 'the reality of the building lies in the space within it, to be lived in.' And he quotes Coleridge: 'Such as the life is, such is the form.' (Emerson says in his essay 'Poetry and Imagination', 'Ask the fact for the form.') The *Oxford English Dictionary* quotes Huxley (Thomas, presumably) as stating that he used the word organic 'almost as an equivalent for the word "living".'

In organic poetry the metric movement, the measure, is the direct expression of the movement of perception. And the sounds, acting together with the measure, are a kind of extended onomatopoeia—i.e., they imitate not the sounds of an experience (which may well be soundless, or to which sounds contribute only incidentally), but the feeling of an experience, its emotional tone, its texture. The varying speed and gait of different strands of perception within an experience (I think of strands of seaweed moving within a wave) result in counterpointed measures.

Thinking about how organic poetry differs from free verse, I wrote that 'most free verse is failed organic poetry, that is, organic poetry from which the attention of the writer had been switched off too soon, before the intrinsic form of the experience had been revealed.' But Robert Duncan pointed out to me that there is a 'free verse' of which this is not true, because it is written not with any desire to seek a form, indeed perhaps with the longing to avoid form (if that were possible) and to express inchoate emotion as purely as possible.* There is a contradiction here, however, because if, as I suppose, there is an

* See, for instance, some of the forgotten poets of the early 20s—also, some of Amy Lowell—Sandburg—John Gould Fletcher. Some Imagist poems were written in 'free verse' in this sense, but by no means all.

inscape of emotion, of feeling, it is impossible to avoid presenting something of it if the rhythm or tone of the feeling is given voice in the poem. But perhaps the difference is this: that free verse isolates the 'rightness' of each line or cadence—if it seems expressive, then never mind the relation of it to the next; while in organic poetry the peculiar rhythms of the parts are in some degree modified, if necessary, in order to discover the rhythm of the whole.

But doesn't the character of the whole depend on, arise out of, the character of the parts? It does; but it is like painting from nature: suppose you absolutely imitate, on the palette, the separate colours of the various objects you are going to paint; yet when they are closely juxtaposed in the actual painting, you may have to lighten, darken, cloud, or sharpen each colour in order to produce an effect equivalent to what you see in nature. Air, light, dust, shadow, and distance have to be taken into account.

Or one could put it this way: in organic poetry the form sense or 'traffic sense', as Stefan Wolpe speaks of it, is ever present along with (yes, paradoxically) fidelity to the revelations of meditation. The form sense is a sort of Stanislavsky of the imagination: putting a chair two feet downstage there, thickening a knot of bystanders upstage left, getting this actor to raise his voice a little and that actress to enter more slowly; all in the interest of a total form he intuits. Or it is a sort of helicopter scout flying over the field of the poem, taking aerial photos and reporting on the state of the forest and its creatures—or over the sea to watch for the schools of herring and direct the fishing fleet toward them.

A manifestation of form sense is the sense the poet's ear has of some rhythmic norm peculiar to a particular poem, from which the individual lines depart and to which they return. I heard Henry Cowell tell that the drone in Indian music is known as the horizon note. Al Kresch, the painter, sent me a quotation from Emerson: 'The health of the eye demands a horizon.' This sense of the beat or pulse underlying the whole I think of as the horizon note of the poem. It interacts with the nuances or forces of feeling which determine emphasis on one word or another, and decides to a great extent what belongs to a given line. It relates the need of that feeling-force which dominates the cadence to the needs of the surrounding parts and so to the whole.

Duncan also pointed to what is perhaps a variety of organic poetry: the poetry of linguistic impulse. It seems to me that the absorption in language itself, the awareness of the world of multiple meaning revealed in sound, word, syntax, and the entering into this world in the poem, is as much an experience or constellation of perceptions as the instress of nonverbal sensuous and psychic events. What might make the poet of linguistic impetus appear to be on another tack entirely is that the demands of his realization may seem in opposition to truth as we think of it; that is, in terms of sensual logic. But the apparent distortion of experience in such a poem for the sake of verbal effects is actually a precise adherence to truth, since the experience itself was a verbal one.

Form is never more than a *revelation* of content.

'The law—one perception must immediately and directly lead to a further perception' (Edward Dahlberg, as quoted by Charles Olson in 'Projective Verse', *Selected Writings*). I've always taken this to mean, 'no loading of the rifts with ore', because there are to be no rifts. Yet alongside this truth is another truth (that I've learned from Duncan more than from anyone else)—that there must be a place in the poem for rifts too—(never to be stuffed with imported ore). Great gaps between perception and perception which must be leapt across if they are to be crossed at all.

The *X*-factor, the magic, is when we come to those rifts and make those leaps. A religious devotion to the truth, to the splendour of the authentic, involves the writer in a process rewarding in itself; but when that devotion brings us to undreamed abysses and we find ourselves sailing slowly over them and landing on the other side—that's ecstasy.

PHILIP LEVINE

THE POET IN NEW YORK IN DETROIT

In the winter of 1953 I was working at Chevrolet Gear and Axle, a factory in Detroit long ago dismantled and gone to dust. I worked the night shift, from midnight to eight in the morning, then returned by bus to my apartment, slept for a time, and rose to try to write poetry, for I believed even then that if I could transform my experience into poetry I would give it the value and dignity it did not begin to possess on its own. I thought too that if I could write about it I could come to understand it; I believed that if I could understand my life—or at least the part my work played in it—I could embrace it with some degree of joy, an element conspicuously missing from my life. No, I was not a young Werther seeking some outlet for my romantic longings for the world. I was a humiliated wage slave employed by a vast corporation I loathed. The job I worked at each night was difficult, boring, and stupefying, for there in the forge room the noise was oceanic and the heat in our faces ferocious. And the work was dangerous; one older man I worked with lost both hands to a defective drop forge, and within a few hours—after a cursory inspection—the machine was back in operation being tended by another man equally liable to give his body for General Motors. A friend had given me a copy of Goethe's saga. I'd read it and merely laughed. If you had the time to survey the mountains and the sky, what was the problem? Oh, yes, you had to embrace the world in all its splendour, you had to reach with aching arms to hold the ungraspable, the sublime. I nicknamed the book *Stormy Werther* and threw it away. I too had aching arms, a thickened back, swollen wrists, and a heart full of emotions I couldn't deal with, fury and rage at a world that seemed already to have defeated me.

Since I worked only eight hours a day and slept only five or six each morning, I had plenty of time to attack my poems. My inspiration at that time was Keats, but though he knew a world at least as difficult as mine it scarcely entered his poetry clothed in the terms in which he encountered it. It was there barely disguised in the third stanza of the 'Ode to a Nightingale', which I would recite over and over to myself:

Fade far away, dissolve, and quite forget
What thou among the leaves hast never known,
The weariness, the fever, and the fret
Here, where men sit and hear each other groan;
Where palsy shakes a few, sad, last grey hairs,
Where youth grows pale, and spectre-thin, and dies;
Where but to think is to be full of sorrow
And leaden-eyed despairs,
Where Beauty cannot keep her lustrous eyes,
Or new Love pine at them beyond tomorrow.

Unquestionably his life had been far harder than mine, and yet he had made immortal poetry out of it. He had struggled against poverty, trying his best to support two younger brothers and a sister; I had only myself and my impossible first wife. He—as a student surgeon—had walked among the sick and dying, at twenty-three he had nursed an eighteen-year-old brother to his death, and even with the first unmistakable signs of TB in his own body—the disease that had killed his brother—he had gone on transforming his life into poetry. I had my health, my strength, and a whole undiscovered continent to write about, and yet I sat at the kitchen table each afternoon failing to complete a single poem that satisfied me, one that could capture the rage I felt at a world that reduced men to what I had become. Of course he had the advantage of being a genius, and another advantage too: he had inherited a tradition that by age twenty-three he knew intimately, one that showed him how to achieve Beauty. He also knew something that I wouldn't learn for years: that Beauty mattered, that it could transform our experience into something worthy, that like love it could redeem our lives. I wanted fire and I wanted gunfire, I wanted to burn down Chevrolet and waste the government of the United States of America.

On weekends I would often go to the Detroit Institute of Arts to try to enter another world, if only for an afternoon. There I found what at first I thought might be the model for the poetry I hoped to write, Diego Rivera's famous frescoes, especially those panels which depict the making of an automobile at Ford's River Rouge empire. I knew no other great art that dealt with my working life. Dos Passos' *U.S.A.* contained a mediocre chapter concerned with assembly-line workers in Detroit as well as a brilliant portrait of Henry Ford, one a worker could love. I thought Céline, in his fury, might show me the way in *Journey to the End of the Night*, but, reading the book, I discovered he clearly was not familiar with industrial labour. It was Rivera, the sworn enemy of my enemies, or no one.

From a distance the frescoes were a miracle of design that left me breathless. As the weeks passed I began to discover why his images were not helping me with my poetry. As I drew closer I found the bodies beautiful, their gestures like those of dancers as they moved in concert, and although their faces were often averted, turned away from the eye of the beholder as though shamed by peonage, those I could see were calm, dignified, and concentrated upon their tasks. The bodies tended to be elongated, the limbs long and slender, turning on their narrow waists as they lifted in unison. And the tones, dominated by warm earth colours, were wrong, far brighter and more vivid than those of the actual world I knew. When I closed my eyes I saw it all in black and white, black men and white men and white fire. And the actual bodies I knew were otherwise, so heavily muscled they seemed earthbound like Blake's Newton, perhaps made of earth, certainly thickened with earth and the metals of the earth. The habitual gaze of those of us who worked at Chevy was downward too, as though whatever stood above us was stunning and victorious and not to be gazed at for fear it could kill, this strange God of the underworld, for surely we were in the underworld. I wondered seriously if Rivera had seen a different world, the Ford plant at River Rouge, then the world's largest industrial complex, could be that different from Chevy.

Some months later, employed as a driver for a company that repaired electric motors, I entered Ford Rouge—because of Ford's notorious anti-Semitism I refused to seek a job there—to pick up a burned-out motor on the assembly line, and found the same world I knew at Chevy, black and white and grey. I heard the same deafening roar, and saw the same men, stunted and isolated by their labours. Rivera's great design, his beautiful dance, was nonsense; automobiles were produced by a colossal accident that shattered men and women. It was what I'd known it was: a world that must be raged against with all the eloquence and fury a poet could muster. And then, by one of those magical strokes of luck that come to the poet in need, I read,

I denounce everyone
who ignores the other half,
the half that can't be redeemed,
who lift their mountains of cement
where the hearts beat
inside forgotten little animals
and where all of us will fall
in the last feast of pneumatic drills.
I spit in all your faces.

I had known García Lorca only as the author of the 'gypsy poems', a writer of lovely, exotic poems that meant little to me. But now one Saturday afternoon became a miracle as I stood in the stacks of the Wayne University library, my hands trembling, and read my life in his words. How had this strange young Andalusian, later murdered by his countrymen, come to understand my life, how had he mastered the language of my rage? This poet of grace and 'deep song' had somehow caught my emotions in a way I never had, and suddenly he opened a door for me to a way of speaking about my life. I accepted his gift. That's what they give us, the humble workers in the fields of poetry, these amazingly inspired geniuses, gifts that change our lives. I later read that upon first entering New York he had cried, 'I don't understand, I don't understand,' as I had cried in the face of Detroit. Months later, taken by a friend to view Wall Street at midnight in moonlight, he had cried, 'I do understand.' What I knew even on the first afternoon in the library was that, before understanding had come poetry had come.

I dove into the *Poet in New York* and everything I could find about its author. 'Gongorism', 'surrealism', 'obscurity': the critics' terms were useless to me. What I was reading made perfect sense to me and at the same time no sense at all. I had discovered the poet could live in the tiny eye at the centre of chaos and write. I had at last discovered the true meaning of what my earlier hero, Keats, had called Negative Capability, 'when man is capable of being in uncertainties, Mysteries, doubts without any irritable reaching after fact and reason.'

What an extraordinary gift to receive in my twenty-fifth year. I would like to be able to say that immediately my own poems flowed from his model and his inspiration, but that was not so. He was a genius, I was a humble and dedicated worker. My one great mentor, John Berryman, had already taught me that certain poets were too much themselves to allow you to imitate them with impunity; he had said that when warning me away from that other great poet of New York, Hart Crane, and towards the influence of Hardy and Frost. What Lorca gave me as no other poet had was a validation of my own emotions, which meant a validation of what I was trying and failing to write. As Wilfred Owen's poetry eight years before had taught me that I was a worthy human being even though I hated and feared the possibility of killing or being killed in war, García Lorca's *Poet in New York* taught me I was a worthy human being although I was filled with hatred for the life I was living, for what capitalist, industrialized America had reduced me to. I saw also in this great book that, if I were able to remain true to my own personal vision of this America, sooner or later my poetry would come—certainly not a poetry as amazing as his, but nonetheless a poetry no one else could write.

Never in poetry written in English had I found such a direct confrontation of one image with another or heard such violence held in abeyance and enclosed in so perfect a musical form. What in my work had been chaotic rant was in his a stately threnody circling around a centre of riot. Here was the first clue to what my poetry would have to become if I were to capture my experience. Had I not read

> *A wooden wind from the south, slanting through the black mire,*
> *spits on the broken boats and drives tacks into shoulders.*
> *A south wind that carries*
> *tusks, sunflowers, alphabets,*
> *and a battery with drowned wasps*

I could not have written

> *Out of burlap sacks, out of bearing butter,*
> *Out of black bean and wet slate bread,*
> *Out of the acids of rage, the candor of tar,*
> *Out of creosote, gasoline, drive shafts, wooden dollies,*
> *They Lion grow.*

I had to work another thirteen years before I was able to begin to realize his gift to me, which is not really very long when you consider the life of a poem that means something. This is not to suggest that my poems mean anything to anyone else or will outlive me. I do know my poems are themselves, and tributes both to the people I shared my life with way back then and to this amazing visitor to our shores, whose voice for me rings as truly today as it did that Saturday almost forty years ago when I first read

No, no: I denounce it all.
I denounce the conspiracy
of these deserted offices
that radiate no agony,
that erase the forest's plans,
and I offer myself as food for the cows wrung dry
when their bellowing fills the valley
where the Hudson gets drunk on oil.

ROBERT LOWELL

FROM AN INTERVIEW*

INTERVIEWER. But in *Lord Weary's Castle* there were poems moving toward a sort of narrative calm, almost a prose calm—'Katherine's Dream', for example, or the two poems on texts by Edwards, or 'The Ghost'—and then, on the other hand, poems in which the form was insisted upon and maybe shown off, and where the things that were characteristic of your poetry at that time—the kind of enjambments, the rhyming, the metres, of course—seem willed and forced, so that you have a terrific log jam of stresses, meanings, strains.

LOWELL. I know one contrast I've felt, and it takes different forms at different times. The ideal modern form seems to be the novel and certain short stories. Maybe Tolstoy would be the perfect example—his work is imagistic, it deals with all experience, and there seems to be no conflict of the form and content. So one thing is to get into poetry that kind of human richness in rather simple descriptive language. Then there's another side of poetry: compression, something highly rhythmical and perhaps wrenched into a small space. I've always been fascinated by both these things. But getting it all on one page in a few stanzas, getting it all done in as little space as possible, revising and revising so that each word and rhythm though not perfect is pondered and wrestled with—you can't do that in prose very well, you'd never get your book written. 'Katherine's Dream' was a real dream. I found that I shaped it a bit, and cut it, and allegorized it, but still it was a dream someone had had. It was material that ordinarily, I think, would go into prose, yet it would have had to be much longer and part of something much longer.

* From *Writers at Work: The Paris Review Interviews*, Second Series, ed. by Malcolm Cowley. The interviewer is Frederick Seidel.

INTERVIEWER. I think you can either look for forms, you can do specific reading for them, or the forms can be demanded by what you want to say. And when the material in poetry seems under almost unbearable pressure you wonder whether the form hasn't cookie-cut what the poet wanted to say. But you chose the couplet, didn't you, and some of your freest passages are in couplets.

LOWELL. The couplet I've used is very much like the couplet Browning uses in 'My Last Duchess', in *Sordello*, run-on with its rhymes buried. I've always, when I've used it, tried to give the impression that I had as much freedom in choosing the rhyme word as I had in any of the other words. Yet they were almost all true rhymes, and maybe half the time there'd be a pause after the rhyme. I wanted something as fluid as prose; you wouldn't notice the form, yet looking back you'd find that great obstacles had been climbed. And the couplet is pleasant in this way—once you've got your two lines to rhyme, then that's done and you can go on to the next. You're not stuck with the whole stanza to round out and build to a climax. A couplet can be a couplet or can be split and left as one line, or it can go on for a hundred lines; any sort of compression or expansion is possible. And that's not so in a stanza. I think a couplet's much less lyrical than a stanza, closer to prose. Yet it's an honest form, its difficulties are in the open. It really is pretty hard to rhyme each line with the one that follows it.

INTERVIEWER. Did the change of style in *Life Studies* have something to do with working away from that compression and pressure by way of, say, the kind of prose clarity of 'Katherine's Dream'?

LOWELL. Yes. By the time I came to *Life Studies* I'd been writing my autobiography and also writing poems that broke metre. I'd been doing a lot of reading aloud. I went on a trip to the West Coast and read at least once a day and sometimes twice for fourteen days, and more and more I found that I was simplifying my poems. If I had a Latin quotation I'd translate it into English. If adding a couple of syllables in a line made it clearer I'd add them, and I'd make little changes just impromptu as I read. That seemed to improve the reading.

INTERVIEWER. Can you think of a place where you added a syllable or two to an otherwise regular line?

LOWELL. It was usually articles and prepositions that I added, very slight little changes, and I didn't change the printed text. It was just done for the moment.

INTERVIEWER. Why did you do this? Just because you thought the most important thing was to get the poem over?

LOWELL. To get it over, yes. And I began to have a certain disrespect for the tight forms. If you could make it easier by adding syllables, why not? And then when I was writing *Life Studies*, a good number of the poems were started in very strict metre, and I found that, more than the rhymes, the regular beat was what I didn't want. I have a long poem in there about my father, called 'Commander Lowell', which actually is largely in couplets, but I originally wrote perfectly strict four-foot couplets. Well, with that form it's hard not to have echoes of Marvell. That regularity just seemed to ruin the honesty of sentiment, and became rhetorical; it said, 'I'm a poem'—though it was a great help when I was revising having this original skeleton. I could keep the couplets where I wanted them and drop them where I didn't; there'd be a form to come back to.

INTERVIEWER. Had you originally intended to handle all that material in prose?

LOWELL. Yes. I found it got awfully tedious working out transitions and putting in things that didn't seem very important but were necessary to the prose continuity. Also I found it hard to revise. Cutting it down into small bits, I could work on it much more carefully and make fast transitions. But there's another point about this mysterious business of prose and poetry, form and content, and the reasons for breaking forms. I don't think there's any very satisfactory answer. I seesaw back and forth between something highly metrical and something highly free; there isn't any one way to write. But it seems to me we've gotten in a sort of Alexandrian age. Poets of my generation and particularly younger ones have gotten terribly proficient at these forms. They write a very musical, difficult poem with tremendous skill, perhaps there's never been such skill. Yet the writings seem divorced from culture somehow. It's become too much something specialized that can't handle much experience. It's a craft, purely a craft, and there must be some breakthrough back into life. Prose is in many ways better off than poetry. It's quite hard to think of a young poet who has the vitality, say, of Salinger or Saul Bellow. Yet prose tends to be very diffuse. The novel is really a much more difficult form than it seems; few people have the wind to write anything that long. Even a short story demands almost poetic perfection. Yet on the whole prose is less cut off from life than poetry is. Now, some of this Alexandrian poetry is very brilliant, you would not have it changed at all. But I thought it was getting increasingly stifling. I couldn't get any experience into tight metrical forms.

INTERVIEWER. So you felt this about your own poetry, your own technique, not just about the general condition of poetry?

LOWELL. Yes. I felt that the metre plastered difficulties and mannerisms on what I was trying to say to such an extent that it terribly hampered me.

INTERVIEWER. This then explains, in part anyway, your admiration for Elizabeth Bishop's poetry. I know that you've said the qualities and the abundance of its descriptive language reminded you of the Russian novel more than anything else.

LOWELL. Any number of people are guilty of writing a complicated poem that has a certain amount of symbolism in it and really difficult meaning, a wonderful poem to teach. Then you unwind it and you feel that the intelligence, the experience, whatever goes into it, is skin-deep. In Elizabeth Bishop's 'Man-Moth' a whole new world is gotten out and you don't know what will come after any one line. It's exploring. And it's as original as Kafka. She's gotten a world, not just a way of writing. She seldom writes a poem that doesn't have that exploratory quality; yet it's very firm, it's not like beat poetry, it's all controlled.

• • •

INTERVIEWER. Do you revise a very great deal?

LOWELL. Endlessly.

INTERVIEWER. You often use an idiom or a very common phrase either for the sake of irony or to bear more meaning than it's customarily asked to bear—do these come late in the game, do you have to look around for them?

LOWELL. They come later because they don't prove much in themselves, and they often replace something that's much more formal and worked-up. Some of my later poetry does have this quality that the earlier doesn't: several lines can be almost what you'd say in conversation. And maybe talking with a friend or with my wife I'd say, 'This doesn't sound quite right', and sort of reach in the air as I talked and change a few words. In that way the new style is easier to write; I sometimes fumble out a natural sequence of lines that will work. But a whole poem won't come that way; my seemingly relaxed poems are just about as hard as the very worked-up ones.

INTERVIEWER. That rightness and familiarity, though, is in 'Between the Porch and the Altar' in several passages which are in couplets.

LOWELL. When I am writing in metre I find the simple lines never come right away. Nothing does. I don't believe I've ever written a poem in metre where I've kept a single one of the original lines. Usually when I was writing my old poems I'd write them out in blank verse and then put in the rhymes. And of course I'd change the rhymes a lot. The most I could hope for at first was that the rhymed version wouldn't be much inferior to the blank verse. Then the real work would begin, to make it something much better than the original out of the difficulties of the metre.

INTERVIEWER. Have you ever gone as far as Yeats and written out a prose argument and then set down the rhymes?

LOWELL. With some of the later poems I've written out prose versions, then cut the prose down and abbreviated it. A rapidly written prose draft of the poem doesn't seem to do much good, too little pain has gone into it; but one really worked on is bound to have phrases that are invaluable. And it's a nice technical problem: how can you keep phrases and get them into metre?

• • •

INTERVIEWER. So you feel that the religion is the business of the poem that it's in and not at all the business of the Church or the religious person.

LOWELL. It shouldn't be. I mean, a religion ought to have objective validity. But by the time it gets into a poem it's so mixed up with technical and imaginative problems that the theologian, the priest, the serious religious person isn't of too much use. The poem is too strange for him to feel at home and make any suggestions.

INTERVIEWER. What does this make of the religious poem as a religious exercise?

LOWELL. Well, it at least makes this: that the poem tries to be a poem and not a piece of artless religious testimony. There is a drawback. It seems to me that with any poem, but maybe particularly a religious one where there are common interests, the opinion of intelligent people who are not poets ought to be useful. There's an independence to this not getting advice from religious people and outsiders, but also there's a narrowness. Then there is a question whether my poems are religious, or whether they just use religious imagery. I haven't really any idea. My last poems don't use religious imagery, they don't use symbolism. In many ways they seem to me more religious than the early ones, which are full of symbols and references to Christ and God. I'm sure the symbols and the Catholic framework didn't make the poems religious experiences. Yet I don't feel my experience changed very much. It seems to me it's clearer to me now than it was then, but it's very much the same sort of thing that went into the religious poems—the same sort of struggle, light and darkness, the flux of experience. The morality seems much the same. But the symbolism is gone; you couldn't possibly say what creed I believed in. I've wondered myself often. Yet what made the earlier poems valuable seems to be some recording of experience, and that seems to be what makes the later ones.

INTERVIEWER. So you end up saying that the poem does have some integrity and can have some beauty apart from the beliefs expressed in the poem.

LOWELL. I think it can only have integrity apart from the beliefs; that no political position, religious position, position of generosity, or what have you, can make a poem good. It's all to the good if a poem *can* use politics, or theology, or gardening, or anything that has its own validity aside from poetry. But these things will never *per se* make a poem.

INTERVIEWER. The difficult question is whether when the beliefs expressed in a poem are obnoxious the poem as a whole can be considered to be beautiful—the problem of the *Pisan Cantos*.

LOWELL. The *Pisan Cantos* are very uneven, aren't they? If you took what most people would agree are maybe the best hundred passages, would the beliefs in those passages be obnoxious? I think you'd get a very mixed answer. You could make quite a good case for Pound's good humour about his imprisonment, his absence of self-pity, his observant eye, his memories of literary friends, for all kinds of generous qualities and open qualities and lyrical qualities that anyone would think were good. And even when he does something like the death of Mussolini, in the passage that opens the *Pisan Cantos*, people debate about it. I've talked to Italians who were partisans, and who said that this is the only poem on Mussolini that's any good. Pound's quite wily often: Mussolini hung up like an ox—his brutal appearance. I don't know whether you could say the beliefs there are wrong or not. And there are other poems that come to mind: in Eliot, the Jew spelled with a small j in 'Gerontion', is that anti-Semitism or not? Eliot's not anti-Semitic in any sense, but there's certainly a dislike of Jews in those early poems. Does he gain in the fierceness of writing his Jew with a small j? He says you write what you have to write and in criticism you can say what you think you should believe in. Very ugly emotions perhaps make a poem.

INTERVIEWER. You were on the Bollingen Committee at the time the award was made to Pound. What did you think of the great ruckus?

LOWELL. I thought it was a very simple problem of voting for the best book of the year; and it seemed to me Pound's was. I thought the *Pisan Cantos* was the best writing Pound had ever done, though it included some of his worst. It is a very mixed book: that was the question. But the consequences of not giving the best book of the year a prize for extraneous reasons, even terrible ones in a sense—I think that's the death of art. Then you have Pasternak suppressed and everything becomes stifling. Particularly in a strong country like ours you've got to award things objectively and not let the beliefs you'd like a man to have govern your choice. It was very close after the war, and anyone must feel that the poetry award was a trifling thing compared with the concentration camps. I actually think they were very distant from Pound. He had no political effect whatsoever and was quite eccentric and impractical. Pound's social credit, his fascism, all these various things, were a tremendous gain to him; he'd be a very Parnassan poet without them. Even if they're bad beliefs—and some were bad, some weren't, and some were just terrible, of course—they made him more human and more to do with life, more to do with the times. They served him. Taking what interested him in these things gave a kind of realism and life to his poetry that it wouldn't have had otherwise.

• • •

INTERVIEWER. Have many of your poems been taken from real people and real events?

LOWELL. I think, except when I've used myself or occasionally named actual people in poems, the characters are purely imaginary. I've tried to buttress them by putting images I've actually seen and in direct ways getting things I've actually experienced into the poem. If I'm writing about a Canadian nun the poem may have a hundred little bits of things I've looked at, but she's not remotely anyone I've ever known. And I don't believe anybody would think my nun was quite a real person. She has a heart and she's alive, I hope, and she has a lot of colour to her and drama, and has some things that Frost's characters don't, but she doesn't have their wonderful quality of life. His Witch of Coös is absolutely there. I've gathered from talking to him that most of the *North of Boston* poems came from actual people he knew shuffled and put together. But then it's all-important that Frost's plots are so extraordinary, so carefully worked out though it seems that they're not there. Like some things in Chekhov, the art is very well hidden.

INTERVIEWER. Don't you think a large part of it is getting the right details, symbolic or not, around which to wind the poem tight and tighter?

LOWELL. Some bit of scenery or something you've felt. Almost the whole problem of writing poetry is to bring it back to what you really feel, and that takes an awful lot of manoeuvring. You may feel the doorknob more strongly than some big personal event, and the doorknob will open into something that you can use as your own. A lot of poetry seems to me very good in the tradition but just doesn't move me very much because it doesn't have personal vibrance to it. I probably exaggerate the value of it, but it's precious to me. Some little image, some detail you've noticed—you're writing about a little country shop, just describing it, and your poem ends up with an existentialist account of your experience. But it's the shop that started it off. You didn't know why it meant a lot to you. Often images and often the sense of the beginning and end of a poem are all you have—some journey to be gone through between those things; you know that, but you don't know the details. And that's marvellous; then you feel the poem will come out. It's a terrible struggle, because what you really feel hasn't got the form, it's not what you can put down in a poem. And the poem you're equipped to write concerns nothing that you care very much about or have much to say on. Then the great moment comes when there's enough resolution of your technical equipment, your way of constructing things, and what you can make a poem out of, to hit something you really want to say. You may not know you have it to say.

DON MCKAY

SOME REMARKS ON POETRY AND POETIC ATTENTION

Things occur to me, in the midst of writing, following my nose into whatever, and I'll pass some of these along. There's an affable iffiness to these in the original sniffing and browsing, which I will allow to diminish in the interests of shape. Also, I don't want them getting pushed around by the big-bullying theories of the schoolyard.

—I suspect that the quality of attention surrounding a poem is more important to me than poetry. A species of longing that somehow evades the usual desire to possess. Or, I should add, to use.

—Art comes across; it occurs as tools attempt to metamorphose into animals. Language, for example, opens its ear to the other. Once you have tools plus longing, you have poetic attention.

—Probably these notions incubate during bird-watching, which in my experience involves a mental set nearly identical to writing: a kind of suspended expectancy, tools at the ready, full awareness that the creatures cannot be compelled to appear. (Bad writing: a trip to the zoo.)

—Poetic attention registers with me as a different form of knowing from the commodity sold in schools. When Martin Heidegger speaks of 'tarrying alongside' whatever it is we're 'knowing', he shifts the relationship away from knowledge as ownership, and catches reverberations with both visiting and distance. And, underlying this, a sense of shared mortality you don't get when you're Knowing with a capital K. You swim awhile with a fellow creature of time.

—But language, you might say, has a life of our own, and a writer can start there instead, with the energies of the prison-house, or house of being, or mother tongue, body speech, animal music, or word-as-such. All these various linguistics interest me, but less and less the closer you get to solipsism, which comes about from spending too much time indoors. I need a linguistics I can talk with. The meetings of experience and language—

negotiation, abrasion, dominion, cross-pollination, intercourse, infection; the 'wondrously tedious monotony and variety of the world' (Francis Ponge); wildness invading language as music, which occurs as soon as syntax is seen as energy rather than enthroned as order: this boundary is not a line but a planet rich with ecosystems. I'm not wild about the taste of paper or the narcissism of the 'signifier', however free or ideologically correct the play may seem in those salons of the spirit where it is pursued. I don't believe that 'reference' is a consequence of imperialism, late capitalism, or the patriarchy. Freeing words from the necessity to refer is equivalent to freeing Tundra swans from the necessity to migrate, or, getting down to it, freeing any creature from its longing for another.

—I suspect, too, that poetry brings us back to that longing, back to poetic attention.

—In one version of our evolution as a species, we become outfitted with a capacity for poetry (all the arts, maybe) as a natural check on our genius for technology: for making things, for control and reduction, for converting the world to human categories. Poetry, that wonderful useless musical machine, performs the actions of technology but undoes the consequences. In this version, Auden gets modified; poetry makes nothing *happen*.

September 1988
Ilderton, Ont.

DAPHNE MARLATT

musing with mothertongue

the beginning: language, a living body we enter at birth, sustains and contains us. it does not stand in place of anything else, it does not replace the bodies around us. placental, our flat land, our sea, it is both place (where we are situated) and body (that contains us), that body of language we speak, our mothertongue. it bears us as we are born in it, into cognition.

language is first of all for us a body of sound. leaving the water of the mother's womb with its one dominant sound, we are born into this other body whose multiple sounds bathe our ears from the moment of our arrival. we learn the sounds before we learn what they say: a child will speak baby-talk in pitch patterns that accurately imitate the sentence patterns of her mothertongue. an adult who cannot read or write will speak his mothertongue without being able to say what a particular morpheme or even word in a phrase means. we learn nursery rhymes without understanding what they refer to. we repeat skipping songs significant for their rhythms. gradually we learn how the sounds of our language are active as meaning and then we go on learning for the rest of our lives what the words are actually saying.

in poetry, which has evolved out of chant and song, in riming and tone-leading, whether they occur in prose or poetry, sound will initiate thought by a process of association. words call each other up, evoke each other, provoke each other, nudge each other into utterance. we know from dreams and schizophrenic speech how deeply association works in our psyches, a form of thought that is not rational but erotic because it works by attraction. a drawing, a pulling toward. a 'liking.' Germanic *līk-*, body, form; like, same.

like the atomic particles of our bodies, phonemes and syllables gravitate toward each other. they attract each other in movements we call assonance, euphony, alliteration, rhyme. they are drawn together and echo each other in rhythms we identify as feet—lines run on, phrases patter like speaking feet. on a macroscopic level, words evoke each other in movements we know as puns and figures of speech (these endless similes, this continuing fascination with making one out of two, a new one, a similitude). meaning moves us deepest the more of the whole field it puts together, and so we get sense where it borders on nonsense ('what is the sense of it all?') as what we sense our way into. the sentence. ('life.') making our multiplicity whole and even intelligible by the end-point. intelligible: logos there in the gathering hand, the reading eye.

hidden in the etymology and usage of so much of our vocabulary for verbal communication (contact, sharing) is a link with the body's physicality: matter (the import of what you say) and matter and by extension mother; language and tongue; to utter and outer (give birth again); a part of speech and a part of the body; pregnant with meaning; to mouth (speak) and the mouth with which we also eat and make love; sense (meaning) and that with which we sense the world; to relate (a story) and to relate to somebody, related (carried back) with its connection with bearing (a child); intimate and to intimate; vulva and voluble; even sentence which comes from a verb meaning to feel.

like the mother's body, language is larger than us and carries us along with it. it bears us, it births us, insofar as we bear with it. if we are poets we spend our lives discovering not just what we have to say but what language is saying as it carries us with it. in etymology we discover a history of verbal relations (a family tree, if you will) that has preceded us and given us the world we live in. the given, the immediately presented, as at birth—a given name a given world. we know language structures our world and in a crucial sense we cannot see what we cannot verbalize, as the work of Whorf and ethnolinguistics has pointed out to us. here we are truly contained within the body of our mothertongue. and even the physicists, chafing at these limits, say that the glimpse physics now gives us of the nature of the universe cannot be conveyed in a language based on the absolute difference between a noun and a verb. poetry has been demonstrating this for some time.

if we are women poets, writers, speakers, we also take issue with the given, hearing the discrepancy between what our patriarchally-loaded language bears (can bear) of our experience and the difference from it our experience bears out—how it misrepresents, even miscarries, and so leaves unsaid what we actually experience. can a pregnant woman be said to be 'master' of the gestation process she finds herself within—is that her relationship to it? (see Julia Kristeva, *Desire in Language*, p. 238.) are women included in the statement 'God appearing as man' (has God ever appeared as a woman?) can a woman ever say she is 'lady of all she surveys' or could others ever say of her she 'ladies it over them'?

so many terms for dominance in English are tied up with male experiencing, masculine hierarchies and differences (exclusion), patriarchal holdings with their legalities. where are the poems that celebrate the soft letting-go the flow of menstrual blood is as it leaves her body? how can the standard sentence structure of English with its linear authority, subject through verb to object, convey the wisdom of endlessly repeating and not exactly repeated cycles her body knows? or the mutuality her body shares embracing other bodies, children, friends, animals, all those she customarily holds and is held by? how can the separate nouns mother and child convey the fusion, bleeding womb-infant mouth, she experiences in those first days of feeding? what syntax can carry the turning herself inside out in love when she is both sucking mouth and hot gush on her lover's tongue?

Julia Kristeva says: 'If it is true every national language has its own dream language and unconscious, then each of the sexes—a division so much more archaic and fundamental than the one into languages—would have its own unconscious wherein the biological and social program of the species would be ciphered in confrontation with language, exposed to its influence, but independent from it' (*Desire in Language*, p. 241). i link this with the call so many feminist writers in Quebec have issued for a language that returns us to the body, a woman's body and the largely unverbalized, presyntactic, postlexical field it knows. postlexical in that, as Mary Daly shows, with intelligence (that gathering hand) certain words (dandelion sparks) seed themselves back to original and originally-related meaning. this is a field where words mutually attract each other, fused by connection, enthused (inspired) into variation (puns, word play, rime at all levels) fertile in proliferation (offspring, rooting back to *al-*, seed syllable to grow, and leafing forward into *alma*, nourishing, a woman's given name, soul, inhabitant.)

inhabitant of language, not master, not even mistress, this new woman writer (Alma, say) in having is had, is held by it, what she is given to say. in giving it away is given herself, on that double edge where she has always lived, between the already spoken and the unspeakable, sense and non-sense. only now she writes it, risking nonsense, chaotic language leafings, unspeakable breaches of usage, intuitive leaps. inside language she leaps for joy, shoving out the walls of taboo and propriety, kicking syntax, discovering life in old roots.

language thus speaking (i.e., inhabited) relates us, 'takes us back' to where we are, as it relates us to the world in a living body of verbal relations. articulation: seeing the connections (and the thighbone, and the hipbone, etc.). putting the living body of language together means putting the world together, the world we live in: an act of composition, an act of birthing, us, uttered and outered there in it.

bpNichol

Some thots on THE MARTYROLOGY BOOK VI—Half-way thru

THE MARTYROLOGY Book VI began in 1978 before I had even finished Book V. This in itself threw me off. Since the structure of much of what I am doing evolves processually in a journal-like fashion, I had grown used to the poem clearly announcing itself in chronological order. But of course the chaining structure that was Book V meant certain thrusts in the narrative of the piece ended much sooner than others and became, therefore, available for articulation in the next book of the work even tho the previous book was still writing itself. I wrote the opening parts of the first text in Book VI, *IMPERFECTION:*

A PROPHECY, & then, a year later, Book V was still in progress, I began *THE BOOK OF HOURS*. I began to think I was writing a new work, a work I called **A COUNTING**, but in fact the counting was really a marking of time until Book V was finished &/or a structural departure from my own method of composition. With hindsight I can see that my compositional method had to change as a consequence of the decentralized narrative of Book V. I was free to work with chronology but was no longer bound to it processually. Which is to say I could work on a number of initiatives at the same time (each with their own secret narrative [a strict chronological one]) but who jumped & moved in time as a reading experience.

CONTINENTAL TRANCE, the third text in Book VI partakes of this interruption. It is, of course, absolutely governed by the narrative of the rail trip from Vancouver to Toronto, a journey that recurs again and again in **THE MARTYROLOGY** & even earlier in **JOURNEYING & the returns**. Chronologically however it falls between Hours 17 & 18 in *THE BOOK OF HOURS*, as the first three parts of *INCHOATE ROAD* (the fourth text in Book VI) fall between Hours 19 & 20. The effect of all this is the effect of flashback, usually achieved by a more conscious manipulation of the sequentiality of materials but here arrived at simply by a decentralization of the narrative, its simultaneous appearance in multiple texts. This is much how we as people are perceived by friends who know this or that element of our lives but receive this information at indeterminate points in an informational sequence over which we do not necessarily have control. The interruptions continue.

bpNichol
September 1982

'After Reading the Chronology'

A record that absolutely influenced my writing was Ornette Coleman's *Free Jazz*. I'd been following his work anyway, and when that album appeared it really cleaned my ears and made me rethink the whole notion of what was possible in improvisation. I thought of this while reading the chronology because on the main compositional principles i've always used in *The M* is exactly that: the notion that i'm improvising. I'd been impressed by Kerouac's sentences and the notion that a line of writing could be like a saxophone solo. Ornette Coleman's saxophone solos showed me the kind of writing i was interested in achieving. A lot of my early writings are different attempts to find different ways of structuring a piece. Hence the exploration of hinge rhyme, schizophrenic logic, texts that drop out of other texts, etc. Thus, in the compositional moment, which is an improvisational moment, i would have a vast range of techniques to call upon, different ways of convening emotions, ideas, etc.

The point of *The M* being open-ended is simply a consequence of taking the notion of open form writing to its logical extreme. It's not open if i'm boundaried by a notion of closure. And a useful way, therefore, to think of such a text is as an improvisation. But i was influenced here too by the internal logic of the solos of Ornette Coleman (and other jazz saxophists like Charlie Christian, etc.) and Fred Astaire's choreography of his dance solos. I'm thinking at the moment of the one from *Funny Face* which begins as a classic lover sings to his beloved on the balcony, and then how the hat and coat he's wearing become used as props to direct traffic—a passing truck with a cow in it—and then become elements in a bull-fight sequence—led into by the presence of the cow. Those kinds of jumps he makes are more usual in choreography than writing but they're exactly the kinds of leaps of mind that interest me in an improvisation. And the way in which they arise logically, as it were, out of the materials at hand (language, in my case), and the ideas and images which inform the body of *The M*.

So in those early years the first problem was to get my chops together, which i think i've done. Now the problem is to keep pushing at my own limitations and attempting to uncover and undermine my own developing clichés. It's a long process.

February 10, 1988

NARRATIVE IN LANGUAGE: THE LONG POEM

1. At a certain point you decide to start with what's in front of you. There's no point despairing of a subject, or carrying on some misguided search for a 'great' theme when all you have to do is start with what's in front of you: the blue lines, the ink, the pen, the letters the pen shapes, the words the letters make, the table, the window, those leafless trees, these leaves in this notebook in front of me, you—the stuff of poetry.

2. Ordinary language is the hardest to write. Ordinary life is the hardest to live. The minute you write or say the word 'ordinary' you draw too much attention to it & it ceases to be; ordinary that is. Extraordinary when you point to it.

3. The extra has to do with singling it out. So that what is extraordinary in language is how what is ordinary is ordinarily transparent or invisible to us. Which includes its narratives too, or possible narratives, stories you see & find there if you choose to.

4. Of course the alphabet is a narrative—that movement thru your ABC. And any word you write is a displacement of that primary narrative. So that all writing always deconstructs some given even as it notes another given down. Or let's say that what's given is that the given shifts depending on how you choose to look at it, has more than one face, more than one aspect. Or to write is to continually reshape the given, watch it flicker in & out of different focii before your, or just after your, very eyes.

5. What's interesting then is not simply to tell the story but rather to find the story that's out there in the midst of all that flickering, let it reveal itself. You already know the story you set out to tell, there's no hurry with that one, so really why not start by listening? This sounds paradoxical but isn't. When I set out to tell a story I begin by listening. When I set out to write one I begin by reading. You're always waiting for the ordinary to shift & reveal yet another face. And to glimpse the face of the ordinary is, in fact, to be given something. To grasp the given we have to stand still long enough to receive it. You just never grab at the first thing that's held out to you. That was a lesson my maw taught me when I was five and I tried to grab all the presents off my friends as they came thru the door to my birthday party. 'Don't grab at the present,' said Maw, 'wait till it's given to you.'

6. Once you realize that the given is constantly reshaping itself, that its new orders, the words in this sentence say, are essentially arbitrary, a useful set of conventions, then the notion of narrative becomes one more element that shifts in the telling. I always liked the way my great aunts & uncles, my grandmothers, told their stories. The stories were always funny, even the saddest ones, and they were constantly jumping forward & backward in time on a purely associative basis. When you were with them, listening, you went with them, gave yourself up to the pleasure of the story. And that's how you get the given. You give in.

7. 7 given things that totally influenced me and that I thot of as part of everyone's ordinary experience but that people now tell me are part of what makes my long poem, *The Martyrology*, difficult & inaccessible:

1) the habit of mentioning personal names in telling a story even when the people don't know the person. As in: 'I was going on this trip with Fred, an old friend of mine, when suddenly. . . .'

2) the scene in Disney's *Alice in Wonderland* where the caterpillar makes letters out of smoke which float thru the air as he sings the vowels in the alphabet.

3) sitting in a movie theatre with my friends watching the horror movie about kids sitting in a movie theatre with their friends watching a horror movie when The Blob rolls in thru the projection booth and everyone in our movie theatre & everyone in their movie theatre turning around & looking up at the projection booth.

4) singing 'I Got a Gal in Kalamazoo' with my sister, especially the part that went:

'A B C D E F G H
I got a gal in
Kalamazoo'

and then later

'Hi there Mr Jackson
Everything's O
K A L A M A Z O
O what a gal!
A real piparoo!'

Those connections & shifts. Which we sang over & over again.

5) watching *Duck Amuck* starring Daffy Duck, where everything that's usually given in the cartoon world, background, foreground, figure, soundtrack, keeps shifting & disappearing on Daffy.

6) the fact that in Wildwood Park in Winnipeg the different streets &/or sections were named after the letters of the alphabet so that when I was first learning the alphabet I was also learning my way home.

7) hearing the crows sing 'When I See an Elephant Fly' in Disney's *Dumbo*, & memorizing all the lyrics because the puns in it were such a revelation to me:

'I saw a peanut stand
Heard a rubber band
Saw a polka dot railroad tie
Etc.'

The ordinary made extra-ordinary again.

8. When we write as we write we are always telling a story. When I write as I write I am telling the story of how I see the world, how it's been given to me, what I take from it. In the long poem I have the time to tell you that in all its faces or, at least, in as many faces as I've seen so far. Even when I'm not telling a specific story, I'm telling you *that* story. A narrative in language. The long poem. How I see the world.

CHARLES OLSON

PROJECTIVE VERSE*

(projectile (percussive (prospective

vs.

The NON-Projective

(or what a French critic calls 'closed' verse, that verse which print bred and which is pretty much what we have had, in English & American, and have still got, despite the work of Pound & Williams:

it led Keats, already a hundred years ago, to see it (Wordsworth's, Milton's) in the light of 'the Egotistical Sublime'; and it persists, at this latter day, as what you might call the private-soul-at-any-public-wall)

Verse now, 1950, if it is to go ahead, if it is to be of essential use, must, I take it, catch up and put into itself certain laws and possibilities of the breath, of the breathing of the man who writes as well as of his listenings. (The revolution of the ear, 1910, the trochee's heave, asks it of the younger poets.)

I want to do two things: first, try to show what projective or OPEN verse is, what it involves, in its act of composition, how, in distinction from the non-projective, it is accomplished; and ii, suggest a few ideas about what stance toward reality brings such verse into being, what that stance does, both to the poet and to his reader. (The stance involves, for example, a change beyond, and larger than, the technical, and may, the way things look, lead to new poetics and to new concepts from which some sort of drama, say, or of epic, perhaps, may emerge.)

I

First, some simplicities that a man learns, if he works in OPEN, or what can also be called COMPOSITION BY FIELD, as opposed to inherited line, stanza, over-all form, what is the 'old' base of the non-projective.

(1) the *kinetics* of the thing. A poem is energy transferred from where the poet got it (he will have some several causations), by way of the poem

* From *Selected Writings of Charles Olson*, ed. by Robert Creeley.

itself to, all the way over to, the reader. Okay. Then the poem itself must, at all points, be a high energy-construct and, at all points, an energy-discharge. So: how is the poet to accomplish same energy, how is he, what is the process by which a poet gets in, at all points energy at least the equivalent of the energy which propelled him in the first place, yet an energy which is peculiar to verse alone and which will be, obviously, also different from the energy which the reader, because he is a third term, will take away?

This is the problem which any poet who departs from closed form is specially confronted by. And it involves a whole series of new recognitions. From the moment he ventures into FIELD COMPOSITION—puts himself in the open—he can go by no track other than the one the poem under hand declares, for itself. Thus he has to behave, and be, instant by instant, aware of some several forces just now beginning to be examined. (It is much more, for example, this push, than simply such a one as Pound put, so wisely, to get us started: 'the musical phrase', go by it, boys, rather than by, the metronome.)

(2) is the *principle*, the law which presides conspicuously over such composition, and, when obeyed, is the reason why a projective poem can come into being. It is this: FORM IS NEVER MORE THAN AN EXTENSION OF CONTENT. (Or so it got phrased by one, R. Creeley, and it makes absolute sense to me, with this possible corollary, that right form, in any given poem, is the only and exclusively possible extension of content under hand.) There it is, brothers, sitting there, for USE.

Now (3) the *process* of the thing, how the principle can be made so to shape the energies that the form is accomplished. And I think it can be boiled down to one statement (first pounded into my head by Edward Dahlberg): ONE PERCEPTION MUST IMMEDIATELY AND DIRECTLY LEAD TO A FURTHER PERCEPTION. It means exactly what it says, is a matter of, at *all* points (even, I should say, of our management of daily reality as of the daily work) get on with it, keep moving, keep in, speed, the nerves, their speed, the perceptions, theirs, the acts, the split second acts, the whole business, keep it moving as fast as you can, citizen. And if you also set up as a poet, USE USE USE the process at all points, in any given poem always, always one perception must must must MOVE, INSTANTER, ON ANOTHER!

So there we are, fast, there's the dogma. And its excuse, its usableness, in practice. Which gets us, it ought to get us, inside the machinery, now, 1950, of how projective verse is made.

If I hammer, if I recall in, and keeping calling in, the breath, the breathing as distinguished from the hearing, it is for cause, it is to insist upon a part that breath plays in verse which has not (due, I think, to the smothering of the power of the line by too set a concept of foot) has not been sufficiently observed or practised, but which has to be if verse is to advance to its proper force and place in the day, now, and ahead. I take it that PROJECTIVE VERSE teaches, is, this lesson, that that verse will only do in which a poet manages to register both the acquisitions of his ear *and* the pressures of his breath.

Let's start from the smallest particle of all, the syllable. It is the king and pin of versification, what rules and holds together the lines, the larger forms, of a poem. I would suggest that verse here and in England dropped this secret from the late Elizabethans to Ezra Pound, lost it, in the sweetness of metre and rime, in a honey-head. (The syllable is one way to distinguish the original success of blank verse, and its falling off, with Milton.)

It is by their syllables that words juxtapose in beauty, by these particles of sound as clearly as by the sense of the words which they compose. In any given instance, because there is a choice of words, the choice, if a man is in there, will be, spontaneously, the obedience of his ear to the syllables. The fineness, and the practice, lie here, at the minimum and source of speech.

> O western wynd, when wilt thou blow
> And the small rain down shall rain
> O Christ that my love were in my arms
> And I in my bed again

It would do no harm, as an act of correction to both prose and verse as now written, if both rime and metre, and, in the quantity words, both sense and sound, were less in the forefront of the mind than the syllable, if the syllable, that fine creature, were more allowed to lead the harmony on. With this warning, to those who would try: to step back here to this place of the elements and minims of language, is to engage speech where it is least careless—and least logical. Listening for the syllables must be so constant and so scrupulous, the exaction must be so complete, that the assurance of the ear is purchased at the highest—40 hours a day—price. For from the root out, from all over the place, the syllable comes, the figures of, the dance:

> 'Is' comes from the Aryan root, *as*, to breathe. The English 'not' equals the Sanskrit *na*, which may come from the root *na*, to be lost, to perish. 'Be' is from *bhu*, to grow.

I say the syllable, king, and that it is spontaneous, this way: the ear, the ear which has collected, which has listened, the ear, which is so close to the mind that it is the mind's, that it has the mind's speed . . .

it is close, another way: the mind is brother to this sister and is, because it is so close, is the drying force, the incest, the sharpener . . .

it is from the union of the mind and the ear that the syllable is born.

But the syllable is only the first child of the incest of verse (always, that Egyptian thing, it produces twins!). The other child is the LINE. And together, these two, the syllable *and* the line, they make a poem, they make that thing, the—what shall we call it, the Boss of all, 'Single Intelligence'. And the line comes (I swear it) from the breath, from the breathing of the man who writes, at the moment that he writes, and thus is, it is here that, the daily work, the WORK, gets in, for only he, the man who writes, can declare, at every moment, the line its metric and its ending—where its breathing, shall come to, termination.

The trouble with most work, to my taking, since the breaking away from traditional lines and stanzas, and from such wholes as, say, Chaucer's *Troilus* or S's *Lear*, is: contemporary workers go lazy RIGHT HERE WHERE THE LINE IS BORN.

Let me put it baldly. The two halves are,

the HEAD, by way of the EAR, to the SYLLABLE
the HEART, by way of the BREATH, to the LINE

And the joker? that it is in the 1st half of the proposition that, in composing, one lets-it-rip; and that it is in the 2nd half, surprise, it is the LINE that's the baby that gets, as the poem is getting made, the attention, the control, that it is right here, in the line, that the shaping takes place, each moment of the going.

I am dogmatic, that the head shows in the syllable. The dance of the intellect is there, among them, prose or verse. Consider the best minds you know in this here business: where does the head show, is it not, precise, here, in the swift currents of the syllable? can't you tell a brain when you see what it does, just there? It is true, what the master says he picked up from Confusion: all the thots men are capable of can be entered on the back of a postage stamp. So, is it not the PLAY of a mind we are after, is not that that shows whether a mind is there at all?

And the threshing floor for the dance? Is it anything but the LINE? And when the line has, is, a deadness, is it not a heart which has gone lazy, is it not, suddenly, slow things, similes, say, adjectives, or such, that we are bored by?

For there is a whole flock of rhetorical devices which have now to be brought under a new bead, now that we sight with the line. Simile is only one bird who comes down, too easily. The descriptive functions generally have to be watched, every second, in projective verse, because of their easiness, and thus their drain on the energy which composition by field allows into a poem.

Any slackness takes off attention, that crucial thing, from the job in hand, from the *push* of the line under hand at the moment, under the reader's eye, in his moment. Observation of any kind is, like argument in prose, properly previous to the act of contemporary to the acting-on-you of the poem? I would argue that here, too, the LAW OF THE LINE, which projective verse creates, must be hewn to, obeyed, and that the conventions which logic has forced on syntax must be broken open as quietly as must the too set feet of the old line. But an analysis of how far a new poet can stretch the very conventions on which communication by language rests, is too big for these notes, which are meant, I hope it is obvious, merely to get things started.

Let me just throw in this. It is my impression that *all* parts of speech suddenly, in composition by field, are fresh for both sound and percussive use, spring up like unknown, unnamed vegetables in the patch, when you work it, come spring. Now take Hart Crane. What strikes me in him is the singleness of the push to the nominative, his push along that one arc of freshness, the attempt to get back to word as handle. (If logos is word as thought, what is word as noun, as, pass me that, as Newman Shea used to ask, at the galley table, put a jib on the blood, will ya.) But there is a loss in Crane of what Fenollosa is so right about, in syntax, the sentence as first act of nature, as lightning, as passage of force from subject to object, quick, in this case, from Hart to me, in every case, from me to you, the VERB, between two nouns. Does not Hart miss the advantages, by such an isolated push, miss the point of the whole front of syllable, line, field, and what happened to all language, and to the poem, as a result?

I return you now to London, to beginnings, to the syllable, for the pleasures of it, to intermit:

> If music be the food of love, play on
> give me excess of it, that, surfeiting,
> the appetite may sicken, and so die.
> That strain again. It had a dying fall,
> o, it came over my ear like the sweet sound
> that breathes upon a bank of violets,
> stealing and giving odour.

What we have suffered from, is manuscript, press, the removal of verse from its producer and its reproducer, the voice, a removal the poem, and, if allowed in, must be so juxtaposed, apposed, set in, that it does not, for an instant, sap the going energy of the content toward its form.

It comes to this, this whole aspect of the newer problems. (We now enter, actually, the large area of the whole poem, into the FIELD, if you like, where all the syllables and all the lines must be managed in their relations to each other.) It is a matter, finally, of OBJECTS, what they are, what they are inside a poem, how they got there, and, once there, how they are to be used. This is something I want to get to in another way in Part ii, but, for the moment, let me indicate this, that every element in an open poem (the syllable, the line, as well as the image, the sound, the sense) must be taken up as participants in the kinetic of the poem just as solidly as we are accustomed to take what we call the objects of reality; and that these elements are to be seen as creating the tensions of a poem just as totally as do those other objects create what we know as the world.

The objects which occur at every given moment of composition (of recognition, we can call it), are, can be, must be treated exactly as they do occur therein and not by any ideas or preconceptions from outside the poem, must be handled as a series of objects in field in such a way that a series of tensions (which they also are) are made to *hold*, and to hold exactly inside the content and the context of the poem which has forced itself, through the poet and them, into being.

Because breath allows *all* the speech-force of language back in (speech is the 'solid' of verse, is the secret of a poem's energy), because, now, a poem has, by speech, solidity, everything in it can now be treated as solids, objects, things; and, though insisting upon the absolute difference of the reality of verse from that other dispersed and distributed thing, yet each of these elements of a poem can be allowed to have the play of their separate energies and can be allowed, once the poem is well composed, to keep, as those other objects do, their proper confusions.

Which brings us up, immediately, bang, against tenses, in fact against syntax, in fact against grammar generally, that is, as we have inherited it. Do not tenses, must they not also be kicked around anew, in order that time, that other governing absolute, may be kept, as must the space-tensions of a poem, immediate, by one, by two removes from its place of origin *and* its destination. For the breath has a double meaning which latin had not yet lost.

The irony is, from the machine has come one gain not yet sufficiently observed or used, but which leads directly on toward projective verse and its consequences. It is the advantage of the typewriter that, due to its rigidity and its space precisions, it can, for a poet, indicate exactly the breath, the pauses, the suspensions even of syllables, the juxtapositions even of parts of phrases, which he intends. For the first time the poet has the stave and the bar a musician has had. For the first time he can, without the convention of rime and metre, record the listening he has done to his own speech and by that one act indicate how he would want any reader, silently or otherwise, to voice his work.

It is time we picked the fruits of the experiments of cummings, Pound, Williams, each of whom has, after his way, already used the machine as a scoring to his composing, as a script to its vocalization. It is now only a matter of the recognition of the conventions of composition by field for us to bring into being an open verse as formal as the closed, with all its traditional advantages.

If a contemporary poet leaves a space as long as the phrase before it, he means that space to be held, by the breath, an equal length of time. If he suspends a word or syllable at the end of a line (this was most cummings's addition) he means that time to pass that it takes the eye—that hair of time suspended—to pick up the next line. If he wishes a pause so light it hardly separates the words, yet does not want a comma—which is an interruption of the meaning rather than the sounding of the line—follow him when he uses a symbol the typewriter has ready to hand:

> What does not change / is the will to change

Observe him, when he takes advantage of the machine's multiple margins, to juxtapose,

> Sd he:
>   to dream takes no effort
>   to think is easy
>   to act is more difficult
>   but for a man to act after he has taken thought, this!
>   is the most difficult thing of all

Each of these lines is a progressing of both the meaning and the breathing forward, and then a backing up, without a progress or any kind of movement outside the unit of time local to the idea.

There is more to be said in order that this convention be recognized, especially in order that the revolution out of which it came may be so forwarded that work will get published to offset the reaction now afoot to return verse to inherited forms of cadence and rime. But what I want to emphasize here, by this emphasis on the typewriter as the personal and instantaneous recorder of the poet's work, is the already projective nature of verse as the sons of Pound and Williams are practising it. Already they are composing as though verse was to have the reading its writing involved, as though not the eye but the ear was to be its measurer, as though the intervals of its composition could be so carefully put down as to be precisely the intervals of its registration. For the ear, which once had the burden of memory to quicken it (rime & regular cadence were its aids and have merely lived on in print after the oral necessities were ended) can now again, that the poet has his means, be the threshold of projective verse.

II

Which gets us to what I promised, the degree to which the projective involves a stance toward reality outside a poem as well as a new stance towards the reality of a poem itself. It is a matter of content, the content of Homer or of Euripides or of Seami as distinct from that which I might call the more 'literary' masters. From the moment the projective purpose of the act of verse is recognized, the content does—it will—change. If the beginning and the end is breath, voice in its largest sense, then the material of verse shifts. It has to. It starts with the composer. The dimension of his line itself changes, not to speak of the change in his conceiving, of the matter he will turn to, of the scale in which he images that matter's use. I myself would pose the difference by a physical image. It is no accident that Pound and Williams both were involved variously in a movement which got called 'objectivism'. But that word was then used in some sort of a necessary quarrel, I take it, with 'subjectivism'. It is now too late to be bothered with the latter. It has excellently done itself to death, even though we are all caught in its dying. What seems to me a more valid formulation for present use is 'objectism', a word to be taken to stand for the kind of relation of man to experience which a poet might state as the necessity of a line or a work to be as wood is, to be as clean as wood is as it issues from the hand of nature, to be shaped as wood can be when a man has had his hand to it. Objectism is the getting rid of the lyrical interference of the individual as ego, of the 'subject' and his soul, that peculiar presumption by which western man has interposed himself between what he is as a creature of nature (with certain instructions to carry out) and those other creations of nature which we may, with no derogation, call objects. For a man is himself an object, whatever he may take to be his advantages, the more likely to recognize himself as such the greater his advantages, particularly at that moment that he achieves an humilitas sufficient to make him of use.

It comes to this: the use of a man, by himself and thus by others, lies in how he conceives his relation to nature, that force to which he owes his somewhat small existence. If he sprawl, he shall find little to sing but himself, and shall sing, nature has such paradoxical ways, by way of artificial forms outside himself. But if he stays inside himself, if he is contained within his nature as he is participant in the larger force, he will be able to listen, and his hearing through himself will give him secrets objects share. And by an inverse law his shapes will make their own way. It is in this sense that the projective act, which is the artist's act in the larger field of objects, leads to dimensions larger than the man. For a man's problem, the moment he takes speech up in all its fullness, is to give his work his seriousness, a seriousness sufficient to cause the thing he makes to try to take its place alongside the things of nature. This is not easy. Nature works from reverence, even in her destructions (species go down with a crash). But breath is man's special qualification as animal. Sound is a dimension he has extended. Language is one of his proudest acts. And when a poet rests in these as they are in himself (in his physiology, if you like, but the life in him, for all that) then he, if he chooses to speak from these roots, works in that area where nature has given him size, projective size.

It is projective size that the play, *The Trojan Women*, possesses, for it is able to stand, is it not, as its people do, beside the Aegean—and neither Andromache or the sea suffer diminution. In a less 'heroic' but equally 'natural' dimension Seami causes the Fisherman and the Angel to stand clear in *Hagoromo*. And Homer, who is such an unexamined cliché that I do not think I need to press home in what scale Nausicaa's girls wash their clothes.

Such works, I should argue—and I use them simply because their equivalents are yet to be done—could not issue from men who conceived verse without the full relevance of human voice, without reference to where lines come from, in the individual who writes. Nor do I think it accident that, at this end point of the argument, I should use, for examples, two dramatists and an epic poet. For I would hazard the guess that, if projective verse is practised long enough, is driven ahead hard enough along the course I think it dictates, verse again can carry much larger material than it has carried in our language since the Elizabethans. But it can't be jumped. We are only at its beginnings, and if I think that the *Cantos* make more 'dramatic' sense than do the plays of Mr Eliot, it is not because I think they have solved the problem but because the methodology of the verse in them points a way by which, one day, the problem of larger content and of larger forms may be solved. Eliot is, in fact, a proof of a present danger, of 'too easy' a going on the practice of verse as it has been, rather than as it must be, practised. There is no question, for example, that Eliot's line, from 'Prufrock' on down, has speech-force, is 'dramatic', is, in fact, one of the most notable lines since Dryden. I suppose it stemmed immediately to him from Browning, as did so many of Pound's early things. In any case Eliot's line has obvious relations backward to the Elizabethans, especially to the soliloquy. Yet O. M. Eliot is *not* projective. It could even be argued (and I say this carefully, as I have said all things about the non-projective, having considered how each of us must save himself after his own fashion and how much, for that matter, each of us owes to the non-projective, and will continue to owe, as both go alongside each other) but it could be argued that it is because Eliot has stayed inside the non-projective that he fails as a dramatist—that his root is the mind alone, and a scholastic mind at that (no high *intelletto* despite his apparent clarities)—and that, in his listenings he has stayed there where the ear and the mind are, has only gone from his fine ear outward rather than, as I say a projective poet will, down through the workings of his own throat to that place where breath comes from, where breath has its beginnings, where drama has to come from, where, the coincidence is, all act springs.

SYLVIA PLATH

AN INTERVIEW*

ORR. Sylvia, what started you writing poetry?

PLATH. I don't know what *started* me, I just wrote it from the time I was quite small. I guess I liked nursery rhymes and I guess I thought I could do the same thing. I wrote my first poem, my first published poem, when I was eight-and-a-half years old. It came out in *The Boston Traveller* and from then on, I suppose, I've been a bit of a professional.

ORR. What sort of thing did you write about when you began?

PLATH. Nature, I think: birds, bees, spring, fall, all those subjects which are absolute gifts to the person who doesn't have any interior experience to write about. I think the coming of spring, the stars overhead, the first snowfall and so on are gifts for a child, a young poet.

ORR. Now, jumping the years, can you say, are there any themes which particularly attract you as a poet, things that you feel you would like to write about?

PLATH. Perhaps this is an American thing: I've been very excited by what I feel is the new breakthrough that came with, say, Robert Lowell's *Life Studies*, this intense breakthrough into very serious, very personal emotional experience which I feel has been partly taboo. Robert Lowell's poems about his experience in a mental hospital, for example, interested me very much. These peculiar, private, and taboo subjects, I feel, have been explored in recent American poetry. I think particularly the poetess Anne Sexton, who writes about her experiences as a mother, as a mother who has had a nervous breakdown, is an extremely emotional and feeling young woman and her poems are wonderfully craftsman-like poems and yet they have a kind of emotional

* From *The Poet Speaks*, ed. by Peter Orr.

and psychological depth which I think is something perhaps quite new, quite exciting.

ORR. Now you, as a poet, and as a person who straddles the Atlantic, if I can put it that way, being an American yourself . . .

PLATH. That's a rather awkward position, but I'll accept it!

ORR. . . . on which side does your weight fall, if I can pursue the metaphor?

PLATH. Well, I think that as far as language goes I'm an American, I'm afraid, my accent is American, my way of talk is an American way of talk, I'm an old-fashioned American. That's probably one of the reasons why I'm in England now and why I'll always stay in England. I'm about fifty years behind as far as my preferences go and I must say that the poets who excite me most are the Americans. There are very few contemporary English poets that I admire.

ORR. Does this mean that you think contemporary English poetry is behind the times compared with American?

PLATH. No, I think it is in a bit of a strait-jacket, if I may say so. There was an essay by Alvarez, the British critic: his arguments about the dangers of gentility in England are very pertinent, very true. I must say that I am not very genteel and I feel that gentility has a stranglehold: the neatness, the wonderful tidiness, which is so evident everywhere in England is perhaps more dangerous than it would appear on the surface.

ORR. But don't you think, too, that there is this business of English poets who are labouring under the whole weight of something which in block capitals is called 'English Literature'?

PLATH. Yes, I couldn't agree more. I know when I was at Cambridge this appeared to me. Young women would come up to me and say 'How do you dare to write, how do you dare to publish a poem, because of the criticism, the terrible criticism, that falls upon one if one does publish?' And the criticism is not of the poem as poem. I remember being appalled when someone criticized me for beginning just like John Donne, but not quite managing to finish like John Donne, and I first felt the full weight of English Literature on me at that point. I think the whole emphasis in England, in universities, on practical criticism (but not that so much as on historical criticism, knowing what period a line comes from) this is almost paralysing. In America, in university, we read—what?—T. S. Eliot, Dylan Thomas, Yeats, that is where we began. Shakespeare flaunted in the background. I'm not sure I agree with this, but I think that for the young poet, the writing poet, it is not quite so frightening to go to university in America as it is in England, for these reasons.

ORR. You say, Sylvia, that you consider yourself an American, but when we listen to a poem like 'Daddy', which talks about Dachau and Auschwitz and *Mein Kampf*, I have the impression that this is the sort of poem that a real American could not have written, because it doesn't mean so much, these names do not mean so much, on the other side of the Atlantic, do they?

PLATH. Well now, you are talking to me as a general American. In particular, my background is, may I say, German and Austrian. On one side I am a first generation American, on one side I'm second generation American, and so my concern with concentration camps and so on is uniquely intense. And then, again, I'm rather a political person as well, so I suppose that's what part of it comes from.

ORR. And as a poet, do you have a great and keen sense of the historic?

PLATH. I am not a historian, but I find myself being more and more fascinated by history and now I find myself reading more and more about history. I am very interested in Napoleon, at the present: I'm very interested in battles, in wars, in Gallipoli, the First World War and so on, and I think that as I age I am becoming more and more historical. I certainly wasn't at all in my early twenties.

ORR. Do your poems tend now to come out of books rather than out of your own life?

PLATH. No, no: I would not say that at all. I think my poems immediately come out of the sensuous and emotional experiences I have, but I must say I cannot sympathize with these cries from the heart that are informed by nothing except a needle or a knife, or whatever it is. I believe that one should be able to control and manipulate experiences, even the most terrifying, like madness, being tortured, this sort of experience, and one should be able to manipulate these experiences with an informed and an intelligent mind. I think that personal experience is very important, but certainly it shouldn't be a kind of shut-box and mirror-looking, narcissistic experience. I believe it should be *relevant*, and relevant to the larger things, the bigger things such as Hiroshima and Dachau and so on.

ORR. And so, behind the primitive, emotional reaction there must be an intellectual discipline.

PLATH. I feel that very strongly: having been an academic, having been tempted by the invitation to stay on to become a Ph.D., a professor, and all that, one side of me certainly does respect all disciplines, as long as they don't ossify.

ORR. What about writers who have influenced you, who have meant a lot to you?

PLATH. There were very few. I find it hard to trace them really. When I was at College I was stunned and astounded by the moderns, by Dylan Thomas, by Yeats, by Auden even: at one point I was absolutely wild for Auden and everything I wrote was desperately Audenesque. Now I again begin to go backwards, I begin to look to Blake, for example. And then, of course, it is presumptuous to say that one is influenced by someone like Shakespeare: one reads Shakespeare, and that is that.

ORR. Sylvia, one notices in reading your poems and listening to your poems that there are two qualities which emerge very quickly and clearly; one is their lucidity (and I think these two qualities have something to do one with the other), their lucidity and the impact they make on reading. Now, do you consciously design your poems to be both lucid and to be effective when they are read aloud?

PLATH. This is something I didn't do in my earlier poems. For example, my first book, *The Colossus*, I can't read any of the poems aloud now. I didn't write them to be read aloud. They, in fact, quite privately, bore me. These ones that I have just read, the ones that are very recent, I've got to say them, I speak them to myself, and I think that this in my own writing development is quite a new thing with me, and whatever lucidity they may have comes from the fact that I say them to myself, I say them aloud.

ORR. Do you think this is an essential ingredient of a good poem, that it should be able to be read aloud effectively?

PLATH. Well, I do feel that now and I feel that this development of recording poems, of speaking poems at readings, of having records of poets, I think this is a wonderful thing. I'm very excited by it. In a sense, there's a return, isn't there, to the old role of the poet, which was to speak to a group of people, to come across.

ORR. Or to sing to a group?

PLATH. To sing to a group of people, exactly.

ORR. Setting aside poetry for a moment, are there other things you would like to write, or that you have written?

PLATH. Well, I always was interested in prose. As a teenager, I published short stories. And I always wanted to write the long short story, I wanted to write a novel. Now that I have attained, shall I say, a respectable age, and have had experiences, I feel much more interested in prose, in the novel. I feel that in a novel, for example, you can get in toothbrushes and all the paraphernalia that one finds in daily life, and I find this more difficult in poetry. Poetry, I feel, is a tyrannical discipline, you've got to go so far, so fast, in such a small space that you've just got to turn away all the peripherals. And I miss them! I'm a woman, I like my little *Lares* and *Penates*, I like trivia, and I find that in a novel I can get more of life, perhaps not such intense life, but certainly more of life, and so I've become very interested in novel writing as a result.

ORR. This is almost a Dr Johnson sort of view, isn't it? What was it he said, 'There are some things that are fit for inclusion in poetry and others which are not'?

PLATH. Well, of course, as a poet I would say pouf! I would say everything should be able to come into a poem, but I *can't* put toothbrushes into a poem, I really can't!

ORR. Do you find yourself much in the company of other writers, of poets?

PLATH. I much prefer doctors, midwives, lawyers, anything but writers. I think writers and artists are the most narcissistic people. I mustn't say this, I like many of them, in fact a great many of my friends happen to be writers and artists. But I must say what I admire most is the person who masters an area of practical experience, and can teach me something. I mean, my local midwife has taught me how to keep bees. Well, she can't understand anything I write. And I find myself liking her, may I say, more than most poets. And among my friends I find people who know all about boats or know all about certain sports, or how to cut somebody open and remove an organ. I'm fascinated by this mastery of the practical. As a poet, one lives a bit on air. I always like someone who can teach me something practical.

ORR. Is there anything else you would rather have done than writing poetry? Because this is something, obviously, which takes up a great deal of one's private life, if one's going to succeed at it. Do you ever have any lingering regrets that you didn't do something else?

PLATH. I think if I had done anything else I would like to have been a doctor. This is the sort of polar opposition to being a writer, I suppose. My best friends when I was young were always doctors. I used to dress up in a white gauze helmet and go round and see babies born and cadavers cut open. This fascinated me, but I could never bring myself to disciplining myself to the point where I could learn all the details that one has to learn to be a good doctor. This is the sort of opposition: somebody who deals directly with human experiences, is able to cure, to mend, to help, this sort of thing. I suppose if I have any nostalgias it's this, but I console myself because I know so many doctors. And I may say, perhaps, I'm happier writing about doctors than I would have been being one.

ORR. But basically this thing, the writing of poetry, is something which has been a great satisfaction to you in your life, is it?

PLATH. Oh, satisfaction! I don't think I could live without it. It's like water or bread, or something absolutely essential to me. I find myself absolutely fulfilled when I have written a poem, when I'm writing one. Having written one, then you fall away very rapidly from having been a poet to becoming a sort of poet in rest, which isn't the same thing at all. But I think the actual experience of writing a poem is a magnificent one.

30 October 1962

☙ Ezra Pound

A Retrospect*

There has been so much scribbling about a new fashion in poetry, that I may perhaps be pardoned this brief recapitulation and retrospect.

In the spring or early summer of 1912, 'H.D.', Richard Aldington, and myself decided that we were agreed upon the three principles following:

(1) Direct treatment of the 'thing' whether subjective or objective.

(2) To use absolutely no word that does not contribute to the presentation.

(3) As regarding rhythm: to compose in the sequence of the musical phrase, not in sequence of a metronome.

Upon many points of taste and of predilection we differed, but agreeing upon these three positions we thought we had as much right to a group name, at least as much right, as a number of French 'schools' proclaimed by Mr Flint in the August number of Harold Monro's magazine for 1911.

This school has since been 'joined' or 'followed' by numerous people who, whatever their merits, do not show any signs of agreeing with the second specification. Indeed *vers libre* has become as prolix and as verbose as any of the flaccid varieties that preceded it. It has brought faults of its own. The actual language and phrasing is often as bad as that of our elders without even the excuse that the words are shovelled in to fill a metric pattern or to complete the noise of a rhyme-sound. Whether or no the phrases followed by the followers are musical must be left to the reader's decision. At times I can find a marked metre in 'vers libres' as stale and hackneyed as any pseudo-Swinburnian, at times the writers seem to follow no musical structure whatever. But it is, on the whole, good that the field should be ploughed. Perhaps a few good poems have come from the new method, and if so it is justified.

Criticism is not a circumscription or a set of prohibitions. It provides fixed points of departure. It may startle a dull reader into alertness. That little of it which is good is mostly in stray phrases; or if it be an older artist helping

---

* A group of early essays and notes which appeared under this title in *Pavannes and Divisions* (1918). 'A Few Don'ts' was first printed in *Poetry*, I: 6 (March 1913). From *The Literary Essays of Ezra Pound.*

a younger it is in great measure but rules of thumb, cautions gained by experience.

I set together a few phrases on practical working about the time the first remarks on imagisme were published. The first use of the word 'Imagiste' was in my note to T. E. Hulme's five poems, printed at the end of my *Ripostes* in the autumn of 1912. I reprint my cautions from *Poetry* for March 1913.

A FEW DON'TS

An 'Image' is that which presents an intellectual and emotional complex in an instant of time. I use the term 'complex' rather in the technical sense employed by the newer psychologists, such as Hart, though we might not agree absolutely in our application.

It is the presentation of such a 'complex' instantaneously which gives that sense of sudden liberation; that sense of freedom from time limits and space limits; that sense of sudden growth, which we experience in the presence of the greatest works of art.

It is better to present one Image in a lifetime than to produce voluminous works.

All this, however, some may consider open to debate. The immediate necessity is to tabulate A LIST OF DON'TS for those beginning to write verses. I can not put all of them into Mosaic negative.

To begin with, consider the three propositions (demanding direct treatment, economy of words, and the sequence of the musical phrase), not as dogma—never consider anything as dogma—but as the result of long contemplation, which, even if it is someone else's contemplation, may be worth consideration.

Pay no attention to the criticism of men who have never themselves written a notable work. Consider the discrepancies between the actual writing of the Greek poets and dramatists, and the theories of the Graeco-Roman grammarians, concocted to explain their metres.

LANGUAGE

Use no superfluous word, no adjective which does not reveal something.

Don't use such an expression as 'dim lands *of peace*'. It dulls the image. It mixes an abstraction with the concrete. It comes from the writer's not realizing that the natural object is always the *adequate* symbol.

Go in fear of abstractions. Do not retell in mediocre verse what has already been done in good prose. Don't think any intelligent person is going to be deceived when you try to shirk all the difficulties of the unspeakably difficult art of good prose by chopping your composition into line lengths.

What the expert is tired of today the public will be tired of tomorrow.

Don't imagine that the art of poetry is any simpler than the art of music, or that you can please the expert before you have spent at least as much effort on the art of verse as the average piano teacher spends on the art of music.

Be influenced by as many great artists as you can, but have the decency either to acknowledge the debt outright, or to try to conceal it.

Don't allow 'influence' to mean merely that you mop up the particular decorative vocabulary of some one or two poets whom you happen to admire. A Turkish war correspondent was recently caught red-handed babbling in his dispatches of 'dove-grey' hills, or else it was 'pearl-pale', I can not remember.

Use either no ornament or good ornament.

RHYTHM AND RHYME

Let the candidate fill his mind with the finest cadences he can discover, preferably in a foreign language,[1] so that the meaning of the words may be less likely to divert his attention from the movement; e.g., Saxon charms, Hebridean Folk Songs, the verse of Dante, and the lyrics of Shakespeare—if he can dissociate the vocabulary from the cadence. Let him dissect the lyrics of Goethe coldly into their component sound values, syllables long and short, stressed and unstressed, into vowels and consonants.

It is not necessary that a poem should rely on its music, but if it does rely on its music that music must be such as will delight the expert.

Let the neophyte know assonance and alliteration, rhyme immediate and delayed, simple and polyphonic, as a musician would expect to know harmony and counterpoint and all the minutiae of his craft. No time is too great to give to these matters or to any one of them, even if the artist seldom have need of them.

Don't imagine that a thing will 'go' in verse just because it's too dull to go in prose.

Don't be 'viewy'—leave that to the writers of pretty little philosophic essays. Don't be descriptive; remember that the painter can describe a landscape much better than you can, and that he has to know a deal more about it.

When Shakespeare talks of the 'Dawn in russet mantle clad' he presents something which the painter does not present. There is in this line of his nothing that one can call description; he presents.

---

[1] This is for rhythm, his vocabulary must of course be found in his native tongue. (E.P.)

Consider the way of the scientists rather than the way of an advertising agent for a new soap.

The scientist does not expect to be acclaimed as a great scientist until he has *discovered* something. He begins by learning what has been discovered already. He goes from that point onward. He does not bank on being a charming fellow personally. He does not expect his friends to applaud the results of his freshman class work. Freshmen in poetry are unfortunately not confined to a definite and recognizable class room. They are 'all over the shop'. Is it any wonder 'the public is indifferent to poetry'?

Don't chop your stuff into separate *iambs*. Don't make each line stop dead at the end, and then begin every next line with a heave. Let the beginning of the next line catch the rise of the rhythm wave, unless you want a definite longish pause.

In short, behave as a musician, a good musician, when dealing with that phase of your art which has exact parallels in music. The same laws govern, and you are bound by no others.

Naturally, your rhythmic structure should not destroy the shape of your words, or their natural sound, or their meaning. It is improbable that, at the start, you will be able to get a rhythm-structure sound enough to affect them very much, though you may fall a victim to all sorts of false stopping due to line ends and caesurae.

The Musician can rely on pitch and the volume of the orchestra. You can not. The term harmony is misapplied in poetry; it refers to simultaneous sounds of different pitch. There is, however, in the best verse a sort of residue of sound which remains in the ear of the hearer and acts more or less as an organ-base.

A rhyme must have in it some slight element of surprise if it is to give pleasure; it need not be bizarre or curious, but it must be well used if used at all.

Vide further Vildrac and Duhamel's notes on rhyme in *Technique Poétique*.

That part of your poetry which strikes upon the imaginative eye of the reader will lose nothing by translation into a foreign tongue; that which appeals to the ear can reach only those who take it in the original.

Consider the definiteness of Dante's presentation, as compared with Milton's rhetoric. Read as much of Wordsworth as does not seem too unutterably dull.[2]

If you want the gist of the matter go to Sappho, Catullus, Villon, Heine when he is in the vein, Gautier when he is not too frigid; or, if you have not the tongues, seek out the leisurely Chaucer. Good prose will do you no harm, and there is good discipline to be had by trying to write it.

---

[2] Vide infra. (E.P.)

Translation is likewise good training, if you find that your original matter 'wobbles' when you try to rewrite it. The meaning of the poem to be translated can not 'wobble'.

If you are using a symmetrical form, don't put in what you want to say and then fill up the remaining vacuums with slush.

Don't mess up the perception of one sense by trying to define it in terms of another. This is usually only the result of being too lazy to find the exact word. To this clause there are possibly exceptions.

The first three simple prescriptions will throw out nine-tenths of all the bad poetry now accepted as standard and classic; and will prevent you from many a crime of production.

'...*Mais d'abord il faut être un poète*', as MM. Duhamel and Vildrac have said at the end of their little book, *Notes sur la Technique Poétique*.

Since March 1913, Ford Madox Hueffer has pointed out that Wordsworth was so intent on the ordinary or plain word that he never thought of hunting for *le mot juste*.

John Butler Yeats has handled or man-handled Wordsworth and the Victorians, and his criticism, contained in letters to his son, is now printed and available.

I do not like writing *about* art, my first, at least I think it was my first essay on the subject, was a protest against it.

PROLEGOMENA[3]

Time was when the poet lay in a green field with his head against a tree and played his diversion on a ha'penny whistle, and Caesar's predecessors conquered the earth, and the predecessors of golden Crassus embezzled, and fashions had their say, and let him alone. And presumably he was fairly content in this circumstance, for I have small doubt that the occasional passerby, being attracted by curiosity to know why anyone should lie under a tree and blow diversion on a ha'penny whistle, came and conversed with him, and that among these passersby there was on occasion a person of charm or a young lady who had not read *Man and Superman*; and looking back upon this naïve state of affairs we call it the age of gold.

Metastasio, and he should know if anyone, assures us that this age endures—even though the modern poet is expected to holloa his verses down a speaking tube to the editors of cheap magazines—S. S. McClure, or someone of that sort—even though hordes of authors meet in dreariness and drink healths

[3] *Poetry and Drama* (then the *Poetry Review*, edited by Harold Monro), Feb. 1912. (E.P.)

to the 'Copyright Bill'; even though these things be, the age of gold pertains. Imperceivably, if you like, but pertains. You meet unkempt Amyclas in a Soho restaurant and chant together of dead and forgotten things—it is a manner of speech among poets to chant of dead, half-forgotten things, there seems no special harm in it; it has always been done—and it's rather better to be a clerk in the Post Office than to look after a lot of stinking, verminous sheep—and at another hour of the day one substitutes the drawing-room for the restaurant and tea is probably more palatable than mead and mare's milk, and little cakes than honey. And in this fashion one survives the resignation of Mr Balfour, and the iniquities of the American customs-house, *e quel bufera infernal*, the periodical press. And then in the middle of it, there being apparently no other person at once capable and available one is stopped and asked to explain oneself.

I begin on the chord thus querulous, for I would much rather lie on what is left of Catullus's parlour floor and speculate the azure beneath it and the hills off to Salo and Riva with their forgotten gods moving unhindered amongst them, than discuss any processes and theories of art whatsoever. I would rather play tennis. I shall not argue.

CREDO

Rhythm.—I believe in an 'absolute rhythm', a rhythm, that is, in poetry which corresponds exactly to the emotion or shade of emotion to be expressed. A man's rhythm must be interpretative, it will be, therefore, in the end, his own, uncounterfeiting, uncounterfeitable.

Symbols.—I believe that the proper and perfect symbol is the natural object, that if a man use 'symbols' he must so use them that their symbolic function does not obtrude; so that *a* sense, and the poetic quality of the passage, is not lost to those who do not understand the symbol as such, to whom, for instance, a hawk is a hawk.

Technique.—I believe in technique as the test of a man's sincerity; in law when it is ascertainable; in the trampling down of every convention that impedes or obscures the determination of the law, or the precise rendering of the impulse.

Form.—I think there is a 'fluid' as well as a 'solid' content, that some poems may have form as a tree has form, some as water poured into a vase. That most symmetrical forms have certain uses. That a vast number of subjects cannot be precisely, and therefore not properly rendered in symmetrical forms.

'Thinking that alone worthy wherein the whole art is employed'.[4] I think the artist should master all known forms and systems of metric, and

[4] Dante, *De Volgari Eloquio*. (E.P.)

I have with some persistence set about doing this, searching particularly into those periods wherein the systems came to birth or attained their maturity. It has been complained, with some justice, that I dump my note-books on the public. I think that only after a long struggle will poetry attain such a degree of development, or, if you will, modernity, that it will vitally concern people who are accustomed, in prose, to Henry James and Anatole France, in music to Debussy. I am constantly contending that it took two centuries of Provence and one of Tuscany to develop the media of Dante's masterwork, that it took the latinists of the Renaissance, and the Pleiade, and his own age of painted speech to prepare Shakespeare his tools. It is tremendously important that great poetry be written, it makes no jot of difference who writes it. The experimental demonstrations of one man may save the time of many—hence my furore over Arnaut Daniel—if a man's experiments try out one new rime, or dispense conclusively with one iota of currently accepted nonsense, he is merely playing fair with his colleagues when he chalks up his result.

No man ever writes very much poetry that 'matters'. In bulk, that is, no one produces much that is final, and when a man is not doing this highest thing, this saying the thing once for all and perfectly; when he is not matching Ποικιλοθρον', αθανατ 'Αφροδιτα,[5] or 'Hist—said Kate the Queen', he had much better be making the sorts of experiment which may be of use to him in his later work, or to his successors.

'The lyf so short, the craft so long to lerne.' It is a foolish thing for a man to begin his work on a too narrow foundation, it is a disgraceful thing for a man's work not to show steady growth and increasing fineness from first to last.

As for 'adaptations'; one finds that all the old masters of painting recommend to their pupils that they begin by copying masterwork, and proceed to their own composition.

As for 'Every man his own poet', the more every man knows about poetry the better. I believe in every one writing poetry who wants to; most do. I believe in every man knowing enough of music to play 'God Bless Our Home' on the harmonium, but I do not believe in every man giving concerts and printing his sin.

The mastery of any art is the work of a lifetime. I should not discriminate between the 'amateur' and the 'professional'. Or rather I should discriminate quite often in favour of the amateur, but I should discriminate between the amateur and the expert. It is certain that the present chaos will endure until the Art of poetry has been preached down the amateur gullet,

---

[5] ['Splendid-throned, deathless Aphrodite': the opening line of Sappho's famous invocation.]

until there is such a general understanding of the fact that poetry is an art and not a pastime; such a knowledge of technique; of technique of surface and technique of content, that the amateurs will cease to try to drown out the masters.

If a certain thing was said once for all in Atlantis or Arcadia, in 450 Before Christ or in 1290 after, it is not for us moderns to go saying it over, or to go obscuring the memory of the dead by saying the same thing with less skill and less conviction.

My pawing over the ancients and semi-ancients has been one struggle to find out what has been done, once for all, better than it can ever be done again, and to find out what remains for us to do, and plenty does remain, for if we still feel the same emotions as those which launched the thousand ships, it is quite certain that we come on these feelings differently, through different nuances, by different intellectual gradations. Each age has its own abounding gifts yet only some ages transmute them into matter of duration. No good poetry is ever written in a manner twenty years old, for to write in such a manner shows conclusively that the writer thinks from books, convention, and cliché, and not from life, yet a man feeling the divorce of life and his art may naturally try to resurrect a forgotten mode if he finds in that mode some leaven, or if he thinks he sees in it some element lacking in contemporary art which might unite that art again to its sustenance, life.

In the art of Daniel and Cavalcanti, I have seen that precision which I miss in the Victorians, that explicit rendering, be it of external nature, or of emotion. Their testimony is of the eyewitness, their symptoms are first hand.

As for the nineteenth century, with all respect to its achievements, I think we shall look back upon it as a rather blurry, messy sort of a period, a rather sentimentalistic, mannerish sort of a period. I say this without any self-righteousness, with no self-satisfaction.

As for there being a 'movement' or my being of it, the conception of poetry as a 'pure art' in the sense in which I use the term, revived with Swinburne. From the puritanical revolt to Swinburne, poetry has been merely the vehicle—yes, definitely, Arthur Symon's scruples and feelings about the word not withholding—the ox-cart and post-chaise for transmitting thoughts poetic or otherwise. And perhaps the 'great Victorians', though it is doubtful, and assuredly the 'nineties' continued the development of the art, confining their improvements, however, chiefly to sound and to refinements of manner.

Mr Yeats has once and for all stripped English poetry of its perdamnable rhetoric. He has boiled away all that is not poetic—and a good deal that is. He has become a classic in his own lifetime and *nel mezzo del cammin*. He has made our poetic idiom a thing pliable, a speech without inversions.

Robert Bridges, Maurice Hewlett, and Frederic Manning are[6] in their different ways seriously concerned with overhauling the metric, in testing the language and its adaptability to certain models. Ford Hueffer is making some sort of experiments in modernity. The Provost of Oriel continues his translation of the *Divina Commedia*.

As to Twentieth-century poetry, and the poetry which I expect to see written during the next decade or so, it will, I think, move against poppycock, it will be harder and saner, it will be what Mr Hewlett calls 'nearer the bone'. It will be as much like granite as it can be, its force will lie in its truth, its interpretative power (of course, poetic force does always rest there); I mean it will not try to seem forcible by rhetorical din, and luxurious riot. We will have fewer painted adjectives impeding the shock and stroke of it. At least for myself, I want it so, austere, direct, free from emotional slither.

What is there now, in 1917, to be added?

RE VERS LIBRE

I think the desire for vers libre is due to the sense of quantity reasserting itself after years of starvation. But I doubt if we can take over, for English, the rules of quantity laid down for Greek and Latin, mostly by Latin grammarians.

I think one should write vers libre only when one 'must', that is to say, only when the 'thing' builds up a rhythm more beautiful than that of set metres, or more real, more a part of the emotion of the 'thing', more germane, intimate, interpretative than the measure of regular accentual verse; a rhythm which discontents one with set iambic or set anapæstic.

Eliot has said the thing very well when he said, 'No *vers* is *libre* for the man who wants to do a good job.'

As a matter of detail, there is vers libre with accent heavily marked as a drum-beat (as par example my 'Dance Figure'), and on the other hand I think I have gone as far as can profitably be gone in the other direction (and perhaps too far). I mean I do not think one can use to any advantage rhythms much more tenuous and imperceptible than some I have used. I think progress lies rather in an attempt to approximate classical quantitative metres (NOT to copy them) than in a carelessness regarding such things.[7]

I agree with John Yeats on the relation of beauty to certitude. I prefer satire, which is due to emotion, to any sham of emotion.

---

[6] (Dec. 1911). (E.P.)

[7] Let me date this statement 20 Aug. 1917. (E.P.)

I have had to write, or at least I have written a good deal about art, sculpture, painting, and poetry. I have seen what seemed to me the best of contemporary work reviled and obstructed. Can anyone write prose of permanent or durable interest when he is merely saying for one year what nearly every one will say at the end of three or four years? I have been battistrada for a sculptor, a painter, a novelist, several poets. I wrote also of certain French writers in *The New Age* in nineteen twelve or eleven.

I would much rather that people would look at Brzeska's sculpture and Lewis's drawings, and that they would read Joyce, Jules Romains, Eliot, than that they should read what I have said of these men, or that I should be asked to republish argumentative essays and reviews.

All that the critic can do for the reader or audience or spectator is to focus his gaze or audition. Rightly or wrongly I think my blasts and essays have done their work, and that more people are now likely to go the sources than are likely to read this book.

Jammes's 'Existences' in *La Triomphe de la Vie* is available. So are his early poems. I think we need a convenient anthology rather than descriptive criticism. Carl Sandburg wrote me from Chicago, 'It's hell when poets can't afford to buy each other's books.' Half the people who care, only borrow. In America so few people know each other that the difficulty lies more than half in distribution. Perhaps one should make an anthology: Romains's 'Un Etre en Marche' and 'Prières', Vildrac's 'Visite'. Retrospectively the fine wrought work of Laforgue, the flashes of Rimbaud, the hard-bit lines of Tristan Corbière, Tailhade's sketches in 'Poèmes Aristophanesques', the 'Litanies' of De Gourmont.

It is difficult at all times to write of the fine arts, it is almost impossible unless one can accompany one's prose with many reproductions. Still I would seize this chance or any chance to reaffirm my belief in Wyndham Lewis's genius, both in his drawings and his writings. And I would name an out of the way prose book, the *Scenes and Portraits* of Frederic Manning, as well as James Joyce's short stories and novel, *Dubliners*, and the now well-known *Portrait of the Artist*, as well as Lewis's *Tarr*, if, that is, I may treat my strange reader as if he were a new friend come into the room, intent on ransacking my bookshelf.

ONLY EMOTION ENDURES

'Only emotion endures.' Surely it is better for me to name over the few beautiful poems that still ring in my head than for me to search my flat for back numbers of periodicals and rearrange all that I have said about friendly and hostile writers.

The first twelve lines of Padraic Colum's 'Drover'; his 'O Woman shapely as a swan, on your account I shall not die'; Joyce's 'I hear an army'; the lines of Yeats that ring in my head and in the heads of all young men of my time who care for poetry: Braseal and the Fisherman, 'The fire that stirs about her, when she stirs'; the later lines of 'The Scholars', the faces of the Magi, William Carlos Williams's 'Postlude', Aldington's version of 'Atthis', and 'H.D.'s' waves like pine tops, and her verse in *Des Imagistes* the first anthology; Hueffer's 'How red your lips are' in his translation from Von der Vogelweide, his 'Three Ten', the general effect of his 'On Heaven'; his sense of the prose values or prose qualities in poetry; his ability to write poems that half-chant and are spoiled by a musician's additions; beyond these a poem by Alice Corbin, 'One City Only', and another ending 'But sliding water over a stone'. These things have worn smooth in my head and I am not through with them, nor with Aldington's 'In Via Sestina' nor his other poems in *Des Imagistes*, though people have told me their flaws. It may be that their content is too much embedded in me for me to look back at the words.

I am almost a different person when I come to take up the argument for Eliot's poems.

AL PURDY

AN INTERVIEW*

INTERVIEWER. Somehow your poetry manages to be domestic and historical at the same time. Is this what critics mean by calling it epic?

PURDY. 'Rooms for rent in the outer planets.' Yes, but I don't think it's epic. Epic sounds grandiose to me; and I don't think I'm grandiose. I certainly hope I'm not.

INTERVIEWER. In 'The Country North of Belleville' there is a sense of beauty and terror in the description. Do you find the Canadian landscape hostile?

PURDY. Landscapes hostile to man? I think man is hostile to himself. Landscapes, I think, are essentially neutral.

INTERVIEWER. But you travel a lot, as do many Canadian writers, and write about the places you visit. Is this because it is easier to control the elements of a newer, smaller area?

PURDY. Easier than Canada, you mean? No, it isn't that. I have the feeling that—before I worked at jobs and described the places where I was and the

* This interview with Gary Geddes took place in the summer of 1968.

people that I met, etc.—that somehow or other one uses up one's past. It isn't that when one goes to another country one is consciously seeking for new poems, because it would get to sounding as goddam self-conscious as hell. For instance, if you go to Baffin Island to write poems (which I did, incidentally) . . . well, I don't like to look at it that way. I'm interested in going to Baffin Island because I'm interested in Baffin Island.

INTERVIEWER. And the poems just happen.

PURDY. I write poems like spiders spin webs, and perhaps for much the same reason: to support my existence. I talk, I eat, I write poems, I make love—I do all these things self-consciously. The 'new area' bit . . . well, unless one is a stone one doesn't sit still. And perhaps new areas of landscape awake old areas of one's self. One has seen the familiar landscape (perhaps) so many times that one ceases to really see it. Maybe it's like the expatriate writers, Joyce and so on, who went to foreign countries in order to see their own.

INTERVIEWER. You have been called the great Canadian realist (to drag one from the bottom of the bag). Do you write any poems which *don't* have some base in actual experience?

PURDY. Aren't you talking about poets like Mallarmé? Very few poets do that. I've written poems about things, even doorknobs, but generally speaking it's out of my own life.

INTERVIEWER. Do you feel at ease to 'cook' your experiences for the sake of a poem?

PURDY. After you've lived your whole life writing poetry (and I started writing at thirteen), I think you've always got one ear cocked, listening to know if you're good enough to put it into a poem. Do you mean, to be wholly involved in the experience without seeing it as something else? No, I don't think so, if that's what you mean. I always know what I'm doing or feeling or seeing. I'm self-conscious about being self-conscious about being self-conscious.

INTERVIEWER. In your 'Lament for Robert Kennedy' there seems to be a qualitative difference between the first part of the poem, where you are dependent for the most part upon rhetoric and abstraction, and the second part, where the images and language become personal and concrete. Do you think that your poetry is strongest when it is attached to images from your own landscape?

PURDY. Yes, I think so. I was being pretty propagandist in the early part of that poem; but, also, when you say there's nothing concrete in it, how about the skidrow losers with the bottle of good booze in their hands like a lily? Yes, I generally stick to the concrete or get to it pretty quick. You can start from the concrete, but I don't think you can take off from no stance at all.

INTERVIEWER. I especially like your poem, 'Portrait', about Irving Layton. What did you mean in the last line?

PURDY. I don't remember the last line, frankly. What is it?

INTERVIEWER. 'And then again I'm a bit disappointed.'

PURDY. Well, I think the thought on my mind was that somebody had fixed themselves, pinned themselves down, taken a stance, identified themselves far too fully. I don't think . . . in my own case I like to think of a continual becoming and a changing and a moving. I feel that Irving takes such positive stances that I'm a little disappointed, because I think he could have done much better. For instance, now he's writing poems in *The Shattered Plinths* about various new events, about violence. Violence is a damned interesting subject, but not the way he's treated it somehow. Everything about Irving is positive; if you were to argue with him on any of these points, he'd defend them all vehemently. You wouldn't be able to win the argument, but he'd still be wrong.

INTERVIEWER. Is it a general characteristic of modern poets to *find* themselves too quickly? Creeley, for example, seems to have established a voice or a style which he exploits; one wonders whether the style reflects or *directs* the life-rhythms.

PURDY. I only know a bit about Creeley. I don't *like* his style very much; I don't like the deliberate ambiguities at the ends of his poems. But style is something that I was very hung up on a few years ago, when I kept noticing, or thought I did, that all the critics were insisting that you find your voice, that you find a consistency, and that you stick to it. Now this, of course, is what Creeley has done; and it's apparently something the critics still approve of. I disagree with it all along the line. I don't think that a man is consistent; he contradicts himself at every turn. Housman, for instance, takes a very dim view of life for the most part, is very depressing—but human life isn't like that *all* of the time. You wake up in the morning, the sun is shining and you feel good; this also is a time when Housman could have written a poem. I can't believe he never felt good once in his life. Anyway, I disagree with this consistency bit very strongly.

INTERVIEWER. Would you not say that the success of *The Cariboo Horses* has something to do with *your* having finally found some kind of voice or consistency?

PURDY. As far as I'm concerned, I found a voice (not necessarily a consistent one), but I thought that I was at my best beginning about 1961-2, when *Poems for All the Annettes* was first published; I was sure I had hit a vein in which I could say many more things. I'd been looking for ways and means of doing it; and finally, it got to the point that I didn't care what I said—I'd say anything—as long as it worked for me.

INTERVIEWER. How consciously are you concerned with technique? Do you share the recent technical interests of Williams and Olson, such as concern for the line, the syllable, the process of breathing?

PURDY. My technique, I suppose, takes a bit from Williams, a bit from Olson; for instance, I agree for the most part with using the contemporary, the modern, idiom. On the other hand, if I were writing a certain kind of poem I might avoid colloquialisms, idiosyncrasies, slang, and so on. It just depends; it all has to do with the poem. No, I pay no attention to the breathing bit; and I never compose on a typewriter, as Olson is supposed to do. Most of the time when I'm writing I don't think of how to write the thing at all, consciously; sometimes I do. When I wrote a poem about hockey players, I deliberately put in swift rhythms to simulate the players going down the ice. And there are times when I've mixed up rhythms deliberately. But other times, whatever rhythm you get in there seems accidental; though I don't suppose it is, because a poet writes a lot of poems. I'm concerned with techniques, yes, but I don't consciously spend so much time thinking of them as Williams and Olson do.

INTERVIEWER. What is it that makes a poem work?

PURDY. Technique? The language itself is part of that, also the various methods used to write a poem. But somehow saying that is not enough. There ought to be a quality in a good poet beyond any analysis, the part of his mind that leaps from one point to another, sideways, backwards, ass-over-the-electric-kettle. This quality is not logic, and the result may not be consistent with the rest of the poem when it happens, though it may be. I believe it is said by medicos that much of the human mind has no known function. Perhaps the leap sideways and backwards comes from there. At any rate, it seems to me the demands made on it cause the mind to stretch, to do more than it is capable of under ordinary and different circumstances. And when this happens, or when you think it does, that time is joyous, and you experience something beyond experience. Like discovering you can fly, or that relative truth may blossom into an absolute. And the absolute must be attacked again and again, until you find something that will stand up, may not be denied, which becomes a compass point by which to move somewhere else. I think that when you put such things into words they are liable to sound like pretentious jargon. Such things exist in your mind without conscious thought, perhaps in that unknown area. And sometimes—if you're lucky—a coloured fragment may slip through into the light when you're writing a poem.

INTERVIEWER. How do your poems generally take shape?

PURDY. Well, that's tough. I wrote the title poem of *The Cariboo Horses* in about twenty minutes, revised it a little, and that was about it; and I took about eight years to write another poem in the same book, which still isn't as good as it ought to be. In the hockey-player poem, I wanted a strong contrast between the metrics and prose; and I tried to make several passages about as prosy as possible in order to contrast with the swift metrical rhythms.

INTERVIEWER. Could you describe the evolution of a single poem?

PURDY. Well, there used to be an old grist mill in Ameliasburg village—four stories high with three-foot-thick walls of grey stone. In 1957-8 I explored that mill from top to bottom, trying to visualize the people who used to operate it. Marvelling at the 24-inch-wide boards from nineteenth-century pine forests; peering curiously at wooden cogs and hand-carved gears, flour-sifting apparatus, bits of rotting silk-screens, and so on.

My interest in the mill grew to a strong curiosity about the people who built it—what were they like?—those old farmers, pioneers, dwellers in deep woods, men who worked from dawn to day's end, so tired the whole world wavered and reeled in their home-going vision. Most of the old ones were United Empire Loyalists, come here to the wilderness after the American Revolution because they had no other place to go. The man who built the village mill in 1842 was Owen Roblin. He lived to be ninety-seven, and lies buried in Ameliasburg graveyard near the black millpond, with wife and scattered brood of sons nearby.

I questioned the old people in the village about Owen Roblin. It seems . . . well, out of it all came my poem, 'Roblin's Mills'.

INTERVIEWER. More than thirty poems in *The Cariboo Horses* are open-ended, concluding with a dash or some other punctuation suggesting incompleteness. Is this simply a device?

PURDY. The open-endedness is both device and philosophy, but it doesn't bar formalism if I feel like it: i.e., I reject nothing. No form, that is, *if* I feel like it and the poem agrees. I was doing it a good deal at the time; maybe that owes something to Olson's 'in the field' bit—a line is as long as it's right for it to be. But I don't like periods very much; if I can work a lot using commas and semi-colons I will. It should just be taken as the reader takes it: I don't attach much more to it than just dispensing with punctuation. Its effect, of course, is different from punctuation, but I haven't gone into that. My own poems *without* this give me a peculiar feeling I can't explain.

INTERVIEWER. The experience that goes into a poem is changing even as the poem is written; in fact, the poem *changes* the experience.

PURDY. You mean *fixes* it.

INTERVIEWER. No, I mean that the open-endedness works against the final fixing of the experience.

PURDY. Well, yes, *you* said it. I have thought of that, but not in connection with these poems. One thinks of poems as little bits of life cut out, except that they are as one sees life with one's mind. You have the odd feeling that you can reach back and pick a poem that will take the place of that experience in the past. It does in one's life of course, but there are so many ifs and buts that when I say a thing I'm never sure if I'm right.

INTERVIEWER. Is poetry a way of exploring experience for you?

PURDY. Jesus Christ, that's an awful question! I've no idea. I like to write poetry; I get a kick out of writing poems. I suppose to a limited degree it does explore my own experience; but if anybody else was looking, they would deny that the poem described it, I expect, particularly my wife. I write poetry because I *like* to write poetry. It's much like getting drunk once in a while, especially if you write something you like. Exploring one's experience sounds like such a terrible way to describe a simple thing like writing a poem. Doesn't it though?

INTERVIEWER. As a descriptive poet, what is your response to external objects?

PURDY. In the first place, I don't consider myself any particular kind of poet. About objects in relation to myself, this is as subjective as hell. Any time any poet writes about an object, he's got to be subjective, no matter how objective he appears. I've sometimes thought that everybody sees the same colour differently. One isn't always able to express these differences in words, since words are so limited and have such large potential at the same time. No, I'm far more interested in objects in relation to something, in relation to people.

INTERVIEWER. You once asked Stephen Spender what he thought of Kenneth Patchen. Is Patchen a favourite? And which of your contemporaries do you admire?

PURDY. Did I ask that? That's a tough one, there are so very few. No, Patchen is not a favourite of mine. I like his 'Dirge'; that's about all I can think of. I like a lot of those poets who are producing in a consistent line, exactly as I said I would not like to do. Robert Bly has adopted a particular style and is writing pretty decent poems; but this style becomes very monotonous if he keeps it up—and he does keep it up. Charles Bukowski is writing in a style in which I also write; but that's just about his *only* style. I hope to get out of it once in a while.

There are so damned few. I like some of James Dickey, for instance, quite a bit; but somehow or other, he lives at such intense white heat so much of the time that I don't believe he can possibly exist; he must burn up. He keeps being confounded, rivers keep boiling through his veins, he keeps becoming exalted all of the time.

In Canada? I like Newlove; I think he might have a chance to do something pretty good. Ian Young, George Jonas—maybe. Who else? They all seem to me—when they adopt some special way of writing, like bpNichol and the concrete boys, or the *Tish* imitators of the Black Mountain—to be travelling down a dead end.

But in the world there are several, some living, some dead, that I like: I like Pierre Superveille very much and, of course, Pablo Neruda and Cesar Vallejo and one or two others. *Modern World Poetry*—in translation—is an awfully good book.

INTERVIEWER. What about earlier writers?

PURDY. I hope to find other poets to expend the same enthusiasms on as I did on Dylan Thomas and, to a certain extent, Robinson Jeffers; and also John Donne at one time. But enthusiasms pass. I was tremendously enthused over Layton about 1955; that enthusiasm has pretty well passed. I agree with my own line on Layton, that words no sooner said become clichés, though Layton is not all cliché. Somehow the immortal claptrap of poetry is a cliché.

INTERVIEWER. How much 'research' went into your poems in *North of Summer*?

PURDY. Actually, I didn't do a helluva lot of research. In fact, when I was up there I was reading E.M. Forster's *Passage to India* and about fifteen other pocket books, including that one I mentioned in 'When I Sat Down to Play the Piano', William Barrett's *Irrational Man*. The point at which books you read, or information from books you read, comes into your head is not when you are reading them, but sometime later. I always take off from any point or fact that seems relevant to the situation (in the North, say); I always take off on a personal expedition from there, though I may not know where I'm headed.

INTERVIEWER. I think of your 'In the Wilderness' as a Canadian 'Easter 1916'. Do other poems trigger you off to write?

PURDY. Yes, sometimes. Oddly enough, one poem called 'Dark Landscape', which will be in *Wild Grape Wine*, I twisted around to mean something other than what Vachel Lindsay means in 'Spring Comes on Forever'. That was almost a direct steal, except that I used it differently. Most of the time, when you read someone else's poem, it will give you your own thoughts on the same subject, which is much more valid, I think. This is why and how I wrote the bird poem in *North of Summer*. I think it was some Cuban poet that had written a poem about birds, so I started thinking about birds. And, incidentally, 'The Cariboo Horses' was written because I read in the Introduction to *New British Poetry* two quotes about horses by Ted Hughes and Philip Larkin and I thought they were terrible and that I could do better; so I started to write a poem. I think that if you write poems, your mind just knowingly or unknowingly casts around for subjects all of the time; I don't think a poet is ever not looking for subjects.

ADRIENNE RICH

EXCERPTS FROM WHAT IS FOUND THERE: NOTEBOOKS ON POETRY AND POLITICS (1993)

But I found myself pulled by names: Dire Whelk, Dusky Tegula, Fingered Limpet, Hooded Puncturella, Veiled Chiton, Bat Star, By-the-Wind Sailor, Crumb-of-bread Sponge, Eye Fringed Worm, Sugar Wrack, Frilled Anemone, Bull Kelp, Ghost Shrimp, Sanderling, Walleye Surfperch, Volcano Barnacle, Stiff-footed Sea Cucumber, Leather Star, Innkeeper Worm, Lug Worm. And I felt the names drawing me into a state of piercing awareness, a state I associate with the reading of poems. These names—by whom given and agreed on?—these names work as poetry works, enlivening a sensuous reality through recognition or through the play of sounds (the short i's of Fingered Limper, the open vowels of Bull Kelp, Hooded Puncturella, Bat Star); the poising of heterogeneous images *volcano* and *barnacle, leather* and *star, sugar* and *wrack)* to evoke other worlds of meaning Sugar Wrack: a foundered ship in the Triangle Trade? Volcano Barnacle: Tiny unnoticed undergrowth with explosive potential? Who saw the bird named Sanderling and gave it that caressive, diminutive name? Or was Sanderling the name of one who saw it? These names work as poetry works in another sense as well: they make something unforgettable. You will remember the pictorial names as you won't the Latin, which, however, is more specific as to genus and species. Human eyes gazed at each of all these forms of life and saw resemblance in difference—the core of metaphor, which lies close to the core of poetry itself, the only hope for a humane civil life. The eye for likeness in the midst of contrast, the appeal to recognition, the association of thing to thing, spiritual fact with embodied form, begins here. And so begins the suggestion of multiple, many-layered, rather than singular, meanings, wherever we look, in the ordinary world.

'Woman and bird'

A poem can't free us from the struggle for existence, but it can uncover desires and appetites buried under the accumulating emergencies of our lives, the fabricated wants and needs we have had urged upon us, have accepted as our own. It's not a philosophical or psychological blueprint; it's an instrument for embodied experience. But we seek that experience, or recognize it when it is offered to us, because it reminds us in some way of our need. After that re-arousal of desire, the task of acting on that truth, or making love, or meeting other needs, is ours.

'Voices from the air'

But there's been a missing term. I saw, or thought I saw, that poetry has been held both indispensable and dangerous, one way or another, in every country but my own. The mistake I was making was to assume that poetry really is unwanted, impotent, in the late twentieth-century United States under the system known as 'free' enterprise. I was missing the point that precisely *because* of its recognitive and recollective powers, precisely because in this nation, created in the search for wealth, it eludes capitalist marketing, commoditizing, price-fixing, poetry has simply been set aside, depreciated, denied public space.

'What would we create?'

And perhaps this is the hope: that poetry can keep its mechanical needs simple, its head clear of the fumes of how 'success' is concocted in the capitals of promotion, marketing, consumerism, and in particular of the competition—taught in the schools, abetted at home—that pushes the 'star' at the expense of the culture as a whole, that makes people want stardom rather than participation, association, exchange, and improvisation with others. Perhaps this is the hope: that poetry, by its nature, will never become leashed to profit, marketing, consumerism.

'The space for poetry'

What is political activism, anyway? I've been asking myself.

It's something both prepared for and spontaneous—like making poetry.

When we do and think and feel certain things privately and in secret, even when thousands of people are doing, thinking, whispering these things privately and in secret, there is still no general, collective understanding from which to move. Each takes her or his risks in isolation. We may think of ourselves as individual rebels, and individual rebels can easily be shot down. The relationship among so many feelings remains unclear. But these thoughts and feelings, suppressed and stored-up and whispered, have an incendiary component. You cannot tell where or how they will connect, spreading underground from rootlet to rootlet till every grass blade is afire from every other. This is that 'spontaneity' which party 'leaders', secret governments, and closed systems dread. Poetry, in its own way, is a carrier of the sparks, because it too comes out of silence, seeking connection with unseen others.

'The hermit's scream'

What poetry is made of is so old, so familiar, that it's easy to forget that it's not just the words, but polyrhythmic sounds, speech in its first endeavours (every poem breaks a silence that had to be overcome), prismatic meanings lit by each other's light, stained by each other's shadows. In the wash of poetry the old, beaten, worn stones of language take on colours that disappear when you sieve them up out of the streambed and try to sort them out.

• • •

Someone is writing a poem. Words are being set down in a force field. It's as if the words themselves have magnetic charges; they veer together or in polarity, they swerve against each other. Part of the force field, the charge, is the working history of the words themselves, how someone has known them, used them, doubted and relied on them in a life. Part of the movement among the words belongs to sound—the guttural, the liquid, the choppy, the drawn-out, the breathy, the visceral, the down-light. The theatre of any poem is a collection of decisions about space and time—how are these words to lie on the page, with what pauses, what headlong motion, what phrasing, how can they meet the breath of someone who comes along to read them? And in part the field is charged by the way images swim into the brain through written language: swan, kettle, icicle, ashes, scab, tamarack, tractor, veil, slime, teeth, freckle.

'Someone is writing a poem'

I would rephrase the critic's sentence and say: *The question for a North American poet is how to bear witness to a reality from which the public—and maybe part of the poet—wants, or is persuaded it wants, to turn away*. Then and only then, when this is said, can we talk about the necessity of rejecting false theatricality and maudlinity, and about all the other problems of creating an art rooted in language, a social art, an art that is not mere self-entertainment for the few.

'A clearing in the imagination'

Moving between poetry and blocks of prose in a poem where everything is made concrete and there are no cloudy generalities or abstract pronouncements, [Irena] Klepfisz has written one of the great 'borderland' poems ['*Bashert*', which means 'fated' or 'predestined']—poems that emerge from the consciousness of being of no one geography, time zone, or culture, of moving inwardly as well as outwardly between continents, landmasses, eras of history. . . .

Throughout, this poetry asks fundamental questions about the uses of history. That it does so from a rootedness in Jewish history, an unassimilated location, is one part of its strength. . . . A tension among many forces—language, speechlessness, memory, politics, irony, compassion, hunger for what is lost, hunger for a justice still to be made—makes this poetry crucial to the new unfoldings of history that we begin, in the 1990s, to imagine.

'History stops for no one'

Poetry wrenches around our ideas about our lives as it grows alongside other kinds of human endeavour. But it also recalls us to ourselves—to memory, association, forgotten or forbidden languages.

Poetry will not fly across the sea, against the storms, to any 'new world', any 'promised land', and then fold its wing and sing. Poetry is not a resting on the given, but a questing toward what might otherwise be. It will always pick a quarrel with the found place, the refuge, the sanctuary, the revolution that is losing momentum. Even though the poet, human being with many anxious fears, might want just to rest, acclimate, adjust, become naturalized, learn to write in a new landscape, a new language. Poetry will go on harassing the poet until, and unless, it is driven away.

'Tourism and promised lands'

A revolutionary poem will not tell you who or when to kill, what and when to burn, or even how to theorize. It reminds you (for you have known, somehow, all along, maybe lost track) where and when and how you are living and might live—it is a wick of desire. It may do its work in the language and images of dreams, lists, love letters, prison letters, chants, filmic jump cuts, meditations, cries of pain, documentary fragments, blues, late-night long-distance calls. It is not programmatic: it searches for words amid the jamming of unfree, free-market idiom, for images that will burn true outside the emotional theme parks. A revolutionary poem is written out of one individual's confrontation with her or his own longings (including all that s/he is expected to deny) in the belief that its readers or hearers (in that old, unending sense of *the people*) deserve an art as complex, as open to contradiction as themselves.

Any truly revolutionary art is an alchemy through which waste, greed, brutality, frozen indifference, 'blind sorrow', and anger are transmuted into some drenching recognition of the *What if?*—the possible. *What if?*—the first revolutionary question, the question the dying forces don't know how to ask. The theme of revolutionary art may of necessity be prevailing conditions, yet the art signals other ways and means. In depicting lives ordinarily down-pressed, shredded, erased, this art reveals through fierce attention their innate and latent vitality and beauty. In portraying alienated and exploited labour with delicate, steady concern for the faces and bodies of the labourers, it calls to mind that work is a human blessing, that alienation does not have to be its inseparable companion. In figuring the hunted, whether Indians or slaves or migrants or women, it calls up a landscape where all might be free to travel unmolested. . . . Revolutionary art dwells, by its nature, on edges.

This is its power: the tension between subject and means, between the *is* and what can be. Edges between ruin and celebration. Naming and mourning damage, keeping pain vocal so it cannot become normalized and acceptable. Yet, through that burning gauze in a poem which flickers over words and images, through the energy of desire, summoning a different reality.

• • •

Forms, colours, sensuous relationships, rhythms, textures, tones, transmutations of energy, all belong to the natural world. Before humans arrived, their power was there; they were nameless yet not powerless. To touch their power, humans had to name them: whorl, branch, rift, stipple, crust, cone, striation, froth, sponge, flake, fringe, gully, rut, tuft, grain, bunch, slime, scale, spine, streak, globe. Over so many millennia, so many cultures, humans have reached into preexisting nature and made art: to celebrate, to drive off evil, to nourish memory, to conjure the desired visitation.

The revolutionary artist, the relayer of possibility, draws on such powers, in opposition to a technocratic society's hatred of multiformity, hatred of the natural world, hatred of the body, hatred of darkness and women, hatred of disobedience. The revolutionary poet loves people, rivers, other creatures, stones, trees inseparably from art, is not ashamed of any of these loves, and for them conjures a language that is public, intimate, inviting, terrifying, and beloved.

'What if'

THEODORE ROETHKE

FROM SOME REMARKS ON RHYTHM*

But what about the rhythm and the motion of the poem as a whole? Are there any ways of sustaining it, you may ask? We must keep in mind that rhythm is the entire movement, the flow, the recurrence of stress and unstress that is related to the rhythms of the blood, the rhythms of nature. It involves certainly stress, time, pitch, the texture of the words, the total meaning of the poem.

We've been told that a rhythm is invariably produced by playing against an established pattern. Blake does this admirably in 'A Poison Tree':

> I was angry with my friend,
> I told my wrath, my wrath did end.
> I was angry with my foe,
> I told it not, my wrath did grow.

The whole poem is a masterly example of variation in rhythm, of playing against metre. It's what Blake called 'the bounding line', the nervousness, the tension, the energy in the whole poem. And this is a clue to everything. Rhythm gives us the very psychic energy of the speaker, in one emotional situation at least.

---

* From *On the Poet and his Craft: Selected Prose of Theodore Roethke*, ed. by Ralph J. Mills Jr.

• • •

Curiously, we find this primitiveness of the imagination cropping up in the most sophisticated poetry. If we concern ourselves with more primitive effects in poetry, we come inevitably to consideration, I think, of verse that is closer to prose. And here we jump rhythmically to a kind of opposite extreme. For many strong stresses, or a playing against an iambic pattern to a loosening up, a longer, more irregular foot, I agree that free verse is a denial in terms. There is, invariably, the ghost of some other form, often blank verse, behind what is written, or the more elaborate rise and fall of the rhythmical prose sentence. Let me point up, to use Mr Warren's phrase, in a more specific way the difference between the formal poem and the more proselike piece. Mr Ransom has written his beautiful elegy, 'Bells for John Whiteside's Daughter'; I'd like to read 'Elegy for Jane' on the same theme, a poem, I'm proud to say, Mr Ransom first printed.

I remember the neckcurls, limp and damp as tendrils;
And her quick look, a sidelong pickerel smile;
And how, once startled into talk, the light syllables leaped for her,
And she balanced in the delight of her thought,
A wren, happy, tail into the wind,
Her song trembling the twigs and small branches.
The shade sang with her;
The leaves, their whispers turned to kissing;
And the mold sang in the bleached valleys under the rose.

Oh, when she was sad, she cast herself down into such a pure depth,
Even a father could not find her:
Scraping her cheek against straw;
Stirring the clearest water.

My sparrow, you are not here,
Waiting like a fern, making a spiny shadow.
The sides of wet stones cannot console me,
Nor the moss, wound with the last light.

If only I could nudge you from this sleep,
My maimed darling, my skittery pigeon.
Over this damp grave I speak the words of my love:
I, with no rights in this matter,
Neither father nor lover.

But let me indicate one or two technical effects in my little piece. For one thing, the enumeration, the favourite device of the more irregular poem. We see it again and again in Whitman and Lawrence. 'I remember', then the listing, the appositions, and the absolute construction. 'Her song trembling', etc. Then the last three lines in the stanza lengthen out:

> The shade sang with her;
> The leaves, their whispers turned to kissing;
> And the mold sang in the bleached valleys under the rose.

A kind of continuing triad. In the last two stanzas exactly the opposite occurs, the final lines being,

> Over this damp grave I speak the words of my love:
> I, with no rights in this matter,
> Neither father nor lover.

There is a successive shortening of the line length, an effect I have become inordinately fond of, I'm afraid. This little piece indicates in a way some of the strategies for the poet writing without the support of a formal pattern—he can vary his line length, modulate, he can stretch out the line, he can shorten. It was Lawrence, a master of this sort of poem (I think I quote him more or less exactly) who said, 'It all depends on the pause, the natural pause.' In other words, the breath unit, the language that is natural to the immediate thing, the particular emotion. Think of what we'd have missed in Lawrence, in Whitman, in Charlotte Mew, or, more lately, in Robert Lowell, if we denied this kind of poem. There are areas of experience in modern life that simply cannot be rendered by either the formal lyric or straight prose. We need the catalogue in our time. We need the eye close on the object, and the poem about the single incident—the animal, the child. We must permit poetry to extend consciousness as far, as deeply, as particularly as it can, to recapture, in Stanley Kunitz's phrase, what it has lost to some extent to prose. We must realize, I think, that the writer in freer forms must have an even greater fidelity to his subject matter than the poet who has the support of form. He must keep his eye on the object, and his rhythm must move as a mind moves, must be imaginatively right, or he is lost. Let me end with a simple and somewhat clumsy example of my own ['Big Wind'] in which we see a formal device giving energy to the piece, that device being, simply, participial or verbal forms that keep the action going.

FROM OPEN LETTER*

Rhythmically, it's the spring and rush of the child I'm after—and Gammer Gurton's concision: *mütterkin*'s wisdom. Most of the time the material seems to demand a varied short line. I believe that, in this kind of poem, the poet, in order to be true to what is most universal in himself, should not rely on allusion; should not comment or employ many judgement words; should not meditate (or maunder). He must scorn being 'mysterious' or loosely oracular, but be willing to face up to genuine mystery. His language must be compelling and immediate: he must create an actuality. He must be able to telescope image and symbol, if necessary, without relying on the obvious connectives: to speak in a kind of psychic shorthand when his protagonist is under great stress. He must be able to shift his rhythms rapidly, the 'tension'. He works intuitively, and the final form of his poem must be imaginatively right. If intensity has compressed the language so it seems, on early reading, obscure, this obscurity should break open suddenly for the serious reader who can hear the language: the 'meaning' itself should come as a dramatic revelation, an excitement. The clues will be scattered richly—as life scatters them; the symbols will mean what they usually mean—and sometimes something more.

* From *On the Poet and his Craft: Selected Prose of Theodore Roethke*, ed. by Ralph J. Mills Jr.

GARY SNYDER

POETRY AND THE PRIMITIVE*

NOTES ON POETRY AS AN ECOLOGICAL SURVIVAL TECHNIQUE

BILATERAL SYMMETRY

'Poetry' as the skilled and inspired use of the voice and language to embody rare and powerful states of mind that are in immediate origin personal to the singer, but at deep levels common to all who listen. 'Primitive' as those societies which have remained non-literate and non-political while necessarily exploring and developing in directions that civilized societies have tended to ignore. Having fewer tools, no concern with history, a living oral tradition rather than an accumulated library, no overriding social goals, and consider-

* From *Earth House Hold* by Gary Snyder.

able freedom of sexual and inner life, such people live vastly in the present. Their daily reality is a fabric of friends and family, the field of feeling and energy that one's own body is, the earth they stand on and the wind that wraps around it; and various areas of consciousness.

At this point some might be tempted to say that the primitive's real life is no different from anybody else's. I think this is not so. To live in the 'mythological present' in close relation to nature and in basic but disciplined body/mind states suggests a wider-ranging imagination and a closer subjective knowledge of one's own physical properties than is usually available to men living (as they themselves describe it) impotently and inadequately in 'history'—their mind-content programmed, and their caressing of nature complicated by the extensions and abstractions which elaborate tools are. A hand pushing a button may wield great power, but that hand will never learn what a hand can do. Unused capacities go sour.

Poetry must sing or speak from authentic experience. Of all the streams of civilized tradition with roots in the paleolithic, poetry is one of the few that can realistically claim an unchanged function and a relevance which will outlast most of the activities that surround us today. Poets, as few others, must live close to the world that primitive men are in: the world, in its nakedness, which is fundamental for all of us—birth, love, death; the sheer fact of being alive.

Music, dance, religion, and philosophy of course have archaic roots—a shared origin with poetry. Religion has tended to become the social justifier, a lackey to power, instead of the vehicle of hair-raising liberating and healing realizations. Dance has mostly lost its connection with ritual drama, the miming of animals, or tracing the maze of the spiritual journey. Most music takes too many tools. The poet can make it on his own voice and mother tongue, while steering a course between crystal clouds of utterly incommunicable non-verbal states—and the gleaming daggers and glittering nets of language.

In one school of Mahayana Buddhism, they talk about the 'Three Mysteries'. These are Body, Voice, and Mind. The things that are what living *is* for us, in life. Poetry is the vehicle of the mystery of voice. The universe, as they sometimes say, is a vast breathing body.

With artists, certain kinds of scientists, yogins, and poets, a kind of mind-sense is not only surviving but modestly flourishing in the twentieth century. Claude Lévi-Strauss (*The Savage Mind*) sees no problem in the continuity: '. . . it is neither the mind of savages nor that of primitive or archaic humanity, but rather mind in its untamed state as distinct from mind cultivated or domesticated for yielding a return . . . We are better able to understand today that it is possible for the two to coexist and interpenetrate in the same way that (in theory at least) it is possible for natural species, of which some are in their savage state and others transformed by agriculture and domestication, to coexist and cross . . . whether one deplores or rejoices in the fact, there are still zones in which savage thought, like savage species, is relatively protected. This is the case of art, to which our civilization accords the status of a national park.'

• • •

We all know what primitive cultures don't have. What they do have is this knowledge of connection and responsibility which amounts to a spiritual ascesis for the whole community. Monks of Christianity or Buddhism, 'leaving the world' (which means the games of society) are trying, in a decadent way, to achieve what whole primitive communities—men, women, and children—live by daily; and with more wholeness. The Shaman-poet is simply the man whose mind reaches easily out into all manners of shapes and other lives, and gives song to dreams. Poets have carried this function forward all through civilized times: poets don't sing about society, they sing about nature—even if the closest they ever get to nature is their lady's queynt. Class-structured civilized society is a kind of mass ego. To transcend the ego is to go beyond society as well. 'Beyond' there lies, inwardly, the unconscious. Outwardly, the equivalent of the unconscious is the wilderness: both of these terms meet, one step even farther on, as *one*.

• • •

Poetry, it should not have to be said, is not writing or books. Non-literate cultures with their traditional training methods of hearing and reciting, carry thousands of poems—death, war, love, dream, work, and spirit-power songs—through time. The voice of inspiration as an 'other' has long been known in the West as The Muse. Widely speaking, the muse is anything other that touches you and moves you. Be it a mountain range, a band of people, the morning star, or a diesel generator. Breaks through the ego-barrier. But this touching-deep is as a mirror, and man in his sexual nature has found the clearest mirror to be his human lover. As the West moved into increasing complexities and hierarchies with civilization, Woman as nature, beauty, and The Other came to be an all-dominating symbol; secretly striving through the last three millennia with the Jehovah or Imperator God-figure, a projection of the gathered power of anti-nature social forces. Thus in the Western tradition the Muse and Romantic Love became part of the same energy, and woman as nature the field for experiencing the universe as sacramental. The lovers' bed was the sole place to enact the dances and ritual dramas that link primitive people to their geology and the Milky Way. The contemporary decline of the cult of romantic is linked to the rise of the sense of the primitive, and the knowledge of the variety of spiritual practices and paths to beauty that cultural anthropology has brought us. We begin to move away now, in this interesting historical spiral, from monogamy and monotheism.

SOME YIPS & BARKS IN THE DARK*

A NOTABLE UTTERANCE

The linguist Bloomfield once defined literature as 'notable utterances'. A poem is usually distinguished from other sorts of utterances by some characteristic arrangement of syllabic stress, pitch, vowel length, rhyming words, internal tone patterns, syllable count, initial or final consonants and so forth. In some cases there is a peculiar vocabulary the poem is couched in. All this is what critics call form. Another distinction is made on the basis of the nature of the message. Perhaps something other than 'words' is being communicated. Straight from the deep mind of the maker to the deep mind of the hearer. This is what poets call the Poem.

THE GRAIN OF THINGS

For me every poem is unique. One can understand and appreciate the conditions which produce formal poetry as part of man's experiment with civilization. The game of inventing an abstract structure and then finding things in experience which can be forced into it. A kind of intensity can indeed be produced this way—but it is the intensity of straining and sweating against self-imposed bonds. Better the perfect, easy discipline of the swallow's dip and swoop, 'without east or west'.

Each poem grows from an energy-mind-field-dance, and has its own inner grain. To let it grow, to let it speak for itself, is a large part of the work of the poet. A scary chaos fills the heart as 'spir'itual breath—in'spir'ation; and is breathed out into the thing-world as a poem. From there it must jump to the hearer's under'stand'ing. The wider the gap the more difficult; and the greater the delight when it crosses. If the poem becomes too elliptical it ceases to be a poem in any usual sense. Then it may be a mantra, a koan, or a dharani. To be used as part of a larger walking, singing, dancing, or meditating practice.

* From *Naked Poetry* edited by Stephen Berg and Robert Mezey.

THE POET

The poet must have total sensitivity to the inner potentials of his own language—pulse, breath, glottals nasals & dentals. An ear, an eye and a belly.

He must know his own unconscious, and the proper ways to meet with the beings who live there. As Confucius said, he should know the names of trees, birds, and flowers. From this knowledge and practice of 'body, speech, and mind' the poem takes form, freely.

It is a mistake that we are searching, now, for 'new forms'. What is needed is a totally new approach to the very idea of form. Why should this be? The future can't be seen on the basis of the present; and I believe mankind is headed someplace else.

Gary Snyder
Kyoto 22. VIII. 1966

Wallace Stevens

Selections from Adagia*

Progress in any aspect is a movement through changes of terminology.

•

To give a sense of the freshness or vividness of life is a valid purpose for poetry. A didactic purpose justifies itself in the mind of the teacher; a philosophical purpose justifies itself in the mind of the philosopher. It is not that one purpose is as justifiable as another but that some purposes are pure, others impure. Seek those purposes that are purely the purposes of the pure poet.

•

The poet makes silk dresses out of worms.

•

Authors are actors, books are theatres.

•

Literature is the better part of life. To this it seems inevitably necessary to add, provided life is the better part of literature.

•

After one has abandoned a belief in God, poetry is that essence which takes its place as life's redemption.

* From *Opus Posthumous* by Wallace Stevens.

•

Accuracy of observation is the equivalent of accuracy of thinking.

•

The relation of art to life is of the first importance especially in a skeptical age since, in the absence of a belief in God, the mind turns to its own creations and examines them, not alone from the aesthetic point of view, but for what they reveal, for what they validate and invalidate, for the support that they give.

Life is the reflection of literature.

As life grows more terrible, its literature grows more terrible.

Poetry and materia poetica are interchangeable terms.

•

The real is only the base. But it is the base.

•

The poem reveals itself only to the ignorant man.

The relation between the poetry of experience and the poetry of rhetoric is not the same thing as the relation between the poetry of reality and that of the imagination. Experience, at least in the case of a poet of any scope, is much broader than reality.

•

Not all objects are equal. The vice of imagism was that it did not recognize this.

•

All poetry is experimental poetry.

The bare image and the image as a symbol are the contrast: the image without meaning and the image as meaning. When the image is used to suggest something else, it is secondary. Poetry as an imaginative thing consists of more than lies on the surface.

•

It is the belief and not the god that counts.

What we see in the mind is as real to us as what we see by the eye.

•

There is nothing in life except what one thinks of it.

There is nothing beautiful in life except life.

There is no wing like meaning.

Consider: I. That the whole world is material for poetry; II. That there is not a specifically poetic material.

One reads poetry with one's nerves.

The poet is the intermediary between people and the world in which they live and also, between people as between themselves; but not between people and some other world.

Sentimentality is a failure of feeling.

•

The final belief is to believe in a fiction, which you know to be a fiction, there being nothing else. The exquisite truth is to know that it is a fiction and that you believe in it willing.

All of our ideas come from the natural world: trees = umbrellas.

•

Ethics are no more a part of poetry than they are of painting.

As the reason destroys, the poet must create.

The exquisite environment of fact. The final poem will be the poem of fact in the language of fact. But it will be the poem of fact not realized before.

•

To live in the world but outside of existing conceptions of it.

•

Poetry has to be something more than a conception of the mind. It has to be a revelation of nature. Conceptions are artificial. Perceptions are essential.

•

Money is a kind of poetry.

Poetry is an effort of a dissatisfied man to find satisfaction through words, occasionally of the dissatisfied thinker to find satisfaction through his emotions.

•

The poem is a nature created by the poet.

The aesthetic order includes all other orders but is not limited to them.

Religion is dependent on faith. But aesthetics is independent of faith. The relative positions of the two might be reversed. It is possible to establish aesthetics in the individual mind as immeasurably a greater thing than religion. Its present state is the result of the difficulty of establishing it except in the individual mind.

The ultimate value is reality.

Realism is a corruption of reality.

The world is the only thing fit to think about.

Poetry is a purging of the world's poverty and change and evil and death. It is a present perfecting, a satisfaction in the irremediable poverty of life.

The time will come when poems like Paradise will seem like very *triste* contraptions.

All men are murderers.

There must be something of the peasant in every poet.

Metaphor creates a new reality from which the original appears to be unreal.

Description is an element, like air or water.

Poets acquire humanity.

Thought tends to collect in pools.

Life is not people and scene but thought and feeling.

God is a postulate of the ego.

Poetry must resist the intelligence almost successfully.

Literature is based not on life but on propositions about life, of which this is one.

Life is a composite of the propositions about it.

A change of style is a change of subject.

•

Poetry is a pheasant disappearing in the brush.

We never arrive intellectually. But emotionally we arrive constantly (as in poetry, happiness, high mountains, vistas).

•

The poet represents the mind in the act of defending us against itself.

•

Every poem is a poem within a poem: the poem of the idea within the poem of the words.

•

Poetry is the gaiety (joy) of language.

To be at the end of fact is not to be at the beginning of imagination but it is to be at the end of both.

•

There is a nature that absorbs the mixedness of metaphors.

•

Imagination applied to the whole world is vapid in comparison to imagination applied to a detail.

•

Poetry is a response to the daily necessity of getting the world right.

•

The essential fault of surrealism is that it invents without discovering. To make a clam play an accordion is to invent not to discover. The observation of the unconscious, so far as it can be observed, should reveal things of which we have previously been unconscious, not the familiar things of which we have been conscious plus imagination.

•

French and English constitute a single language.

•

Reality is a cliché from which we escape by metaphor. It is only *au pays de la métaphore qu'on est poète*.

The degrees of metaphor. The absolute object slightly turned is a metaphor of the object.

Some objects are less susceptible to metaphor than others. The whole world is less susceptible to metaphor than a tea-cup is.

There is no such thing as a metaphor of a metaphor. One does not progress through metaphors. Thus reality is the indispensable element of each metaphor. When I say that man is a god it is very easy to see that if I also say that a god is something else, god has become reality.

In the long run the truth does not matter.

•

Poetry creates a fictitious existence on an exquisite plane. This definition must vary as the plane varies, an exquisite plane being merely illustrative.

DYLAN THOMAS

NOTES ON THE ART OF POETRY*

You want to know why and how I just began to write poetry, and which poets or kinds of poetry I was first moved and influenced by.

To answer the first part of this question, I should say I wanted to write poetry in the beginning because I had fallen in love with words. The first poems I knew were nursery rhymes, and before I could read them for myself I had come to love just the words of them, the words alone. What the words stood for, symbolized, or meant, was of very secondary importance. What mattered was the *sound* of them as I heard them for the first time on the lips of the remote and incomprehensible grown-ups who seemed, for some reason, to be living in my world. And these words were, to me, as the notes of bells, the sounds of musical instruments, the noises of wind, sea, and rain, the rattle of milkcarts, the clopping of hooves on cobbles, the fingering of branches on a window pane, might be to someone, deaf from birth, who has miraculously found his hearing. I did not care what the words said, overmuch, nor what happened to Jack and Jill and the Mother Goose rest of them; I cared for the shapes of sound that their names, and the words describing their actions, made in my ears; I cared for the colours the words cast on my eyes. I realize that I may be, as I think back all that way, romanticizing my reactions to the simple and beautiful words of those pure poems; but that is all I can honestly remember, however much time might have falsified my memory. I fell in love—that is the only expression I can think of—at

* Written in the summer of 1951, at Laugharne, in reply to questions posed by a student. From *Texas Quarterly* (winter 1961).

once, and am still at the mercy of words, though sometimes now, knowing a little of their behaviour very well, I think I can influence them slightly and have even learned to beat them now and then, which they appear to enjoy. I tumbled for words at once. And, when I began to read the nursery rhymes for myself, and, later, to read other verses and ballads, I knew that I had discovered the most important things, to me, that could be ever. There they were, seemingly lifeless, made only of black and white, but out of them, out of their own being, came love and terror and pity and pain and wonder and all the other vague abstractions that make our ephemeral lives dangerous, great, and bearable. Out of them came the gusts and grunts and hiccups and heehaws of the common fun of the earth; and though what the words meant was, in its own way, often deliciously funny enough, so much funnier seemed to me, at that almost forgotten time, the shape and shade and size and noise of the words as they hummed, strummed, jugged, and galloped along. That was the time of innocence; words burst upon me, unencumbered by trivial or portentous association; words were their spring-like selves, fresh with Eden's dew, as they flew out of the air. They made their own original associations as they sprang and shone. The words, 'Ride a cock-horse to Banbury Cross', were as haunting to me, who did not know then what a cock-horse was nor cared a damn where Banbury Cross might be, as, much later, were such lines as John Donne's, 'Go and catch a falling star,/Get with child a mandrake root', which also I could not understand when I first read them. And as I read more and more, and it was not all verse, by any means, my love for the real life of words increased until I knew that I must live *with* them and *in* them always. I knew, in fact, that I must be a writer of words, and nothing else. The first thing was to feel and know their sound and substance; what I was going to do with those words, what use I was going to make of them, what I was going to say through them, would come later. I knew I had to know them most intimately in all their forms and moods, their ups and downs, their chops and changes, their needs and demands. (Here, I am afraid, I am beginning to talk too vaguely. I do not like writing *about* words, because then I often use bad and wrong and stale and woolly words. What I like to do is to treat words as a craftsman does his wood or stone or what-have-you, to hew, carve, mould, coil, polish, and plane them into patterns, sequences, sculptures, fugues of sound expressing some lyrical impulse, some spiritual doubt or conviction, some dimly-realized truth I must try to reach and realize.) It was when I was very young, and just at school, that, in my father's study, before homework that was never done, I began to know one kind of writing from another, one kind of goodness, one kind of badness. My first, and greatest, liberty was that of being able to read everything and anything I cared to. I read indiscriminately, and with my eyes hanging out. I could never have dreamt that there were such goings-on in the world between the covers of books, such sand-storms and ice-blasts of words, such slashing of humbug, and humbug too, such staggering peace, such enormous laughter, such and so many blinding bright lights breaking across the just-awaking wits and splashing all over the pages in a million bits and pieces all of which were words, words, words, and each of which was alive forever in its own delight and glory and oddity and light (I must try not to make these supposedly helpful notes as confusing as my poems themselves). I wrote endless imitations, though I never thought them to be imitations but, rather, wonderfully original things, like eggs laid by tigers. They were imitations of anything I happened to be reading at the time: Sir Thomas Browne, de Quincey, Henry Newbolt, the Ballads, Blake, Baroness Orczy, Marlowe, Chums, the Imagists, the Bible, Poe, Keats, Lawrence, Anon., and Shakespeare. A mixed lot, as you see, and randomly remembered. I tried my callow hand at almost every poetical form. How could I learn the tricks of a trade unless I tried to do them myself? I learned that the bad tricks come easily; and the good ones, which help you to say what you think you wish to say in the most meaningful, moving way, I am still learning. (But in earnest company you must call these tricks by other names, such as technical devices, prosodic experiments, etc.)

The writers, then, who influenced my earliest poems and stories were, quite simply and truthfully, all the writers I was reading at the time, and, as you see from a specimen list higher up the page they ranged from writers of schoolboy adventure yarns to incomparable and inimitable masters like Blake. That is, when I began, bad writing had as much influence on my stuff as good. The bad influences I tried to remove and renounce bit by bit, shadow by shadow, echo by echo, through trial and error, through delight and disgust and misgiving, as I came to love words more and to hate the heavy hands that knocked them about, the thick tongues that [had] no feel for their multitudinous tastes, the dull and botching hacks who flattened them out into a colourless and insipid paste, the pedants who made them moribund and pompous as themselves. Let me say that the things that first made me love language and want to work *in* it and *for* it were nursery rhymes and folk tales, the Scottish Ballads, a few lines of hymns, the most famous Bible stories and the rhythms of the Bible, Blake's *Songs of Innocence*, and the quite incomprehensible magical mystery and nonsense of Shakespeare heard, read, and near-murdered in the first forms of my school.

You ask me, next, if it is true that three of the dominant influences on my published prose and poetry are Joyce, the Bible, and Freud. (I purposely say my 'published' prose and poetry, as in the preceding pages I have been talking about the primary influences upon my very first and forever unpublishable juvenilia.) I cannot say that I have been 'influenced' by Joyce, whom I enormously admire and whose *Ulysses*, and earlier stories I have read a great deal. I think this Joyce question arose because somebody once, in print, remarked on the closeness of the title of my book of short stories, *Portrait of the Artist as a Young Dog* to Joyce's title, *Portrait of the Artist as a Young Man*. As you know, the name given to innumerable portrait paintings by their artists is, 'Portrait of the Artist as a Young Man'—a perfectly straightforward title. Joyce used the *painting*-title for the first time as the title of a literary work. I myself made a bit of doggish fun of the painting-title and, of course, intended no possible reference to Joyce. I do not think that Joyce has had any hand at all in my writing; certainly, his *Ulysses* has not. On the other hand, I cannot deny that the shaping of some of my *Portrait* stories might owe something to Joyce's stories in the volume *Dubliners*. But then, *Dubliners* was a pioneering work in the world of the short story, and no good story-writer since can have failed, in some way, however little, to have benefited by it.

The Bible, I have referred to in attempting to answer your first question. Its great stories, of Noah, Jonah, Lot, Moses, Jacob, David, Solomon, and a thousand more, I had, of course, known from very early youth; the great rhythms had rolled over me from the Welsh pulpits; and I read, for myself, from Job and Ecclesiastes; and the story of the New Testament is part of my life. But I have never sat down and studied the Bible, never consciously echoed its language, and am, in reality, as ignorant of it as most brought-up Christians. All of the Bible that I use in my work is remembered from childhood, and is the common property of all who were brought up in English-speaking communities. Nowhere, indeed, in all my writing, do I use any knowledge which is not commonplace to any literate person. I *have* used a few difficult words in early poems, but they are easily looked-up and were, in any case, thrown into the poems in a kind of adolescent showing-off which I hope I have now discarded.

And that leads me to the third 'dominant influence': Sigmund Freud. My only acquaintance with the theories and discoveries of Dr Freud has been through the work of novelists who have been excited by his case-book histories, of popular newspaper scientific-potboilers who have, I imagine, vulgarized his work beyond recognition, and of a few modern poets, including Auden, who have attempted to use psychoanalytical phraseology and theory in some of their poems. I have read only one book of Freud's, *The Interpretation of Dreams*, and do not recall having been influenced by it in any way. Again, no honest writer today can possibly avoid being influenced by Freud through his pioneering work into the Unconscious and by the influence of those discoveries on the scientific, philosophic, and artistic work of his contemporaries: but not, by any means, necessarily through Freud's own writing.

To your third question—Do I deliberately utilize devices of rhyme, rhythm, and word-formation in my writing—I must, of course, answer with an immediate, Yes. I am a painstaking, conscientious, involved, and devious craftsman in words, however unsuccessful the result so often appears, and to whatever wrong uses I may apply my technical paraphernalia. I use everything and anything to make my poems work and move in the direction I want them to: old tricks, new tricks, puns, portmanteau-words, paradox, allusion, paronomasia, paragram, catachresis, slang, assonantal rhymes, vowel rhymes, sprung rhythm. Every device there is in language is there to be used if you will. Poets have got to enjoy themselves sometimes, and the twisting and convolutions of words, the inventions and contrivances, are all part of the joy that is part of the painful, voluntary work.

Your next question asks whether my use of combinations of words to create something new, 'in the Surrealist way', is according to a set formula or is spontaneous.

There is a confusion here, for the Surrealists' set formula *was* to juxtapose the unpremeditated.

Let me make it clearer if I can. The Surrealists—(that is, super-realists, or those who work *above* realism)—were a coterie of painters and writers in Paris, in the nineteen twenties, who did not believe in the conscious selection of images. To put it in another way: they were artists who were dissatisfied with both the realists—(roughly speaking, those who tried to put down in paint and words an actual representation of what they imagined to be the real world in which they lived)—and the impressionists who, roughly speaking again, were those who tried to give an impression of what they imagined to be the real world. The Surrealists wanted to dive into the subconscious mind, the mind below the conscious surface, and dig up their images from there without the aid of logic or reason, and put them down, illogically and unreasonably, in paint and words. The Surrealists affirmed that, as three quarters of the mind was submerged, it was the function of the artist to gather his material from the greatest, submerged mass of the mind rather than from that quarter of the mind which, like the tip of an iceberg, protruded from the subconscious sea. One method the Surrealists used in their poetry was to juxtapose words and images that had no rational relationship; and out of this they hoped to achieve a kind of subconscious, or dream, poetry that would be truer to the real, imaginative world of the mind, mostly submerged, than is the poetry of the conscious mind that relies upon the rational and logical relationship of ideas, objects, and images.

This is, very crudely, the credo of the Surrealists, and one with which I profoundly disagree. I do not mind from where the images of a poem are dragged up; drag them up, if you like, from the nethermost sea of the hidden self; but, before they reach paper, they must go through all the rational processes of the intellect. The Surrealists, on the other hand, put their words down together on paper exactly as they emerge from chaos; they do not shape these words or put them in order; to them, chaos is the shape and order. This seems to me to be exceedingly presumptuous; the Surrealists imagine that whatever they dredge from their subconscious selves and put down in paint or in words must, essentially, be of some interest or value. I deny this. One of the arts of the poet is to make comprehensible and articulate what might emerge from subconscious sources; one of the great main uses of the intellect is to *select*, from the amorphous mass of subconscious images, those that will best further his imaginative purpose, which is to write the best poem he can.

And Question five is, God help us, what is my definition of Poetry?

I myself, do not read poetry for anything but pleasure. I read only the poems I like. This means, of course, that I have to read a lot of poems I don't like before I find the ones I do, but, when I *do* find the ones I do, then all I can say is 'Here they are', and read them to myself for pleasure.

Read the poems you like reading. Don't bother whether they're important, or if they'll live. What does it matter what poetry *is*, after all? If you want a definition of poetry, say: 'Poetry is what makes me laugh or cry or yawn, what makes my toenails twinkle, what makes me want to do this or that or nothing', and let it go at that. All that matters about poetry is the enjoyment of it, however tragic it may be. All that matters is the eternal movement behind it, the vast undercurrent of human grief, folly, pretension, exaltation, or ignorance, however unlofty the intention of the poem.

You can tear a poem apart to see what makes it technically tick, and say to yourself, when the works are laid out before you, the vowels, the consonants, the rhymes and rhythms. 'Yes, this is *it*. This is why the poem moves me so. It is because of the craftsmanship'. But you're back again where you began. You're back with the mystery of having been moved by words. The best craftsmanship always leaves holes and gaps in the works of the poem so that something that is *not* in the poem can creep, crawl, flash, or thunder in.

The joy and function of poetry is, and was, the celebration of man, which is also the celebration of God.

PHYLLIS WEBB

ON THE LINE*

To whom am I talking? The awkward sound of that 'to whom'. Am I talking? No. My mouth is shut. Gary's letter arrives; I feel oppressed. It's Gary who wants the answers, though I put him up to it. Why did I start this dialogue which I now rebel against? On the poetic line. Let me discover the reasons for that as I try to find out to whom I am talking.

Last night, feeling uneasy, I turned again to Adrienne Rich, rereading her essays, 'The Tensions of Anne Bradstreet' and 'When We Dead Awaken: Writing as Re-vision'. I think I am trying to re-vision the approach to the line and all such matters. Gary, in Montreal, during that discussion we didn't tape, gave me the lead, talking about shorelines, tidelines. And Doug Barbour before that with his title *Shore Lines*. Sure lines.

I look again at the yellow dying tulip on the table. It is stretched out on an almost true horizontal. The flower has sliced itself exactly in half. I sympathize. The half tulip, halved tulip, hangs exposed. I was not there to hear the petals fall. They form a curve of yellow on the glass tabletop; they dropped to form a new line, a waxy curvature, unique to the forces that befell them. *Curvature*.

That is what I am coming to, the physics of the poem. Energy/Mass. Waxy splendour, the massive quiet of the fallen tulip petals. So much depends upon: the wit of the syntax, the rhythm and the speed of the fall, the drop, the assumption of a specific light, curved.

The oppression lifts as I draw the line on the page, like this

---

A hair-line, a hair's breadth. The wind in the willow. Hair's breath. Talking to myself on an April afternoon, my birth-day. The opening of that crack, of Duncan's field ('a wild field,' he says, 'I'm sort of interested in wild feelings, wild thoughts—and I don't mean like whoopee—but like wild life.') Or 'a series of fields folded'. Today, the fifty-fourth, the flowers arrive: roses, daisies, carnations, tulips (red), grape hyacinth, dead daffodils. Are falling into line, each one its own line, of its own accord, curved. Is that what we seek in sky, in field, in poem—*curvature*?

* * * * * *

---

* From *Talking* by Phyllis Webb. Gary Geddes's letter, referred to in line 2 above, begins on page 924.

Enjambment: As bad as 'to whom'. Ugly, stupid, door-jamb. For closing. Foreclosing. Squashed.

* * * * * *

The short line is 'for candor', says Duncan. Or terror, say I. Notes Toward a Poetics of Terror. Pull down thy vanity. The tulip is moving horizontally towards the light (tropos), cells burning brightly, dying out. Snuff out the poem. Stuff it. ('For flowers are peculiarly the poetry of Christ'—Christopher Smart.)

* * * * * *

Syntactivity. Under the electron microscope. Oh look and see. Against this, an image pushes through of splicing tape. Janet in the listening room late at night at CBC. Listening room. The poem as listening room. Cut 20 seconds. Hear how they sound! Glossy plastic ribbon on the cutting room floor. Curling.

Ribbon at the end of the race. Break it. Ribbon at ceremonial opening of the bridge. Cut it with big authorial scissors. Champagne all around.

I am out of it. Cut. Splice. Play it again. To whom am I talking? Seriously. A fine line.

'The line has shattered,' Olson gasped in that interview I did with him in '63.

The water is boiling. Kenneth Koch's poem, 'The Boiling Water'. The seriousness of the boiling point for the water. For the tea, for me. The syntactivity (Geddes). So Gary forces me to this ebullience. The dance of the intellect in the syllables, for Olson. Knuckles of the articulate hand.

* * * * * *

Certainties: that the long line (in English) is aggressive, with much 'voice'. Assertive, at least. It comes from assurance (or hysteria), high tide, full moon, open mouth, big-mouthed Whitman, yawp, yawp, and Ginsberg—howling. Male.

* * * * * *

Modulations. Now take Kit Smart in *Jubilate Agno*. Yes, sure of himself, madly hurting. Sore lines. 'Silly Fellow, Silly Fellow.' Blessed. Based on Hebraic long-line psalmistry. (The short line, *au contraire*, private palmistry, heart line, cut to the quick.) Gary, forget the commas, line breaks, caesura (plucked from the womb, untimely), the modes of measuring (though you are right about Levertov's 1/2 comma as frivolous), and look again at that idea: Behold, I am here. Even as the leaves of grass. Sexton *imitates* Smart (Behold, I am *almost* here). She was not able to walk that line alone. Few women are, but they are learning. Anne, you took Christopher right into the poem for company.

In 'For Fyodor', the beetle is aggressive, enraged, monologuing dramatically along the extended line. Poor Fyodor, foaming at the mouth, harangued by this Trickster (yells and chuckles): 'You are mine, Dostoevsky.' Big-mouthed, proletarian, revolting beetle. The balance of power unbalanced. (See also Wayman's industrial poems.) Notes from the Insect Underground. Spider Webb.

* * * * * *

Notes. The musical phrase, go with it, sd. Pound. Another big mouth, or was it really a big ear, delicate as seashell or tulipcup? He changed our borders, changed the shape of the poem, its energy potential, for the 'data grid'? (Ed Sanders) And presented us with the freedom we now mediate. Who are 'we'? To whom, etc.? Emily?

* * * * * *

—Emily—those gasps, those inarticulate dashes—those incitements—hiding what unspeakable—foul breath? But not revolting; *subversive*. Female. Hiding yourself—Emily—no, compressing yourself, even singing yourself—tinily—with compacted passion—a violet storm—

* * * * * *

Compare:

> Now you are sitting doubled up in pain.
> What's that for?
> Doubled up I feel
> small like these poems
> the area of attack
> is diminished.

I did not count the syllables or the ways. A hare's breath.

* * * * * *

Sidelines. I play by ear. And the eye. The yellow tulip stretched on its stem, petals falling, a new moon, a phase.

I drink the tea. The seriousness of the moving line, for me. Detritus, the phenomenal world in Kenneth Koch. He cannot pull the wool over his eyes. Giving up on the weights and measures of the fine line to *hear* the water boiling, to overhear himself. Am I talking? Almost, to K.K. He lays himself bare in anxiety. Kroetsch sees anxiety as central to the short-lined *Naked Poems*—and the post-modern long poem generally. But the long-lined unyawping K.K. (unaggressive, relatively, unhysterical, relatively) fields his anxiety as you sprawl on your carpet, Kenneth, sprawl on the page, talking to me!

Comedian that he is, he throws away his lines. Hooray.

Hook, line and sinker.

* * * * * *

Sound poetry. 'Open wide,' says doctor as he/she depresses your tongue to look down the little red lane.

From whence comes the dragon! Or the Four Horsemen. Whee. Whoa. Woe. Stop. Or that horse-thief Rothenberg. Technicians of the Sacred on the firing line.

But *no lines now*. Notes only. Notation. 'A new alphabet gasps for air'
Actually, an old alphabet
Shamanic
The Gutenberg Galaxy self-destructing under my hand and—
the mystical numbers come through the mail from Gwendolyn MacEwen, April 7, 1981:

1 - The Bond
3 - Divine Interception
5 - Impending Doom
7 - Weakness

'To control reality' when she was a child. Holding the line. The oppression of all that for the wild child.

Verse as numbers. Mystical systems. Music of the spheres. Curvature. Curlicue. Of the tulip of
Heraclitean fire.

'I am learning to be / a poet, caught in the / Divine Storm.' (Bowering, 'The Breath, Releast'.)

* * * * * *

Poundsound. Prosody: The articulation of the total sound of the poem. Or of the tulip, the yellow tulip, P.K.'s 'squeaky' flower.

* * * * * *

And ultimately meaning, as you say, Gary, the movement of the meaning, the syntactivity, radioactivity, power.

When we dead arise.

I once complained about Adrienne Rich's line breaks, but when I read *The Dream of a Common Language*, I felt shame, shame, ashamed, that I had ever been so petty, knowing that, like Marie Curie, your wounds, Adrienne, and your power come from the same source.

* * * * * *

I talk like this only to myself with my mouth shut. Laying it on the line.

Edmonton.
April 8/9, 1981

LETTER FROM GARY GEDDES TO PHYLLIS WEBB

Dear Phyllis:

I'm looking forward to doing the interview with you, by mail and in person hopefully. It will help me formulate my own ideas too on the subject of the line. I think Levertov is right about the importance of the line, but less reliable on the absolute weight in terms of timing that it has. I'd say the weight of an end-line is very relative, depending almost entirely on context, the degree of syntactical activity (syntactivity?) and the momentum of sound and idea to hit the bearing-point of each line. Does a comma plus an end-line therefore equal 1-1/2 commas? If so, what is the real duration of the comma—it all depends on the kind of noise, the buzz, each poem makes.

And the stanza. Lord, how to prescribe for its usage. Does the stanza have to be self-contained, with a closure either given by way of a full-stop or implied by spacing? Obviously not. Good poems break that convention often. And a comma hanging at the end of a stanza, what does that do, beyond keeping those words from sliding into the abyss that follows?

I wish Levertov would tell us more clearly how the line can be best used and then show how that method has been/must be broken to avoid tedium or predictability. I, for example, often separate the noun and adjective, precisely in order to *avoid* the sense of closure, of finality, or the predictability that one associates with the phrasally determined line. The pause in many cases, then, is mainly eliminated or only hinted at. The advantage lies, I believe, in a subtle increase in energy *and* meaning that comes from making the noun and its qualifier appear separated in space but linked in time, thus giving a three-way focus on two words.

So I doubt if Levertov's theory of the line is any more reliable than Olson's breath-unit theory. We need, perhaps, to come at it via Olson, since one man's 4/4 time is another's 2/2 time, and then try to show how the material, the subject itself, calls up a certain momentum, as a lover does to one's pulse and breathing habits; this is where the question of tradition begins to get interesting, because one can see certain poets gaining strength by working against the iambic pentameter line with syllabics or some other mode of measuring.

Your own poem 'Poetics Against the Angel of Death' moves out onto the wide prairie in the last line, as a spacial pun and a manifesto, and in so doing it sits in the tradition of the free 20th and the more ordered 18th centuries. Pope could make the line crawl or leap or dance by virtue of his clever use of punctuation and syntax, so that the end of the line was less important than the main portion. Is that too Aristotelian—happiness of the line is more important—no, the means towards the end of the line is more important than the end itself? I want you 'to put yourself on the line' and say *what a line can't do without*, i.e., something for the ear, eye or mind, preferably all three.

That's all for now. Please drop me a *line* as you feel, the urge. . . .

WILLIAM CARLOS WILLIAMS

A NEW MEASURE*

I have never been one to write by rule, even by my own rules. Let's begin with the rule of counted syllables, in which all poems have been written hitherto. That has become tiresome to my ear.

Finally, the stated syllables, as in the best of present-day free verse, have become entirely divorced from the beat, that is the measure. The musical pace proceeds without them.

* From a letter written to Richard Eberhart, 23 May 1954. From *Selected Letters of William Carlos Williams*, ed. by John C. Thirlwall.

Therefore the measure, that is to say, the count, having got rid of the words, which held it down, is returned to the *music*.

The words, having been freed, have been allowed to run all over the map, 'free', as we have mistakenly thought. This has amounted to no more (in Whitman and others) than no discipline at all.

But if we keep in mind the *tune* which the lines (not necessarily the words) make in our ears, we are ready to proceed.

By measure I mean musical pace. Now, with music in our ears the words need only be taught to keep as distinguished an order, as chosen a character, as regular, according to the music, as in the best of prose.

By its *music* shall the best of modern verse be known and the *resources* of the music. The refinement of the poem, its subtlety, is not to be known by the elevation of the words but—the words don't so much matter—by the resources of the *music*.

To give you an example from my own work—not that I know anything about what I have myself written:

(count):—not that I ever count when writing but, at best, the lines must be capable of being counted, that is to say, measured—(believe it or not).—At that I may, half consciously, even count the measure under my breath as I write.—

(approximate example)

(1) The smell of the heat is boxwood
(2) when rousing us
(3) a movement of the air
(4) stirs our thoughts
(5) that had no life in them
(6) to a life, a life in which

(or)

(1) Mother of God! Our Lady!
(2) the heart
(3) is an unruly master:
(4) Forgive us our sins
(5) as we
(6) forgive
(7) those who have sinned against

Count a single beat to each numeral. You may not agree with my ear, but that is the way I count the line. Over the whole poem it gives a pattern to the metre that can be felt as a new measure. It gives resources to the ear which result in a language which we hear spoken about us every day.

ON MEASURE—STATEMENT FOR CID CORMAN*

Verse—we'd better not speak of poetry lest we become confused—verse has always been associated in men's minds with 'measure', i.e., with mathematics. In scanning any piece of verse, you 'count' the syllables. Let's not speak either of rhythm, an aimless sort of thing without precise meaning of any sort. But measure implies something that can be measured. Today verse has lost all measure.

Our lives also have lost all that in the past we had to measure them by, except outmoded standards that are meaningless to us. In the same way our verses, of which our poems are made, are left without any metrical construction of which you can speak, any recognizable, any new measure by which they can be pulled together. We get sonnets, etc., but no one alive today, or half alive, seems to see anything incongruous in that. They cannot see that poems cannot any longer be made following a Euclidian measure, 'beautiful' as this may make them. The very grounds for our beliefs have altered. We do not live that way any more; nothing in our lives, at bottom, is ordered according to that measure; our social concepts, our schools, our very religious ideas, certainly our understanding of mathematics are greatly altered. Were we called upon to go back to what we believed in the past we should be lost. Only the construction of our poems—and at best the construction of a poem must engage the tips of our intellectual awareness—is left shamefully to the past.

A relative order is operative elsewhere in our lives. Even the divorce laws recognize that. Are we so stupid that we can't see that the same things apply to the construction of modern verse, to an art which hopes to engage the attention of a modern world? If men do not find in the verse they are called on to read a construction that interests them or that they believe in, they will not read your verses and I, for one, do not blame them. What will they find out there that is worth bothering about? So, I understand, the young men of my generation are going back to Pope. Let them. They want to be read at least with some understanding of what they are saying and Pope is at least understandable; a good master. They have been besides scared by all the wild experimentation that preceded them so that now they want to play it safe and to conform.

They have valid reasons for what they are doing—of course not all of them are doing it, but the English, with a man such as Christopher Fry prominent among them, lead the pack. Dylan Thomas is thrashing around somewhere in the wings but he is Welsh and acknowledges no rule—he cannot be of much help to us. Return as they may to the classics for their models it will not solve anything for them. They will still, later, have to tackle the fundamental problems which concern verse of a new construction to conform

* From *Selected Essays of William Carlos Williams*.

with our age. Their brothers in the chemical laboratory, from among whom their most acute readers will come if they know what is good for them, must be met on a footing that will not be retrograde but equal to their own. Though they may recognize this theoretically there is no one who dares overstep the conventional mark.

It's not only a question of daring, no one has instructed them differently. Most poems I see today are concerned with what they are *saying*, how profound they have been given to be. So true is this that those who write them have forgotten to make poems at all of them. Thank God we're not musicians, with our lack of structural invention we'd be ashamed to look ourselves in the face otherwise. There is nothing interesting in the construction of our poems, nothing that can jog the ear out of its boredom. I for one can't read them. There is nothing in their metrical construction to attract me, so I fall back on e.e. cummings and the disguised conventions that he presents which are at least amusing—as amusing as 'Doctor Foster went to Gloucester, in a shower of rain.' Ogden Nash is also amusing, but not amusing enough.

The thing is that 'free verse' since Whitman's time has led us astray. He was taken up, as were the leaders of the French Revolution before him with the abstract idea of freedom. It slopped over into all their thinking. But it was an idea lethal to all order, particularly to that order which has to do with the poem. Whitman was right in breaking our bounds but, having no valid restraints to hold him, went wild. He didn't know any better. At the last he resorted to a loose sort of language with no discipline about it of any sort and we have copied its worst feature, just that.

The corrective to that is forgetting Whitman, for instinctively he was on the right track, to find a new discipline. Invention is the mother of art. We must invent new modes to take the place of those which are worn out. For want of this we have gone back to worn-out modes with our tongues hanging out and our mouths drooling after 'beauty' which is not even in the same category under which we are seeking it. Whitman, great as he was in his instinctive drive, was also the cause of our going astray. I among the rest have much to answer for. No verse can be free, it must be governed by some measure, but not by the old measure. There Whitman was right but there, at the same time, his leadership failed him. The time was not ready for it. We have to return to some measure but a measure consonant with our time and not a mode so rotten that it stinks.

We have no measure by which to guide ourselves except a purely intuitive one which we feel but do not name. I am not speaking of verse which has long since been frozen into a rigid mould signifying its death, but of verse which shows that it has been touched with some dissatisfaction with its present state. It is all over the page at the mere whim of the man who has composed it. This will not do. Certainly an art which implies a discipline as the poem does, a rule, a measure, will not tolerate it. There is no measure to guide us, no recognizable measure.

Relativity gives us the cue. So, again, mathematics comes to the rescue of the arts. Measure, an ancient word in poetry, something we have almost forgotten in its literal significance as something measured, becomes related again with the poetic. We have today to do with the poetic, as always, but a *relatively* stable foot, not a rigid one. That is all the difference. It is that which must become the object of our search. Only by coming to that realization shall we escape the power of these magnificent verses of the past which we have always marvelled over and still be able to enjoy them. We live in a new world, pregnant with tremendous possibility for enlightenment but sometimes, being old, I despair of it. For the poem which has always led the way to the other arts as to life, being explicit, the only art which is explicit, has lately been left to fall into decay.

Without measure we are lost. But we have lost even the ability to count. Actually we are not as bad as that. Instinctively we have continued to count as always but it has become not a conscious process and being unconscious has descended to a low level of the invention. There are a few exceptions but there is no one among us who is consciously aware of what he is doing. I have accordingly made a few experiments which will appear in a new book shortly. What I want to emphasize is that I do not consider anything I have put down there as final. There will be other experiments but all will be directed toward the discovery of a new measure, I repeat, a new measure by which may be ordered our poems as well as our lives.

1953

William Butler Yeats

From Magic*

I cannot now think symbols less than the greatest of all powers whether they are used consciously by the masters of magic, or half unconsciously by their successors, the poet, the musician, and the artist. At first I tried to distinguish between symbols and symbols, between what I called inherent symbols and arbitrary symbols, but the distinction has come to mean little

* From *Ideas of Good and Evil* by William Butler Yeats.

or nothing. Whether their power has arisen out of themselves, or whether it has an arbitrary origin, matters little, for they act, as I believe, because the Great Memory associates them with certain events and moods and persons. Whatever the passions of man have gathered about, becomes a symbol in the Great Memory, and in the hands of him who has the secret it is a worker of wonders, a caller-up of angels or of devils. The symbols are of all kinds, for everything in heaven or earth has its association, momentous or trivial, in the Great Memory, and one never knows what forgotten events may have plunged it, like the toadstool and the ragweed, into the great passions. Knowledgeable men and women in Ireland sometimes distinguish between the simples that work cures by some medical property in the herb, and those that do their work by magic. Such magical simples as the husk of the flax, water out of the fork of an elm-tree, do their work, as I think, by awaking in the depths of the mind where it mingles with the Great Mind, and is enlarged by the Great Memory, some curative energy, some hypnotic command. They are not what we call faith cures, for they have been much used and successfully, the traditions of all lands affirm, over children and over animals, and to me they seem the only medicine that could have been committed safely to ancient hands. To pluck the wrong leaf would have been to go uncured, but, if one had eaten it, one might have been poisoned.

• • •

And surely, at whatever risk, we must cry out that imagination is always seeking to remake the world according to the impulses and the patterns in that Great Mind, and that Great Memory? Can there be anything so important as to cry out that what we call romance, poetry, intellectual beauty, is the only signal that the supreme Enchanter, or some one in His councils, is speaking of what has been, and shall be again, in the consummation of time?

1901

FROM THE SYMBOLISM OF POETRY*

All sounds, all colours, all forms, either because of their preordained energies or because of long association, evoke indefinable and yet precise emotions, or, as I prefer to think, call down among us certain disembodied powers, whose footsteps over our hearts we call emotions; and when sound, and colour, and

* From *Ideas of Good and Evil* by William Butler Yeats.

form are in a musical relation, a beautiful relation to one another, they become, as it were, one sound, one colour, one form, and evoke an emotion that is made out of their distinct evocations and yet is one emotion. The same relation exists between all portions of every work of art, whether it be an epic or a song, and the more perfect it is, and the more various and numerous the elements that have flowed into its perfection, the more powerful will be the emotion, the power, the god it calls among us. Because an emotion does not exist, or does not become perceptible and active among us, till it has found its expression, in colour or in sound or in form, or in all of these, and because no two modulations or arrangements of these evoke the same emotion, poets and painters and musicians, and in a less degree because their effects are momentary, day and night and cloud and shadow, are continually making and unmaking mankind. It is indeed only those things which seem useless or very feeble that have any power, and all those things that seem useful or strong, armies, moving wheels, modes of architecture, modes of government, speculations of the reason, would have been a little different if some mind long ago had not given itself to some emotion, as a woman gives herself to her lover, and shaped sounds or colours or forms, or all of these, into a musical relation, that their emotion might live in other minds. A little lyric evokes an emotion, and this emotion gathers others about it and melts into their being in the making of some great epic; and at last, needing an always less delicate body, or symbol, as it grows more powerful, it flows out, with all it has gathered, among the blind instincts of daily life, where it moves a power within powers, as one sees ring within ring in the stem of an old tree. This is maybe what Arthur O'Shaughnessy meant when he made his poets say they had built Nineveh with their sighing; and I am certainly never sure, when I hear of some war, or of some religious excitement, or of some new manufacture, or of anything else that fills the ear of the world, that it has not all happened because of something that a boy piped in Thessaly. I remember once telling a seeress to ask one among the gods who, as she believed, were standing about her in their symbolic bodies, what would come of a charming but seeming trivial labour of a friend, and the form answering, 'the devastation of peoples and the overwhelming of cities'. I doubt indeed if the crude circumstance of the world, which seems to create all our emotions, does more than reflect, as in multiplying mirrors, the emotions that have come to solitary men in moments of poetical contemplation; or that love itself would be more than an animal hunger but for the poet and his shadow the priest, for unless we believe that outer things are the reality, we must believe that the gross is the shadow of the subtle, that things are wise before they become foolish, and secret before they cry out in the market-place. Solitary men in moments of contemplation receive, as I think, the creative impulse from the lowest of the

Nine Hierarchies, and so make and unmake mankind, and even the world itself, for does not 'the eye altering alter all'?

> Our towns are copied fragments from our breast;
> And all man's Babylons strive but to impart
> The grandeurs of his Babylonian heart.

The purpose of rhythm, it has always seemed to me, is to prolong the moment of contemplation, the moment when we are both asleep and awake, which is the one moment of creation, by hushing us with an alluring monotony, while it holds us waking by variety, to keep us in that state of perhaps real trance, in which the mind liberated from the pressure of the will is unfolded in symbols. If certain sensitive persons listen persistently to the ticking of a watch, or gaze persistently on the monotonous flashing of a light, they fall into the hypnotic trance; and rhythm is but the ticking of a watch made softer, that one must needs listen, and various, that one may not be swept beyond memory or grow weary of listening; while the patterns of the artist are but the monotonous flash woven to take the eyes in a subtler enchantment. I have heard in meditation voices that were forgotten the moment they had spoken; and I have been swept, when in more profound meditation, beyond all memory but of those things that came from beyond the threshold of waking life. I was writing once at a very symbolical and abstract poem, when my pen fell on the ground; and as I stooped to pick it up, I remembered some fantastic adventure that yet did not seem fantastic, and then another like adventure, and when I asked myself when these things had happened, I found that I was remembering my dreams for many nights. I tried to remember what I had done the day before, and then what I had done that morning; but all my waking life had perished from me, and it was only after a struggle that I came to remember it again, and as I did so that more powerful and startling life perished in its turn. Had my pen not fallen on the ground and so made me turn from the images that I was weaving into verse, I would never have known that meditation had become trance, for I would have been like one who does not know that he is passing through a wood because his eyes are on the pathway. So I think that in the making and in the understanding of a work of art, and the more easily if it is full of patterns and symbols and music, we are lured to the threshold of sleep, and it may be far beyond it, without knowing that we have ever set our feet upon the steps of horn or of ivory.

Besides emotional symbols, symbols that evoke emotions alone,—and in this sense all alluring or hateful things are symbols, although their relations with one another are too subtle to delight us fully, away from rhythm and pattern,—there are intellectual symbols, symbols that evoke ideas alone, or ideas mingled with emotions; and outside the very definite traditions of mysticism and the less definite criticism of certain modern poets, these alone are called symbols. Most things belong to one or another kind, according to the way we speak of them and the companions we give them, for symbols, associated with ideas that are more than fragments of the shadows thrown upon the intellect by the emotions they evoke, are the playthings of the allegorist or the pedant, and soon pass away. If I say 'white' or 'purple' in an ordinary line of poetry, they evoke emotions so exclusively that I cannot say why they move me; but if I bring them into the same sentence with such obvious intellectual symbols as a cross or a crown of thorns, I think of purity and sovereignty. Furthermore, innumerable meanings, which are held to 'white' or to 'purple' by bonds of subtle suggestion, and alike in the emotions and in the intellect, move visibly through my mind, and move invisibly beyond the threshold of sleep, casting lights and shadows of an indefinable wisdom on what had seemed before, it may be, but sterility and noisy violence. It is the intellect that decides where the reader shall ponder over the procession of the symbols, and if the symbols are merely emotional, he gazes from amid the accidents and destinies of the world; but if the symbols are intellectual too, he becomes himself a part of pure intellect, and he is himself mingled with the procession. If I watch a rushy pool in the moonlight, my emotion at its beauty is mixed with memories of the man that I have seen ploughing by its margin, or of the lovers I saw there a night ago; but if I look at the moon herself and remember any of her ancient names and meanings, I move among divine people, and things that have shaken off our mortality, the tower of ivory, the queen of waters, the shining stag among enchanted woods, the white hare sitting upon the hilltop, the fool of Faery with his shining cup full of dreams, and it may be 'make a friend of one of these images of wonder', and 'meet the Lord in the air'. So, too, if one is moved by Shakespeare, who is content with emotional symbols that he may come the nearer to our sympathy, one is mixed with the whole spectacle of the world; while if one is moved by Dante, or by the myth of Demeter, one is mixed into the shadow of God or of a goddess. So, too, one is furthest from symbols when one is busy doing this or that, but the soul moves among symbols and unfolds in symbols when trance, or madness, or deep meditation has withdrawn it from every impulse but its own. 'I then saw,' wrote Gérard de Nerval of his madness, 'vaguely drifting into form, plastic images of antiquity, which outlined themselves, became definite, and seemed to represent symbols of which I only seized the idea with difficulty.' In an earlier time he would have been of that multitude whose souls austerity withdrew, even more perfectly than madness could withdraw his soul, from hope and memory, from desire and regret, that they might reveal those processions of symbols that men bow to before altars, and woo with incense and offerings. But being of our time, he has been like Maeterlinck, like Villiers de l'Isle-Adam in *Axël*, like all who are preoccupied with intellectual symbols in our time, a foreshadower of the new sacred book, of which all the arts, as somebody has said, are beginning to dream. How can the arts overcome the slow dying of men's hearts that we call the progress of the world, and lay their hands upon men's heartstrings again, without becoming the garment of religion as in old times?

If people were to accept the theory that poetry moves us because of its symbolism, what change should one look for in the manner of our poetry? A return to the way of our fathers, a casting out of descriptions of nature for the sake of nature, of the moral law for the sake of the moral law, a casting out of all anecdotes and of that brooding over scientific opinion that so often extinguished the central flame in Tennyson, and of that vehemence that would make us do or not do certain things; or, in other words, we should come to understand that the beryl stone was enchanted by our fathers that it might unfold the pictures in its heart, and not to mirror our own excited faces, or the boughs waving outside the window. With this change of substance, this return to imagination, this understanding that the laws of art, which are the hidden laws of the world, can alone bind the imagination, would come a change of style, and we would cast out of serious poetry those energetic rhythms, as of a man running, which are the invention of the will with its eyes always on something to be done or undone; and we would seek out those wavering, meditative, organic rhythms, which are the embodiment of the imagination, that neither desires nor hates, because it has done with time, and only wishes to gaze upon some reality, some beauty; nor would it be any longer possible for anybody to deny the importance of form, in all its kinds, for although you can expound an opinion, or describe a thing, when your words are not quite well chosen, you cannot give a body to something that moves beyond the senses, unless your words are as subtle, as complex, as full of mysterious life, as the body of a flower or of a woman. The form of sincere poetry, unlike the form of the 'popular poetry', may indeed be sometimes obscure, or ungrammatical as in some of the best of the *Songs of Innocence and Experience*, but it must have the perfections that escape analysis, the subtleties that have a new meaning every day, and it must have all this whether it be but a little song made out of a moment of dreamy indolence, or some great epic made out of the dreams of one poet and of a hundred generations whose hands were never weary of the sword.

1900

FROM A GENERAL INTRODUCTION TO MY WORK*

STYLE AND ATTITUDE

Style is almost unconscious. I know what I have tried to do, little what I have done. Contemporary lyric poems, even those that moved me—'The Stream's Secret', 'Dolores'—seemed too long, but an Irish preference for a swift current might be mere indolence, yet Burns may have felt the same when he read Thomson and Cowper. The English mind is meditative, rich, deliberate; it may remember the Thames valley. I planned to write short lyrics or poetic drama where every speech would be short and concentrated, knit by dramatic tension, and I did so with more confidence because young English poets were at that time writing out of emotion at the moment of crisis, though their old slow-moving meditation returned almost at once. Then, and in this English poetry has followed my lead, I tried to make the language of poetry coincide with that of passionate, normal speech. I wanted to write in whatever language comes most naturally when we soliloquize, as I do all day long, upon the events of our own lives or of any life where we can see ourselves for the moment. I sometimes compare myself with the mad old slum women I hear denouncing and remembering; 'How dare you,' I heard one say of some imaginary suitor, 'and you without health or a home!' If I spoke my thoughts aloud they might be as angry and as wild. It was a long time before I had made a language to my liking; I began to make it when I discovered some twenty years ago that I must seek, not as Wordsworth thought, words in common use, but a powerful and passionate syntax, and a complete coincidence between period and stanza. Because I need a passionate syntax for passionate subject-matter I compel myself to accept those traditional metres that have developed with the language. Ezra Pound, Turner, Lawrence wrote admirable free verse, I could not. I would lose myself, become joyless like those mad old women. The translators of the Bible, Sir Thomas Browne, certain translators from the Greek when translators still bothered about rhythm, created a form midway between prose and verse that seems natural to impersonal meditation; but all that is personal soon rots; it must be packed in ice or salt. Once when I was in delirium from pneumonia I dictated a letter to George Moore telling him to eat salt because it was a symbol of eternity; the delirium passed, I had no memory of that letter, but I must have meant what I now mean. If I wrote of personal love or sorrow in free verse, or in any rhythm that left it unchanged, amid all its accidence, I would be full of self-contempt because of my egotism and indiscretion, and foresee the boredom

---

* From *Essays and Introductions* by William Butler Yeats.

of my reader. I must choose a traditional stanza, even what I alter must seem traditional. I commit my emotion to shepherds, herdsmen, camel-drivers, learned men, Milton's or Shelley's Platonist, that tower Palmer drew. Talk to me of originality and I will turn on you with rage. I am a crowd, I am a lonely man, I am nothing. Ancient salt is best packing. The heroes of Shakespeare convey to us through their looks, or through the metaphorical patterns of their speech, the sudden enlargement of their vision, their ecstasy at the approach of death: 'She should have died hereafter', 'Of many thousand kisses, the poor last', 'Absent thee from felicity awhile'. They have become God or Mother Goddess, the pelican, 'My baby at my breast', but all must be cold; no actress has ever sobbed when she played Cleopatra, even the shallow brain of a producer has never thought of such a thing. The supernatural is present, cold winds blow across our hands, upon our faces, the thermometer falls, and because of that cold we are hated by journalists and groundlings. There may be in this or that detail painful tragedy, but in the whole work none. I have heard Lady Gregory say, rejecting some play in the modern manner sent to the Abbey Theatre, 'Tragedy must be a joy to the man who dies.' Nor is it any different with lyrics, songs, narrative poems; neither scholars nor the populace have sung or read anything generation after generation because of its pain. The maid of honour whose tragedy they sing must be lifted out of history with timeless pattern, she is one of the four Maries, the rhythm is old and familiar, imagination must dance, must be carried beyond feeling into the aboriginal ice. Is ice the correct word? I once boasted, copying the phrase from a letter of my father's, that I would write a poem 'cold and passionate as the dawn'.

When I wrote in blank verse I was dissatisfied; my vaguely medieval *Countess Cathleen* fitted the measure, but our Heroic Age went better, or so I fancied, in the ballad metre of *The Green Helmet*. There was something in what I felt about Deirdre, about Cuchulain, that rejected the Renaissance and its characteristic metres, and this was a principal reason why I created in dance plays the form that varies blank verse with lyric metres. When I speak blank verse and analyse my feelings, I stand at a moment of history when instinct, its traditional songs and dances, its general agreement, is of the past. I have been cast up out of the whale's belly though I still remember the sound and sway that came from beyond its ribs, and, like the Queen in Paul Fort's ballad, I smell of the fish of the sea. The contrapuntal structure of the verse, to employ a term adopted by Robert Bridges, combines the past and present. If I repeat the first line of *Paradise Lost* so as to emphasize its five feet I am among the folk singers—'Of mán's first dísobédience ánd the frúit', but speak it as I should cross it with another emphasis, that of passionate prose—'Of mán's fírst disobédience and the frúit', or 'Of mán's fírst dísobedience and the frúit'; the folk song is still there, but a ghostly voice, an unvariable possibility, an unconscious norm. What moves me and my hearer is a vivid speech that has no laws except that it must not exorcise the ghostly voice. I am awake and asleep, at my moment of revelation, self-possessed in self-surrender; there is no rhyme, no echo of the beaten drum, the dancing foot, that would overset my balance. When I was a boy I wrote a poem upon dancing that had one good line: 'They snatch with their hands at the sleep of the skies'. If I sat down and thought for a year I would discover that but for certain syllabic limitations, a rejection or acceptance of certain elisions, I must wake or sleep.

The Countess Cathleen could speak a blank verse which I had loosened, almost put out of joint, for her need, because I thought of her as medieval and thereby connected her with the general European movement. For Deirdre and Cuchulain and all the other figures of Irish legend are still in the whale's belly.

Acknowledgements

JOHN ASHBERY 'The Orioles' from *Some Trees* by John Ashbery. Copyright © 1956 by John Ashbery. First printed by The Ecco Press in 1978. Reprinted by permission. 'Our Youth' from *The Tennis Court Oath* © 1962 by John Ashbery, Wesleyan University Press by permission of University Press of New England. 'Forties Flick', copyright © 1974 by John Ashbery, 'A Man of Words', copyright © 1973 by John Ashbery, from *Self-Portrait in a Convex Mirror* by John Ashbery, are used by permission of Viking Penguin, a division of Penguin Books USA Inc. and Carcanet Press Limited. 'And *Ut Pictura Poesis* is Her Name' by John Ashbery from *Houseboat Days* (New York: Viking Penguin, 1977). Copyright © 1975, 1976, 1977 by John Ashbery, and 'The Absence of a Noble Presence' by John Ashbery from *Shadow Train* (New York: Viking Penguin, 1981). Copyright © 1981 by John Ashbery are reprinted by permission of Georges Borchardt, Inc. and Carcanet Press Limited. 'On the Empress's Mind' and 'The Old Complex' from *Hotel Lautreamont* by John Ashbery. Copyright © 1992 by John Ashbery. Are reprinted by permission of Alfred A. Knopf, Inc. and Carcanet Press Limited.

MARGARET ATWOOD 'It Is Dangerous to Read Newspapers', 'Progressive Insanities of a Pioneer', and 'Backdrop Addresses Cowboy' from *The Animals in That Country* by Margaret Atwood. Copyright © Oxford University Press Canada 1968. 'Death of a Young Son by Drowning' from *The Journals of Susanna Moodie* by Margaret Atwood. Copyright © Oxford University Press Canada 1970. 'Marrying the Hangman' from *Two-Headed Poems* © Margaret Atwood 1978. 'Notes Towards a Poem That Can Never Be Written' from *True Stories* © Margaret Atwood 1981. Reprinted by permission of Oxford University Press Canada. 'Marrying the Hangman' and 'Notes Towards a Poem that Can Never Be Written' from *Selected Poems II: Poems Selected and New.* Copyright © 1987 by Margaret Atwood. Reprinted by permission of Houghton Mifflin Company. All rights reserved. 'You take my hand' from *Power Politics* by Margaret Atwood. Reprinted with the permission of Stoddart Publishing Co. Limited, Don Mills, Ontario. 'Morning in the Burned House' from *Morning in the Burned House* by Margaret Atwood. Copyright © 1995 by Margaret Atwood. Used by permission of the Canadian Publishers, McClelland & Stewart, Toronto, and Houghton Mifflin Company. All rights reserved. And with permission of Curtis Brown Ltd, London on behalf of Margaret Atwood. 'Conversations' reprinted from *Margaret Atwood: Conversations* edited by Earl G. Ingersoll. Copyright © Ontario Review Press. Reprinted by permission.

W.H. AUDEN 'As I Walked Out One Evening', 'Lullaby', 'Musée des Beaux Arts', 'In Memory of W.B. Yeats', and 'The Unknown Citizen' from *Collected Poems* by W.H. Auden edited by Edward Mendelson. Reprinted by permission of Faber and Faber Ltd. 'The Shield of Achilles' from *Collected Poems* by W.H. Auden, edit., E. Mendelson. Copyright 1952 by W.H. Auden. Reprinted by permission of Random House Inc. and Faber and Faber Ltd. Excerpt from 'The Poet and the City' and excerpt from 'The Virgin and the Dynamo' from *The Dyer's Hand and Other Essays* by W.H. Auden. Copyright © 1948, 1950, 1952, 1953, 1954, © 1956, 1957, 1958, 1960, 1962 by W.H. Auden. Reprinted by permission of Random House, Inc. and Faber and Faber Ltd.

MARGARET AVISON 'The Word Still Needs', 'To Professor X, Year Y', 'The Swimmer's Moment', 'Voluptuaries and Others', 'Pace', 'Black-White Under Green: May 18, 1965', 'July Man', and 'In a Season of Unemployment' from *Selected Poems*. Copyright © Margaret Avison 1991. Reprinted by permission of Oxford University Press Canada. 'Oughtiness ousted' and 'We the Poor Who Are Always With Us' from *sunblue* by Margaret Avison. Reprinted by permission of Lancelot Press, Hantsport, N.S.

JOHN BERRYMAN 'The Dispossessed' and 'A Professor's Song' from *Short Poems* by John Berryman. Copyright © 1967 by John Berryman. Dream Songs #1, 8, 14, 26, 29, 40, 49, 50 and 52 from *The Dream Songs* by John Berryman. Copyright © 1969 by John Berryman. Reprinted by permission of Farrar, Straus & Giroux, Inc. and Faber and Faber Ltd.

EARLE BIRNEY 'Vancouver Lights', 'Anglosaxon Street', 'From the Hazel Bough', 'David', and 'Bushed' from *Selected Poems of Earle Birney* by Earle Birney. 'A Walk in Kyoto', 'The Bear on the Delhi Road', and 'Haiku for a Young Waitress' from *Collected Poems of Earle Birney* by Earle Birney. Used by permission of the Canadian Publishers, McClelland & Stewart, Toronto.

ELIZABETH BISHOP 'The Map', 'The Imaginary Iceberg', 'At the Fishhouses', 'Cape Breton', 'Arrival at Santos', 'Questions of Travel', 'Squatter's Children', '12 O'Clock News', and 'Santarem' from *The Complete Poems 1927-1979* by Elizabeth Bishop. Copyright © 1979, 1983 by Alice Helen Methfessel. Reprinted by permission of Farrar, Straus & Giroux, Inc.

ROBERT BLY Reprinted by permission of Robert Bly: 'Driving Toward the Lac Qui Parle River' from *Silence in the Snowy Fields*, Wesleyan University Press, 1962, Copyright 1962 by Robert Bly; 'The Dead Seal' from *The Morning Glory*, Harper & Row, 1975, Copyright 1975 by Robert Bly; and 'Finding the Father' from *This Body Is Made of Camphor and Gopherwood*, Harper & Row, 1977, Copyright 1977 by Robert Bly. Reprinted by permission of HarperCollins Publishers, Inc.: 'Counting Small-Boned Bodies' and 'Driving Through Minnesota During the Hanoi Bombings' from *The Light Around the Body* by Robert Bly. Copyright © 1967 by Robert Bly. Copyright renewed 1995 by Robert Bly; and 'Looking for Dragon Smoke' from *American Poetry: Wilderness and Domesticity* by Robert Bly. Copyright © 1990 by Robert Bly. Used by permission of Doubleday, a division of Bantam Doubleday Dell Publishing Group, Inc.: 'Fifty Males Sitting Together' and 'Snowbanks North of the House' from *The Man in the Black Coat Turns* by Robert Bly. Copyright © 1981 by Robert Bly; and 'In Rainy September', 'Winter Poem', 'What We Provide', and 'The Horse of Desire' from *Loving a Woman in Two Worlds* by Robert Bly. Copyright © 1985 by Robert Bly. 'The Mushroom' by Robert Bly. From *Ten Poems of Francis Ponge Translated by Robert Bly*, and *Ten Poems of Robert Bly Inspired by the Poems of Francis Ponge*. © 1990 by Robert Bly. Used by permission of Owl's Head Press, Alma, New Brunswick.

EAVAN BOLAND Reprinted by permission of W.W. Norton & Company, Inc.: 'Ode to Suburbia', 'Anorexic', 'Mastectomy', and 'Mise Eire', from *An Origin Like Water: Collected Poems 1967-1987* by Eavan Boland. Copyright © 1996 by Eavan Boland; 'The Black Lace Fan My Mother Gave Me' and 'Midnight Flowers' from *Outside History: Selected Poems 1980-1990* by Eavan Boland. Copyright © 1990 by Eavan Boland; and 'Lava Cameo', copyright © 1991 by Eavan Boland, from *In a Time of Violence* by Eavan Boland. Reprinted by permission of Carcanet Press Limited: 'The Politics of Eroticism' from *Object Lessons: The Life of the Woman and the Poet in Our Time* by Eavan Boland (1995); 'Ode to Suburbia', 'Anorexic', 'Mastectony', and 'Mise Eire' from *Selected Poems* (1989) by Eavan Boland; 'The Black Lace Fan My Mother Gave Me' and 'Midnight Flowers' from *Outside History* (1990) by Eavan Boland; and 'Lava Cameo' and 'Time and Violence' from *In a Time of Violence* (1994).

ROO BORSON 'Abundance', 'Talk', 'Waterfront', 'October, Hanson's Field', 'Flowers', 'A Sad Device', 'Spring', 'The Garden', 'Beauty', 'Intermittent Rain', 'Snowlight on the Northwood Path', 'City Lights', 'Rubber Boots', and 'Grove' from *Night Walk: Selected Poems* (Oxford University Press, 1994). Used by permission of the author. 'July' is reprinted from *The Transparence of November/Snow* by permission of Quarry Press, Inc.

LEONARD COHEN 'Elegy', 'Story', 'You have the lovers', 'As the mist leaves no scar', 'Now of Sleeping', 'The Genius', 'Style', 'The Music Crept by Us', and 'Disguise' from *Selected Poems* by Leonard Cohen. 'How to Speak Poetry' from *Stranger Music* by Leonard Cohen. Used by permission of the Canadian Publishers, McClelland & Stewart, Toronto. Stranger Music Inc.

ROBERT CREELEY Reprinted by permission of the Regents of the University of California and University of California Press: 'Je vois dans le hasard tous les biens que j'espère', 'After Lorca', 'The pool', 'For My Mother Jules Creeley', and 'I keep to myself such measures', 'The Awakening', and 'The Rain' from *Collected Poems of Robert Creeley, 1945-1975*. Copyright © 1983 The Regents of the University of California. 'A Sense of Measure' from *Collected Essays of Robert Creeley*. Copyright © 1989 The Regents of the University of California. 'Self Portrait', 'Bresson's Movies', and 'Echoes' from *Selected Poems*. Copyright © 1991 The Regents of the University of California. Reprinted by permission of New Directions Publishing Corp.: 'Epic' from *Windows*. Copyright © 1990 by Robert Creeley.

LORNA CROZIER 'Forms of Innocence', 'The Child Who Walks Backwards', 'Onions', and 'Peas' from *The Garden Going on Without Us* by Lorna Crozier. 'Fathers, Uncles, Old Friends of the Family', 'Angel of Infinity', and 'Mother and I, Walking' from *Angels of Flesh, Angels of Silence* by Lorna Crozier. 'Variation on the Origin of Flight', 'Living Day By Day', 'Inventing the Hawk', 'Last Testaments', and 'Skunks' from *Inventing the Hawk* by Lorna Crozier. 'The Game' from *Everything Arrives At the Light* by Lorna Crozier. Used by permission of the Canadian Publishers, McClelland & Stewart, Toronto. Excerpt from 'Who's Listening', published in *NeWest Review*, February/March 1989. Reprinted by permission of the author.

E.E. CUMMINGS 'Chansons Innocentes', 'my sweet old etcetera', 'i sing of Olaf', 'somewhere i have never travelled, gladly beyond', 'anyone lived in a pretty how town', 'my father moved through dooms of love', 'love is more thicker than forget', 'dying is fine)but Death', and 'i thank You God for most this amazing', Introduction to *New Poems*, and Forward to *Is 5* from *Complete Poems: 1904-1962* by E.E. Cummings, Edited by George J. Firmage. Copyright © 1923, 1925, 1926, 1931, 1935, 1938, 1939, 1940, 1944, 1945, 1946, 1947, 1948, 1949, 1950, 1951, 1952, 1953, 1954, 1955, 1956, 1957, 1958, 1959, 1960, 1961, 1962, 1963, 1966, 1967, 1968, 1972, 1973, 1974, 1975, 1976, 1977, 1978, 1979, 1980, 1951, 1982, 1983, 1984, 1985, 1986, 1987, 1988, 1989, 1990, 1991 by the Trustees for the E.E. Cummings Trust. Copyright © 1973, 1976, 1978, 1979, 1981, 1983, 1985, 1991 by George James Firmage. 'A Poet's Advice to Students', copyright © 1955, 1965 by the Trustees for the E.E. Cummings Trust. Copyright © 1958, 1965 by George J. Firmage, from *A Miscellany Revised* by E.E. Cummings, Edited by George J. Firmage. All poems reprinted by permission of Liveright Publishing Corporation.

RITA DOVE 'Nigger Song: An Odyssey', 'The Secret Garden', 'The House Slave', and 'Adolescence—II' from *The Yellow House on the Corner* by Rita Dove (Carnegie Mellon University Press). Copyright © 1980 by Rita Dove. 'Boccaccio: The Plague Years' from *Museum* by Rita Dove (Carnegie Mellon University Press). Copyright © 1983 by Rita Dove. 'The Event', 'Variation on Pain', 'The Stroke', 'Thomas at the Wheel', 'Taking in Wash', 'Daystar', and 'The Great Palaces of Versailles' from *Thomas and Beulah* by Rita Dove (Carnegie Mellon University Press). Copyright © 1986 by Rita Dove. Reprinted by permission of the author. 'Pastoral', 'After Reading *Mickey in the Night Kitchen* for the Third Time Before Bed', and 'Canary' from *Grace Notes* copyright © 1989 by Rita Dove. Reprinted by permission of the author and W.W. Norton & Company, Inc.

CAROL ANN DUFFY 'Standing Female Nude', 'War Photographer', and 'A Healthy Meal' are taken from *Standing Female Nude* published by Anvil Press Poetry in 1985. 'Model Village', 'Psychopath', 'Foreign', and 'Warming Her Pearls' are taken from *Selling Manhattan* published by Anvil Press Poetry in 1987. 'Girlfriends' and 'The Kissing Gate' are taken from *The Other Country* published by Anvil Press Poetry in 1990. 'Prayer' is taken from Mean Time published by Anvil Press Poetry in 1993.

T.S. ELIOT 'The Love Song of J. Alfred Prufrock', 'Preludes', 'The Hollow Men', 'Journey of the Magi', and 'Burnt Norton' from *Collected Poems 1909-1962* by T.S. Eliot. 'Tradition and the Individual Talent' and excerpt from 'Hamlet and his Problems' from *Selected Essays* by T.S. Eliot. Harcourt Brace & Company. Excerpt from 'The Music of Poetry' from *On Poetry and Poets* by T.S. Eliot. Reprinted by permission of Faber and Faber Ltd. Farrar, Straus & Girous, Inc.

LAWRENCE FERLINGHETTI 'In Goya's greatest scenes we seem to see', 'Don't let that horse eat that violin', 'Constantly risking absurdity and death', 'The pennycandystore beyond the El', and 'Junkman's Obbligato' from *A Coney Island of the Mind*. Copyright © 1958 by Lawrence Ferlinghetti. Reprinted by permission of New Directions Publishing Corp. 'Modern Poetry Is Prose (But It Is Saying Plenty)' from *These Are My Rivers: New and Selected Poems 1955-1993*. Reprinted by permission of New Directions Publishing Corp.

ROBERT FROST 'Mending Wall', 'After Apple-Picking', 'Birches', 'Fire and Ice', 'Stopping by Woods on a Snowy Evening', 'Acquainted with the Night', 'Departmental', 'Desert Places', 'Neither Out Far Nor In Deep', 'Design', 'Provide, Provide', 'One Step Backward Taken', and 'Directive' from *The Poetry of Robert Frost* edited by Edward Connery Lathem. Copyright 1936, 1951 © 1956 by Robert Frost. Copyright © 1964 by Lesley Frost Ballantine. Copyright 1923, 1928, 1947 © 1969 by Henry Holt and Co. Inc. 'The Figure a Poem Makes' from *Selected Prose of Robert Frost* edited by Hyde Cox and Edward Connery Lathem. Copyright 1939 © 1967 by Henry Holt and Co., Inc. Reprinted by permission of Henry Holt and Co., Inc. and Jonathan Cape Ltd.

GARY GEDDES All poems used by permission of the author.

ALLEN GINSBERG all lines from 'Howl' from *Collected Poems 1947-1980* by Allen Ginsberg. Copyright © 1955 by Allen Ginsberg. All lines from 'A Supermarket in California' from *Collected Poems 1947-1980* by Allen Ginsberg. Copyright © 1955 by Allen Ginsberg. Copyright renewed. All lines from 'America' from *Collected Poems 1947-1980* by Allen Ginsberg. Copyright © 1956, 1959 by Allen Ginsberg. Copyright renewed. Reprinted by permission of HarperCollins Publishers, Inc. 'Notes for Howl and Other Poems' from *Fantasy* (LP Recording 7006). Wylie, Aitken & Stone Inc.

LOUISE GLÜCK 'For My Mother' from *The House on Marshland* by Louise Glück. Copyright © 1971, 1972, 1973, 1974, 1975 by Louise Glück. First published by The Ecco Press in 1975. 'Epithalamium' and 'Dedication to Hunger' from *Descending Figure* by Louise Glück. Copyright © 1976, 1977, 1978, 1979, 1980 by Louise Glück. First published by The Ecco Press in 1980. 'Mock Orange', 'Legend', and 'Horse' from *The Triumph of Achilles* by Louise Glück. Copyright © 1985 by Louise Glück. First published by The Ecco Press in 1985. 'Brown Circle' from Ararat by Louise Glück. Copyright © 1990 by Louise Glück. First published by The Ecco Press in 1990. 'The Wild Iris', 'Trillium', 'End of Winter', 'Witchgrass', and 'Retreating Light' from *The Wild Iris* by Louise Glück. Copyright © 1992 by Louise Glück. First published by The Ecco Press in 1992. Reprinted by permission of the Ecco Press and Carcanet Press Limited.

ROBERT HASS 'Song' from *Field Guide* (1973) by Robert Hass. Reprinted by permission of Yale University Press. 'Meditation at Lagunitas' from Praise by Robert Hass. Copyright © 1974, 1975, 1976, 1977, 1978, and 1979 by Robert Hass. First published by The Ecco Press in 1979. 'A Story About the Body', 'Human Wishes', and 'Natural Theology' from *Human Wishes* by Robert Hass. Copyright © 1989 by Robert Hass. First published by The Ecco Press in 1989. Reprinted by permission. 'My Mother's Nipples' from *Best American Poetry*. © Robert Hass. Reprinted by permission of the author.

SEAMUS HEANEY 'Digging', 'Death of a Naturalist', 'Mid-Term Break', and 'Personal Helicon' from *Death of a Naturalist* by Seamus Heaney. 'Requiem for the Croppies' and 'Bogland' from *Door into the Dark* by Seamus Heaney. 'Summer Home' from *Wintering Out* by Seamus Heaney. 'Bog Queen' from *North* by Seamus Heaney. 'Feelings into Words' from *Preoccupations: Selected Prose 1968-1978* by Seamus Heaney. 'From the Frontier of Writing' from *Selected Poems 1966-1987* by Seamus Heaney. Copyright © 1990 by Seamus Heaney. Reprinted by permission of Farrar, Straus & Giroux, Inc. and Faber and Faber Ltd.

TED HUGHES 'The Thought-Fox', 'Six Young Men', and 'Invitation to Dance' from *The Hawk in the Rain* by Ted Hughes. 'Hawk Roosting' and 'Pike' from *Lupercal* by Ted Hughes. 'A Childish Prank', 'Crow's First Lesson', and 'A Disaster' from *Crow: From the Life and Songs of the Crow* by Ted Hughes. 'Dehorning' from *Moortown Diary* by Ted Hughes. Reprinted by permission of Faber and Faber Ltd. 'On Poetry' from *Ted Hughes: The Unaccommodated Universe*. Copyright © 1980 by Edbert Faas and reprinted with the permission of Black Sparrow Press.

GALWAY KINNELL 'First Song' from *What a Kingdom It Was*. Copyright © 1960, renewed 1988 by Galway Kinnell. 'The Bear' from *Three Books*. Copyright © 1993 by Galway Kinnell. First published in *Body Rags* (1967). 'Under the Maud Moon' from *The Book of Nightmares*. Copyright © 1971 by Galway Kinnell. 'After Making Love We Hear Footsteps' from *Three Books*. Copyright © 1993 by Galway Kinnell. First published in *Mortal Acts, Mortal Words* (1980). Reprinted by permission of Houghton Mifflin Co. All rights reserved. 'When One Has Lived a Long Time Alone' from *When One Has Lived a Long Time Alone* by Galway Kinnell. Copyright © 1990 by Galway Kinnell. Reprinted by permission of Alfred A. Knopf, Inc.

A.M. KLEIN 'Heirloom', 'Autobiographical', 'Political Meeting', 'Lone Bather', and 'Portrait of the Poet as Landscape' from *Complete Poems* by A.M. Klein, Zailig Pollack, ed. Copyright © University of Toronto Press 1990. Reprinted by permission of the University of Toronto Press Incorporated.

ROBERT KROETSCH 'Seed Catalogue' © 1989 Robert Kroetsch. From *Complete Field Notes: The Long Poems of Robert Kroetsch* (McClelland & Stewart). Used by permission of Westwood Creative Artists Ltd.

PATRICK LANE 'Ten Miles in from Horsefly', 'Elephants', 'Passing Into Storm', 'Stigmata', 'Albino Pheasants', 'The Carpenter', and 'A Murder of Crows' from *Selected Poems*, 'The Measure' from *The Measure*, 'There Is a Time' from *Old Mother*, and 'Fathers and Sons' from *Mortal Remains*. Reprinted by permission of the author.

PHILIP LARKIN 'Lines on a Young Lady's Photograph Album', 'Wants', 'Church Going', 'Toads', 'Poetry of Departures', and 'If, My Darling' are reprinted from *The Less Deceived* by permission of The Marvell Press, England and Australia. 'Faith Healing' from *The Whitsun Weddings* by Philip Larkin. Reprinted by permission of Faber and Faber Ltd.

IRVING LAYTON All poems from *Collected Poems* by Irving Layton. Used by permission of the Canadian Publishers, McClelland & Stewart, Toronto.

DENISE LEVERTOV 'A Map of the Western Part of the County of Essex in England', 'Come into Animal Presence', 'The Ache of Marriage', 'Hypocrite Women', 'Second Didactic Poem' from *Poems 1960-1967*. Copyright © by Denise Levertov. 'An Interim', 'He-Who-Came-Forth' from *Poems 1968-1972*. Copyright © by Denise Levertov. 'The Poem Rising By Its Own Weight' from *The Freeing of the Dust*. Copyright © by Denise Levertov. 'She and the Muse' from *Candles in Babylon*. Copyright © by Denise Levertov. 'Brother Ivy' from *Evening Train*. Copyright © by Denise Levertov. 'Some Notes on Organic Form' from *New and Selected Essays*. Copyright © 1973 by Denise Levertov. Reprinted by permission of New Directions Publishing Corp. and Laurence Pollinger Limited.

PHILIP LEVINE 'For Fran', 'Coming Home, *Detroit*, 1968', 'Late Moon', 'Starlight', 'Lost and Found', 'Let Me Begin Again', 'The Fox', 'The Voice', 'A Theory of Prosody', 'What Work Is', 'Gin', and 'The Simple Truth' from *New and Selected Poems* by Philip Levine. Copyright © 1991 by Philip Levine. 'The Poet in New York in Detroit' from *The Bread to Time: Toward an Autobiography*. Copyright © by Philip Levine. Reprinted by permission of Alfred A. Knopf, Inc.

TIM LILBURN 'Names of God' and 'Pumpkins' from *Names of God*, Oolichan Books, 1986. Used by permission of the author. 'Touching An Elephant In A Dark Room' from *Tourist to Ecstasy* © Tim Lilburn. Reprinted by permission of Exile Editions Ltd. 'In the Hills', 'Watching', 'Learning a Deeper Courtesy of the Eye', 'Discipline of Secrecy', 'How To Be Here?', and 'Restoration' from *Moosewood Sandhills* by Tim Lilburn. Used by permission of the Canadian Publishers, McClelland & Stewart, Toronto.

ROBERT LOWELL 'Mr. Edwards and the Spider', 'The Quaker Graveyard in Nantucket', 'After the Surprising Conversions', 'Christmas in Black Rock', and 'The Holy Innocents' from *Lord Weary's Castle*, copyright 1946 and renewed 1974 by Robert Lowell, reprinted by permission of Harcourt Brace & Company. 'Memories of West Street and Lepke' and 'Skunk Hour' from *Life Studies* by Robert Lowell. Copyright © 1956, 1959 by Robert Lowell. Copyright renewed © 1987 by Harriet Lowell, Sheridan Lowell, and Caroline Lowell. 'For the Union Dead' from *For the Union Dead* by Robert Lowell. Copyright © 1964 by Robert Lowell. Copyright renewed © 1992 by Harriet Lowell, Sheridan Lowell, and Caroline Lowell. Reprinted by permission of Farrar, Straus & Giroux, Inc. and Faber and Faber Ltd. Excerpt from the interview 'Robert Lowell' edited by George Plimpton, *Writers at Work, Second Series* by George A. Plimpton, editor, introduction by Van Wyck Brook. Copyright © 1963 by The Paris Review. Used by permission of Viking Penguin, a division of Penguin Books USA Inc.

GWENDOLYN MacEWEN 'Poems in Braille', 'Manzini: Escape Artist', 'Poem Improvised Around a First Line', 'The Red Bird You Wait For', 'The Discovery', 'Dark Pines Under Water', 'Memoirs of a Mad Cook', and 'The Child Dancing' from *Magic Animals*. Reprinted with the permission of Stoddart Publishing Co. Limited, Don Mills, Ont., Canada.

'Apologies', 'Nitroglycerine Tulips', 'Deraa', 'Ghazala's Foal', 'Tall Tales', and 'Notes from the Dead Land' from *The T.E. Lawrence Poems* by Gwendolyn MacEwen, © 1995 Third Printing, published with the permission of Mosaic Press, 1252 Speers Road, Units 1 & 2, Oakville, ON L6L 5N9. 'The Transparent Womb', 'The Loneliness of the Long Distance Poet', and 'You Can Study it if You Want' from *Afterworlds* by Gwendolyn MacEwen. Used by permission of the Canadian Publishers, McClelland & Stewart, Toronto, and the author's family.

DAPHNE MARLATT 'Alcazar, Cecil, Belmont, New Fountain, names stations of the way, to' from *Vancouver Poems* (Coach House Press, 1972). 'Imagine: a town' and 'A by-channel; a small backwater' from *Steveston*, Daphne Marlatt, Talonbooks, 1974 and Longspoon Press, 1984. Reprinted with permission of the author. 'Vacant, Lots' and 'Listen' from *Net Work: Selected Writings*, Daphne Marlatt, edited by Fred Wah, Talonbooks 1980. 'yes', 'healing', and 'musing with mothertongue' from *Two Women in a Birth* by Daphne Marlatt and Betsy Warland, Guernica Editions, 1994. Reprinted by permission of Daphne Marlatt and Guernica Editions. 'The difference three makes: a narrative' and 'Seeing it go up in smoke' from *Salvage* by Daphne Marlatt. Copyright © 1991. Reprinted by permission of Red Deer College Press.

DON McKAY 'The Great Blue Heron', 'Fridge Nocturne', 'Adagio for a Fallen Sparrow', 'Esthétique du Chien', 'The Poem, to be Slow as Evening', and 'Listen at the Edge' from *Birding, or desire* by Don McKay. 'Via, Eastbound' from *Sanding Down this Rocking Chair* by Don McKay. 'Waking at the Mouth of the Willow River', 'Meditation on Snow Clouds Approaching the University from the North-West', and 'Song for the Restless Wind' from *Night Field* by Don McKay. Used by permission of the Canadian Publishers, McClelland & Stewart, Toronto. 'Some Remarks on Poetry and Poetic Attention' is reprinted by permission of the author.

ERIN MOURÉ 'Empire, York Street' © Erin Mouré. Reprinted with the author's permission. 'The Cooking' from *Sheepish Beauty, Civilian Love* by Erin Mouré appears with the permission of the publisher, Véhicule Press. 'Post-Modern Literature', 'Divergences', 'Being Carpenter', 'Public Health', 'Tropic Line', 'Toxicity', 'Hooked', 'Miss Chatelaine', 'Betty', and 'Gorgeous' reprinted with the permission of Stoddart Publishing Co. Limited, Don Mills, Ontario M3B 2T6.

bpNICHOL 'Blues', from 'The Captain Poetry Poems', 'Allegory #6', 'What is Can Lit?', 'Landscape: I', and 'The Mouth' from *An H in the Heart* by bp Nichol. Used by permission of the Canadian Publishers, McClelland & Stewart, Toronto. 'continental trance' from *Continental Trance*, Oolichan Press, 1982. 'Some thots on the Martyrology Book VI Half-way thru', 'After Reading the Chronology', and 'Narrative in Language: The Long Poem' from *Tracing the Paths*, Line/TalonBooks, 1988. © The Estate of bp Nichol. Reprinted by permission.

SHARON OLDS 'Indictment of Senior Officers', 'First Night', 'Station', and 'Fishing Off Nova Scotia' from *Satan Says*, by Sharon Olds, © 1980. Reprinted by permission of the University of Pittsburgh Press. 'The Death of Marilyn Monroe', 'Miscarriage', and 'The Connoisseuse of Slugs' from *The Dead and the Living* by Sharon Olds. Copyright © 1983 by Sharon Olds. 'Summer Solstice, New York City', 'Still Life', and 'The Green Shirt' from *The Gold Cell* by Sharon Olds. Copyright © 1987 by Sharon Olds. 'The Glass', 'The Lifting', 'The Exact Moment of His Death', 'The Swimmer', 'I Wanted to Be There When

My Father Died', and 'My Father Speaks to Me from the Dead' from *The Father* by Sharon Olds. Copyright © 1992 by Sharon Olds. Reprinted by permission of Alfred A. Knopf, Inc.

CHARLES OLSON 'The Kingfishers' and 'As the Dead Prey Upon Us' from *Selected Writings of Charles Olson*. Copyright © 1951, 1966 by Charles Olson. 'Projective Verse' from *Selected Writings of Charles Olson*. Copyright © 1951, 1966 by Charles Olson. Reprinted by permission of New Directions Publishing Corp. 'Maximus, to Himself' from *The Maximus Poems*, trans./ed. by George Butterick. Copyright © 1983 The Regents of the University of California. Reprinted by permission of the University of California Press.

MICHAEL ONDAATJE 'Elizabeth', 'Letters & Other Worlds', 'White Dwarfs', 'Bearhug', and 'Light' from *The Cinnemon Peeler* by Michael Ondaatje (McClelland and Stewart, Canada), (Alfred A. Knopf, Inc. USA), (Picador, UK). Excerpt from 'Billy the Kid' from *Billy the Kid* by Michael Ondaatje. 'In a Yellow Room' and 'Red Accordion' from *Secular Love* by Michael Ondaatje. 'A Gentleman Compares his Virtues to a Jade' appeared in the magazine *Salmagundi*. The author would like to acknowledge the book *A History of Private Life* by Aries and Duby for two phrases in the poem. All poems reprinted by permission of the author.

P.K. PAGE All poems © P.K. Page. Reprinted by permission of the author.

SYLVIA PLATH 'Two Views of a Cadaver Room', 'The Colossus', 'Black Rook in Rainy Weather', 'Blue Moles', and 'The Disquieting Muses' from *The Colossus and Other Poems* by Sylvia Plath. 'Lady Lazarus', 'Tulips', and 'Ariel' from *Ariel* by Sylvia Plath. Reprinted by permission of Faber and Faber Ltd. 'Lady Lazarus', from *Ariel* by Sylvia Plath. Copyright © 1963 by Ted Hughes. Copyright Renewed. 'Tulips', and 'Ariel' from *Ariel* by Sylvia Plath. Copyright © 1965 by Ted Hughes. Copyright Renewed. Reprinted by permission of Harper Collins Publishers, Inc. 'An Interview' from *The Poet Speaks* edited by Peter Orr. Reprinted by permission of the British Council.

EZRA POUND 'Portrait d'une Femme', 'The Garden', 'Commission', 'Dance Figure', 'In a Station of the Metro', 'Alba', 'L'Art, 1910', 'The Tea Shop', 'The River-Merchant's Wife: A Letter', 'From *Hugh Selwyn Mauberley*: E.P. Ode pour l'élection de son sépulchre', and 'Mr. Nixon' from *Personae*. Copyright © 1926 by Ezra Pound. 'Canto I' and 'Canto XIII' from *The Cantos of Ezra Pound*. Copyright © 1934, 48, 1934, 1938 by Ezra Pound. 'A Retrospect' from *The Literary Essays of Ezra Pound*. Copyright © 1935 by Ezra Pound. Reprinted by permission of New Directions Publishing Corp.

ALFRED PURDY 'The Cariboo Horses', 'Song of the Impermanent Husband', 'Eskimo Graveyard', 'Arctic Rhododendrons', 'Lament for the Dorsets', and 'Poem' from *Selected Poems* by Al Purdy. Used by permission of the Canadian Publishers, McClelland & Stewart, Toronto. 'Grosse Isle' and 'An Interview' are reprinted by permission of the author.

ADRIENNE RICH 'At a Bach Concert', 'Snapshots of a Daughter-in-Law', 'The Burning of Paper Instead of Children', 'Diving into the Wreck', 'The Phenomenology of Anger', and 'Frame' from *The Fact of a Doorframe: Poems Selected and New, 1950-1984* by Adrienne Rich. Copyright © 1984 by Adrienne Rich. Copyright © 1975, 1978 by W.W. Norton & Company, Inc. Copyright © 1981 by Adrienne Rich. 'North American Time' from *Your Native Land, Your Life: Poems* by Adrienne Rich. Copyright © 1986 by Adrienne Rich. Selected excerpts from *What Is Found There: Notebooks on Poetry and Politics* by Adrienne Rich.

Copyright © 1993 by Adrienne Rich. Reprinted by permission of the author and W.W. Norton & Company, Inc. and Little, Brown and Company (UK) Ltd.

THEODORE ROETHKE 'Prayer', copyright 1935 by Theodore Roethke. 'Big Wind', copyright 1947 by The United Chapters of Phi Beta Kappa. 'Dolor', copyright 1943 by Modern Poetry Association, Inc. 'Praise to the End!', copyright 1950 by Theodore Roethke. 'The Waking', copyright 1953 by Theodore Roethke. 'I Knew a Woman', copyright 1954 by Theodore Roethke. 'The Far Field', copyright © 1962 by Beatrice Roethke, Administratrix of the Estate of Theodore Roethke. 'In a Dark Time', copyright © 1960 by Beatrice Roethke, Administratrix of the Estate of Theodore Roethke. From *The Collected Poems of Theodore Roethke* by Theodore Roethke. Used by permission of Doubleday, a division of Bantam Doubleday Dell Publishing Group, Inc. and Faber and Faber Ltd. Excerpts from 'Some Remarks on Rhythm' and 'Open Letter' from *On the Poet and His Craft: Selected Prose of Theodore Roethke*, edited by Ralph J. Mills, Jr. Copyright © University of Washington Press. Used with permission of the University of Washington Press.

GARY SNYDER 'Piute Creek' and 'Riprap' from *Riprap and Cold Mountain: Poems* © Gary Snyder. 'Journeys (Section Six)' from *Six Sections from Mountain and Rivers Without End* © Gary Snyder. 'Some Yips & Barks in the Dark' © Gary Snyder. 'Front Lines' © Gary Snyder. Reprinted by permission of the author. 'Song of the Taste' and 'Kai, Today' from *Regarding Wave*. Copyright © 1970 by Gary Snyder. 'Poetry and the Primitive' from *Earth House Hold*. Copyright © 1969 by Gary Snyder. Reprinted by permission of New Directions Publishing Corp.

WALLACE STEVENS 'The Emperor of Ice-Cream' from *Collected Poems* by Wallace Stevens. Copyright 1923 and renewed 1951 by Wallace Stevens. 'Sunday Morning' from *Collected Poems* by Wallace Stevens. Copyright 1923 and renewed 1951 by Wallace Stevens. 'The Idea of Order at Key West' from *Collected Poems* by Wallace Stevens. Copyright 1936 by Wallace Stevens and renewed 1964 by Holly Stevens. 'The Man on the Dump' from *Collected Poems* by Wallace Stevens. Copyright 1942 by Wallace Stevens and renewed 1970 by Holly Stevens. 'The Motive for Metaphor' from *Collected Poems* by Wallace Stevens. Copyright 1947 by Wallace Stevens. 'Credences of Summer' from *Collected* Poems by Wallace Stevens. Copyright 1947 by Wallace Stevens. 'The Poem That Took the Place of a Mountain' from *Collected Poems* by Wallace Stevens. Copyright 1952 by Wallace Stevens. Selections from 'Adagia' from *Opus Postumous* by Wallace Stevens. Copyright © 1957 by Elsie Stevens and Holly Stevens. Reprinted by permission of Alfred A. Knopf Inc. and Faber and Faber Ltd.

SHARON THESEN All poems copyright © Sharon Thesen. Reprinted by permission of the author.

DYLAN THOMAS All poems from *The Poems* published by J.M. Dent. 'Notes on the Art of Poetry' from *Texas Quarterly*, Winter 1961. Reprinted by permission of David Higham Associates.

DEREK WALCOTT 'A Far Cry from Africa', 'Orient and Immortal Wheat', 'Islands', 'The Castaway', 'A Map of Europe', 'Crusoe's Island', 'Sea Grapes', 'North and South', 'Early Pompeian', and section XV from 'Midsummer' from *Collected Poems 1948-1984* by Derek Walcott. Copyright © 1986 by Derek Walcott. Reprinted by permission of Farrar, Straus & Giroux, Inc.

BRONWEN WALLACE 'The Woman in this Poem', 'All That Uneasy Spring', and 'A Simple Poem for Virginia Woolf' are reprinted from *Signs of the Former Tenant*, 'Common Magic' and 'Thinking With the Heart' are reprinted from *Common Magic* by permission of Oberon Press. 'Particulars' from *The Stubborn Particulars of Grace* by Bronwen Wallace. Used by permission of the Canadian Publishers, McClelland & Stewart, Toronto.

PHYLLIS WEBB All poems are reprinted by permission of the author.

WILLIAM CARLOS WILLIAMS 'Aux Imagistes', 'Danse Russe', 'This is Just to Say', 'To Waken an Old Lady', 'Tract', 'Spring and All', 'The Red Wheelbarrow', 'Nantucket', and 'The Yachts' from *Collected Poems: 1909-1939, Volume I*. Copyright © 1938, 1944,45, 1938, 1938, 1938 by New Directions Publishing Corp. 'The Dance', 'The Rewaking', and 'To a Dog Injured in the Street' from *Collected Poems 1939-1962, Volume II*. Copyright © 1953, 1948, 1962 by William Carlos Williams. 'On Measure—Statement for Cid Corman' from *Selected Essays of William Carlos Williams*. Copyright © 1954 by William Carlos Williams. Reprinted by permission of New Directions Publishing Corp. and Carcanet Press Limited. 'A New Measure' from *Selected Letters of William Carlos Williams*. Copyright © by William Carlos Williams. Reprinted by permission of New Directions Publishing Corp.

Every effort has been made to determine and contact copyright owners. In the case of any omissions, the publisher will be pleased to make suitable acknowledgement in future editions.

Author Title Index

Theatricalities — Nov. 14/16 Kilmer

Those wonderful plays
that [illegible] near to [illegible]
to feel the [illegible] the stage
all set to being thrilled
[illegible] found [illegible]
of yearning as we [illegible]
Shakespeare to get a whole
as life under the great Bard
of human [illegible]
Imaginations and characters
we [illegible] spelling experience [illegible]
[illegible] the theatre and
then forgetting we realize the
pleasure [illegible] perceptions
that our companion [illegible]
in recognizing expectations.

copied, extended & edited.

Simplification of my writing — Nov. 14 2016 Kilmer

Don't what I don't write
That's what reading of it
and what school [illegible] so far!

copied.